Environmental Law in Bosnia & Herzegovina

Environmental Law in Bosnia & Herzegovina

Dragoljub Todić
Mladenka Ignjatić
Vid Vukasović†

This book was originally published as a monograph in the International Encyclopaedia of Laws/Environmental Law.

Founding Editor: Roger Blanpain
General Editor: Frank Hendrickx
Volume Editor: Kurt Deketelaere

Wolters Kluwer

Published by:
Kluwer Law International B.V.
PO Box 316
2400 AH Alphen aan den Rijn
The Netherlands
E-mail: lrs-sales@wolterskluwer.com
Website: www.wolterskluwer.com/en/solutions/kluwerlawinternational

Sold and distributed by:
Wolters Kluwer Legal & Regulatory U.S.
7201 McKinney Circle
Frederick, MD 21704
United States of America
E-mail: customer.service@wolterskluwer.com

Printed on acid-free paper

ISBN 978-94-035-1556-4

e-Book: ISBN 978-94-035-1236-5
web-PDF: ISBN 978-94-035-1246-4

Printed in the United Kingdom.

The Authors

Dr Dragoljub Todić was born in 1958 in Lopare, Republic of Srpska (Bosnia and Herzegovina). He received his Doctorate and Magisterium at the Faculty of Law of Belgrade University (Serbia) and Diploma of the Faculty of Political Sciences from Belgrade University.

Currently, he is employed at the Institute of International Politics and Economics, Belgrade (Serbia). He was a professor at the Faculty of Public Administration and Management, and Faculty of International Economics in Belgrade (2001–2012). Before that, he was engaged in the former federal state administration competent for the environmental issues.

Todić's fields of interest include Environmental Law and Policy, EU Environmental Policy and Law, EU Integration, Sustainable Development, International Law, State Administration, Human Rights and Migration Law. He is a member of the Serbian International Law Association, the Serbian Association of Lawyers and several NGOs active in the environmental and European integration fields.

His published books are: (with V. Vukasovic) 'Medjunarodne organizacije i medjunarodna saradnja u oblasti zastite zivotne sredine' (*International Organizations and International Cooperation in the Field of the Environment*), published by 'Prometej', Novi Sad, 1999; Editor-in-Chief of 'Zakonodavstvo Evropske unije o zivotnoj sredini i zemlje u tranziciji' (*The EU Environmental Legislation and Countries in Transition*), published by the Federal Ministry for Development, Science and the Environment, Belgrade, 2000; Coordinator of the project (and one of Editors) 'Pravo na adekvatnu zivotnu sredinu – pravo na informisanje i ucesce u odlucivanju prema Arhuskoj konvenciji' (*The Right to Adequate Environment: Right to Environmental Information and to Public Participation According to the Aarhus Convention and to Yugoslav Legislation*) Regional Environmental Centre for Central and Eastern Europe, Belgrade Office, Belgrade, 2001; Edited (with V. Vukasovic) Zaštita životne sredine u međunarodnom i unutrašnjem pravu (*Protection of the Environment in International and National Law*), Uprava za zastitu zivotne sredine Ministarstva zdravlja i zivotne sredine Republike Srbije, Beograd, 2001; Monograph (with V. Vukasović), Serbia and Montenegro, Environmental Law, *International Encyclopaedia of Laws*, Supplement 37, Kluwer Law International, The Hague, London, New York, 2002; (with V. Vukasovic) 'Ekološka kriza u svetu i odgovor međunarodne zajednice (izbor najznačajnijih međunarodnih dokumenata i jugoslovenskih propisa)', Savezni sekretarijat za rad, zdravstvo i socijalno staranje, Institut za medjunarodnu politiku i privredu, Belgrade, 2002; (One of authors) 'Enciklopedija – Životna sredina – Održivi razvoj', Ecolibri, Beograd, Zavod za udžbenike i nastavna sredstva, Srpsko Sarajevo, 2003; (with V. Vukasović) Zbirka propisa u oblasti životne sredine, Megatrend univerzitet, Belgrade 2007. Ekološki menadžment u uslovima globalizacije *(Environmental Management in Circumstances of Globalization)*, Megatrend, Belgrade, 2008; Savremena politika i pravo životne sredine *(Contemporary Environmental Policy and Law)*, Megatrend Univerzitet, Beograd, 2008. Vukasović, V., Todić, D., Environmental Law (Serbia), in *International Encyclopedia of Laws*, edited by Kurte Deketelaere. Alphen aan den Rijin, NL: Kluwer Law International BV, The Netherlands, 2009. Todić, D., Environmental Law (Montenegro), in *International Encyclopedia of Laws*, Suppl. 70 (December 2009), Monograph; Kluwer Law International BV, The Netherlands, 2009. Todić, D., *Vodič kroz EU politike – životna sredine* (EU policy guide – Environment), Belgrade, European Movement in Serbia, 2011. Todić, D, Ignjatić, M., Katić, M, Plavšić, P, 2012, *Nadležnost i kapaciteti lokalne samouprave i organizacija civilnog društva za primenu evropskih standarda u oblasti životne sredine*, (The Competence and Capacity of Local Self-Governments and Civil Society Organizations for the Implementation of European Environmental Standards) Beograd: Evropski pokret u Srbiji. Vukasović, V., Todić, D., *Environmental Law in Serbia*, Wolters Kluwer, Law &Business, 2012. Grbić, V., M. Antevski, Todić, D., *Finansiranje i zajedničke politike Evropske unije (Financing and Common Policies of the European Union)*, Institute for International Politics and Economics, 2013. Todić, D., 'Montenegro' in *International Encyclopaedia of Laws: Environmental Law*, edited by Kurt Deketelaere, Alphen aan den Rijin, NL: Kluwer Law International, 2013. Todić, D., Grbić, V., Antevski M., *Pridruživanje Evropskoj Uniji i održivi razvoj (Accession to the European Union and Sustainable Development)*, Institute of International Politics and Economics, Belgrade, 2014. Todić D., *Klimatske promene u pravu i reforma sistema upravljanja (Climate Change in Law and the Reform of the Governance System)*, Institute of International Politics and Economics, Belgrade, 2014. Todić, D. *Ujedinjene nacije, međunarodni ugovori i životna sredina (United Nations, International Treaties and Environment)*, Institute of International Politics and Economics, Belgrade, 2018.

Besides the mentioned books, he has also published more than 200 articles and other shorter works in various periodicals.

He has participated in a number of conferences in Serbia and abroad and in several domestic and international (EU, OSCE, UNDP, WB, REC) projects.

He participated in the scientific project No. 179029 financed by the Ministry of Education and Science of the Republic of Serbia (2011–2018).

The Authors

MA Mladenka Ignjatić completed her studies at Faculty of Geo-economy in Belgrade. She received her Master's from the Faculty of International Economics at Megatrend University Belgrade. The subject of her master thesis was: *Influence of Renewable Energy Sources on Sustainable Development of EU and Republic of Serbia.*

From 1998 to 2007, she worked for NGO World Vision International in Banja Luka, Republic of Srpska. From 2007 to 2011, she worked at Megatrend University, Belgrade. Presently, she works as an Independent Consultant on environmental issues. She has participated in a number of international and national conferences in Serbia.

Published books: Todić, D., Ignjatić, M., Katić, M., Plavšić, P., *Nadležnosti ikapacitetilokalnesamouprave i organizacijacivilnog društva za primenuevropsk ihstandarda u oblasti životne sredine* (*The Competencies and Capacities of the Local Self-Governments and Civil Society Organizations for the Implementation of European Environmental Standards*), published by the European Movement in Serbia, Belgrade, 2012.

Assistant in writing the following books: Vukasović, V., Todić D., *Environmental Law in Serbia,* Kluwer Law International BV, The Netherlands Monograph in the International Encyclopaedia of Laws/Environmental Law, 2012; *Guidebook Through European Politics: Environmental Politic,* The European Movement in Serbia, Belgrade, 2011.

She has also published the below articles:

- Ignjatić, M. *Assessment and capacity strengthening of the local governments for the implementation of European standards in the field of the environment*, The Ambassadors of sustainable development and the environment and the Serbian Chamber of Commerce, pp. 24–29.
- Todić, D., Vukasović. V., Ignjatić, M., Čavoški, A. '*International treaties in the field of environment in function of European integration-region of Southeast Europe*', The European Movement in Serbia, Belgrade, October 2011.
- Ignjatić, M. 'Directive of the European Parliament and of the Council on promotion of the use of energy from renewable sources', *European legislation*, No: 35–36, pp. 106–115.

Dr Vid Vukasović† completed studies at the Faculty of Law of Belgrade University; he received his Master's and his Doctorate at the same University. He received his Diploma in Air and Space Law from McGill University (1968, Montreal, Canada).

From 1968 to 2006, he was Research Fellow of the Institute of International Politics and Economics (Senior Research Staff from 1974), Belgrade. He was the Head of the International Law Department (1984–1987) and Chairman of the Scientific Council of the Institute (1984–1995 and 2000–2005).

He was a member of International Council of Environmental Law (ICEL), the International Law Association (ILA), the Serbian International Law Association and the Serbian Association of Lawyers.

He has participated in a number of important international conferences and projects, for example, in the work of the Intergovernmental Working Group of experts on natural resources shared by two or more States which drafted the principles concerning the shared natural resources (Geneva 1976, Nairobi 1977); the Ad Hoc Meeting of Senior Government Officials Expert in Environmental Law (Geneva 1981 and Montevideo 1981) on which the System Wide Medium Term Environment Programme (SWMTEP) was drafted; the Mediterranean Action Plan (MAP) project 'Blue Book'; Project concerning the interrelation between human rights and the development of science and technology commissioned by the United Nations University (Tokyo) in 1988–1990; various UNEP's working groups, sessions of the UNEP's Governing Council, a number of conferences dealing with the protection of the Mediterranean Sea, etc.

His books include *International Law and the Development of Science and Technology* (in Serbian, with summaries in English and Russian), Belgrade 1978; *Protection and Improvement of the Environment-International Legal Regulation* (in Serbian with a summary in English), Belgrade, 1980; *Environmental Protection and the United Nations* (in Serbian, with a summary in English), Belgrade, 1985; (with D. Todić) *International Organizations in the Field of Environmental Protection* (in Serbian) 'Prometej', Novi Sad, 1999; Edited (with D. Todić) 'Pravo na adekvatnu zivotnu sredinu – pravo na informisanje i ucesce u odlucivanju prema Arhuskoj konvenciji' *(The Right to Adequate Environment – Right to Environmental Information and to Public Participation according to the Aarhus Convention and to Yugoslav legislation)*, Regional Environmental Centre for Central and Eastern Europe, Belgrade Office, Belgrade, 2001; Edited (with D. Todić), 'Zastita zivotne sredine u medjunarodnom i unutrasnjem pravu' (*Protection of the Environment in International and National Law*), Uprava za zastitu zivotne sredine Ministarstva zdravlja i zivotne sredine Republike Srbije, Belgrade, 2001; Monograph (with D. Todić), *Serbia and Montenegro, Environmental Law, International Encyclopedia of Laws*, Supplement 37, Kluwer Law International, The Hague, London, New York, 2002; (with D. Todić) 'Ekološka kriza u svetu i odgovor međunarodne zajednice (izbor najznačajnijih međunarodnih dokumenata i jugoslovenskih propisa)', Savezni sekretarijat za rad, zdravstvo i socijalno staranje, Sektor za zivotnu sredinu i Institut za medjunarodnu politiku i privredu, Belgrade, 2002; (One of authors) 'Enciklopedija – Životna sredina – Održivi razvoj', Published by: ECOLIBRI, Beograd, Zavod za udzbenike i sredstva, Srpsko Sarajevo, 2003; (with D. Todić), Zbirka propisa u oblasti životne sredine, Megatrend univerzitet, Belgrade 2007. Vukasović, V., Todić, D., *Environmental Law in Serbia*, Wolters Kluwer, Law & Business, 2012.

Besides the mentioned books, he has published more than 300 articles and other shorter works in various periodicals. He has lectured in Serbia and abroad. For example, he lectured at the Specialized Course in High Administration and Comparative Governance 2003–2004, the University of Bari and the Institute of International Politics and Economics, Bari and Belgrade and lectured at the Specialized Course 'The Law of Energetic', Faculty of Law, Belgrade 2005 and 2006, etc.

Table of Contents

Table of Contents

List of Abbreviations

APREF	Action Plan for using of Renewable Energy sources in the Federation BiH
BAM	Bosnian Convertible Mark
BAT	Best Available Techniques
BD	Brčko District of BiH
BHAS	Agency for Statistics of Bosnia and Herzegovina
BHMAC	Bosnia and Herzegovina Mine Action Centre
BiH	Bosnia and Herzegovina
CARDS	Community Assistance for Reconstruction, Development and Stabilization
CBC	Central Bosnia Canton
CEC	Commission of the European Communities
CEFTA	Central European Free Trade Agreement
CLP	Classification, Labelling and Packaging
CO	Carbon Dioxide
CoE	Council of Europe
DEI	European Integrations Directorate
DSPPA	Department of Spatial Planning, and Property Affairs of Brčko District BiH
DU	Depleted Uranium
EAS	Environmental Approximation Strategy
EBRD	European Bank for Reconstruction and Development
EC	European Commission
ECT	Energy Charter Treaty
ECtHR	European Court of Human Rights
EEA	European Environment Agency
EIA	Environmental Impact Assessment
EIS	Environmental Impact Study
EMAS	Environmental Management System
EPBD	Energy Performance of Buildings Directive

List of Abbreviations

EPI	Environmental Performance Index
EU	European Union
FAO	Food and Agriculture Organization
FBiH	Federation of Bosnia and Herzegovina
FDI	Foreign Direct Investment
FMAWMF	FBiH Ministry of Agriculture, Water and Forestry
FMET	Federal Ministry of Environment and Tourism
FSA	The Food Safety Agency
GDP	Gross Domestic Product
GEF	Global Environment Facility
GHG	Greenhouse Gases
GLP	Good Laboratory Practice
GMO	Genetically Modified Organisms
GNI	Gross National Income
HDI	Human Development Index
IAEA	International Atomic Energy Agency
IDA	International Development Association
IDPs	Internally Displaced Persons
IUCN	International Union for Conservation of Nature
MDG	Millennium Development Goals
MEAs	Multilateral Environmental Agreements
MFTER	Ministry of Foreign Trade and Economic Relations of BiH
NAPRES	National Action Plan for Use of Renewable Energy Sources
NATO	The North Atlantic Treaty Organization
NATURA2000	EU Network of Nature Protected Areas
NEAP	National Environmental Action Plan
NEEAP	National Energy Efficiency Plan
NGO	Non-Governmental Organization
NHDR	National Human Development Report
Nox	Nitrogen oxides
ODA	Official Development Aid
OG BDBiH	Official Gazette of the Brčko District of Bosnia and Herzegovina
OG BiH	Official Gazette of the Bosnia and Herzegovina
OG FBiH	Official Gazette of the Federation of Bosnia and Herzegovina
OG RS	Official Gazette of the Republic of Srpska
OHR	Office of the High Representative in Bosnia and Herzegovina
OSCE	Organization for Security and Cooperation in Europe

PHPA	The Plant Health Protection Administration
PRSP	Poverty Reduction Strategy Paper
PRTR	Pollutant Release and Transfer Registers
REC	Regional Environmental Centre for Central and Eastern Europe
RENA	Regional Environmental Network for Accession
RES	Renewable Energy Sources
RS	Republic of Srpska
RSMoAFWM	Ministry of Agriculture, Forestry and Water Management, Republic of Srpska
RSMoSPCEE	Ministry of Spatial Planning, Civil Engineering and Ecology of RS
SAA	Stabilization and Association Agreement
SC	Sarajevo Canton
SDS	Safety Data Sheet
SEA	The Strategic Environmental Assessment
SFRY	Socialist Federal Republic of Yugoslavia
SO	Sulphur Dioxide
SR BiH	Socialist Republic of Bosnia and Herzegovina
SY FBiH	Statistical Yearbook of FBiH
SY RS (Stat. Yearb. of Rep. Srpska)	Statistical Yearbook of RS
TC	Tuzla Canton
UN	United Nations
UNDP	United Nations Development Programme
UNECE	United Nations Economic Commission for Europe
UNEP	United Nations Environment Programme
UNESCO	United Nations Educational, Scientific and Cultural Organization
UNHCR	UN High Commissioner for Refugees
UNICEF	United Nations Children's Fund
USAID	United States Agency for International Development
USC	Una-Sana Canton
UXO	Unexploded Ordnance
WB	World Bank
WHC	West-Herzegovina Canton
WSSD	The World Summit on Sustainable development
WTO	World Trade Organization
ZDC	Zenica-Doboj Canton

List of Abbreviations

General Introduction

§1. General Information

I. Geography and Population

A. Geography

1. Bosnia and Herzegovina (BiH) is located at the western part of Balkan Peninsula, and it has 51,209.2 km^2.[1] The land covers 51,197 km^2, and sea covers 12.2 km^2.[2] Federation of Bosnia and Herzegovina (FBiH) has 26,110.5 km^2,[3] Republic of Srpska (RS) 24,641 km^2,[4] and Brčko District of Bosnia and Herzegovina (BD) 493.3 km^2.[5] North, west and south-west boundary lines divide BiH from the Republic of Croatia, and east and south boundary lines from the Republic of Serbia and the Montenegro. BiH has a small exit to the sea, stretching over about 21 km long coastline, near Neum town.[6]

2. 'According to its geographical position, BiH belongs to the Adriatic and Black Sea Basins. It is primarily a mountainous country covered by forests. The

1. Agency for Statistics of Bosnia and Herzegovina, *Bosnia and Herzegovina in Figures 2020*, Sarajevo, 2021, p. 5. http://www.bhas.gov.ba/data/Publikacije/Bilteni/2021/NUM_00_2020_TB_1_EN.pdf (19 February 2021). Geographical coordinates of the extreme points: North geographical latitude (North: 45° 16'30'; South: 42°. 33' 00'; East: 44°. 03' 00'; West: 44°. 49'30'); East geographical longitude (North: 16°.55' .56'; South: 18°. 32' .24'; East: 19°. 37' .41'; West 15°. 44' .00'). Institute for Statistics of FBiH. *Statistical Yearbook of the Federation of Bosnia and Herzegovina 2020.* Sarajevo, 2020, p. 33. https://docs.google.com/gview?url=http://fzs.ba/wp-content/uploads/2020/12/Godisnjak2020.pdf (19 Feb. 2021).
2. *See*: EEA, European Environment Agency, https://www.eea.europa.eu/soer/2010/countries/ba/country-introduction-bosnia-and-herzegovina (18 Jul. 2022).
3. Federal Office of Statistics, *Statistical Yearbook 2021, ('SY FBiH 21')*, Sarajevo, 2021, p. 34. http://fzs.ba/index.php/publikacije/statisticki-godisnjaciljetopisi/ (18 Jul. 2022).
4. Republic of Srpska Institute of statistic, *Statistical Yearbook of Republic of Srpska, 2021*, Banja Luka, November 2021, p. 14. https://www.rzs.rs.ba/static/uploads/bilteni/godisnjak/2021/StatistickiGodisnjak_2021_WEB_II.pdf (18 Jul. 2022). 'Data on the surface area of Republic of Srpska is temporary. Final surface area will be determined after reaching the agreement on entity borderline and on international border of BH. Length of boundaries should also be used conditionally'. *Ibid.*, p. 17.
5. Strategija razvoja Brčko Distrikta BiH za period 2021–2027. godina [Development Strategy of the Brčko District BiH for the period 2021 to 2027. year], Brčko, 2 Jul. 2021. p. 2. http://www.vlada.bdcentral.net/Content/Read/strategije (18 Jul. 2022).
6. *See*: https://www.vijeceministara.gov.ba/osnovne_informacije_o_bih/default.aspx?id=95&langTag=en-US (18 Jul. 2022).

average altitude is 500 meters, with the highest peak being the Maglić Mountain (2,387 m). Out of its total surface area, 42% consists of mountains, 24% of hills, 29% of karst areas and 5% of lowlands.'[7]

3. 'General climate characteristics of the country are greatly influenced by characteristics of Adriatic Sea, local topography-especially the Dinarides Mountains, which are located NW to SE parallel to the coast. The climate of BiH varies from a temperate continental climate in the northern Pannonia lowlands along the Sava River and in the foothill zone, to an alpine climate in the mountain regions, and a Mediterranean climate in the coastal and lowland areas of the Herzegovina region in the south and southeast.'[8]

B. Population

4. According to the results of the 2013 Census in BiH, the total number of enumerated persons is 3,531, 159,[9] out of which: in the FBiH 2, 219, 220 persons[10]; in the RS 1,170, 342 persons,[11] and in BD BiH 82,410 persons.[12] 'Whereas the RS covers predominantly Serb areas, the FBiH governs parts of the country that are mostly Croat and Bosnian Muslim.'[13] Available figures (2014) give a life expectancy of 79.03 years for women and 73.96 years for men. The country's fertility rate

7. BiH MFTER, *State of the environment Report of the Bosnia and Herzegovina 2012*, Ministry of Foreign Trade and Economic Relations, Millennium Development Goals Achievement Fund, Sarajevo. 2012, p. 41.
8. BiH MFTER, Ministry of Physical Planning, Civil Engineering and Ecology of Republic of Srpska, Federal Ministry of Environment and Tourism, UNDP, *Initial National Communication of Bosnia and Herzegovina under the United Nations Framework Convention on Climate Change*, Banja Luka, 2009. p. 28. http://unfccc.int/resource/docs/natc/bihnc1.pdf (28 Jul. 2022). In the lowlands in the northern part of the country, air temperature generally ranges between -1°C and -2°C in January and between 18 and 20°C in July. In highlands with the altitude above 1000m, the average temperature ranges from -4°C to -7°C in January to 9°C to 14°C in July. On the Adriatic coast and in the lowland regions of Herzegovina, air temperature ranges from 3 to 9°C in January to 22 to 25°C in July. Extremes of -41.8°C (the lowest) and 42.2°C (the highest) have been recorded. *Ibid.*, p. 28. For more information *see also*: UNDP in Bosnia and Herzegovina. *Third National Communication and Second Biennial Update Report on Greenhouse Gas Emissions of Bosnia and Herzegovina under the United Nations Framework Convention on Climate Change*, GEF, UNDP, MFTER, MSPCEE, FMET, DSPPA BD, July 2016. https://www.undp.org/bosnia-herzegovina/publications/third-national-communication-tnc-and-second-biennial-update-report-greenhouse-gas-emissions-sbur-bosnia-and (18 Jul. 2022).
9. Agency for Statistic of Bosnia and Herzegovina, Demography 2020, Sarajevo, 2021, p. 17.
10. Institute for Statistics of F BiH, Statistical Yearbook of the Federation of Bosnia and Herzegovina 2021, Sarajevo, 2021, p. 89.
11. Republika Srpska Institute of Statistics, *Statistical Yearbook of Republic of Srpska 2021*, Banja Luka, 2021, p. 5.
12. Brčko District of BiH, *Development Strategy of Brčko District BiH 2021-2027*, Brčko 2020, p. 10.
13. EBRD, *Commercial Law of Bosnia and Herzegovina, An Assessment by the EBRD*, October 2010, European Bank for Reconstruction and Development, p. 3. http://www.ebrd.com/downloads/sector/legal/bosnia.pdf (19 Jul. 2020).

was 1.27 in 2008 and decreased slightly to 1.26 in 2014, which is lower than in any other of the western Balkan countries and also lower than the European Union (EU) average of 1.54 in 2014.[14]

5. BiH has three major population groups: Bosniaks, Serbs and Croats.[15]'All are ethnically South Slavs and the primary difference between them is their religion. Bosniaks are generally Sunni Muslims; Croats are Roman Catholics, while Serbs are traditionally Orthodox Christians.'[16]'According to the 2013 census, Bosniaks constitute 50.11% of the population, Serbs 30.78% and Croats 15.43%, while the remaining 2.73% either did not declare their ethnicity or did not answer.'[17]

6. 'Demographically, rural communities tend to be older than urban and have smaller proportions of people to work and drive the local economy. There is also a gradual migration of people from rural to urban areas; the share of the population living in rural areas probably falls by about 10% every generation. Economically, the big divide is not between urban and rural areas but actually between the six main cities and the rest of BiH.'[18] According to the WB Report, 'demographic trends are at the core of the development challenges for BiH, which faces several demographic trends that pose a significant threat to its ability to grow'.[19]

---

14. UNECE, *3rd Environmental Performance Review, Bosnia and Herzegovina*, United Nations, New York, Geneva, 2018. p. 1.
15. In the Preamble of the Constitution, the Bosniacs, Serbs and Croats are described as the 'constitutive peoples'.
16. UNECE, *2nd Environmental Performance Review, supra* p. 2. There are seventeen recognized national minorities in the BiH, according to the Art. 3 of the Law on the Protection of Rights of National Minorities in BiH (Official Gazette of BiH, No. 12/03, and 76/05). For more information *see also* Law on the Protection of Rights of National Minorities in RS (Official Gazette of BiH, No. 2/04), and the Law on the Protection of Rights of National Minorities in FBiH (Official Gazette of BiH, No. 56/08). *See also*: Nagradić, S. National minorities in legislation of Bosnia and Herzegovina, *Politea*, 10/2015, 181-207. https://scindeks-clanci.ceon.rs/data/pdf/2232-9641/2015/2232-96411510181N.pdf (26 Jul. 2022).
17. UNECE. *3rd Environmental Performance Review, Bosnia and Herzegovina*, p. 1.
18. Official statistics show that Sarajevo, Banja Luka Tuzla, Zenica, Mostar and Bijeljina, each of which has at least 100,000 inhabitants, have almost 40% lower unemployment (*six main cities 31% v. towns and villages 50%*), 25% higher wages (*six cities 895 BAM v. towns and villages 715 BAM*) and over twice the *per capita* GDP than the rest of the country (*six main cities 10,460 BAM v. towns and villages 4,730 BAM*) all of which stimulates a significant movement of people to the cities. Hodžić-Kovač E., (Ed) *Progress towards the Realisation of Millennium Development Goals in Bosnia and Herzegovina 2013*, Ministry of Finance and Treasury of Bosnia and Herzegovina, Office of the UN Resident Coordinator in Bosnia and Herzegovina, Sarajevo, 2013, pp. 24, 25. For more details, *see* UNDP, *Rural development in Bosnia and Herzegovina: myth and reality*, National Human Development Report 2013, United Nations Development Programme (UNDP) in Bosnia and Herzegovina, Sarajevo, 2013. https://hdr.undp.org/content/rural-development-bosnia-and-herzegovina-myth-and-reality (19 Jul. 2022).
19. World Bank Group, Bosnia and Herzegovina, Systematic Country Diagnostic Update, Report No. 148573-BA, Washington, 2020, p. 18. 'These trends include rapid outward migration, a rapidly aging population, a declining birth rate, and loss of human capital due to deficiencies in healthcare and education.' Ibid.

7. The period between 1992 and 1995 is characterized by war migrations. In addition to those who left during the war, it is estimated that approximately another 110,000 citizens emigrated after the war, out of which around 43,000 have permanently changed their citizenship.[20]

8. Bosnia and Herzegovina (BiH) experienced a substantial increase in mixed movement arrivals from 2018 (over 85,000 at the end of 2021). In 2021, the BiH authorities registered the asylum claims of 167 individuals, a 32% decrease from the 245 claims registered in 2020, which was already a significant decrease compared to 2018 (1,572) and 2019 (785). In 2021, most asylum-seekers were coming from Turkey, Afghanistan and Iran.[21]

According to the EC Progress Report for 2021, 'the authorities detected 16,183 arrivals, compared to 29,302 in 2019, a 40 decrease primarily due to the impact of the pandemic on global mobility'.[22]

9. By the end of September 2021, the country had recorded 227,579 cases and 10,606 deaths related to the COVID-19 pandemic. Bosnia and Herzegovina does not have a countrywide vaccine strategy, and the entities (the Republic of Srpska and the Federation of BiH) have proceeded with their own separate vaccine procurement.[23]

II. Legal and Political Structure

A. Bosnia and Herzegovina

10. The current governmental structure of Bosnia and Herzegovina has its origins in the General Framework Agreement for Peace in Bosnia and Herzegovina, usually referred to as Dayton Peace Agreement of 1995, which ended the country's civil war.[24] The Dayton Agreement included the BiH Constitution as one of its

---

20. BiH MFTER, *State of the environment Report of the Bosnia and Herzegovina 2012*, *supra* p. 49.
21. UNHCR, Bosnia and Herzegovina, https://www.unhcr.org/bosnia-and-herzegovina.html (19 Jul. 2022).
22. EC. *Bosnia and Herzegovina 2021 Progress Report*, p. 39. 'Overall, the top three declared countries of origin were Afghanistan, Pakistan and Bangladesh. ... However, facilities remain insufficient to ensure shelter and protection to those in need.' *Ibid.*, p. 40.
23. *Ibid.*, p. 3. Fore more information, see: https://www.phi.rs.ba/index.php?view=kategorija&id=45 (19 Jul. 2022); https://www.zzjzfbih.ba/covid-19/ (19 Jul. 2022); https://covid19.who.int/region/euro/country/ba (26 Jul. 2022).
24. The Office of the High Representative (OHR) is 'an *ad hoc* international institution responsible for overseeing implementation of civilian aspects of the Peace Agreement ending the war in Bosnia and Herzegovina'. The position of High Representative was created under the Dayton Peace Agreement. Art. II of Annex 10 of the Dayton Peace Agreement directs the High Representative to: Monitor the implementation of the peace settlement; Maintain close contact with the parties to the Agreement, to promote their full compliance with all civilian aspects of the Agreement; Coordinate the activities of the civilian organizations and agencies in Bosnia and Herzegovina to ensure the efficient implementation of the civilian aspects of the peace settlement. The High Representative shall respect their autonomy within their spheres of operation while as necessary giving general guidance to them about the impact of their activities on the implementation of the peace settlement; Facilitate, as the High

annexes. The Constitution establishes a limited central state that includes two fairly autonomous entities: The Republic of Srpska and The Federation of Bosnia and Herzegovina.[25] Originally, Dayton Constitution accorded the central state of BiH jurisdiction over foreign policy and foreign trade, customs and monetary policy, as well as jurisdiction in policy matters regulating the issues of immigration, refugees and asylum, and the control of its airspace. However 'the process of 'defragmentation' – mainly under the auspices or by way of direct intervention by representatives of the international community in BiH (the Office of the High Representative – OHR) 'returned' to Bosnia and Herzegovina jurisdiction over defence (2005), civil affairs (the number of institutions of the state of BiH increased from just a few in 1995 to more than fifty in 2010), and indirect taxation (2006)'.[26]

11. Each of these entities has its own government and civil structure. Generally speaking, Bosnia and Herzegovina has fourteen different government levels and types: the state level; two entities – Federation of BiH and the Republic of Srpska; ten cantons;[27] one district, and a municipality level. 'Altogether these considerations make BiH's overall institutional environment uniquely complex.'[28]'The overarching Bosnian state is confederal in character, exerting virtually no authority; the federating units (the two entities) rather than the federal government are constitutionally empowered.'[29] The capital of BiH is Sarajevo (Article I.5 of the Constitution of BiH).

Representative judges necessary, the resolution of any difficulties arising in connection with civilian implementation; Participate in meetings of donor organizations; Report periodically on progress to the United Nations, European Union, United States, Russian Federation and other interested governments, parties and organizations; Provide guidance to the United Nations International Police Task Force (IPTF). *See*: http://www.ohr.int/?page_id=63269 (19 Jul. 2022).

25. EBRD, *Commercial Law of BiH*, An Assessment by the EBRD, *supra* p. 3.
26. 'The same process was also a means to achieve the establishment of the Court of Bosnia and Herzegovina (2002), the High Judicial and Prosecutorial Council (2002), and sets of laws were passed to, among other things, determine a unique framework for matters of criminal law and family law in BiH, as well as laws that established intelligence and security agencies at the state level'. Gratz, D. Incomplete Bosnia and Herzegovina and the capacity of state institutions, in Bassuener K. (pr) *Bosna i Hercegovina: između paketa mjera za EU-integraciju i izlazne strategije međunarodne zajednice* [Bosnia and Herzegovina: between EU-integration toolbox and international community's exit strategy], Sarajevo: Fondacija Heinrich Böll, Ured za Bosnu i Hercegovinu, 2010. p. 64.
27. According to the World Bank 'in BiH, the term "state government" refers to what would be considered the national or federal government in other federal systems. The term "entity governments" is analogous to "state or provincial governments" in other federal systems. The canton governments in the Federation also resemble state or provincial governments'. World Bank. '*Bosnia and Herzegovina, from aid dependency to fiscal self-reliance, a public expenditure and institutional review*', WB Report No. 24297-BIH, Poverty Reduction and Economic Management Unit Europe and Central Asia Region: The World Bank, 2002. p. 5. Apart from the term 'state government' in the documents, reports and articles, authors use the formulations 'BiH level,' 'national level', etc.
28. Efendic A., Pugh G., Adnett N. Confidence in formal institutions and reliance on informal institutions in Bosnia and Herzegovina-An empirical investigation using survey data, *Economics of Transition*, Vol. 19, No. 3/2011, p. 523. DOI: 10.1111/j.1468-0351.2010.00408.x.
29. Fagan A, Global–Local Linkage in the Western Balkans: The Politics of Environmental Capacity Building in Bosnia-Herzegovina, *Political Studies*, Vol. 56. No. 3/2008, p. 640, doi: 10.1111/j.1467-9248.2007.00711.x. *See also*, Bose, S. 'The Bosnian State a Decade after Dayton', in D. Chandler (ed.), 'Peace Without Politics? Ten Years of International State-Building in Bosnia', *International Peacekeeping*, Vol. 12, No. 3/2005, pp. 322–55.

12. The BiH Parliamentary Assembly has two chambers, the House of Representatives[30] and the House of Peoples.[31] According to the Article IV.4. of the Constitution of BiH the Parliamentary Assembly shall have responsibility for: (a) enacting legislation as necessary to implement decisions of the Presidency or to carry out the responsibilities of the Assembly under this Constitution; (b) deciding upon the sources and amounts of revenues for the operations of the institutions of BiH and international obligations of BiH; (c) approving a budget for the institutions of BiH; (d) deciding whether to consent to the ratification of treaties; and (e) such other matters as are necessary to carry out its duties or as are assigned to it by mutual agreement of the Entities.[32]

13. The Presidency of BiH consists of three Members: one Bosniac and one Croat, each directly elected from the territory of the Federation, and one Serb directly elected from the territory of the Republic of Srpska (Article V of the Constitution of BiH).[33] All three have equal rights. They serve for four years. The chairmanship of the Presidency rotates every eight months.[34]

In accordance with the Article V.4 of the Constitution of BiH, the Presidency shall nominate the Chair of the Council of Ministers, who shall take office upon the approval of the House of Representatives. The Chair shall nominate a Foreign Minister, a Minister for Foreign Trade and other Ministers as may be appropriate, who shall take office upon the approval of the House of Representatives. Together the

30. The House of Representatives has 42 directly elected members. Two-thirds of them are elected from the entity of Federation of BiH and one-third from the entity of Republic of Srpska (Art. IV.2 of the Constitution). *See* details on the Parliamentary Assembly of BiH (House of Representatives) website (https://www.parlament.ba/Content/Read/58?title=Op%C4%87ipodaci (19 Jul. 2022).
31. The House of Peoples has fifteen members, five Croats, five Serbs and five Bosniaks, elected by the parliaments of the entities (ten FBiH, five RS). *See* details on the Parliamentary Assembly of BiH (House of Peoples) website https://www.parlament.ba/Content/Read/36?title=Op%C4%87ipodaci&lang=en (19 Jul. 2022).
32. *See*: https://www.parlament.ba/Content/Read/25?title=FunkcijeParlamentarneskup%C5%A1tineBiH (19 Jul. 2022).
33. Pursuant to the Art. V.3 of the Constitution of BiH the Presidency shall have responsibility for: (a) Conducting the foreign policy of BiH; (b) Appointing ambassadors and other international representatives of BiH, no more than two-thirds of whom may be selected from the territory of the Federation; (c) Representing BiH in international and European organizations and institutions and seeking membership in such organizations and institutions of which BiH is not a member; (d) Negotiating, denouncing, and, with the consent of the Parliamentary Assembly, ratifying treaties of BiH; (e) Executing decisions of the Parliamentary Assembly; (f) Proposing, upon the recommendation of the Council of Ministers, an annual budget to the Parliamentary Assembly; (g) Reporting as requested, but not less than annually, to the Parliamentary Assembly on expenditures by the Presidency; (h) Coordinating as necessary with international and non-governmental organizations in BiH; and (i) Performing such other functions as may be necessary to carry out its duties, as may be assigned to it by the Parliamentary Assembly, or as may be agreed by the Entities.
34. 'The history of the Presidency of BiH begins in 1974, when the Constitution of the then Socialist Republic of BiH, in the framework of the Socialist Federal Republic of Yugoslavia, established a new institution in the socio-political system. At that time, the Presidency consisted of 9 Members, but after first multiparty elections in December 1990, it had 7 Members – two Bosniac, two Serbs, two Croats, and one Member representing the rest of the people.' For more information *see*: http://www.predsjednistvobih.ba/hron/default.aspx?id=10074&langTag=en-US (19 Jul. 2022).

Chair and the Ministers shall constitute the Council of Ministers,[35] with responsibility for carrying out the policies and decisions of BiH in the fields referred to in Article III(1), (4) and (5)[36] and reporting to the Parliamentary Assembly (including, at least annually, on expenditures by BiH) (Article V.4a).

B. The Republic of Srpska

14. The Republic of Srpska was proclaimed on 9 January 1992 and verified as a state entity of Bosnia and Herzegovina on 14 December 1995 by the Dayton Peace Agreement and peace ratification in Paris. Today, the Republic of Srpska is a parliamentary republic with limited international subjectivity.[37] Banja Luka is the administrative capital of the Republic of Srpska, the second largest city in Bosnia and Herzegovina.

15. RS has a unified governmental structure, a unicameral People's Assembly and a directly elected president.[38]'The structure of the National Assembly of the Republic of Srpska, in accordance to modern parliamentary principles, is composed of eighty-three deputies, elected by the people at direct parliamentary elections. Until 2002 the deputies in the National Assembly of the Republic of Srpska were elected for a mandate which lasted two years, and from 2002, in accordance to a new legal regulation, they are elected for a mandate lasting four years.'[39] The Government of the Republic of Srpska has sixteen ministries, including the Ministry of Spatial Planning, Civil Engineering and Ecology.[40]

35. The Council of Ministers is a body of executive authority of Bosnia and Herzegovina, exercising its rights and carrying out its duties as governmental functions, according to the Constitution of BiH, laws and other regulations of Bosnia and Herzegovina. The Council of Ministers of BiH comprises the Chairman and the following Ministers: Minister of Foreign Affairs, Minister of Foreign Trade and Economic Relations, Minister of Finance and Treasury, Minister of Communications and Transport, Minister of Civil Affairs, Minister of Human Rights and Refugees, Minister of Justice, Minister of Security, and Minister of Defence. *See*: https://www.vijeceministara.gov.ba/default.aspx?pageIndex=1&langTag=en-US (19 Jul. 2022).
36. Article III(1) relates to the responsibilities of the Institutions of BiH (*See* the s. 4. Role of government institutions in the shaping and administration of environmental law and policy, I. Governmental Institutions and Their Competencies); Art. III(4) relates to the 'inter-Entity coordination on matters not within the responsibilities of BiH as provided in this Constitution.' Art. III(5) relates to 'Additional Responsibilities'.
37. Republic of Srpska, Institute of statistic, *Statistical Yearbook of Republic of Srpska, 2018*, p. 14. 'The Dayton negotiations bear out what can be frequently discerned in international practice, namely that entities which exercise de facto control over a specific territory may be regarded as subjects of international law, even if they enjoy a limited international personality'. For details, *see* Gaeta P. The Dayton Agreements and International Law, *European Journal of International Law*, Vol. 7, No. 2/1996, p. 158.
38. *See*: https://www.predsjednikrs.net/en/ (19 Jul. 2022).
39. *See*: http://www.narodnaskupstinars.net/?q=en/national-assembly/about-national-assembly (19 Jul. 2022).
40. For more information *see*: http://www.vladars.net/eng/Pages/default.aspx (19 Jul. 2022).

16. RS has fifty-five municipalities and nine cities.[41] A municipality is the main territorial unit of local self-government, formed for a part of a settlement, for one settlement or more of them. A city is a territorial unit which is a coherent geographic, historical, administrative, social and economic whole, adequately developed.[42]

C. *The Federation of Bosnia and Herzegovina*

17. The Federation of Bosnia and Herzegovina is constituted on the basis of the Washington Agreement signed in 1994[43] 'which brought an end to violent conflict between Croats and Bosniacs in a region of Bosnia and Herzegovina'.[44]

18. The Federation of Bosnia and Herzegovina has its constitution, a bicameral parliament[45] and a government headed by a Prime Minister,[46] who is nominated by the parliament. The Government of the Federation of Bosnia and Herzegovina has sixteen ministries, including Ministry of Environment and Tourism.[47] The political structure of FBiH is divided into three levels: the entity level, the cantonal level and the municipal level. Sarajevo is the capital of the Federation of Bosnia and Herzegovina entity.

19. An expert working group was set up with support from the US and the EU and drafted recommendations for reform of the Federation's Constitution. 'The recommendations also aim to address the costly and complex governance structures with certain overlapping competences between the Federation, the Cantons and the municipalities as currently entailed in the Federation Constitution.'[48]

41. Republic of Srpska, Institute of statistic, *Statistical Yearbook of Republic of Srpska,* 2021, *supra* p. 14.
42. *See* Arts 8 and 10 of the Law on local self-government (Official Gazette of RS, No. 97/16, 36/19, 61/21).
43. 'The Framework Agreement establishing a Federation in the Areas of the Republic of Bosnia and Herzegovina with a Majority Bosniacs and Croat Population'. *See*: Letter dated 3 Mar. 1994 from the permanent representatives of Bosnia and Herzegovina and Croatia to the United Nations Addressed to the Secretary General, S/1994/255, UN Security Council, 4 Mar. 1994.
44. *Negotiating Justice? Human Rights and Peace Agreements*, International Council on Human Rights Policy, Geneva, Switzerland, 2006, p. 130.
45. *See*: http://parlamentfbih.gov.ba/ (19 Jul. 2022). The House of Representatives is composed of ninety -eight members, while House of Peoples is composed of fifty eight members.
46. *See*: https://fbihvlada.gov.ba/ (19 Jul. 2022).
47. For more information *see*: https://fbihvlada.gov.ba/bs/ministarstva-vlade-federacije-bosne-i-hercegovine (19 Jul. 2022).
48. EC, *Bosnia and Herzegovina 2013 Progress Report,* accompanying the document, Communication from the Commission to the European Parliament and the Council, Enlargement Strategy and Main Challenges 2013–2014, COM(2013) 700 final, European Commission, Brussels, 16 Oct. 2013, pp. 5, 6. On 26 Aug. (2013), the Federation Government decided to form a high level working group dealing with the constitutional reform in cooperation with the experts. No draft amendments have yet been put into the legislative procedure.

1. Cantons

20. 'Canton is a federal unit of the Federation which includes the cities and municipalities within the canton in accordance with federal regulation. The cantons are formed taking into account ethnic, economic and functional, natural-geographic and communication principles.' 'Canton area is defined area of related municipalities and settlements.'[49] 'At cantonal level, each of the 10 cantons has its own parliamentary assembly with the power to adopt cantonal laws and appoint the cantonal government.' These are the following: Sarajevo, Una-Sana, Posavina, Tuzla, Zenica-Doboj, Bosna-Podrinje, Central Bosnia, Herzegovina-Neretva, West Herzegovina and Canton 10. Cantons are divided into municipalities.

21. The third political level in the FBiH is the municipal one, where each self-governing municipality has its own municipal council and administrative structures.[50] FBiH has seventy-nine municipalities.[51] The municipality is a unit of local government which is based on meeting the prescribed criteria established by the law (Law on the principles of Local Self-Government of the FBiH; Official Gazette of FBiH, No. 49/06, and 51/09).[52]

D. Brčko District of Bosnia and Herzegovina

22. Brčko District (a third administrative unit) is under international administration.[53] In March 2009, the Constitution of BiH was amended to define Brčko District on the basis of the awards of the Arbitral Tribunal and to ensure the district effective access to the Bosnia and Herzegovina Constitutional Court.

23. Pursuant to Article 1 of Statute of the Brčko District of Bosnia and Herzegovina (7 December 1999)[54]'the Brčko District (hereinafter, the 'District') is a single administrative unit of local self-government existing under the sovereignty of Bosnia and Herzegovina' (point 1). The District is based on the division of powers. The legislative power is exercised by the District Assembly. The executive power is exercised by the District Government. The judicial power is exercised by the District Courts (Article 20).

---

49. Law on federal units (Cantons) (Official Gazette of FBiH, No. 9/96, 30 Jun. 1996). *See also*: SY FBiH 2012, pp. 35–38.
50. UNECE, *3rd Environmental Performance Review, supra* p. 4.
51. *See*: Institute for Statistics of FBiH, *Federation of Bosnia and Herzegovina in Figures*, Sarajevo, 2017. p. 16.
52. *See also* canton's laws on self-government (Law on Local Self-Government of the West Herzegovina Canton, Official Gazette of West Herzegovina Canton, No. 3/09, 18/11; Law on Local Self-Government, Official Gazette of Zenica-Doboj Canton, No. 13/98, 8/00, 2/05; Law on Local Self-Government, Official Gazette of Canton 10, 4/98, 13/00, 10/05).
53. In accordance with the decision by the Arbitrary Commission for Brčko, it becomes a separate district under the authority of BiH. *See* Decision on the establishment of the Brčko District of BiH: http://www.ohr.int/?p=67147 (19 Jul. 2022). https://www.skupstinabd.ba/images/dokumenti/ba/arbitrazna-odluka.pdf (19 Jul. 2022).
54. *See*: https://www.skupstinabd.ba/images/dokumenti/ba/statut-brcko-distrikta.pdf (19 Jul. 2022).

III. Economic Characteristics

24. 'Based on the available macroeconomic indicators for the period 2006-2016, it can be concluded that the BiH economy has marked significant economic progress from year to year. In the period prior to the crisis in 2009, BiH recorded extremely high GDP growth rates of around 6% annually ... ' 'In the period from 2011-2016, the average growth rate of GDP in BiH was 1,8% y/y, whereby in the two last years the economic growth has further intensified, with the growth rate at around 3%.'[55]

25. Bosnia and Herzegovina is a country which had a medium level of economic development before the 1992–1995 war. 'Before the war Bosnia and Herzegovina had a diversified economic structure: Industrial production (43%), Agriculture and Forestry (18%) and Mining (14%) were important and produced the main part of the GDP. Tourism was also well developed. Yugoslavia's military industries were heavily concentrated there, and producing about 40% of Yugoslavia's armaments, were a significant part of the economy.'[56]

26. 'The economy of BiH is based on natural resources and, as such, it has often been environmentally unsustainable. Pollution of water, air and land, cutting of forests and unsustainable mining are the results of such an economy and use of unclean technologies.'[57]

27. The war caused immense human and material losses.[58]'In the post-war period, BiH was going through a triple transition: from war to peace; from international finance aid to sustainable development and from a planned economy and political monopoly towards market economy and democracy.'[59]

'In the post-war period of 1995 to 2000 BiH received large amounts of financial aid intended for humanitarian assistance, economic recovery and reconstruction as well as other forms of assistance (support to democratization, institutional building, etc.). BiH's experience of that period indicates the need to increase the efficiency of international assistance. An important basis for that is stronger reliance on national

---

55. Directorate for European Integration, *Answers to the Questionnaire, Chapter 27, Environment and climate change, Economic criteria*, 27 Feb. 2018.
56. UNECE, *Environmental Performance Review, Bosnia and Herzegovina*, United Nations, New York, Geneva, 2004. p. 5. http://www.unece.org/fileadmin/DAM/env/epr/epr_studies/bosnia_and_herzegovina.pdf (19 Jul. 2022).
57. BiH MFTER, *State of the environment Report of the Bosnia and Herzegovina 2012*, *supra*, p. 53. 'The main challenges which BiH faces and which inevitably affect sustainable production and consumption, are: a high level of unemployment, underdeveloped private sector, unstable institutions and non-existence of institutions, underdeveloped infrastructure – particularly transport infrastructure, insufficient investment into research and development, an educational system not adjusted to market needs, as well as irrational use of energy'. *Ibid.*, p. 53.
58. ' The economy is among the least competitive in the region.' *See*: *The CIA World Factbook Bosnia and Herzegovina*, https://www.cia.gov/the-world-factbook/countries/bosnia-and-herzegovina/ (19 Jul. 2022).
59. Nixon N., (Ed) *Progress towards the Realization of the Millennium Development Goals in Bosnia and Herzegovina 2010*, the Ministry of Finance and Treasury of Bosnia and Herzegovina and the United Nations Country Team in Bosnia and Herzegovina., Sarajevo, 2010., p. 6.

stakeholders as well as better coordination among different donors. At the beginning of this decade, the official development aid (ODA) was very large, accounting for over 10% of GDP in 2001.'[60]

According to the World Bank classification, BiH belongs to the group of 'upper middle income' countries with GNI per capita USD 6,770 (Atlas method, current USD).[61]

28. The privatization programme in Bosnia and Herzegovina has been developed to assist in the economic and social transition. The privatization has had mixed economic and social results at best. According to government officials and representatives of nongovernmental organizations, public opinion of the privatization process is generally negative. Privatization is perceived to have brought very few benefits so far. In particular, the revenues from privatization are low and unemployment remains high.[62] 'Unemployment is particularly high for youth, which at 39 percent remains among the highest in the region.'[63]

29. 'The level of foreign direct investment (FDI) grew from almost zero in 1999 to USD 2 billion in 2007 and although the annual amount dropped to USD 1 billion in 2008, the FDI accumulated between 1999 and 2008 stood at USD 6.3 billion.'[64]

'At the end of the third quarter of 2011, the total balance of the external debt amounted to KM 6.49 billion, which is by KM 199.4 million or 3.2% more than at the end of 2010. Out of the total external debt, the debt to the World Bank – IDA amounted to KM 1.75 billion or 26.9%, which is the largest share of the external debt. In addition to this, the debt to the Paris Club (debt incurred prior to 1992) amounts to KM 825.1 million or 12.7% and the debt to the International Monetary Fund amounts to KM 765.0 or 11.8%.'[65]

30. The economic development of the country shows regional differences, although these disparities are between the municipalities rather than at the entity level. 'Since the last EPR, the differences in per capita net wages between the entities have disappeared. In 2008, the average net wages in the … FBiH and in … RS were almost identical – KM 751 and KM 755 KM per month respectively. GDP per capita almost doubled (1.92 times) between 1997 and 2008 from KM 2,470 to KM 4,758 (in 2005 prices), noticeably increasing the affluence of the population.'[66]

60. *Ibid.*, p. 51.
61. *See*: https://data.worldbank.org/indicator/NY.GNP.PCAP.CD?view=chart&locations=BA (19 Jul. 2022).
62. UNECE, *Environmental Performance Review, Bosnia and Herzegovina, supra* pp. 34, 35.
63. World Bank Group. *Bosnia and Herzegovina, Systematic Country Diagnostic Update*, Report No. 148573-BA, Washington, 2020, p. 34.
64. 'How much of this has been used for environmental projects is unclear, but the inflow of investments has definitely had an effect on the country's post-war economic development and prosperity.' UNECE, *2nd Environmental Performance Review, supra* p. 64.
65. BiH MFTER, *State of the environment Report of the Bosnia and Herzegovina, supra* p. 56.
66. UNECE, *2nd Environmental Performance Review, supra* p. 64.

31. Despite progress in poverty reduction earlier in the decade, poverty was estimated at 14% in 2007.[67] While more recent poverty estimates are not available, other indicators such as unemployment suggest a deterioration in living standards due to the crisis and, as expected, a reversal in poverty reduction. More than 50% of the population report receiving reduced remittances, and almost 40% reduced wages.[68] 'The latest data from 2015 shows that the poverty rate has fallen from 17.9% to 16.9%.'[69]

32. Occupying eighty-first place out of 186 BiH, as captured by the HDI, lags behind countries in the region: Croatia is ranked forty-seventh (belonging to the group of countries with Very High Human Development), Montenegro fifty-second, Serbia sixty-fourth, Albania seventieth, and FYRoM is in seventy-eighth place. In other international comparisons, BiH is also not ranking well: the country is ranked ninety-eighth out of 167 countries in the world in terms of democracy, 126th out of 185 countries in terms of ease of doing business (2013) and seventy-second out of 176 countries in terms of perceptions of corruption (2012).[70]

According to World Bank figures, 'the remittances peaked at US$2.662 billion in 2008, dropping by one-third in two years to US$1.775 billion in 2010 and since then fluctuating at this lower level – the latest available figure, for 2015, was US$1.741 billion'.[71]

67. In 2007, 193,692 households (18.4% of the total number of households) or 627,903 citizens in BiH (18.2% of the total population) lived in relative poverty. This data is a result of different living conditions in three geographic areas in the country. Out of 100 poor households, 55.4% live in the FBiH where almost every sixth household lives in poverty, while in the RS almost every fifth child is poor, while in the BD almost every forth household is poor. BiH MFTER, *State of the environment Report of the Bosnia and Herzegovina, supra* p. 52. *See also*: WB. https://data.worldbank.org/indicator/SI.POV.NAHC?locations=BA (26 Jul. 2022).

68. World Bank Group – Bosnia and Herzegovina, Partnership Country Program Snapshot, April 2013, p. 4. After two years of fragile recovery from the global recession, Bosnia and Herzegovina (BH) experienced a double-dip recession in 2012. After growing by about 1% annually in 2010–11, BH's GDP is estimated to have shrunk by 0.7% in 2012. BH's growth outlook remains subdued. Over the medium term, economic growth is projected to gradually increase from 0.5% in 2013 to 3.5% in 2015. The growth forecast for 2013 remains low, owing to weakening external demand – from the European Union (EU) and the region – caused by the prolonged sovereign debt crisis. *Ibid.*, p. 2. *See also* EC–Directorate-General for Economic and Financial Affairs. *2013 Economic and Fiscal Programmes of Albania and Bosnia and Herzegovina: EU Commission's overview and country Assessments*, Occasional Papers 157, European Commission, Directorate-General for Economic and Financial Affairs, Brussels, July 2013. pp. 20–28.

69. BiH, *Implementation of Agenda 2030 and the Sustainable Development Goals in Bosnia and Herzegovina, Voluntary Review*, April 2019, p. 38. https://sustainabledevelopment.un.org/content/documents/23345VNR_BiH_ENG_Final.pdf (26 Jul. 2022). ' … there are still no countrywide strategies on poverty reduction, social inclusion and protection or a system at state level for monitoring policy implementation'. EC, *Bosnia and Herzegovina 2021 Progress Report*, p. 23.

70. Hodžić-Kovač E., (Ed) *Progress towards the Realisation of Millennium Development Goals in Bosnia and Herzegovina 2013*, Ministry of Finance and Treasury of Bosnia and Herzegovina, Office of the UN Resident Coordinator in Bosnia and Herzegovina, Sarajevo, 2013, p. 14.

71. UNECE. *3rd Environmental Performance Review, Bosnia and Herzegovina, supra* p. 2. 'The level of foreign direct investment (FDI) has declined even more dramatically than remittances. FDI decreased by 74.56 per cent between 2008 and 2015, from US$0.965 billion to US$0.245 billion.' *Ibid.*, p. 2.

IV. Social and Cultural Characteristics

33. Bosnia and Herzegovina is 'based on respect for human dignity, liberty, and equality' (First paragraph of the Preamble of the Constitution). However, in 2007, 193,692 households (18.4% of the total number of households) or 627,903 citizens in BiH (18.2% of the total population) lived in relative poverty:[72]

> it is evident that the social position of the population of BiH is extremely difficult. The burden of poverty particularly affects those who belong to marginalized groups, above all – refugees and displaced persons, older persons, youth, persons with disabilities, the Roma, who are most numerous marginalized group in BiH, but also the most vulnerable population groups and others.[73]

34. The link between poverty and a poor economic state and degradation of the environment in BiH is primarily reflected in an inadequate discharge and treatment of wastewater, inadequate waste management (inadequate disposal of municipal waste and waste from industrial plants), influences of old abandoned industrial waste disposal sites from earlier periods that have not been remediated, pollution of air by emissions from traffic and industrial plants with old technological processes, deforestation caused by commercial exploitation and cutting firewood, etc.[74] However, 'there are indications that society at large and policymakers have come to understand that developing the economy, solving numerous social problems and protecting the environment must be considered simultaneously and do not have to be mutually exclusive'.[75]

35. According to the Situation Analysis on Human Resources at the Labour Market in BiH, the level of education is low, in comparison to EU standards. It has been estimated that 41.8% (30.6% men and 53% of women) have a low qualifications level, 47.4% (56.8% men and 38% of women) have medium fifty-two qualifications level, while 10.8% (12.6% men and 9% of women) have a high qualifications level. The level of education of women in BiH is especially low – when compared to EU standards. From the gender perspective, this is alarming evidence. Groups with low education levels lack some of the basic skills, vocational capacities and the basis for lifelong learning.[76]

---

72. *See also* Hodžić-Kovač E., (Ed) *Progress towards the Realisation of Millennium Development Goals in Bosnia and Herzegovina 2013, supra* p. 23. The poverty rate in 2015 was 17%, a 1-point reduction from 2011: Today over 170,000 households and half a million people in BiH are living below the BiH poverty line. *Bosnia and Herzegovina and the United Nations Sustainable Development Cooperation Framework, A Partnership for Sustainable Development, 2021-2025*, Sarajevo 2021, p. 19. https://unece.org/sites/default/files/2021-05/2021-2025_UNSDC_BiH.pdf (27 Jul. 2022).
73. Ministry of Human Rights and Refugees, *The Second Periodic Report of Bosnia and Herzegovina on International Covenant on Economic, Social and Cultural Rights*, Sarajevo, 2010, p. 29.
74. BiH MFTER, *State of the environment Report of the Bosnia and Herzegovina 2012, supra* p. 53.
75. UNECE, *Environmental Performance Review, Bosnia and Herzegovina, supra* p. 26.
76. Nixon N., (Ed) *Progress towards the Realization of the Millennium Development Goals in Bosnia and Herzegovina 2010, supra* p. 24.

36. The educational system is financed from the entity, cantonal and municipal budgets. The share of educational funding from the state budget is small. RS allocates about 4% of GDP for education, while the FBiH allocates about 6% of total GDP, and in the Brčko District is allocated 11.2% of the District budget.[77]

37. The goal from Poverty Reduction Strategy Paper (PRSP) for 2007 was to achieve a 12% preschool enrolment rate and to achieve a 25% enrolment rate by 2015. The percentage of children attending preschool institutions in 2006 was 6.4% with a somewhat higher rate for girls (8%) compared to boys (4.7%). For the purpose of reaching Millennium Development Goals 2 (MDG2), the PRSP set the expected primary education enrolment rate at 99% in 2007 and 100% in 2015. The net primary school enrolment rate in 2001 was between 92.8% and 98.9%, depending on the data source. The net primary education attendance rate in 2006 was 97.9% implying that there are 1% to 2% of children of primary school age in BiH not attending primary school. According to 2001 data, the secondary education enrolment rate ranged from 56.8% to 68.3%, depending on the source of data, and according to 2006 data, from 80.3% to 89.3%, while the attendance rate was 79.3%.[78]

The higher education enrolment rate in 2001 was 19.8%. In the period from 2001 to 2010, the number of students at the higher education institutions almost doubled.[79]

38. 'The official languages of the Republic of Srpska are: the language of the Serb people, the language of the Bosniak people and the language of the Croat people. The official scripts are Cyrillic and Latin. In regions inhabited by groups speaking other languages, their languages and alphabet shall also be in official use, as specified by law.' (Article 7. of the Constitution of RS, Official Gazette of RS, Nos. 6/92, 8/92, 15/92, 19/92, 21/92, 28/94, 8/96, 13/96, 15/96, 16/96, 21/96, 36/00, 31/02, 69/02, 31/03, 98/03).[80]

Pursuant to Article 6 of the Constitution of FBiH (Official Gazette of FBiH, Nos. 1/94, 13/97, 16/02, 22/02, 52/02, 60/02, 18/03, 63/03) 'the official languages of the Federation of BiH shall be: Bosnian language, Croat language and Serb language. The official scripts shall be Latin and Cyrillic. ... Other languages may be used as a means of communication and instruction'.

V. Main Environmental Problems

39. The main environmental problems stem from several factors, including the following: the characteristics of the economic structure of Bosnia and Herzegovina

77. Bratović E., Lepić S., *Education for Sustainable Development, Bosnia and Herzegovina, Research Report*, Promente, Sarajevo, 2011. p. 12.
78. Nixon N., (Ed) *Progress towards the Realization of the Millennium Development Goals in Bosnia and Herzegovina 2010, supra* p. 23.
79. *Ibid.*, p. 24.
80. *See also*: Republic of Srpska Institute of statistic, *Statistical Yearbook of Republic of Srpska*, 2013, *supra* p. 29.

and its position in the former Yugoslavia (heavy industry), massive war destruction, slow recovery after the war, the current level of economic development, the consequences of privatization and so on. BiH today is 'still suffering from a legacy of environmental neglect and deterioration resulting from a governance system that failed to take into account the sustainability of economic and infrastructure developments, the impact of economic deterioration and conflict in the region. Initially in the immediate aftermath of the regional conflict, environmental protection was not generally perceived to be of high importance'.[81] 'Environmental standards have remained low and are often neglected, leading to high levels of pollution, impeding the health (and thus productivity) of the country's labour force and constituting an additional factor supporting the brain drain.'[82]

40. The major cause of pollution in BiH lies in the sphere of energy and industry. At the same time, a specific characteristic is an energy-intensive economy.[83] Alignment with the EU acquis on industrial pollution control and risk management remains very limited.[84]

Within the framework of the planned strategic development of BiH, as an integral federal unit of former Yugoslavia, it was envisaged to provide raw materials and energy for economic development of the country and space for the development of basic and military industries.[85]'Therefore, the intensive exploitation of natural resources, for which mainly obsolete and highly polluting technologies were used, and the resulting degradation of environment, along with the fact that it was the state (and not the market) that dictated the prices of raw materials and energy, did not offer chances for balanced development in which economy and environment would be in harmony, in other words, did not open the prospects for sustainable development of Bosnia and Herzegovina.'[86]

---

81. BiH MFTER. *Environmental Approximation Strategy of Bosnia and Herzegovina*, EAS – BiH, Ministry of Foreign Trade and Economic Relations of Bosnia and Herzegovina, May 2017, p. 25.
82. EC, *Bosnia and Herzegovina 2021 Progress Report*, p. 54.
83. For more information *see also*: https://www.eea.europa.eu/soer/2015/countries/bosnia-and-herzegovina (19 Jul. 2022).
84. EC, *Bosnia and Herzegovina 2021 Progress Report*, p. 104. BiH has reported on the implementation of the national emissions reduction plan (NERP) in 2020 to the Energy Community Secretariat (EnCS), and the EnCS 'initiated a dispute settlement procedure against Bosnia and Herzegovina for not meeting their NERP ceilings for emissions of certain pollutants into the air from large combustion plants for the reporting years 2018 and 2019.' *ibid.*
85. 'Even prior to the war, the economy of B&H was characterized by the indiscriminate consumption of resources, making it the one of the most polluted regions of Yugoslavia.' Thompson, S. Status of the environment in Bosnia and Herzegovina: current assessment. *Georgetown International Environmental Law Review,* 12(1)/1999, pp. 247–268.
86. Bosnia and Herzegovina, *Assessment of sustainable development in Bosnia and Herzegovina,* The Report of BiH for The World Summit on Sustainable development (WSSD), Project of preparation of Bosnia and Herzegovina for participation on The World Summit on Sustainable Development Rio+10, Johannesburg 28 Aug.–04 Sept. 2002, Sarajevo, Banja Luka, Mostar – June 2002. p. 6. Relatively large hydro and thermal energy potentials and large supplies of coal and metal ores, enabled it to produce more than half of the Yugoslav output in coal, 70% of the output in metal ores, iron, aluminium, lead and zin and almost 50% of the electric energy. Also, substantial part of former Yugoslavia's chemical industry (which used nitrogen and chlorine as basis) was situated in Bosnia and Herzegovina.

41. 'The level of social and economic environmental pressures in BiH in the last two decades has been predetermined by the country's development characterized by war-time aftermaths, transition process and introduction of European standards necessary for accession to the European Union (EU).'[87] The privatization has had mixed economic and social results and impact on the state of environment and environmental policy. The stated goals of privatization include economic recovery, post-war reconstruction and transition to the market economy; social stability; settlement of outstanding claims; increased employment; and liquidation of domestic and foreign debts accumulated by enterprises, banks and the State. They do not mention improving the environmental situation at the privatized enterprises or any other environmental considerations.[88] The promotion of environmental investments in the privatization process has been made by introducing clauses on past liabilities and requirements on environmental compliance plans, as recommended. However, there is still a large presence of an often unprofitable and inefficient public sector, which is involved in a wide range of activities, discouraging private capital flows.[89]

42. Before the war overall air quality was poor: large energy and metallurgy plants, built for the needs of the former Yugoslavia, generated much pollution. The overall recession and the decline in activity in particular in the industrial sector, as a result of the war, have significantly relieved pressure on air quality.[90]

Air pollution in BiH generally arises from industrial activities and traffic. Industrial process emissions have decreased compared to the pre-war period and as pre-war production levels have not yet been reached, air quality status in BiH is better than it was prior to the 1990s. However, a constant increase in traffic leads to rising traffic emissions which mostly affect major urban centres. Due to specific climate conditions and temperature inversions, air pollution is significantly pronounced in the winter months in larger urban areas, and especially in cities located in valleys where emissions become 'trapped' for longer periods of time.[91] It is estimated that about 3,300 people die prematurely every year as a result of exposure to ambient PM2.5 air pollution in BiH. About 16% of this health burden is carried by Sarajevo and Banja Luka.[92]

---

87. BiH MFTER, *State of the environment Report of the Bosnia and Herzegovina 2012*, *supra* p. 32. The State of the Environment Report of BiH 2012 (Report) is the first report on the state of the environment of the country of BiH and it presents one of the founding documents on environmental protection in BiH. *Ibid.*, 27. Apart from that Report on the state of the environment in the Federation of Bosnia and Herzegovina-2010 was published. *See*: FMET, *State of the environment in Federation of Bosnia and Herzegovina-2010 Report*, Federal Ministry of Environment and Tourism, Sarajevo, June 2010. Republic of Srpska has not published a report on the state of the environment.
88. UNECE, *Environmental Performance Review, Bosnia and Herzegovina*, *supra* p. 34.
89. UNECE. *3rd Environmental Performance Review, Bosnia and Herzegovina*, *supra* p. 235.
90. UNECE, *Environmental Performance Review, Bosnia and Herzegovina*, *supra.*, p. 69.
91. BiH MFTER, *State of the environment Report of the Bosnia and Herzegovina 2012*, *supra* pp. 36, 37.
92. WB. *Air Pollution Management in Bosnia and Herzegovina*. Report No: AUS0001227, October 2019. https://documents1.worldbank.org/curated/en/117281576515111584/pdf/Air-Quality-Management-in-Bosnia-and-Herzegovina.pdf (1 Aug. 2022), p. V.

43. BiH is highly vulnerable to climate change. Exposure to threats from climate change will be considerable. The country also has a high sensitivity to these threats because of the economic role of 'climate-sensitive' sectors, such as agriculture and forestry (and the role of hydropower in the energy sector to a lesser extent), with significant secondary impacts. Finally, BiH has very limited adaptive capacity to address climate risks.[93] BiH 'remains heavily reliant on lignite coal and still plans to increase its energy generation based on fossile fuels, jeopordising its commitments to decarbonisation and climate neutrality by 2050'.[94]

Greenhouse gas (GHG) emissions in BiH are estimated to grow by almost 30% between 2005 and 2030, driven by the increase in CO2 emissions. Currently, 73% of GHG emissions originate from the energy sector, followed by 13.5% from agriculture, and 10.4% from industry. The energy sector of BiH is mostly based on coal, which represented around 45% of total primary energy supply in 2005, followed by liquid fuels (21%), renewable energy (20%), and hydropower (10%). The impact of land use change and forestry represents almost 22% of gross national emissions.[95] BiH was among the first countries to submit in April 2021 its revised NDC for 2020–2030 to the UNFCCC.[96] It plans to reduce GHG emissions for slightly more than one-third by 2030, and almost two-thirds (about 66%) by 2050 compared to 1990.[97]

44. Waste is generally one of the most significant environmental issues in BiH. 'Inappropriately placed and unprotected waste dumpsites pose a serious threat to the environment and public health in BiH and, possibly, also to neighbouring States. Treatment facilities for medical and hazardous waste are still lacking. There are also only limited attempts to reduce and recycle industrial and municipal waste. Improving the treatment of industrial and medical waste, municipal waste management, and reduction and recycling of waste still remains a challenge, although there are signs of progress in the development of policies and laws, and modest investments in appropriate infrastructure have been made.'[98]

---

93. BiH MFTER, Ministry of Physical Planning, Civil Engineering and Ecology of Republic of Srpska, Federal Ministry of Environment and Tourism, UNDP, *Initial National Communication of Bosnia and Herzegovina under the United Nations Framework Convention on Climate Change, supra* p. 16. For more information *see also*: Knežević, A., Kaplina, A., Husika, A., Carrington, D., Arnautović Aksić, D., Jordan, G., Trbić, G., Stritih, J., Tabaković, L., Kotur, M. Cupać, R. *Strategija prilago avanja na klimatske promjene i niskoemisionog razvoja za Bosnu i Hercegovinu*[Climate Change Adaptation and Low Emission Development Strategy for BiH], juni 2013. http://www.unfccc.ba/site /publikacije/spkp.pdf (19 Jul. 2022). http://www.ba.undp.org/content/bosnia_and_herzegovina/en/ home/library/environment_energy/climate-change-adaptation-and-low-emission-development-strategy-.html (19 Jul. 2022).
94. EC, *Bosnia and Herzegovina 2021 Progress Report*, p. 95.
95. UNECE, *Environmental Performance Review, Bosnia and Herzegovina, supra* p. XXVII, 79–86.
96. EC, *Bosnia and Herzegovina 2021 Progress Report*, p. 105.
97. For more information, *see*: BiH. Nationally Determined Contribution of Bosnia and Herzegovina (NDC) for the period 2020-2030. https://www.vladars.net/sr-SP-Cyrl/Vlada/Ministarstva/mgr/ Documents/NDC%20BiH%20_170460761.pdf (29 Jul. 2022); https://unfccc.int/sites/default/files/ NDC/2022-06/NDC%20BiH_November%202020%20FINAL%20DRAFT%2005%20Nov%20 ENG%20LR.pdf (29 Jul. 2022).
98. UNECE, *2nd Environmental Performance Review, supra* p. 103.

'Since 2003, generated municipal waste in BiH has been constantly increasing, and in 2010 it amounted to 332 kg per capita. The level of service coverage is 68%. Waste collection is generally performed by municipal utility companies entirely or partially state-owned or in some cases, by private companies contracted by municipalities. Reliable statistical data on generation of packaging waste in BiH is non-existent, but estimates indicate that annual quantities of packaging waste amount to approximately 240,000 tones.'[99]

45. Soil degradation is increasing, and land use changes and loss of agricultural land are caused by sudden urbanization, industrialization, and changes to commercial development. Opencast mining or opencast exploitation of mineral ores has resulted in approximately 15,000 ha of damaged land in BiH, while disposals of fly ash and slag occupy an area of approximately 250 ha.[100]

'Land degradation stands out as one of the most critical environmental problems in Bosnia and Herzegovina.'[101]

'Most anthropogenic pressures on water are caused by urban zones without sewerage and wastewater treatment plants (WWTPs) or uncontrolled leachates from solid waste sites without proper treatment.'[102]

46. The population in BiH covered by public water supply services is 58%. Losses in the water supply network are estimated between 30% and 50%, and the uncharged water level is between 25% and 75%. According to estimates from strategic documents, only 33% of the population is connected to public sewage systems, while only some municipalities in the FBiH and one in the RS have functioning wastewater treatment plants. The rest is directly discharged into receiving water bodies.[103]

47. A number of problems have been created in the coastal area as a consequence of a permanent and strong pressure of competitive demands for land on the coast. However, 'the Bosnian part of the Adriatic is still one of the best-preserved regions in the European part of the Mediterranean. But, wastewaters flowing from the hinterland into the sea are the biggest polluters ... '[104] In the whole coastal area, there is no suitable landfill for controlled disposal of solid waste or its processing. Illegal construction, often followed by the lack of qualitative spatial plans, which, among others, do not include environment as an integral development component, poses a big threat to coastal area.[105]

---

99. BiH MFTER, *State of the environment Report of the Bosnia and Herzegovina 2012*, *supra* p. 34.
100. *Ibid.*, p. 35.
101. UNECE. *3rd Environmental Performance Review, Bosnia and Herzegovina*, *supra* p. 88.
102. *Ibid.*, p. xxvi.
103. BiH MFTER, *State of the environment Report of the Bosnia and Herzegovina 2012*, *supra* pp. 35, 36.
104. UNEP, PAP, PC, *National Report on Current Policy, Procedures, Legal Basis and Practice of Marine Spatial Planning in Bosnia and Herzegovina*, Mostar, May 2007. p. 29.
105. *Ibid.*, p. 30.

48. With respect to biological diversity, BiH is rich in terms of genetic and species diversity, as well as diversity of ecosystems. However, 'there are no accurate and up-to-date general and specific data on status of biological diversity in BiH. Systematic gathering and analysis of data on biodiversity and monitoring status of biological diversity is almost non existent'.[106]

'Despite one of the highest levels of biodiversity in Europe, BiH is still the country with the lowest expanse of protected areas among European countries. The majority of external and domestic sources give a figure of 0.55% coverage of the total territory (although some sources give a figure of as much as 2.2%).'[107]

It is possible to identify pressures on different levels of biodiversity. On the level of genetic and species diversity the most intensive pressures are: habitats conversion, unsustainable use of resources, permanent pollution of all environmental spheres, devastation and destruction of ecosystems, degradation and fragmentation of ecosystems, disturbance in wilderness, logging, hunt and poaching, unsustainable gathering of economically important species, uncontrolled use of pesticides and fertilizers, uncontrolled introduction of alien species, uncontrolled introduction and manipulation with GMOs.[108]

49. Public health from the environmental aspect is still an insufficiently explored area in BiH. Public health institutes report on epidemiological data, but no data directly linking environmental factors and human health (air pollution, summer heat waves, etc.) exist. A lack of targeted research regarding specific environmental pollution and its consequences on human health is evident.[109]

For BiH, the annual mortality rate (per 100,000 people) attributed to household and ambient air pollution is estimated by the WHO at 223.6 in 2012 (World Health Statistics, 2016), which is one of the highest mortality rates by air pollution in the world.[110]

50. The presence of depleted uranium 'became a concern in BiH, since depleted uranium was used in the shelling at around 11 locations between 1994 and

106. MFTER, *Sixth National Report of Bosnia and Herzegovina to the Convention on Biological Diversity*, Ministry of Foreign Trade and Economic Relations of Bosnia and Herzegovina, 2019, p. 211.
107. Based on the data collected from different sources during the second EPR mission, protected areas which are designated in line with current legislation (including virgin forests) cover 0.84% of the national territory (FBiH, 0.85% and RS, 0.83%). Although this figure is higher than that provided by other sources, it still leaves the country at the very bottom of the European list and far below EU requirements (Habitat Directive). Existing significant variations in data stress the need to undertake a full national inventory and cadastre of protected areas. UNECE, *Environmental Performance Review, Bosnia and Herzegovina, supra* p. 129.
108. *Bosnia and Herzegovina Fourth Report to the United Nations Convention on Biological Diversity*, 2010 Biodiversity Targets National Assessments, April 2010, p. 16.
109. Even though there is still no systematic reporting on toxic chemicals and substances in all segments of the environment, there are information sources which clearly state that water, soil, and food in BiH contain certain concentrations of harmful substances. BiH MFTER, *State of the environment Report of the Bosnia and Herzegovina 2012, supra* p. 37.
110. UNECE. *3rd Environmental Performance Review, Bosnia and Herzegovina, supra* p. 135.

1995'.[111] 'A total of 11 sites known to be attacked in 1994-1995 by A-10 planes using 30 mm DU ammunition was published by NATO … '[112] DU was found at three sites; the former Tank Repair Facility and former Ammunition Storage Depot in Hadzici, Han Pijesak Artillery Storage and Barracks. Clear and unambiguous findings of penetrators or contamination points on the ground and soil were found at each of these sites, as well as water contamination at one site, air contamination at two sites, and in botanical samples taken at three sites.[113]

51. From the aspect of environmental and human safety, landslides, wildfires and floods represent a significant issue in BiH. The experiences with floods and landslides in 2014 in BiH, but also in the wider area of the Balkans, 'clearly indicate the need to improve regulation and practices in disaster risk management'.[114] Aside from this, it is estimated that 'total minefield contamination amounts to 1,176.5 square kilometres or 2.3% of the total surface area of the country'.[115] As regards landmines from the 1992–1995 conflict, implementation of the mine action strategy has been slow. … Since September 2013, six people have been killed and nine injured in landmine accidents. '[116] Mine Action Strategy in Bosnia and Herzegovina for the period 2018–2025 has been adopted at 165th session of BiH Ministry Council. [117]

§2. Basic Principles of Environmental Law

I. Basic Principles

52. The basic principles of environmental law are defined in the environmental protection laws of the Republic of Srpska (Articles 6–13), the Federation of Bosnia and Herzegovina (Articles 5–11) and the Brčko District of Bosnia and Herzegovina (Articles 5–11), as follows:

(a) Sustainable development principle.
(b) Principles of precaution and prevention.
(c) Substitution principle.
(d) Principle of integration.
(e) Principle of cooperation and division of responsibilities.

111. BiH MFTER, *State of the environment Report of the Bosnia and Herzegovina 2012, supra* p. 191.
112. UNEP, *Depleted Uranium in Bosnia and Herzegovina Post-Conflict Environmental Assessment*, Nairobi, March, 2003, p. 23.
113. *Ibid.*, p. 29.
114. For more information *see*: Abolmasov, B. *Landslide Risk Management Study in Bosnia and Herzegovina*, UNDP, 2016.
115. UNDP in Bosnia and Herzegovina, *Human Development Report 2016, Risk-Proofing the Western Balkans: Empowering People to Prevent Disasters*, Sarajevo, 2016, p. 52. https://hdr.undp.org/system/files/documents//riskproofingthewesternbalkanspdf.pdf (19 Jul. 2022).
116. EC. *Bosnia and Herzegovina 2014 Progress Report*, p. 22.
117. For the text of Bosnia and Herzegovina Mine Action Strategy 2018 – 2025, See: http://bhmac.org/?page_id=624&lang=en (27 Jul. 2022).

(f) Public participation and access to information.
(g) 'Polluter pays' principle.[118]

II. Constitutional Providers

A. Bosnia and Herzegovina

53. The BiH Constitution does not contain explicit provisions on environmental protection and sustainable development. Environmental policies and natural resource use are the responsibility of entity and BD governments which regulate environmental matters through laws, regulations and standards. However, according to the Article IV.4a of the Constitution of BiH:

> the Parliamentary Assembly shall have responsibility for: a) Enacting legislation as necessary to implement decisions of the Presidency or to carry out the responsibilities of the Assembly under this Constitution.

B. The Republic of Srpska

54. Pursuant to Article 35 of the Constitution of RS (Official Gazette of RS, Nos 21/92 – revised text, 28/94, 8/96, 13/96, 15/96, 16/96, 21/96, 21/02, 26/02, 30/02, 31/02, 69/02, 31/03, 98/03, 115/05 and 117/05) 'everyone shall have the right to a healthy environment' and 'everyone shall be bound, in accordance with law and within his possibilities, to protect and improve the environment' (Article 35).[119] Apart from that, the Constitution defines that the RS organizes and provides environmental protection (Amendment XXXII, item 13) (Article 68) and 'protects and encourages' 'the rational use of natural resources with the view of protecting and improving the quality of life and protecting and reviving the environment to the general benefit' (Article 64).

C. Federation of Bosnia and Herzegovina

55. According to the Constitution of FBiH (Official Gazette of FBiH, Nos 1/94, 13/97, 16/02, 22/02, 52/02, 63/03, 9/04, 20/04, 33/04, 71/05, 72/05 and 88/08), Chapter III, Article 2, paragraph (c), the environmental protection policy is in the joint responsibility of the FBiH and cantons. In the Constitution of FBiH, there is

118. For more information *see also*: Directorate for European Integration, *Answers to the Questionnaire, Chapter 27, Environment and climate change*, 27 Feb. 2018, pp. 11–13.
119. Free enterprise may exceptionally be restricted by law for the purposes of protecting the interest of the Republic, the human environment, health and security of people (Art. 52). The use and exploitation of property of special cultural, scientific, artistic or historical significance, or significant for the protection of nature or the environment, may be restricted against a full compensation to the owner (Art. 59).

no explicit provision which defines the responsibility for sustainable development, however, items (d) and (i) of Chapter III, Article I are relevant to this responsibility and therein it is specified that the FBiH is exclusively responsible for defining the economic and energy policy.

D. Statute of Brčko District of Bosnia and Herzegovina

56. The responsibility of the BD for environmental protection is defined in Article 8 of the Statute of the BD – 7 December 1999 (Official Gazette of BD BiH, Nos 17/08 and 39/09).

§3. Historical Background of Environmental Law

57. Bosnia and Herzegovina has a long and rich history and a cultural heritage which is a mix of different influences. 'Spatial diversity and its processes have been influenced by a series of historical circumstances. At the crossroad between East and West, BiH has always been the meeting place of different cultures, nations and civilizations.'[120]'For centuries, different social and political systems have succeeded one another in BiH, starting from the feudal state, through the Ottoman, Austro-Hungarian to the Socialist Republic of BiH in the framework of the Socialist Federal Republic of Yugoslavia.'[121]

58. 'In November 1943, a partisan congress in Jajce, proclaimed a new federal Yugoslavia. BiH with its mixed multi-ethnic Serb, Bosniak (Muslim) and Croat populations was established as one of six constituent republics of Yugoslavia.'[122] It had that status until 1991, with a population of 4,377,000 (1990) and USD 2,429 GDP per capita.[123]

59. The United States and the EU recognized the independence of the BiH on 6 April 1992, 'but a war erupted the same week, escalating to a conflict in which all three ethnic groups tried to consolidate their control over the country'.[124]

Following the successful negotiation of the Dayton Peace Agreement in November 1995,[125] a Peace Implementation Conference was held in London on 8–9

120. BiH MFTER, *State of the environment Report of the Bosnia and Herzegovina 2012*, *supra* p. 32.
121. *Ibid.*, p. 43. For more information on history *see*: Filipović O. (Ed) *Parliamentary Assembly of Bosnia and Herzegovina*, Sarajevo: Parliamentary Assembly of Bosnia and Herzegovina, 2010.
122. UNECE, *Environmental Performance Review, BiH*, *supra* p. 3.
123. Bosnia and Herzegovina, *Assessment of Sustainable Development in BiH*, 2002. *supra* p. 5.
124. UNECE, *Environmental Performance Review, BiH*, *supra* p. 3.
125. For more information on The General Framework Agreement for Peace in BiH *see*: http://www.ohr.int/?page_id=1258 (19 Jul. 2022). The Constitution of BiH is an Annex to the General Framework Agreement for Peace in BiH (Dayton Peace Accords). Constitution of BiH is part of the Dayton Peace Agreement.

December 1995, to mobilize international support for the Agreement. The meeting resulted in the establishment of the Peace Implementation Council.[126]

The Peace Agreement defined the Constitution of BiH and established a complex state, composed of two entities (FBiH and RS) to which, later on, following the international arbitration decision, Brčko District of BiH was added as an independent administrative unit within BiH.[127]

60. 'Recent developments in the history of BiH have also had an extremely strong impact on the area of natural resource management. In the period before 1992, the 1965 Law on Nature Protection provided protection to 144 areas of different sizes and levels of protection in the territory of BiH.'[128]

Under the Dayton Agreement, all laws from the former Socialist Republic of BiH that are not inconsistent with the 1995 Constitution may remain in force. In terms of the environment, this was particularly relevant for several years of application of the Law on Physical Planning of 1987.[129] This law was replaced by FBiH's 2002 Law on Physical Planning (OG FBiH 52/2002) and the RS's Law on Physical Planning (OG RS 84/2002).

61. 'BiH started accession negotiations with the European Union (EU) in November 2005 and is at present a potential candidate for membership.'[130] The Stabilization and Association Agreement between Bosnia and Herzegovina and the EU was ratified in 2011 but has not yet entered into force. 'All EU Member States have ratified the Stabilization and Association Agreement (SAA) signed in June 2008, but the Council has refrained from taking a decision on its entering into force due to the country's failure to implement the Sejdić-Finci ruling of the European Court of Human Rights (ECtHR).'[131] The country submitted its application for EU membership in February 2016. Following the recognition of meaningful progress in the implementation of the Reform Agenda, in September 2016 the EU Council invited

126. *See*: http://www.ohr.int/?page_id=1220 (19 Jul. 2022).
127. 'The major part of the competences or responsibilities for social, economic, educational, health care issues and industrial development, and for use of the country's natural resources, including the authority to grant concessions on exploitation of natural resources to domestic or foreign concessionaires, i.e., the fundamental factors for controlling the sustainable development, are practically in the hands of the entities; furthermore, the BiH Federation additionally shares the powers with lower administrative units i.e., cantons, which have significant competences'. BiH, *Assessment of Sustainable Development in BiH*, 2002., *supra* p. 6.
128. This Law established sixteen strict nature reserves, nine administered (managed) nature reserves, two national parks, six special reserves, ten reserves of natural landscapes and even 110 nature monuments, among which there were numerous BiH's waterfalls, streams, springs, wells, mountain lakes, grottoes and caves. *BiH Fourth Report to the United Nations Convention on Biological Diversity*, 2010, *supra* p. 32.
129. Juelich R. *Progress in Environmental Law Drafting in South Eastern Europe*, Regional Environmental Centre, Szentendre, Hungary, December 2005, p. 73.
130. *See*: https://ec.europa.eu/neighbourhood-enlargement/enlargement-policy/bosnia-and-herzegovina_en (19 Jul. 2022). *See also*: BiH Council of Ministers, *EU Integration Strategy of Bosnia and Herzegovina*, Directorate for European Integration. 2004.
131. EC, *Bosnia and Herzegovina 2013 Progress Report,* 2013, *supra* p. 4. 'Bosnia and Herzegovina's Constitution remains in breach of the European Convention on Human Rights (ECHR), following the Sejdić-Finci and related cases.' EC, *Bosnia and Herzegovina 2021 Progress Report,* 2021, p. 4.

the European Commission to submit its opinion on Bosnia and Herzegovina's application for EU membership.[132] In December 2016 the European Commission handed over its Questionnaire as official document by which the EU assessed the readiness of a country to begin accession process. BiH submitted answers to the questions from the EC Questionnaire (February 2018),[133] received follow-up questions from the EC Questionnaire (June 2018),[134] and submitted its answers to additional questions (March 2019).[135] After all that, the European Commission issued its Opinion on Bosnia and Herzegovina's application for EU membership (29 May 2019).[136]

62. 'BiH is also negotiating its entry into the World Trade Organization (WTO) and since April 2010, has been a candidate for NATO membership. It has been a member of the Council of Europe since 24 April 2002 and was a founding member of the Mediterranean Union upon its establishment on 13 July 2008. In 2006, the country signed the Central European Free Trade Agreement (CEFTA) with neighbouring countries.'[137]

63. New environmental legislation has been prepared through the EU project, 'Preparation of Environmental Law and Policy in BiH'.[138] The environmental laws include: Law on the Protection of the Environment, Law on the Protection of the Waters, Law on the Protection of the Nature, Law on Waste Management and Law on the Protection of the Air. The environmental laws were passed in the Republic of Srpska in September 2002, in addition to the Law on the Waters. In the Federation of BiH, the environmental laws were passed in July 2003. These laws are very similar in both entities, although not identical, and reflect the goals and principles of EC environmental directives. 'Differences lay mainly in the allocation of responsibilities to the different public authorities in charge of environmental protection, given the different organisational structure of the two entities. Drafting of these six laws began in 1998 and mostly concluded in 2001.'[139]

64. The National Environmental Action Plan (NEAP) for BiH was completed at the beginning of 2003 supported by World Bank, and adopted by the entities' Governments after open public discussion.[140] NEAP identified eight priorities: water resource management and wastewater treatment, waste and waste management, sustainable development in rural areas, environmental management, protection of biological and landscape diversity, economy and sustainable development, public health and demining.

132. EC. *Bosnia and Herzegovina 2016 Progress Report*, p. 75.
133. https://www.dei.gov.ba/en/odgovori-na-upitnik-ek (7 Feb. 2022)
134. https://www.dei.gov.ba/uploads/documents/follow-up-questions_1615884049.pdf (7 Feb. 2022)
135. https://www.dei.gov.ba/en/odgovori-na-dodatna-pitanja-iz-upitnika (7 Feb. 2022).
136. EC, *Commission Opinion on Bosnia and Herzegovina's application for membership of the European Union*, 2019.
137. UNECE, *2nd Environmental Performance Review, supra* p. 3.
138. Regional Environmental Centre for BiH. 2002. *Regional Centre report on the status and needs of the environmental legislation in BiH.* 25 Jan–15 Mar. 2002.
139. Juelich R. *Progress in Environmental Law Drafting in South Eastern Europe, supra* p. 73.
140. NEAP is a key and first document for BiH to identify and prioritize environmental issues. *See*: http://web.worldbank.org/archive/website00983A/WEB/PDF/BOSNIA_N.PDF (19 Jul. 2022).

§4. The Role of Governmental Institutions in the Shaping and Administration of Environmental Law and Policy

I. Bosnia and Herzegovina

65. 'Bosnia and Herzegovina is a decentralized country with a high level of legislative autonomy given to the entities and BD of BiH. In the context of environmental protection, BiH authorities have very limited competence, as it was noted earlier, and most of the EU legal requirements have been transposed or will be transposed by the entities and BD of BiH legislation.'[141] Specific jurisdictions are assigned to BiH Ministry of Foreign Trade and Economic Relations (MFTER) over protection of the environment under the Law on Ministries and other administrative bodies of BiH (Official Gazette of BiH, Nos 5/03, 42/03, 26/04, 42/04, 45/06, 88/07, 35/09, 59/09, 103/09, 87/12, 6/13 and 19/16).[142] The Plant Health Protection Administration of BiH (PHPA)[143] is an administrative organization of the MFTER, responsible for the protection of plant health, production and sale of seed and seedling, protection of new varieties, market and use of phytopharmaceutical products (PPP) and mineral fertilizers.[144] The Veterinary Office of BiH was established by the decision of the Council of Ministers of 18 December 2000.[145]

66. The Food Safety Agency of BiH (FSA)[146] is an independent administrative organization established by the decision 60 of the Council of Ministers, the authority for food safety and quality, for application of international conventions and agreements in the field of food safety and animal feed which are binding for the country.[147]

67. An Inter-Entity Environmental Protection Body was established in 2006 with the purpose of cooperation and coordination between entities and BD BiH in realization of common goals and protection of environmental interests.[148] It deals

141. BiH MFTER. *Environmental Approximation Strategy of Bosnia and Herzegovina*, EAS – BiH, Ministry of Foreign Trade and Economic Relations of Bosnia and Herzegovina, May 2017, p. 108.
142. Pursuant to the relevant sublegal act of the Ministry, 16 civil servants and 2 non-civil service staff members are currently employed in the Division for Water Resources, Tourism and Environmental Protection. Division includes three sections: Office of Assistant Minister, Section for Water Resources, Section for Tourism, and Section for Environmental Protection. Directorate for European Integration, *Answers to the Questionnaire, Chapter 27, Environment and climate change*, p. 49. https://www.dei.gov.ba/en/odgovori-na-upitnik-ek (19 Jul. 2022).
143. *See* details on the website: http://uzzb.gov.ba/sr/sr (6 Feb. 2022).
144. By the Decision of the Council of Ministers of BiH–the Plant Health Protection Administration has been appointed to coordinate the implementation of the Rotterdam Convention in BiH.
145. *See*: http://vet.gov.ba/v2/?lang=en (6 Feb. 2022).
146. *See*: https://fsa.gov.ba/fsa/sr/ (6 Feb. 2022).
147. Pursuant to the Law on Food (Official Gazette of BiH, No 50/04), the Food Safety Agency is responsible for risk analysis (assessment, management and communication of risk), initiation, preparation, drafting and proposing regulations on food, as well as other tasks from this area.
148. *See* the Art. 41 of the Law on environment protection of the FBiH, and Art. 41 of the Law on Environmental Protection of the RS. The Body meets at least six times a year and reaches decisions by consensus. The BiH Ministry of Foreign Trade and Economic relations is regularly informed about

with all environmental protection issues which require a harmonized approach of both Entities and is competent for harmonizing environmental laws, regulations, standards and actions plans, international treaties addressing environmental issues and their implementation; participation in international processes and cooperation with international organizations; monitoring of the environment, information systems and information exchange as well as transboundary and inter-entity environmental issues.[149]

68. Concerning mechanisms and policy instruments for the implementation of sustainable development, it should be noted that according to the Conclusions of the sixty-sixth session of the BiH Council of Ministers of 16 May 2002, a Steering Committee for Sustainable Development was established, which held a few sessions, followed by establishment of advisory bodies for environmental protection and sustainable development at the entity level.[150]

69. Several other institutions that have some competencies relevant for achieving environmental policy and law goals include: Ministry of Finance and Treasury of BiH (MFT), Ministry of Human Rights and Refugees of BiH (MHRR), Ministry of Security (MoS), Ministry of Civil Affairs (MoCA), Ministry of Communication and Transport (MoCT), Ministry of Foreign Affairs (MoFA), Ministry of Justice (MoJ), Agency for Statistics of Bosnia and Herzegovina (BHAS), BH Mine Action Center (BHMAC), etc.

II. The Republic of Srpska

70. In accordance with the Law on Administration in the Republic of Srpska (Official Gazette of RS, No. 115/18, 111/2021) activities in the environmental field is under the jurisdiction of several administrative bodies of the RS.[151] These are the following:

– RS Ministry of Spatial Planning, Construction and Ecology.[152]
– RS Environmental Protection and Energy Efficiency Fund.
– RS Ministry of Agriculture, Forestry and Water Management.
– Public institution 'Vode Srpske' Bijeljina.
–
– RS Hydrometeorological Institute.

---

meetings of the Inter-Entity Body, for coordination and cooperation purposes. BiH Council of Ministers, *Answers to the List of EU Questions on Chapter 27, Environment, supra* p. 12.

149. This Committee consists of eight members, four nominated by the Government of the Republic of Srpska and four nominated by the Government of the Federation of Bosnia and Herzegovina, who meet at least six times a year.

150. *See*: BiH Council of Ministers, *Answers to the List of EU Questions on Chapter 27, Environment, supra* p. 10.

151. For more information *see*: *Ibid.*, pp. 34–51.

152. *See*: https://www.vladars.net/sr-SP-Cyrl/Vlada/Ministarstva/mgr/Pages/default.aspx (3 Feb. 2022).

– Public Forestry Company 'Šume Republike Srpske'.
– RS Ministry of Energy and Mining.
– RS Ministry of Health and Social Welfare.
– RS Public Health Institute.
– RS Administration for Inspection Affairs.

III. Federation of Bosnia and Herzegovina

71. Environmental policy and natural resource use are the joint responsibility of the Federation of BiH and the cantons.[153] In accordance with the Article III.4 of the Constitution of FBiH where responsibility is not expressly granted to FBiH, the cantons have full responsibility for the provision of public services, local energy production facilities, local land use and cantonal tourism.

At the level of FBiH the several institutions are responsible for the adoption, implementation and enforcement of regulations and policies in the field of environment. These are the following:

– FBiH Ministry of Environment and Tourism.[154]
– FBiH Ministry of Agriculture, Water Management and Forestry.
– FBiH Hydrometeorology Institute.
– FBiH Agropedology Institute.
– FBiH Forestry Administration.
– Agency for Water Area of the River Sava.
– Agency for Water Area of the Adriatic Sea.
– FBiH Environment Protection Fund.
– National park 'Una'.
– FBiH Public Health Institute.[155]
– FBiH Administration for Inspection Affairs.[156]

A. Cantons

72. All of the ten cantons in FBiH have their own environmental bodies. 'There is no unique form of organization for ministries dealing with environmental issues

153. 'Both the Federation Government and the Cantons are to have responsibilities for the following: (a) Guaranteeing and enforcing human rights; (b) Health; (c) Environmental policy; (d) Infrastructure for communications and transport, according to the Constitution of Bosnia and Herzegovina; (e) Social welfare policy; (f) Implementing laws and regulations concerning citizenship; (g) Implementing laws and regulations concerning citizenship and passports of citizens of Bosnia and Herzegovina from the Federation territory, and on foreigners staying and movement; (h) Tourism; and (i) Use of natural resources' (Art. III.2 of the Constitution).
154. *See*: https://www.fmoit.gov.ba/bs/ (3 Feb. 2022).
155. In addition to the Cantonal Public Health Institute.
156. In addition to eight cantonal administrations for inspection affairs and two cantonal ministries with inspection services.

at the cantonal level.'[157] The following institutions are responsible for the adoption, implementation and enforcement of environmental legislation and policy:

- *Una – Sana Canton.*
- Ministry of Construction, Physical Planning and Environmental Protection.[158]
- *Posavina Canton.*
- Ministry of Transport, Communications, Tourism and Environmental Protection.[159]
- *Tuzla Canton.*
- Ministry of Physical Planning and Environmental Protection.[160]
- *Zenica – Doboj Canton.*
- Ministry of Physical Planning, Transport and Communications and Environmental Protection.[161]
- *Bosna – Podrinje Canton.*
- Ministry of Urbanism, Physical Planning and Environmental Protection.[162]
- *Central Bosnia Canton.*
- Ministry of Physical Planning, Reconstruction and Return.[163]
- *Herzegovina-Neretva Canton.*
- Ministry of Trade, Tourism and Environmental Protection.[164]
- *West Herzegovina Canton.*
- Ministry of Physical Planning, Construction and Environmental Protection.[165]
- *Sarajevo Canton.*
- Ministry of Communal Economy, Infrastructure, Physical Planning, Construction and Environmental Protection[166]
- *Canton 10.*
- Ministry of Construction, Reconstruction, Physical Planning and Environmental Protection.[167]

157. For more information, *see*: UNECE. *3rd Environmental Performance Review, Bosnia and Herzegovina*. p. 35.
158. *See*: http://vladausk.ba/v4/index/ministarstvo-za-gradjenje-prostorno-uredjenje-i-zastite-okolisa/5 (3 Feb. 2022).
159. *See*: https://www.zupanijaposavska.ba/ministarstvo-prometa-veza-turizma-i-zastite-okolisa/ (3 Feb. 2022).
160. *See*: http://www.vladatk.kim.ba/ministarstva-tk/ministarstvo-prostornog-uredenja-i-zastite-okolice (3 Feb. 2022).
161. *See*: https://www.zdk.ba/ministarstva/item/2986 (3 Feb. 2022).
162. *See*: http://mu.bpkg.gov.ba/ (3 Feb. 2022).
163. *See*: http://www.sbk-ksb.gov.ba/bs/ministarstvo-prostornog-ure%C4%91enja,-gra%C4%91enja,-za%C5%A1tite-okoli%C5%A1a,-povratka-i-stambenih-poslova.html (3 Feb. 2022).
164. *See*: http://mtto-hnz-k.ba/ (3 Feb. 2022).
165. *See*: http://www.vladazzh.com/detaljno.aspx?id=20 (3 Feb. 2022).
166. *See*: http://mkipgo.ks.gov.ba/ (3 Feb. 2022).
167. *See*: http://www.vladahbz.com/ministarstvo-graditeljstva-obnove-prostornog-uredenja-i-zastite-okolisa/ (3 Feb. 2022).

IV. Brčko District of Bosnia and Herzegovina

73. The Department of Physical Planning and Property Legal Affairs of Brčko District of BiH Government has administrative jurisdiction over the environmental protection.[168] The Department of Agriculture, Forestry and Water Management of BD Government is responsible for agriculture, forestry and water management and administrative capacities are defined by the organizational plan of the Government of BD BiH.[169]

§5. Sources of Environmental Law

I. International Sources of Environmental Law

A. Constitutional Provisions

74. Pursuant to the Article II.7 of the Constitution, Bosnia and Herzegovina shall remain or become party to the international agreements listed in Annex I to this Constitution.[170] Bosnia and Herzegovina and both entities shall ensure the highest level of internationally recognized human rights and fundamental freedoms. To that end, there shall be a Human Rights Commission for Bosnia and Herzegovina as provided for in *Annex 6* to the General Framework Agreement (Article II.1).[171] According to the Constitution of BiH 'the Presidency shall have responsibility for: … negotiating, denouncing, and, with the consent of the Parliamentary Assembly, *ratifying treaties of Bosnia and Herzegovina* [emphasis added]' (Article V.3.d),

168. *See*: http://ppipo.bdcentral.net/Content/Read/o_odjeljenju?lang=en (6 Feb. 2022).
169. *See*: http://psv.bdcentral.net/?lang=bs (6 Feb. 2022). Department of Municipal Affairs is responsible for the issues related to water supply and solid waste. *BiH Answers to the Questionnaire*, p. 133.
170. Annex I: Additional Human Rights Agreements To Be Applied In Bosnia And Herzegovina 1. 1948 Convention on the Prevention and Punishment of the Crime of Genocide 2. 1949 Geneva Conventions I-IV on the Protection of the Victims of War, and the 1977 Geneva Protocols I-II thereto, 3. 1951 Convention relating to the Status of Refugees and the 1966 Protocol thereto, 4. 1957 Convention on the Nationality of Married Women, 5. 1961 Convention on the Reduction of Statelessness, 6. 1965 International Convention on the Elimination of All Forms of Racial Discrimination, 7. 1966 International Covenant on Civil and Political Rights and the 1966 and 1989 Optional Protocols thereto, 8. 1966 Covenant on Economic, Social and Cultural Rights, 9. 1979 Convention on the Elimination of All Forms of Discrimination against Women, 10. 1984 Convention against Torture and Other Cruel, Inhuman or Degrading Treatment or Punishment, 11. 1987 European Convention on the Prevention of Torture and Inhuman or Degrading Treatment or Punishment, 12. 1989 Convention on the Rights of the Child, 13. 1990 International Convention on the Protection of the Rights of All Migrant Workers and Members of Their Families, 14. 1992 European Charter for Regional or Minority Languages, 15. 1994 Framework Convention for the Protection of National Minorities.
171. The rights and freedoms set forth in the European Convention for the Protection of Human Rights and Fundamental Freedoms and its Protocols shall apply directly in Bosnia and Herzegovina. These shall have priority over all other law (Art. II.2). BiH has ratified all major European and international human rights instruments, most of which are included in its Constitution. However, 'there was no systematic follow-up to the 204 accepted recommendations from the November 2019 Universal Periodic Review.' EC, *Bosnia and Herzegovina 2021 Progress Report*, p. 25.

and the Parliamentary Assembly shall have responsibility for 'deciding whether to consent to the *ratification of treaties* [emphasis added]' (Article IV.4.d).[172]

75. Each entity may enter into agreements with states and international organizations with the consent of the Parliamentary Assembly. The Parliamentary Assembly may prescribe by law that certain types of agreements do not require such consent (Article III.2.d).[173] Besides that, the entities shall have the right to establish special parallel relationships with neighbouring states consistent with the sovereignty and territorial integrity of Bosnia and Herzegovina (Article III.2.a).[174]

B. Multilateral Environmental Agreements

76. Bosnia and Herzegovina became a party to the following conventions by succession, as a successor state of Former Yugoslavia:[175]

(1) Convention on Wetlands of International Importance Especially as Waterfowl Habitat, Ramsar, 1971, 1 March 1992.
(2) Convention on Long-range Transboundary Air Pollution Geneva, 1979, 1 September 1993.
(3) Protocol on Long-term Financing of the Cooperative Programme for Monitoring and Evaluation of the Long-range Transmission of Air Pollutants in Europe (EMEP), Geneva, 1984, 1 September 1993.
(4) Convention on International Maritime Organizations Geneva, 1948, 16 July 1993.
(5) Convention on International Civil Aviation, annex 16 – aircraft noise Chicago, 1944, 13 January 1993.
(6) Convention on Ozone Protection Vienna, 1985, 1 September 1993.
(7) Protocol on Substances that Deplete the Ozone Layer Montreal, 1987, 1 September 1993.
(8) Amendments to Montreal Protocol agreed by the parties at the second meeting London, 1990, 11 August 2003.
(9) Amendments to Montreal Protocol agreed by the parties at the fourth meeting Copenhagen, 1992, 11 August 2003.

---

172. Detailed information about relations between Constitution of BiH and international law can be found in: Ademović N., Marko J., Marković G. *Ustavno pravo Bosne i Hercegovine* [Constitutional Law of Bosnia and Herzegovina], Fondacija 'Konrad Adenauer', Predstavništvo u Bosni i Hercegovini, Sarajevo, 2012. pp. 38–41.
173. For more information *see*: Todić, D. Zaključivanje i izvršavanje međunarodnih ugovora u pravnom sistemu BiH, Crne Gore i Hrvatske [Conclusion and Implementation of International Treaties in the Legal Systems of BiH, Montenegro, and Croatia], *Strani pravni život*, 2/2018, pp. 103–119, https://www.stranipravnizivot.rs/index.php/SPZ/article/view/425 (19 Jul. 2022).
174. Web sites of many governmental bodies are not regularly updated, therefore authors have faced some problems in finding valid laws and other documents needed for preparation of this monograph.
175. In addition, BiH has also concluded bilateral agreements on environmental and sustainable development cooperation with the Republic of Serbia and the Republic of Croatia (Official Gazette of the BiH – MU, No. 2/16, and 2/17).

(10) Amendments to Montreal Protocol agreed by the parties at the ninth meeting, Montreal, 1997, 11 August 2003.
(11) Amendments to Montreal Protocol agreed by the parties at the eleventh meeting Beijing, 1999 (Not adopted).
(12) UN Convention on the Law of the Sea Montego Bay, 1982, 12 January 1994.
(13) Convention for the Protection of the Mediterranean Sea Against Pollution Barcelona, 1976, 1 March 1992.
(14) Protocol for the prevention of pollution of the Mediterranean Sea by dumping from ships and aircraft. Barcelona, 1976, 1 March 1992.
(15) Protocol concerning cooperation in combating pollution of the Mediterranean Sea by oil and other harmful substances in cases of emergency. Kuwait, 1978, 1 March 1992.
(16) Protocol for the protection of the Mediterranean Sea against pollution from land-based sources (LBS), Athens, 1980, 22 October 1994.
(17) Protocol concerning Mediterranean specially protected areas. Geneva, 1982, 22 October 1994.
(18) Protocol concerning specially protected areas and biological diversity in the Mediterranean Barcelona, 1995, 12 December 1999.
(19) Convention on Protection of the World Cultural and Natural Heritage Paris, 1972, 12 July 1993.
(20) Convention Concerning the Use of White Lead in Painting Geneva, 1921, 2 June 1993.
(21) European Agreement Concerning the International Carriage of Dangerous Goods by Road (ADR), Geneva, 1957, 1 September 1993.
(22) Protocol Amending Article 14 of the European Agreement Concerning the International Carriage of Dangerous Goods by Road (ADR), New York, 1975, 1 September 1993.
(23) Convention on the Physical Protection of Nuclear Material Vienna, 1979, 30 June 1998.
(24) Convention on Fishing and Conservation of Living Resources of the High Seas, Geneva, 1958, 12 January 1994.
(25) Convention on the Territorial Sea and the Contiguous Zone Geneva, 1958, 1 September 1993.
(26) Convention on Continental Shelf Geneva, 1958, 12 January 1994.
(27) Convention on the High Seas Geneva, 1958, 1 September 1993.
(28) Convention on Protection of Employees against Occupational Hazards in the Working Environment Due to Air Pollution, Noise and Vibration Geneva, 1977, 2 June 1993.
(29) Treaty on the Prohibition of the Emplacement of Nuclear Weapons and other Weapons of Mass Destruction on the Sea-Bed and the Ocean Floor and in the Subsoil Thereof. London, Moscow, Washington D.C., 1971, 15 August 1994.
(30) Treaty on the Non-proliferation of Nuclear Weapons New York, 1968, 15 August 1994.
(31) Convention on Early Notification of a Nuclear Accident Vienna, 1986, 30 June 1998.
(32) Convention on Assistance in the Case of a Nuclear Accident or Radiological Emergency Vienna, 1986, 30 June 1998.

(33) Convention on the Prohibition of the Development, Production and Stockpiling of Bacteriological (Biological) and Toxin Weapons and on their Destruction, London, Moscow, Washington D.C., 1972, 15 August 1994.

77. Multilateral environmental treaties ratified by BiH in accordance with the State Law on the Procedures for the Conclusion and Implementation of International Agreements (Official Gazette of BiH No. 29/00, and 32/13) are the following:

(1) Kigali amendment to the Montreal Protocol on substances that deplete the ozone layer (Kigali, 2016), 2021.
(2) Convention on the Conservation of Migratory Species of Wild Animals (Bon, 1979), 2017.
(3) Paris Agreement on Climate Change (Paris, 2015), 2017.
(4) UN Framework Convention on Climate Change (Rio de Janeiro, 1992), 2000.
(5) Kyoto Protocol Kyoto, 1997, 2007.
(6) International Convention on Plant Protection (Rome, 1951), 2003.
(7) Convention on Control of Transboundary Movements of Hazardous Wastes and Their Disposal (Basel, 1989), 2001.
(8) UN Convention on Biological Diversity (Rio de Janeiro, 1992), 2002.
(9) Cartagena Protocol on Biosafety (Cartagena, 2000), 2009.
(10) UN Convention on Combat Desertification in Those Countries Experiencing Serious Drought and/or Desertification, Particularly in Africa (Paris, 1994), 2002.
(11) Convention on Cooperation for the Protection and Sustainable use of the Danube River (Sofia, 1994), 2005.
(12) Convention for the Establishment of the European and Mediterranean Plant Protection Organization, (Paris, 1955), 2005.
(13) UNECE Convention on Access to Information, Public Participation in Decision-making and Access to Justice in Environmental Matters (Aaarhus, 1998), 2008.
(14) Protocol on Pollutant Release and Transfer Registers (PRTR) (Kiev, 2003), 2003.
(15) Convention on Persistent Organic Pollutants (Stockholm, 2001), 2010.
(16) Convention on the Prior Informed Consent Procedure for Certain Hazardous Chemicals and Pesticides in International Trade (Rotterdam, 1998), 2007.
(17) Convention on International Trade in Endangered Species of Wild Fauna and Flora (CITES) (Washington DC, 1973), 2009.
(18) Convention on Environmental Impact Assessment in Transboundary Context (Espoo, 1991), 2009.
(19) Protocol on Strategic Environmental Assessment (Kiev, 2003), 2017.
(20) Convention on the Conservation of European Wildlife and Natural Habitats (Bern, 1979), 2008.
(21) Framework Agreement on the Sava River Basin (Kranjska Gora, 2002), 2003.
(22) Convention on the Protection and Use of Transboundary Watercourses and International Lakes (Helsinki, 1992), 2009.
(23) Protocol on Water and Health to the Convention on the Protection and Use of Transboundary Watercourses and International Lakes (London, 1999), 2011.

(24) Changes to Articles 25 and 26 of the Convention on the Protection and Use of Transboundary Watercourses and International Lakes (Madrid, 2003), 2010.
(25) Convention on the Transboundary Effects of Industrial Accidents Helsinki, 1992, 2012.
(26) Council of Europe Framework Convention on the Value of Cultural Heritage for Society (Faro, 2005), 2009.
(27) Agreement on Energy Charter (Lisbon, 1994), 2001.
(28) Energy Charter – Protocol on Energy Efficiency and Related Environmental Aspects, (Lisbon, 1994), 2001.
(29) Convention on Safety and Health in Mines (Geneva, 1995), 2010.
(30) Convention on Safety and Health in Agriculture (Geneva, 2001), 2010.
(31) Convention Concerning Work in the Fishing Sector (Geneva, 2007), 2010.
(32) Convention Concerning the Prevention of Major Industrial Accidents (Geneva, 1993) 2010.
(33) The European Landscape Convention (Florence, 2000), 2010.
(34) Convention on the Prohibition of the Use, Stockpiling, Production and Transfer of Anti-Personnel Mines and on their Destruction (Oslo, 1997), 1998.
(35) Convention on the Prior Informed Consent Procedure for Certain Hazardous Chemicals and Pesticides in International Trade, (Rotterdam, 1998), 2007.
(36) Amendment to Convention on International Trade in Endangered Species of Wild Fauna and Flora (Article XI), (Bonn, 1979), 2009.
(37) European Framework Convention on Transboundary Cooperation between Territorial Communities or Authorities, (Madrid, 1980), 2008.
(38) Convention Concerning International Carriage of Goods by Rail (Bern, 1980), 1996.

78. Despite the progress achieved by BiH in ratification or accession to global and regional multilateral environmental agreements, there are still a number of MEAs that have been signed but are still awaiting ratification.[176]

Since 2011, the BiH became party to the several MEAs. However, 'the improvement of Bosnia and Herzegovina's performance vis-à-vis international and regional

176. For instance, Protocol on Access to Genetic Resources and the Fair and Equitable Sharing of Benefits Arising from their Utilization, GMO amendment to the Convention on Access to Information, Public Participation in Decision-making and Access to Justice in Environmental Matters, Protocol to Abate Acidification, Eutrophication and Ground-level Ozone and its 2012 amended version, Protocol on Persistent Organic Pollutants (POPs) and its 2009 amended version, and Protocol on Heavy Metals and its 2012 amended version, to the Convention on Long-range Transboundary Air Pollution, etc. The Protocol on Civil Liability and Compensation for Damage Caused by the Transboundary Effects of Industrial Accidents on Transboundary Waters, to the Convention on the Protection and Use of Transboundary Watercourses and International Lakes, were signed during the Fifth Ministerial Conference 'Environment for Europe' (Kiev, 2003) but have still not been ratified. In addition, BiH is not a member of Convention on the Protection of the Environment through Criminal Law, Convention on Civil Liability for Damage from Activities Dangerous for the Environment, Convention on Mercury, Convention on the Law of Non-navigational Uses of International Watercourses, etc. For more information, See: Todić D. Multilateral Environmental Agreements and EU Integration of Western Balkan States (Status of Bosnia and Herzegovina, Montenegro, Serbia and Croatia in Multilateral Environmental Agreements), *European Energy and Environmental Law Review*, February 2019, Vol. 28, No. 1, pp. 17–27.

environmental agreements and the 2030 Agenda for Sustainable Development requires a coordinated and joint endeavour among different parts of the administration'.[177]

II. National Sources of Environmental Law

A. Levels and Procedure of Adoption of Laws

79. There are several levels of legislative bodies and procedures in Bosnia and Herzegovina (the Parliamentary Assembly at the level of Bosnia and Herzegovina, the two Entity-level legislatures representing the Republic of Srpska and the Federation of BiH), Brčko District level and cantonal level (in the framework of the FBiH). Each of these legislative bodies has its own competencies and procedures in accordance with constitutions.[178] However, there is no general environmental law in BiH. In accordance with the prescribed competencies, environmental laws and relevant sublegal acts have been adopted in the RS, FBiH, BDBiH and cantons (in FBiH).[179]

B. The List of Basic National Environmental Laws

1. The Republic of Srpska

80. The following basic laws have been adopted:

(1) The Law on Environmental Protection (Official Gazette of RS No. 71/12, 79/15, 70/20).
(2) The Law on Fund and financing of the environment (Official Gazette of RS No. 117/11, 90/16).
(3) The Law on Nature Protection (Official Gazette of RS No. 20/14).
(4) The Law on National Parks (Official Gazette of RS No. 75/10).
(5) The Law on Air Protection (Official Gazette of RS No. 124/11, and 46/17).
(6) The Law on Waste Management (Official Gazette of RS Nos 111/13, 106/15 and 16/18).
(7) The Law on Chemicals (Official Gazette of RS No. 21/18).
(8) The Law on Biocides (Official Gazette of RS No. 37/09).
(9) The Law on Waters (Official Gazette of RS Nos 50/06, 92/09 and 121/12).

177. UNECE. *3rd Environmental Performance Review, Bosnia and Herzegovina*, p. 103. In addition, 'there is a general absence of information provided by the Bosnia and Herzegovina environmental authorities to the public on the status of Bosnia and Herzegovina's participation in global, regional and bilateral agreements and on the implementation of those agreements, including the reports submitted'. *Ibid.*, p. 104.

178. *Legislative Advocacy Resource Guide, Promoting Human Rights in Bosnia and Herzegovina*, Global Rights, Washington, 2005.

179. For more information *see*: Directorate for European Integration, *Answers to the Questionnaire, Chapter 27, Environment and climate change*, pp. 4–11.

(10) The Law on Forests (Official Gazette of RS Nos 75/08 and 60/13).
(11) The Law on Forest Trees Reproductive Material (Official Gazette of RS No. 70/09).
(12) The Law on Agricultural Land (Official Gazette of RS Nos 93/06, 86/07, 14/10 and 5/12).
(13) The Law on Agriculture (Official Gazette of RS No. 70/06, 20/07, 86/07, 71/09).
(14) The Law on Plant Protection Products (Official Gazette of RS No. 52/10).
(15) The Law on Mineral Fertilisers (Official Gazette of RS No. 24/12).
(16) The Law on Fishery (Official Gazette of RS No. 72/12).
(17) The Law on Hunting (Official Gazette of RS No. 60/09 and 50/13).
(18) The Law on Tobacco (Official Gazette of RS No. 72/12).
(19) The Law on Spatial Planning and Construction (Official Gazette of RS Nos 40/13, 106/15 and 3/16).
(20) The Energy Law (Official Gazette of RS No. 49/09).
(21) The Law on Mining (Official Gazette of RS No. 62/18).
(22) The Law of Geological Exploration (Official Gazette of RS Nos 110/13 and 91/17).
(23) The Law on Oil and Oil Derivatives (Official Gazette of RS Nos 36/09 and 102/12).
(24) Law on Pipeline Transportation of Gaseous and Liquid Hydrocarbons and Distribution of Gaseous Hydrocarbons (Official Gazette of RS No. 52/12).
(25) The Law on Gas (Official Gazette of RS No. 22/18).
(26) The Law on Tourism (Official Gazette of RS No. 45/17).
(27) The Law on Utility Activities (Official Gazette of RS No. 124/11, 100/17).
(28) The Law on GMO (Official Gazette of RS No. 103/08).
(29) The Law on concessions (Official Gazette of RS No. 59/13).
(30) The Law on renewable energy sources (Official Gazette of RS No. 16/22).
(31) The Law on energy efficiency (Official Gazette of RS No. 59/13).

2. Federation of Bosnia and Herzegovina and Cantons

81. The following basic laws represent elements that define the legal framework:[180]

---

180. Some issues cantons autonomously regulate and they have (in some elements) specific legislation. For example, Sarajevo Canton has following environmental laws, *inter alia*: Law on noise (Official Gazette of Canton Sarajevo, No. 26/07), Law on environmental protection fund (Official Gazette of Canton Sarajevo, No. 41/08), Law on Promulgation of Nature Monument 'Spring of Bosnia' (Official Gazette of Canton Sarajevo, No. 6/10), Law on protected landscape 'Trebević' (Official Gazette of Canton Sarajevo, No. 15/14), Law on spatial planning (Official Gazette of Canton Sarajevo, No. 7/05), Regulation of the strategic assessment of plans and programs on the environment (Official Gazette of Canton Sarajevo, No. 32/11), Rulebook of plants that can be built and put into operation only if the environmental permit (Official Gazette of Canton Sarajevo, No. 8/11), Decision on the protection and improvement of air quality in the Canton of Sarajevo (Official Gazette of Canton Sarajevo, No. 1/13), Decision on the establishment of cantonal public institutions for

(1) The Law on Environmental Protection (Official Gazette of FBiH No. 15/21).
(2) The Law on Air Protection (Official Gazette of FBiH Nos 33/03, and 04/10).
(3) The Law on Waste Management (Official Gazette of FBiH Nos 33/03, a 72/09, and 92/17).
(4) The Law on Chemicals (Official Gazette of FBiH No. 77/20).
(5) The Law on Environmental Protection Fund of FBiH (Official Gazette of FBiH No. 33/03).
(6) The Law on Waters (Official Gazette of BiH No. 70/06).
(7) The Law on Noise Protection (Official Gazette of FBiH No. 110/12).
(8) Law on Nature Protection (Official Gazette of FBiH No. 66/13).
(9) Decree on Forests (Official Gazette of FBiH Nos 83/09, 26/10, 33/10, 38/10).[181]
(10) Law on Freshwater Fishing (Official Gazette of FBiH No. 64/04).
(11) Law on Spatial Planning and Land Use (Official Gazette of FBiH Nos 2/06, 72/07, 32/08, 4/10, 13/10 and 45/10).
(12) Law on Hunting (Official Gazette of FBiH Nos 4/06, 8/10 and 81/14).
(13) Law on Agriculture (Official Gazette of FBiH Nos 88/07, 4/10, 27/12 and 7/13).
(14) Law on Una National Park (Official Gazette of FBiH No. 44/08).
(15) Law on Agricultural Land (Official Gazette of FBiH No. 52/09).
(16) Law on Geological Survey (Official Gazette of FBiH Nos 9/10 and 14/10).
(17) Law on Mining (Official Gazette of FBiH No. 26/10).
(18) Law on Seeds and Planting Materials for Forest and Horticultural Trees and Bushes (Official Gazette of FBiH Nos 71/05, 8/10).
(19) Law on Concessions (Official Gazette of FBiH Nos 40/02, 61/06).
(20) Law on Health Protection (Official Gazette of FBiH No. 46/10, 75/13).
(21) The Law on renewable energy sources (Official Gazette of FBiH No. 70/13).

---

protected natural areas (Official Gazette of Canton Sarajevo, No. 14/11), etc. For more information, *see*: https://mkipgo.ks.gov.ba/legislativa (19 Jul. 2022). Canton West Herzegovina adopted following environmental regulations: Law on environmental protection (Official Gazette of West Herzegovina Canton, No. 8/13), Rulebook on plants that can be built and operate only if they have the environmental permit (Official Gazette of West Herzegovina Canton, No. 2/06). *See*: https://www.mpugzo-zzh.com/hr/zastita-okolisa (19 Jul. 2022). Bosnian-Podrinje Canton adopted, *inter alia*: Law on environmental protection (Official Gazette of Bosnian-Podrinje Canton, No. 5/05, 11/10, 8/11), Law on protection against noise (Official Gazette of Bosnian-Podrinje Canton, No. 5/05), Rulebook on deadlines for applying for environmental permits for plants for which permits had been issued before the enactment of Law on Environmental Protection, Rulebook on energy certification of buildings (Official Gazette of Bosnian-Podrinje Canton, No. 8/13), etc. *See*: http://mu.bpkg.gov.ba/preuzmanja/71/zakoni-i-propisi (19 Jul. 2022).

181. The Law on Forests (Official Gazette of FBiH no. 20/02, 29/03, 37/04) was made null and void on 27 Nov. 2009, since the Parliament of the Federation of BiH did not act upon the verdict of the Constitutional Court of the Federation of BiH. *See*: UNEP, *Desk Review of the Legal and Institutional Framework of Environmental Protection in Bosnia and Herzegovina*, [FINAL DRAFT], UNEP Bosnia and Herzegovina, April 2011. p. 20.

3. Brčko District of Bosnia and Herzegovina

82. The following basic laws have been adopted:

(1) The Law on Environmental Protection of the Brčko District of BiH (Official Gazette of BD BiH Nos 24/04, 19/07, 1/05 and 9/09).
(2) The Law on Air Protection of the Brčko District of BiH (Official Gazette of BD BiH Nos 25/04, 19/07, 1/05, 9/09, 17/22).
(3) The Law on Waste management of the Brčko District of BiH (Official Gazette of BD BiH Nos 25/04, 19/07, 1/05, 2/08, 9/09, 22/18).
(4) The Law on Water Protection of the Brčko District of BiH (Official Gazette of BD BiH Nos 25/04, 01/05 and 19/07).
(5) The Law on nature protection (Official Gazette of BD BiH Nos 24/04, 01/05, 19/07 and 09/09).
(6) The Law on Spatial Planning and Construction of the Brčko District of BiH (Official Gazette of BD BiH No. 29/08, 18/17, 48/18, 54/18, 10/20, 29/20, and 40/20).
(7) The Law on Utility Activities of the Brčko District of BiH (Official Gazette of BD BiH Nos 30/04 and 24/07, 09/13, 3/18, 25/20).
(8) The Law on Forests of the Brčko District of BiH (Official Gazette of BD BiH No. 14/10 and 26/16).
(9) The Law on Hunting of the Brčko District of BiH (Official Gazette of BD BiH No. 1/15, 52/18, and 26/21).
(10) The Law on Tourist Activities of the Brčko District of BiH (Official Gazette of BD BiH Nos 30/06, 19/07, and 11/20).
(11) The Law on Agricultural Land of the Brčko District of BiH (Official Gazette of BD BiH Nos 32/04, 20/06, 19/07).[182]
(12) The Law on Renewable Energy Sources and Effective Cogeneration of the Brčko District of BiH (Official Gazette of BD BiH No. 22/22).

---

182. *See also*: Nalog supervizora o urbanističkom planiranju [Supervisory Order on urban planning], (Official Gazette of BD BiH No. 10/07).

Part I. Pollution Control

§1. Strategic Documents

83. The Environmental Approximation Strategy of BiH (EAS) (supplemented by Environmental Approximation Programmes for the Federation of Bosnia and Herzegovina, Republika Srpska and Brčko District) was developed with support from the EnvIS project in 2014.[183] The National Human Development Report/BiH Millennium Development Goals (NHDR/MDG) was developed in 2003 for the 2003–2015 period. The document contains a set of policy proposals aimed at achieving progress towards the full realization of the relevant Millennium Development Goals at the local level, including eighteen specific goals for BiH.[184] The National Action Plan for the Protection of the Environment in BiH – NEAP is adopted in 2003.[185]

84. The Republic of Srpska has not adopted *Environmental Protection Strategy*, but there are other strategic frameworks for this field (The Nature Protection Strategy of 2011, The Air Protection Strategy of 2011, The Strategy for Agricultural Development of the Republic of Srpska by 2015, dated from 2006, The Republic of Srpska Chemical Safety Strategy for the 2012–2016 period, The Republic of Srpska Energy Development Strategy by 2030, dated from 2012, etc.).

85. In accordance with the FBiH Law on Environmental Protection, the FBiH Environmental Strategy was adopted, together with an action plan for the 2008–2018 period (Strategy of FBiH), consisting of: FBiH Nature Protection Strategy, FBiH Air Protection Strategy, FBiH Waste Management Strategy, FBiH Water Management Strategy.

---

183. For more information, *see*: BiH MFTER. *Environmental Approximation Strategy of Bosnia and Herzegovina*, EAS – BiH, Ministry of Foreign Trade and Economic Relations of Bosnia and Herzegovina May 2017. http://www.mvteo.gov.ba/data/Home/Dokumenti/Vodni%20resursi/Environmetal.pdf (19 Jul. 2022).
See also: UNECE. *3rd Environmental Performance Review, Bosnia and Herzegovina*. p. 19.
184. For more information, *see*, BiH Council of Ministers, *Answers to the List of EU Questions on Chapter 27, Environment, supra* pp. 9, 10. For detailed information, *see* Bosnia and Herzegovina, *Assessment of Sustainable Development in Bosnia and Herzegovina*, 2002, *supra;* Nixon N., (Ed) *Progress towards the Realization of the Millennium Development Goals in Bosnia and Herzegovina 2010, supra.*
185. *See*: Council of Ministers, 2012, *Answers to the List of EU Questions on Chapter 27, Environment, supra,* p. 15.

86. Brčko District Development Strategy for the 2008–2017 period was adopted.[186]

186. For detailed information, *see, Ibid.*, pp. 16–18.

Chapter 1. General Law

87. The first set of environmental laws in BiH was prepared with the financial and technical assistance of the EU Community Assistance, Reconstruction, Development and Stabilization Programme (CARDS).[187] The intention was to develop laws that would be in line with the relevant EU Directives and harmonized for both entities and the Brčko District. These laws were adopted in the Republic of Srpska in 2002, in the Federation of Bosnia and Herzegovina in 2003 and in the Brčko District in 2004.[188]

§1. Laws on Environment

88. The laws on environmental protection of the Republic of Srpska, the Federation of Bosnia and Herzegovina, and the Brčko District of Bosnia and Herzegovina, as well as other relevant laws, are the founding legal acts that govern the sector.

I. The Republic of Srpska

A. The Law on Environmental Protection

89. The basic legal act regulating environmental[189] protection in the Republic of Srpska is the Law on Environmental Protection[190] (Official Gazette of the RS, No. 71/12, 79/15, 70/20). It has the following fifteen parts: Part I – General Provisions (Articles 1–14), Part II – Protection of the Environmental Elements (Articles 15–24), Part III – Environmental Information and Education (Articles 25–32), Part IV – Public Participation and Access to Information Related to the Environment (Articles 33–42), Part V – Planning and Environmental Protection (Articles 43–47), Part VI – Strategic Environmental Impact Assessment (Articles 48–59), Part VII – Environmental Impact Assessment (Articles 60–79), Part VIII – Environmental Permits Issuing and Preventing of Large-Scale Disaster (Articles 80–110), Part IX –

187. This set of laws was considered and approved by the Inter-Entity Environmental Steering Committee and it comprises the following laws: the Framework Law on Environmental Protection, the Law on the Environmental Fund, the Law on Water Protection, the Law on Air Protection, the Law on Waste Management, and the Law on Nature Protection. UNEP, *Desk Review of the Legal and Institutional Framework of Environmental Protection in Bosnia and Herzegovina*, *supra* p. 19.

188. 'The contents of such laws are not identical for both Entities and the Brčko District, but are very similar and there are no critical differences between them. However, the Law on Water Protection is no longer in force and has been replaced in both Entities by a new Law on Water in 2006'. *Ibid.*

189. *Environment* is a set of natural and created values whose complex interrelationships make the environment, i.e., space and living conditions (Art. 14, point ž).

190. The provisions of this Law are related to the (Art. 4): (a) all the elements of the environment (air, water, land, flora and fauna, landscape and built environment) and (b) all types of activities that use natural resources and burden the environmental, i.e., impact the environment so that present a risk for the environment pollution, which polluting the environment, or that have a negative impact on the environment (such as noise, vibration, radiation, excluding nuclear radiation, waste, etc.).

Eco-Labelling, Management and Environmental Control System (Articles 111–115a), Part X – Financing of the Environmental and Economic Instruments (Articles 116–117), Part XI – Civil Liability for Environmental Damage (Articles 118–126), Part XII – Inter-Entity cooperation (Articles 127–128), Part XIII – Supervision (Articles 129–131a), Part XIV – Penalties (Articles 132–133), Part XV – Transitional and Final Provisions (Articles 134–138).

90. According to Article 1, the Law on Environmental Protection regulates the environmental protection[191] for its conservation, to reduce the risk to life and health, ensuring and improving quality of life, the protection of all environmental elements,[192] information and access to information in the field of environmental protection, planning and environmental protection, strategic impact assessment and environmental impact assessment,[193] environmental permits[194] issuing process and large-scale disaster prevention, an eco-labelling system and environmental management, financing activities related to the environment, responsibility for environmental damage, and the rights and obligations of legal entities and natural persons engaged in activities under this law.

1. Environmental Protection, Implementation and Principles

91. The environmental protection[195] is implemented in order to (Article 2): (a) usage[196] reducing, overloading prevention, environmental pollution[197] and degradation, improve and restore of the damaged environment; (b) human health protection

---

191. *Environment protection* includes all relevant activities and measures aimed to prevention of danger, harm or pollution of the environment, reduce and eliminate the caused damage, and return to the state before the caused damage (Art. 14, point l).
192. *Environmental elements* are land, air, water, biosphere, as well as constructed (artificial) environment, which is a result of human activity factor, as an integral part of the environment (Art. 14, point dj).
193. *Environmental impact assessment* is the identification, description and appropriate assessment in relation to each single case, in accordance with the provisions of this law, the direct and indirect effects of a project on the following elements and factors: population and human health, biological, geological and landscape diversity, soil, water, air, climate, material goods, cultural-historical and natural heritage, landscape and interaction of the above factors. (Art. 14, point av).
194. *Environmental permit* is a decision of the competent authority issued in the form of a decision establishing that the facility meets the specific requirements for the construction and operation of the entire facility or parts of facility, and may cover one or more installations on the same site operated by the same responsible person (Art. 14, point d).
195. According to the Art. 3, Every person has the right on healthy environment (Art. 3, para. 1), Every person has the right to live in the environment eligible for health and well-being, therefore it is an individual and collective responsibility to protect and improve the environment for the benefit of present and future generations (Art. 3, para. 2).
196. Use of the environment is organized and conducted in a manner that (Art. 8, para. 2): (a) result in the lowest possible level of the environment pressure and usage, (b) to prevent environmental pollution and (c) to prevent damage to the environment. According to the Art. 8, para. 3, the environmental usage must be complied with the precaution principle, i.e., carefully management and economically use of the environmental elements, and to reduced waste production to the minimum by applying waste recycling, i.e., reuse of natural and artificial materials. *Use of the environment* is an activity that causes changes in the environment, so it uses the environment as a whole or some

and improving of the environmental conditions for quality of life; (c) sustainable management, conservation and protection of the natural resources,[198] rational resources usage and such the economy that ensures resource recovery; (d) compliance of social, economic and other interests of the Republic of Srpska with the requirements of environmental protection; (e) international cooperation in environmental protection; (f) providing opportunities for initiatives and public[199] participation in the environment protection activities; (g) economic coordination and integration of social and economic development in accordance with the prescribed standards for environmental protection; and (h) to establish and develop institutions for the protection and preservation of the environment.

92. According to Article 6, the principles of the environmental protection are: (a) the sustainable development principle; (b) the precaution and prevention principle; (c) the substitution principle; (d) the integrated approach principle;[200] (e) the cooperation and shared responsibility principle; (f) the public participation and access to information principle; and (g) the polluter pays principle.

93. The environment protection and improvement provide, within its authorities, the Republic of Srpska,[201] local government units, companies, entrepreneurs, associations and foundations, as well as other legal entities and natural persons, professional organizations and other public services (Article 5, paragraph 1).[202]

2. Protection of the Environmental Elements

94. The protection of the environment elements involves protection of the quality, quantity and their stock, as well as the preservation of natural processes within the elements and their natural balance (Article 15, paragraph 1). The environmental elements must be protected individually and in conjunction with other elements of

---

of its elements as a natural resource or emitting substances, i.e., energy into the environment or environmental elements within the regulations governing protection of the environment (Art. 14, point p).

197. *Pollution* is the direct or indirect introduction of substances, vibrations, heat or noise into the air, water or land caused by human activity that can be harmful to human health or to the quality of the environment and can cause damage to material goods, or to violate or interfere enjoyment, as well as the other legitimate uses of the environment (Art. 14, point z).

198. *Natural resource* is a component of the natural environment, i.e., an integral part of the natural environment that can be used to meet the needs of the society, with the exception of an artificial environment (Art. 14, point adj).

199. *Public* is one or more natural persons or legal entities and their associations, organizations or groups (Art. 14, point o).

200. The purpose of the integrated approach principles is to prevent or reduce to a minimum the risk of damage to the environment as a whole (Art. 10, para. 2).

201. The Republic of Srpska establishes cooperation and coordination with the Federation of Bosnia and Herzegovina and with the Brčko District within the framework of common goals and environmental protection interests (Art. 5, para. 3). The Republic participates in international cooperation in the field of environmental protection (Art. 5, para. 4).

202. The subjects from para. 1 of this article are obliged to protect and improve the environment (Art. 5, para. 2).

the environment, taking into account their interdependent relationships (Article 15, paragraph 2). The specific areas of protection and preservation of environmental elements, a method of burdening[203] and using of the elements and protection from the impact[204] that pose a threat[205] to the environment, are governed by special regulations (Article 15, paragraph 3).

95. Soil protection includes the protection of the soil surface and subsurface soil layers and is achieved by implementing measures and activities in planning, management, use, monitoring and protection from soil pollution and degradation in order to preserve its natural properties and functions (Article 16, paragraph 1).[206] Water can be used and loaded. The wastewater can be discharged into the water with appropriate treatment, in a manner and to a level that does not pose a threat to natural processes or for the restoration of water quality and quantity, and that does not diminish the ability of their versatility usage (Article 17, paragraph 1).

96. Air protection[207] is achieved by taking measures of systematic monitoring[208] of air quality, reduction of air pollutants below the prescribed limits and taking technological and other necessary measures to reduce emissions,[209] monitoring of the effect of air pollution to human health and the environment. Air protection measures provide preservation of atmospheric air in its entirety with all its processes and climate characteristics (Article 18, paragraph 1).

97. The biosphere preservation includes the protection of organisms, their communities and their habitats, including the preservation of natural processes and natural balance in the ecosystem, while ensuring their sustainability (Article 19,

203. *Burdening* of the environment is the emission of substances or energy into the environment (Art. 14, point dž).
204. *Environmental impact* is the change in the environment caused by loading and using the environment (Art. 14, point am).
205. *The threat* is an internal characteristic of hazardous substances or physical condition that can cause damage to human health or the environment (Art. 14, point h).
206. In the case of a large-scale incident or accident in which land has been polluted, the environmental inspector orders emergency measures (Art. 16a, para. 1). In order to rehabilitate, i.e. improve the state of polluted and degraded land to a level that is safe for use in accordance with its intended purpose, appropriate measures and activities, i.e. remediation and/or land recultivation, are implemented (Art. 16b, para. 1). The provisions of this law relating to land protection do not apply to agricultural, forest and water land, the protection of which is governed by special regulations (Art. 16g, para. 1).
207. Planning of air protection, emission sources, air protection, monitoring, public participation and financing of air protection is conducted in accordance with separate air protection regulations (Art. 18, para. 2).
208. *Monitoring* is the system of monitoring environmental conditions, i.e., environmental pollution, monitoring of emissions and imissions, and natural phenomena (Art. 14, point c).
209. *Emission* is the direct or indirect release of substances in the form of vibration, radiation, heat, odour, or noise produced by one or more sources and releases to air, water or land (Art. 14, point e).

paragraph 1). The biodiversity[210] protection and biological resources usage is based on this law and other regulation governing the nature protection (Article 19, paragraph 3).

98. The construction zones at specific locations are determined by Spatial Plan depending on the degree of contamination of the environment and building purposes in certain locations (Article 20, paragraph 1). The performing of certain activities in certain areas where there is a protective distance or protective area is permitted in the manner prescribed in separate regulations governing the degree of contamination of the environment in accordance with the nature of the environment loading and in accordance with this law (Article 20, paragraph 2).[211]

99. Management of hazardous substances,[212] i.e., protection from organic and inorganic substances with hazardous properties, as well as planning, organizing and preventive and remedial measures are carried out under the conditions and in a manner that provides reduction of risks to the environment and to the human health, and providing of adequate response to environmental threats (Article 21, paragraph 1).

100. Protection from the harmful effects of waste on the environment includes all kinds of substances and products, including packaging materials and material for packaging of those substances, i.e., all kinds of disposed products or that are planned to be disposed of (Article 22, paragraph 1).[213]

101. The user of noise sources can use noise sources with the application of protective measures that reduce noise emissions, i.e. the use of facilities, devices, machines, means of transport and devices that cause noise (Article 23, paragraph 1).[214]

102. Radiation protection is implemented by using a system of measures to prevent environmental degradation and risk on human health from effects of radiation

---

210. *Biological diversity (biodiversity)* is the totality of all living organisms, which are integral parts of ecosystems, and includes a variety of living organisms from all sources including *inter alia*, terrestrial and aquatic ecosystems and the ecological complexes to which they belong. This includes diversity within species, between species, habitats and ecosystems (Art. 14, point a).
211. The green areas, as well as the safety belt zone on the territory of the local self-government shall be regulated by special regulations (Art. 20, para. 3).
212. *Hazardous substance* is a substance prescribed by the regulation, mixture of substances or preparations in the form of raw materials, products, by-products, residue or intermediate, including those substances for which it is reasonably expected that could arise in the case of an accident (Art. 14, point c).
213. Waste management planning, waste management licences, monitoring of waste management, activities and responsibilities of waste management, transboundary movements of waste and compensation are regulated by special rules (Art. 22, para. 3).
214. Protection against noise is regulated by a regulation, issued by the minister, which prescribes in detail the limit values of noise intensity in areas of the natural and built environment in accordance with the established purpose of the area, the method of measuring noise outdoors and indoors, as well as the spatial distribution of the area (zone) (Art. 23, para. 2).

emanating from ionizing and non-ionizing sources and eliminates the effects of radiation emissions that radiation sources emit or that may emit (Article 24, paragraph 1).

3. Information and Education in the Field of Environmental Protection

103. The competent authorities and other authorized organizations are obliged to regularly, timely and objectively inform the public[215] about the state of the environment, i.e., on the trends under emissions and immissions[216] monitoring, as well as a cautionary measure or spreading of pollution that can pose a threat to life and health in accordance with this law and other regulations (Article 25, paragraph 1).

104. The Ministry in charge for urban planning, construction and ecology in cooperation with the Ministry responsible for Education and Culture, as well as with the Ministry responsible for science and technology develops and acts in accordance with the annual education plans in the field of environmental protection, which improve education and public awareness on environmental protection in the curriculum and in non-curriculum programme (Article 28, paragraph 1).[217]

4. Public Participation and Access to Information Relating to the Environment

105. Each individual and organization must have appropriate access to information concerning the environment that is held by the Government, including information on hazardous materials and activities in their communities, and the opportunity to participate in decision-making (Article 12, paragraph 1).[218]

106. The Ministry, independently or in cooperation with associations and foundations, promotes environment protection and provides environmental information in a transparent manner, using publications in printed and in electronic form, which are easily accessible to the public, as well as using the media (Article 33, paragraph 1). In the case of an immediate threat to human health or the environment, the Ministry independently or in cooperation with associations and foundations promptly

215. The public has a right of access to prescribed records or evidences containing information and data in accordance with this Law (Art. 25, para. 2).
216. *Imission* is a concentration of substances in a particular place at a particular time in the environment (Art. 14, point n).
217. The Ministry in cooperation with the Ministry responsible for Education and Culture and the Ministry responsible for science and technology provides continuous cooperation, joint activities and support to programs and activities, as well as regular training of associations and foundations representatives (Art. 28, para. 3).
218. The Ministry and local government units (hereinafter, 'the competent authorities') are required to help develop public awareness and facilitating the availability of information to the general public (Art. 12, para. 2).

deliver to the interested public[219] of the affected areas all information in its possession, in order to take measures to prevent or mitigate damage arising from certain danger (Article 33, paragraph 2).

107. The public[220] has a right to participate in the proceedings conducted in accordance with this law and other regulations (Article 12, paragraph 3).[221] Public access to information, participation in decision-making and the environmental protection[222] have all physical persons regardless of citizenship, nationality or place of residence and legal entities regardless of the company headquarter (Article 35, paragraph 1). A request for access to environmental information must be in writing. It is not necessary that request state the reasons for requesting the information (Article 36, paragraph 2). The answer to the request must be in writing, except in the cases mentioned in Article 36, paragraph 3.[223]

5. Planning and Environmental Protection

108. In accordance with Article 43 of the Republic of Srpska issued the following planning documents on environmental protection:[224] the Environmental Protection Strategy (hereinafter, 'The Strategy') and the Environmental Protection Plan of Local government units (hereinafter, 'the Local plan').

109. The Strategy is prepared by the Ministry in cooperation with other relevant Ministries (Article 44, paragraph 3). The strategy is adopted by the Government at the proposal of the Ministry (Article 44, paragraph 4).[225]

110. The competent authority of the local government is obliged to prepare and to adopt Local plans[226] in accordance with the Strategy (Article 46, paragraph 1).

---

219. *Interested public* is the public affected or could be affected by the decisions on the issuance or revision and renewal of a permit or permit conditions or having an interest in making such decisions. In terms of this definition, it shall be deemed that associations and foundations have an interest to promote environmental protection (Art. 14, point k).
220. Any interested person who believes that their rights were violated under para. 3 of this article shall have the right for protection in administrative and court proceedings (Art. 12, para. 4).
221. The competent authorities must ensure that environmental information are available to the public, as well as a copy of the documents containing such information (Art. 36, para. 1).
222. The competent authorities shall ensure public participation in: (a) Proceedings of projects impact assessment to the environment and (b) proceeding of environmental permitting issuance (Art. 39, para. 1).
223. The possible reasons for rejecting of the request for access to environmental information are stipulated under Art. 37, para. 1. Cost for providing the information is to be covered by the applicant for access to environmental information (Art. 38, para. 1).
224. All environmental protection planning documents shall be adopted for a period of ten years (Art. 43, para. 7).
225. The Strategy implementation is made by an Action plan, adopted by the Government (Art. 45, para. 1).
226. Content of the Local plan is prescribed in Art. 46, para. 3.

The Local plan includes long-term measures and environmental protection activities, which are of interest and under the responsibility of the local governments (Article 46, paragraph 2).

111. The Report[227] on the state of the environment is prepared every two years for the purpose of achieving the objectives of the Strategy and of the Action Plan, as well as for the purpose of the complete insight into the state of the environment (Article 47, paragraph 1).

6. Strategic Environmental Impact Assessment

112. Strategic Environmental Impact Assessment (hereinafter, 'the Strategic assessment')[228] is made for plans, programmes and basics (hereinafter, 'the Plans and Programmes')[229] in the field of spatial and urban planning, land use, agriculture, forestry, fisheries, hunting, energy, industry, transport, waste management, water management, telecommunications, tourism, conservation of natural habitats and flora and fauna, which set a framework for the approval of future development projects of certain regulations governing the assessment of environmental impact (Article 48, paragraph 1).

113. The Strategic assessments made at various levels for Plans and Programmes must be mutually compatible, consistent with the project impact assessment to the environment, as well as with environment protection Plans and Programmes (Article 50, paragraph 1).[230]

114. The authority responsible for the preparation of Plans and Programmes submits a Report on the strategic assessment[231] under Article 53 of this law to interested agencies and organizations for review (Article 54, paragraph 1). The

227. Content of the Report is prescribed in Art. 47, para. 2.

228. *Strategic Environmental Assessment* is a systematic evaluation process of the consequences of proposed plans, programs or strategies to the environment with the aim that environmental consideration are included at an early stage of decision-making together with economic and social considerations (Art. 14, point aj).

229. *Plans and programs* are all development and other plans and programs, the basics, including their amendments, prepared and/or adopted by an authority at national or local level, or which the competent authority prepares for the adoption procedure in the National Assembly of the Republic of Srpska or the Government of the Republic of Srpska (hereinafter, 'the Government'), i.e., in the local governments, as well as plans and programs prepared on the basis of special regulations (Art. 14, point š).

230. The Plan or Program which establishes a framework for the development of a particular sector, i.e., its features, objectives and geographic coverage make the basis for the strategic assessment (Art. 50, para. 2).

231. Report on the Strategic Environmental Assessment is a document that accompanies the Plan or Program and includes the identification, description and assessment of the likely significant environmental impacts due to the implementation of the plan and program, as well as the variations discussed and adopted on the basis of the objectives and extent of the Plan and Program (Art. 14, point nj).

authorities and organizations shall submit their opinion within thirty days of receipt of the Report and supporting documents (Article 54, paragraph 2).

The authority responsible for preparation of Plans and Programmes provides public participation in the process of reviewing the Report on the strategic assessment before submitting the Report to the Ministry for review (Article 55, paragraph 1).[232] The Ministry within thirty days of receipt of the Report on the Strategic Assessment and the Report on the consultations conducted in accordance with Articles 54–56 of this law, gives the opinion, taking into account the interests of the protection, preservation and improvement of the environment (Article 57, paragraph 1).

7. Environmental Impact Assessment

115. In the environmental impact assessment, the direct and indirect significant impact of the project on the following elements and factors is determined, described and evaluated in an appropriate manner, considering each individual case: (a) population and human health, (b) biological diversity (biodiversity), with special attention focused on species and habitats protected in accordance with a special regulation, (c) geological and landscape diversity, (g) soil, water, air and climate, (d) material assets, cultural-historical and natural heritage, (f) interaction of the aforementioned factors in points (a) to (d) of this article. Also, it is necessary to obtain a certificate on approval of the environmental impact study (hereinafter, 'decision on approving the study') in accordance with the law (Article 61, paragraph 1). The assessment of the impact on the environment is not carried out for projects intended for the security of the Republic, projects to mitigate and eliminate the consequences of natural disasters (paragraph 2).[233]

116. The Minister shall issue the decision on determining the liability of the Impact Assessments and scope of the Impact Assessment and decision on approval of the study for certain projects according to the procedure stipulated by this law (Article 62, paragraph 1).[234]

---

232. The authority responsible for the preparation of the plan and program submits to the Ministry a report on the strategic assessment of the impact on the environment and a report on the consultations carried out, in order to give an opinion. The reports from para. 1 of this article shall be submitted in written form in the original (one copy) and in electronic form (one copy) (Art. 55a).

233. Environmental Impact Assessment (hereinafter, 'the Impact Assessment') is conducted in two phases: 1) in the preliminary assessment procedure, deciding on:–the obligation on conducting Environmental Impact Assessment,–the scope of the Impact Assessment, if the Impact Assessment implementation is required; 2) in the Environment Impact Assessment procedure (Art. 61, para. 3).

234. *See*: Decree on projects for which an environment impact assessment is underway and on the criteria for deciding on the obligation to conduct an environment impact assessment and on the scope thereof (Official Gazette of RS No. 124/12); Manual on the contents of the environment impact study (Official Gazette of RS No. 108/13).

117. Impact Study contains[235] a special section that refers to the possible impact of the project on the environment of another entity, on the environment of Brčko District or that might have possible transboundary impacts, in accordance with Article 75 paragraph 1, and Article 79 of this Law (Article 68, paragraph 4).

Project holder[236] organizes a public hearing on impact assessment study in the local government which is the location of the project (Article 70, paragraph 1). It is mandatory that the Ministry representative participate in public hearing, as well as to hold a public hearing (Article 70, paragraph 2).[237]

8. Environmental Permits Issuing and Preventing of Large-Scale Disaster

118. An environmental permit[238] prescribes measures to prevent or, when it is not feasible, to reduce emissions into air, water and soil, as well as to prevent the waste production, in order to achieve a high level of the environmental protection as a whole (Article 80, paragraph 1). An environmental permit contains the basic obligations of the responsible person and the measures prescribed by the laws which provisions are related to the facility (Article 90, paragraph 1).[239]

An environmental permit may include two or more facilities operated by the same responsible person[240] at one location. That environmental permit includes measures to ensure that every single facility[241] meets the requirements prescribed by this law (Article 82, paragraph 1). A person responsible for the facility is obliged to contribute to the achievement of environmental quality standards[242] to minimize transboundary pollution, as well as to effectively protect the environment as a whole (Article 83, paragraph 1).

235. The Minister shall issue regulation defining the contents of the Environmental Impact Study (Art. 68, para. 1).
236. The project holder is a natural or legal person, including republican and other authorized institutions, upon whose request the procedure for preliminary environmental impact assessment and/or the procedure for approving the environmental impact study is initiated, (Art. 14. Point u). Costs of informing and facilitating of public participation to be involved in the Environmental Impact Assessment procedures and the impact study audit costs shall be borne by the project holder (Art. 74, para. 1).
237. The interested public may, within fifteen days from the date of the public hearing, submit comments and opinions regarding the request and the impact study to the project holder and the Ministry in writing (para. 5).
238. Environmental Permit shall not be issued for research activities, development activities, as well as for the testing of new products and processes (Art. 80, para. 2).
239. The Minister shall issue a regulation that determines the facilities that can be built and put into operation only if they have an environmental permit (Art. 81, para. 1).
240. *Responsible person* means any natural person or legal entity who, in whole or in part manage or control the facility or person to which it transferred the authority to make economic decisions in the field of technical functioning of the facility or installation (Art. 14, point f).
241. *Facility* includes one or more drives, one or more technical units in one place for performing activities that may have adverse effects on the environment or where hazardous substances are located. The facility includes any activity which is directly linked to the performance of technical activities at the facility site, and which may have an impact on the level of emissions and pollution (Art. 14, point ad).
242. *Environmental quality standard* prescribes requirement that must be met in a certain period, in a certain area or a certain part, as prescribed by this Law or by other Laws (Art. 14, point az).

The authority responsible for issuing of environmental permits performs every five years review, as well as the renewal of an issued environmental permit by changing the conditions from the permit, as required (Article 94, paragraph 1).[243] The competent authority for issuing environmental permits establishes and maintains the register of environmental permits (Article 101, paragraph 1).[244] The Minister shall issue a regulation setting forth the content and manner of keeping the register (Article 101, paragraph 3).

119. Article 84 provides that environmental quality standards are achieved using the best available techniques[245] in order to prevent or to reduce to a minimum the negative impacts of drives and facilities or activities, and in particular: (a) by establishing limiting emission values[246] for pollutants, (b) applying of environmental protection technical standards for certain product, operation, installation or device, equipment and manufacturing process that may result in a risk or danger to the environment and (c) by determining the requirements for measuring and monitoring.

120. The responsible person for the facility is obliged to provide the competent authority with all information necessary for the review of the conditions from the environmental permit, involving monitoring results and other data (Article 94, paragraph 2).

The Republic Hydrometeorological Institute keeps the register[247] of realized and transferred pollutants (Article 102, paragraph 1). The person responsible for the facility for which an environmental permit has been issued is required to submit a report to the Republic Hydrometeorological Institute on releases and transfers of pollutants off-site facilities (Article 102, paragraph 2).

121. The responsible person of a facility which can cause large-scale disaster is obliged to take all measures necessary to prevent large-scale accidents[248] and limit their effects on humans and the environment (Article 103, paragraph 1). Also, that

---

243. The renewal of the environmental permit is carried out at the request of the responsible person, which is submitted to the competent authority no later than three months before the expiration of its term, accompanied by the evidence required for the purpose of renewing and revising the conditions of the said permit (para. 2).
244. The local government unit shall submit to the Ministry an annual report of licences issued for smaller facilities that threaten or may threaten the environment (Art. 101, para. 2).
245. *Best available techniques* are the most effective and the most advanced stage in the development of activities and manner of their performance, which indicate the practical suitability of particular techniques in order to provide the basis for emission limit values and other requirements from environmental permits prescribed to prevent, or if not feasible, to reduce emissions and the impact on the environment as a whole (Art. 14, point t).
246. *Emission limit values* are expressed in terms of mass of specific parameters, concentration and / or level of emissions that will not be exceeded during a specified period or for specified periods (Art. 14, point v).
247. The Minister shall issue a regulation on the keeping of this Register (Art. 102, para. 4).
248. *Large-scale disaster/accident* is a large-scale emission, fire or explosion due to uncontrollable events that occurred during the operation of the plant, which poses a serious threat to human health or the environment, immediate or delayed, inside or outside the plant, which includes one or more hazardous substances (Art. 14, point dj).

person is obliged to prepare a plan to prevent large-scale disaster through authorized institutions (hereinafter, 'the Plan') as well as to ensure proper implementation of the Plan (Article 105, paragraph 1).[249] The Plan must ensure that it is guaranteed a high level of protection for people and the environment by the appropriate means, structures and management system (Article 105, paragraph 2).

For facility which may cause large-scale disaster, the responsible person prepare the plan for internal intervention for measures to be taken within the facility and submit it to the competent authorities for treatment in emergency situations, the necessary information for making external intervention plans, before beginning of operation of the facility (Article 108, paragraph 1).[250]

9. Eco-Labelling, Management and Environmental Control

122. The eco-label awarding system is set up to encourage the development, production, marketing and use of products with reduced environmental impact compared to the total duration of the product, and for better informing of the consumers about the impact of the product on the environment (Article 111, paragraph 1).[251] The system of the eco-label awarding shall be in compliance with health and safety conditions and requirements for environmental protection (Article 111, paragraph 3).

123. The Minister shall prescribe a system and procedure for eco-label awarding,[252] the bodies responsible for the management of the eco-label and so on (Article 111, paragraph 5). Eco-label is an emblem which is determined in accordance with the provisions of paragraph 5 of this article and is awarded to products and services (Article 111, paragraph 4) for a period of three years (Article 114, paragraph 3).[253]Eco-label can be assigned to products available in the Republic of Srpska, which comply with the basic requirements for protection of the environment and the eco-label criteria established according to product groups[254] (Article 112, paragraph 1).

---

249. Plan for facilities specified in para. 1 this article, including warehouses is submitted to the competent inspection and to the Ministry together with the application for an environmental permit (Art. 105, para. 3).
250. The responsible person shall apply without delay the internal and external emergency plans in case of large-scale disaster or in case of an uncontrolled accident that could lead to a major or significant accident (Art. 108, para. 4).
251. Environmental impacts are determined based on the testing of the product interaction with the environment, including the use of energy and natural resources, in comparison to the total life cycle of the product (Art. 111, para. 2).
252. The Ministry, in accordance with the bylaw from Art. 111, para. 5 of this Law governs the eco-label award system from choosing of the label product groups and their ecological criteria to the eco-label award and concluding the contract relating to the conditions for use of the label (Art. 113, para. 1).
253. The Ministry makes a decision on the eco-label award after checking whether the conditions of ecological criteria for that product group are met (Art. 114, para. 2).
254. *A product group* is any type of product or service with similar purposes and as such is equal in terms of usage and perceptions of consumers (Art. 14, point g).

124. Eco-label cannot be placed on substances that are classified as highly toxic and dangerous to the environment or that are carcinogenic, toxic for reproduction or which are mutagenic, or for products that are made in the process which are likely that are extremely hazardous to human health or the environment, or that their normal application could be harmful to consumers (Article 112, paragraph 3).[255]

Eco-label is awarded on the basis of voluntary applications submitted by producers, importers, suppliers of services and retailers (Article 114, paragraph 1). Eco-label cannot be used, nor can it be invoked on eco-label in advertising, until the label awarding. After the award, it can only be used for such kind of product that has been assigned for (Article 114, paragraph 6).[256]

10. Financing of the Environmental Protection and Economic Instruments

125. The funds for environmental protection shall be provided in the budget of the Republic of Srpska, in the budget of the local governments, the Fund for Environmental Protection and Energy Efficiency of the Republic of Srpska (hereinafter, 'the Fund'), as well as from other sources in accordance with the law (Article 116, paragraph 1). Other sources of funds are grants, loans, international aid, funding of foreign projects, programmes, as well as investments designed to protect the environment and other resources prescribed by a separate law (Article 116, paragraph 2).[257]

Environmental polluter[258] (hereinafter, 'the polluter') pays fee for environmental pollution in accordance with the regulations governing the financing of environmental protection, when their activities cause or may cause environmental pollution, i.e., if produce, use or place on the market raw materials, semi-finished products or products containing harmful substances to the environment (Article 13, paragraph 1).

126. In accordance with the regulations governing the financing of the environmental protection, the Fund collects and distributes financial means for environmental protection in the Republic of Srpska, which are used in particular for the following purposes: (a) Support the implementation of obligations arising from the obligations and responsibilities to the international community in the field of environmental protection, (b) Prevention of environmental damage in the case when it cannot be applied the responsibility for performing damage to a certain person, (c)

255. Awarding of eco-labels for food, beverage, pharmaceutical or medical products, is regulated by a special Law (Art. 112, para. 4).

256. Legal entities and natural persons in the Republic of Srpska may voluntarily participate in the environmental management system (EMAS), which was at the European Union level established with the aim to improve the operations of legal entities and natural persons to the environment and to provide relevant information to the public and interested parties (Art. 115, para. 1).

257. The funds for environmental protection are used for the preservation, protection and improvement of the environment (Art. 116, para. 3).

258. The polluter, in accordance with the provisions of para. 1 of this article covers the total costs of measures for pollution prevention and reduction, which include the costs of environmental risks and the costs of disposing of the damage caused to the environment (Art. 13, para. 2).

The cost of preventing or repairing the damage to the environment that requires immediate intervention, (d) Support for measures to protect the environment, especially in the development and financing of information system, education and information dissemination, research and public activities related to environmental protection and (e) Preservation of protected natural areas (Article 117, paragraph 1).

11. Civil Liability for Environmental Damage

127. Article 118 provides that any legal entity or natural person is obliged to ensure the protection of the environment in performing its activities, as follows: (a) by the implementation and enforcement of regulations on environmental protection, (b) by sustainable use of natural resources, goods and energy, (c) by introduction of energy-efficient technologies and the use of renewable natural resources, (d) by use of products, processes, technologies and practices that less threaten the environment, (e) by taking measures to prevent or eliminate the effects of threats and damage to the environment, (f) by keeping track of raw materials and energy, discharge of pollutants and energy, classification, characteristics and quantities of waste, (g) by controlling of facility activities and operation that may pose a risk or cause danger to the environment and human health and (h) by other measures in accordance with the law.[259]

12. Inter-entity Cooperation and Monitoring

128. The establishment of cooperation and coordination from Article 5 paragraph 3 of this law perform inter-entity body for environmental protection (hereinafter, 'inter-entity body'), established by the Government of the Republic of Srpska, Government of the Federation of Bosnia and Herzegovina and the Brčko District (Article 127, paragraph 1). The inter-entity body has four members of the Republic of Srpska, four members from the Federation of Bosnia and Herzegovina and two members from the Brčko District (Article 127, paragraph 2).[260]

129. The Ministry performs administrative supervision over the implementation of this law and regulations issued on the basis of it (Article 129, paragraph 1). Inspection supervision of the enforcement of the provisions of this law and the other regulations adopted on the basis of it are performed by inspectors responsible for environmental protection of the Republic Administration for Inspection Affairs and local government units (hereinafter, 'competent inspectors') (Article 130, paragraph 1).

259. Legal entities and natural persons perform these environmental protection measures independently or through an authorized legal entity (Art. 118, para. 2). For more information on civil liability *see* Part IV (Liability questions).

260. Inter-entity body meets at least six times a year and makes decisions by consensus (Art. 127, para. 4).

B. Other Relevant RS Regulations

130. The following secondary environmental regulations were adopted:

(1) Regulation on projects for which an environment impact assessment is carried out and on the criteria for deciding on the obligation to conduct and on the scope of an environment impact assessment (Official Gazette of RS No. 124/12).[261]
(2) Regulation on plants that can be constructed and commissioned only if an environmental permit has been issued (Official Gazette of RS No. 124/12).
(3) Instruction on the contents of the environment impact study (Official Gazette of RS No. 108/13).
(4) Rule book on the requirements for performing operations in the field of environmental protection (Official Gazette of RS No. 28/13, 74/18).
(5) Rulebook on activities and method of making the best available techniques (Official Gazette of the RS, No. 108/13).
(6) Rule book on eco-labels and on the manner of governing eco-labelling (Official Gazette of RS No. 108/13).
(7) Rulebook on the content and manner of keeping a register of issued environmental permits (Official Gazette of RS, No. 108/13).
(8) Rulebook on the procedure for revision and renewal of environmental permits (Official Gazette of RS, Nos. 28/13 and 104/17).
(9) Rule book on the methodology and manner of keeping a register of plants and pollutants (Official Gazette of RS No. 92/07).
(10) Rule book on the manner of establishing and managing information systems for environmental protection and monitoring system ('Official Gazette of the RS' No. 85/05).
(11) Rulebook on the Appearance of the Nature Protection Sign (Official Gazette of RS, No 50/16)
(12) Regulation on compensation for the cost of issuing licenses in the field of environmental protection (Official Gazette of RS, No. 19/16).
(13) Rulebook on conditions and manner of taking the professional exam for carrying out activities in the field of environmental protection (Official Gazette of RS, No. 105/16, 37/22)
(14) Rulebook on criteria for deciding on the need to conduct a strategic environmental impact assessment (Official Gazette of RS, 28/13).
(15) Rulebook on the content of the strategic environmental impact assessment report (Official Gazette of RS, 28/13).
(16) Rulebook on the content of the remediation and recultivation project (Official Gazette of RS, 97/20).

---

261. *See*: http://www.vladars.net/sr-SP-Cyrl/Vlada/Ministarstva/mgr/PAO/Pages/Akti.aspx (10 July 2022).

II. Federation of Bosnia and Herzegovina

A. The Law on Environmental Protection

131. Basic legal act regulating environmental protection[262] in the Federation of Bosnia and Herzegovina is the Law on Environmental Protection (Official Gazette of FBiH, No 15/21). It has the following eighteen parts: Part I – General Provisions (Articles 1–4),[263] Part II – Principles of the Environmental Protection (Articles 5–11), Part III – Protection of the Environmental Components (Articles 12–21), Part IV – Competence (Articles 22–27), Part V – Informing and Education on the Environment (Articles 28–33), Part VI – Access to the Information and Public Participation (Articles 34–43), Part VII – Planning of the Environment Protection (Articles 44–47), Part VIII – Strategic Environmental Assessment (Articles 48–63), Part IX – Environmental Impact Assessment (Articles 64–81), X – Issuing of the Environmental Permits (Articles 82–101), XI – Prevention of Large Scale Accidents (Articles 102–113), XII – Financing of the Environmental Protection (Articles 114–122), XIII – Eco-Labeling System and Eco-Management and Audit Scheme (EMAS) (Articles 123–124), XIV – Inter-Entity Cooperation (Articles 125–127), XV – Environmental Monitoring (Articles 128–131), XVI – Supervision (Article 132-140), XVII – Misdemeanor Provisions (Articles 141–145), Part XVIII – Transitional and Final Provisions (Articles 146–149).

132. Article 1 provides that the objectives of this Law are: (a) reduced use, prevention of loading and environmental pollution, prevention of disturbances, as well as improvement and restoration of the damaged environment; (b) improvement of environmental conditions, protection of human health, including the right to a healthy life; (c) conservation and protection of natural resources, rational use of resources and such a way of economy which ensures the renewal of resources; (d) harmonization of social, economic and other interests of the Federation of BiH with the requirements for environmental protection; (e) realization and improvement of international cooperation in environmental protection; (f) public animation and public participation in activities aimed at environmental protection; (g) coordination of the economy and integration of social and economic development in accordance with the requirements of environmental protection, and (h) establishment and development of institutions for environmental protection and preservation (paragraph 2).

262. *Environmental protection* – all appropriate actions and measures aimed at the prevention of danger, damage or pollution of the environment, reduction or removal of caused damage, and return to the state prior to the damage (Art. 4, para. 1).

263. According to the Art. 1, para. 1, this Law regulates: a) the principles of environmental protection; b) protection of environmental components; c) competence in the field of environmental protection; d) information and education on the environment; e) access to environmental information and public participation in the field of environmental protection; f) environmental planning; g) strategic environmental assessment; h) establishing environmental quality standards; i) environmental impact assessment; j) environmental permit; k) prevention of large-scale accidents; l) financing of environmental protection; m) civil liability for environmental damage; n) eco-labelling and environmental management system; o) inter-entity cooperation in the field of environmental protection; p) administrative and inspection supervision and r) misdemeanour provisions..

133. According to Article 2 provisions of this law are related to the following: (a) all components of the environment (air, water, soil, world of plants, animals and fungi, landscape, built environment); (b) all types of activities whose purpose is to use and burden natural resources, i.e., the impact on the environment that means the risk of pollution during the activity or have a negative impact on the environment (such as noise, vibration, radiation, excluding nuclear radiation, waste, light pollution); (c) rights and responsibilities of legal and natural persons performing activities determined by law; (d) tasks in the field of environment arising from international conventions (Article 2,).

134. The right to a healthy and ecologically friendly environment for everyone is recognized as a basic human right, so it is an individual and collective duty to protect and improve the environment for the benefit of present and future generations (Article 3, paragraph 1). Entities that ensure environmental protection are the Federation of Bosnia and Herzegovina, cantons and local self-government units in accordance with this Law and other regulations (paragraph 2).

1. Principles of the Environmental Protection

135. The Environmental sustainable development principle. Sustainable development in the field of environment includes: (a) preservation of environmental components and strengthening of their ecological functions; (b) that emissions of pollutants do not exceed the capacity of air, water and soil and their ability to absorb and self-purify, and (c) continuous preservation of biological diversity, human health and air, water and soil quality to standards that are always sufficient for human, plant and animal life of the world (Article 5).

The precaution and prevention principle prescribes that when there is a threat of irreversible damage, lack of full scientific base cannot be used as a reason for delaying of introduction of precaution and prevention measures in order to prevent further environmental degradation (Article 6, paragraph 1).[264] For prevention purpose, the best available techniques[265] are applied during using of the environment (Article 6, paragraph 4). If the damage was caused as a result of past activities of the user, the user is obliged to eliminate and repair the incurred damage (Article 6, paragraph 5).

264. The use of the environment shall be organized and performed in a manner that: a) results in the lowest possible degree of burden and use of the environment; b) prevents environmental pollution and c) prevents damage to the environment. The use of resources (raw, and materials) must respect the precautionary principle, i.e. carefully manage and economically use environmental components, and minimize the generation of waste by recycling and / or reuse of natural and artificial materials.

265. *Best available techniques* – the most effective and advanced stage in development of activities and their methods of operation which indicate at the practical suitability of application of certain technologies (for insurance of limiting emission values) in order to prevent and where is not practicable, reduce emissions into the environment (Art. 4, para. 1). Best available techniques include both the technology applied and the way the plant is designed, built, maintained, used and decommissioned;

The replacement principle prescribes that it is necessary to replace any activity that might have harmful effects on the environment with another activity that has significantly less risk. Replacement of the activities shall be performed, as well as in case that the costs of such activities are higher than the value to be protected (Article 7, paragraph 1).[266]

Purpose of *The principle of integrated approach* is to prevent or reduce to a minimum the risk of damage to the environment as a whole (Article 8, paragraph 2).[267] The principle of integrated approach includes the following (Article 8, paragraph 3):

(1) Taking into account the whole life cycle of substances and products.
(2) Prediction of the consequences in all components of the environment as a result of interaction of substances and activities (new and existing).
(3) Reduction of waste generation and harmful effects of waste to a minimum.
(4) Application of general methods for assessment and comparison of the environmental problems.
(5) The complementary application of measures in relation to the consequences, such as quality objectives of the environmental protection and measures that are aimed at the sources, in terms of emissions.[268]

The principle of cooperation and sharing of responsibility prescribes that sustainable development can be achieved through cooperation and joint action of all entities in order to protect the environment, each within its jurisdiction and responsibilities (Article 9, paragraph 1).[269]

The principle of public participation and access to information prescribes that environmental issues are realized through the participation of citizens.[270] Every individual and organization must have appropriate access to environmental information that are held by the administrative bodies, including and information on hazardous materials and activities in their communities,[271] as well as the possibility of participation in the decision-making process (Article 10, paragraph 1). Regulatory bodies and bodies responsible for environmental protection are obliged to assist and develop public awareness, as well as to encourage participation in decision-making,

---

266. The provisions of para. 1 of this article shall apply in the use of products, parts of facilities, equipment and application of production processes with mandatory limiting of the environmental pollution at the source (Art. 7, para. 2).
267. Requirements for a high level of environmental protection and improvement of environmental quality are an integral part of all policies aimed at environmental development, and are ensured in accordance with the principle of sustainable development.
268. *Emissions* – means the release into the environment of substances, compounds, organisms or microorganisms resulting from human activities and, as well as vibrations, heat, odours, noise or light produced by one or more sources in an installation and released into the air, water, soil (Art. 4).
269. Implementation of environmental objectives is achieved through cooperation and coordination in the Federation of BiH, inter-entity cooperation and cooperation with the Brčko District of BiH, bilateral or multilateral international agreements on environmental protection, as well as providing information and assistance on environmental protection, especially in relations with neighbouring countries (para. 2).
270. The public has the right to participate in proceedings conducted at the request of operators and investors in accordance with the provisions of this Law or other regulations (Art. 10, para. 3).
271. Every individual has the right to equal access to environmental information regardless of gender, age, religion and race (Art. 10, para. 5).

enabling the availability of information to the general public (Article 10, paragraph 2). In order to obtain compensation or legal protection, every interested party has the right to protection in administrative and judicial proceedings (Article 10, paragraph 4).

The polluter pays principle prescribes that the polluter pays the costs of monitoring and prevention of pollution, as well as compensation for damage done to the environment, regardless of whether the costs are incurred as a result of the imposition of liability due to pollution emissions, compensation determined by appropriate financial instruments or as an obligation determined by the regulation on reducing the environmental pollution (Article 11, paragraph 1). The polluter, from paragraph (1) of this article, is responsible for all activities that have an impact on the environment in accordance with this Law and other regulations (Article 11, paragraph 2).

2. Protection of the Environmental Components

136. Integrated protection of the environmental components[272] means that the environment components must be protected individually and within other components of the environment, taking into account their interdependent relationships. Accordingly, it also determines the way of loading and usage of the environment components (Article 12, paragraph 1).[273]

The soil preservation includes surface and subsurface layers of the soil, soil, formations of rocks and minerals, as well as its natural and transitional forms and processes (Article 13, paragraph 1). The land conservation includes preservation of productivity, structure, balance of water and air, as well as soil biota (Article 13, paragraph 2).[274] During and before the implementation of projects (construction, exploitation of ores, etc.), appropriate separation, disposal and protection of the surface layer of the soil as well as protection and use of agricultural and forest land must be ensured (Article 13, paragraph 4).[275]

The water protection involves preservation of surface and ground waters, reserves, regulation of the water quality and quantity, riverbed protection, coastal areas of the inland waters and aquifer (Article 14, paragraph 1). Water protection is implemented through general prohibitions and restrictions, the obligation to drain and treat wastewater, control compliance with prescribed limit values for wastewater discharge, achieving good water status and environmental quality standards for

272. Protection of the environment components means protecting of the quality, quantity and their stocks, as well as conservation of natural processes within the components and their natural balance (Art. 12, para. 2).
273. The protection of environmental components means the protection of quality, quantity and their stocks, as well as the preservation of natural processes within the components and their natural balance (para. 2). The special regulations regulate the particular areas of protection and conservation of the environmental components and protection from the impact that pose a threat to the environment (para. 3).
274. Land protection is defined by special regulations governing the field of agricultural, forestry and other soil in the Federation of BiH (Art. 13, para. 7).
275. Upon completion of activities involving land use, the user shall ensure the restoration of the area according to the reclamation project (Art. 13, para. 5).

water, incident management, ensuring conditions for achieving environmental acceptable flow and the establishment of protected areas.[276]

Protection of the sea and coastal area from pollution includes: management of the coastal area, seabed and subsoil and marine environment based on ecosystem approach, reduction or removal of pollution or burdens in the marine and coastal environment, preservation of protected and ecologically significant areas at sea and coastal zone, protection, conservation and restoration of marine resources and structures and functions of marine and coastal ecosystems, systematic monitoring and control of marine and coastal ecosystems, based on the ecosystem approach (Article 14, paragraph 3).[277]

The air protection includes preservation of the atmosphere complete with all its processes, preserving its structure and climate characteristics (Article 15, paragraph 1).[278] When planning the introduction of activities and the establishment of facilities, as well as the production and use of products, it is necessary to take measures to reduce the level of air pollutants to a minimum.[279]

The biosphere preservation includes protection of living organisms, their communities and habitats, taking also into account conservation of natural processes within their habitats and natural balance while ensuring sustainability of the ecosystem (Article 16, paragraph 1).[280]

Preservation of the built environment means that developing plan defines the zones of construction in certain locations depending on the degree of environmental loads and building purposes within certain parts at specific locations (Article 17, paragraph 1).[281]

Protection from harmful impact of hazardous substances[282] includes protection from usage of all natural and artificial substances that were used, produced or distributed by the users of the environment during conducting of activities, which are

---

276. Water protection is regulated by a special regulation governing the field of water in the Federation of BiH (Art. 14, para. 5).

277. Protection and management of the coastal zone includes measures for the protection of coastal ecosystems and sustainable and integrated management of coastal resources and coordination activities related to improving the harmonization of activities of all entities responsible for coastal areas by applying the integrated coastal zone management approach (Art. 13, para. 4).

278. The air must be protected from the burden of any artificial influences on the air or on other environmental components through transmission of radioactive, liquid, gaseous or solid matters if there is a danger that it will have harmful effect on air quality or will have harmful effect on human health (Art. 15, para. 2).

279. Air protection planning, emission sources, air protection, supervision, public participation and financing of air protection are prescribed by a special regulation regulating air protection in the Federation of BiH (Art. 15, para. 4).

280. Using of the biosphere cannot be done in a way that violates natural processes and conditions of biodiversity and poses a threat to their sustainability (Art. 16, para. 2). Protection and use of the biosphere shall be performed on the basis of this Law and special regulations governing nature protection in the Federation of BiH (Art. 16, para. 3).

281. Green areas within local self-government units shall be regulated in the manner determined by the Law on Principles of Local Self-Government in the Federation of BiH and local self-government acts on communal order (Art. 17, para. 3).

282. *Hazardous substance* – refers to a substance, mixture of substances or preparation determined by implementing regulation, which is present as a raw material, product, by-product, residue or intermediate product, including those substances for which it is expected to be incurred in case of an accident (Art. 4, para. 1).

by their quantity or quality, explosive, flammable, radioactive, toxic, corrosive, causing infection, eco-toxic, mutagenic, carcinogenic, or irritating, or may cause such effects in contact with other substances (Article 18, paragraph 1).

Protection from the harmful impact of waste on the environment includes protection from all kinds of substances, products, including packaging and packing materials for these substances, i.e., all kinds of products that are disposed of or that are planned to be disposed of (Article 19, paragraph 1).[283]

Protection from noise and vibration in the environment includes protection from all kinds of artificially produced energy emissions that cause load by undesirable, unpleasant noise, i.e., vibrations that may endanger the health or that might have adverse effect on health (Article 20, paragraph 1).[284]

Protection from harmful radiation impact on the environment includes protection from artificially produced and natural ionization, non-ionizing radiation and thermal radiation of all types in accordance with laws and other regulations (Article 21, paragraph 1). Protection against light pollution includes measures to protect against unnecessary, useless or harmful light emissions into space in the zone and outside the zone to be illuminated, and measures to protect the night sky from excessive lighting (paragraph 2).[285]

3. Environmental Information and Education

137. The Federal Ministry shall establish an environmental information system and order monitoring of the state of the environment, activities of measurement, collection, processing, and recording of environmental data, as well as enable all collected data to be available (Article 28, paragraph 1). The information system shall be formed and organized, and the manner of collecting and submitting data is defined in more detail in Article 129 of this Law (paragraphs 2 and 4).[286]

283. The waste holder is obliged to take appropriate waste management measures and other waste disposal measures prescribed by the regulation on waste management in the Federation of BiH, and provide basic measures to prevent waste generation, recycling and treatment of waste for reuse and possible use waste for energy generation and safe disposal (Art. 19, para. 2).
284. Protection against noise and vibration is defined by this Law and special regulations on protection against noise and vibration in the Federation of BiH (Art. 20, para. 3).
285. The competent federal ministry shall regulate the measures of protection against light pollution (Art. 21, para. 4).
286. The Federal Water Agency, the Federal Hydrometeorological Institute, the Federal Institute of Agropedology, the Environmental Protection Fund of the Federation of BiH, the Federal Institute of Statistics, the Federal Institute of Geology and other federal administrative organizations and cantons shall ensure the collection, processing and recording of appropriate data and information (Art. 28, para. 3).

138. Environmental users are required to make measurements of loading and usage of the environment as a result of their activities in a way determined by special regulations, to confirm it and to record them in accordance with its technical capabilities and to allow access to these data to the responsible authorities (Article 29, paragraph 1).[287]

139. Determined factual state, the extent and nature of permanent damage to the environment, determined by the decision of the competent authority or court, are recorded in the Land Registry as a temporary registration, as well as in Real Estate Cadastre (Article 30, paragraph 1).[288]

140. The Federal Ministry is obliged to cooperate with administrative bodies and ministries responsible for the environment and education in order to provide professional education on the environment (Article 32, paragraph 2), and every citizen has the right to acquire and improve knowledge about the environment.[289]

141. Environmental education programmes are included in curricula and extracurricular programmes (Article 32, paragraph 4), and the Federal Ministry have to organize training of interested legal entities dealing with environmental issues.

4. Access to the Environmental Information and Public Participation

142. The Federal Ministry shall maintain electronic registers of pollutants, pollutions and facilities containing dangerous substances that are the basis for reporting in accordance with legal obligations and international agreements, including those arising from the Kiev Protocol and the Aarhus Convention on Access to Information (Article 34, paragraph 1).[290] Electronic registers on pollutants, pollution and facilities in which dangerous substances are present are available to the public via the website of the Federal Ministry (paragraph 5), and any person may request access to the electronic register and provision of data from the electronic register (paragraph 6).

143. Upon request for access to environmental information, the Federal Ministry, cantonal ministries and other administrative bodies and legal entities exercising

287. The competent authority shall publish this information on its website for the purpose of informing the public.
288. The Federal or Cantonal Ministry shall *ex officio* request the entry of data in the case when the responsibility has been determined by a court (para.2).
289. Entities ensuring environmental protection shall, in accordance with the possibilities in their budgets, provide funds for education and promotion on environmental protection (Art. 32, para. 6).
Federal, cantonal administrative bodies and municipal administrative services provide support to educational institutions, religious communities, scientific institutions, professional organizations and associations in order to be able to more effectively carry out their education and training activities in the field of environmental protection (Art. 33, para. 3).
290. The electronic register shall contain data on facilities and installations from federal and cantonal jurisdiction that endanger or may endanger the environment.

public authority and possessing environmental information[291] shall ensure that such information is available to the public (Article 38, paragraph 1). The environmental information referred to in paragraph (1) of this article shall be made available as soon as possible, and no later than fifteen days from the date of submission of the request, except in cases where the content and complexity of the information justify extending this deadline to one month (paragraph 3). Rejection of requests for environmental information is regulated by Article 39 of the Law.

144. At the request of the public, the Federal and Cantonal Ministries shall, within fifteen days, submit information on the environment or make it publicly available through the Ministry's website, of which it shall inform the applicant in writing (Article 41, paragraph 1).

145. The public has access to information, opportunity to participate in decision-making and protection of rights before administrative and judicial bodies on environmental protection without discrimination based on citizenship, nationality or place of residence and in the case of legal entities without discrimination based on their place enrolment or activity centre (Article 37, paragraph 1).

146. According to Article 40 of the Law, the Federal and Cantonal Ministries shall ensure public participation in decision-making in the conduct of all proceedings concerning environmental decision-making (paragraph 1). The Federal Ministry shall ensure the public participation in the decision-making for: (a) projects for which a preliminary assessment and/or environmental impact assessment is performed, in the form of a public hearing; (b) all existing installations and new installations that do not require an environmental impact assessment, in the form of public inspection; and (c) closure, or demolition of facilities and installations, in the form of a public hearing.[292] A public hearing shall also be held for plants and facilities within the cantonal jurisdiction, if the activities in question are dangerous for the environment in accordance with Article 116 of this Law (paragraph 8).[293]

After initiating the administrative procedure, the competent ministry shall inform the public (Article 40, paragraph 2), and the public may, within thirty days from the

---

291. Environmental information includes all information in written, visual, oral, audio, electronic or other form on: (a) the state of environmental components, landscape and natural location, biodiversity and its components, including genetically modified organisms and the interaction between these components; (b) substances, energy, noise and radiation, and activities and measures, including administrative measures, environmental agreements, policies, legislation, plans and programs, relating to environmental components under point a) of this Article, cost-effectiveness and other economic analyzes; and assumptions used in environmental decision-making; (c) the state of human health and safety, living conditions, cultural sites and construction structures, ... (Art. 36).
292. The provisions of this article shall not apply in the case of decisions on activities serving the defense and security (para. 3).
293. In addition to the right to participate in permitting and environmental impact assessment procedures, members of the public have the right to initiate proceedings to protect their rights before a competent court (Art. 53).

day of publication of the information, submit in writing remarks, information, analysis, or opinion that it considers important for resolving in the subject procedure (paragraph 6).[294]

5. Competences

147. Pursuant to Article 22 of the Law, the environmental competences are exercised at the level of the Federation of BiH and the cantons.[295]

> The Federal Ministry of Environment and Tourism (hereinafter, 'Federal Ministry'):
> a) plans, proposes and implements strategic documents, policies, financial plans and programs in the field of environmental protection, and programs and regulations in the field of prevention, rehabilitation and development of environmental protection; b) monitor, analyze and evaluate the state of the environment and the implementation of environmental protection, as well as experiences gained in the field of protection, use and development of the environment; c) establishes and manages the system of reporting and information on the environment in the Federation of BiH; d) issue environmental permits within its competence in accordance with the provisions of this Law and other regulations; e) keep a register on pollutants and pollution of all components of the environment which is available to the public; f) organizes activities aimed at preventing or reducing harmful effects on the environment; g) participates with other competent bodies in the development of programs and plans for the use of natural resources, development and implementation of a special plan and qualification system and decides on appeals against decisions of cantonal ministries made under federal law and other federal regulations and performs other environmental tasks and tasks within the competence of the Federation of BiH; h) provide the necessary assistance to the competent state bodies in the implementation of international obligations undertaken by BiH and cooperate with the competent ministry of the Republika Srpska, the competent authority of the Brčko District of BiH and the institutions of BiH (Article 23).

148. The Cantonal ministry in charge of the environment (a) prepares draft regulations and planning documents in the field of environmental protection, which are harmonized with federal regulations, strategies and other planning documents in this field; (b) analyses and evaluate the state of the environment and environmental protection activities by exchanging experiences gained in the field of environmental protection and use; (c) performs tasks and duties determined by federal law and

294. The results of public participation shall be taken into account in final decision process (para. 7).
295. The Parliament of the Federation of BiH adopts the environmental protection strategy and other plans necessary to preserve the interests of environmental protection and evaluates their implementation every two years based on the implementation of the environmental protection strategy (Art. 6 – acts of the Parliament of the Federation of Bosnia and Herzegovina). In case of caused damage or danger of damage to the environment, the provisions of the Criminal Code of the Federation of BiH, the Criminal Procedure Code of the Federation of BiH and other regulations in force in the Federation of BiH shall apply (Art. 27 – role of the judiciary in environmental protection).

other federal regulations; (d) establishes and manages the environmental information system in the canton; (e) issues licenses within its competence; (f) organizes activities aimed at preventing or reducing harmful effects on the environment; (g) supervises the implementation of cantonal regulations and planning documents in the field of environmental protection; (h) establishes and implements a system of prohibition of movement of motor vehicles of certain eco categories when it is assessed that this is a necessary measure in environmental protection; (i) performs other tasks determined by the cantonal regulation (Article 24).

149. The Environmental Advisory Council (hereinafter, 'the Advisory Council') is established to provide scientific and professional support to the Federal Minister of Environment and Tourism and the Government of the Federation of Bosnia and Herzegovina in the field of environmental protection (Article 25, paragraph 1) The Advisory Council has a consultative and advisory role, consisting of the eighteen members taking into account gender equality.[296]

150. The Advisory Council shall harmonize the strategic planning and programming documents and environmental policies. The Advisory Council also considers issues of inter-cantonal cooperation and coordination in the field of environmental protection (Article 25, paragraph 4).

6. Strategic Environmental Assessment

151. Strategic assessment must be conducted for strategies, plans and programmes in the following areas: spatial planning or land use, agriculture, forestry, fisheries, hunting, energy, industry, transport, waste management, water management, telecommunications, tourism, nature conservation habitats of flora and fauna, which establish a framework for approving future development projects[297] (Article 48, paragraph 2).[298]

152. Pursuant to Article 50 the strategic assessment is carried out in the following phases: (a) The phase of determining the scope and content of the strategic study. (b) Strategic study evaluation phase by the expert commission (hereinafter,

296. Members of the Advisory Council shall be appointed by the Government of the Federation of BiH for a period of four years (Art. 25, para. 5). If necessary, representatives of employers' associations and certain branches of industry may be invited to the sessions of the Council, depending on the agenda. Invited representatives can give proposals and suggestions, but they do not have the right to vote in decision-making (Art. 25, para. 3).
297. *Strategic environmental assessment*– a systematic process of evaluating of the environmental consequences of proposed plans and programs, including health, consisting of determining the scope of the strategic assessment report and its preparation, ensuring public hearings and consultations, in order to include environmental considerations in the early stages of decision-making, in addition to economic and social considerations (Art. 4, para. 1).
298. Strategies, plans and programs that serve exclusively for the needs of defense and civil protection, declaration of state of emergency, protection and rescue, flood risk management plans and financial and budgetary strategies are not subject to strategic assessment (Art. 49).

'the strategic assessment commission'). (c) Phase of consultations on the draft strategy, plan and programme and strategic study which includes: participation of interested bodies and organizations; public participation; consultations with interested bodies, organizations and the public of another entity, i.e., Brčko District of BiH, or other country, if the implementation of the plan, programme or strategy may have an impact on the environment of another entity, Brčko District of BiH or other country; and report on results of interested bodies both organization and public. (d) Phase of evaluation of the draft strategy, plan and programme and strategic study, which includes issuing an opinion of the Federal Ministry on the draft strategy, plan and programme, which takes into account the results of evaluation of the strategic study by the expert commission, consultations with bodies and organizations, and the public; in particular consultations with representatives of another entity, the Brčko District of BiH or another state. (e) Adoption of the report of the body responsible for the preparation of the strategy, plan and programme.[299]

153. The law also regulates the following issues: competence for conducting strategic assessment, determining the scope, content and evaluation of the strategic study, manner of conducting strategic assessment, preparation of strategic study, body responsible for the selection of the holder of the strategic study, Strategic Study Evaluation Commission, obtaining the opinion of interested administrative bodies and administrative organizations, public participation in the strategic assessment procedure, obtaining the opinion of an entity, Brčko District of BiH or another state, assessment of strategic study, opinion of the ministry responsible for environmental protection, harmonization with the opinion of the ministry responsible for environmental protection, funds for strategic assessment (Articles 51-63).

7. Environmental Impact Assessment

154. Pursuant to Article 64 of the Law, environmental impact assessment includes identification, description, assessment, direct and indirect impact of projects on: (a) people, flora and fauna and the world of fungi; (b) soil, water, air, climate and landscape; (c) material goods and cultural heritage and (d) interaction of factors listed in points (a) to (c) of this paragraph.[300] The Federal Ministry shall conduct an environmental impact assessment procedure, and stakeholders, competent authorities, citizens' associations and the interested public shall be involved in the impact assessment procedure (Article 65).

155. In accordance with Article 67 the impact assessment is carried out in two phases (1) the preliminary impact assessment procedure, in which a decision is made on: (a) the need to conduct an impact assessment, (b) the scope of the impact

299. Consultations with representatives of another state, as well as procedures for obtaining and giving opinions in this regard, shall be conducted through the institutions of Bosnia and Herzegovina responsible for foreign policy and environment and implementation of the Convention on Environmental Impact Assessment in a Transboundary Context (para. 2).

300. Projects that serve exclusively for defense purposes or projects whose sole purpose is to respond to civil emergencies are not subject to environmental impact assessment (Art. 64, para. 2).

assessment, if the conduct of an impact assessment is mandatory, and (2) the preparation of an environmental impact assessment study. The Government of the Federation of BiH shall issue a regulation determining: (a) projects for which an impact assessment is mandatory and (b) projects for which the competent ministry decides on the obligation to conduct an impact assessment based on criteria in individual cases (Article 68).[301]

156. In addition, the law also regulates the following issues in detail: Initiation of the procedure for preliminary environmental impact assessment, Article 69; Mandatory inspection for preliminary environmental impact assessment, Article 70; Decision on preliminary environmental impact assessment, Article 71; Conducting environmental impact assessment, Article 72; Holders of the Study and electronic register, Article 73; Content of the Study, Article 74; Manner of submitting the Study and informing the public, Article 75; Public hearing, Article 76; Public hearing procedure, Article 77; Expert Commission, Article 78; Approval of the Study, Article 79; Costs incurred in the environmental impact assessment procedure, Article 80, and Probability of transboundary environmental impacts of neighbouring states, Republika Srpska and/or Brčko District of BiH, Article 81.

8. Environmental Permits

157. Environmental permits shall be issued for the purpose of complete environmental protection by providing measures for prevention and reduction of industrial emissions into air, water, soil, reduction of impact on population, flora and fauna and prevention of waste and noise generation in order to achieve a high level of environmental protection as a whole. In addition, an environmental permit shall also be issued in the event of a significant change in the operation of the plant and plant (Article 82, paragraphs 1 and 2).[302]

158. The competence for issuing environmental permits is divided into three levels: the government, the federal ministry, and the cantonal ministry (Article 83).[303]

---

301. In addition to projects determined by the regulation referred to in paragraph (1) of this article, environmental impact assessment is required for: (a) significant changes in projects, determined by Art. 95 of this Act, whereby the project change reaches the prescribed thresholds of this article, (b) projects whose production growth, energy use, water use, space use, emissions or waste production exceeds 25% of the originally determined values, and (c) cessation of operation, demolition and closure of facilities referred to in paragraph (1) of this article and facilities and plants that are subject to the obligation to obtain an environmental permit, in accordance with the bylaw referred to in para. (1) of Art. 83 of this Law (Art. 68 para. 2).
302. An environmental permit shall not be issued for research activities, development activities or for testing new products and processes. For research activities referred to in para. 3 of this article, an environmental impact assessment is mandatory. The Federal Ministry shall issue an environmental permit for a period of five years (Art. 82, paras 3–5).
303. The Government of the Federation of BiH shall issue a regulation determining the plants and facilities that may be built and put into operation only if they have an environmental permit issued in

159. In addition, the law regulates the following issues in detail: General obligations of the operator related to environmental protection, Article 84; Unification of environmental permit, Article 85; Application for issuance of environmental permit, Article 86; Procedure upon receipt of an application for an environmental permit, Article 87; Public participation, Article 88; Issuance of environmental permit, Article 89; Delivery of environmental permit and right to appeal, Article 90; Obligations of the operator after obtaining the environmental permit, Article 91; Rejection of the application for the issuance of an environmental permit, Article 92; Renewal of environmental permit, Article 93; Reconsideration and amendments to the environmental permit, Article 94; Change in work, Article 95; Termination of work, Article 96; Termination of environmental permit, Article 97; Existing plants and facilities, Article 98; Emission limit values, Article 99; Best Available Techniques, Article 100; and Register of Environmental Permits, Article 101.

9. Preventing Large-Scale Accidents

160. Pursuant to Article 102 of the Law the operator of plants and facilities, including warehouses that may cause large-scale accidents (due to the presence of hazardous substances in quantities above the quantities specified in the implementing regulation issued by the Federal Minister) shall: (a) submit to the Ministry information on all in the environment or on the suspicion of such an imminent danger; (b) take the necessary preventive measures; (c) seek guidance on the necessary preventive measures to be taken. The operator shall at any time present to the ministry and the competent inspectorate evidence of the measures taken.[304]

161. The operator of the plant or plant or warehouse referred to in paragraph (1) of Article 102 of this Law shall submit to the Federal Ministry a notification with the following information: (a) name of the responsible person and full address of the plant, (b) registered place of business; with full address, (c) information on hazardous substances present or category of substances in plant and plant or warehouse, (d) quantity and physical form of hazardous substances in plant and plant or warehouse, (e) description of plant and plant and storage area, and (f) immediate environment plants and facilities or warehouses that may cause a major accident or exacerbate its consequences (Article 104, paragraph 1).[305]

---

accordance with the provisions of this Law. The Federal Ministry is responsible for issuing environmental permits for plants and facilities above the thresholds determined by the regulation referred to in paragraph (1) of this article. The Cantonal Ministry is responsible for plants and facilities below the thresholds determined by the regulation referred to in paragraph (1) of this article.

304. If the ministry cannot determine the operator or the operator does not bear responsibility in accordance with Art. 117 of this Law, the ministry shall take the necessary measures (Art. 102, para. 3). The Federal Ministry is responsible for the plants and facilities referred to in para. (1), Art. 102 of this Law (Art. 103).

305. The data referred to in paragraph (1) of this article shall be submitted to the Federal Ministry with the application for the issuance of an environmental permit (para. 3).

162. The plant and plant operator shall, as soon as possible, inform the Civil Protection Information and Alert Center, and then the Federal Ministry, of the large-scale accident, and submit data on: (a) the circumstances of the accident; (b) hazardous substances present; (c) assessment of the impact of the accident on people and the environment, and (d) emergency measures taken (Article 105, paragraph 1). The operator is obliged to inform the ministry about the measures taken to mitigate the consequences of the accident and prevent the occurrence of new accidents. If the operator receives additional data related to the accident, he is obliged to submit them to the Federal Ministry.[306]

163. In addition, the Law regulates the following issues in detail: Article 106 Large-scale accident prevention plan, Article 106; Security Status Report, Article 107; Changes in the operation of the plant, Article 108; Termination procedure, Article 109; Information on security measures, Article 110; Register of large-scale accidents, Article 111; Domino effect, Article 112; Internal and external intervention plans, Article 113.

10. Eco-Labelling System and EMAS

164. According to Article 123 of the Law, the eco-labelling system shall be established to promote the manufacture, production, marketing and use of products with reduced environmental impact in relation to the total duration of that product and to better inform consumers about the environmental impact of products.[307] Environmental impacts shall be determined on the basis of an examination of the interaction of the product with the environment, including the use of energy and natural resources, in relation to the total life cycle of the product. The eco-label award system must comply with existing and emerging health, safety and environmental requirements (paragraph 3).[308]

165. Legal and natural persons in the Federation of BiH may voluntarily participate in the Environmental Management System (EMAS), established at the European Union level to assess and improve the impact of legal and natural persons on the environment and provide relevant information to the public and stakeholders

306. Natural or legal persons have the right to submit to the Ministry all objections related to cases of environmental damage or danger of damage known to them, as well as to require the Federal Ministry to act under this Law: (a) which are affected or likely to be affected by environmental damage; (b) which have a sufficient interest in making environmental decisions relating to the damage or, alternatively (c) which allege infringement (Art. 105, para. 4).
307. The eco-label is an emblem determined by the implementing regulation referred to in paragraph (4) of this Article and awarded to products and services (para. 2).
308. The Federal Minister shall, by an implementing regulation, prescribe the system and procedure for awarding eco-labels, bodies responsible for managing the eco-label system, from the selection of product groups and their ecological criteria to the award of eco-labels and the conclusion of contracts, which enables voluntary participation of legal and natural persons whose products and services meet the requirements of this system (para. 4).

(Article 124, paragraph 1).[309] The procedure for submitting an application for registration, the amount of the fee, the content and manner of keeping the register, the reason for refusing entry, temporary or permanent deletion from the register, education and promotion of EMAS, and other issues shall be determined by a special regulation issued by the Federal Minister (paragraph 3). In addition, the Law also prescribes the conclusion of voluntary agreements. Voluntary agreements may be concluded between bodies and organizations representing certain interests, groups of potential polluters or individual polluters and competent bodies (paragraphs 4–7).

11. Financing Environmental Damages and Liability for Environmental Damage

166. Pursuant to Article 114 the Environmental Protection Fund of the Federation of BiH is established by a special law with the aim of improving the development of economic organization favourable to the environment, preventing environmental damage, implementing measures to eliminate environmental damage; conservation of protected natural areas; motivating and improving the use of best available techniques or alternative solutions favourable to environmental protection; improving and developing public awareness of environmental protection and environmental research.[310]

167. An operator performing an activity dangerous to the environment[311] shall be liable for damage caused by that activity to people, property and the environment (Article 116). The possibility that an activity dangerous to the environment causes damage shall be assessed on the basis of the mode of operation, facilities

309. The aim of the system referred to in paragraph (1) of this article is to promote continuous improvement in the operation of organizations on the environment: (a) establishing and implementing management systems by organizations, (b) systematic, objective and periodic assessment of improving in the field of environmental protection, (c) providing information on environmental impact and enabling the exchange of information with the public and stakeholders and (d) active participation of employees in the organization in establishing and implementing environmental management systems (para. 2).

310. Legal and natural persons are obliged to ensure environmental protection in the performance of their activities, namely: (a) application and implementation of regulations on environmental protection, (b) sustainable use of natural resources, goods and energy, (c) introduction of more energy-efficient technologies and renewable natural resources, (d) using products, processes, technologies and practices that pose less risk to the environment, (e) taking measures to prevent or eliminate the consequences of endangerment and damage to the environment, (f) keeping records of raw materials and energy consumption, pollutants and energy, classification, characteristics and quantities of waste, (g) control of activities and operation of facilities that may pose a risk or cause danger to the environment and human health, (h) other measures in accordance with this Law (Art. 115).

311. Plants and plants such as mines, mineral oil or refinery deposits, gas supply and smelting plants, thermal power plants, coke ovens, metal and mineral production and processing plants, chemical plants, treatment plants, heat treatment and storage wastewater treatment plants, slaughterhouses, dyehouses and tanneries, papermaking plants, dams and hydropower infrastructure, gas or oil pipelines and storage facilities and liquefied atmospheric gases are hazardous to the environment due to the way they are managed, the materials they use or the activities which is performed in them (para. 3).

used, type and concentration of substances used or generated by that activity, use of genetically modified organisms or microorganisms, meteorological conditions and time and place of damage.[312]

168. However, the operator is not responsible for damage caused by: (a) war; (b) natural disaster or other force majeure; (c) by a third party intending to cause harm; or (d) due to the implementation of special orders and measures of the competent authorities that affected the occurrence of damage (Article 117). In addition, the operator shall be released from liability for damage if he proves that he has applied appropriate protection measures in order to prevent or mitigate the damage (paragraph 2).[313]

169. If a hazardous activity damages the environment, the operator is obliged to reimburse the costs of damage assessment and the costs of measures to return to the condition immediately before the damage or mitigation of environmental damage and compensation for damage to persons and property caused by hazardous activities (Article 120).[314] If the damage caused to the environment cannot be remedied by appropriate measures, the person who caused the damage shall be responsible for compensating the damage in the amount of the value of the destroyed property (Article 121). The amount of compensation should be close to the economic and ecological value of the destroyed property. If this value cannot be determined by the usual economic methods, the court will determine the amount of damage on the basis of equality, taking into account the necessary costs of remediation, the degree of individual responsibility and the benefits gained from damaging the environment.[315]

12. Inter-entity and International Cooperation

170. Inter-entity body for the environment is set up by decisions of the Government of the FbiH, the Government of the Republic of Srpska, and the Brčko District BiH (Article 125, paragraph 1).[316] The Inter-Entity Environmental Body shall deal with all environmental issues requiring harmonized access of the Entities, as

312. If several operators perform an activity dangerous to the environment together, they shall bear joint responsibility. The last operator shall be responsible for the remediation of the location where the plant and the plant have stopped working or the activity has been permanently stopped (paras 4 and 5).
313. A legal or natural person who considers that he has suffered damage as a result of performing an activity dangerous to the environment may always request information on circumstances that affect the proof that the given activity caused the damage (Art. 118).
314. However, the provisions of this article shall not apply to activities whose main purpose is national defense or international security, nor to activities whose sole purpose is protection against natural disasters (para. 3).
315. The Federation of BiH reserves the right to compensation if there are no other persons who have that right (para. 3).
316. The Inter-Entity Environmental Body shall have four members from the Republika Srpska, four members from the Federation of BiH, and two members from the Brčko District of BiH, taking into account equal gender representation (Art. 125, para. 2).

well as other issues transferred to the Inter-Entity Environmental Body by the Entities, this Law, Entity, and other regulations, in particular: (a) international agreements and programmes in the field of environmental protection; (b) coordinating the implementation and enactment of laws and other regulations; (c) coordinating the monitoring of the implementation of environmental protection standards and procedures; (d) making recommendations for the establishment of harmonized environmental quality standards at the entity level; (e) coordination of entity action plans and other programmes and plans in the field of environmental protection; (f) coordination of monitoring and information systems; (g) collection and exchange of information and (h) inter-entity body also considers issues initiated by the canton regarding the border negative impact of plants and facilities (Article 126, paragraph 1).

The inter-entity body for the environment is obliged to ensure that the interests of both entities, the Brčko District of BiH and Bosnia and Herzegovina, are taken into account when planning and implementing projects that may have a corresponding mutual impact on the environment, both within Bosnia and Herzegovina, i.e., between the entities and the Brčko District of BiH, as well as in a cross-border context (Article 126, paragraph 3).[317]

171. Members of the Inter-Entity Body for the Environment from the Federation of Bosnia and Herzegovina submit a report to the Federal Ministry after each meeting (Article 127).

B. Other Relevant FBiH Regulations

172.

(1) Rule book on projects for which environmental impact assessment is mandatory and projects for which authority has to decide on the need for environmental impact assessment (Official Gazette of FBiH No. 51/21).
(2) Decree determining the plants and facilities that must have an environmental permit (Official Gazette of FBiH No. 51/21).
(3) Rule book on plants, and warehouses where dangerous substances are present that can lead to large-scale accidents (Official Gazette of FBiH No. 51/21).
(4) Rule book on the manner of formation and work of expert commissions for the evaluation of studies on environmental impact assessment in the process of issuing environmental permits for plants for the production of hydroelectric energy (Official Gazette of FBiH No. 9/21).
(5) Rule book on determining the conditions and criteria for inclusion in the list of experts who may be appointed to expert commissions for the assessment of environmental impact studies (Official Gazette of FBiH No. 63/21).
(6) Rule book on the content of environmental impact assessment (Official Gazette of FBiH No. 63/21).

---

317. The Inter-Entity Environment Body shall provide expert assistance to the competent entity ministries (Art. 26, para. 2).

(7) Regulation on action in case of transboundary and inter-entity impact of the project on the environment (Official Gazette of FBiH No. 105/21).
(8) Rule book on drafting annual/semi-annual inspection programmes for environmental protection (Official Gazette of FBiH No. 68/05).
(9) Rule book on the contents of the report on the state of safety, the content of information about safety measures and contents of internal and external intervention plans (SEVESO) (Official Gazette of FBiH No. 68/05).
(10) Rule book on the requirements for applying for the issuance of an environmental permit for plants and facilities for which permits were issued before the Law on Environmental Protection came into force (Official Gazette of FBiH No. 68/05).
(11) Rule book on the deadlines for submitting for applying for issuance of an environmental permit for plants and facilities for which permits were issued before the Law on Environmental Protection came into force (Official Gazette of FBiH Nos 68/05 and 31/2012).
(12) Rule book on the requirements and criteria that project leaders in charge of developing the Environmental Impact Study must meet and on rates of fees and other costs incurred during the environmental impact assessment (Official Gazette of FBiH Nos 68/05, 92/07, 29/08 and 33/12).
(13) Rule book on registries of plants and pollution (Official Gazette of FBiH No. 82/07).
(14) Rule book on passing the best available techniques (BAT) for achieving environmental quality standards (Official Gazette of FBiH No. 92/07).
(15) Rule book on eco-labels and on the manner of governing eco-labelling (Official Gazette of FBiH No. 92/07).[318]

III. Brčko District of Bosnia and Herzegovina

A. The Law on Environmental Protection

173. Basic legal act regulating environmental protection[319] issues in Brčko District of Bosnia and Herzegovina is the Law on Environmental Protection (Official Gazette of BD BiH, Nos 24/04, 01/05, 19/07 and 09/09). It has the following nineteen parts: Part I – General Provisions (Articles 1–3), Part II – Definitions (Article 4), Part III – Principles of the Environmental Protections (Articles 5–11), Part IV – Protection of the Environmental Components (Articles 12–21), Part V – Information and Education in the Field of the Environmental Protection (Articles 22–29), Part VI – Public Participation and Access to Information Related to the Environment[320] (Articles 30–37), Part VII – Competencies (Articles 38–43), Part VIII –

318. *See*: https://www.fmoit.gov.ba/bs/zakoni/zakoni-na-razini-fbih (7 Feb. 2022).
319. *Environmental protection*-all appropriate activities and measures aimed at the prevention of danger, damage or pollution of the environment, the reduction or elimination of caused damage and return to the state prior to the caused damage (Art. 4, para. 1).
320. *Environment*-implies components of the environment, certain systems, processes, and structure of the environment (Art. 4, para. 1).

Planning of the Environmental Protection (Articles 44–51), Part IX – Study on the Environmental Impact (Articles 52–62), Part X – Issuing of the Environmental Permits and Preventing of the Large-Scale Accidents (Articles 63–80), Part XI – Determining of Conditions for Plants and Standards for Quality of the Environment (Articles 81–82), Part XII – Supervision (Articles 83–88), Part XIII – Eco-Labelling System and Management of the Environment (Articles 89–94), Part XIV – Voluntary Agreements (Articles 95–96), Part XV – Financing of the Environmental Protection and Economic Instruments (Articles 97–98), Part XVI – Civil Liability for Damage Caused to the Environment (Articles 99–107), Part XVII – Inter-entity Cooperation and Inter-entity Relations (Articles 108–111), Part XVIII – Penalty Provisions (Article 112), Part XIX – Transitional and Final Provisions (Articles 113–114).[321]

174. According to Article 1, paragraph 1, this law regulates:

(1) Conservation, protection, restoration and enhancement of the environmental quality and capacity of the environment as well as life quality.
(2) Measures and conditions for management, conservation and rational use of nature resources.
(3) Framework of legal measures and institutions for the preservation, protection and improvement of the environment.
(4) Financing of activities related to the environment.
(5) Tasks and duties of the District prescribed by the law and bylaws, as well as obligations of the District.

175. The aims of this law are following (Article 1, paragraph 2):

(1) Reduced usage, preventing of the loading and pollution of the environment, preventing of the disruptions, as well as improvement and restoration of the damaged environment.
(2) Human health protection and improvement of environmental conditions for life quality.
(3) Conservation and protection of natural resources, rational use of resources and such way of economy to ensure the resources recovery.
(4) Compliance of other interests of the District with the requirements for environmental protection.
(5) International cooperation in environmental protection.
(6) Initiatives by the public[322] and public participation in activities aimed at protection of the environment.
(7) Coordinating of the economy and integration of social and economic development in accordance with the requirements of environmental protection.

---

321. The inspection supervision over the implementation of provisions of this Law and regulations adopted there under shall be performed by inspectors for the environmental protection within their jurisdiction (Art. 84, para. 1).

322. *Public*-natural persons and legal entities and their associations, organizations or groups (Art. 4, para. 1).

(8) Establishment and development of institutions for the protection and preservation of the environment.

176. Every person has the right to a healthy and ecologically acceptable environment as a fundamental constitutional right (Article 3. paragraph 1). Every human being has the right to live in the environment which is conducive for the health and for well-being. Therefore, the individual and collective responsibility is to protect and to improve the environment for the benefit of present and future generations (Article 3. paragraph 2).

177. According to this law, principles of the environmental protection are following: sustainable development principle; principle of precaution and prevention; principle of substitution; principle of an integrated approach; principle of cooperation and shared responsibility; and public participation and access to information and the 'polluter pays' principle (Articles 5–11).

1. Protection of the Environmental Components

178. Environmental components must be protected individually and as part of other components of the environment, taking into account their interdependent relationships. In accordance with this, the way of loading and using of the environmental components are determined (Article 12, paragraph 1). Protection of the environmental components implies protecting of the quality, quantity and their stocks, as well as preservation of natural processes within the components and their natural balance (Article 12, paragraph 2).

Soil protection covers a surface area and subsurface soil layers, rock formations and minerals as well as their natural and transitional forms and processes (Article 13, paragraph 1).

Water protection covers protection of water sources, protection of surface and ground waters and supplies; regulation of water quality and quantity; protection of riverbeds, coastal areas and inland waters, as well as protection of aquasphere (Article 14, paragraph 1).

Air protection encompasses the atmosphere protection as a whole, with all its processes, as well as its structure and climatic characteristics (Article 15, paragraph 1).

The biosphere protection encompasses protection of living organisms, their communities and habitats: taking into account the protection of natural processes within their habitats; taking into account the protection of natural processes within their habitats and natural balance, with ensuring of ecosystem sustainability (Article 16, paragraph 1).

Regarding preserving of the *built environment,* zones for building in certain locations, in a certain area, depending on the degree of the environmental loading[323] and building purposes within certain parts at certain locations, are determined in spatial plans (Article 17, paragraph 1).

323. *Burdening of the environment*-emissions of substances or the energy into the environment (Art. 4, para. 1).

Protection from harmful effects of *hazardous substances*[324] encompasses the use of all natural and artificial substances that are used, produced or distributed by users of the environment during conducting of activities which are, according to their quantity or quality, explosive, flammable, radioactive, toxic, drying, corrosive, infectious, eco-toxic, mutagenic, carcinogenic or irritating, or that may cause such effects in contact with other substances (Article 18, paragraph 1).

Protection from the harmful *waste* effects to the environment includes treating of all kinds of substances and products-including packaging and packaging material of these substances, i.e., all kinds of products that are disposed of or that are planned to be disposed of (Article 19, paragraph 1).

Protecting the environment from *noise and vibration* includes all kinds of protection from artificially produced emissions[325] of energies that cause adverse health effects (Article 20, paragraph 1).

Protection from harmful effects of *radiation* to the environment includes protection from artificially and naturally produced ionization and thermal radiation (Article 21, paragraph 1).

2. Information and Education in the Field of the Environmental Protection

179. The Government of Brčko District of Bosnia and Herzegovina (hereinafter, 'the Government') is obliged through bylaws to establishes a system of informing on the environment and to enable implementation of environmental monitoring, as well as activities of measurement, data collection, processing and recording of data on the usage and loading of the environment (Article 22, paragraph 1).

180. Users of the environment are obliged to perform measurements of loading and utilization of the environment resulting from their activities in a way determined by this law, i.e., to confirm and to record them in accordance with prescribed technical possibilities, as well as to provide access to data to the competent Government department (hereinafter, 'competent department') (Article 23, paragraph 1).

181. Every citizen has the right to acquire and to improve knowledge about the environment (Article 26, paragraph 1). The dissemination and improvement of knowledge about the environment are the primary responsibilities of the competent department (Article 26, paragraph 1). The competent department keeps a register of facilities and contaminants (Article 28, paragraph 1).

324. *Hazardous substance*-a substance, mixture of substances or preparations which meet the criteria prescribed by the bylaw, which are present as a raw material, product, by-product, residue or intermediate product, including those substances which are expected that might arise in case of an accident (Art. 4, para. 1).

325. *Emissions* –direct or indirect release of substances, vibrations, heat, odour or noise produced by one or more sources in the facility and released it into the air, water, land (Art. 4, para. 1).

3. Access to Environmental Information and Education

182. Provisions of this law provide access to information to the public, the possibility to participate in decision-making and access to justice in matters related to the environmental protection, regardless of citizenship, nationality or place of residence and for legal entities regardless of residence (Article 30, paragraph 1).

183. Pursuant to Article 35 the competent department shall ensure public participation in: – Procedures for projects assessment to the environment (Chapter IX of this law); – Procedures for the issuing of ecological permits for facilities that excess the thresholds prescribed by bylaw (paragraph 1).

184. In instituted proceedings, the competent department will at the request of the public concerned[326] in the shortest period of time allow free access to all information relevant for making decision, i.e., information available at the time of the public participation process, which does not affect the right to refuse the disclosure of certain information (Article 36, paragraph 1).

185. The competent department prepares an annual educational plan in the field of environmental protection and complies in accordance to it. Educational plans for environmental protection improve education and public awareness of environmental protection in the curricular and in the extracurricular programme (Article 31, paragraph 1). The competent department must ensure that environmental information is available to the public, as well as copies of documents containing such information (Article 32, paragraph 1).

4. Planning of the Environmental Protection

186. The strategic plan for environmental protection shall be adopted in the District (Article 44, paragraph 1). Strategic Plan for Brčko District contains the following: General elements for protection and management of the environment from Article 46 of this law; Strategic documents on protection of water, air and nature, management of waste and management of other integral components of the environment and impacts on the environment,[327] adopted on the basis of special laws (Article 47, paragraph 1).

---

326. *The public concerned* – public that is affected or that is likely to be affected by, or which have an interest in the decision-making related to environmental protection, due to the location of the project or because of the nature of that case; nongovernmental organizations promoting environmental protection and meeting the requirements (Art. 4, para. 1).

327. *Environmental impact*-changes in the environment resulting from the use and from the loading of the environment (Art. 4, para. 1).

187. For the environmental protection planning purpose, at Bosnia and Herzegovina state level, Brčko District concludes an agreement with the entities, i.e., the competent authority at the level of the Council of Ministers of Bosnia and Herzegovina (paragraph 2).

It is necessary to obtain a Strategic environmental impact assessment[328] during the adoption of regulations and decisions by the competent department, the Government or the District Assembly, which may have an adverse effect on the quality of the environment and on human health (Article 50, paragraph 1).

Companies adopt programmes for environmental protection management within their needs and interests (Article 49, paragraph 1).

188. Environmental protection measures established in planning documents on environmental protection[329] must be consistent with economic, social and spatial planning documents on the development of Brčko District, as well as with other development plans of all sectors of the economy (Article 45, paragraph 1).

5. The Environmental Impact Assessment

189. The Environmental Impact Assessment involves identifying, describing and analysing of the direct and indirect effects of a project on the following elements and factors:

- People, flora and fauna.
- Soil, water, air, climate and space.
- Material assets and cultural heritage.
- Interaction of factors set forth in paragraphs one, two and three (Article 52, paragraph 1).

190. Rules relating to the environmental impacts assessment also apply in the following cases: – In case of possibility that the project will have a significant impact on the environment of another entity; – When the state is bound by international treaties, as well as on the basis of bilateral agreements, reciprocity or other reasons (Article 60, paragraph 1).

328. Content of the Strategic Environmental Impact Assessment is prescribed in Art. 51, para. 1. *Environmental impact assessment*-the identification, characterization and assessment (in particular case), in an appropriate manner, in relation to each single case and in accordance with the articles of this Chapter, the direct and indirect influence of some project to the following elements and factors (Art. 4, para. 1): People, flora and fauna; Land, water, air, climate and landscape; Material assets and cultural heritage; Interaction of the factors listed in subparagraphs one, two and three.
329. All planning documents on environmental protection shall be adopted for a period of 10 years (Art. 45, para. 2). Content of the planning documents on environmental protection is prescribed in Art. 46, para. 1.

6. Issuing of the Environmental Permits and Preventing of Large-Scale Accidents

191. Activities or facilities that threaten or that may threaten the environment or which have or which may have a negative impact on the environment are put under a special regime of control (Article 63, paragraph 1). Control is implemented through the following:

- Special obligations and conditions prescribed for these activities or facilities.
- The conditions prescribed for obtaining of environmental permits.
- Documentation in the registry/cadastre on environmental pollution.
- Regular inspection controls.
- Remedial measures to prevent contamination (paragraph 2).

192. In bylaws, adopted on the base of this law, are listed facilities that can be built and put into operation only if they have an environmental permit issued by the competent department, as prescribed in Article 67 of this law. Rules for the adoption of environmental permits shall be prescribed in bylaw (Article 65, paragraph 1).

193. The objective of the environmental permit[330] is a high level of environmental protection as a whole, including the protection of air, water and land. If adopting of other permits for facilities is prescribed by special law, this permit will be issued together with the environmental permit (Article 65, paragraph 2).

194. Responsible person of the facility in which dangerous substances are present must take all preventive measures necessary to prevent large-scale accidents[331] and limit their impact on people and on the environment. The responsible person must always (and especially during inspection supervision), present to the competent department, that he/she has taken the necessary measures prescribed by this law (Article 69, paragraph 1).

195. If the operation of the facility can cause significant adverse effects on the territory of another state, entity or on Brčko District or if other country, Entity or Brčko District so requests, the request for the issuance of the environmental permits will be delivered to another entity or to Brčko District through the competent department, and to other state at the same time when it becomes available to the public (Article 70, paragraph 1).

---

330. The content of the Request for issuing of the environmental permit is prescribed in Art. 66, para. 1. The content of the Environmental permit is prescribed in Art. 67, para. 3.

331. *Large-scale accidents*– phenomena of large-scale emission, fire or explosion due to uncontrolled changes occurred during facility operation which pose a serious threat to human health or the environment, immediate or delayed, inside or outside of the facility, which include one or more hazardous substances (Art. 4, para. 1).

7. Setting of Conditions for Facilities and Standards for Environmental Quality

196. Government, at the proposal of the Head of the Department responsible for the environmental protection, adopts the following bylaws prescribing:[332]

- Special conditions concerning the documents to be submitted during the procedure of issuing of the environmental permits.
- The conditions which must be fulfilled by authorized institutions for preparation of documentation prescribed by this law.
- Additional provisions for the prevention of large-scale accidents (Article 81, paragraph 1).

197. Head of the Department responsible for the environmental protection enacts the following bylaws prescribing:

- Rules for procedure for issuing of the environmental permits.
- Requirements related to the issuance of the environmental permits for specific types of facilities, especially concerning the best available technologies[333] and limiting values of emissions[334] and technical measures in accordance with the rules for establishing of the standards.
- Environmental Quality Standards (Article 81, paragraph 2).

8. Eco-Labelling System and Environmental Management System

198. The system of eco-label awarding is established to foster development, production, marketing, as well as use of products with reduced impact on the environment during the total product life period, as well as for the purpose of better informing of consumers about the impact of the products on the environment. Eco-label is awarded to products and to services (Article 89, paragraph 1).

Eco-label is an emblem which is determined by a special regulation. The environmental impacts are determined on the basis of testings and interactions between products and the environment, including the use of energy and natural resources, in relation to the total product life cycle (Article 89, paragraph 2).

Eco-label can be issued for products that are in compliance with environmental requirements and eco-label criteria which are established according to a group of products (Article 90, paragraph 1). Eco-label is awarded on the basis of the request

332. *Environmental quality standard* – prescribed requirements that must be met within a certain period of time, in a given environment or in a specific part, as prescribed by this Law or by other Laws, for example related to air or water quality (Art. 4, para. 1).

333. *Best available technology* – The most effective and advanced stage in the development of technologies and their methods of operation which indicate at the practical suitability of the application of certain technologies (for providing of the limiting emission values) in order to prevent and, where it is not feasible, to reduce emissions into the environment as a whole (Art. 4, para. 1).

334. *Limiting emission values* – level of concentration of certain pollutants in the air determined in the regulation (Art. 4, para. 1).

submitted by the manufacturer, importer, services supplier and merchant (Article 92, paragraph 1). The decision on awarding of the label is made for a period of three years (Article 92, paragraph 3).

199. Environmental management system encompasses organizational structure, obligations, procedures and resources of organizations which are implementing systematic measures for environmental protection (Article 93, paragraph 1). The main objectives of this system are to carry out assessment and improvement of activities concerning the environmental protection, and to provide adequate information to the public, as well as to continue with constant and continuous improvement of operational activities in the field of environmental protection (Article 93, paragraph 2).

200. Persons who represent certain interests of some groups using potential pollutants or certain pollutants may conclude agreements with the competent authorities in order to meet environmental requirements in an environmentally acceptable and economically efficient way (Article 95, paragraph 1). Conditions and procedures for the voluntary agreement and in accordance with the terms set out herein will be prescribed in bylaws (Article 95, paragraph 1).

9. Financing of the Environmental Protection and Economic Instruments

201. According to Article 97 Brčko District budget provides fund for the following:

- Support in the implementation of obligations arising from the obligations and responsibilities to the international community in the field of the environmental protection.
- Combating the damage to the environment, where it cannot be applied responsibility for causing damage to a specific person.
- The costs for preventing or remediation of damage to the environment that requires immediate intervention.
- Support for measures in order to protect the environment, particularly in the area of development and operation of information systems, control by the public administration, education and dissemination of information, research and activities of the public related to environmental protection.

202. Fund for the Environmental Protection (hereinafter, 'the Fund') shall be established by the Law with the aim of collecting and distributing of funds for environmental protection in the area of Brčko District, and will be used specifically for the following purposes: – Support in implementation of obligations arising from the obligations and responsibilities to the international community in the field of the environment; – Combating the damage to the environment where it cannot be applied responsibility for causing damage to a certain person:

- The costs of preventing or minimizing of damage to the environment that requires immediate intervention; – Support for measures in order to protect the environment, particularly in areas of development and financing of information system, education and dissemination of information, research and activities of the public related to the environmental protection; – Improving development of the economic structure that is favourable to the environment.
- Preservation of protected natural areas; – Promotion of environmental awareness of the public and exploration of the environment (Article 98, paragraph 1).

10. Civil Liability for Damage to the Environment

203. In order to prevent causing damage to the environment and ensuring adequate fees, this law establishes: responsibility for activities dangerous to environment, remediation of the damage done to the environment, the burden of proof, access to information about the responsible persons, the rules for granting rights to NGOs and duties of the responsible persons to compensate for damages (Article 99, paragraph 1).

204. Legal entity engaged in activities harmful to the environment, is responsible for the damage caused by this activity to the people, property and the environment (Article 100, paragraph 1).[335] If more than one person performs a dangerous activity at the same location, then they share the responsibility for the damages (Article 100, paragraph 6).

Anyone who claims to have suffered damage due to some activities dangerous to the environment may require information on the circumstances in order to prove that the activity caused the damage (Article 102, paragraph 1).

205. If a dangerous activity caused damage to the environment, the legal entity shall reimburse the costs of damage assessment and the cost for measures to restore to the original state (Article 105, paragraph 1). If the damage inflicted to the environment cannot be remediated by appropriate measures, then the person who caused the damage is responsible for compensation in the amount of destroyed property (Article 106, paragraph 1).[336]

335. Activities dangerous to the environment are those activities that pose a significant risk to people, property or the environment. Activities dangerous to the environment are the following: managing locations that are hazardous to the environment; the release of genetically modified organisms and the release of microorganisms (Art. 100, para. 2).
336. The amount of compensation should be approximate to the economic and ecological value of destroyed property from the environment (Art. 106, para. 2).

11. Inter-entity Cooperation and Relationships

206. Brčko District Government establishes cooperation and coordination with Republic of Srpska and Federation of Bosnia and Herzegovina within the framework of common goals and interests for environmental protection by establishing inter-entity body for environmental protection (Article 108, paragraph 1).[337] Brčko District and entities, with the mediation of inter-entity body for environment participate in international cooperation in the field of environmental protection (Article 111, paragraph 1).

207. Inter-entity body for environmental protection deals with issues concerning the environment that require harmonized approach of Brčko District of Bosnia and Herzegovina and of entities, as well as with other issues that were transferred from Brčko District of Bosnia and Herzegovina and the entities to the inter-entity bodies for environmental protection of Brčko District of Bosnia and Herzegovina and entities, this law and with other regulations (Article 109, paragraph 1).

Inter-entity body for environmental protection enact inter-entity programme for environmental protection (Article 110, paragraph 1). Inter-entity programme for environmental protection encompasses issues which require a harmonized approach of Brčko District of Bosnia and Herzegovina and of entities, paying special attention to cooperation at the international level and to international obligations (Article 110, paragraph 2).

§2. Laws on the Funds and Financing of the Environmental Protection

208. Generally speaking, in Bosnia and Herzegovina, the main environmental fees are levied on water resources, forests, air pollution, wastes and land uses under different regulations.[338]

I. The Republic of Srpska

A. The Law on the Fund and Financing of the Environmental Protection in the Republic of Srpska

209. Basic legal act regulating the Fund and financing of the environmental protection is the Law on the Fund and financing of the environmental protection in the Republic of Srpska (Official Gazette of RS, No. 117/11, 63/14 and 90/16).

337. Inter-entity body for environmental protection is to be established by decisions of the Government of Republic of Srpska and Government of Federation of Bosnia and Herzegovina (Art. 108, para. 2).

338. For more information, *see*: UNECE. *3rd Environmental Performance Review, Bosnia and Herzegovina*, p. 51.

210. According to Article 1, this law regulates the status, activities, organizations, income and way of use of the Fund's financial resources for environmental protection and energy efficiency[339] of the Republic of Srpska as well as the conditions, procedures and way of funding of environmental protection and energy efficiency.

1. Establishing of the Fund

211. The Republic of Srpska is the founder[340] of the Fund (Article 2, paragraph 1). The Ministry responsible for environmental protection (hereinafter, 'the Ministry') is monitoring the work of the Fund and application of the provisions of this law (Article 2, paragraph 3). The Fund adopts a medium-term programme of work,[341] financial and annual plan of operations[342] (Article 11, paragraph 1). The Government approves the annual operating plan and financial plan of the Fund, obtaining prior opinion of the Ministry and the Ministry in charge for energy and the Ministry responsible for water management (Article 11, paragraph 5).

The general acts of the Fund are Statute[343] and other documents which in a general way regulate certain issues (Article 12, paragraph 1). The Fund's bodies are the Board of Directors[344] and Managing Director (Article 14, paragraph 1).

2. Reporting

212. The annual report[345] on the realization of the work plan and financial plan, the Fund submits to the Government for approval through the Ministry not later than 31 March of the current year for the previous year, with the previously obtained opinion of the Ministry in charge for energy and the Ministry responsible for affairs of water management (Article 11, paragraph 6).

339. *Energy efficiency*, in terms of this Law, is the development and application of technologies and measures for achieving energy savings with the aim of reduction of depletion of fossil fuels and reducing of negative impacts on the environment (Art. 9, para. 1).
340. The rights and responsibilities of the founder are done by the Government of the Republic of Srpska (Art. 2, para. 2).
341. The medium-term program of work determines the direction, dynamic and development policy of the Fund for a period that cannot be less than three years (Art. 11, para. 2). The Government gives approval on the medium-term program of work, obtaining prior opinion of the Ministry and the ministries in charge for energy affairs and the Ministry responsible for affairs of water management (Art. 11, para. 3).
342. The Fund adopts the annual work plan and financial plan, in which it plans activities for the next calendar year, and shall be made no later than 15 Dec. of the current year for the next calendar year (Art. 11, para. 4).
343. The Fund Statute is enacted by the Governing Board of the Fund for the prior approval of the Ministry (Art. 12, para. 2). The Government gives approval on the Fund Statute (Art. 12, para. 3).
344. Board of Directors has three members, appointed and dismissed by the Government (Art. 14, para. 2).
345. The report must contain quantitative overview of the realised goals from the field of the environmental protection, the amount of the saved energy and money, as well as reduced emissions of the pollutants (Art. 11, para. 7).

In the work programme, in the financial plan and in reports, projects and programmes for environmental protection are separately shown from the projects and programmes from the field of energy efficiency and renewable energy sources (Article 11, paragraph 8).[346]

3. Financing of the Fund

213. The Fund manages and disposes of with resources for the tasks and purposes set out in this law on behalf of the Republic of Srpska (Article 4, paragraph 1). For its obligations, the Fund is liable by its assets[347] (Article 4, paragraph 2).

214. In carrying out its activities, the Fund provides financial support for achievement of the objectives and principles of environmental protection and the improvement of energy efficiency, defined in the republican strategic documents and in local environmental action plans of the local government units, in order to raise quality of systematic and integrated environmental protection, conservation of natural community and rational use of natural resources and energy, as the basic conditions for sustainable development, and realization of human rights to a healthy environment (Article 10, paragraph 1).

215. Resources for financing of the Fund, environment, energy efficiency and renewable energy sources in accordance with this law are provided from the following sources:

(a) Fees paid by environment polluters.
(b) Fees for burdening of the environment by the waste.
(c) Fee for water protection paid by the owners of the transport means using petroleum or petroleum products in accordance with the Law on Waters ('Official Gazette of RS' No. 50/06 and 92/09).
(d) The funds generated from international programmes, projects and other activities in the area of environmental protection, energy efficiency and renewable energy sources.
(e) Contributions, donations, gifts and grants.
(f) From other sources in accordance with the law (Article 17, paragraph 1).

216. Environmental pollutants, liable to pay compensation under Article 17, points (a) and (b) of this law are: (a) Legal entities and natural persons[348] whose actions directly or indirectly cause environmental pollution in terms of the Law on

346. The Fund shall submit to the National Assembly the report on its activities, as well as the financial report for the previous year, no later than 30 Apr. of the current year (Art. 11, para. 9).
347. Fund assets are assets, rights and other assets of the founder, as well as other means that the Fund generates otherwise in accordance with Law (Art. 5, para. 1).
348. Individuals referred to in para. 1 of this article are entrepreneurs performing activity in its own name and for its own account for purpose of making profit in accordance with the regulation governing handicraft entrepreneurial business (Art. 18, para. 2).

the Environmental Protection, other laws and international regulations; (b) Legal entities and natural persons producing or importing products/goods, which are harmful substances or which contain such substances, in accordance with the Law on the Environmental Protection, other regulations and international regulations, i.e., products/goods that can significantly burden the environment; (c) Legal entities and natural persons who produce or import products/goods that after using become a special waste flow; (d) Energy entities which in performing energy activities emit in the atmosphere carbon dioxide (CO), sulphur dioxide (SO), nitrogen oxides (NOx) and solid particles; (e) Legal entities and natural persons that are burdening the environment by waste disposal (Article 18, paragraph 1).

217. The taxpayer[349] has the right to return the fees already paid for the waste disposal, accompanied by a customs declaration that the goods is exported from the territory of the Republic of Srpska (Article 22, paragraph 1).

The Fund is required to keep a record on obligors for payment of fees (hereinafter, 'the taxpayer') (Article 26, paragraph 1).

4. The Fund's Public Authorities and Activities

218. In performing activities, the Fund has public authorities:

(a) To issue the decision for taxpayers to pay the fees prescribed by the law regulating the sustainable management of natural resources and environmental protection (hereinafter, 'fee').
(b) To determine the detailed conditions which must be met by all users of Fund resources, conditions and manners of assigning resources, criteria and standards for the evaluation of project proposals, i.e., applications for fund allocation which must be in accordance with the strategic plans of state and local authorities, performing project implementation supervision, ways of monitoring the proper use of funds and contractual rights and obligations, as well as other activities relevant to the allocation and use of Fund resources, in accordance with this law.
(c) To take measures to Fund users for illegitimate funds usage and failure to meet contractual rights and obligations (Article 7, paragraph 1).

219. Fund's activities are including the activities related to the collection of funds, as well as financing of preparation, implementation and development of programmes, projects and similar activities in the field of conservation, sustainable use, protection and improvement of the environment, and in the field of energy efficiency and renewable energy sources[350] usage (Article 8, paragraph 1).[351]

---

349. At the request of the taxpayer, the Fund shall issue a decision on return of fees in accordance with the regulations governing general administrative procedure (Art. 22, para. 2).

350. *Renewable energy sources,* in terms of this Law, are: Forms of energy that can be found naturally in the free form (biomass, rivers, sun, wind, geothermal energy, aerothermal energy, bio-gas, etc.)

5. Allocation of the Fund's Financial Resources

220. The users of the Fund's financial resources are all natural persons and legal entities having headquarters or domicile on the territory of the Republic of Srpska (hereinafter, 'users') (Article 24, paragraph 1).

221. The Fund's financial means[352] shall be awarded to users in order to finance the programmes, projects and similar activities by means of: (a) grants; (b) subsidy; (c) credit funds; loans and guarantees (Article 24, paragraph 2).

The method of allocation and criteria for the allocation of funds referred to in paragraph 2 of this article shall be determined by the general acts of the Fund in accordance with this Law (Article 24, paragraph 4). The method of use of Fund resources shall be determined by the general acts of the Fund in accordance with this Law (Article 24, paragraph 6).

222. According to Article 23, paragraph 1, the Fund's financial resources shall be used to fund environmental protection, energy efficiency and renewable energy sources, in accordance with the law, the statute, the work programme of the Fund, as well as with the strategic documents of the Republic of Srpska, and especially for:[353]

(a) The protection, preservation and improvement of the air, water, soil and forests quality, as well as mitigation of the climate change effects and ozone layer protection.
(b) Remediation of landfills, encouraging reduction of waste generation, reusing and recycling of waste.
(c) Encouraging the introduction of technological processes that reduce or completely eliminate negative impacts on the environment.
(d) The protection and conservation of biodiversity and geodiversity.
(e) The promotion of sustainable use of protected areas.
(f) The promotion of sustainable development of rural areas.
(g) Encouraging the improvement of energy efficiency.
(h) Encouraging the realization of energy efficiency and renewable energy projects in the public sector.

---

and are used locally to increase energy efficiency; Electrical, thermal or mechanical energy produced from solar energy, biomass, geothermal energy, bio-gas, wind or water flows, which is not intended for sale and is not covered by some of the stimulus measures, and is used locally in the house/building in which is partially or completely produced (Art. 9, para. 1).

351. More detailed Fund activities are listed in Art. 8, para. 1, points a–e.

352. The Fund's financial means under para. 2 of this article shall be awarded on the basis of (a) open competition published by the Fund (b) Government decisions on granting subsidies and (c) Government decision on the co-financing of programs, projects and similar activities in the implementation of strategic documents of the Government (Art. 24, para. 3).

353. The Fund may participate in the financing of programs, projects and other activities on the territory of the Republic for the purposes specified in para. 1 of this article which are organized and funded by international organizations, financial institutions and bodies or other foreign entities (Art. 23, para. 2).

(i) Encouraging the use and research of the renewable energy and their use in order to increase energy efficiency.
(j) Encouraging cleaner transport.
(k) Encouraging of education, research, innovating and development studies, programmes and projects in the field of environmental protection.
(l) Funding of environmental education programme and public awareness about the issues of environmental protection and sustainable development.

223. The work of the Fund is open to the public (Article 27, paragraph 1). The Fund promptly and accurately, and in a manner prescribed by the Fund Statute, informs the public about the activities for which it was established (paragraph 2).[354] The Fund may withhold giving the information if it is prescribed as an official or business secret (paragraph 4).

B. Other Relevant RS Regulation

224.
(1) Law on energy efficiency (Official Gazette of RS No. 59/13).
(2) Rule book on the manner of and criteria for allocating funds for environmental protection programmes and projects (Official Gazette of RS No. 2/14).
(3) Rulebook on the form, content and manner of keeping records of the payer of fees (Official Gazette of RS No. 34/12).
(4) Decision on environmental pollution fees for motor vehicles (Official Gazette of RS No. 116/18).[355]

II. Federation of Bosnia and Herzegovina

A. The Law on the Fund for Environmental Protection of the Federation of Bosnia and Herzegovina

225. Basic legal act regulating the Fund for the environmental protection of the Federation of Bosnia and Herzegovina is the law on the Fund for environmental protection of the Federation of Bosnia and Herzegovina (Official Gazette of FBiH, No. 33/03). It has the following nine parts: Part I – General Provisions (Articles 1–5), Part II – Organization of the Fund (Articles 6–9), Part III – Organizing and Management of the Fund (Articles 10–17), Part IV – Financing (Articles 18–27), Part V – Asset and Financial Operations of the Fund (Articles 28–33), Part VI – Publicity of the Fund's Work (Article 34), Part VII – Administrative Supervision (Article 35), Part VIII – Penalty Provisions (Articles 36–41), Part IX – Transitional and Final Provisions (Articles 42–46).

354. The Fund is obliged on the request of the public and the media to provide them with information about the performance of its activities, as well as to provide access to the requested documentation, in accordance with the Law on freedom of access to information (Art. 27, para. 3).
355. *See*: http://ekofondrs.org/ofondu/zakonskiokvir.html (19 Jul. 2022).

226. According to Article 1, paragraph 1, this law establishes the Fund for Environmental Protection of the Federation of Bosnia and Herzegovina (hereinafter, 'the Fund'), establishes the structure, organization and management of the Fund, the assets and activities of the Fund, sources, purpose and way of use of the Fund's resources, and also regulates other questions related to the acquisition and management of the Fund's resources.[356]

1. Activity of the Fund

227. Article 3 provides that the activity of the Fund is to collect and distribute financial resources for environmental protection on the territory of the Federation of Bosnia and Herzegovina, and will be used in particular for the following purposes:

- Support to the execution of tasks arising from the obligations and responsibilities to the International community in the field of environmental protection.
- Suppression of damage to the environment in case when it is not possible to apply the principle of responsibility for performing the damage to a particular person (polluter pays).
- The costs of preventing or eliminating the damage to the environment that requires immediate intervention.
- Support with measures with the aim to protect the environment, particularly in the area of the development and financing of the information system, education and dissemination of information.
- Improving the development of economic structure favourable to the environment.
- Preservation of protected natural areas.
- Improving of environmental awareness of the public and environmental research.
- Conservation, sustainable use, protection and improvement the state of the environment.
- Financing of preparation of making, implementation and development of programmes documents and similar activities in the areas of conservation, sustainable use, protection and improvement of renewable energy sources.

228. Activity of the Fund includes activities related to the acquisition of the resources, encouraging and financing of the preparation, implementation and development of programmes, projects and similar activities in the field of conservation, sustainable use, protection and improvement of the state of the environment and the use of renewable energy sources (hereinafter, 'the financing of environmental protection'), and in particular:[357]

356. The Fund is a financial organization and a legal entity. It is registered at the Court Register. Questions related to the foundation, activities, management and organization of the Fund relevant to the Cantons and their organs are regulated by the Cantonal Laws (Art. 2, para. 1).
357. The Fund may also perform other activities determined by Statute used for performing activities from para. 1 of this article (Art. 4, para. 2).

- Professional and other activities related to the acquisition, management and use of the Fund's resources.
- Intermediating in relation to the financing of the environmental protection from the foreign countries funds, international financial institutions and bodies, as well as from domestic and foreign legal entities and natural persons.
- Providing of professional services in relation to the financing of environmental protection.
- Maintaining a database about the programmes, projects and similar activities in the field of the environmental protection, as well as necessary and available financial resources for their realization.
- Promotion, establishment and realization of cooperation with international and domestic financial institutions and other legal entities and natural persons to finance environmental protection in accordance with the Federal strategy for environmental protection.
- Environmental protection plans adopted on the base of the Strategy, the international treaties which is Bosnia and Herzegovina Member State, as well as other programmes and documents in the field of environmental protection.
- Carrying out other activities related to encouraging and financing of the environmental protection established by the Statute of the Fund (Article 4, paragraph 1).

229. In carrying out its activities, the Fund applies the principles of transparency and publicity, objectivity and responsibility in decision-making and application of internationally recognized standards of good practice (Article 4, paragraph 4).

In carrying out its activities, the Fund promotes the goals and principles of environmental protection in order to achieve systematic and comprehensive quality preservation of all environmental components, preservation of natural communities and rational use of natural resources and energy as basic conditions for sustainable development, with the aim of achieving the fundamental right of citizens to a healthy environment (Article 5, paragraph 1).

2. The Structure, Organizing and Management of the Fund

230. The Fund is the legal entity with rights, obligations and responsibilities determined by this law, other laws and the Statute of the Fund (Article 6, paragraph 2). The Fund is a non-profit legal entity and has one bank account (Article 6, paragraph 3). The work of the Fund is open to the public (Article 6, paragraph 4). The Fund manages and disposes of with earmarked funds, established by this law (Article 8, paragraph 1). The Fund has a Statute and other general acts, in accordance with law and the Fund Statute (Article 9, paragraph 1).

231. The Steering Committee manages with the Fund (Article 10, paragraph 1). The Steering Committee consists of seven members who are appointed and dismissed by the Government of the Federation of Bosnia and Herzegovina taking into account regional representation of its members (Article 10, paragraph 1). The Supervisory Board performs supervision of the Fund's work (Article 13, paragraph 1).

232. The Fund is engaged in professional, administration and other activities to achieve the Fund's activities prescribed in Articles 3 and 4 of this law (Article 17, paragraph 1). Funding for performing professional, administrative and other jobs of the Fund shall be provided from the total income of the Fund (Article 17, paragraph 2).

3. Income of the Fund and Payers

233. Income of the Fund to finance environmental protection, in accordance to this law, shall be provided from:

- Fee from environment polluters.
- Fee from environment users.
- Special fee for environment to be paid at each motor vehicle registration (Article 18, paragraph 1).

234. Incomes of the Fund are provided from:

- Funds provided on the basis of international bilateral and multilateral cooperation, and cooperation in the country on joint programmes, projects and similar activities in the field of environmental protection.
- Budget of the Federation.
- Bank loans.
- Funds from loans and other lendings from other legal entities and financial institutions.
- The grants and other forms of support.
- Operations of the Fund (fee for performing of the services, repayment of principal, interest, etc.).
- Other sources of funds determined by a special law, other regulations or contracts (Article 18, paragraph 2).

235. Environmental polluters, liable to pay fees from Article 18, paragraph 1, subparagraph 1 of this law are:

- Legal entities and natural persons whose actions directly or indirectly causing environmental pollution in terms of the Law on Environmental Protection, other environmental laws and/or international regulations.
- Legal and natural persons who produce or import products/goods that are harmful substances or which contain harmful substances, according to the Law on Environmental Protection, other regulations and/or international regulations, i.e., products/goods which may have a significant burden on the environment.
- Energy entities which pollute the environment during performing energy activities, and legal entities which pollute the environment during using of the energy (Article 19, paragraph 1).

4. The Financial Resources and Asset of the Fund

236. The Fund adopts a decision on fees within the framework of delegated public authorities (Article 20, paragraph 1). Funds raised in the Fund will be distributed between the Federation and the Cantons in relation to 30% versus 70% (The Federation 30% – Canton 70%) (Article 25, paragraph 1).

237. According to Article 26 the Fund's resources are used to finance environmental protection, in particular:

- The protection, preservation and improvement of the quality of air, soil, water and sea and mitigation of changes and protection of the ozone layer.
- Rehabilitation, supporting of the avoiding and reducing of waste generation.
- Use of valuable characteristics and waste treatment.
- The protection and conservation of biological and landscape diversity.
- Implementation of energy programmes.
- Demining programmes.
- Upgrading and construction of infrastructure for environmental protection.
- Improving the monitoring and assessment of the state of the environment, and the introduction of environmental management systems.
- Encouraging the sustainable use of natural resources.
- Encouraging sustainable economic activities, i.e., sustainable economic development.
- Encouraging research, development studies, programme projects and other activities, including demonstration activities (Article 26, paragraph 1).[358]

238. Financial resources of the Fund are allocated to legal entities and natural persons, beneficiaries, in order to finance the purposes prescribed in Article 26, paragraph 1 of this law, through loans and borrowings, subsidies, guarantees, donations, on the basis of Fund's public competition or on other way prescribed by the Fund Statute (Article 27, paragraph 1).[359]

239. Fund's asset are items, rights and other resources acquired by the founders, the resources which Fund acquire in performing of its activities or in any other way prescribed by this law (Article 28, paragraph 1).[360] The Fund adopted the work programme and financial plan for each business year with the approval of the Federation Government (Article 30, paragraph 1).

---

358. The Fund may participate in co-financing of programs, projects and similar activities for the purposes referred to in para. 1 of this article, organized and financed by international financial institutions and organizations (Art. 26, para. 2).
359. The Fund is required when allocating resources to apply the principle to achieve the greatest overall benefit to the environment with available resources (Art. 27, para. 2).
360. The Steering Committee and Director of the Fund dispose with the asset of the Fund in accordance to the Law and Fund's Statute (Art. 28, para. 2).

5. Publicity of the Fund's Work and Supervision

240. The work of the Fund is open to the public (Article 34, paragraph 1). The Fund will submit to the Government of the Federation the Report on work and the Report on realization of the financial plan and programmes for the past year within the time limit specified in the Fund's Statute (Article 34, paragraph 2).[361] Pursuant to Article 35 the administrative supervision over the legality of the work and of general acts of the Fund is conducted by the Federal Ministry of Spatial Planning and Environment (hereinafter, 'the Federal Ministry') (paragraph 1). Supervision of the implementation of provisions of this law and other regulations adopted pursuant to this law is performed by the Inspection for Environmental Protection within its jurisdiction (paragraph 2).[362]

B. Other Relevant FBiH Regulations

241. Following bylaws have been adopted:

(1) Rule book on allocation of funds from the Revolving Fund for water protection projects and waste recycling (Official Gazette of FBiH No. 99/17).
(2) Rule book on allocation of funds from the revolving fund for energy efficiency projects (Official Gazette of FBiH No. 10/17, 99/17).
(3) Rule book on the procedure for issuing calls for proposals and on selecting beneficiaries of the proceeds of the Environmental Protection Fund of the Federation of Bosnia and Herzegovina (Official Gazette of FBiH No. 74/17, and 63/18).
(4) Rule book on the criteria for evaluating applications for allocating proceeds of the Fund, i.e., programmes, projects and similar activities (Official Gazette of FBiH No. 74/17).
(5) Rule book on the manner of monitoring the use of dedicated funds and contractual rights and obligations (Official Gazette of FBiH No. 73/10).
(6) Rule book on the requirements that beneficiaries of the proceeds of the Environmental Protection Fund of the Federation of Bosnia and Herzegovina must meet (Official Gazette of FBiH No. 75/10).
(7) Rule book on the requirements and manner of allocating credits, loans and other proceeds of the Fund (Official Gazette of FBiH No. 75/10, and 74/17).
(8) Regulation on fees for plastic bags (Official Gazette of FBiH No. 9/14).
(9) Regulation on types of remuneration and criteria for calculating compensation for air pollutants (Official Gazette of FBiH No. 66/11, 107/14).
(10) Regulation on special environmental fees payable on registration of motor vehicles (Official Gazette of FBiH No. 14/11).

361. Fond informs the public about its work in a timely and truthful way, in a manner specified in the Fund's Statute (Art. 34, para. 3).
362. The Federal Ministry of the Finance performs supervision over the calculation and payment of the fees and other assets of the payers, in accordance to this Law (Art. 35, para. 3).

(11) Rulebook on cross-border movement of waste (Official Gazette of FBiH, No. 7/11, 39/15, 25/19 and 19/21).
(12) Rulebook on packaging and packaging waste management (Official Gazette of FBiH, No. 88/11, 28/13, 8/16, 54/16, 103/16, 84/17, and 85/20).[363]

§3. Enforcement and Control

242. According to the EC 2021 Progress Report:

> Significant efforts are needed on implementation and enforcement … The legal framework regulating environmental inspections and its enforcement needs to be improved in line with the relevant EU *acquis*.[364]

The activities on inspection are regulated by the general laws on inspections of the two entities (RS, FBiH), and BDBiH, and related legislation. There are no specific laws on environmental inspections. At the level of BiH, there is no active monitoring system to verify compliance with regulations concerning the environment and state of the environment. There is also no environmental inspection.[365] There are four regional units in the Federation of Bosnia and Herzegovina, with about 150 inspectors. Republika Srpska has six units with 250 inspectors. The entities' administrations of inspection services consolidate and coordinate the inspections of these units. However, the number of environmental inspectors remains small: both entities have five environmental inspectors.[366]

Mechanisms for monitoring the compliance with environmental legislation and their implementation are prescribed by a set of environmental laws and relevant bylaws (supervision, rights and duties of inspector, minor offence in the case of noncompliance, etc.).[367]

I. The Republic of Srpska

243. The main mechanism for monitoring compliance with regulations on protection of the environment inspections is carried out in the RS by the Bureau for Inspection Affairs of the RS – the Inspectorate and the competent inspectors in the local self-governance bodies.[368]

363. For more information *see*: https://fzofbih.org.ba/uredbe/; https://fzofbih.org.ba/pravilnici/(19 Jul. 2022).
364. EC, *Bosnia and Herzegovina 2021 Progress Report*, p. 102.
365. For more details, *see*: Directorate for European Integration, *Answers to the Questionnaire, Chapter 27, Environment and climate change*, 27 Feb. 2018, 151–183.
366. *See* UNECE, *3rd Environmental Performance Review, supra* pp. 43–45.
367. *See*: UNECE. *3rd Environmental Performance Review, Bosnia and Herzegovina, supra* pp. 41–50.
368. *See*: http://www.inspektorat.vladars.net/ (4 Jan. 2019).

244. The Inspectorate is an independent administration which carries out inspection activities on the territory of RS and which is established by the Law on Inspection in the Republic of Srpska ('Official Gazette of RS', Nos. 113/05, 1/08, 74/10, 109/12 and 44/16).[369]

245. In the local self-government units the following positions are performing tasks of inspection supervision: food inspector, market inspector, agricultural inspector, veterinary inspector, water inspector, traffic inspector, urban – construction inspector, environmental inspector,[370] health inspector, labour inspector (Article 3, paragraph 2).

246. Since its establishment (1 March 2006) RS Inspectorate has been keeping records of executed controls and measures taken for all inspection agencies that deal with particular segments of the environment protection.[371] In the period from 2009 to 2011, the Inspectorate conducted 1037 inspection checks in the area of environment protection (four RS environment inspectors), and irregularities were found in 381 cases or 36.7%. After these irregularities had been found, the inspection primarily acted preventively and ordered their removal. In the course of checks which resulted in ordering the removal of the irregularities, minor offence measures were imposed to entities that had not removed irregularities within the prescribed time limit, i.e., fifty-four minor offence orders were issued in the amount of BAM 55,000.[372]

369. The Inspectorate carries out activities organized through the following inspection services: (a) Food Safety Inspection Service, (b) Market Inspection Service, (c) Agricultural Inspection Service, (d) Forestry Inspection Service, (e) Veterinary Inspection Service, (f) Water Inspection Service, (g) Technical Inspection Service, (h) Traffic Inspection Service, (i) Urban Planning and Construction and Environmental Inspection Service, (j) Labour Inspection Service, (k) Health Inspection Service, (l) Education Inspection Service and (m) Fire Safety Inspection Service.

370. The environmental inspector performs inspection regarding compliance with the regulations related to environmental protection, ecology, waste management and in other administrative areas, as determined by a special regulation (Art. 25, para. 2). *See also*: Directorate for European Integration, *Answers to the Questionnaire, Chapter 27, Environment and climate change*, 27 Feb. 2018, p. 85.

371. BiH Council of Ministers. *Answers to the List of EU Questions on Chapter 27, Environment.* Sarajevo. 2012, p. 105.

372. *Ibid.*, p. 113. In the same period, municipal environment inspectors, who perform inspection supervisions in the local self-government units, according to the principle of functional connection with the inspections, conducted 6572 checks and found irregularities in 2575 cases or in 39.2%. In the course of the execution checks which resulted in ordering the removal of irregularities the city/municipal environment inspections imposed minor offence measures i.e., issued 39 minor offence orders to entities that had not removed irregularities within the prescribed time limit. In the said period there were no crime charges and no second instance appeals decisions issued by environment inspectors, which indicates that facts were determined in realistic and quality way and that inspectors respected legislative provisions.

II. Federation of Bosnia and Herzegovina

247. Performing the inspection controls in FBiH in order to ensure the enforcement of the laws and other regulations and general acts is defined by the Law on Inspection Services in FBiH, ('Official Gazette of FbiH', No. 73/14). On the basis of this law, the inspection control in Federation is done by the inspection bodies organized by the FBiH Administration for Inspection Affairs (FBiH Administration).[373]

248. 'FBiH inspectors in the last three years issued 186 minor offence charges in the area of air and waste management. The fines were ranging from BAM 1000+200 to BAM 3000+300. Out of that, the entities which were subject to the control paid fines in 124 cases, and in 37 cases after final judgements, while in 25 cases fines were not collected.'[374]

249. Besides that, monitoring compliance in the area and the state of the environment in accordance with the Law on Environmental Protection is done in the Canton by the Cantonal inspection body, especially concerning environmental licences. Oversight over the implementation of some environmental laws (e.g., Law on waste management) is carried out by the municipal inspection body.[375]

III. Brčko District of Bosnia and Herzegovina

250. The BD Inspectorate is an organizational unit that performs inspection, administrative, professional and other activities, promotes social discipline in enforcing laws and regulations. In terms of organizational hierarchy, it is situated within the Office of the Mayor. The Inspectorate is managed by the Head of Inspectorate, and the departments of the Inspectorate are managed by general inspectors.[376] The Government of BD has adopted The Law on Inspections in BDBiH in 2008 (Official Gazette of BD Nos 24/08, 25/08, 20/13 and 16/18).

---

373. FBiH Administration consists of the several federal inspection bodies: 1. Trade Inspection Service; 2. Sanitary, Health Inspection Service; 3. Labour Inspection Service; 4. Urban Planning and Environmental Inspection Service; 5. Traffic Inspection Service; 6. Agricultural Inspection Service; 7. Forestry Inspection Service; 8. Water Inspection Service; 9. Veterinary Inspection Service, etc. *See*: http://www.fuzip.gov.ba/stranica/33/pregled (19 Jul. 2022).

374. BiH Council of Ministers. *Answers to the List of EU Questions on Chapter 27, Environment.* Sarajevo. 2012., p. 118. For detailed data on cantonal inspection's activities, *see Ibid.*, pp. 118–122.

375. *Ibid.*, pp. 84–90. For more accurate information, *see*: Directorate for European Integration, *Answers to the Questionnaire, Chapter 27, Environment and climate change*, 27 Feb. 2018, 164–183.

376. The Inspectorate consists of three departments: Department for business activities inspection consists of three inspection services (1. Market Inspection Service, 2. Labour and Labour Relations Inspection Service, 3. Education Inspection Service), Department for health and environment protection inspection consists of eight inspection services (1. Phytosanitary Inspection Service, 2. Health Inspection Service, 3. Sanitary Inspection Service, 4. Veterinary Inspection Service, 5. Inspection Service for Environment Protection, 6. Inspection Service for Water Management, 7. Agricultural Inspection Service, 8. Forestry Inspection Service), Department for inspection of occupation activities consists of eight inspection services (1. Communal Inspection Service, 2. Traffic

§4. Harmonization with EU Legislation

251. Negotiations over the Stabilization and Association Agreement between Bosnia and Herzegovina and the EU officially commenced in November 2005.[377] The Parliamentary Assembly of BiH adopted in 2008 the Resolution on the Acceleration of the Process of Admission of BiH to the EU. By virtue of signing the Stabilization and Association Agreement between BiH and the EU in July 2008, BiH entered its first contractual relationship with the EU.[378]

252. 'Over the last decade BiH has increased its efforts to address environmental challenges and has harmonised the legal aspects of environmental protection in each of the entities through a set of environmental laws prepared in accordance with European Union directives.'[379] The accession process 'is one of the main driving forces in the environment sector reform, which, for the most part, applies to harmonization of domestic legislation with the *acquis communautaire*'.[380] In the period between 2002 and 2004, the RS, the FBiH, and the BD adopted a set of environmental laws that are a basis for drafting subordinate legislation at all levels.

253. On the basis of Article 18 of the law on Law on Ministries and Other Administrative Bodies of BiH, the Directorate for European Integration is in charge of coordination of all activities in the process of integration of BiH to the EU.[381] In the field of harmonization of legislation, the Directorate for European Integration is responsible for coordination of activities on the harmonization of the BiH legal system with the EU legislation, compliance checking of drafts/legislative proposals submitted to the Council of Ministers by the ministries and administrative bodies,

---

Inspection Service, 3. Urban Planning and Construction Inspection Service, 4. Occupational Safety Inspection Service, 5. Fire Protection Inspection Service, 6. Electricity Inspection Service, 7. Thermal energy Inspection Service, 8. Road Inspection Service). *See*: http://kg.bdcentral.net/Content/Read/inspektorat (19 Jul. 2022).

377. For information on key dates, *see*: http://europa.ba/?page_id=496 http://europa.ba/?page_id=496 (19 Jul. 2022).

378. Filipović O. (Ed) *Parliamentary Assembly of Bosnia and Herzegovina, supra* p. 133.

379. Hodžić-Kovač E., (Ed) *Progress towards the Realisation of Millennium Development Goals in Bosnia and Herzegovina 2013, supra* p. 116.

380. BiH MFTER, *State of the environment Report of the Bosnia and Herzegovina 2012, supra* p. 38.

381. Joint Committee on European Integration (Parliamentary Assembly of BiH) considers issues in light of: general issues related to EU integration, monitoring the implementation of BiH's rights and obligations arising from international treaties in view of CoE membership; coordinating the work of working bodies related to EU integration and submitting opinions, recommendations and warnings to these bodies; analysing the impact of integration strategy for BiH and drafting comprehensive reports; supervising the drafting of the feasibility study and monitoring the implementation of the pre-accession (Stabilization and Association Agreement) and accession strategies of BiH; supervising the harmonization of BiH legislation with the *acquis communautaire* (applicable EU legislation) when the Committee meets all the requirements; cooperation with institutions of BiH (particularly with the BiH Directorate for EU Integration), organizing public opinion debates on integration issues; supervising the use of funds allocated by the EU; and also considers other issues related to EU integration. For more information *see* https://www.parlament.ba/committee/read/39?lang=en (19 Jul. 2022).

and participates in drafting of legal act to be harmonized with the EU legislation.[382] However, the most important activity of harmonizing legislation and policies takes place at the level of entities and Brčko District.

In the preparation of legislation, regulations and strategic documents, authorities at three levels (BiH level, RS and FBiH levels, and BDBiH level) are required to identify relevant *acquis* and to harmonized these documents. The legislation that ensures alignment is as follows: Decision on the procedure for alignment of the BiH legislation with EU *acquis* (Official Gazette of BiH, No. 75/16), Decision on the procedure for alignment of the BiH legislation with EU *acquis* and legal acts of the Council of Europe (Official Gazette of RS, No. 46/11, 1/14, 9/14), Decree on the procedure for alignment of the FBiH legislation with EU *acquis* (Official Gazette of BiH, No. 98/16), and Decision on the procedure for alignment of the BiH legislation with EU *acquis* (Official Gazette of BDBiH, No. 49/14).[383]

254. According to the European Commission Report (2021) BiH is 'at an early stage of preparation / has achieved some level of preparation in the area of environment and climate change. … The country needs to ensure an even, countrywide harmonised and consistent approach in strategic planning and alignment with the EU *acquis* at all levels of government. Significant efforts are needed on implementation and enforcement'.[384]

Horizontal legislation is, to a limited extent, aligned with the EU *acquis*.[385]

Enforcing SEA and EIA provisions needs to be strengthened together with the necessary improvements in access to information and the participation of the public in the decision-making process on planned investments.[386] Regarding the climate change 'the level of alignment with the EU climate *acquis* remains limited'.[387]

EU provided financial support for drafting the EAS through implementation of the IPA Project EnvIS (2011–2014). Due to its composite constitutional features, the BiH environmental approximation approach comprises a set composed of four strategic planning documents – one applicable in the entire territory of the country and

382. According to the Decision on the Directorate for European Integration, the Directorate acts as a permanent and independent professional body that performs tasks and duties related to the coordination of activities of the BiH authorities; it supervises the implementation of decisions adopted by competent BiH institutions concerning activities relevant for the European integration process. *See* details on the website https://www.dei.gov.ba/en/o-nam (19 Jul. 2022). *See also* BiH Council of Ministers, *Answers to the List of EU Questions on Chapter 27, Environment, supra* pp. 19–21. 'The role and capacity of the Directorate for European Integration will need to be further strengthened.' EC, *Bosnia and Herzegovina 2018 Progress Report, supra* p. 5. 'The executives have little capacities for coordination and policy planning, including on EU matters. This requires effectively implementing the legislation on coordination of EU matters, including the coordination mechanism, and strengthening the Directorate for European Integration.' EC, *Bosnia and Herzegovina 2021 Progress Report,* p. 9.

383. For more information, *see*: Directorate for European Integration, *Answers to the Questionnaire, Chapter 27, Environment and climate change*, 27 Feb. 2018, pp. 19–23.

384. EC, *Bosnia and Herzegovina 2021 Progress Report*, p. 102.

385. *Ibid.*, p. 102.

386. *Ibid.*, p. 102.

387. *Ibid.*, p. 105.

three covering the territories of the two BiH entities (Republika Srpska and Federation of BiH) and Brčko District of BiH.[388]

§5. Critical Evaluation of the Efficiency of the Existing Environmental Laws

255. 'The 2010 Yale Index ranks BiH 98th out of 163 countries, achieving 55.9% of its environmental objectives. This performance placed it below its geographic group average result (59%), ranking the country far behind Albania (23rd place), Serbia (29th), Croatia (35th), and the Former Yugoslav Republic of Macedonia (73rd). According to this ranking, BiH is distinguishing itself for excellent results in forestry and water management, but has unfortunately achieved a very low success rate in biodiversity protection.'[389]

256. BiH has fourteen legal systems, thirteen constitutions, thirteen prime ministers, five levels of administration, and over 150 ministries (including in each canton within the Federation of Bosnia and Herzegovina). The structure entails very high administrative costs, which have been estimated at 50% of gross domestic product (GDP), while the state-wide fragmentation of administrative and legislative systems and processes has distinctly negative effects on efficiency in all sectors. Furthermore, issues of mandate and jurisdiction combine with ethnic sensitivities and political positioning to make coordination very complex.[390]

257. 'Despite the success so far achieved in certain areas, BiH faces major challenges in fulfilling set goals in the field of environmental protection.' Several of them may be recognized as 'basic obstacles which might impede the implementation of environmental reform', such as a lack of subordinate legislation and funds for certain significant measures to implement environmental policy, non-existence of unified data collection and processing, problems in coordination, etc.):[391]

> the fact that transposition of certain aspects of analyzed EU environmental acquis is lagging behind has consequences on the institutional aspects. This

388. *See*: BiH MFTER. *Environmental Approximation Strategy of Bosnia and Herzegovina*, EAS – BiH, Ministry of Foreign Trade and Economic Relations of Bosnia and Herzegovina, May 2017. *See also*: http://www.mvteo.gov.ba/Content/Read/vodni-resursi-zastita-okoline-strateski-dokumenti?lang=sr (19 Jul. 2022).
389. The Environmental Performance Index (EPI) of Yale University ranks countries according to how well they have achieved their environmental policy goals. EPR, 2011, p. 3.
390. UNDP, *Assessment of Development Results, Evaluation of UNDP Contribution, Bosnia and Herzegovina*, May 2009. p. 7. 'The existing legislation is not harmonized vertically (there are many gaps between state and Entity level laws and between laws at the level of Cantons and the Federation of BiH), let alone horizontally (environmental legislation differs in the two Entities and all relevant laws in both Entities and the Brčko District have not been adopted)'UNEP, *Desk Review of the Legal and Institutional Framework of Environmental Protection in Bosnia and Herzegovina, supra* p. 25.
391. BiH MFTER, *State of the environment Report of the Bosnia and Herzegovina 2012, supra* p. 38.

> means that the competent authorities have not been specifically designated for all analyzed EU legal instruments. However, it seems that they will not be in position to take over most of the institutional responsibilities in regards to the currently not transposed legal instruments. Necessity for (re)-organization and strengthening of most of them, at all administrative levels, seems obvious.[392] The efficiency and effectiveness of the system of regulation and compliance have not changed since 2011. There is still inadequate vertical coordination and communication between cantons/municipalities and entities but also insufficient horizontal coordination at the inter-entity and intercantonal and intermunicipal levels.[393]

Little progress has been made since 2011 in developing a cohesive and comprehensive monitoring system or developing an environmental information system at the state level, including the development of a central database for environmental information.[394]

258. 'The existing protected areas do not fully implement the system of protection, monitoring and sustainable use. The reason for this in the lack of the budgetary allocations, inadequate structure of employees, the lack of management plans, failure to appoint the institution responsible for the management of the protected areas ... '[395]

259. 'Laws on SD do not exist as such neither on cantonal, entity or national level. Sustainable development is incorporated in existing laws on agriculture, forestry, water, energy, regional development, nature protection but they are not linked to educational system and educational process. Thus, SD as such is not a component of educational process.'[396]

260. In the forthcoming period it is necessary to strengthen environmental protection institutions and human and technical capacities at all levels including inspectorates. Proper management of environmental issues and risks requires decision-making that needs to be based on science and adequate evidence. Improved environmental data collection and application, based on reliable and timely inputs and information, is a prerequisite for adequate planning, monitoring and reporting.[397]

---

392. BiH MFTER. *Environmental Approximation Strategy of Bosnia and Herzegovina*, EAS – BiH, Ministry of Foreign Trade and Economic Relations of Bosnia and Herzegovina, May 2017, p. 205.
393. UNECE, *3rd Environmental Performance Review, supra* p. 46. In addition, the shortage of staff and funding to carry out tasks and activities in environmental permitting, assessment and inspection is today still much the same challenge as it was in 2011.
394. UNECE, *3rd Environmental Performance Review, Bosnia and Herzegovina. supra* p. 71.
395. BiH MFTER, UNEP, GEF. *Strategy and Action Plan for Protection of Biological Diversity in Bosnia and Herzegovina (2015–2020), supra* p. 74.
396. Bratović E., Lepić S. *Education for Sustainable Development, Bosnia and Herzegovina, Research Report, supra* p. 9.
397. Hodžić-Kovač E., (Ed) *Progress towards the Realisation of Millennium Development Goals in Bosnia and Herzegovina 2013, supra* p. 125. 'For long-term environmental protection sustainable

261. Since the end of the war in 1995, BiH has made progress in its international environmental cooperation at bilateral, regional, European and global levels. However, there is still important work to be done, in particular in clarifying institutional responsibilities. One issue of concern is the lack of a systematic, strategic approach to international cooperation.[398]

BiH does not have in place 'effective institutional mechanisms to oversee and coordinate the implementation of all international environmental agreements to which the country is a party'.[399]

262. '… The legal framework regulating environmental inspections and its enforcement needs to be improved in line with the relevant EU *acquis*. Institutional capacities need to be considerably strengthened.'[400] In the process of the EU integration 'special attention' should be paid to free access to environmental information and public participation in decision-making on environmental matters.[401]

---

sources of financing are required, which includes efforts to prioritise and coordinate investment programmes and also fully utilise already available funds (such as in the water sector). Finally, comprehensive environmental protection can only be ensured through the inclusion of environmental protection needs in planning and development processes of all sectors that exercise environmental pressures'. *Ibid.*, p. 125.

398. RSMoAFWM, *First national report on the implementation of the United Nations Convention to Combat Desertification/Land Degradation in Bosnia and Herzegovina*, Ministry of Agriculture, Forestry and Water Management, Republic of Srpska, Banja Luka, 2007. p. 14.

399. For more information, *see*: UNECE· *3rd Environmental Performance Review, Bosnia and Herzegovina. supra* pp. 102–104.

400. EC. *Bosnia and Herzegovina 2021 Progress Report*, p. 102. 'Countrywide harmonised efforts are still required in transposing the provisions' of EIA and SEA 'in the legislation at all levels of government and across relevant sectors to ensure a consistent alignment.' Ibid. 102. In addition, BiH 'needs to align with the new EU climate *acquis* in a countrywide harmonised manner and establish a consistent legal framework.', Ibid, p. 105.

401. BiH MFTER. *Environmental Approximation Strategy of Bosnia and Herzegovina, supra* p. 206. For more details, *see also*: UNECE· *3rd Environmental Performance Review, Bosnia and Herzegovina*, pp. 74–77; Directorate for European Integration, *Answers to the Questionnaire, Chapter 27, Environment and climate change*, 27 Feb. 2018, pp. 255–286.

Chapter 2. Air Pollution

§1. State of Air Pollution and Monitoring

263. 'Air quality in urban areas deteriorate during the winter period, due to emissions from stationary sources (small furnaces) and mobile sources (transport), combined with the location of cities in the valleys. Concentrations of SO_2 and PM_{10} exceed limit values in winter period, accompanied with heavy smog.'[402]

264. At present, there are 10 locations in Bosnia and Herzegovina that conduct air quality measurements. These locations include automated measuring stations to provide continuous monitoring in both urban and suburban environments, covering 16 automatic air quality measurement stations in the Federation of Bosnia and Herzegovina and 12 in Republika Srpska. The air quality monitoring system covers the following parameters: SO_2, NO, NO_2, NOx, O_3, PM10.[403]

§2. Competencies

265. Air quality management is under the jurisdiction of entity ministries responsible for environment. Certain activities regarding air quality monitoring are carried out by the entity meteorological institutes.[404]

§3. Legislation

266. Air protection and air quality standards are stipulated in entity-level legislation and legislation of BDBiH.

The Climate Change Adaptation and Low-Emission Development Strategy for BiH has been developed alongside the Second National Communication of Bosnia and Herzegovina to the United Nations Framework Convention on Climate Change (UNFCCC) coordinated by the United Nations Development Programme (UNDP) in Bosnia and Herzegovina.[405] In addition, the Third National Communication and

402. *See*: https://www.eea.europa.eu/soer-2015/countries/bosnia-and-herzegovina (19 Jul. 2022).
403. UNECE· *3rd Environmental Performance Review, supra* p. 71.
404. Until 2007, the responsibility for the air quality monitoring network was not given to anyone. Measuring of air quality in BiH is done by the Federal Hydrometeorological Institute and responsible cantonal bodies in the FBiH, the Republic Hydrometeorological Institute in the RS, a responsible department in the BD Government, and in certain cases even the municipalities. BiH MFTER, *State of the environment Report of the Bosnia and Herzegovina 2012, supra,* p. 166. 'Even though progress has been made since 2011, monitoring of air quality is limited and done according to different methodologies. For instance, the Hydrometeorological Institute of the Federation of Bosnia and Herzegovina uses the CORINAIR methodology, while the Hydrometeorological Institute of Republika Srpska uses the IPCC methodology. There is consequently no aggregated air quality data available for the entire country.' UNECE, *3rd Environmental Performance Review, Bosnia and Herzegovina*. New York, Geneva: United Nations, 2018, p. 71.
405. For more information *see*: Knežević, A., Kaplina, A., Husika, A., Carrington, D., Arnautović Aksić, D., Jordan, G., Trbić, G., Stritih, J., Tabaković, L., Kotur, M. Cupać, R. *Strategija prilag*

Second Biennial Update Report on Greenhouse Gas Emissions of Bosnia and Herzegovina under the United Nations Framework Convention on Climate Change was adopted by the BiH Council of Ministers on 23 May 2017 and submitted to the UNFCCC Secretariat in Bonn.[406]

I. The Republic of Srpska

A. The Law on Air Protection

267. Basic legal act regulating air protection in the Republic of Srpska is the Law on the Air Protection (Official Gazette of RS, No. 124/11, and 46/17). It has the following twelve parts: Part I – General Provisions (Articles 1–4), Part II – Air Quality Control (Articles 5–17), Part III – Values of Air Quality (Articles 18–25), Part IV – Strategy, Plans and Programmes (Articles 26–39), Part V – Measures for Air Quality Improvement (Articles 40–57), Part VI – Activities of Emissions Measures and Levels of Air Pollutants in the Air (Articles 58–63), Part VII – Informing and Reporting (Articles 64–66), Part VIII – Information Systems (Articles 67–69), Part IX – Financing of Protection and Improvement of Air Quality (Articles 70–71), Part X – Supervision (Articles 72–74), Part XI – Penalties (Articles 75–78), Part XII – Transitional and Final Provisions (Articles 79–86).

268. According to Article 1, the Law on Air[407] Protection[408] regulates air protection and management of air quality and determines measures, way of organization, as well as control of the implementation of protection and air quality improvement as a natural resource of common interest which has special protection.

269. Article 2 provides that air protection is achieved by:

a. Establishing, maintaining and developing a unified system of air quality management on the territory of the Republic of Srpska (hereinafter, 'the Republic').
b. Maintaining and improving the air quality through identification and implementation of measures in the field of protection in order to prevent or reduce harmful effects on human health and/or environment.
c. Avoiding, preventing and reducing pollution that affects ozone depletion and climate change.

---

odavanja na klimatske promjele i niskoemisionog razvoja za BoInu i Hercegovinu[Climate Change Adaptation and Low Emission Development Strategy for BiH], juni 2013. http://www.unfccc.ba/site/publikacije/spkp.pdf (19 Jul. 2022). http://www.ba.undp.org/content/bosnia_and_herzegovina/en/home/library/environment_energy/climate-change-adaptation-and-low-emission-development-strategy-.html (19 Jul. 2022).

406. See: https://unfccc.int/sites/default/files/resource/TNC%20AND%20SBUR%20ENG.pdf (26 Jul. 2022).

407. *Air* is air in the troposphere, i.e., outdoor air, which does not include indoor air (Art. 3, point a).

408. The provisions of this Law shall not apply to the pollution caused by radioactive substances, industrial accidents and natural disasters (Art. 1, para. 2).

d. Monitoring, collecting and evaluating relevant air quality data, based on measurements and standardized methods.
e. Ensuring the availability of air quality data.
f. Performing obligations in accordance with recognized international treaties.
g. Establishing international cooperation in the field of protection and improvement of air quality, and providing access of such data to the public.

270. The air protection and improvement is provided, within its mandate, by the Republic of Srpska, and by local government units, companies, entrepreneurs, as well as other legal entities and natural persons (Article 4, paragraph 1). The companies, other legal entities and entrepreneurs which in performing their operations affect or which may affect air quality are required to: provide technical measures to prevent or reduce emissions[409] to the air;[410] to plan costs for air protection from pollution within the investment and production costs; monitor the impact of its activities on air quality, provide other protection measures, in accordance with this law and other laws governing the environmental protection (Article 4, paragraph 2).

1. The Air Quality Monitoring and Control

271. Zones[411] and agglomerations[412] are determined on the basis of the air quality assessment, depending on the defined upper[413] and lower limits of the evaluation[414] (Article 6, paragraph 1). In order to control, maintenance of the state and/or improvement of air quality, the Government defines zones and agglomerations on the Republic of Srpska territory (Article 6, paragraph 4). Determination of the zones and agglomerations is reviewed at least once every five years,[415] according to the

---

409. *'Emission'* means the discharge of pollutants in gaseous, liquid or solid physical state from the sources of pollution in the air (Art. 3, point j).
410. Monitoring of air quality and air emissions monitoring is performed by the competent authorities and legal entities that are licensed for this activity (Art. 4, para. 3).
411. *Zone* is a part of the territory with defined borders, determined in order to evaluate and to manage the air quality that from the standpoint of control, maintenance and/or improvement of the air quality, produces a characteristic functional unit (Art. 5, para. 1).
412. *Agglomeration* is a zone with more than 250,000 inhabitants (Art. 5, para. 2). Agglomeration can be a zone with a smaller population, if the population density in this area is higher than prescribed, therefore it is a justifiable a need for the assessment and management of air quality (Art. 5, para. 3).
413. *Upper limit of evaluation* is a prescribed level of pollutants below which the evaluation can be performed in a combination of measurements and estimation methods on the bases of the mathematical models and/or other appropriate estimation methods (Art. 3, point g).
414. *'Lower limits of evaluation'* is prescribed level of pollutants below which the assessment can be done only by using estimation methods on the base of the mathematical models and/or other methods of assessment (Art. 3, point ž).
415. Determination of the zones and agglomerations referred to in para. 1 of this article is reviewed in a shorter period, in the case of changing of activities important for increasing the concentration of pollutants (Art. 6, para. 3).

monitoring conditions specified in the act of the Republic of Srpska Government (hereinafter, 'Government') from Article 9, paragraph 3 of this law (Article 6, paragraph 2).

272. The air quality is assessed in the Republic with regard to the level of pollutants[416] depending on the upper and lower limits of assessment, namely:

(a) In all zones and agglomerations where the level of pollutants exceeds the upper limit of evaluation for these pollutants, the data obtained by fixed measurements[417] that can be complement with data obtained by the techniques of modelling and/or indicative measurements[418] are used for the air quality assessment.[419]
(b) In all zones and agglomerations where the level of pollutants is below the upper limit of assessment established for these pollutants, a combination of fixed measurements and modelling techniques and/or indicative measurements for air quality assessment can be used.
(c) In all zones and agglomerations where the level of pollutants is below the lower limit of assessment established for that pollutants, modelling techniques and/or valuation techniques[420] are used for assessment of air quality (Article 7, paragraph 1).

273. For the purpose of efficient air quality management, a unified functional system of monitoring and control the level of air pollution and maintenance a database on air quality (hereinafter, 'the air quality monitoring') is introduced (Article 9, paragraph 1). The Republic and local government units, within their authority determined by the law,[421] provide air quality monitoring (Article 9, paragraph 2).

Air quality monitoring is performed by Republican and local network of measuring stations and/or measurement points for fixed measurements (Article 10, paragraph 1). Republican network of measuring stations and/or measurement sites

416. *'The level of pollutants'* is the concentration of pollutants in the air or depositing them on the surface in a given period, expressing the air quality (Art. 3, point c).
417. *'Fixed measurements'* are measurements made at fixed locations, by continuous or periodic sampling with the aim to determine the level of pollutants in accordance with the relevant objectives of data quality (Art. 3, point ae).
418. *'Indicative measurements'* are measurements for which are set less strict requirements in terms of data quality than those required for fixed measurements (Art. 3, point m).
419. *'Air quality assessment'* means any method used for the measurement, calculations, forecasts and estimates of the pollutants level in order to determine the areas in accordance to the level of contamination (Art. 3, point c).
420. Notwithstanding from para. 1, item c) of this article, the measurements are carried out on the basis of rural locations, away from major air pollution sources, in order to provide the minimum level of information on pollutant substances level (Art. 7, para. 2).
421. The Government shall, on the proposal of the Ministry, adopt a regulation that establishes requirements for air quality monitoring on the territory of the Republic of Srpska (Art. 9, para. 3). The Government shall at the proposal of the Ministry, within a period of one year from the date of enactment of this Law, issue: (a) the regulations on conditions for monitoring of air quality on the territory of the Republic of Srpska from Art. 9, para. 3 of this Law (Art. 79, point a).

(hereinafter, 'the Republican network') are established to monitor air quality at the Republic level (Article 11, paragraph 1).[422]

274. In case of regional and cross-border atmospheric transport of pollutants in the air and in air-sediments within the international obligations, it can be established one or several common measuring stations, covering neighbouring zones in the Republic of Srpska and in neighbouring countries, in order to obtain the necessary spatial resolution (Article 11, paragraph 4).

275. Republican network consists of measuring stations and/or test points for measuring:

(a) Regional and cross-border transfer of atmospheric pollutants in the air and in air-sediment within international obligations.
(b) The air quality in residential areas, industrial and uninhabited areas.
(c) Air quality in protected natural resources and protected environment of immovable cultural property.
(d) The air quality in areas affected by specific pollution source, including mobile sources.[423]
(e) Allergenic pollen (Article 12, paragraph 1).

276. A local government unit in its territory establishes a local network of measuring stations and/or measurement sites (hereinafter, 'local area network') to monitor air quality (Article 14, paragraph 1). Monitoring of air quality in the local network is performed in accordance to the regulation which a local government authority adopts for its territory, which shall be in accordance with the provisions of Article 11, paragraph 3 of this law (Article 14, paragraph 3).[424]

277. The funds for realization of the air quality control programmes in the local network are provided from the budget of the local government units (Article 15, paragraph 1). The competent authority of the local government unit is obliged to publish data on the results of air quality monitoring and submit them to the Republican administrative organization in charge for hydrological and meteorological affairs (Article 15, paragraph 5).

278. In case that there is reasonable doubt that there was air pollution that can damage human health and/or the environment, levels of polluting substances[425]

---

422. The Republican network is financed from the Republican budget (Art. 11, para. 2).
423. *'Mobile pollution source'* is the internal combustion engine installed in the transport vehicle or in operating machines (Art. 3, point ž).
424. The local government shall issue a regulation on air quality control at the local level, which determines the number and distribution of measurement stations and/or measurement stations in the specific zones and agglomerations, as well as the volume, type and frequency of measurements with the prior approval of the Ministry (Art. 14, para. 4).
425. *'Polluting substance'* means any substance (introduced into the air directly or indirectly by men), present in the air, which has adverse effects on human health and the environment in general (Art. 3, point l).

must be properly measured (Article 16, paragraph 1). After that, the Ministry makes a decision on measuring of special purposes which contain modalities and deadlines for measurements, as well as the type of polluting substances which will be measured (Article 16, paragraph 2).[426]

279. The competent authority of the local government unit and authorized legal persons[427] are required to submit air quality data to the national administrative organization in charge for hydrological and meteorological activities up to 15 of the month for the previous month, and the annual report not later than sixty days after expiry of the calendar year for the previous year. These data are obtained during air quality control from the local network, as well as the results of measurements of specific purposes[428] (Article 17, paragraph 1).

2. The Air Quality Values

280. The air quality values[429] are numerical values of limited values of pollutants level in the air, the lower and upper limits of air quality assessment, critical levels,[430] the tolerance limits,[431] and the tolerance values,[432] targeted values[433] and

426. The Ministry or the competent authority of the local government unit carries out measurements of special purposes through the competent authorities of the Republican administration or the authorized legal entity (Art. 16, para. 3).
427. *'Authorized legal entity'* is a professional organization accredited as a testing laboratory, which has a licence for carrying out air monitoring and/or measurement of emissions, issued by the ministry responsible for environmental protection (hereinafter, 'the Ministry') (Art. 3, point ć).
428. Data from the para. 1 of this article shall be used for the air quality assessment, as well as for preparation of reports on the state of air quality. Also, these data are an integral part of the air quality information system (Art. 17, para. 3). The Republican administration organization responsible for hydrological and meteorological affairs and relevant local government unit's authority are required to make the data specified in para. 1 of this article available to the public and to publish them in the media, in electronic media, as well as on their web sites (Art. 17, para. 2).
429. The Government, at the proposal of the Ministry, prescribes the values of air quality in order to control the air quality (Art. 18, para. 2). The Government, at the proposal, within a period of one year from the date of enactment of this Act, shall issue Regulations for the control of air quality and value under Art. 11, para. 3 and Art. 18, para. 2 of this Law (Art. 79, point b). The regulation referred to in para. 2 of Art. 18 defines the deadlines for reaching the limiting and/or targeted values, in case that they are exceeded (Art. 18, para. 3). Short-term action plans may be adopted, for the purpose to protect human health and/or the environment, if necessary, in case that there is a risk of exceeding one or more limiting or targeted values for certain pollutants, established in Art. 18, para. 2 of this Law (Art. 33, para. 2).
430. *'Critical level'* is the level of pollutant based on scientific knowledge, above which may appear direct adverse effects on some receptors, such as trees, other plants or natural ecosystems, but not to humans (Art. 3, point p).
431. *'Tolerance limit'* is the percentage of allowed overdraft limits under the prescribed conditions (Art. 3, point d).
432. *'Tolerance value'* is the limiting value increased for the margin of tolerance (Art. 3, point ad).
433. *'Target value'* is the level of pollutant determined in order to avoid, prevent or reduce harmful effects on human health and/or the environment as a whole, which will be achieved within the specified time (Art. 3, point az).

long-term goals[434] of pollutants in the air, the concentration dangerous to human health[435] and concentration to be reported to the public[436] (Article 18, paragraph 1).

In case of concentration exceeding to be reported to the public, stipulated in the act referred to in Article 18, paragraph 1 of this law, or the concentration of certain pollutants harmful to human health, the Ministry and the competent authority of the local government are obliged to inform the public via radio, television, newspapers, the Internet and/or by other suitable means (Article 23, paragraph 1).

281. According to the level of contamination, starting from the prescribed limit and tolerance values, based on the measurement results, the following categories of air quality are determined:

(a) First category – clean or slightly polluted air where the limited levels are not exceeded for any pollutant substance.
(b) Second category – moderately polluted air where the limit values are exceeded for the level of one or more polluting substances, but not above the tolerance value of any pollutant substance.
(c) Third category – excessive air pollution where the tolerance values are exceeded for one or more pollutant substances (Article 21, paragraph 1).[437]

3. Strategies, Plans and Programmes

282. The policy and planning instruments of the air protection are:[438]

(a) Air Protection Strategy.
(b) Air quality plans.
(c) Short-term action plans.
(d) The Republican programme for the gradual reduction of maximum annual emissions[439] of the pollutants.

---

434. *'Long-term goal'* is the level of pollutants, set as the target for a longer period, if it is not possible to reach limiting value within a set deadline by using appropriate means (Art. 3, point i).
435. *'Concentration dangerous to human health'* is the level of polluting substance which an excess pose a risk to human health from short exposure. It is urgently need to take appropriate prescribed measures in case of appearance of these concentrations (Art. 3, point o).
436. *'Concentration to be reported to the public'* is the level of pollutant which exceedance poses a risk to the health, especially of vulnerable population from the short-term exposure. It is necessary urgently and in appropriate way to inform public about that (Art. 3, point nj). *'Public'* is one or more natural persons or legal entities, their associations, organizations or groups (Art. 3, point n).
437. The Minister shall annually bring a list of zones and agglomerations where the limited values of air quality are established, originating from the natural sources (Art. 24, para. 1).
438. *'Plans and programs'* are instruments that establish measures in order to reach the limiting and targeted values, in case that they are exceeded (Art. 3, point č).
439. *'Maximum emission'* is the maximum amount of pollutants expressed in kilotonnes that can be emitted in the Republic of Srpska in a calendar year in accordance with recognized international treaties (Art. 3, point r).

(e) The operator's[440] plans to reduce emissions from stationary plants (Article 26, paragraph 1).

283. Air Protection Strategy (hereinafter, 'The Strategy') is the basic document for bringing air quality plans, short-term action plans and programmes for the reduction of air pollutants emissions and which must be in compliance with the Strategy (Article 27, paragraph 1). The Strategy is coordinated with other Republican, municipal and sectoral plans and policies (Article 27, paragraph 2).[441]

Strategy is a document that provides conditions for establishment of an institutional system on which are taken measures for avoiding, preventing or reducing air pollution and harmful consequences to human health and/or the environment as a whole, in the territory of the Republic of Srpska[442] (Article 28, paragraph 1).

Realization of the Strategy is implemented by adopting an action plan[443] for the air protection,[444] the atmosphere and combating of climate change, adopted by the Government (Article 29, paragraph 1). The Ministry in cooperation with other relevant authorities is drafting the plan (Article 29, paragraph 3).

The Government shall submit a report on implementation of the Strategy to the National Assembly of the Republic of Srpska every three years (Article 30, paragraph 1). The Government shall make available this report to the public in accordance with the provisions of this law. Public opinion is taken into consideration when making a decision on review and correcting of strategic decisions (Article 30, paragraph 2).

284. The competent local government authority adopts the Air Quality Plan[445] in the zones and agglomerations where the air is of third category, i.e., when air pollution exceeds the effects of the taken measures, or when the capacity of the environment is in danger or when there is a constant air pollution in a particular area, in order to achieve the appropriate limiting values[446] or target values determined by the act referred to in Article 18, paragraph 2 of this law (Article 32, paragraph 1).

440. *'Operator'* means any legal entity, other legal entity or entrepreneur that owns an environmental permit issued in accordance with the regulation governing the environmental protection and which manages the facility, controls it or is authorized to make economic decisions in the field of technical functioning of the facility (Art. 3, point u).
441. The Government is preparing a Strategy proposal adopted by the National Assembly of the Republic of Srpska for a six years period (Art. 27, para. 3).
442. Mandatory content of the Strategy is set out in Art. 28, para. 2.
443. The content of the Action plan is listed in Art. 29, para. 2.
444. The content of the Air quality plans is listed in Art. 31, para. 1.
445. The Air Quality Plan shall be made on the basis of the air quality assessment and shall include all major pollutants and the major air pollution sources that led to the pollution (Art. 32, para. 2). The Ministry approves the Air Quality Plans (Art. 32, para. 4).
446. *The limiting value* is the highest allowed level of pollutants in the air, determined on the basis of scientific knowledge, in order to avoid, prevent or reduce harmful effects to human health and/or the environment. Once reached, it is not allowed to exceed that limiting value (Art. 3, point dj).

285. According to Article 33 the competent authority of the local government adopts short-term action plans[447] in the zone or in agglomeration located in their territory if:

(a) there is a risk that the air pollutants levels exceed one or more concentrations hazardous to human health, set forth in regulation from Article 18, paragraph 2 of this law;
(b) there is a risk to exceed the concentration of ground level ozone[448] dangerous to human health, established under Article 18, paragraph 2 of this law, if the competent authority assesses, taking into account the geographical, meteorological and economic conditions, that there is significant potential to reduce the risk, duration and severity of such excess.

Short-term action plans must include short-term measures taken to reduce the risk or duration of such excess (Article 34, paragraph 1). Depending on each individual case, effective measures to control the activities that contribute to the occurrence of the risk of exceeding the appropriate limiting or targeted values or concentrations dangerous to human health can be taken by short-term action plan. If necessary, these activities can be temporarily stopped (Article 34, paragraph 2).[449]

286. The competent local government authority shall notify the Ministry[450] immediately if any of the limiting value, a critical level, tolerance limit, the targeted value and the long-term goal, the concentration dangerous to human health or the concentration to be notified to the public are exceeded due to the significant cross-border transfer of air pollutants substances or their precursor (Article 36, paragraph 1).[451]

287. The Republican programme for gradually reduction of the maximum Republican annual emission of pollutants (hereinafter, 'the Republican programme') is adopted by the Government for a period of four years (Article 37, paragraph 1). The content of the Republican programme is prescribed in Article 37, paragraph 2. The Republican programme must be available to the public and to the interested public[452] (Article 37, paragraph 3).

---

447. Ministry approves the short-term action plans (Art. 33, para. 3).
448. *'Ground level ozone'* is ozone located in the lowest layers of the troposphere (Art. 3, point ab).
449. Short-term action plans and information on their application must be available to the public and to interested organizations, such as organizations dealing with the protection of the environment, the organization representing the interests of sensitive population groups, health organizations and associations of entrepreneurs (Art. 35, para. 1).
450. The Ministry informs the public in cases from paras 1 and 2 of Art. 36 (Art. 36, para. 4).
451. In case of exceeding the concentration hazardous to the human health and the concentration notified to the public in zones or agglomerations near the entity boundaries, the Ministry shall promptly notify the competent authority of the neighbouring country (Art. 36, para. 3).
452. *'Interested public'* is a public at which the installations work and performing of activities are affecting or may to affect, including non-governmental organizations dealing with the environmental protection and which are registered at the competent authority (Art. 3, point lj).

The Republican plan for reduction of emissions from the existing combustion plants[453] is part of the Republican programme from Article 37 of this law (Article 38, paragraph 1).

288. In the area where a third category of air quality is established, the authority responsible for environmental protection requires to the operator to produce a plan for reduction of emissions from stationary air pollution sources[454] and sets a deadline for drafting the plan (Article 39, paragraph 1).

4. The Air Quality Improvement Measures

289. Measures to prevent and reduce air pollution and improve air quality include:

(a) Prescribing limiting emission levels of pollutants from stationary sources of pollution.
(b) Prescribing limiting emission levels of pollutants from mobile sources of pollution.
(c) Complying with the maximum republican emission after its determination for certain pollutants.
(d) Prescribing of the allowed amount of certain pollutants in certain products.
(e) Reducing emissions of greenhouse gases.[455]
(f) Gradually reducing the use of substances that deplete the ozone layer.[456]
(g) Other measures to prevent and reduce pollution (Article 40).

290. The Minister shall in special regulation[457] establish measures for prevention and reduction of air pollution and air quality improvement, which include: (a) Limiting emission values of pollutants in the air, (b) The methods, procedures, frequency and methodology of measuring the emission of pollutants, (c) Establishing

453. The content of the Republican plan to reduce emissions from existing combustion plants is specified in Art. 38, para. 2 of this Law. *'Combustion plant'* is a technical system (furnace) in which fuel is oxidized in order to use the heat thus produced (Art. 3, point š).

454. The content of the operators Plan for reduction of emissions from stationary air pollution sources is prescribed in the Art. 39, para. 3. Approval on the Plan gives the authority that ordered drafting of the Plan (Art. 39, para. 4). *'Stationary pollution source'* means a stationary technical unit, including combustion, in which one or more activities that can lead to air pollution are performed, as well as any other activity having a technical connection with the activities carried out in that place and that can produce emissions and pollution (Art. 3, point ag).

455. *'Emissions of greenhouse gases'* is the release of greenhouse gases from the individual and/or from diffuse sources into the air (Art. 3, point k).

456. *'Substances that deplete the ozone layer'* are substances that have the potential to damage the ozone layer greater than zero (Art. 3, point av).

457. In the act from para. 1 of this article, it can be prescribed for existing air pollution sources, allowed emissions limiting values of certain pollutants and set a deadline in which these values should be reduced to the level of emission limits (Art. 41, para. 2). The Ministry prescribes limiting emission values of pollutants from the existing combustion plants. *'Limiting emission value'* is the maximum allowed value of the pollutants concentration in waste gases from stationary and mobile sources of pollution that can be released into the air in a given period (Art. 3, point e).

criteria for establishment of the measuring points for emission measurement, (d) The procedure to validate the results of emission measurement and compliance with the prescribed standards, (e) The content of the report on performed emissions measurements and emission balance and (f) The manner of data submission on emissions for the information system[458] purposes and data submission deadlines (Article 41, paragraph 1).

291. In order to protect and preserve the air quality, are performed emission controls of volatile organic compounds from installations for storage and distribution of petroleum products from the terminals to petrol stations, as well as from the technological processes and activities in which volatile organic compounds are used as solvents (Article 43, paragraph 1).

292. Legal entities and entrepreneurs engaged in storage, distribution and placing on the market of petroleum and petroleum products are required to apply the regulation on technical measures in order to reduce emissions of volatile organic compounds (Article 44, paragraph 1).

A legal entity or entrepreneur which in their production process use organic solvents are obliged to implement measures to reduce the emission of volatile organic compounds below the prescribed limit (Article 45, paragraph 1).[459] The Government shall adopt a Regulation establishing: (a) a method of gradual excluding use of substances that damage the ozone layer, (b) treatment of these substances, substitute substances and new controlled substances, (c) treatment of products containing substances or that are produced by these substances, (d) the method of checking the emission and control of emissions of these substances, (e) treatment of such substances after the cessation of the product use and equipment containing them, (f) the manner of their collection, renewal and processing and (g) the procedure for issuing consent for import, export and placing on the market ozone-depleting substances[460] (Article 51, paragraph 1).

For the performance of production, maintenance and/or repair and banned from use of products and equipment containing substances that deplete the ozone layer, legal persons and entrepreneurs must have the permission of the Ministry (Article 51, paragraph 3).

---

458. The information system of the air quality will be established within five years from the date of enactment of this Law (Art. 82, para. 2).
459. The Minister shall issue a regulation that determines: (a) a method for preventing or reducing the direct or indirect consequences of emissions of volatile organic compounds to the environment, in particular emissions into the air; (b) limiting values for emission of volatile organic compounds from installations and activities using organic solvents; (c) requirements for installations that use these compounds, as well (d) Schemes for reducing emissions of volatile organic compounds (Art. 45, para. 2).
460. The Government, at the proposal of the Ministry, within a period of one year from the date of enactment of this Act, issue provision on treatment with substances that deplete the ozone layer, and substitute substances referred to in Art. 51, para. 1 of this Law (Art. 79, point v).

293. Mobile pollution sources[461] can be used and placed on the market if the pollutants in the exhaust gases from these sources do not exceed the emission limit values specified in technical regulations, in accordance with the law (Article 46, paragraph 1).

A special Regulation regulates: (a) technical requirements relating to the quality of the fuel placed on the market and used in stationary and mobile sources of pollution, (b) the permissible amount of pollutants in the fuel, (c) methods of fuel testing, (d) the method of determining the quality and proving compliance with the prescribed limit values, as well (e) technical measures that are applied in order to reduce the emissions of volatile organic compounds resulting from the process of storage and distribution of petroleum products (Article 48, paragraph 1).

In order to reduce emissions of volatile organic compounds from paints and varnishes it is prescribed the maximum permissible content of certain volatile organic compounds in paints and varnishes[462] (Article 49, paragraph 1).

294. Article 50 provides that the prevention and reduction of air pollution affecting climate change is implemented through: (a) Application of measures to reduce emissions of greenhouse gases[463] and (b) Monitoring of greenhouse gases[464] emissions from the sources and by monitoring of removed quantities of these gases by sinks.[465]

295. Data on unintentionally emitted persistent organic pollutants[466] makes inventory on unintentionally emitted persistent organic pollutants, kept by the Republic administrative organization in charge for hydrological and meteorological activities (Article 51, paragraph 4).

296. It is prohibited on the territory of the Republic of Srpska:

---

461. Emissions from mobile sources of pollution are controlled during normal, special and technical inspection in accordance with the relevant technical regulations and Laws governing traffic safety (Art. 46, para. 2).

462. The maximum permissible content of volatile organic compounds in paints and varnishes was determined in regulations governing the chemicals (Art. 49, para. 2).

463. These measures shall be accomplished by (Art. 50, para. 3): (a) The development and use of cleaner technologies to prevent or reduce emissions of greenhouse gases, (b) Encouraging the use of renewable energy sources, (c) Promote energy efficiency and (d) Activities to increase the removal of greenhouse gases from the atmosphere. Also, these measures can be realised in the Clean Development Mechanism under the Kyoto Protocol (Art. 50, para. 4).

464. *Greenhouse gases* are gases that absorb and retransmit infrared radiation. Greenhouse gases come to the atmosphere as a result of natural processes, but also as result of human activities (Art. 3, point b).

465. Data on emissions and removed quantities of greenhouse gases consists of an Inventory of greenhouse gas emissions (Art. 50, para. 7). These data are public (Art. 50, para. 9). The Republican administration organization responsible for hydrological and meteorological activities keeps Inventory of greenhouse gases emissions (Art. 50, para. 8).

466. *'Unintentionally omitted persistent organic pollutants'* are substances that are persistent, bioaccumulative and toxic, emitted from stationary and mobile polluting sources, such as: polychlorinated dibenzofurans and polychlorinated dibenzodioxins, polycyclic aromatic hydrocarbons, polychlorinated biphenyls and hexachlorobenzene (Art. 3, point t).

(a) Production of substances that deplete the ozone layer.
(b) Import and/or export of substances that deplete the ozone layer, set by an ratified international treaty, i.e., products and equipment containing these substances from the countries or in countries that are not signatory of the treaty.
(c) Import and/or export and placing on the market without the permission of substances that deplete the ozone layer and substitute substances.[467]
(d) Import and/or export and placing on the market of new products and equipment containing controlled substances, and ozone-depleting substances, except chlorofluorohydrocarbons.
(e) Releasing substances that deplete the ozone layer and substitute substances.
(f) Filling of products and equipment containing substitute substances with substances that deplete the ozone layer.
(g) Rinsing with substances that deplete the ozone layer.
(h) Import and/or export, placing on the market and usage of single-use reservoir for storing of the substances that deplete the ozone layer and substitute substances.
(i) Placing on the market in retail of the substances that deplete the ozone layer and substitute substances.
(j) Import and/or export and placing on the market of used products and equipment containing substances that deplete the ozone layer (Article 53, paragraph 1).

297. Legal entities and entrepreneurs who have obtained the license referred to in Article 52 of this Law shall keep records of the types and quantities of collected and used substances that damage the ozone layer and substitute substances, as well as the quantities of recovered and /or processed ozone-depleting substances (Article 54, paragraph 1).

298. The facility must be designed, constructed and/or produced, equipped, used and maintained so that it does not emit pollutants into the air in quantities greater than the emission limit values (Article 55, paragraph 1).

If there is a device malfunction used to ensure the implementation of prescribed protection measures, or disruption of the technological process, leading to exceeding of emission limit values, the operator is required to eliminate the defect or disorder, or adapt to the new situation and work to stop the technological process, to reduced emission to permitted limits as soon as possible (Article 55, paragraph 2).[468]

---

467. 'Substitute substances' are fluorinated gases with a greenhouse effect including: fluorocarbons, perfluorocarbons and sulphur hexafluorides which potential of the ozone layer damage is equal to zero (Art. 3, point až).

468. In case of exceeding the limiting values of pollutants in the air, operator is obliged, when he notices exceeding of the limiting values or at the direction of the competent inspector, to undertake technical and technological measures or to suspend technological process, in order to reduce the concentration of pollutants to prescribed limiting values (Art. 55, para. 3).

The newly built or reconstructed stationary pollution source may begin its working if it obtains an environmental permit,[469] in accordance with regulations on environmental protection (Article 56, paragraph 1).

299. Pursuant to Article 57 the operator is obliged to:

a. Submit to the Republican administrative organization in charge for hydrological and meteorological affairs and the competent authority of the local government information on the stationary pollution source and its every change (reconstruction).
b. Ensure regular monitoring of emissions and to keep records on it.
c. Provide continuous measurements of emissions if it is prescribed for certain pollutants and/or for sources of pollution alone, by automatic device for continuous measurement, with the approval of the Republican administrative organization in charge for hydrological and meteorological affairs.
d. Provide control measurements over an authorized legal entity, if emission measurements are performed independently.
e. Ensure prescribed periodic measurements of emission, through an authorized legal person, twice a year, if it does not carry out measuring of emissions continuously.
f. Provide air quality monitoring inspection by order of a competent inspection authority, either independently or through an authorized legal entity.
g. Keep records of measurements performed with data on measurement locations, results of the measurement frequency and deliver data in a report format prescribed by the Republican administrative organization in charge for hydrological and meteorological affairs and the competent authority of the local government, including: (1) For the measurements from the paragraph 1, point (b) and (c) of this article – a quarterly basis within fifteen days from the quarter, (2) For the measurements from the paragraph 1, point d) of this Article – within thirty days from the date of such measurements, (3) For annual measurements – in the form of an annual report no later than 31 January of the current year for the previous calendar year.
h. To keep records of the type and quality of raw materials, fuels and waste incineration process.
i. To keep a record on the work of unit for preventing or reducing pollutant emissions, as well as the measuring device for measuring emissions (paragraph 1).[470]

469. It is prohibited to work newly constructed or reconstructed stationary sources of air pollution, as well as performing other outdoor activities that can lead to uncontrolled release of pollutants, until obtaining an environmental permit (Art. 56, para. 2).

470. The operator is obliged to, at its expense, implement measures to reduce emissions of pollutants defined in a plan for their stationary air pollution sources (Art. 57, para. 2).

5. Emissions Measurement, Information and Reporting

300. The authorized legal entities[471] obtaining air quality monitoring licence[472] are required to measure the air quality in accordance with the provisions of Article 9, paragraph 3 and Article 18, paragraph 2 of this law (Article 58, paragraph 1).

The authorized legal entities possessing licence for the measurement of emissions from stationary sources of pollution are obliged to perform emission measurements in accordance with the provisions of Articles 41 and 42 of this law (Article 58, paragraph 2).[473]

301. The competent authority is obliged to notify the other agencies and organizations, and the public through electronic and printing media in at least one journal that is distributed on the whole territory of the Republic of Srpska, about: (a) Air quality, (b) Plans on air quality and waste disposal for some time, to achieve the limiting values for nitrogen dioxide, benzene and particulate matter PM10, (c) Plans for achieving the target values in the zones and agglomerations where the targeted value has been exceeded, and (d) The annual report on all pollutants that are covered by this law (Article 64, paragraph 1).

302. In the case of exceeding the concentration dangerous to human health and the concentration to be notified to the public, the competent authority shall inform the public about: location or area of exceeding; kind of concentration that is exceeded (the concentration to be notified to the public or which is hazardous to human health), starting time and duration of the exceeding, the highest one-hour concentration, i.e., the highest eight hour middle concentration in the case of ground ozone, the geographical area in which is expected excess concentration to be notified to the public and/or which is dangerous to human health; forecasts for the future period with the expected pollution changes with assessment of changes, the data for the vulnerable groups of the population, possible health effects and recommended behaviour (data on vulnerable groups, a description of possible symptoms, taking

471. Authorized legal entities referred to in Art. 58, paras 1 and 2 of this Law may carry out measurements after obtaining a license from the competent Ministry, if they meet the requirements for personnel, equipment and space, and if they are technically qualified according to the requirements of the standard BAS ISO/IEC 17025 in accordance with a special regulation (Art. 59, para. 1). The Minister, on the initiative of the inspector, shall revoke the licence from Art. 59, para. 1 of this Law, i.e., a licence from Art. 60, para. 2 of this Law (Art. 62, para. 1). A review of licences issued is performed annually or at the request of an authorized legal person or operator (Art. 63, para. 1). The Minister shall prescribe detailed requirements for the issuance of a licence under para. 1 of this article, as well as requirements to be met by a legal person under Art. 15, para. 4 of this Law (Art. 59, para. 2).

472. Licences for air quality measuring and/or emissions shall be forfeited if the authorized legal person ceases to meet the requirements and if it is determined that an authorized entity does not perform these duties in accordance with the licence and the provisions of Art. 9, para. 3, Art. 18, para. 2 of this Law, and Arts 41 and 42 of this Law (Art. 59, para. 3).

473. The legal entity referred to in Art. 15, para. 4 is obliged to perform the automatic monitoring stations data collection in accordance with the provisions of Art. 9, para. 3 and Art. 18, para. 2 of this Law (Art. 58, para. 3).

the recommended measures, new information about the course of events) and data on preventive measures to reduce the pollution (Article 65, paragraph 2).

303. The competent authority shall inform the public about:

(a) The air quality, in the form of an annual report on the state of air quality, until 31 July of the current year for the previous year.
(b) Air quality plans and delay for some time of achieving of targeted values for nitrogen dioxide or benzene and particulate matter PM10, within eight days from the date of approval.
(c) Plans for achieving the targeted values in the zones and agglomerations where targeted values are exceeded, within eight days from the date of adoption (Article 66, paragraph 1).

The annual report on the state of air quality in the Republic of Srpska is prepared and published by the Republican administrative organization in charge for hydrological and meteorological activities (Article 66, paragraph 2).[474]

6. Information System

304. The air quality information system is an integral part of a unified information system for environmental protection and it includes:

(a) Republic and local networks data for air quality monitoring, and data obtained in the measurement by the operators.
(b) Data on substances that deplete the ozone layer.
(c) The data from the inventory of emissions of GHG and removed quantities of these gases by sinks.
(d) The data from the inventory from accidental discharges of persistent organic pollutants.
(e) Measures and plans for the protection and improvement of air quality.
(f) Measures and plans to mitigate climate change.
(g) Measures and plans for the protection of the ozone layer.
(h) Data on the excess of concentration dangerous to human health and measures to protect human health and the environment in such cases.
(i) Data on the Republic's administration and about the authorized legal persons performing air quality monitoring and measuring levels of pollutants and emissions.
(j) The data from the register of air pollution.
(k) Information on the completed inspection supervision and imposed measures.

474. The Republican administration organization responsible for hydrological and meteorological affairs publishes a monthly report on the state of air quality, based on data from the local networks (Art. 66, para. 3).

(l) Other information relevant to air quality (Article 67, paragraph 1).[475]

305. Data from the air quality information system is used to share information about the measurement sites in the national and local network through measurement techniques, as well as for the exchange of data obtained by monitoring the air quality in the national and local networks and data on emissions from the air pollution sources for reporting purposes in accordance with undertaken international obligations[476] (Article 68).

7. Economic Instruments, Funding of the Air Protection and Supervision

306. Funds for financing the air quality protection and improvement are provided in the budget of the Republic of Srpska and in the local government budget from income from the fund responsible for the protection and financing of the environment, as well as from the revenues collected from the obligations of operators, and in accordance with the laws governing the protection and financing of the environment, as well as by this law (Article 70, paragraph 1).

307. The Ministry performs the administrative supervision over the implementation and application of this law, as well as over the regulations adopted for its implementation (Article 72, paragraph 1). Inspection monitoring over the compliance of this law and the regulations adopted for its implementation performs the Republican administration for inspection by the competent government inspectors and inspectors from the local government units (hereinafter, 'the inspector') (Article 73, paragraph 1).

B. Other Relevant RS Regulations

308.

(1) Rulebook on waste management containing asbestos (Official Gazette of RS, No 47/18).
(2) Rulebook on the conditions for issuing a license for air quality monitoring (Official Gazette of RS, Nos. 3/18 and 57/18).
(3) Rulebook on measures for the prevention and reduction of air pollution and air quality improvement (Official Gazette of RS, No. 3/15, 51/15 and 47/16).
(4) Decree on the conditions for monitoring of the air quality (Official Gazette of RS, No 124/12).

475. The information system of air quality for the Republic of Srpska keeps the Republican administration organization responsible for hydrological and meteorological activities (Art. 67, para. 2).

476. The Republican administrative organization responsible for hydrological and meteorological affairs is the Republic reference centre for air quality, air emissions and climate change mitigation, which exchanges data on air quality and emissions for reporting purposes, in accordance with the assumed international obligations, with the prior consent of the Ministry (Art. 69).

(5) Decree on the Establishment of the Republic network of measuring stations and measuring points (Official Gazette of RS, No 124/12).
(6) Decree on Air Quality Values (Official Gazette of RS, No 124/12).
(7) Rulebook on the methodology and method for keeping a Register of plants and polluters (Official Gazette of the RS No. 92/07).
(8) Decree on emission limiting values of polluting substances into the air (Official Gazette of RS No. 39/05).
(9) Decree on gradual exclusion of ozone-depleting substances (Official Gazette of RS No. 94/05).
(10) Rule book on monitoring air quality (Official Gazette of RS No. 124/12).
(11) Rule book on air quality limit values (Official Gazette of RS No. 124/12).
(12) Rule book on limiting emissions from biomass combustion plants (Official Gazette of RS No. 85/05).
(13) Rule book on the emission of vapourizing organic compounds (Official Gazette of RS No. 39/05).

II. Federation of Bosnia and Herzegovina

A. The Law on Air Protection

309. Basic legal act regulating air[477] protection in the Federation of Bosnia and Herzegovina is the Law on Air Protection (Official Gazette of FBiH, Nos 33/03 and 04/10). It has the following nine parts: Part I – General Provisions (Article 1), Part II – Terms and Definitions (Articles 2–3), Part III – Planning (Articles 4–15), Part IV – Special Sources[478] of Emissions[479] (Articles 16–25), Part V – The Cadastre of Emissions (Article 26), Part VI – The Air Quality[480] (Articles 27–32), Part VII – Supervision (Articles 33–34), Part VIII – Penalty Provisions (Articles 35–36), Part IX – Transitional and Final Provisions (Articles 37–39).

310. According to Article 1, paragraph 1, this law regulates the technical requirements of measures to prevent or reduce air emissions caused by human activities that have to be respected in the production process, on the territory of Federation of Bosnia and Herzegovina, planning the protection of air quality, the specific sources of emissions, cadastre of emissions, air quality, supervision and penalties for offences for natural persons and legal entities.

311. The measures referred to in paragraph 1 of this article shall be undertaken using the following principle:

---

477. *Air* – means outdoor air in the atmosphere, not including working premises (Art. 2, para. 1).
478. *Source* – means any origin releasing of substances into the air, including stationary sources from industry and households, as well as mobile sources such as motor vehicles and pointing sources and diffuse sources (Art. 2, para. 1).
479. *Emissions* mean the discharge of substances from any source into the air (Art. 2, para. 1).
480. *The Air Quality* means the concentration of pollutants in the air or the deposition on the surface during a certain period (Art. 2, para. 1).

- *An integrated approach to environmental protection*, including air, water and soil as well as the obligation to reduce emissions to a minimum using the best available techniques.
- *Polluter pays*, which ensures that the costs for reducing of air pollution[481] shall be borne by the operators of emission sources of polluting substances.[482]
- *Compliance* of occupational safety with rules for environmental protection.
- *Improving the air quality* also out of the territory of the Federation of Bosnia and Herzegovina (Article 1, paragraph 2).

312. Protection and improvement of air quality is performed, within their authorizations, by: the Federation, cantons, local government units, business entities and other legal entities and natural persons (Article 1, paragraph 3).[483] Authorities of the Federation, cantons and municipalities, operators of emission, business entities and other legal entities and natural persons are obliged to cooperate to each other in order to protect and improve air quality (Article 3, paragraph 1).

The operators of emission sources are obliged to implement obligations prescribed by the law and bylaws adopted on the base of this law (Article 3, paragraph 2).[484]

1. Planning

313. To achieve the objectives of this law, the Federal Ministry of Spatial Planning and Environment (hereinafter, 'Federal Ministry') and cantonal ministries responsible for environmental affairs (hereinafter, 'the cantonal ministry') are obliged to coordinate and harmonize plans regarding air quality (Article 4, paragraph 1).[485]

The air quality protection must be taken into account in preparation of spatial planning documents and other plans. A plan cannot be adopted if it does not comply

481. *Air pollution* means the direct or indirect introduction of substances into the air by a man resulting in such adverse effects that endanger human health, which harm living resources and ecosystems, as well as material goods (Art. 2, para. 1).
482. *Polluting substances* means any substance which man directly or indirectly entries in the air and which is likely to cause an adverse effect on human health and/or the environment as a whole, including odours (Art. 2, para. 1).
483. Responsible Federal and cantonal authorities are responsible for ensuring public participation in preparation of spatial planning documents and other plans that affect the air quality, as well as in preparation of air quality policies and action plans on the air, in determining the location, procedures for permit issuing and inspections of emissions sources (Art. 1, para. 4).
484. It is forbidden causing of significant air pollution or causing harm to the environment through emissions (Art. 3, para. 3).
485. Parliament of the Federation of Bosnia and Herzegovina (hereinafter, 'the Federation Parliament') adopts the Federal Strategy for air protection for a period of at least ten years as part of the Federal Environmental Protection Strategy, which aims to improve air quality. In addition to measures for preserving air quality, this strategy covers the issue of climate change (Art. 4, para. 3).

with determined the Federal Environmental Protection Strategy and the Federal Strategy for Air Quality Protection (Article 5, paragraph 1).[486]

314. The Federal Ministry in cooperation with the competent Ministry from the Republic of Srpska determines emission quotas in 2010 and 2020 year for gases whose emissions is regulated by international treaties, conventions and protocols relating to transboundary air pollution (Article 4, paragraph 6).

The Federal Minister of Environment and Tourism (hereinafter, 'the Federal Minister') shall prescribe the emission limiting values (Article 6, paragraph 2). According to Article 6 each emission source must meet the following requirements:

- That emissions of air pollutant substances, as well as the emission of odours, reduced to a minimum with the use of best available techniques in the stages of planning, design and putting into operation and operation.
- That emission quotas[487] and emission limiting values[488] are not exceeded (paragraph 1).

315. Air emissions that originate from sources of emissions for which there is obligation of environmental impact assessment and obtaining of the environmental permit is regulated by the environmental permit (Article 7, paragraph 1). Operator of stationary source of emissions from Article 7, paragraph 1 of this law shall submit an annual report[489] to the responsible Ministry (Article 13, paragraph 1).

For new emission sources that require an environmental permit, as well as in cases when it is estimated that they may have adverse effects on human health and/or the environment as a whole, at the request of the competent Federal or cantonal Ministry, the applicant shall made a study in which anticipated air emissions and their impact on the environment will be described in detail (Article 7, paragraph 2). The content of the environmental permit issued in accordance to Article 71 of the Law on Environmental Protection and Article 7 of this law are prescribed in Article 12, paragraph 1.[490] The competent Ministry shall be informed of any change in the project, plan or in operation of an emission source (Article 11, paragraph 1).

Study on the air is prepared by a company that meets the requirements and criteria set forth in the provisions of Article 59, paragraph 5 of Law on Environmental Protection (Article 10, paragraph 1). Costs of conducting studies on air are born by the applicant for the issuance of the permit (Article 10, paragraph 2).

---

486. The Federal Ministry and cantonal ministries, each within its jurisdiction, create a list of areas where cannot be located any new point source emissions, which is particularly related to facilities, facilities with combustion and facilities for waste incineration (Art. 5, para. 2).
487. *Emission allowances of pollutant substances* means the total allowed annual amount of emissions (expressed in units of mass in a specified time) from one or more sources together, i.e., from certain areas and/or in the territory of the Federation of Bosnia and Herzegovina (Art. 2, para. 1).
488. *Emission limiting values* means the concentration and/or amount of pollutant substances in emissions from some source during a specified period, which may not be exceeded (Art. 2, para. 1).
489. The report contains data on emissions from a given source, on the consumption of energy and fuel, as well as general information about the potential impact on health, which may have a substance which emits given source (Art. 13, para. 2).
490. The Federal Minister shall prescribe in special regulation monitoring of emissions and monitoring of air quality (Art. 12, para. 2).

2. The Special Emission Sources

316. The provisions of Articles from 7 to 15 of this law do not apply to air emissions from household activities or from home combustion sources whose thermal power is less than 250 kW (Article 16, paragraph 1).[491] In the house emission sources may be used only fuel specified in standards set forth by the Institute for Standards of Bosnia and Herzegovina (Article 17, paragraph 1).

317. Questions related to emissions from combustion installations with a nominal thermal power equal to or greater than 10 MW, as well as the nominal thermal power less than 10 MW shall be regulated by the implementing regulation arising from this law (Article 18, paragraph 1).

Conditions for working of waste incineration plants will be regulated by the implementing regulation in accordance with this law (Article 19, paragraph 1).

Emissions from motor vehicles as non-stationary point pollution sources are regulated with special regulations, which regulate regular annual inspection of motor vehicles (Article 20, paragraph 1).[492]

Heavy oil in which the sulphur content exceeds 1.00% by weight cannot be used as fuel for combustion plants from 1 January 2010. Fuel for motor vehicles must comply with the quality standards published by the Institute for Standards of Bosnia and Herzegovina (Article 22, paragraph 1). Leaded gasoline will not be sold as of 1 January 2010 (Article 22, paragraph 2).

318. The provisions of this law shall apply to buildings, facilities, vehicles, railroad and vessels used for storage, loading and transport of petrol from one warehouse to another, or from the main storage to the gas station (Article 23, paragraph 1). Emissions of volatile organic compounds shall be determined by the implementing regulation in accordance with this law (Article 24, paragraph 1).[493]

319. The protection of ozone layer refers to substances that deplete the ozone layer, products and equipment containing these substances (Article 25, paragraph 1). Conditions and procedure for the gradual exclusion from the use of substances that deplete the ozone layer and their replacement with alternative substances that have significantly less harmful impact on the environment and procedure for handling with products that contain or which are made of substances that deplete the ozone layer will be regulated by the implementing regulation in accordance with this law (Article 25, paragraph 2).

491. District heating plants are not considered as household sources (Art. 16, para. 2).

492. The competent authority cannot register the vehicle which exceeds a certain limiting emissions values (Art. 20, para. 2).

493. Use of organic compounds in the activities and facilities must be reduced to a minimum (Art. 24, para. 2).

3. The Emissions Registry and Air Quality Monitoring

320. In the Register of facilities and environmental pollution, which is established on the basis of the Law on the Environment Protection, it is also kept a Register on air emissions that records data on the sources of air emissions, their legal entities and polluting substances that sources emit into the air (Article 26, paragraph 1).

The Federal Ministry prepares and regularly updates Emissions Register[494] that includes all data on emissions of key sources (Article 26, paragraph 5).[495]

Inter-entity body for the environment in April of each year brings together the Report on air emissions for the year before last, on the basis of information provided by the entity Ministries. The consolidated Report shall be submitted to the Council of Ministers of Bosnia and Herzegovina to be sent to the competent authorities of international agreements of which Bosnia and Herzegovina is a signatory (Article 26, paragraph 9).[496]

321. For the purpose of air quality monitoring (to determine the level of contamination) and to take measures in order to prevent and reduce pollution, the limiting values of air quality for certain polluting substances in the air and long-term objectives for ozone are prescribed (Article 27, paragraph 1).

The Federal Ministry ensures regular monitoring of air quality (Article 28, paragraph 2).[497]

As part of air quality monitoring, it is an established network of measuring stations for systematic measurement of air quality including: federal, cantonal, municipal, pollution source and special areas (Article 28, paragraph 4). Locations of stations in the federal network, at the proposal of the Federal Ministry, prescribe the Government of the Federation (Article 28, paragraph 5).

Expert institutions[498] authorized by the Federal Ministry and the Federal Ministry of Health establish and monitor the air quality in accordance with the implementing regulation (Article 28, paragraph 6). In cases where there is reasonable doubt that there was an air pollution which can be harmful to human health, quality of life and/or adversely affect to any part of the environment, measurements for special purposes or to perform an assessment of the level of contamination must be carried out (Article 28a, paragraph 1).

---

494. *Emissions Registry* means a collection of data on the type, quantity, method, spatial distribution, the place of discharge and introduction of pollutants into the air (Art. 2, para. 1).
495. The Federal Ministry in January of each year publishes a Report on emissions of polluting substances into the air for the year before last for the Federation of Bosnia and Herzegovina (Art. 26, para. 6). The Federal Ministry provides access to information on emissions through public disclosure (Art. 26, para. 7).
496. The Reports must be prepared in accordance with the requirements for issuing the Reports determined in international treaties to which Bosnia and Herzegovina is a signatory (Art. 26, para. 10).
497. For the purpose of efficient air quality management a unique functional system of air quality monitoring is established (Art. 28, para. 1).
498. These expert institutions keep database on air quality monitoring (Art. 28, para. 7).

4. Information and Supervision

322. In accordance with Article 28 of this law, institutions and authorities responsible for assessment of air quality, submit to Federal Ministry necessary information for the Report, while Federal Ministry submits them to inter-entity body responsible for the environmental protection (Article 31, paragraph 1). Professional institutions from Article 28 of this law ensure that updated information on concentration of polluting substances in the air regularly are provided to the public and to relevant organizations such as: the Organization for the Environment protection, the consumer's organizations, organizations representing vulnerable groups of the population and other relevant bodies dealing with health protection (Article 32, paragraph 1).[499]

323. Canton within two years adopts Cantonal action plan for the protection of air quality in areas where the limited values of air quality of one or more polluting substances are exceeded (Article 29, paragraph 1). If the limiting values are exceeded in two or more cantons, the Federal Ministry coordinates among the cantons (Article 29, paragraph 2). The plan[500] must be made available to the public for comments before its adoption (Article 29, paragraph 5).

Canton adopts intervention plan when there is a risk of exceeding of the threshold alerts indicating the measures to reduce the risk of exceeding and limiting the duration of such phenomenon (Article 30, paragraph 1).[501]

324. Supervision over the implementation of provisions of this law and the regulations adopted thereunder performs the Federal Ministry (Article 33, paragraph 1).

The inspection activities carry out the Federal and Cantonal inspectors within their jurisdiction (Article 33, paragraph 2).[502] The inspector in performing of the inspection supervision prepares Inspection Report on the findings of the inspection (Article 33, paragraph 6).[503]

B. Other Relevant FBiH Regulations

325.

(1) Rule book on air quality limiting values (Official Gazette of FBiH No. 12/05).
(2) Rule book on air quality monitoring (Official Gazette of FBiH No. 1/12).
(3) Rule book on emission limiting values (Official Gazette of FBiH No. 12/05).

---

499. Information is done through radio, television, press, display or electronically (Art. 32, para. 2).
500. Content of the Plan is prescribed in Art. 29, para. 6.
501. Plans can provide control measures, suspension of activities, including motor traffic, which contribute to the threshold alerts (Art. 30, para. 2).
502. Inspector in line of duty performs inspection supervision to verify whether the emissions are in accordance with the relevant limiting emission values and with the other conditions from the environmental permit, which is issued for a given emission source (Art. 33, para. 3).
503. The inspector submits to operator of emission sources Inspection Report of supervisory inspection within one month from the performed inspection (Art. 33, para. 7).

(4) Rule book on monitoring the emission of polluting substances into the air (Official Gazette of FBiH No. 12/05).
(5) Rule book on the requirements for the operation of waste incineration plants (Official Gazette of FBiH No. 12/05, and 102/12).
(6) Rule book on limiting values for air emissions from combustion plants (Official Gazette of FBiH No. 3/13).
(7) Rule book on the emission of volatile organic compounds (Official Gazette of FBiH No. 12/05).
(8) Rule book on the conditions of measurement and control of sulphur content in fuel (Official Gazette of FBiH No. 6/08).
(9) Rule book on gradual exclusion of ozone-depleting substances (Official Gazette of FBiH No. 39/05).
(10) Regulation on the types, content and quality of biofuels in motor fuels (Official Gazette FBiH No. 29/08).
(11) Regulation on special environmental fees payable on the registration of motor vehicles according to the Law on Environmental Protection Fund in FBiH (Official Gazette of FBiH No. 14/11).
(12) Regulation on the Method of Accounting and Payments of Taxes and Deadlines for the Computation and Payment of Taxes for Polluting Air Matters under the Law on the Environmental Protection Fund in FBiH (Official Gazette of FBiH No. 66/11).
(13) Rulebook on the content, methods and deadlines for the establishment and maintenance of a register of pollutants that pay taxes on polluting substances in accordance with the Law on Environmental Protection Fund in the FBiH (Official Gazette FBiH No. 56/12).

III. Brčko District of Bosnia and Herzegovina

A. *The Law on Air Protection*

326. Basic legal act regulating air[504] protection in Brčko District of Bosnia and Herzegovina is the Law on Air Protection (Official Gazette of BD, Nos 25/04, 01/05, 19/07 and 09/09). It has the following seven parts: Part I – General Provisions (Articles 1–5), Part II – Planning of the Air Protection (Articles 6–10), Part III – Sources[505] of Emissions[506] (Articles 11–36), Part IV – The Air Protection (Articles 37–42), Part V – Supervision (Article 43), Part VI – Penalty Provisions (Article 44), Part VII – Transitional and Final Provisions (Articles 45–48).

504. *Air* – means outdoor air (set of all gasses) in the atmosphere, not including working premises (Art. 4, para. 1).
505. *Source* – means any origin releasing of substances into the air, including stationary sources from industry and households, as well as mobile sources such as motor vehicles and pointing sources and diffuse sources (Art. 4, para. 1).
506. *Emissions* mean the discharge of substances from any source into the air (Art. 4, para. 1).

327. According to Article 1, paragraph 1, this law regulates the air protection from pollution in order to protect human health, climate and environment from the harmful effects of polluted air (Article 1, paragraph 1).[507]

1. Objectives of the Air Protection

328. According to this law, the Air Protection shall provide:

- The protection of air quality[508] in order to avoid, prevent or reduce, the harmful effects of air pollution[509] on human health, climate and environment as a whole.
- Control of air pollution originating from human activity and limiting the intensity of air pollution at the source of pollution.
- Maintaining the current state of air quality in areas of unpolluted (of clean) air.
- Improving the value of air quality in areas where the air is polluted.
- The process of air protection, as part of the environmental protection system, with established rights, obligations and responsibilities of natural persons and legal entities.
- Informing the population about values of air quality, as well as about measures for preserving and improving of air quality.
- Public participation in process of air protection.
- Realizing other objectives of the air protection in accordance with this law (Article 2, paragraph 1).

2. The Air Protection Principles

329. Starting from the basic principles of environmental protection, air protection is based on the following:

- The protection of air, water and soil as well as the basic components and the potential of the environment.
- Limiting the discharge of pollutants into the air to a minimum, using the best available technology.
- The polluter pays principle which ensures that the costs to implement measures to improve the state of the air will be borne by legal entities or natural persons which discharge pollutants into the air.
- The principle that the measures and procedures for the air protection cannot be implemented if it would have a negative impact on the environment outside the

507. The air protection from pollution caused by radioactive substances, industrial accidents and natural disasters is regulated by a special Law (Art. 1, para. 2).
508. *Air quality*-means the concentration of polluting substances in the air during a certain period (Art. 4, para. 1).
509. *Air pollution* means the direct or indirect introduction of substances into the air by a man and results in such adverse effects that endanger human health, harm living resources, ecosystems, material property and that deplete and affect the leisure and other types of the legal use of the environment (Art. 4, para. 1).

Brčko District of Bosnia and Herzegovina (hereinafter, 'the District') or would be contrary to the strict regulations on safety at work.
- Public participation in the process of establishing policies and adopting plans and programmes for the air protection, issuing of approvals and permits, inspection supervision and other procedures of the air protection process.

330. All entities whose activities have an impact on air are required to cooperate on environmental issues (Article 5, paragraph 1).[510]

3. Planning of the Air Protection

331. The strategies for air protection with the action plan for management of air quality and other plans and programmes that are adopted and realized in the manner and under the conditions set forth in this law are determined in the District in order to achieve the objectives of air pollution prescribed by this law (Article 6, paragraph 1).

332. Article 7 provides that in the District the following planning documents from the field of air protection are adopted:

- Strategy for the air protection of Brčko District with the Action plan of air quality management (hereinafter, 'Strategy for air protection of the District').
- Reports on the execution of Plans and Programmes (paragraph 1).

At the Mayor's proposal, the Assembly of Brčko District adopts the Strategy for air protection, for a period of ten years (Article 8, paragraph 2).[511] The Strategy for air protection of Brčko District is an integral part of the Strategy of District, as well as of the Action plan for environmental protection, which at the process of preparation and adoption will be harmonized with the relevant planning document at the level of Bosnia and Herzegovina (Article 8, paragraph 3).

The Mayor at the proposal of the Government submits at least once every two years to the Assembly of the Brčko District the Report[512] about implementation of the policy set out in the Strategy for air protection of the District for consideration (Article 9, paragraph 1).

510. It is forbidden to discharge or intake into the air of pollutants in quantities that could endanger human health and the environment (Art. 5, para. 2).

511. The Strategy for air protection of Brčko District shall determine the policies for air protection and management of air quality. Strategy for air protection of the District is prepared by relevant Government departments, in the manner prescribed by the Law on the Environmental Protection for preparation of the Strategy for air protection of the District and Action Plan for environmental protection (Art. 8, para. 1).

512. The content of the Report is prescribed in Art. 9, para. 2.

333. During space planning, policy, measures and restrictions determined in planning documents from the area of air protection, represent one of the required basis for the preparation and making of spatial plans (Article 10, paragraph 1).[513]

4. Sources of Emissions and Permits

334. According to Article 11, a legal entity that release hazardous substances into the air from their plant, machinery and other sources, which pollute or which may pollute the air are required to:

- Perform measurement and monitoring of emissions.
- Reduce to a minimum, emissions of polluting substances and odours in the air, using the best available technology.
- Do not exceed the limiting values of emissions.[514]

335. On the base of the environmental impact study, environmental permit determines whether the air emissions that come from sources for which construction and use is necessary to obtain the environmental permit, can have an impact on the environment that can be determined (Article 12, paragraph 1).

Whether the air emissions that come from sources[515] for which construction and use environmental permit is not required, could have an impact on the environment which may be allowed, will be determined by the urban planning consent, construction approval and approval for use, on the basis of the air studies (Article 13, paragraph 1).[516] The legal entity of the stationary source emissions from Article 13 of this law shall submit the Report to the competent Government departments once a year (Article 21, paragraph 1). The Report contains data on energy and fuel consumption, emissions from sources, as well as general information about impact on human health that might have substances that are released into the air (Article 21, paragraph 2).

---

513. A list of protected areas is determined for the area of the District. It is not allowed to build any new point source of emissions, especially plants and facilities, plants with incineration and plants for waste incineration, and also cannot be made significant expansion of existing activities at these areas (Art. 10, para. 2).

514. The limiting values of emissions prescribe Government in bylaw (Art. 12, para. 2). *Limiting value of emissions*-means the concentration and/or the amount of polluting substances in emissions from a source in a given period, which shall not be exceeded (Art. 4, para. 1). *Polluting substance*-means any substance that is directly or indirectly entered into the air by men, which is likely to cause an adverse effect on human health and/or the environment as a whole, including odours (Art. 4, para. 1).

515. The Department responsible for issuing of the environmental permits and the population of the endangered area shall be notified on large-scale disasters originating from the source of emissions from Art. 13 of this Law (Art. 25, para. 1). In that case, the Inspector for Environmental Protection is obliged to suspend the operation of emission sources until remediation of excessive discharge of pollutants that threaten human health and the environment, as well as the consequences of the accident (Art. 25, para. 2).

516. Conditions and data that make up the content of the Permit from Arts 13 and 14 of this Law are prescribed by the Law on the Environmental Protection and the Law on Spatial Planning (Art. 19, para. 1).

336. Relevant Government departments cannot issue a Permit, Consent or Approval[517] from Articles 13 and 14 of this law, if according to the study of the environmental impact, i.e., the air study, the air emissions from a source may have adverse effects on human health and the climate or the environment to a significant extent (Article 14, paragraph 1).

A legal entity as source of emissions from Article 14 of this law is obliged to notify the competent departments for issuing the permit if release in the air of amount of pollutants exceeds the established limiting values (Article 23, paragraph 1).

In case of failure on the emission sources from Article 14 of this law, the responsible person is obliged to reduce duration or to stop work until the source of emissions is safe for operation (Article 24, paragraph 1).[518]

337. Relevant Government departments will issue to a legal entity, as emission sources, approval to start business activities, stating that the conditions in terms of technical equipment, safety at work, protection and improvement of the environment, as well as other prescribed conditions (hereinafter, 'the Approval for work')[519] are met, in the manner and under the conditions laid down by special regulations (Article 15, paragraph 1). In any change of the project, plan or in work of some emission source, the legal entity is required to apply for changing of the approval (Article 18, paragraph 1).

338. The Chief of the Responsible Division prescribes the method for regular monitoring of emissions of air pollutants, sampling and measuring of air parameters and observing of changes in air quality and their impact on human health and the environment (Article 20, paragraph 1).

5. The Special Limitations

339. General restrictions determined by this law (Articles 13–20) do not apply to emissions into the air from household activities or from household combustion sources with thermal power of less than 250 kW (Article 26, paragraph 1). In the household, emission sources may be used only species and liquid fuels specified in the standards of organization responsible for standardization, measurement and patents (Article 27, paragraph 1).

340. Emissions from combustion facility with a nominal thermal power less, equal to or greater than 50 MW, prescribes the Head of the relevant department

517. Permit, Consent or Approval shall not be issued if it is certain that a source will release substances into the air above the emission limiting values prescribed on the base of this Law (Art. 14, para. 2).

518. In the circumstances referred to in para. 1 of this article, the operation of emission sources cannot last continuously for more than eight hours, and the total annual work duration cannot be longer than ninety-six hours (Art. 24, para. 2).

519. Approval for the work of the legal entity as air emission sources is issued each time at the commencement of the operations (in case of interruption of work, changing of conditions for performing of their activity, changes of activity, etc.) (Art. 15, para. 4).

(Article 28, paragraph 1). Conditions for working of the waste incineration plant provide Head of the competent Department in accordance with this law (Article 29, paragraph 1).

341. Emissions from motor vehicles shall be regulated by bylaw, which governs the regular annual technical inspection of motor vehicles (Article 30, paragraph 1). The competent authority cannot register the vehicle, which exceeds the prescribed emission limiting values (Article 30, paragraph 1). Fuels for motor vehicles must comply with the standards prescribed by the organization responsible for standardization, measurement and patents (Article 32, paragraph 1). The traffic of leaded gasoline is forbidden from 1 January 2010 (Article 32, paragraph 2).

342. Heavy oils, in which the sulphur content exceeds 1.00% by weight, cannot be used as fuels for combustion facilities from 1 January 2010 (Article 31, paragraph 1).

343. Emissions of volatile organic compounds prescribe Government by a special regulation in accordance with this law (Article 34, paragraph 1).[520]

344. The Government prescribes conditions and procedure for the gradual excluding from the use of substances that deplete the ozone layer and their replacement with alternative substances that have significantly less harmful impact on the environment, as well as procedures for handling with products that contain or are made of substances that deplete the ozone layer (Article 35, paragraph 1).

345. The Government of Brčko District of Bosnia and Herzegovina, in accordance with this law, prescribes limiting values, targeting values and threshold alerts for polluting substances that are released into the air (Article 37, paragraph 1).

An Expert Institution, authorized by the Head of the relevant Department, establishes and performs monitoring of air quality in accordance with conditions determined in Article 21 and Article 26, paragraph 1 of this law (Article 38, paragraph 1 and paragraph 2).

6. Emissions Registry

346. In the Register of plants and environmental pollution, which is established on the base of the Law on Environmental Protection, shall be also kept Register of air emissions for recording data on air emission sources, their legal entities and polluting substances that source emits into the air (Article 36, paragraph 1)On the basis of data from the Register of air emissions, the Government of Brčko District of Bosnia and Herzegovina publishes in January of each year the Report on emissions of air pollutants, including emissions from natural sources in the District area for the year before last (Article 36, paragraph 4).

---

520. Use of organic compounds referred to in para. 1 of this article in the activities and in propulsions must be reduced to a minimum (Art. 34, para. 1).

B. Other Relevant BDBiH Air Quality Regulations

347.

(1) Rule book on the emission of volatile organic compounds (Official Gazette of BDBiH No. 30/06).
(2) Rule book on air quality monitoring (Official Gazette of BDBiH No. 30/06). Rule book on monitoring the emission of polluting substances into the air (Official Gazette of BDBiH No. 30/06).
(3) Rule book on air quality limiting values (Official Gazette of BDBiH No. 30/06).
(4) Rule book on gradual exclusion of ozone-depleting substances (Official Gazette of BDBiH No. 30/06).
(5) Rule book on limiting emissions from biomass combustion plants into the air (Official Gazette of BDBiH No. 30/06).
(6) Rule book on the requirements for the operation of waste incineration plants (Official Gazette of BDBiH No. 30/06).
(7) Rulebook on conditions for the operation of waste incineration plant (Official Gazette of the BD BiH No. 30/06).
(8) Rulebook on limits and targeted air quality values, information thresholds and alerts (Official Gazette BD BiH No. 18/11).

§4. Harmonization with EU Legislation

348. In the air protection and climate change sectors the several activities should be implemented 'in order to achieve full compliance with EU environmental acquis and by BiH accepted international obligations.'[521] Generally, 'the level of alignment with the EU climate *acquis* remains limited'.[522] In addition, 'alignment with the EU *acquis* on air quality remains limited'.[523] There has been no progress in aligning with the EU *acquis* on reducing the sulphur content of certain liquid fuels (the country remains in 'serious and persistent breach of the Energy Community Treaty', and sanctions have been applied since January 2021).

---

521. BiH MFTER. *Environmental Approximation Strategy of Bosnia and Herzegovina*, EAS – BiH, Ministry of Foreign Trade and Economic Relations of Bosnia and Herzegovina, May 2017, p. 209. For more details, *see*: RS MoSPCEE. *Program usklađivanja zakonodavstva Republike Srpske sa pravnom tekovinom EU u oblasti zaštite životne sredine*, [Program of approximation of the Republika Srpska Legislation with the EU environmental *acquis*], Banja Luka, November 2016, pp. 73–85. FMET. *Program aproksimacije propisa Federacije Bosne i Hercegovine sa pravnom stečevinom EU u oblasti okoliša*, [Program of approximation of the Federation of Bosnia and Herzegovina Legislation with the EU environmental *acquis*] Sarajevo, December 2016, pp. 47–52. BD. *Strategija aproksimacije propisa pravnoj stečevini EU u oblasti zaštite životne sredine/okoliša Brčko distrikta BiH*[Strategy for harmonisation of Brčko District BiH environmental legislation with EU *acquis*], EAS Brčko Distrikta, February 2017, pp. 50–56.
522. EC, *Bosnia and Herzegovina 2016 Progress Report, supra* p. 105. BiH 'should develop a national strategy on progressive decarbonisation and clean energy transition in line with its commitments on depollution under the 2020 Sofia declaration on the Green agenda for the Western Balkans.' Ibid.
523. EC, *Bosnia and Herzegovina 2021 Progress Report,* p. 103.

Chapter 3. Water Pollution

§1. Water Availability and Use

349. Bosnia and Herzegovina has rich mineral water resources, but has only developed these to a limited extent. Mineral and thermal water have good economic potential especially in the areas of eco-tourism and health care. Some investments were made in this sector before the war (e.g., 'Hotel Reumal' and 'Medical rehabilitation centre' – Fojnica, spa resort 'Banja Vruæica' – Tesliæ) but little has been done to repair them after the war and no new investments have been forthcoming.[524]

350. The annual precipitation varies from 800 l/m^2 in the north-east of Bosnia and Herzegovina to 1500 l/m^2 in the south, with an average of 1250 l/m^2.[525] Bosnia and Herzegovina is therefore rich in water resources compared to the European average of 1000 l/m^2. The total outflow from the territory of Bosnia and Herzegovina is 1155 m^3/s, or 57% of total precipitation. Water from the Sava basin, which covers 75.7% of the country, drains to the Black Sea. The main rivers in the Sava basin are the Una-Sana, Vrbas, Bosna, Drina and Sava, with a mean discharge of 722 m^3/s.[526]

351. In 2011, total water intake was 329,954,000 m3, which is 3% less than in 2010. In the structure of the total water intake, 45.9% of water came from underground sources, 36.8% came from surface sources, 15.1% came from river courses, 0.8% came from reservoirs, and 1.3% came from lakes. In 2011, the amount of water delivered from public water supply systems was 150,834,000 m3, which is 8.4% less than in the preceding year. The structure of water consumption shows that households were the largest water consumers, consuming 76.3% of the water delivered by public water supply systems. Outlets of untreated wastewater, access to drinking water and flood management remain key issues in this sector.[527]

---

524. RSMoAFWM, *First national report on the implementation of the United Nations Convention to Combat Desertification/Land Degradation in Bosnia and Herzegovina, supra* p. 33.
525. Or, according to the *State of the environment Report of the Bosnia and Herzegovina 2012*, the total annual water resources from precipitation in BiH amount to 63.9 km3/yr20, while internal renewable water resources amount to 36.4 km3/yr. If we take into account the quantity of water flowing in from other countries (through the Sava and the Drina rivers), the total annual renewable water resources amount to 64.5 km3/yr. BiH MFTER, *State of the environment Report of the Bosnia and Herzegovina 2012, supra* p. 127. *See also*, Zavod za vodoprivredu, *Water Management Strategy of the Federation of Bosnia and Herzegovina*, Zavod za vodoprivredu, Sarajevo, Mostar, Sarajevo, March 2012. p. 44.
526. UNECE, *Environmental Performance Review, Bosnia and Herzegovina, supra* p. 89.
527. RSMoSPCEE, *Second National Communication of Bosnia and Herzegovina under the United Nations Framework Convention on Climate Change*, Ministry for Spatial Planning, Construction and Ecology, Banja Luka, 2013. pp. 34, 35.

§2. MONITORING

352. After the breakdown of the former Hydrometeorology Service in the early 1990s, State-level services have never been restored and no hydrological study has been prepared for the last two decades for BiH as a whole. Consequently, there is no collection and processing of hydrological data at the national level, so decision makers and managers in the water sector are obliged to use historical climate data (i.e., data generated before 1990) to design water infrastructure and guide their management decisions. At the same time, conditions are constantly changing, due in part to climate change and changes in land use, and extreme hydrological situations are becoming more frequent.[528]

353. 'Monitoring of inland and coastal bathing water quality is not carried out systematically, but according to immediate needs and available funds, while systematic monitoring of groundwater quality is not performed in a satisfactory manner.'[529]

§3. COMPETENCIES

354. Field of integrated water resources management is regulated through a legal framework at the level of entities, RS, FBiH and BD BiH.[530]

355. FBiH Ministry of Environment and Tourism and the FBiH Ministry of Agriculture, Water-Management and Forestry have responsibilities of water management and water protection. FBiH Ministry of Health has the authority to make regulations pertaining to quality of water and chemicals, noting that regulations for chemicals have not yet been enacted.[531]

356. Water management competences in the RS belong to following ministries and other institutions: Ministry of Agriculture, Forestry and Water Management,

---

528. UN[EC]E, *2nd Environmental Performance Review, supra* p. 88. Those areas where there is a lack of hydrological information include the following: The water balances and water regimes of small and medium-sized catchments, Extreme flows and distribution of water quantity over longer periods, The water regimes, definition of underground bodies and underground communicating water zones in certain areas of karsts, A more detailed study of spatial variations of the underground Adriatic–Black Sea watershed, A comparative analysis of potential coincidence of hydrological phenomena in the main water courses of the Adriatic Sea basin and the Black Sea basin in the country.
529. BiH MFTER, *State of the environment Report of the Bosnia and Herzegovina 2012, supra* p. 36.
530. BiH Council of Ministers, *Answers to the List of EU Questions on Chapter 27, Environment, supra* pp. 210–250. For more information *See also*: Bogdanović, S. Water Law After Dayton, *Water International*, 25(4)/2000, pp. 534–543.
531. BiH Council of Ministers, *Answers to the List of EU Questions on Chapter 27, Environment, supra* p. 73. Responsibilities related to water monitoring is shared by the Water Agencies and the FBiH Hydrometeorology Institute. Agencies organize, finance and maintain the system of the network of hydrological stations, while the FBiH Hydrometeorology Institute performs the control, processing and archiving of data, preparation of water balance and hydrological yearbooks.

i.e., the agencies within its structure and the RS Hydrometeorology Institute;[532] the Ministry of Spatial Planning, Civil Engineering and Ecology, the Ministry of Health and Social Welfare, the Ministry of Industry, Energy and Mining and the Ministry of Transport and Communications of RS, as well as local communities.

357. The Department of Agriculture, Forestry and Water Management of BD Government is responsible for agriculture, forestry and water management and administrative capacities are defined by the organizational plan of the Government of BD BiH.

§4. LEGISLATION

I. Republic of Srpska

A. The Law on Water Protection

358. Basic legal act regulating water[533,534] protection in the Republic of Srpska is the Law on Water Protection (Official Gazette of RS, No. 50/06 and the Law on amendments to the Law on Water Protection, No. 92/09, 121/12 and 74/17). It has the following fourteen parts: Part I – General Provisions (Articles 1–4), Part II – Characterization of Water, Water Resource and Water Facilities (Articles 5–20), Part III – Water Management (Articles 21–47), Part IV – Water Usage (Articles 48–56), Part V – Water Protection (Articles 57–84), Part VI – Watercourse Regulation and Other Waters and Protection from the Harmful Water Effects (Articles 85–109), Part VII – Information System (Articles 110–119), Part VIII – The Water Legal Acts (Articles 120–164), Part IX – The Limitation of the Owner's Right and Land Users (Articles 165–175), Part X – Organisation of the Water Management (Articles 176–187), Part XI – Financing of the Water Management (Articles 188–195), Part XII – Inspection Supervision (Articles 196–208), Part XIII – Penalty Provisions (Articles 209–214), Part XIV – Transitional and Final Provisions (Articles 215–232).[535]

---

532. Public institution 'Vode Srpske' is a public institution that manages water, public water resources and hydraulic engineering structures and systems, rivers, streams, lakes, in the manner prescribed by law, in the Republic of Srpska in accordance with the provisions of the Law on Water protection and other relevant regulations. *See* the website for more details: http://www.voders.org/o-nama/pravni-status/ (19 Jul. 2022).
533. In addition to internal legislation, it should be borne in mind that Bosnia and Herzegovina is a member of key international treaties in the field of water (*See* the chapter dedicated to the Sources of Environmental Law). For more information on international water treaties in regional context: *see also*: Todić, D., Zlatić, M. Transboundary cooperation of Western Balkan states in the field of water resources management: Between the existing treaties and a new international treaty, Environmental Science & Policy, Vol. 89/November 2018, pp. 67–72.
534. *Water* – means all the water inside the Republic of Srpska that is static or flowing on the Earth's surface and each ground water closer to the country along the base line of the territory border (Art. 4, para. 1, point 1).
535. The purpose of this Law is to ensure integrated water management, in particular: To achieve good water condition and prevention of its degradation; To achieve sustainable water use; Ensuring fair

359. The provisions of this law regulate the manner of integrated water management[536] within the territory of the Republic of Srpska (Article 1, paragraph 1). In addition, this law regulates financing of business activities, administrative bodies, public services and institutions in the water sector, water facilities and plants, and other problems related to integrated water management in the Republic of Srpska (Article 1, paragraph 3).

1. Basic Principles

360. According to Article 3, the water management must be based on the following general principles):

a. Water is not a commercial product like any other products, but heritage which must be protected, defended and treated as such.
b. Water usage and water management is done in a rational and sustainable manner so as to prevent unnecessary water use and that water usage does not exceed the natural resource recovery.
c. Water must be used in a manner that provides the functionality of natural processes of aquatic ecosystems, terrestrial ecosystems and wetland areas, which directly depend on the water, and which areas are determined in accordance with this Law.
d. To ensure cost recovery of water services, including the costs for environmental protection and resources, according to an economic analysis conducted according to the Annex 3 of the EU Water Framework Directive[537] and in particular according to *'the polluter pays principle.'*
e. An adequate economic compensation for used quantity of water must be provided from the user of that resource, in accordance to *'the user pays principle'* (paragraph 1).

---

access to water; Incitement of social and economic development; Providing protection of aquatic, semi-aquatic and terrestrial ecosystems that are dependent on water; Organizing of flood protection, and other adverse effects that water may cause; To ensure public participation in decision-making related to water, including public access to complete, accurate and timely information on the state of water, on the activities undertaken by persons who use or pollute the water and on the activities undertaken by the competent authorities and institutions; The prevention and resolution of conflicts related to the protection and water use, and (a) Meeting the obligations of international agreements that are binding for Bosnia and Herzegovina (Art. 2, para. 1).

536. Water management involves an integrated approach, including: water protection, water usage, protection from harmful water effect, regulation of the watercourse, other water bodies, as well as regulation of the public good (Art. 1, para. 2).

537. *The Water Framework Directive*-means Directive 2000/60/EC of 23 Oct. 2000 year ('Official Gazette of the EC', No. L 327 of 22 Dec. 2000) of the European Parliament and of the Council on establishing a framework for EU action in the field of water policy (Art. 4, para. 1, point 37).

2. Characterization of Water

361. The waters are common goods (Article 8, paragraph 1). The waters are under the special protection of the Republic of Srpska, as constituent part of Bosnia and Herzegovina (Article 8, paragraph 2).

362. Identification of location and structure boundaries and surface water[538] bodies, as well as their initial characterization according to the methodology given in the Water Framework Directive shall be carried out for the purpose of water management (Article 5, paragraph 1).

The structure and body of surface water[539] within the river basin district[540] shall be identified so that it falls under one of the following categories of the surface water-rivers,[541] lakes,[542] or as artificial structures and the surface water body, or drastically modified the structure and the body of surface water (Article 5, paragraph 2).[543] For the purpose of water management, characterization[544] of all the structures and groundwater bodies will be developed to assess their use and the risk degree of not meeting the standards for each structure and the groundwater body (Article 6, paragraph 1).[545]

363. Public Institution 'Waters of Srpska' is responsible for organizing monitoring and implementation of the necessary measures to prevent derogation of the surface waters and ground waters status in accordance with this law and the Water Framework Directive (Article 7, paragraph 1).

---

538. *Surface waters* mean all waters on the surface of the Republic of Srpska territory, except ground waters (Art. 4, para. 1, point 2).
539. *Water body of surface waters*-means separated, specially observed element of surface water such as a lake, stream, river or channel, part of a stream, river or part of a channel (Art. 4, para. 1, point 17). *Water body of ground waters*-means separated, specially observed quantities of groundwater within one or more aquifers (Art. 4, para. 1, point 19).
540. *River basin district (District)*-means the area of land consisting of one or more neighbouring river basins together with their associated ground waters, which are identified by a special decision of the competent authority of the Republic of Srpska, pursuant to the Art. 3. (1) of the Directives 2000/60/EC of 23 Oct. 2000 year ('Official Gazette of the EC', No. L 327 of 22 Dec. 2000), which represent the main unit for management of river basins (Art. 4, para. 1, point 15).
541. *River*-means a water body within the Republic of Srpska territory, which mostly flows on the surface of the Earth, but part of its course can flow underground (Art. 4, para. 1, point 4).
542. *The lake* means water body of standing surface water within the Republic of Srpska (Art. 4, para. 1, point 5).
543. For each surface water category, the relevant structures and the surface water body will be sorted according to the type of 'B' system, as specified in the Water Framework Directive (Art. 5, para. 3).
544. The further characterization, as well as the characterization mentioned in para. 1 of this article, will be done according to The Water Framework Directive (Art. 6, para. 2).
545. The Ministry and Public Institution 'Waters of Srpska' are responsible for organizing implementation of the activities referred to in Art. 5 and Art. 6 of this Law. Within nine years, after the year in which this Law enters into force, full coordination of activities from this Chapter with the Water Framework Directive will be done, according to the dynamics which will be defined by special decisions of the Ministry in accordance with the provisions of this Law (Art. 6, para. 3).

3. Water Resources and Water Facilities

364. Water resources,[546] in terms of this law, is water land,[547] water and water facilities, which because of their special significance are goods of general interest and are under special protection (Article 9, paragraph 1). The water resource belongings, in accordance with this law and its ownership background, are defined in the Ministry Decision (Article 9, paragraph 3).

Public water resource[548] consists of all segments of water resources, such as: soil particles, water or hydro technical objects, rivers and streams with defined morphological, geological and hydrological content, which up to the date of enactment of this law, have been registered in the Land Registry, i.e., Cadastre property as a public water resource of a general interest or which were defined in other public documents, i.e., which became state property on the base of the law (Article 10, paragraph 1).

365. Water facilities and systems, together with accompanying equipment that make up the technical, i.e., technological unity, are used for regulation of watercourses and other waters, protection from harmful water effect, water tapping for their intended use, water state monitoring, for water protection from pollution[549] and maintenance of aquatic ecosystems (Article 14, paragraph 1).

366. Article 15 provides that water facilities[550] considering their purpose are the following:

a. Flood protection facilities include:[551] embankments, bank revetments, regulated river beds-watercourses, drainage channels, peripheral (lateral) channels for protection from outside water, drain tunnels, dams with reservoirs, floodgates, retention basins, pumping stations for flood defence and other related facilities.

---

546. Water resource, as a good of public interest, is managed in the manner prescribed by the provisions of this Law and on the basis of it by other regulations or decisions of the competent authorities (Art. 9, para. 2).
547. *The water land* means a set of land plots that make up the beds of rivers, lakes and reservoirs, as well as their coast to the centennial water level, i.e., to the highest level for accumulations (Art. 4, para. 1, point 6).
548. Public water resource is resource of general interest and is the property of the Republic of Srpska (Art. 10, para. 2).
549. *Pollution* means directly or indirectly introduction of substances or heat into the water, land or into the air, caused by human activity, which may be harmful to human health or to the quality of aquatic or semi-aquatic ecosystems, of which the main substances are listed in Annex 8, Directive 2000/60/EC of 23 Oct. 2000 year (Art. 4, para. 1, point 28).
550. Water facilities from Art. 15 of this Law are properties of interest for the Republic of Srpska (Art. 16, para. 1).
551. Water protection facilities from Art. 15, para. 1, point a) of this Law are owned by the Republic of Srpska and others if it is determined by a special Ministry decree (Art. 16, para. 2). Notwithstanding from the provisions of para. 2, Art. 16, water facilities from Art. 15, para. 1, points b), c), d) and e) can be owned by the local government as well, i.e., can be owned by natural persons and legal entities that own the land on which water facility was built, as established by special acts of the local government unit, the owner and the Ministry (Art. 16, para. 3).

b. Facilities for erosion protection and torrents.
c. Water facilities for drainage.
d. Water facilities for water usage and utilization.
e. Water facilities for water protection from pollution.[552]

4. Water Management

367. The Republic of Srpska manages waters in the manner prescribed by this law and fulfils the obligations that Bosnia and Herzegovina has as an international legal entity (Article 21, paragraph 1).

368. The framework policy of integrated water management is defined in the Water Management Strategy[553] (Article 25, paragraph 1). The Ministry prepares the Water Management Strategy and submits it to the Government (Article 25, paragraph 3). The National Assembly of the Republic of Srpska, on the Government proposal, adopts the Integrated Water Management Strategy for the Republic of Srpska (Article 25, paragraph 4).

369. The Public Institution 'Waters of Srpska' will provide public access, at least for a six months period, for comments in writing for every general act for which the local authority is in territorial jurisdiction, in accordance with this law, special regulations and the current regulations on public participation. Public access must be allowed to the documents and information that were used for preparation of Draft river basin management plan, which is published in the 'Official Gazette of the RS' (Article 29, paragraph 1).

5. River Basin Management

370. The basic unit for water management is the river basin district (District) (Article 23, paragraph 1). For the purpose of water management in the Republic of Srpska the following river basin districts are determined (Article 23, paragraph 2): (a) Sava river district basin and (b) Trebišnjica river district basin.

371. River basin management plan[554] is to be prepared for each river basin district, in accordance with this law and with the Water Framework Directive (Article 26, paragraph 1). The programme of measures for each river basin district is to be established in order to achieve the objectives of environmental protection in accordance with the Water Framework Directive and with this Law, taking into account

552. Maintenance of aquatic facilities referred to in Art. 15 of this Law shall be carried out in accordance to the Rulebook referred to in Art. 16, para. 8 of this Law, and according to the program adopted by the entity that manages the facility (Art. 17, para. 1).
553. The content of the Water Management strategy is prescribed in Art. 25, para. 2.
554. The content of the River basin management plan is prescribed in Art. 26, para. 2.

the results of the economic analysis on which that directive indicates. The programme of measures[555] is established by river basin management plans (Article 27, paragraph 1).

372. The overall objectives of the water management in the river basin[556] district are implementation of the integrated management principle, protection, improvement and restoration of surface water and groundwater,[557] in order to achieve at least good status of surface waters and ground waters, and to prevent deterioration of their status (Article 22, paragraph 1).

373. During the preparatory work for planning in the field of water basin management, the Public Institution 'Waters of Srpska' will conduct regular consultations with relevant agencies in the Federation of Bosnia and Herzegovina, in order to coordinate plans for river basins management in two entities (Article 31, paragraph 1).[558]

The Public Institution 'Waters of Srpska' will prepare a proposal for a coordinated management plan for the river basin, and it shall submit that plan to the Ministry within the timeframe specified in this law (Article 32, paragraph 1).[559] The River Basin District management plans are prepared by Public Institution 'Waters of Srpska' and submitted for approval to the Ministry (Article 33, paragraph 1). After obtaining the approval from the Ministry,[560] the Government adopts the River Basin District Management Plan (Article 33, paragraph 2).

374. Article 36 provides that water body of surface waters may be determined in the River Basin Management plan as artificial or very modified, when changes of the hydro morphological characteristics of that body, which are necessary for achieving of good ecological status, would have significant adverse effects on: (a) wider space of the environment; (b) navigation, including port plants, or recreation; (c) the activities for which water is stored, such as water supply, energy production and irrigation; (d) water regulation, flood protection, drainage; (e) other equally

555. The content of the Programme of measures is prescribed in Art. 27, para. 2.
556. *River basin*-means the land area over which flow all surface flows through streams, rivers and possibly lakes into the sea through one river estuary, armlet or through delta (Art. 4, para. 1, point. 13).
557. *Groundwater* means all water under the Earth's surface in the saturation zone, that are in direct contact with the land surface or sub layer (Art. 4, para. 1, point 3).
558. Coordination of river basin management plans in international river basins can be regulated by international agreements which are binding for Bosnia and Herzegovina (Art. 31, para. 3).
559. The Ministry will be engaged in consultations with relevant Ministry in the Federation of Bosnia and Herzegovina, to ensure coordination of proposed river basin management plans (Art. 32, para. 2).
560. The Ministry is in charge for publishing of basic elements of The River basin district management plan in 'The Official Gazette of the RS' (Art. 33, para. 4).

important sustainable human development activities (paragraph 1).[561] Determination of characteristics of water bodies of surface water and groundwater, for the purposes of river basin management, will be performed in accordance with the methodology established in accordance with Articles 5 and 6 of this law (Article 40).

6. Water Status and Usage

375. Water bodies of surface water and groundwater will be classified on the basis of the level of changes caused by human-anthropogenic impacts and changes in the values of the elements of physical-chemical, biological and hydro morphological quality and quantity of the type of structure and water body in comparison to the type under undisturbed conditions (Article 41, paragraph 1).

376. Classification of the quality element value of the ecological status of each category of surface water is carried out as a high status, good status, moderate status, insufficient status and bad status, in accordance with the Water Framework Directive and the bylaw prescribed by the Ministry, in accordance with Article 7, paragraph 2 of this law (Article 41, paragraph 2).[562]

Monitoring the state – status of surface water and groundwater is based on the monitoring programme that will provide a clear and comprehensive overview of water status within each river basin (Article 44, paragraph 1).[563]

377. The Public Institution 'Waters of Srpska' is responsible for implementation of water status monitoring programme.[564] Only specialized institutions for the water sector and the environment sector, which meet prescribed technical criteria, can implement all activities of water status monitoring or just some of them (Article 44, paragraph 3).

378. Everyone is allowed to use water under the conditions stipulated by this law (Article 49, paragraph 1).[565] Water must be used rationally and economically.

561. Beside the requirements from para. 1 of Art. 36, it is necessary to prove that the beneficial objectives to which serve the artificial or changed and modified characteristics of the water body, for technical reasons or due to disproportionate cost, cannot be achieved by other means, which would be significantly milder in its impact on the environment (Art. 36, para. 2).
562. Classification of groundwater status is done by monitoring of parameters for the classification of groundwater quantitative and chemical status, in accordance with para. 2 of Art. 41 (Art. 41, para. 3).
563. Water monitoring program takes into account protection of aquatic and terrestrial ecosystems and species which directly depend on water (Art. 44, para. 2).
564. Water status monitoring is based on the Water state-status monitoring program adopted by the Ministry (Art. 46, para. 1).
565. The water usage, in accordance with the provisions of this Law, shall be: (a) Abstraction, pumping and usage of surface and groundwater for various purposes (drinking water supply, sanitary and technological needs, irrigation, etc.); (b) The use of water power to generate electricity and other operating needs; (c) The use of water for fish farming; (d) The use of water for navigation; (e) The use of water for sport, swimming, recreation, and other similar purposes (Art. 48, para. 1).

Every water user is obliged to use water in a manner and to the extent that prevents wastage of water and harmful changes of its properties, and that does not interfere to other legal rights concerning use of water (Article 49, paragraph 2). The water permit or approval, in accordance with the provisions of this law, is required for any water use beyond the scope of general use stipulated in Article 50 of this law (Article 51, paragraph 1).

7. Water Protection

379. The discharge of used water into surface waters shall be permitted only in the manner and under the conditions set by this law and bylaws enacted on the base of this law (Article 57, paragraph 1). It is forbidden the discharge wastewater[566] in natural lakes, ponds, wetlands and other natural water reservoirs, which have continuous or an occasional inflow or outflow of surface or ground water, as well as in the water reservoirs which are made due to extraction or exploitation of mineral resources, or other similar operations (Article 57, paragraph 2). It is also forbidden to use water in a way that could cause threaten of water ecological or chemical state (Article 57, paragraph 3). Besides that, it is forbidden to directly discharge wastewater into the groundwater (Article 57, paragraph 4).[567]

380. It is prohibited to produce, handle, store, and dispose of hazardous materials[568] and waste in water and in water resource (Article 62, paragraph 1). Transportation and reloading of hazardous materials and substances on surface waters is regulated in accordance with regulations concerning the transport of dangerous goods and from the area of e area of and road traffic, in order to exclude or to reduce to a minimum possibility of an uncontrolled discharge (Article 63).

381. The Ministry shall by special bylaw, in cooperation with the Ministry be responsible for the environment, establish rules of good agricultural practices to be applied in areas where the waters are polluted by nitrates and by plant protection products, or in areas with risk of such contamination (Article 59, paragraph 1).[569]

The Government shall determine the individual surface water or parts of surface waters were navigation of ships on oil derivatives is prohibited (Article 60, paragraph 1).[570]

The local community on certain area is obliged to ensure and organize wastewater treatment directly and by help of the services and subjects formed for special purposes (Article 58, paragraph 2).

566. *Wastewater* means water which changed its original physical, chemical or biological properties as a result of human activities (Art. 4, para. 1, point 29).
567. Indirect discharging of the wastewater in the groundwater is allowed only in a way and under conditions stipulated by this Law and bylaws adopted on the base of this Law (Art. 57, para. 5).
568. *Hazardous materials*-means substances or group of substances those are toxic or persistent or liable for accumulation (Art. 4, para. 1, point 27).
569. It is forbidden to use fertilizers or plant protection products at water resource (Art. 59, para. 4).
570. The discharge of wastewater from vessels is forbidden, except unpolluted cooling water or for load-balancing (Art. 60, para. 3).

The Ministry, in accordance with the provisions of this law, shall adopt regulations on limiting values for pollutants in wastewater and other requirements regarding wastewater discharge to surface water, land, public sewer system, as well as other hazardous substances which are prohibited to be released into the water, into the land belonging to the water resources, to forest and agricultural land (Article 67, paragraph 1).

All persons are required to discharge wastewater into the public sewer system or to other systems in a way that is consistent with the provisions of Article 67 of this law, as determined by specific decisions on wastewater drainage (Article 68, paragraph 1).

382. If due to a sudden case of failure or for other reasons, there is a danger of water pollution, operator or person whose act or omission created such threat, shall immediately take all necessary measures to prevent or mitigate the effects caused by the incident, and that prevent recurrence of the incident, and then, without delay, to inform the nearest police station, water inspection or a Public Institution 'Waters of Srpska' (Article 64, paragraph 1). Also, any person aware that there was a situation referred to in paragraph 1 of Article 64, is in charge to inform nearest police station, water inspection or Public Institution 'Waters of Srpska' (Article 64, paragraph 2).

383. This law establishes basis for establishment and functioning of a the reference laboratory for the purpose of monitoring of water status, verification of the work results of accredited laboratories and for carrying out the responsibilities of the Ministry and the Public Institution 'Waters of Srpska' (Article 69, paragraph 1).

8. Protected Areas

384. Article 70 provides that the protected areas are those that require special protection in accordance with this law and other regulations (paragraph 1). The protected areas include:

(a) The areas designated for the abstraction of drinking water.
(b) The areas of water bodies intended for protection of the species important for economy.
(c) Water intended for recreation, including areas designated for swimming.
(d) The areas susceptible to eutrophication and areas sensitive to nitrates.
(e) The areas intended for the protection of habitats or species where the maintenance or improvement of state of water is an essential condition for their survival and reproduction (Article 70, paragraph 2).

385. Notwithstanding the protected areas mentioned in Article 70 of this law, the Public Institution 'Waters of Srpska' may establish protected areas of water reserves, regardless of their future purpose, in accordance with the provisions of Article 73, paragraph 3, of this law (Article 71, paragraph 1).

386. For source of water important for future human use,[571] or for use of the source of mineral,[572] thermal[573] or thermo-mineral,[574] or other ground water, the Public Institution 'Waters of Srpska' will propose adoption of decision on temporary protection of the area where the source is located (Article 72, paragraph 1).

387. Areas where sources of drinking water and for human consumption are located, and which according to the quantity and quality can be used or are used in a public way, shall be protected from contamination, and from other factors which might have negative influence on the sanitary safety of water or on source yield (Article 73, paragraph 1). Sanitary protection zones established by the decision on the protection of water sources, as well as area reserved for the sanitary protection zones for which no decision was made are showed in the water management plan (Article 74, paragraph 1). Sanitary protection zones and protective measures are determined in accordance with the provisions of Article 73, paragraph 3 of this law by a local government unit in which territory are located source protection zones or user of that source (Article 75, paragraph 1).[575]

388. Beaches are places intended for organized swimming and places where swimming is not prohibited, and where is traditionally practiced (Article 77, paragraph 1). The Ministry, in cooperation with the Ministry in charge for field of health, prescribes detailed criteria for areas designed for swimming (Article 77, paragraph 6).

9. The Sensitive Areas and Regulation of Watercourses and Other Waters

389. In order to protect water resources, the areas susceptible to eutrophication and areas sensitive on nitrates, may be classified as sensitive and less sensitive (Article 78, paragraph 1). The Ministry in its act declares sensitive or less sensitive areas on the Republic of Srpska territory (Article 79, paragraph 1).

The areas intended for the protection of habitats or species where the maintenance or improvement of water state is an essential condition for their survival or reproduction shall be determined in accordance with regulations on environmental

571. *Water intended for human consumption* – is water intended for human consumption which is in accordance to the regulations from the field of food safety, as well as meanings according to the Directive 80/778/EEC, amended by Directive 98/83/EC (Art. 4, para. 1, point 20).
572. *Mineral water* – means groundwater containing more than 1g/l of dissolved mineral salts (Art. 4, para. 1, point 21).
573. *Thermal water* – means groundwater which temperature is equal to or greater than 20°C (Art. 4, para. 1, point 22).
574. *Thermomineral water* means water which content at the same time meets the established criteria of thermal and mineral waters (Art. 4, para. 1, point 23).
575. Protection of water body's areas intended for the protection for nature important aquatic species shall be performed in accordance with the bylaw of the Ministry for Physical Planning, Civil Engineering and Ecology, which regulates this area (Art. 76, para. 1).

protection and nature protection (Article 80, paragraph 1). Enhanced water state monitoring in sensitive areas is obligatory (Article 82, paragraph 1).[576]

390. Regulation of watercourses[577] and other waters are activities and actions which during their implementation obligatory need special security measures in accordance with this law, as well as regarding the activities on the facilities stipulated in Articles 16 and 17 of this law (Article 85, paragraph 1). The Republic of Srpska and local government units provide, in accordance with this law, the regulation of watercourses and other waters, in the manner specified in Article 5 of this law (Article 89, paragraph 1).[578]

10. Protection from Harmful Water Effects

391. The protection from the harmful water effects means the implementation of activities and measures in order to reduce or to prevent threat to the people and property from harmful water effects, and elimination of the consequences of their actions (Article 90, paragraph 1).[579]

392. In order to reduce the level of vulnerability of people and property, and the implementation of measures and activities for protection from harmful water effects, an area is determined[580] as threatened due to (Article 91, paragraph 1): (a) Flood (water flooded area);[581] (b) Erosion of surface water (erosion area).[582] In order to protect against harmful water effect and flood, planning of activities, measures and

576. The Ministry shall prescribe the method of the water state monitoring in sensitive areas. Water state monitoring includes activities on water and activities in the sensitive area (Art. 82, para. 2).
577. *Watercourse*-means a riverbed space which consists of set of land plots over which continuously or intermittently the water flows, with the water of stream water level of occurrence probability of once in 50 years (Art. 4, para. 1, point 7).
578. The Republic of Srpska and local government units, within their competence, manage water resources, as resources of public interest and protect them from the damage, destruction, or unconscientiously and illegal use in accordance with this and with special Laws (Art. 89, para. 3).
579. Protection from harmful water effects is related to flood and ice protection on watercourses, and protection from erosion and flood (Art. 90, para. 2), as well as protection measures and elimination of consequences caused by water pollution in incidents (Art. 90, para. 3).
580. The areas from para. 90 (the affected areas) are determined by the Government, at the proposal of the Ministry, taking into account the nature possibilities of the occurrence of harmful water effects, the number of potentially affected population and size of possible damage to land, buildings and properties (Art. 91, para. 2).
581. Water flooded area is the area along to watercourse that may be flooded during flood events if water is poured out over the water land to a wider area, regardless of whether the area is protected with water protection facilities (Art. 92, para. 1).
582. The erosive area, in accordance with this Law is the land area in which changes occurs in the surface layer of the soil relief, by erosion or denudation, i.e., stripping, as a consequence of the rain, running water, ice or snow avalanches. There can be several types of erosion processes, depending on the cause of this phenomenon on the erosion area, such as: (a) Fluvial erosion-running water erosion; (b) Pluvial erosion-erosion by rain; (c) Glacial erosion-erosion by ice and snow avalanches; (d) Abrasion erosion-erosion combined by water and wind force (Art. 93, para. 1).

works that are necessary to prevent or mitigate the consequences of harmful water effect is carried out (Article 95, paragraph 1).[583]

393. The Republic of Srpska ensures, in accordance to the law, protection from natural and other disasters, natural and other phenomena, performing of activities of water state monitoring, and other activities related to the protection from harmful water effect, and in particular: (a) Monitoring and forecasting of emergency hydrological conditions and other natural phenomena such as floods, occurrence of water flooded waves, torrent and erosion and ice on watercourse. (b) Monitoring of the state of high barriers on the basis of the data of the propulsion monitoring of state of water facilities or devices referred to in Article 15 of this law (Article 100, paragraph 1).[584]

394. Mitigation of consequences of harmful water effects on water, coastal or other land, or on the affected land area, water infrastructure and water facilities or on water devices is performed on the basis of the remediation programme (Article 103, paragraph 1).[585]

11. Information System and Water Cadastres

395. For the purpose of optimal possibility of collection, usage and connection of the basic groups of data that makes the basis for an integrated water management at the river basin level, the Information System is established at the level of river basins district, including: (a) The information system for river basin district 'Sava'.

583. Activities from item 1 of this article refer but are not limited to: (a) Maintenance, reconstruction and building of protection facilities and plants, (b) Maintenance of main canal network, secondary canal network, tertiary canal network, which serves for drainage and passage of all categories pertaining to the system, (c) Maintenance of stability of defensive embankments, (d) Maintenance and prevention of stability disturbance of banks of water course bed, accumulation, retention, dams and similar, (e) Measures to be taken before and in case of flood danger or harmful water effect, (f) Data about equipment and materials which will be prepared for implementation of activities, (g) Allocation of duties and appointment of responsible persons and competent legal persons established by this Law, (h) Responsibilities and authorizations with regard to taking certain actions and ways of communication in connection with other sector participants, (i) Designation of regional river basin, basin, water course, sector and section where operations for protection of harmful water effect are conducted, (j) Measures to be taken at the time and before flood defence, (k) Water level or height of water level in individual sectors and sections, where preparation and implementations of measures for flood defence is started, (l) Ways of informing competent authorities (m) Ways to keep the connections, and similar (Art. 95, para. 2).

584. During the increased level of vulnerability due to harmful water effect, the Republic of Srpska and local government units, in accordance with their responsibilities, through the competent authorities ensure the implementation of measures and activities of active defence from harmful water effect (Art. 101, para. 1).

585. The Ministry prepares remediation program, taking into account the water management plans and the results of the work of the Commission for assessing the damage. Commission for assessing the damage prepares proposals for the elimination of consequences of harmful water effects in accordance to the water regulations and regulations on the protection of natural and other disasters. The Government, at the proposal of the Ministry, adopts remediation program, no later than 6 months after the end of harmful water effects (Art. 103, para. 6).

(b) The information system for basin district 'Trebisnjica' (Article 117, paragraph 1). Public Institution 'Waters of Srpska' is obliged to organize, establish and manage the Information system for the Regional River Basins of the Republic of Srpska (Article 117, paragraph 2).[586]

The Republican Water Information System (hereinafter, 'Information System') is an integral part of information system of the Republic of Srpska, and is established and organized in accordance with this law and with special laws which define the basis and structure of establishing of such a system (Article 110, paragraph 1).

396. The water cadastres are (Article 113, paragraph 1): (a) Water cadastre;[587] (b) The cadastre of water resource and water buildings; (c) The cadastre of arrangement and protection from harmful water effect; (d) The cadastre of water usage; (e) The cadastre of water protection; (f) The cadastre of the other water infrastructure.

397. The evidence on issued water guidelines, water consents, water permits and orders shall be recorded in the Water Book (Article 114, paragraph 1). The Water Books keep authorities in charge for issuing of water documents (Article 114, paragraph 3).[588]

12. Types of Water Legal Acts and Revoking of Water Legal Acts

398. In order to ensure water management and for the purpose of fair access to water of all persons, this law regulates the way of use of water rights by issuing the following water legal acts: (a) guidelines; (b) compliance; (c) permits (Article 120, paragraph 1).

The water legal acts for the activities referred to in Article 120 of this law, shall be issued for a limited period, in accordance with the provisions of this law. Depending on the technological complexity of the facility, the water permit may be issued for a shorter period of time than stipulated in this law (Article 149, paragraph 1).

399. In order to resolve the conflict of interest and public participation in the work, the competent authority, before issuing the water legal act, must inform interested parties. On request it informs the public at the territory in which it operates, through a notice on the bulletin board of the competent authority, by the advertising in the public media, and in case of inter-entity impact, in at least two public media that are available to the public in the Republic of Srpska and the Federation of Bosnia and Herzegovina (Article 130, paragraph 1).

---

586. Ministry adopts bylaws about technical details, elements, activities and other significant procedures when establishing Information System and manages, and manages integral water information system of Republic of Srpska (Art. 117, para. 3).
587. The water cadastre contains data on surface waters and ground waters (Art. 113, para. 2).
588. The Ministry, in accordance with this and with special regulations, keeps a Register of concessions on water and on water resources in which are entered the data on the preparation of the concession by the Ministry, on decisions of the competent authorities and concession agreements on water and on water resource (Art. 115, para. 1).

400. For failure of issued order, according to the decision referred to in Article 155 of this law, water legal act to the legal person, as well as the right in relation to it, may be temporary or permanently revoked (Article 161, paragraph 1).[589]

Water legal act shall be revoked permanently: (a) If within a specified time, the user does not perform activities, does not make investments or if the user refrain from some activities stated in the issued order due to which water legal act was temporarily revoked; (b) If the execution of the issued order could result in serious and immediate threat to life or health or to economic disturbances (Article 163, paragraph 1).[590]

13. Property Easement as Limitations of Land Owners

401. For the purpose of implementing the provisions of this law, the right is established on property easement, as a land owner's property right, that he can for the purpose of that good perform certain actions on the property, the servient estate, of another owner or to require from the owner of servient estate to refrain from performing certain actions that regularly would be entitled to be performed on the property (Article 165). The property easement can be determined by a special act of the relevant authority for the enforcement of this law, for a certain period of time or for a certain period of the year (Article 166, paragraph 1).

14. The Public Institution 'Waters of Srpska'

402. For the activities prescribed by this Law and the bylaws adopted on the basis of it, the Public Institution 'Waters of Srpska' shall be established, as an organization that integrates water management in accordance with this Law. The headquarters of the Public Institution 'Waters of Srpska' is in Bijeljina. The territory where the Public institution 'Waters of Srpska' performs duties in accordance with this Law and other relevant regulations is the territory of the Republic of Srpska (Article 176, paragraphs 1–3).

403. Jobs and activities of the Public Institution 'Waters of Srpska' are professional and independent performing of the jobs of general interest and other tasks defined by this law, the law which was applied for establishing the Public Institution 'Waters of Srpska', as well as by bylaws and other acts adopted on the base of those regulations (Article 177, paragraph 1). Article 178 provides that *s*ome of the tasks which the Public Institution 'Waters of Srpska' carries out on the territory of Republic of Srpska under its authority are the following: (a) Organize collection,

589. The water legal act, shall be revoked for a period of six months, during which period the beneficiary will be deprived of the rights acquired on the base of that act and in which the user is required to perform the activity for which water legal act was revoked (Art. 162, para. 2).

590. The beneficiary to whom is water legal act revoked, may apply for a new water act if he fulfils the required conditions, set forth in the provisions of Art. 120, para. 4 of this Law (Art. 163, para. 2).

management and distribution of the data on water resources. (b) Organize water state monitoring, in relation to the hydrological state of water, qualitative state of water, the ecological state of surface water and groundwater state. (c) Prepare the river basin management plans for their river basin district and performs other duties related to the water planning as prescribed by this law. (d) Prepare plans, studies and projects to prevent and reduce the harmful effects that are caused by floods, severe droughts, coastal erosion of water bodies and organizes the implementation of the plans. (e) Issue water legal acts[591] in accordance with this law. (f) Participate in cooperation in relation to coordination during preparation and implementation of integrated water management plans with the relevant organizations from the Federation of Bosnia and Herzegovina for the needs of Bosnia and Herzegovina, i.e., with the competent international bodies for the area of international river basins, etc.

15. Council of Water District and Public Enterprises in the Field of Water

404. The council of Sava River Basin District and the Council of Trebišnjica River Basin District (hereinafter, 'the Council') are established as the highest advisory body in order to consider systemic questions from the water sector of importance for a certain river basin district, consideration of the different needs and interests, and to propose measures for the development and improvement of functioning of the water sector in the particular river basin district (Article 184, paragraph 1).[592]

405. Jobs and activities of general interest are: preparation and implementation of flood defence, arrangement of river beds and shores, management of water facilities and systems of interest for the Republic of Srpska, assessment and management of flood risks, as well as other tasks prescribed by this Law (Article 187, paragraph 1).

16. Financing of Water Management

406. Funds for performing of jobs and tasks in accordance with this law, the functioning and maintenance of real estate and water facilities of common interest, the preservation of values of built water facilities and systems, taking measures of public investment and capital construction of water facilities, according to this law, shall be provided from:

591. *The water legal acts* are acts which in a general or in special administrative procedure establish some right, obligation or legal interest for a third natural person or for legal entity, the Government-Republican or local Government authority (Art. 4, para. 1, point 35).
592. The organization, composition, activities, way of working and the number of Council members for a certain river basin district shall be prescribed by an act issued by the Public Institution 'Waters of Srpska', taking into account the characteristics of the River Basin District, the number of municipalities that belong to a certain river basin district, number of population and the state of the industry in the municipality, the importance of different types of water usage, and other specificities of River Basin Districts (Art. 184, para. 2).

(a) Special water fees.
(b) Income from the lease of public water resources.
(c) The general part of the Republic of Srpska budget and of the local government unit's budget.
(d) Donations (Article 188, paragraph 1).

407. Pursuant to Article 189 the special water fees are the following: Fees for the abstraction of surface and ground waters; Fees for electricity production from the use of hydropower; Fees for water protection; Fees for exploiting of material from watercourses; Fees for protection from the water (paragraph 1). The rates of special water fees from Article 189 of this law are prescribed by the Government, at the proposal of the Ministry, except for the cases provided in point (d) of sub-points (1) and (2) of paragraph 1 of said article, which is the income of the local Government in whose area that land is situated and, as such, shall be prescribed by that administration (Article 190, paragraph 1).[593]

17. Inspection Supervision

408. Inspection supervision over the enforcement of this law and bylaws and other acts based on it, performs the Republican administration for inspection activities (Article 196, paragraph 1). The Republic Water Inspection supervises the enforcement of this law in terms of its application, and in particular respecting ways of using water rights and respecting Water legal acts referred to in Article 120 hereof, and actions that are criminal offence or civil offence (Article 198, paragraph 1).[594] Water Inspection of Local Governments performs supervision over the enforcement of this law, particularly in the areas and cases from Article 121 of this law, as well as in cases in which it is authorized on its territory, respecting the jurisdiction of issuing water legal acts (Article 199, paragraph 1).

409. Water inspectors from both entities have the right to jointly carry out the inspection in the following cases:

(a) In case of an accidental contamination of water and water resources which consequences are evident on the territory of another entity.
(b) In case of facilities with such mode of work which effects are evident on the territory of both entities.
(c) For activities which impact is evident in the territory of both entities.

593. Water fees from Art. 189 and the revenue generated from the lease of public water resources, the Ministry monitors for each river basin district separately, and the competent authority, the fees from the said article, except those in point c) sub-point 1), 2) and 3), para. 1 of Art. 189, allocate as follows: (a) 70% to the account for special purposes for water; 30% to the account for special purposes to the local government budget on whose territory are realised activities for which a special water charge is prescribed (Art. 194).

594. Republic water inspection supervises implementation of provisions of this law on the whole territory of Republic, in the way prescribed by this law, as well as special regulations referring to operation of inspection, if they are not in conflict with provisions of this law (Art. 198, para. 2).

(d) In other cases, when it was agreed (Article 205, paragraph 1).

410. The Public Institution 'Waters of Srpska' is obliged, when it is necessary in order to monitor the implementation of this law to undertake inspection measures, at the request of water inspector, regardless of his level:

(a) To provide the necessary information, acts or documents.
(b) To prepare the appropriate expertise.
(c) To carry out water quality testing.
(d) To perform any other necessary actions (Article 208, paragraph 1).

B. Other Relevant RS Regulations

411.

(1) Rule book on the conditions and method of renting aquatic land (Official Gazette of RS No. 105/17, 83/18).
(2) Rulebook on the conditions and method of dislocation and extraction of materials from the watercourse (Official Gazette of RS No. 24/17, 40/17).
(3) Rulebook on protection measures, manner of determining, maintaining and marking sanitary protection zones (Official Gazette of RS No. 76/16).
(4) Decree on the manner, procedure and deadlines for calculating and paying special water fees (Official Gazette of RS No. 7/14).
(5) Rule book on the requirements for discharging wastewater into the public sewer (Official Gazette of RS No. 44/01).
(6) Rule book on protection measures, manner of defining and maintaining sanitary protection zones and strips, areas with springs as well as water facilities and water intended for human use (Official Gazette of RS No. 7/03).
(7) Decision on defining boundaries of river basin districts and basins on the territory of the Republic of Srpska (Official Gazette of RS No. 98/06).
(8) Regulation on the manner, procedures and deadlines for calculating and paying special water fees (Official Gazette of RS Nos 53/11 and 16/12).
(9) Regulation on the manner of public participation in water management (Official Gazette of RS No. 35/07).
(10) Rule book on the treatment and drainage of wastewater in town and residential areas lacking a public sewer system (Official Gazette of RS No. 68/01).
(11) Rule book on the manner of maintaining river beds and water grounds (Official Gazette of RS Nos 34/03, 22/06).
(12) Rule book on the manner and methods of determining the degree of water pollution (Official Gazette of RS Nos 79/11, 25/12 and 36/12).
(13) Decision on the rates of special water fees (Official Gazette RS No. 53/11).
(14) Rule book on requirements that must be met by water management laboratories (Official Gazette of RS No. 44/01).

(15) Regulation on classification of water and water flow categorization (Official Gazette of RS No. 42/01).[595]

II. Federation of Bosnia and Herzegovina

412. The first Law on Waters of the Federation of BiH was adopted in 1998 (Official Gazette of FBiH, No. 18/98). During the time of effectiveness of this law, the Cantons adopted their first laws on water and other water regulations falling under their competence. The Law on Water Protection of the Federation of BiH was adopted in 2003 (Official Gazette of FBiH, Nos 33/03 and 54/04). The new Law on Waters adopted in 2006 (Official Gazette of the FBiH, No. 70/06), In accordance with 2006 Law on Waters the Cantons are obliged to harmonize the provisions of the Cantonal laws on waters with the provisions of the latest Law.[596]

A. The Law on Waters

413. Basic legal act regulating water issues in the Federation of Bosnia and Herzegovina is the Law on waters (Official Gazette of FBiH, No. 70/06). It has the following fifteen parts: Part I – General Provisions (Articles 1–2), Part II – Basic Principles and Definitions (Articles 3–4), Part III – Classification of Surface Waters, Water Resource and Water Facilities (Articles 5–20), Part IV – Water Management (Articles 21–43), Part V – Water Usage (Articles 44–52), Part VI – Water Protection (Articles 53–79), Part VII – Regulation of Watercourses and Other Waters and Protection from Harmful Water Effects (Articles 80–97), Part VIII – Information System of Waters (Articles 98–106), Part IX – Water Acts (Articles 107–139), Part X – Limitation of Land Owners and Users (Articles 140–151), Part XI – Organization of Water Management (Articles 152–167), Part XII – Financing of Water Management (Articles 168–178), XIII – Supervision over the Implementation of this Law (Articles 179–203), Part XIV – Penalty Provisions (Articles 204–206), Part XV – Transitional and Final Provisions (Articles 207–224).[597]

According to Article 1, paragraph 1, this law regulates the water management[598] within the territory of the Federation of Bosnia and Herzegovina (hereinafter, 'the Federation'). Apart from that, this law regulates: water resource and public water

---

595. *See*: http://www.vladars.net/sr-SP-Cyrl/Vlada/Ministarstva/mps/%D0%B1.%D0%BA%D0%B5%D1%86%D0%BC%D0%B0%D0%BD/Pages/default.aspx (19 Jul. 2022).

596. For more information *see*: Zavod za vodoprivredu, *Water Management Strategy of the Federation of Bosnia and Herzegovina*, *supra* pp. 88–91.

597. Purpose of this Law is to ensure water management with the aim of: Reducing water pollution, achieving good water status and preventing water degradation; Achieving sustainable water use; Ensuring equitable access to water; Encouraging social and economic development; Protection of ecosystems; Reducing flooding risk and other adverse water impacts; Ensuring public participation in decision-making related to water; Prevention and resolution of conflicts related to water protection and usage; Fulfilment of obligations from international agreements that are binding for Bosnia and Herzegovina (Art. 2, para. 1).

598. Water management includes: water protection, water usage, protection from harmful water effects, regulation of water courses and other waters (Art. 1, para. 2).

resource, water facilities, legal entities and other institutions responsible for specific water management issues and other issues related to waters in the Federation (Article 1, paragraph 3).

1. General Principles

414. Waters are public good and as such are under the special protection of Bosnia and Herzegovina, the Federation, cantons, cities and municipalities (Article 3, paragraph 1).

415. Water management is based on the following principles (Article 3, paragraph 2):

- *Non commercialism*, according to which water is basically not a commercial product, but the legacy that must be stored, protected and treated in accordance to it.
- *Integrity*, which takes into account the natural processes and dynamics of waters and interconnectedness and interdependence of water and water-related ecosystems.
- *Long-term quality protection and rational use* of the available amount of water.
- *Ensuring protection against harmful water effects* on people and their property, taking into account the influence of natural processes.
- *Economic valuation of waters*, which includes the cost of loading, protection and water regulation and protection from harmful water effects.
- *Public participation* in adoption of water management plans.
- Taking into account the *best available technology, scientific achievements* and the *best environmental practices.*

2. Classification of Surface Waters, Water Resource, and Water Facilities

416. Surface waters,[599] according to the importance which they have for the water management are divided into waters of I category[600] and waters of II category (Article 5, paragraph 1).

Surface waters include running waters and standing waters (Article 6, paragraph 1). Running waters are natural watercourses[601] such as torrents, streams and rivers, regardless of whether they have permanent or occasional stream (Article 6, paragraph 2). Running waters involve regulated watercourses, watercourses resulting

599. *Surface waters*-means all inland waters, except groundwater, transitional and coastal sea waters, except sea waters that belong to territorial waters (Art. 4, para. 1).
600. Waters of I Category are listed in Art. 5, para. 2, while all other waters are waters of II Category (Art. 5, para. 2).
601. *Watercourse* means a riverbed of running water along with coast and water that flows through it continuously or periodically (Art. 4, para. 1).

from the relocation of the natural watercourse or by partial water abstraction from natural watercourses (Article 6, paragraph 3).

Standing waters are: coastal sea waters, natural lakes, including those that periodically dry up, swamps, wetlands and other natural water reservoirs that have a permanent or temporary inflow or outflow of surface or groundwater[602] (Article 6, paragraph 4). Standing waters are also water reservoirs made by damming of running waters or by other interventions in the area (Article 6, paragraph 5).

417. Water resource, according to this law, is a set of land plots (Article 7, paragraph 1).[603] Water resource[604] can be owned by the Federation, cantons, cities, municipalities, legal entity or natural person (Article 7, paragraph 3). In case of sale of a land plot owned by a legal entity or natural person which belongs to the water resource, right of priority purchase have the Federation, canton, city, i.e., municipality (Article 7, paragraph 4).

Public water resource consist of land plots from Article 7, paragraph 1 of this law which by the date of the enactment of this law were registered in the Land Registry as a public property, state property or property of the city or municipality, i.e., which became state property on the base of the law (Article 9, paragraph 1).[605]

418. Water facilities are buildings or groups of buildings which, together with related devices, make technical, i.e., technological unit and are used for protection from the harmful water effects, water abstraction for intended use and water protection from pollution (Article 13, paragraph 1). Water facilities with regard to their purpose, are following: (1) protective facilities; (2) drainage facilities, basic and detailed drainage canal network, pumping stations for drainage and other associated facilities; (3) facilities for water utilization and (4) facilities for water protection from pollution (hereinafter, 'Water facilities for water protection') (Article 14, paragraph 1).[606]

---

602. *Groundwaters* means all water under the ground in the saturation zone and which are in direct contact with the surface and underground layers of the land (Art. 4, para. 1).
603. The Federal Minister of Agriculture, Water Management and Forestry (hereinafter, 'the Federal Minister') shall issue a regulation on the method of determining the boundaries of water resources from Art. 7, para. 1 of this Law and about the process for determining of belonging of a land plot to the public water resource from Art. 9, paras 1 and 2 of this Law (Art. 8, para. 1).
604. It is not allowed to perform interventions on water resource, except in cases listed in Art. 12, para. 1.
605. Authorizations for management of public water resource is performed by the authorities, legal entities and other institutions to the extent and in the manner prescribed by this Law or other acts of the competent authorities to which is transferred the right to manage with public water resources (Art. 9, para. 4).
606. Water facilities from this article can be at the same time used for several purposes – multi-purpose water facilities (Art. 14, para. 2).

3. Water Management Objectives and Water Areas

419. Water management is under responsibility of Bosnia and Herzegovina, the Federation, canton, city and municipality in the way prescribed in this law (Article 21, paragraph 1).

Water management objectives are the following: to achieve good status, i.e., good ecological potential of surface waters and groundwaters, i.e., water and water-related ecosystems, reduction of damages caused by various adverse water effects, ensuring necessary amount of water of adequate quality for a variety of uses and encouraging of sustainable water use, taking into account the long-term protection of available water sources and their quality (Article 22, paragraph 1).

420. The basic territorial unit for water management is the water area (Article 23, paragraph 1). For the purpose of water management on the territory of Bosnia and Herzegovina, i.e., the Federation, it shall be determined the following water areas:[607] Water area of Sava river and Water area of Adriatic Sea (Article 23, paragraph 2).

4. Strategy for Water Management and the Programme of Measures

421. Water management policy is determined by Water Management Strategy (Article 24, paragraph 1).[608] The Federal Ministry prepares proposal of the Water Management Strategy, with the consent of the Federal Ministry responsible for the environment (Article 24, paragraph 2). The Federal Ministry is obliged to establish and to ensure coordination of all activities with the Ministry of the Republic of Srpska responsible for waters in order to ensure adoption of uniform Water Management Strategy for whole Bosnia and Herzegovina (Article 24, paragraph 6).

Water Management Strategy adopts, at the proposal of the Government of the Federation, Parliament of the Federation of Bosnia and Herzegovina (hereinafter, 'the Federation Parliament'), i.e., the Parliamentary Assembly of Bosnia and Herzegovina for the period to twelve years (Article 24, paragraph 7). The Water Management Plans[609] for the water area of Sava river and the water area of Adriatic Sea shall be adopted for implementation of the Strategy (Article 25, paragraph 1).

607. *River basin (district)*-means an area of land and sea that consists of one or more neighbouring river basins (catchments) and together with their associated groundwaters and coastal sea waters and is designated as the basic unit for water management (Art. 4, para. 1).

608. The content of the Water Management Strategy is prescribed in Art. 24, para. 3. The Water Management Strategy is part of the Strategy for the environmental protection (Art. 24, para. 9).

609. Mandatory content of the Water Management Plan is prescribed in Art. 25, para. 2.

422. Programme of measures[610] includes basic measures needed to achieve goals related to water protection, water regulation and protection from harmful water effects and water usage (Article 26, paragraph 1).[611]

5. The Water Agency and Water Management Plans

423. Article 29 provides that the responsible Water Agency from Article 152 of this law:

1. Prepares an analysis of characteristics of water area.
2. Prepares review of the impact of human activity on the status of surface waters and groundwaters.
3. Prepares an economic analysis of water use.
4. Establishes a register of protected areas referred to in Article 65 of this law, as well as areas with special protection determined by decision of the Government of the Federation.
5. Establishes a register of water bodies that are used or intended to be used for water abstraction for human consumption.
6. Prepares classification of the ecological, chemical and quantitative status of water.
7. Prepares programme and organizes monitoring of water state.
8. Prepares a water management plan and programme of measures.

424. Implementation of the programme of measures identified in the Water Management Plans ensures:

(1) Preventing of deterioration of state of water bodies of surface water[612] and groundwater,[613] and achieving at least its good status.
(2) Achieving of good ecological potential and good chemical status of artificial or heavily modified water bodies.
(3) Protection, improvement and restoration of water bodies of surface waters in order to achieve the state from items 1 and 2, paragraph 1 of this article, the latest for six years after the adoption of the first Water Management Plan.
(4) Protection, improvement and restoration of water bodies of groundwaters in order to achieve the state from item 1 of this paragraph, the latest for six years from the adoption of the first Water Management Plan.

---

610. Program of measures is part of the plan for water management (Art. 26, para. 6) in which are determined the priorities for realization of the certain measures referred to in para. 2, item 2 of this article (Art. 26, para. 4).
611. Basic measures from Program of measures are the following: 1. Measures related to the water protection; 2. Measures related to water regulation and protection from the harmful water effects; 3. Measures related to the use of water (Art. 26, para. 2).
612. *State of the surface water* means the status of a water body of surface water that is determined by its ecological or chemical status, taking that which is worse (Art. 4, para. 1).
613. *State of the groundwater* means the state of a water body of groundwater which is determined by its quantitative or chemical state, taking that which is worse (Art. 4, para. 1).

(5) Implementation of the progressive pollution reduction of water bodies of surface waters with priority substances.
(6) Gradual pollution reduction of water bodies of groundwaters caused by human activities.
(7) Harmonization of standards and objectives for water protection in the protected zones according to which are established certain protected areas from item 4, paragraph 1 of this Article, with the international standards for such protection the latest within the next six years from the adoption of the first Water Management Plan (Article 30, paragraph 1).
(8) Characteristics of the Water Bodies Types and Classification of State of Waters.

425. In order to achieve and maintain good status or good ecological potential, characteristics of the water body types will be determined (Article 31, paragraph 1).[614] Determination of the characteristics of water bodies of surface waters and groundwaters is carried out in accordance with the methodology set forth in the bylaw referred to in Article 43, paragraph 1, point 1 of this law. For the initial determination of the characteristics, water bodies can be grouped (Article 31, paragraph 5).

In the field of water management, water body of surface waters[615] can be declared as artificial or heavily modified under conditions prescribed in Article 33, paragraph 1. Commitment for designating a water body of surface water for artificial or for heavily modified, as well as the reasons for it, are especially stated in the water management plans and are reviewed every six years (Article 33, paragraph 2).

426. Classification of state of water bodies of surface waters and groundwaters shall be determined on the basis of the level of change caused by human activities (Article 32, paragraph 1).[616] The ecological state of a water body of surface water is classified as high, good, moderate, poor and bad (Article 32, paragraph 3).[617] Chemical status of a water body of surface waters is classified as good or bad (Article 32, paragraph 4). State of a water body of groundwater is determined by its quantitative and chemical state depending on which one is worse (Article 32, paragraph 5).

---

614. Water bodies of surface waters in the water area shall be classified into one of the following types: rivers, lakes, transitional waters and coastal sea waters or as artificial or heavily modified water bodies (Art. 31, para. 2).
615. *Body of surface water* means an isolated and special part of the observed surface water such as a lake, stream, river or canal, part of a stream, river or canal, a transitional water or a stretch of coastal waters (Art. 4, para. 1).
616. The state of a water body of surface waters is determined by its ecological and chemical status, depending on which one is worse (Art. 32, para. 2).
617. For artificial and heavily modified water bodies of surface waters shall be applied the criteria for determining of the ecological state of water bodies of surface waters referred to in para. 3 of this article, taking one that is the most similar (Art. 32, para. 6).

6. Plans for Water Management and Other Plans

427. The Agency for water area, referred to in Article 152 of this law, notifies in writing the Advisory Council for Water referred to in Article 164 of this law, canton, city and municipality about beginning of preparation of the plan for water management and through the public media informs legal entities and natural persons which have their headquarters or domicile in the territory of the water area for which is prepared the plan, for at least three years before the beginning of the period to which the plan applies (Article 38, paragraph 1).[618] After conclusion of the procedures from this article, the Agency for Water area prepares the Proposal Plan (Article 38, paragraph 10).

428. During development of a Water Management Plan referred to Article 25 of this law, authorized institution for development of the plan establishes and ensures coordination of all activities with appropriate institution responsible for developing of the plan for the same water area from the Republic of Srpska and Brčko District of Bosnia and Herzegovina (hereinafter, 'Brčko District') in order to ensure adoption of a unique plan for water management of the water area in Bosnia and Herzegovina (Article 39, paragraph 1).

Plans from Article 25 of this law may be supplemented by preparation of more detailed programmes and plans for water management for certain sub-basins, certain water categories and particular water management issues (Article 41, paragraph 1).[619]

429. The plan for water management of the water area adopts the Government of the Federation on the proposal of the Federal Minister, in accordance with the provision from Article 25, paragraph 4 of this law. Decision on adopted plan shall be published in the 'Official Gazette of the Federation of Bosnia and Herzegovina' (Article 40, paragraph 1).

7. Water Usage

430. According to Article 44 water usage includes:

1. Abstraction, pumping and use of surface waters and groundwaters for various purposes (drinking water supply, sanitation and technological needs, irrigation, etc.).
2. Use of water power for production of electricity and other propulsion purposes.

---

618. Legal entities and natural persons referred to in para. 1 of this article can submit to the Agency for water area written remarks on the draft Plan within six months after its publication (Art. 38, para. 6).

619. Plans referred to in para. 1 of Art. 41 adopts the Government of the Federation on the proposal of the Federal Minister, in accordance with the regulation from Art. 25, para. 4 of this Law. Decision on adopted Plan shall be published in the 'Official Gazette of the Federation of Bosnia and Herzegovina' (Art. 41, para. 6).

3. Use of water for fish farming.
4. Use of water for navigation.
5. Use of water for sports, swimming, recreation and other similar purposes (paragraph 1).

431. Everyone is allowed to use water under conditions specified by this law (Article 45, paragraph 1). Water must be used rationally and economically. Each water user is obliged to use water in a manner and to the extent that keeps the water from wasting and harmful changes of its properties (quality) and provides a legal right of water use to other persons (Article 45, paragraph 2).

Everyone is allowed to use the water, usually in a way that does not require special devices and does not exclude others from the same water use (general use of water) (Article 46, paragraph 1). For each water use that exceeds the scope of the general use of Article 46 of this law, a water permit is required, in accordance with this law (Article 47, paragraph 1).

432. Quality of drinking water (water supply) must comply with the conditions prescribed in the regulation on drinking water quality issued by the Federal Minister responsible for Health (Article 48, paragraph 1). The use of water from sources and groundwaters, except for the general use of water, may be approved only if water research works have been previously carried out (Article 49, paragraph 1).

8. Water Protection

433. The discharge of wastewater into surface waters is permitted only in the manner and under conditions specified in this law and bylaw referred to in Article 55, paragraph 1 of this law (Article 53, paragraph 1). It is prohibited to discharge wastewater[620] directly into groundwater[621] (Article 53, paragraph 4). A natural person or legal entity is obliged to discharge wastewater into the public sewerage system or otherwise, in accordance with decision on wastewater drainage (Article 54, paragraph 1).

It is forbidden to wash a vehicle (car, truck and other machinery and equipment) in surface water and on land belonging to water resource (Article 58, paragraph 1). It is prohibited to produce, handling, storing and disposing of hazardous substances and waste on waters and on water resource (Article 59, paragraph 1).

434. The Government of the Federation of Bosnia and Herzegovina adopts a regulation on limiting values for polluting substances in wastewater and on other

620. *Wastewater* means water that has changed its natural, physical, chemical or biological properties as a result of human activities (Art. 4, para. 1).

621. *Direct discharge to groundwater* means the discharge of pollution into groundwater without filtration throughout the surface or subsurface layers of the soil (Art. 4, para. 1).

requirements about discharge of wastewater to surface waters and indirect discharge of wastewater into groundwater, as well as regulation on dangerous and priority substances[622] on the proposal of the Federal Minister responsible for the environment (Article 55, paragraph 1).[623]

The Federal Minister, with the consent of the Federal Minister responsible for the environment, adopts a regulation on rules of good agricultural practice to be applied in areas where the water is polluted by nitrates and pesticides, or in areas where exists the risk of such pollution (Article 56, paragraph 1).[624]

The Government of the Federation, on the proposal of the Federal Minister determines individual surface waters or parts of surface waters that are banned of vessels fuelled by petroleum products (Article 57, paragraph 1). Protection of coastal sea waters from pollution caused by vessels shall be regulated in accordance with special regulations governing the field of maritime transport (Article 57, paragraph 3).

435. In the regulations relating to the transport and transhipment of dangerous goods on inland waters[625] and at sea are governed by the conditions of transport and transhipment of materials in order to exclude the possibility of water pollution or to reduce it to a minimum (Article 60, paragraph 1).

If due to the accidental cases, malfunction or other reasons there is a danger of water pollution, natural person and legal entity which act or omission caused the risk, must immediately take all necessary measures to prevent or mitigate the impact caused by the incident, and prevent recurrence of the incident, and then, without delay, notify the nearest police department, water inspection, federal inspection in charge for environmental protection, the agency for water area or the operating centre of civil protection (Article 61, paragraph 1). The costs of measures taken (elimination of consequences) bear the legal entity and natural person whose act or omission caused the pollution or threat of pollution (Article 61, paragraph 8).[626]

436. Extraction of materials from the river is allowed to the extent and in a manner that does not significantly alter natural processes, does not disturb the natural balance of the ecosystem or stimulate harmful water effect (Article 63, paragraph 1).

437. For monitoring of water status, verification of the results of work of accredited laboratories and for performing tasks within the jurisdiction of the Federal Ministry, the Federal Ministry responsible for the environment, the Cantonal Ministries

---

622. Before making Regulations from para. 1 of this article, the Government of the Federation shall ensure, in consultation with the Government of the Republic of Srpska, its complete harmonization with the relevant regulations of the Republic of Srpska (Art. 55, para. 3).
623. The Government of the Federation adopts regulation referred to in para. 1 of this article, only if the Council of Ministers of Bosnia and Herzegovina did not adopt such Regulation (Art. 55, para. 2).
624. It is forbidden the use of fertilizers and the use of pesticides on the water resource (Art. 56, para. 4).
625. *Inland waters*-means all standing or running waters on the surface of the land and all groundwaters on the landward side from the baseline from which is measured the breadth of the territorial sea (Art. 4, para. 1).
626. The Federal Minister responsible for the environment, with the consent of the Federal Minister, prescribes the procedure and measures to be taken in case of an accident (Art. 61, para. 9).

in charge of Water and Environment and the Agency for water area, the reference laboratory is in charge (Article 64, paragraph 1). Until the establishment of the reference laboratory at the state level, the activities and tasks of the reference laboratory may be awarded to one of the approved laboratories (Article 64, paragraph 2).

9. Protected Areas

438. For the purpose of establishment of special protection of surface water and groundwater, habitats of plant and animal species or aquatic species areas and water bodies can be declared as protected areas (Article 65, paragraph 1). According to the paragraph 2 of this article protected areas are:

(1) Areas intended for the abstraction of drinking water.
(2) Areas designated for the protection of economically significant aquatic species.
(3) Surface water bodies intended for recreation, including areas designated for swimming.
(4) Areas subject to eutrophication and areas sensitive to nitrates.
(5) Areas designated for protection of habitats of plant and animal species or aquatic species where the maintenance or improvement of water is an essential condition for their survival and reproduction.

439. The area where there is a source of water which according to quantity and quality can be used or is used for public water supply must be protected from pollution and other adverse impacts on the health safety of water or abundance of its sources (Article 66, paragraph 1). In addition to the protected areas referred to in Article 66 of this law, the Agency for Water Area may also determine protected areas of reserves of inland waters, regardless of their future use (Article 69, paragraph 1) which shall be determined on the basis of identified reserves of inland waters, which due to their chemical, physicochemical and microbiological characteristics are classified in the highest order (Article 69, paragraph 2).

440. Sanitary protection zones determined by the decision on the protection of water source, as well as space reserved for establishment of sanitary protection zones for sources that are used, and for which decision is not yet adopted, shall be entered into the Water Management Plan (Article 67, paragraph 1).

441. The protection of areas used for farming of economically important aquatic species is done by establishing of special protection from pollution and other adverse impacts on some aquatic species (Article 71, paragraph 1).

442. In order to protect water, areas prone to eutrophication and areas sensitive to nitrates are divided into sensitive and less sensitive areas (Article 73, paragraph 1).[627]

The Federal Minister responsible for the environment declares sensitive areas in the territory of the Federation of Bosnia and Herzegovina (Article 74, paragraph 1). Sensitive areas that extend on the territory of the Federation of Bosnia and Herzegovina and on the territory of the Republic of Srpska declare the Ministry of Bosnia and Herzegovina in charge for water, at the proposal of the Ministers of the Federation and of the Republic of Srpska in charge for water and environment (Article 74, paragraph 2). Sensitive areas that extend on the territory of Bosnia and Herzegovina and on neighbouring countries are declared by the authority of Bosnia and Herzegovina determined by regulation of Bosnia and Herzegovina (Article 74, paragraph 3).

Monitoring of sensitive areas is required and includes water monitoring and monitoring of activities (Article 76, paragraph 1). The Federal Minister responsible for the environment, with the consent of the Federal Minister, adopts a regulation on the method of monitoring of sensitive areas (Article 76, paragraph 2).

10. Regulation of Watercourses and Other Waters and Protection from Harmful Water Effects

443. Regulation of watercourses and other waters, according to this law, is maintenance of watercourse and water resource, as well as other works that enable controlled and harmless water flow (Article 80, paragraph 1).

Protection from harmful water effects means implementation of activities and measures aimed at reducing or preventing the risk to people and property from harmful water effects and elimination of consequences of their effects (Article 85, paragraph 1). Protection from harmful water effects is related to defence from flood and ice on watercourses and protection from erosion and flood (Article 85, paragraph 2).[628]

444. To reduce the level of vulnerability of people and property and for enforcement of measures and activities of protection from harmful water effects, it is determined the area that is at risk by: (1) floods (hereinafter, 'flooded area'); (2) erosion of surface waters (hereinafter, 'erosive area') (Article 86, paragraph 1).[629]

In order to protect from harmful water effects, the Federation, cantons, cities and municipalities in the affected areas ensure, each within its jurisdiction according to provisions of this law, the planning of protective measures, construction and management of flood protection facilities, and in particular the construction of the

627. The Federal Minister responsible for the environment, with the consent of the Federal Minister, makes regulation for identification of sensitive and less sensitive areas, as well as protection measures, prohibitions and restrictions in sensitive area (Art. 73, para. 2).

628. In addition to that, protection from harmful water effects also includes protection measures and elimination of consequences caused by emergency water pollution (Art. 85, para. 3).

629. The Federal Minister shall issue a regulation on ways of determining of vulnerable areas and classification of land into risk categories (Art. 86, para. 4).

embankment, dams, barriers, objects to stabilize the bottom and banks, facilities for drainage of internal water, etc. (Article 89, paragraph 1).

445. The scope of protection from the harmful water effects and necessary measures is determined by the following plans: special plans for protection from flood and ice, plans for protection from erosion and floods and plans for protection from emergency water pollution (Article 90, paragraph 1). The Government of the Federation of Bosnia and Herzegovina, on the proposal of the Federal Minister shall adopt a regulation on the types and content of the Plans referred to in paragraph 1 of this article (Article 90, paragraph 3).

446. Remediation of harmful water effects is carried out based on a remediation programme (Article 94, paragraph 1). If the consequences of the harmful water effects are incurred on the water, coastal or on other land or on water infrastructure or on other water facility and device owned by the Federation, financial resources for their remediation are provided by the Federation (Article 94, paragraph 2).[630]

447. On the water resource and in coastal land are prohibited activities and interventions in the area which can:

(1) Threaten the stability of the water and coastal land.
(2) Reduce the level of protection from the harmful water effect.
(3) Prevent the normal water flow, sediment sand mud.
(4) Disable the survival and reproduction of water and water-related organisms (Article 95, paragraph 1).

448. On the floodplain, except to the prohibition from Article 12 of this law, are also forbidden all activities that can during floods have a harmful effect on water, water resource, coastal land and protective objects (Article 96, paragraph 1).

11. Information System on Waters and Water Cadastre

449. Pursuant to Article 98 the general objectives of establishing the Information System on Waters are the following:

(1) Rationalization, integration and optimization of the decision-making in the water sector through the process of using of information and communication technologies.
(2) Exchange and integration of information internally – within the water sector and externally – with external and international institutions (paragraph 1).

630. If the consequences of the harmful water effects are incurred on the water facility or device intended for special use of water and water resource which is not owned by the Federation, the remediation shall provide the owner or operator (Art. 94, para. 3).

450. Specific objectives of establishing of the Information System on Waters are the following:

(1) Improving of accuracy and reliability of information from water management systems.
(2) Reducing the time of availability of information to the water management systems.
(3) Establishing of a basis for continuous monitoring changes in the water management system.
(4) Using rationally and protecting the water resources.
(5) Increasing of the quality in making development decision.
(6) Increasing of intellectual capital.
(7) Promoting of a positive image on the water management based on professional and responsible work.

451. Water Cadastre consists of the following cadastres: (1) water; (2) water resource and water facilities; (3) regulation and protection from the harmful water effects; (4) water use; (5) water protection; and (6) other water documents (Article 100, paragraph 1).[631]

12. Water Acts

452. In order to ensure water management and to ensure equitable access of water to all legal entities and natural persons, it is prescribed in this law the manner of exercising the right to water by issuing Water Acts.[632] Water Acts, in terms of this law, are the following:

(1) Preliminary water consent.
(2) Water consent.
(3) Water permit (Article 107, paragraph 1).[633]

453. In preliminary water consent it shall be decided on the existence of the conditions for realizing right to water of the applicant, as well as on the way of realizing that right, and the conditions which documentation is needed for building of new, reconstruction or removal of existing buildings and other activities that are not considered as construction, and which can be permanently, occasionally or temporarily affected at change in the water regime (Article 111, paragraph 1).

631. All information on issued water acts and orders shall be recorded in the Water Book (Art. 101, para. 1).
632. The content of the Water Act is prescribed in Art. 108, para. 1.
633. Water acts are administrative acts and are issued in the form of Decision, if this Law does not prescribe otherwise (Art. 107, para. 2).

454. Environmental permit for plants and facilities for which is necessary to obtain an environmental permit, in accordance with the law on environmental protection, is issued on the basis of preliminary water consent for objects for which is by this law prescribed obligation to obtain the prior water consent (Article 112, paragraph 1).

455. It is determined in Water Consent that the documents attached to the application for issuing the water consent are in accordance to the prior water consent, water legislation and planning documents (Article 114, paragraph 1).[634]

456. Water permit is required for all facilities and activities for which this law prescribes issuing water consent, except for the extraction of material from the water courses from Article 63 and regulation of watercourses from Article 80 of this law (Article 115, paragraph 1). Water permit establishes the purpose, method and conditions of water usage, operating mode of the objects and facilities, way and conditions for wastewater discharge, manner and conditions for disposal of solid and liquid wastes and other conditions (Article 116, paragraph 1).

457. A Water Act may be permanently or temporarily revoked from a legal entity (Article 135, paragraph 1). The decision on a permanent or temporary revoking of a Water Act adopts the authority which issued the Water Act (Article 135, paragraph 2). According to this law, limitations of land owners and users are the following: Easements, The right to cross over land, Decision on temporary land occupation, Temporary use of land for the protection of water, Using of materials for flood protection, Restrictions on ownership rights and compensation, Drainage of precipitation and drainage of water, Transition and land use to monitor water (Articles 140–151).

13. The Water Agencies and Financing of the Water Management

458. This law establishes the agencies for water areas (hereinafter, 'the Water Agencies') for conducting of water management tasks which by this law and the regulations based on this law are placed under their jurisdiction (Article 152, paragraph 1).[635] Tasks of the Water Agencies are permanent and smooth conducting of water management activities to the extent set forth in Article 160, paragraphs 1 and 2, item 2 of this law and in accordance with the funds which shall be provided for this purpose on the base of this law (Article 155, paragraph 1).[636]

634. Consent for construction of new or rehabilitation of existing buildings, in terms of Regulation on the physical planning, issued on the base of the water consent for buildings for which is by this Law prescribed obligation for obtaining of water permit (Art. 114, para. 2).

635. Water Agencies referred to in para. 1 of this article are the following: 1. The Agency for water area of Sava River and 2. The Agency for water area of the Adriatic Sea (Art. 152, para. 2).

636. For performing activities of public interest the Water Agency has, in accordance with this Law, prescribed authorities within which brings administrative and other Laws, and decide on the issues relevant to water management (Art. 155, para. 2).

459. Funding for performing of activities and tasks set out in this law shall be provided from:

(1) General water fees.
(2) Special water fees.
(3) Revenues derived from the lease of public water resources.
(4) Budget of the Federation, cantonal budgets, as well as budgets of towns and municipalities.
(5) Credit funds.
(6) Funds provided by special Law.
(7) Donations and other funds in accordance with the Law (Article 168, paragraph 1).

14. Supervision

460. The Federal Ministry performs administrative supervision over implementation of this Law and the regulations adopted on the base of this law, as well as the administrative supervision on work of the Water Agency in performing activities delegated to the Water Agency by this law (Article 179, paragraph 1).

The Federal Ministry shall supervise the legality of the water acts adopted by the Water Agencies, as well as cantonal, town and municipal authorities responsible for water management in resolving administrative matters on the rights and obligations of natural persons and legal entities which are in this law prescribed as jurisdiction of the Water Agency, i.e., jurisdiction of cantonal, town and municipal administrative body responsible for water (Article 181, paragraph 1).

B. Other Relevant FBiH Water Regulations

461. The following secondary legislation adopted on the basis of the Water Law is in force:

(1) Rule book on Method of calculation, Procedures and Deadlines for calculation, Payments and Control of settlement of liabilities on the basis of General Water fees and Special Water fees (Official Gazette of FBiH No. 92/07, 46/09, 79/11 and 88/12).
(2) Rule book on Content, Form, Requirements and way of Issuing and Keeping of Water Acts (Official Gazette of FBiH No. 31/15).
(3) Regulation on the manner of granting the right to extract material from watercourses (Official Gazette FBiH No. 58/15).
(4) Federal Operational Flood Protection Plan (Official Gazette of FBiH No. 97/15).
(5) Rule book on Requirements and Criteria to be met by Legal Entities for the Development of Documentation Serving as the Basis for Issuing of Water Acts (Official Gazette of FBiH Nos. 17/08 and 38/12).

(6) Rule book on Content and way of Keeping the evidence and Submission of Data on the Quantities of Abstracted Water (Official Gazette of FBiH No. 83/08).
(7) Rule book on Procedures for determining of Water resource boundary and procedure for determining belonging of land plot to public water resource (Official Gazette of FBiH No. 26/09).
(8) Rule book on manner and conditions of limited right to use public water resource (Official Gazette of FBiH No. 26/09).
(9) Rule book on Requirements and Criteria to be Met by Authorized Legal Entity for Carrying out Professional and Technical Activities Falling under the Competence of the Water Agencies, including the Procedures for Issuing of Authorizations (Official Gazette of FBiH Nos. 75/09 and 43/10 and 66/13).
(10) Regulation on Types and Contents of Plans for the Protection against Harmful Effects of Water (Official Gazette of FBiH No. 26/09).
(11) Rule book on Procedures and Measures in case of Accidents on Waters and Coastal Water land (Official Gazette of FBiH No. 71/09).
(12) Rule book on Establishing the Eutrophication-susceptible and Nitrate-sensitive Areas (Official Gazette of FBiH No. 71/09).
(13) Rule book on Monitoring in the Areas Susceptible to Eutrophication and Sensitive to nitrates (Official Gazette of FBiH No. 71/09).
(14) Rule book on the Establishment and Management of Water Information System (Official Gazette of FBiH No. 77/09).
(15) Rule book on Requirements to be met by Reference or Authorized Laboratories for Water Testing, Content and way of giving authorizations (Official Gazette of FBiH Nos. 14/10 and 14/13 and 26/14).
(16) Decision on Establishing and Nominating the Members for the Advisory Council of the Adriatic Sea Basin District (Official Gazette of FBiH, No. 80/09).
(17) Decision on Establishing and Nominating the Members for the Advisory Council of the Sava River Basin District (Official Gazette of FBiH, No. 77/09).
(18) Decision on Borders of River Basins within the Territory of Federation BiH (Official Gazette of FBiH No. 41/07).
(19) Decision on Levels of Special Water Fees (Official Gazette of FBiH No. 46/07, and 10/14).
(20) Decision amending the Decision on Levels of Special Water Fees (Official Gazette of FBiH No. 10/14).
(21) Decision on Characterization of Surface and Ground Waters, Reference Requirements and Parameters for the Assessment of Water Status and Water Monitoring (Official Gazette of FBiH No. 1/14).
(22) Decision on Types and Levels of Operating Costs of Advisory Councils of water areas (Official Gazette of FBiH, No. 75/09).
(23) Rule book on Drinking Water Safety (Official Gazette of BiH Nos 40/10 and 30/12).
(24) Instruction on Issuing Water Acts for the Repair and Maintenance water-courses Works (Official Gazette of FBiH, No. 04/11).

(25) Rule book on Requirements and Criteria to be met by Specialized and Authorized Legal Entity to carry out Measures to Remove or Prevent Water Pollution in case of Sudden Water Pollution or Risk of Sudden Water Pollution, including the Methods of issuing authorizations (Official Gazette of FBiH, Nos 06/11 and 90/13).
(26) Regulation on Requirements for Wastewater Discharge into Natural Recipients and Public Sewerage Systems (Official Gazette of FBiH, No. 4/12).
(27) Rule book on Requirements for Determination of Sanitary Protection Zones and Protection Measures for Water Sources Used for Public Water Supply (Official Gazette of FBiH, No. 88/12).
(28) Rule book on method for Determining of Environmentally Acceptable Flow (Official Gazette of FBiH, No. 4/13).[637]

462. Pending the adoption of new secondary legislation, the following secondary legislation adopted on the basis of earlier laws is still in force: Rule book on Minimum Content of a General Document on Maintenance; Use and Monitoring of Water Management Facilities (Official Gazette of FBiH No. 18/07); Regulation on Classification of Waters and Coastal Sea Waters within the Borders of Former Socialist Republic of Bosnia and Herzegovina (Official Gazette of SR BiH No. 18/80); Regulation on Watercourse Categorization (Official Gazette of SR BiH No. 43/67).[638]

III. Brčko District of Bosnia and Herzegovina

A. The Law on Waters Protection

463. Basic legal act regulating water[639,640] protection in Brčko District of Bosnia and Herzegovina is the Law on Waters Protection (Official Gazette of BD BiH, Nos 25/04, 01/05 and 19/07). It has the following ten parts: Part I – General Provisions (Articles 1–6), Part II – Definitions (Article 7), Part III – Planning of Water Protections (Articles 8–17), Part IV – Protection of Waters and Water Ecosystems (Articles 18–22), Part V – Organisation of Water Protection (Articles 49–54), Part VI – Supervision (Articles 55–60), Part VII – Public Participation (Article 61), Part VIII – Financing (Article 62), Part IX – Penalty Provisions (Article 63), Part X – Transitional and Final Provisions (Articles 64–66).

637. *See*: https://fmpvs.gov.ba/vode-propisi/ (19 Jul. 2022).
638. For more information, *see*: FMET. *Program aproksimacije propisa Federacije Bosne i Hercegovine sa pravnom stečevinom EU u oblasti okoliša*, [Program of approximation of the Federation of Bosnia and Herzegovina Legislation with the EU environmental *acquis*] Sarajevo, December 2016, pp. 33–41.
639. A new Law on Waters is in the procedure of adoption in BD BiH. *See*: BD. *Strategija aproksimacije propisa pravnoj stečevini EU u oblasti zaštite životne sredine/okoliša Brčko distrikta BiH-* [Strategy for harmonisation of Brčko District BiH environmental legislation with EU *acquis*], EAS Brčko Distrikta, February 2017, p. 44.
640. *Water* means – all natural and artificial surface water and groundwater (Art. 7, para. 1).

464. According to Article 1, paragraph 1, this law regulates water protection from pollution[641] and from unreasonable use (Article 1, paragraph 1). Water protection includes maintenance and regulation of required amount of water, good condition, maintenance of the shore and the water land[642] and making decisions on achievement of rational-sustainable utilization (Article 1, paragraph 2).

465. Water protection ensures sustainable use of waters in order to preserve and improve their quality, preservation of natural processes and natural balance of water, plant and animal species and their habitats that depend on water (hereinafter, 'aquatic ecosystems'), and providing the necessary amount of water for various uses (Article 2, paragraph 1).

1. The Principles of Water Protection

466. According to Article 3 water protection is based on the following principles:

- Economic approach to water, implementation of policy that the user pays a realistic compensation for the use of water, and that the polluter compensates damage caused by water.
- Integrity of river basins, taking into account the dynamics of water and natural processes as well as harmony and interdependence of aquatic ecosystems within the river basin.
- The application of best available technologies and new scientific knowledge in ecology.
- Sustainable use of water, based on ensuring functioning of natural process and maintenance of the natural balance of aquatic ecosystems and the long-term protection and rational use of available water resources.
- The precautionary principle, according to which, where there are threats of serious and irreversible damages, lack of full scientific safety will not be used as a reason for postponing of measures to prevent environmental degradation.
- Preventing overburdening of water and improving of sustainable use of water (paragraph 1).

641. *Pollution* is a direct or indirect introduction of substances or heat into the air, water or land, as a result of human activities that can be harmful to human health or the quality of water and soil ecosystems which directly depend on aquatic ecosystems, resulting in damage of material property, or which disrupts or affects the enjoyment or other types of legal use of the environment (Art. 7, para. 1).

642. *Water land* means land which is permanently or periodically covered by inland waters. Such land therefore represents specific hydrological, geomorphological and biological conditions that define aquatic ecosystems and that reach the coast. Water land also means abandoned riverbeds and gravel areas that water occasionally inundates. Land of occasional lakes does not mean the water land (Art. 7, para. 1).

2. Planning and Implementation of Water Protection

467. Water protection of an unreasonable use and pollution, including shores and water land in protected and in endangered areas, is planned and is carried out in a way to ensure the preservation of natural processes, natural balance of aquatic ecosystems, protected natural resources and areas, as well as of landscape features of water in accordance with this law (Article 5, paragraph 1).

468. In order to ensure an integrated and coherent water protection, taking into account the hydrological features, uniqueness and coherence of the water regime[643] in the District, this law stipulates river basins, sub-basins and parts of sub-basins, as a territorial basis for planning and achieving water protection in the District (Article 8, paragraph 1). It shall be determined the river basins of the following rivers on the territory of the District: Sava, Brka and Tinja river basins which are divided into river sub-basins (Article 9, paragraph 1).

469. The Government adopts regulations on water protection strategy, as well as plans for protection of river basins, river sub-basins and parts of the river sub-basins (Article 11, paragraph 1). Content of a plan for protection of the river basin areas[644] is prescribed in Article 14, paragraph 1.

The Government determines limiting values for chemical, physicochemical and biological parameters of water for swimming, water intended for water supply and for mineral, thermal and thermo-mineral water (Article 22, paragraph 1).

470. The water protection policy shall be determined by Water Protection Strategy of the District (Article 12, paragraph 1).[645] The Water Protection Strategy of the District is adopted by the Assembly of the Brčko District of Bosnia and Herzegovina on Mayor's proposal previously approved by the Government for a period of at least ten years (Article 13, paragraph 1).

471. Protection of water and aquatic ecosystems includes the classification of surface and groundwater, prohibitions and restrictions related to the water load, specific prohibitions and restrictions in protected areas, control and data collection for water protection and other measures prescribed by this Law (Article 18, paragraph 1).[646]

643. *Water regime* means a group of natural or artificial hydrological, chemical and biological characteristics related to surface and groundwater in a specific area during a certain period of time (Art. 7, para. 1).

644. *River basin area* means an area of land consisting of one or more neighbouring river basins together with their groundwater and coastal waters (Art. 7, para. 1).

645. The content of the Water Protection Strategy is prescribed in Art. 12, para. 2.

646. The objectives of water quality protection are: ensuring of good status of water and of the environment, protection of human health and consumers' interests (Art. 19, para. 1).

3. General Measures for Water Protection

472. Wastewater discharge and emissions of heat in surface water and absorption of heat from surface water can be done only in the manner and under conditions determined in this law (Article 23, paragraph 1). It is prohibited to direct discharge of wastewater into groundwater (Article 23, paragraph 2).

It is forbidden to wash vehicles and other machinery and equipment in surface waters, on the shores or on the water land (Article 26, paragraph 1). It is forbidden to discharge, laying and disposal in water of substances or objects, which due to their shape, physical, chemical or biological properties or other characteristics, may endanger the life or health of humans and aquatic ecosystems, to hinder flow of water or to threaten water facilities and equipment (Article 27, paragraph 1).

473. Fertilization or use of plant protection products on the coastal land is prohibited in land width of 10 meters from the coast border of the inland waters (Article 24, paragraph 1).

474. Transport of cargos by vessels which are fuelled by oil is prohibited in inland waters, except in emergency cases of water protection, rescue of people, animals and property, conducting of policing tasks in cases of military defence (Article 25, paragraph 1).[647]

475. Construction of plants or equipment on the water land, intended for the production process containing hazardous substances, plant or equipment for handling of hazardous substances or for their storage, as well as systems or equipment for waste disposal, is forbidden (Article 28, paragraph 1).

476. A person who causes or is a witness of discharges, disposal or deposit of hazardous or harmful substances[648] in the water or on the coastal land or water land, or on land that is located in a protected area, as well as in case of imminent danger of these activities, is obliged to immediately inform the competent organization of river basin about the event or about immediate danger. In accordance with the regulations on the protection of natural or other disasters, the relevant river basin organization must ensure that harmful effects on the environment are reduced to the minimum (Article 29, paragraph 1).

4. Special Measures for Water Protection

477. Relevant organizations of river basin determine protected areas in order to protect watercourses or parts of watercourses, through which groundwater flows

647. It is forbidden to discharge wastewater directly from vessels other than unpolluted cooling water (Art. 25, para. 3).

648. *Hazardous substances* means substances or groups of substances that are toxic, persistent and liable to bioaccumulation, and other substances or groups of substances that cause the same level of concern (Art. 7, para. 1).

towards the river basin to be used for public drinking water supply, bottling of natural water for drinking, or for the use of mineral, thermal or thermo-mineral water for drinking production, protection against pollution or other types of loading of water, which could affect the health suitability of water and its amount, and to protect the area above the flow of water from which surface water drains or flows into the water stream (Article 34, paragraph 1).[649]

478. In case of discovery of water source that is essential for drinking water supply, or a source of mineral, thermal or thermo-mineral water or other groundwater for the production of beverages, Government at the proposal of the relevant river basin organization may make decision on temporarily protection of the area where the source is located (Article 35, paragraph 1).[650]

479. In protected water area may be restricted or prohibited activities that may endanger the quantitative and qualitative status of water sources. Obligations to carry out or to allow the implementation of measures to protect the quantity and quality of water sources can be determined to the owners or other land holders in protected water area (Article 36, paragraph 1).

Protected areas and baths must be marked (Article 40, paragraph 1). In order to improve the disturbed natural balance of aquatic ecosystems of surface water, the competent organization performs its renaturation, in accordance with the plans of the river basin and river sub-basins (paragraph 2).

5. Water Protection Consent, Information System and Financing of Water Protection

480. Water protection consent[651] is issued by the competent Government Department for the areas of the river basin. Water protection consent is issued:

- If the use of water is possible on the basis of the water protection plan of the river basin.
- If water use does not degrade, restrict or obstruct realization of the right on water to other users (Article 46, paragraph 1).[652]

481. The competent organization of river basin is obliged to create and maintain an information system for water protection in its territory (Article 48, paragraph 1).

649. In order to establish different levels of protection, protected water area can be classified in protected water belts (Art. 34, para. 2).
650. In addition to the protected areas referred to in Arts 34 and 35 of this Law, the competent organization of river basins can determine protected areas of reserves of surface water (Art. 37, para. 1).
651. The content of the Water protection Consent is prescribed in Art. 47, para. 1.
652. Waterproof consent cannot be issued for existing plants and devices that discharge wastewater or hazardous and harmful substances in the water, the atmosphere or in land (Art. 46, para. 2).

482. Financing of activities prescribed by this law is ensured from the Fund for Environmental Protection of the District budget, in accordance with the Fund for Environmental Protection (Article 62).

6. Supervision of Water Protection and the Public Participation

483. Administrative supervision over implementation of provisions of this law and of regulations adopted on the basis of it, is conducted by the competent Government department (Article 55).[653] The inspection supervision of the implementation of this law and regulations adopted on the basis of it performs Inspector for Environmental Protection of Brčko District (hereinafter, 'Inspector') (Article 56).

484. The provisions of the Law on Environmental Protection and the provisions of this law are applied with public participation and access to information in the process of water protection according to this law (Article 61, paragraph 1).[654]

§5. HARMONIZATION WITH EU LEGISLATION

485. BiH 'lacks a consistent and harmonised countrywide strategy and sustainable investment plan on water management and urban waste water management. Specific plans for implementing EU legislation on drinking water, urban waste water and flood risk management are still to be adopted. A roof report on river basin management plans remains to be adopted.'[655] An action plan for flood protection and river management in Bosnia and Herzegovina for 2014–2017 is being implemented. Flood hazards and risks are being mapped for the entire country.[656]

---

653. The competent organization of the river basin area manages with protection of waters of the river basin in the manner and under conditions determined by this Law (Art. 49).
654. Relevant organization of river basin supports public monitoring *inter alia* through the providing of regular training, equipment and professional support for those who carry out this type of public participation (Art. 61, para. 2).
655. EC, *Bosnia and Herzegovina 2021 Progress Report,* p. 103.
656. Ibid.

Chapter 4. Waste

§1. Waste Pollution

486. 'The predominant method for waste disposal in Bosnia and Herzegovina is land filling. According to the Agency for Statistics of Bosnia and Herzegovina, between 2011 and 2015, the rate of waste permanently disposed of in landfills varied between 67 per cent and 79 per cent. The recovery rate was increasing during this period, but it did not reach 1 per cent by 2015.'[657]

§2. Waste Monitoring

487. Waste monitoring and management, performed by the Agency for Statistics of BiH, the FBiH Office of Statistics, the Republic of Srpska Institute of Statistics, are based on the statistical form completed by public utility companies. The data are predominantly estimates since waste monitoring is not performed frequently and waste quantification is usually done by visual assessment and not by measurement. As a result, the total volume of generated and disposed waste as reported is questionable.[658]

§3. Competencies

488. The responsibility for waste management policy and legislation is shared between entity ministries responsible for the environment and corresponding cantonal ministries in the Federation of Bosnia and Herzegovina.

489. At entity level, the RS Ministry of Spatial Planning, Civil Engineering and Ecology is in charge of waste management issues. In FBiH the Ministry of Environment and Tourism is in charge.[659] Municipalities are responsible for the development of waste management plans and the organization of waste collection through the establishment of municipal enterprises, which can be public, private or private-public, which collect and dispose of waste. There is also an Inter-Entity

657. UNECE. *3rd Environmental Performance Review, Bosnia and Herzegovina.* New York, Geneva: United Nations, 2018, p. xxvii. For more details, *see*: *Ibid.*, pp. 169–186.

658. BiH MFTER, *State of the environment Report of the Bosnia and Herzegovina 2012*, *supra* p. 214. 'Data collection on municipal solid waste in Bosnia and Herzegovina has improved since 2011 and datasets from 2011 onwards are available for several aspects of municipal solid waste generation and collection at the national level.' UNECE. *3rd Environmental Performance Review, Bosnia and Herzegovina, supra* p. 169.

659. In FBiH all responsibility for waste issues was transferred to the cantonal level, in line with Art. 11 of the Law on Waste Management. The respective cantonal ministries responsible for physical planning and the environment are also responsible for the development of cantonal waste management strategies, laws and regulations, issuing permits to business entities for handling waste (up to a certain size), and monitoring.

Environmental Steering Committee that was established in 1998, consisting of government officials, professionals and academics, to coordinate environmental policy on harmonizing waste laws and joint project implementation between the entities.[660]

§4. LEGISLATION

490. Both FBiH and RS have a Law on Waste Management and the two laws are 'harmonized'.[661] Brčko District has Law on Waste Management, too. These are framework laws and include general provisions for the overall concept of waste management, while specific issues are dealt with in bylaws.

I. The Republic of Srpska

A. The Law on Waste Management

491. Basic legal act regulating waste[662] management[663] in the Republic of Srpska is the Law on Waste Management (Official Gazette of the RS, No. 111/13, 106/15 and 16/18). It has the following fourteen parts: Part I – General Provisions (Articles 1–12), Part II – Types and Classification of Waste (Articles 13–14), Part III – Waste Management Planning (Articles 15–22), Part IV – Subjects of Waste Management (Articles 23–29), Part V – Activities and Responsibilities of Waste Management (Articles 30–36), Part VI – Organisation of Waste Management (Articles 37–51), Part VII – Management of Special Waste Streams (Articles 52–63), Part VIII – Permits for Waste Management (Articles 64–74), Part IX – Transboundary Waste Movement (Articles 75–78), Part X – Reporting on Waste and Data Base (Articles 79–81), Part XI – Financing of Waste Management (Articles 82–87), Part XII – Supervision (Articles 88–91), Part XIII – Penalty Provisions (Articles 92–95), Part XIV – Transitional and Final Provisions (Articles 96–105).

492. Purpose of this Law is to provide and ensure conditions for: (a) waste management in a way that does not endanger human health and the environment; (b) prevention of waste generation, in particular development of cleaner technologies and rational use of natural resources, and elimination of danger of its harmful effects on human health and the environment; (c) re-utilization and recycling of waste, separation of secondary raw materials from waste and use of waste as energy

660. UNECE, *2nd Environmental Performance Review, supra* p. 111.

661. *Ibid.*, p. 110.

662. *Waste-means* any substance or item contained in the List of waste categories (Q-list) that the owner throw away, intends or must to throw away, in accordance to the Law (Art. 6, para. 1, point s).

663. *Waste management* is an activity of general interest, which implies implementation of prescribed waste management measures consisting of collection, transport, storage, treatment and disposal of waste, including supervision of those activities and care of waste management facilities after closure (Art. 2).

source; (d) development of methods and procedures for waste disposal, (e) rehabilitation of unregulated landfills, (f) monitoring condition of existing and newly formed waste landfills and (g) Developing of waste management awareness (Article 3).[664]

493. Waste management is carried out in a way to minimize the risk of endangering human health and environmental, by controlling and mitigation of following measures: (a) pollution of water, air and soil, (b) threats to the flora and fauna, (c) risk of accident, explosion or fire, (d) negative impacts on landscapes and natural resources of special values and (e) levels of noise and unpleasant smells (Article 4).

1. The Waste Management Hierarchy

494. The waste management hierarchy represents the order of the priority in waste management practice, which is: (a) prevention of waste generation and reduction, i.e., reduction in the use of resources and reduction of quantities and/or hazardous characteristics of generated waste, (b) reuse or reuse of products for the same or other purpose, (c) recycling or treatment of waste for the purpose of obtaining a raw material for the production of the same or other product, (d) utilization or use of waste values (composting, burning with the use of energy and others) and (e) Disposal of waste by land filling or incineration without the use of energy, if there is no other appropriate solution (Article 10).

2. Basic Principles

495. According to Article 7 the principles of waste management are the following: (a) the principle of choosing the most suitable option for the environment, (b) the principle of proximity and common approach to the waste management, (c) the principle of waste management hierarchy, (d) the responsibility principle and (e) the 'polluter pays' principle.[665]

---

664. Provisions of this Law shall not apply to: (a) Radioactive waste; (b) Gases emitted in the atmosphere; (c) Wastewater, except liquid waste; (d) Sludge from sewage systems and waste from septic tanks, except sludge from facilities for sludge treatment; (e) Waste of animal origin (includes carcasses of animal origin and their parts, components of animal bodies which are not designed or safe for human consumption and offal); (f) Waste from mining generated by exploration, mining, processing and storage of mineral resources, as well as waste from mines the quarry; (g) Waste resulting from the search, excavation, transportation and final treatment or destruction of mines-explosives devices and other numerous means and explosives; (h) Straw and other non-hazardous agricultural or forest material found in nature and used in agriculture, forestry or for production of energy from such biomass by processes or methods that do not have a detrimental effect on the environment and do not endanger human health (Art. 5).

665. For more details *see* Arts 8–12.

3. Types and Classification of Waste

496. Types of waste within the meaning of this Law are: (a) municipal waste (household waste); (b) commercial waste and (c) industrial waste. The waste, depending on the hazardous characteristics that affect human health and the environment, can be: (a) inert, (b) non dangerous and (c) dangerous (Article 13, paragraphs 1 and 2).

497. Waste is classified according to the waste catalogue (Article 14, paragraph 1).[666] Hazardous waste is classified according to the origin, characteristics and composition that makes it hazardous (Article 14, paragraph 3).

The owner of the waste or the responsible person, shall classify the waste in the prescribed manner, in accordance to this Law (Article 14, paragraph 4). In order to determine the composition and hazardous characteristics of waste, the owner of the waste or the responsible person, shall be obliged to carry out examination of hazardous waste, as well as to determine waste which according to its origin, composition and characteristics may be hazardous waste (Article 14, paragraph 5).[667]

4. Planning of Waste Management

498. In order to plan waste management in the Republic of Srpska, the following planning documents are drawn up: (a) Waste management strategy (hereinafter, 'Strategy'), (b) The Republic Waste Management Plan (hereinafter, 'the Republic Plan'), (c) joint waste management plan, (d) local waste management plan and (e) waste management plan at a facility having an environmental permit issued (Article 15, paragraph 1).

499. The Strategy is basic document that evaluates the state of waste management, determines the long-term goals of waste management and provides conditions for rational and sustainable waste management. The Strategy shall be prepared by the Ministry in cooperation with the competent Ministries and department responsible for environmental protection in the local self-government unit. The Strategy shall be adopted by the National Assembly of Republika Srpska upon proposal of the Government of Republika Srpska (hereinafter, 'the Government') for a period of ten years (Article 16, paragraphs 1–3).[668]

---

666. The waste catalogue is a summary list of non-hazardous and hazardous waste according to the place of origin, origin and according to the prescribed method of treatment (Art. 14, para. 2).
667. The Minister in charge for environmental affairs (hereinafter, 'the Minister') shall adopt the regulations prescribing: (a) waste catalogue, (b) list of waste categories (Q-list), (c) list of hazardous waste categories according to the origin and composition (Y-list), (d) List of hazardous waste characteristics (H-list), (e) list of waste components for which waste is considered hazardous (C-list), (f) the concentration of limit values of hazardous components in waste, (g) list of procedures and method of disposal and re-utilization of waste (D-list and R-list), (h) type, content and form of the waste test report, (i) types of parameters for waste testing needed for thermal treatment, (j) method and procedure for waste classification (Art. 14, para. 6).
668. Content of the Strategy is prescribed in Art. 17.

500. The Republic Plan is a document that determines and directs management waste based on the analysis of the current state and goals of waste management established by the Strategy (Article 18, paragraph 1).[669] The Republic Plan shall be prepared by the Ministry in cooperation with local self-government units (Article 18, paragraph 3). The Republic Plan shall be adopted by the Government for a period of ten years and revised, if necessary (Article 18, paragraph 4). Report on the implementation of the Republic Plan is prepared by the Ministry and submit to the Government for adoption every three years (Article 18, paragraph 6).

501. The Assembly of two or more local self-government units with at least 200,000 inhabitants shall, upon obtaining the approval of the Ministry, jointly manage the Waste Management Plan, defining the common goals for waste management in accordance with the Strategy (Article 19, paragraph 1). A joint Waste Management Plan may also be adopted by two or more local self-government units with less than 200,000 inhabitants, according to a pre-feasibility study for the adoption of a joint plan. The Ministry gives its consent on feasibility study (Article 19, paragraph 2). Waste management in the area of two or more local self-government units shall be carried out in accordance to joint and Local Waste Management Plan (Article 19, paragraph 4). The Assembly of the local self-government unit shall adopt a Local Waste Management Plan defining the objectives of waste management in its area in accordance with the Strategy, as well as the measures and bearers of the activities for achieving the goals, upon the previously obtained approval from the Ministry (Article 20, paragraph 1). Waste management plans[670] shall be adopted for a period of five years (Article 21, paragraph 1).

502. For all facilities for which an environmental permit is issued, waste management plan shall be prepared and adopted (Article 22, paragraph 1). The waste management plan, together with other evidence, shall be attached to the application for the issuance of an environmental permit, in accordance with the regulation that regulates the environmental protection. The waste management plan shall be updated every five years (Article 22, paragraphs 3–4).

5. Subjects of Waste Management

503. The entities responsible for waste management are: (a) The Government, (b) The Ministry, (c) Fund for Environmental Protection and Energy Efficiency of Republika Srpska, (d) local self-government units and (e) expert organizations for waste testing (Article 23, paragraph 1).

504. The Government, through the competent authorities and organizations, provides waste management for the territory of the Republic (Article 24, paragraph 1). The Ministry is competent to: (a) prepares the Strategy in cooperation with the competent authorities, (b) propose to the Government Republic Plan, (c) monitor the

669. Content of the Plan is prescribed in Art. 18, para. 2.
670. The plans must be in compliance with the Republic plans (Art. 21, para. 3).

situation, coordinate and perform waste management matters of importance to the Republic, (d) approve joint and local waste management plans, (e) issue licenses, approvals and other acts prescribed by this Law; (f) determine the authorized organizations in accordance with this Law (Article 24, paragraph 2).

505. The Fund for Environmental Protection and Energy Efficiency of Republika Srpska (hereinafter, 'the Fund') performs tasks related to: (a) collection of fees for management of special waste streams, (b) waste collection and treatment services and coordination of waste management system participants; (c) maintenance and updating of waste management database, (d) information on waste quantities, (e) reporting on waste management, (f) financing of preparation, implementation and development of programmes, projects and similar activities in the field of conservation, sustainable use, protection and improvement of the environment, and in the field of energy efficiency and use of renewable energy sources in accordance with the special regulation and (g) other tasks determined by a special regulation (Article 25, paragraph 1).

506. Local self-government unit: (a) adopt a local waste management plan and a common waste management plan, (b) regulate, provide, organize and implement municipal waste management on its territory (c) regulate procedure for collection of services in the field of municipal waste management (Article 26, paragraph 1).[671] Two or more local self-government units jointly provide and conduct waste management, under the conditions and in the manner defined by the Law, Strategy and agreement of local self-government units (Article 27, paragraph 1).

6. Activities and Responsibilities of Waste Management

507. Producer or importer whose product becomes hazardous waste after use shall be obliged to take over such waste after use, without compensation of costs and shall treat it in accordance with this Law and other regulations (Article 30, paragraph 2).

508. The waste producer shall: (a) prepare a waste management plan referred to in Article 22 of this Law, (b) Provide a report on waste testing, (c) Ensure application of waste management hierarchy principles, (d) collect waste separately in accordance with the need for future treatment, (e) store waste in a way that minimizes human health and the environment, (f) keep records of the waste that is generated, collected or disposed, (g) determine the person responsible for waste management (Article 31, paragraph 1).

---

671. The local self-government unit, by its act, determines the authorities and services in charge for performing these tasks (Art. 26, para. 2).

509. The owner of the waste is responsible for all waste management costs (Article 32, paragraph 1).[672]

7. Organising of Waste Management

510. Waste management shall be organized in a way that does not pose a danger to human health and the environment in accordance with the Law (Article 37, paragraph 1). The Minister may impose additional measures on the management of certain types of waste, if: (a) treatment of waste endangers or may endanger human health and the environment; and (b) in case of additional requirements for implementation provisions of international treaties that are binding on Bosnia and Herzegovina and the Republic (Article 37, paragraph 2).[673]

511. Storage, treatment or disposal of waste may be carried out by a company, enterprise or other legal entity or entrepreneur performing storage, treatment or disposal of waste in accordance with this Law (Article 38, paragraph 1).

512. In waste management plants, waste can only be stored, treated or disposed of in accordance with the issued permits (Article 38, paragraph 5). Waste treatment shall be carried out using the best available techniques and technologies in accordance with this Law. Waste treatment facilities and equipment may be stationary or mobile. The treatment of waste in a stationary or mobile facilities shall be carried out in accordance with a permit for treatment issued pursuant to this Law (Article 42, paragraphs 1–3).

513. Disposal of waste to the landfill shall be done if there is no other appropriate solution, in accordance with the principle of waste management hierarchy (Article 47, paragraph 1). Waste shall be disposed of at a landfill having technical, technological and other conditions and requirements, in accordance with the permit issued pursuant to this Law (paragraph 2). Before disposal waste shall be treated in accordance with the provisions of this Law and other regulations (paragraph 4). Waste landfills are divided into three classes, depending on the type of waste disposed on them, which are: (a) landfills for inert waste, (b) landfills for non-hazardous waste and (c) landfill for hazardous waste (paragraph 5).[674]

514. Municipal waste shall be collected, treated and disposed of in accordance with this Law and special regulations governing utility activities (Article 48, paragraph 1)

---

672. Waste transport can only be carried out between physical persons and legal entities that keep documentation in accordance with this Law (Art. 32, para. 2).
673. If the legal entity or natural person treats waste contrary to this Law and consequently threat or risk to human health and the environment, the Republic shall take urgent measures to protect human health and the environment, surface and ground water, air, soil, plants and animals (Art. 37, para. 4).
674. Joint disposal of hazardous waste with other types of waste at the same location is not permitted, except in the cases stipulated by the regulation referred to in Art. 47, para. 7 (Art. 47, para. 6).

515. The treatment of hazardous waste shall have priority in relation to the treatment of other waste and shall be carried out only in facilities that have a permit for the treatment of hazardous waste in accordance with this Law. When collecting, sorting, storing, transporting, reusing and disposing, hazardous waste is packaged and labelled in a manner that ensures safety for human health and the environment (Article 49 paragraphs 1–2).

516. The mixing of different categories of hazardous waste or mixing of hazardous waste with non-hazardous waste is prohibited, except in the procedure of hazardous waste treatment. It is forbidden to dispose of hazardous waste without prior treatment, which significantly reduces hazardous waste characteristics (Article 49 paragraphs 4–5).[675]

517. Transport of hazardous waste follows a separate document on the transport of hazardous waste, which is completed by producer, owner and everyone who takes over hazardous waste (Article 51, paragraph 1). The Minister shall issue a rulebook that prescribes form of document on the movement of hazardous waste and the instruction for its filling (Article 51, paragraph 9).

8. Management of Special Waste Streams

518. The circulation of batteries and accumulators containing more than 0.0005% of the weight of the mercury shall be prohibited unless otherwise provided by this Law (Article 52, paragraph 1).

519. Waste oils, for the purposes of this law, are all mineral or synthetic oils or lubricants that are unusable for originally intended purpose (Article 53, paragraph 1). It is prohibited: (a) discharge or spillage of waste oils into the soil or land, surface and ground water and into the sewage system, (b) disposal of waste oils and uncontrolled release of residues from processing of waste oils, (c) mixing of waste oils during collection and storage with PCBs, (d) any type of waste oil treatment that pollutes air at concentrations above the prescribed limit values (Article 53, paragraph 2).

520. The person who collects, stores and treats waste oils must have the permit, keep records of waste oils and the amount collected, stored or treated and the final disposal of residues after treatment and shall submit data to the Fund (Article 53, paragraph 5). Waste edible oil produced by catering and tourism activities, in industry, trade and other similar activities in which more than 50 meals are prepared daily is collected for processing and obtaining biofuels (Article 53, paragraph 6).[676]

675. The Minister shall issue a regulation prescribing the manner of storage, packaging and labelling of hazardous waste (Art. 49 para. 7).

676. The Minister shall issue a Regulation prescribing the conditions, manner and procedure for waste oils management (Art. 53, para. 8).

521. Waste tires, within the meaning of this Law, are tires of motor vehicles (cars, buses, trucks, motorcycles, etc.), agricultural and construction machinery, trailers, towing machines, etc. after the expiry date of their use (Article 54, paragraph 1). A person engaged in the collection, transport, treatment or disposal of waste tires must have a permit (Article 54, paragraph 2).[677]

522. The waste from electrical and electronic products cannot be mixed with other types of waste. The disposal of waste from electrical and electronic products is prohibited without prior treatment (Article 55, paragraphs 1–2). Producer or importer of electrical or electronic products shall identify the recyclable components of these products (Article 55, paragraph 5). A person who collects, treats or disposes of waste from electrical and electronic products must have a license, keep a record of the quantity and type of electrical or electronic products taken over, and submit the data to the Fund (Article 55, paragraph 8).[678]

523. Waste fluorescent tubes containing mercury shall be collected separately. It is forbidden to dispose of waste fluorescent tubes containing mercury without prior treatment (Article 56, paragraphs 1–2).[679]

524. Waste containing PCBs is collected separately (Article 57, paragraph 1). The owner of PCB and PCB waste shall be obliged to secure their disposal or decontamination (Article 57, paragraph 3). All PCB-containing devices and premises or installations in which they are located, as well as decontaminated devices must be labelled. A person who collects, treats, decontaminates or disposes of PCB waste must have a permit (Article 57, paragraphs 7–8).[680]

525. POPs waste, for the purposes of this law, is waste consisting of, contained or contaminated with long lasting organic pollutants (POPs substances) (Article 58, paragraph 1). The owner of POPs waste shall be obliged to report to the Ministry the type and quantity of POPs waste.[681]

526. The asbestos-containing waste shall be separately collected, packaged, stored and disposed at the landfill in a clearly marked place intended for the disposal of asbestos-containing waste (Article 59, paragraph 1). The owner of the

677. The Minister shall issue a Regulation prescribing the manner and procedure for the management of waste tires (Art. 54, para. 3).
678. The Minister shall issue a regulation prescribing a list of electrical and electronic products, prohibiting measures and restrictions on the use of electrical and electronic equipment containing hazardous substances, the manner and procedure for waste management from electrical and electronic products (Art. 55, para. 10).
679. The Minister shall issue a regulation prescribing the method and procedure for management of waste fluorescent tubes containing mercury (Art. 56, para. 5).
680. The Fund keeps a register of devices in use that contain PCBs (Art. 57, para. 9).
681. The Minister shall issue a rulebook which shall prescribe the list of POPs substances, the manner and procedure for the management of POPs waste and the concentration limit of POPs substances related to the disposal of waste containing or contaminated with POPs substances (Art. 58, paras 3–4).

asbestos-containing waste shall be obliged to keep a record of the quantities of waste that is stored or disposed of and shall submit the data to the Fund.[682]

527. Waste and/or useless vehicles are motor vehicles or parts of vehicles that are waste and which the owner wants to dispose or their owner is unknown (Article 60, paragraph 1). The owner of the waste vehicle (if known) shall be obliged to provide taking over of the vehicle to a person having a permit for collection or treatment (Article 60, paragraph 4).[683]

528. Medical waste from facilities in which health care is performed must be classified at the site of origin to hazardous and non-hazardous waste. Persons managing those facilities shall be obliged to develop a medical waste management plan and appoint a responsible person for the management of medical waste who shall be obliged to keep records of the quantities of medical waste and shall submit the data to the Fund. The Minister, in cooperation with the Minister in charge of health, shall issue a rulebook that prescribes the manner and procedure for the management of medical waste (Article 61, paragraphs 1–4).

529. Titanium dioxide wastes are all types of waste generated during the production of titanium dioxide, which the producer disposes or is obligated to dispose in accordance with this Law, as well as the residue resulting from the treatment of this type of waste. Titanium dioxide waste disposal operations may not be carried out without the permit of the Ministry. The producer and owner of the waste shall be obliged to have a permit, to keep records of the quantities of this type of waste that has been collected, stored, treated or delayed and shall submit the data to the Fund (Article 62, paragraphs 1–3).[684]

530. Packaging waste, for the purposes of this Law, means manufactured and imported packaging or packaging in which the product is packaged which becomes packaging waste after use (Article 63, paragraph 2). The producer, importer, packer or wholesaler shall ensure the proper management of packaging and packaging waste through an operator in accordance with this Law and the regulations adopted

682. The Minister shall issue a regulation prescribing the manner of packaging, criteria, conditions and manner of final disposal of waste containing asbestos and other measures to prevent the spread of asbestos fibres and dust in the environment (Art. 59, paras 3–4).
683. The Minister shall issue a regulation prescribing the manner and procedure for management of waste vehicles (Art. 60, par. 8).
684. The Minister shall issue a regulation prescribing the manner and procedure for waste management from titanium dioxide, as well as environmental monitoring measures at the site (Art. 62, para. 5).

pursuant to this Law (Article 63, paragraph 3). For manufactured or imported packaging that becomes waste packaging after use, which is not disposed of in accordance with paragraph 2 of this Article, the charge for loading the environment with packaging waste shall be paid (hereinafter, 'compensation') (Article 63, paragraph 4).[685]

9. Permits for Waste Management

531. Permits for obtaining one or more activities in the field of waste management shall be obtained, and they can be: (a) a permit for waste collection, (b) a permit for waste transport, (c) a permit for waste storage, (d) a permit for waste treatment and (e) a permit for waste disposal (Article 64, paragraph 1).

532. One permit may be issued for performing several activities of one responsible person and shall be issued by the Ministry.[686] The permit for the collection and transport of hazardous waste shall be issued in accordance with Article 74 of this Law and other regulations (Article 64, paragraphs 2–3).

533. Permit shall not be issued for: (a) movement of waste within the location of the waste producer, (b) containers for household waste in public places (c) the waste movement between different plants or locations of the same producer, with the exception of hazardous waste, (d) the transport of waste by the manufacturer himself with his own means of transport to the site or waste management facility for which he has a permit, and if quantities of waste do not exceed 1000 kilograms per consignment, excluding hazardous waste, (e) returning packaging or used products to traders and (f) natural persons, or individual waste collectors, collecting non-hazardous waste in the territory of the local self-government unit (Article 65, paragraph 1).

534. Application for the issuance of a permit for collection, transport, storage, treatment and disposal of waste shall be submitted to the Ministry (Article 67, paragraph 1). Permit determines conditions for performing of activity of responsible person in the facility for storage, treatment and disposal of waste (Article 68, paragraph 1).

535. The permit for a mobile waste treatment facility shall include obligation of the responsible person to inform the Ministry of any change of location and submit the location approval. The Minister shall issue a regulation prescribing the content and appearance of the license (Article 68, paragraphs 4–5).

---

685. Conditions for the design, production and use of packaging, management packaging and packaging waste, special conditions for the issuance of a license for operators, as well as forms of report on management of packaging and packaging waste, are regulated by a special regulation of the Government (Art. 63z).

686. The permit referred to in paras 1 and 2 of Art. 64 shall be issued for the performance of activities in the field of waste management (Art. 64, para. 5).

536. The permit decision for collection, transport, storage and treatment of waste shall be issued for a period of five years and for the disposal of waste for a period of ten years. After the expiration of that deadline, a request for renewal or revision of the permit conditions in accordance with this Law shall be submitted. The application for renewal of the permit shall be submitted four months before the validity of the permit expiration, in order to ensure the continuity validity of the permit (Article 70, paragraphs 1–3).

537. The permit shall cease to be valid if: (a) expiration of the deadline for issuing it, (b) during inspection supervision it is determined that the responsible person does not fulfil the conditions prescribed by the permit and does not act within the deadline after measures ordered by the inspector, (c) a bankruptcy procedure has been initiated and the activities are not continued by other entity, (d) the responsible person does not submit the evidence prescribed in Article 70, paragraph 5 of this Law (Article 71, paragraph 1).[687]

538. The Ministry shall inform public about issued permit through the Ministry's website (Article 73, paragraph 1).

539. The permit for the collection and transport of waste shall be issued to a person registered for the performance of the collection activity, that is, the person who has the capacity of the carrier in accordance with the Laws regulating the transport in public transport or the domestic carrier, in accordance with the Laws regulating international public transport, except in the cases defined in Article 65 of this Law (Article 74, paragraph 1). The permit shall determine the mandatory measures for the collection, transport of inert, non-hazardous and hazardous waste in accordance with the provisions of this Law and other regulations. The permit shall be issued for a period of five years and may be renewed. If the legal entity or natural person fails to comply with the conditions prescribed by the permit, the Ministry shall issue a decision on termination of the permit in accordance with Article 71 of this Law (Article 74, paragraphs 1–5).

10. Transboundary Waste Movement

540. The transboundary waste movement shall be carried out in accordance with this Law and other regulations. The transboundary waste movement shall be accompanied by documentation on the movement from the place where the movement started to the final destination in accordance with this Law and bylaws adopted on the basis thereof, as well as international regulations relating to cross-border traffic. If the Republic of Srpska does not have technical facilities and facilities for waste treatment or disposal in an environmentally acceptable and efficient manner, such waste will be exported (Article 75, paragraphs 1–3).

---

687. The Decision on termination validity of the permit shall determine measures and activities that need to be implemented after termination of the work of responsible person, in order to avoid the risk to the environment, human health and material goods (Art. 71, para. 2).

541. Non-hazardous waste may be imported for the purpose of treatment provided that there is a facility for treatment of such waste. Import of waste for the purpose of disposal and exploitation for energy purposes in accordance with this Law shall be prohibited. Import of hazardous waste is prohibited, but certain types of hazardous waste required as secondary raw materials to the processing industry in the Republic, in accordance with the objectives of processing these waste, may be imported on the basis of a permit issued by the Ministry (Article 75, paragraphs 4–7).

542. Transboundary waste movement is carried out provided the waste is packaged, marked and transported in a way to ensure conditions for the least risk to human health and the environment (Article 75, paragraph 9).[688]

543. Application for issuance of permit for import, export and transit of waste shall be submitted to the Ministry in accordance with the Law (Article 76, paragraph 1). The permit for import, export and transit of waste to which the cross-border movement is subject to the control procedure prescribed by ratified international agreement shall be issued within 60 days from the date of receipt of the request referred to in paragraph 1 of Article 76. The import, export and transit of waste that is carried out in several consignments shall be valid for up to one year (Article 76, paragraphs 5–6).

544. In case of hazardous waste movement due to the delay between the Republic, the Federation of Bosnia and Herzegovina and the Brčko District of BiH, a notification shall be required from the Ministry responsible for environmental protection of the entity or Brčko District of BiH from which the waste is transported to the Ministry responsible for environmental protection of the entities or Brčko District of BiH in which the disposal of hazardous waste is carried out (Article 78, paragraph 1).

11. Reporting on Waste and Database

545. For the purpose of achieving the objectives of the Strategy, and due to a complete insight into the state of the environment, a report on waste management is prepared on the territory of the Republic, which is an integral part of the Environmental Report and is submitted once in two years to the National Assembly of the Republic of Srpska, in accordance with regulation on environmental protection. Two or more local self-government units that have adopted a joint waste management plan shall consider the report on the implementation plan once in three years and at the expiration of the validity period of the common waste management plan and submit the report to the Ministry and the Fund (Article 79, paragraphs 1–2).

---

688. The Government shall adopt a Regulation determining certain types of hazardous waste that may be imported as secondary raw materials (Art. 75, para. 11).

546. The local self-government unit shall consider the report on implementation of local waste management plan once in three years and after the expiration of the validity period of the local waste management plan and submit the report to the Ministry and the Fund (Article 79, paragraph 3).[689]

547. Legal person or entrepreneur who participate in the waste transport shall be obliged to submit to the Fund data on the type and quantity of waste, including secondary raw materials that are placed on the market in the prescribed manner (Article 80, paragraph 2).

548. The local self-government unit shall keep records of collected municipal waste, as well as a list of unregulated landfills and shall submit the data to the Fund. The Fund shall keep the original waste records for at least 25 years for the needs of the Republic of Srpska's waste production statistics (Article 80, paragraphs 5–6).[690]

549. The register of issued licenses is established and kept by the Ministry. Data from the register are submitted to the Fund. The registry of issued licenses is a database in which data on issued waste management permits and permits for import, export and transit of waste are recorded (Article 81, paragraphs 1–2). The Minister shall issue a rulebook prescribing the content, manner of keeping and appearance of the registry of issued waste management permits (Article 81, paragraph 4).

12. Financing of Waste Management

550. Waste management costs are determined according to the quantity and characteristics of waste in accordance to the 'polluter pays' principle and include: (a) the costs of separate waste collection, (b) the cost of waste transport, (c) costs of other waste management measures that are not covered by revenues generated from the trafficking of waste, (d) waste removal costs that unknown person has disposed outside the landfill and (e) the costs of designing and constructing a facility for storage, treatment and disposal of waste, plant operating costs, closure costs and subsequent maintenance after the termination of its operation.

551. The producer or owner of waste shall bear the costs for collection, transport, storage, treatment and disposal of waste in accordance with the Law. The costs of removing waste disposed outside of landfill, whose origin or ownership cannot be determined, shall be borne by the local self-government unit (Article 83, paragraphs 1–2).[691]

689. The Minister shall issue a regulation prescribing the contents and form of the report on implementation of joint and local waste management plan (Art. 79, para. 5).

690. The Fund shall, once a year, by 31 May of the current year at the latest, as well as on demand, or upon request, provide to the Ministry information on the collected data and data from the submitted reports (Art. 80, para. 7).

691. Households bear the costs of waste management in accordance with the regulations governing utility services (Art. 83, para. 3).

552. A producer or importer of products that becomes special waste streams after the use, pays compensation in accordance with this Law and special regulations and shall be obliged to keep daily record of the quantity and type of manufactured and imported products, or to submit a regular annual report to the Fund (Article 84, paragraphs 2–3).

553. Implementation of the Waste Management Strategy and Plans, as well as construction of facilities for storage, treatment and disposal of waste, is financed from the Fund's special funds in accordance with Fund's regulations, as well as from loans, donations and funds of legal entities and natural persons managing waste, from fees and other sources of funding, in accordance with the Law (Article 85, paragraph 1).

554. Implementation of joint and local waste management plans, as well as construction of facilities for storage, treatment and disposal of waste shall be financed from the special funds of the Fund, in accordance with the regulations on the Fund, as well from special funds of the local self-government units budgets, loans, donations and funds of legal entities and natural persons managing waste, from fees and other sources of financing, in accordance with the Law (Article 85, paragraph 2).[692]

13. Supervision

555. Inspection supervision over the implementation of provisions of the Law on Waste Management and bylaws adopted on the base of it shall be performed by the Republican Administration for inspection affairs over the Republican environmental inspectors and inspectors in the local Government units (Article 89).

556. The administrative supervision over the application of the provisions of this Law and the regulations adopted on the basis of it, as well as the supervision over the work of the Fund and authorized legal entities in the performance of entrusted tasks, shall be carried out by the Ministry (Article 88).

B. Other Relevant RS Regulations

557. In accordance with the Law on Waste Management, a large number of secondary legislation has been adopted, as follow:

(1) Decree on thermal treatment of waste (Official Gazette of RS No. 54/17).
(2) Decree on the management of packaging and packaging waste (Official Gazette of RS No. 58/18).
(3) Decree on the waste disposal in landfills (Official Gazette of RS No. 36/15).

---

692. Payment of administrative fees for issuing permits prescribed by this Law shall be carried out in accordance with the regulations on administrative fees (Art. 87).

(4) Rulebook on categories, testing and classification of waste (Official Gazette of RS No. 19/15, 79/18).
(5) Rulebook on the content, manner of keeping and appearance of the registry of issued waste management licenses (Official Gazette of RS No. 43/15, 14/18).
(6) Rulebook on waste management containing asbestos (Official Gazette of RS No. 47/18).
(7) Rulebook on general and special documentation submitted with the application for issuing the license for import, export and transit of waste (Official Gazette of RS No. 5/16).
(8) Rulebook on the methodology for collecting data on waste and their records (Official Gazette of RS No. 71/15).
(9) Rulebook on conditions and manner of collection, transport, storage and treatment of waste used as secondary raw material or for obtaining energy (Official Gazette of RS No. 61/15).
(10) Rulebook on the application form for the issuance of a permit for the storage, treatment and disposal of waste (Official Gazette of RS No. 18/15).
(11) Rulebook on the content and appearance of a waste management license (Official Gazette of RS No. 43/15).
(12) Rulebook on the content of programme measures with adjustment dynamics for the operation of existing landfills (Official Gazette of RS No. 41/15).
(13) Rulebook on the form of the document on the hazardous waste movement and the instructions for filling in (Official Gazette of RS No. 21/15).
(14) Rulebook on the manner of storage, packaging and labelling of hazardous waste (Official Gazette of RS No. 20/12).
(15) Rulebook on the waste tires management (Official Gazette of RS No. 20/12).
(16) Rule book on financial guarantees for insuring transboundary waste transport (Official Gazette of RS No. 86/05).
(17) Rule book on medical waste management (Official Gazette of RS No. 90/06).[693]

II. Federation of Bosnia and Herzegovina

A. The Law on Waste Management

558. Basic legal act regulating waste[694] management[695] in the Federation of Bosnia and Herzegovina is the Law on Waste Management (Official Gazette of the

693. For more details, *see*: RS MoSPCEE. *Program usklađivanja zakonodavstva Republike Srpske sa pravnom tekovinom EU u oblasti zaštite životne sredine*, [Program of approximation of the Republika Srpska Legislation with the EU environmental *acquis*], Banja Luka, November 2016, pp. 64–72.

694. *Waste* means any substances or objects which the owner disposes, intends to dispose of or is required to be disposed of in accordance with one of the categories of waste listed in the list of wastes outlined in the implementing regulation (Art. 4, para. 1).

695. *Waste management*-means a system of activities and actions related to waste, including prevention of waste generation, reduction of waste quantity and its hazardous characteristics, waste treatment, planning and control of activities and processes of waste management, waste transport, setting up,

FBiH, Nos 33/03, 72/09 and 92/17). It has the following ten parts: Part I – General Provisions (Articles 1–3), Part II – Definitions (Article 4), Part III – Basic Principles (Article 5), Part IV – Planning of the Waste Management (Articles 6–14), Part V – Responsibilities in Waste Management and Activities (Articles 15–37), Part VI – Transboundary Waste Movement (Articles 38–47), Part VII – Supervision of Waste Management (Articles 48–51), Part VIII – Penalty Provisions (Articles 52–53), Part IX – Compensation for Damages (Article 54), Part X – Transitional and Final Provisions (Articles 55–60).

559. According to Article 1, paragraph 1, this law regulates: all categories of waste, except waste referred to in paragraph 3 of this article;[696] all kinds of activities in waste management, operations and facilities.

560. The provisions of this law shall apply on: waste generated during recourses research, extraction, treatment[697] and utilization of mineral resources and in the working of quarries; liquid waste; animal waste and other non-hazardous materials of natural origin that can be used for agricultural purposes; delayed explosives, unless it is not regulated by a specific regulation (Article 1, paragraph 2).

561. The aim of this law is to encourage and to ensure the most important conditions for prevention of waste generation, waste processing for reuse and recycling, separation of raw materials and their use for energy production and safe waste disposal (Article 2, paragraph 1).

562. To achieve the goal and prevention of pollution and reduction of consequences for human health and the environment, waste management shall be made in a way to ensure:

- Minimal waste generation, especially reducing of hazardous characteristics of such waste to a minimum.
- Reduction of generated waste by volume, especially taking into account the waste streams.
- Waste treatment in a way that ensures return of the raw materials from it.
- Incineration or disposal on landfills[698] in an environmentally friendly way those types of waste that are not subject to return of components, reuse or energy production (Article 3, paragraph 1).[699]

---

operation, closure and maintenance of devices for waste treatment after closure, monitoring, counselling and education in relation to activities and actions on waste management (Art. 4, para. 1).

696. The provisions of this Law shall not apply on radioactive waste, gases released into the atmosphere, and on wastewater (Art. 1, para. 3).

697. *Treatment*-means the physical, thermal, chemical or biological processes, including sorting, that change characteristics of waste in order to reduce quantity or hazardous waste characteristics, that facilitate handling or that increase return of waste components (Art. 4, para. 1).

698. *Landfill*-means a waste disposal site for the purpose of final disposal on the surface or below the surface of land, *including*: Inner disposal sites (e.g., landfills where waste producer dispose of their own waste at the place of generation), and permanent locations (e.g., for more than one year) which are used for long-term waste disposal, *but excluding*: objects where is not allowed waste storage,

1. Basic Principles

563. According to Article 5, principles of waste management are the following:

- *Prevention* – avoiding of waste generation or reducing of quantity and harmfulness of generated waste in order to reduce the risk to human health and the environment and to avoid environmental degradation.
- *Precaution measures* – preventing of danger or damage to the environment caused by waste, taking measures, even if the complete scientific base is not available.
- *Responsibility of waste producers* – Producer is responsible for choosing the most acceptable environmental solution according to the product characteristics and production technology, including product life cycle and usage of the best available technology.
- *Polluter pays principle* – waste producer or holder shall bear all costs of prevention, treatment and disposal of waste, including care after usage and monitoring. The waste producer or holder is financially responsible for preventive and remediation measures for environmental damage caused by him or to be likely caused by him.
- *Proximity*-waste treatment or disposal should be done at the nearest appropriate facility or location, taking into account the environmental and economic profitability.
- *Regionality* – development of waste treatment and construction of facilities for its disposal should be done in a way that covers the needs of the region and enables sustainability of built objects.

2. Federal Waste Management Plan and Strategy

564. Federal Waste Management Plan is the implementing document of the Strategy referred to in Article 8 of this law and shall be adopted by the Government of the Federation of Bosnia and Herzegovina, on the proposal of the Federal Ministry of environment and tourism (hereinafter, 'the Ministry') for a period of five years. In order to manage with certain waste categories, Government of the Federation of Bosnia and Herzegovina can also adopt individual plans (Article 6, paragraph 2 and 3).

Supervision over implementation of the Federal Waste Management Plan performs the Ministry, annually, by 30 June of the current year for the previous year.

---

and waste is ready for further transport in order to be reused, for treatment or disposal elsewhere, previously storing of waste for reuse or treatment for a period less than three years, or previously storing of waste for disposal for a period less than one year (Art. 4, para. 1).

699. Waste management shall be made in the way to take all necessary measures which ensure waste treatment and disposal without endangering human health and without causing harm or significant risk to the environment, and in particular: without risk to water, air, soil, plants and animals; without creating disturbance through noise or odours; without harmful impact to the nature or places of special interest (Art. 3, para. 3).

The Ministry submits to the Government of the Federation of Bosnia and Herzegovina a report on the enforcement of established commitments and effectiveness of taken measures from the Waste Management Plan (Article 6, paragraph 5).

565. Inter-entity body for the environment, in addition to powers stipulated by the Environmental Protection Law, is authorized for coordination on the entity level during preparation of the Waste Management Strategy (Article 7, paragraph 1). The Waste Management Strategy is adopted by the Parliament of the Federation of Bosnia and Herzegovina (hereinafter, 'the Federation Parliament') for a period of ten years, on proposal of the Government of the Federation of Bosnia and Herzegovina (Article 8, paragraph 1).[700] The Government of the Federation of Bosnia and Herzegovina will submit Report on implementation of the Strategy to the Parliament of the Federation of Bosnia and Herzegovina (Article 8, paragraph 5) every two years.

3. Cantonal Waste Management Plans and Financial Guarantees

566. Each canton shall adopt Waste Management Plan for its area (Article 9, paragraph 1) which must be harmonized with Waste Management Strategy of the Federation of Bosnia and Herzegovina, as well as with the Federal Plan for Waste Management (Article 9, paragraph 2).[701]

By Cantonal regulation will be determined tasks for municipalities concerning drafting Plans for Waste Management (Article 10, paragraph 1) which will be submitted to the cantonal Ministry responsible for environmental issues (hereinafter, 'Cantonal Ministry') (Article 10, paragraph 3).

567. Waste management activities within jurisdiction of the Federation of Bosnia and Herzegovina are performed by the Federal Ministry in cooperation with Federal Ministry for Health and with other relevant Ministries (Article 11, paragraph 1).[702]

568. For performing activities for waste management and disposal it is necessary to obtain the permit[703] unless this law prescribes otherwise (Article 12, paragraph 1). By implementing legislation will be regulated issuance of permits for small business activities in waste management (Article 13, paragraph 4). The permit is issued for a period of five years and may be renewed for the same period of time if there are no changes in conditions under which the licence was issued (Article 13, paragraph 4).

700. Professional and other activities in preparation of the Waste Management Strategy performs the Federal Ministry of Environment and Tourism (hereinafter, 'the Ministry') (Art. 8, para. 2).
701. Conditions for planning of waste management in the municipalities will be regulated by Cantonal regulations (Art. 9, para. 4).
702. Activities of transboundary waste movement and activities for management of waste and a facility for waste treatment, which include area of two or more cantons, are performed by the Federal Ministry (Art. 11, para. 2).
703. The content of the Request for obtaining the permit is prescribed in Art. 13, para. 1, while content of the permit is prescribed in Art. 13, para. 3.

569. Financial and other guarantees to cover risk costs from possible damage, remediation and after-closing operations are paid into Cantonal fund on which territory is located landfill (Article 14, paragraph 1). Financial guarantee shall be proportionate to the amount of waste, to the expected costs and risks occurrence (Article 14, paragraph 2). Financial guarantee or a part for operation of the landfill shall be valid until needed and at least thirty years after the closure of the landfill (Article 14, paragraph 3).

4. General Requirements and Responsibilities for Waste Management

570. All activities should be undertaken so that they have very little impact on the environment and human health, that reduce loading and usage of environmental resources, that do not endanger human health or pollute the environment, that reduce the amount of harmful waste effects, that improve waste reuse and recycling (material recovery) and safe waste disposal (Article 15, paragraph 1). In order to prevent waste production and reduction of the amount and harmful waste effects it will be stimulated:

- Rational use of materials and energy.
- Storing of materials and residues within the process of production and consumption as much as possible.
- Production of products that produce the least amount of waste and produce the least harmful impact.
- Replacement of materials that cause a risk when they become waste (Article 15, paragraph 2).[704]

571. Waste is disposed of only if it is not possible to use its material and/or energy in existing technical and economic conditions, and if the costs of reuse are unreasonably high in comparison with the costs of disposal (Article 15, paragraph 5). It is forbidden to leave, accumulate, dispose or treat waste without supervision as well as to mix different types of waste, unless if it enables row material recovery and/or disposal (Article 15, paragraph 7).

572. The producer will design a product and packaging, to use of technology and to develop production in a way that most efficiently uses materials and energy, that stimulates products reuse and recycling, and that at the end of the product life cycle promotes environmentally sustainable treatment, usage and disposal (Article 16,

704. Waste reuse, waste recycling, substitution of raw materials with waste in the aim of using material or energy from waste, will be stimulated. If this is not possible, the use of waste will be stimulated as an energy source (Art. 15, para. 3).

paragraph 1). The producer is obliged to use such raw materials and basic materials, semi-finished products and packaging that reduce usage of energy and materials, and which usage reduces waste production and use of long lasting packaging and do not threaten the environment when it becomes waste (Article 16, paragraph 2).[705]

573. The producer is obliged to notify the seller and the consumer about important characteristics of the product and packaging in terms of waste management, as well as about the method of treatment in case of the end of the product life cycle and waste produced from it (Article 17, paragraph 1). Waste producers and owners are required to collect, to take care on the reuse and recycling or disposal of waste which was produced by their actions or by waste which they possess (Article 24, paragraph 1).[706]

574. The producer and importer of products is socially and financially responsible for the environmental impact that can be caused by products placed on the market of the Federation of BiH, and which after usage become special categories of waste. Special categories of waste include: packaging waste, waste vehicles, waste oils, waste batteries and vehicle batteries, waste tires, electrical and electronic waste, waste containing asbestos, PCB waste, waste from the production of titanium dioxide, medical waste, animal waste and construction waste (Article 18a, paragraph 1). Fee for special categories of waste will be paid in Fond for environmental protection of Federation BiH (Article 18b, paragraph 1). The Fund distributes collected funds to the cantons in the amount defined by the Law on the Fund for Environmental Protection, for projects and management activities for special categories of waste. The Fund is obliged to adopt an annual management plan and a financial plan for special categories of waste, which will be approved by the Government of FBiH, with the prior consent of the Federal Ministry (Article 18b, paragraphs 2–4).

575. In accordance with the Law on Environmental Protection, operator of the facility that requires an environmental permit prepares Plan on Waste Management (Article 19, paragraph 1). The operator of the facility for which is needed an environmental permit, as a producer, must designate a person responsible for waste management activities (Article 20, paragraph 1).

576. The seller of goods and services (hereinafter, 'the seller') is obliged to return and/or to reimburse deposits, to collect in a selective way and to deliver products and packaging which are at the end of life cycle to producer or to operator authorized to provide waste management services if it is determined by a special

705. Residues of the technological process which will be introduced again into the technological process, as well as products that can be used again for their original purposes without further treatment, become waste only when they are moved out from this production cycle (Art. 16, para. 3).
706. Waste producers and owners are obliged, before disposal and reuse of waste, to store the waste in an environmentally acceptable manner (Art. 24, para. 2).

regulation (Article 21, paragraph 1).[707] Producer and seller can transfer obligations from Article 16, paragraph 1 and Article 21, paragraph 1 of this law on operator of the system for waste collection through an agreement or contract (Article 22, paragraph 1). The system for waste collection can be established by the producer and/or by vendor or operator for waste management (Article 23, paragraph 1).

5. Waste Collecting, Transport, Disposal, Treatment and Usage

577. The public service activities[708] include: collection of waste from households and other premises which produce communal waste; treatment of communal waste, including management of raw material recovery and/or disposal; sites for selective waste collection (Article 26, paragraph 2).

578. Collection and treatment of communal waste[709] is carried out in accordance with a special regulation on communal activities (Article 25, paragraph 1). By cantonal regulation will be regulated the establishment and operation of utility companies and obligations of the municipalities in providing of utility services (Article 25, paragraph 2), as well as performing of public service activities, especially service for selective waste treatment (Article 26, paragraph 1).

579. Households are obliged to collect the waste they have produced and to hand it over to utility companies for waste, while hazardous waste[710] they are obliged to hand it over to the certain collection points, or to the person who is responsible for providing waste management services (Article 25, paragraph 3).[711]

The operator of the facility for waste treatment will be considered as waste generator if waste is produced during the treatment (Article 29, paragraph 1).[712]

580. Waste producer or owner shall collect waste selectively in accordance with the need of future treatment (Article 30, paragraph 1). Waste collection within the

---

707. The seller may return to the producer or to compensate packaged goods or waste generated from them when the seller is responsible for treatment, reuse and recycling of waste in accordance with special regulations (para. 2).

708. The public services activities performs the operator for waste management who gets a job through tender (Art. 27, para. 1). Tender can be given for all waste management activities or just for one or more waste management activities (Art. 27, para. 2).

709. *Communal waste* means waste from households as well as other waste which, because of its nature or composition, is similar to the waste from households (Art. 4, para. 1).

710. *Hazardous waste* means any waste which is determined by a special regulation and which has one or more characteristics, which poses a risk to human health and the environment due to its origin, composition or concentration, as well as the waste that is listed in the list of waste as hazardous and that is regulated by the implementing regulation (Art. 4, para. 1).

711. The producers are not obliged to use the services of waste companies if they collect and treat their waste in accordance with environmental regulations, and if they hand over their waste to the authorized waste management operators (Art. 25, para. 5).

712. The operator shall keep record of data on waste which is taken for the treatment, as well as on the waste that is generated during treatment, and shall notify the competent authority at least once a year in accordance with a special regulation (Art. 29, para. 2).

sites of producer or owner in a way that excludes risk to the environment is time limited and does not require a special permit (Article 30, paragraph 2).[713]

581. The waste will be transported in a way that excludes environmental pollution (Article 32, paragraph 1). In case of pollution generated during transport, the carrier will be responsible for cleaning and bringing into original condition the polluted area (Article 32, paragraph 2).[714]

582. Pursuant to Article 33 method of waste disposal and treatment can be the following: disposal at a landfill site; thermal treatment; other chemical, biological or physical treatments (paragraph 1). Priority in issuing necessary permits for new landfills has a regional landfill (paragraph 2).[715]

583. Waste can also be used by recovery of materials and energy (Article 31, paragraph 1). Waste will be used in a way that the products resulting from the waste usage will not cause greater environmental loading than the products from primary raw materials (Article 31, paragraph 2).

6. Landfills, Cadastre of Polluters and Waste Incineration

584. In accordance with Article 13, paragraph 3 of this law, the following will be determined in the permit:

- Class of the landfill (landfill for hazardous waste, landfill for non-hazardous waste, landfill for inert waste).[716]
- A list of defined types and the total amount of waste that is allowed to be disposed of in a landfill.
- Requirements for the preparation of landfill, activities of disposal, monitoring and control, including contingency plans, as well as temporary requirements for landfills closure and procedures after closing.
- Requirements for waste acceptance procedures.
- Obligation of the applicant to report at least annually to the competent authority on types and quantities of waste disposed of and of the monitoring programme results (Article 34, paragraph 1).

713. Operator for waste collection collects waste from producers and owners and transports it to the place for waste collection, to the transfer-station or to the place for reuse and recycling, treatment or final disposal (Art. 30, para. 3).

714. Hazardous waste must be labelled and packaged during transport in accordance with special regulation. Transportation of hazardous wastes must comply with the general requirements for transport of dangerous goods (Art. 32, para. 6).

715. An integral part of the landfills are waste management centres (Art. 33, para. 3).

716. *Inert waste*-means waste that does not undergo to any significant physical, chemical or biological changes. Inert waste will not be dissolved, burned or otherwise physically or chemically processed, biodegraded or to have adverse effect on other substances with which it comes into contact in a way to cause pollution of the environment or endangering of human health (Art. 4, para. 1).

585. Each landfill must be registered in the Real Estate Cadastre and in Cadastre of polluters (hereinafter, 'Cadastre') (Article 37, paragraph 1). Existing landfill sites or those that are closed as a result of reviewing of the adjustment plan are registered in the Cadastre on the base of the decision of the competent authority for environmental protection (paragraph 2).[717]

586. In accordance with Article 13, paragraph 3 of this law, an issued licence must contain the following:

– The same categories of waste that can be treated.
– Data on the total capacity of waste incineration facility.
– Specified procedure of sampling and measurement for fulfilment of the obligations of periodic measurements for each air and water polluters (Article 35, paragraph 2).[718]

7. Transboundary Waste Movement

587. Transboundary waste movement is carried out provided that:

– The state of Bosnia and Herzegovina-Federation of Bosnia and Herzegovina as an exporter does not have technical capacities and necessary facilities, capacities or suitable sites for waste disposal for the purpose of waste disposal in an environmentally acceptable and efficient manner, or waste is used as raw material for recycling industry or components recovery in the state, entity-importer.
– Compliance for the transboundary waste movement is issued.
– Wastes are packaged, labelled and transported in a way that prevents environment pollution according to best available practice.
– There is adequate documentation about the movement from the point where its movement started by the time of disposal, in accordance with national and international standards and relevant international standards and relevant international rules and requirements relating to the beginning of transboundary traffic, to the point of disposal (Article 38, paragraph 1).[719]

717. The landfill owner is obliged after the closure of the landfill to prepare environmental impact assessment and to submit it to the competent authority (Art. 37, para. 3).

718. Permit issued by the competent authority for facilities for incineration of hazardous waste shall contain: quantities of the different categories of hazardous waste that can be treated; specification of the minimum and maximum mass flows of those hazardous wastes, their minimum and maximum calorific values and their maximum content of polluting substances (PCB, PCP, chlorine, fluorine, sulphur, heavy metals) (Art. 35, para. 3).

719. The Federal Minister will regulate the transboundary movement of waste by the implementing regulation (Art. 38, para. 2).

588. In the case of transboundary waste movement when the Federation of Bosnia and Herzegovina is an exporter, producer or exporter is obliged to submit a written request[720] to the Federal Ministry about intended waste export (Article 39, paragraph 1).

589. The import of waste for disposal in the Federation of Bosnia and Herzegovina is prohibited (Article 40, paragraph 1). Waste can be imported into the Federation of Bosnia and Herzegovina only for the purpose of return of materials or energy (Article 40, paragraph 2). In case of transboundary waste movement, when the Federation of Bosnia and Herzegovina is an importer, provisions of Article 39 of this law shall be applied (Article 40, paragraph 3).[721]

590. Instead of individual consents, general consent may be given in case of regular waste shipping, waste with the same physical and chemical characteristics, the same disposer, via the same customs office at the exit from the country and at the entrance in a country that imports, in a case of transit via the same customs office at the entrance or exit from the transit country or countries, (Article 42, paragraph 1).[722]

8. Financial Guarantees for Transboundary Waste Movement

591. By special regulation shall be determined the types of financial guarantees that can ensure transboundary waste movement (Article 44, paragraph 1).

When transboundary waste movement with authorization cannot be done in accordance with the provisions of the agreement, an exporting country ensures that wastes are returned to the exporting country if another solution cannot be found for waste disposal in an environmentally acceptable way, within ninety days from arrival of waste at the destination (Article 45, paragraph 1).

592. In case of transport of hazardous waste for disposal between entities of Bosnia and Herzegovina, it is necessary to obtain notification[723] of the competent entity Ministry from which the waste is exported for the Ministry of the entity that imports the waste (Article 47, paragraph 1).

---

720. Content of the Request is prescribed in Art. 39, para. 2).
721. In the case of transboundary waste movements when the Federation of Bosnia and Herzegovina is transit country, the provisions of Art. 39 of this Law will be applied (Art. 41, para. 1).
722. Consent under para. 1, Art. 42 gives the Federal Ministry for a period not exceeding twelve months (Art. 42, para. 2).
723. Content of the Notification is prescribed in Art. 47, para. 2.

9. Supervision over the Waste Management

593. Waste producers and facility operators are obliged annually to make a report on meeting the conditions from the permit and other information determined by the implementing regulation (Article 48, paragraph 1).

594. Supervision over activities of waste management and fulfilling of conditions from the permit in accordance with the provisions of this law and regulations adopted thereunder performs environmental inspectors and market, tourism-catering inspector, at the federal level – Federal Inspector and at the cantonal level – Cantonal Inspector (hereinafter, 'the inspector') (Article 49, paragraph 1).

10. Compensation for Damages

595. Federation of Bosnia and Herzegovina is responsible for taking emergency measures or clearing activities, if it is not possible to identify the responsible perpetrators and the interests of protecting human health, animal and plant world require a direct and fast action (Article 54, paragraph 1).[724]

596. In order to prevent greater damage and limiting of further harmful effects on the environment, the Federal Minister and the Cantonal Minister may undertake all measures in order to prevent and limit further damage or distortion at the expense of a damage perpetrator (Article 54, paragraph 3).

B. Other Relevant FBiH Waste Management Regulations

597. During the last several years the following sublegal acts have been adopted:[725]

(1) Rule book on issuing permits for activities of small business enterprises dealing with waste management (Official Gazette of FBiH No. 9/05).
(2) Rule book on categories of waste together with lists (Official Gazette of FBiH No. 9/05).
(3) Rule book defining the handling of hazardous waste not included in the list of waste or which content is unknown (Official Gazette of FBiH No. 33/03).
(4) Rule book on the necessary requirements for assigning liabilities from manufacturers and vendors to the system operators for waste collection (Official Gazette of FBiH No. 9/05).
(5) Rule book on the contents of the plan for adjusting waste management in terms of existing waste treatment or disposal plants and on activities undertaken by the competent authority (Official Gazette of FBiH No. 9/05).

---

724. This provision from para. 1 of this article does not exclude the seeking for a remedial action and recovery of costs.
725. *See*: http://www.fmoit.gov.ba/bs/okolis/upravljanje-otpadom(19 Jul. 2022).

(6) Decree on the mandatory submission of the annual report on meeting the requirements set out in the water management permit (Official Gazette of FBiH No. 31/06).
(7) Decree on financial guarantees for insuring transboundary waste transport (Official Gazette of FBiH No. 41/05).
(8) Decree on financial and other guarantees for covering costs related to risks of possible damages, rehabilitation and processes after closing down landfills (Official Gazette of FBiH No. 39/06).
(9) Decree on selective gathering, packaging and labelling of waste (Official Gazette of FBiH No. 38/06).
(10) Rule book on the form, contents and process of notification, carried out by the manufacturer, of important product characteristics and packaging (Official Gazette of FBiH No. 8/08).
(11) Rule book on animal waste and other non-hazardous natural materials that can be used in agriculture (Official Gazette of FBiH No. 8/08).
(12) Rule book on packaging and packaging waste management (Official Gazette of FBiH No. 88/11, 28/13, 8/16 and 54/16).
(13) Rule book on medical waste management (Official Gazette of FBiH No. 77/08).
(14) Rule book on waste management from electrical and electronic products (Official Gazette FBiH No. 87/12, 107/14, 8/16 and 79/16).
(15) Decree on fees for plastic bags (Official Gazette of FBiH No. 9/14).
(16) Decree on Waste Management Information System (Official Gazette of FBiH No. 97/18).[726]

III. Brčko District of Bosnia and Herzegovina

A. *The Law on Waste Management*

598. Basic legal act regulating waste management in Brčko District of BiH is the Law on Waste Management (Official Gazette of BD BiH, Nos 25/04, 01/05, 19/07, 02/08, 09/09 and 10/18). It has the following eleven parts: Part I – General Provisions (Articles 1–3), Part II – Definitions (Article 4), Part III – The Basic Principles (Article 5), Part IV – Planning of Waste Management (Articles 6–10), Part V – The Permit for Waste Management (Articles 11–17), Part VI – Supervision of Waste Management (Articles 18–21), Part VII – Activities and Responsibilities of Waste Management (Articles 22–44), Part VIII – Transboundary Movement of Waste (Articles 45–54), Part IX – Compensation for Damages (Article 55), Part X – Penalty Provisions (Article 56), Part XI – Transitional and Final Provisions (Articles 57–61).

726. For more details, *see*: FMET. *Program aproksimacije propisa Federacije Bosne i Hercegovine sa pravnom stečevinom EU u oblasti okoliša*, [Program of approximation of the Federation of Bosnia and Herzegovina Legislation with the EU environmental *acquis*] Sarajevo, December 2016, pp. 41–46.

599. This Law regulates: all categories of waste, except radioactive waste, gases released into the atmosphere and wastewater; all kind of activities, operations and facilities in waste management (Article 1, paragraph 1 and paragraph 3).[727]

600. The objective of the Law on Waste Management is to encourage and ensure the most important requirements for the following: prevention of waste generation; waste processing for reuse and recycling; the extraction of raw materials from waste and its use for the production of energy, and safe waste disposal (Article 2, paragraph 1).[728]

601. The basic principles of waste management are the following: prevention principle, precautionary principle, responsibility principle, polluter pays principle, proximity principle, regionality principle (Article 5, paragraph 1, points 1–6).

1. The Planning of Waste Management and the Strategy for Waste Management

602. The competent department is obliged to prepare Waste Management Plans within the time prescribed by this law (Article 6, paragraph 1). The Assembly of Brčko District on the Mayor's proposal shall adopt Solid Waste Management Strategy for the period of ten years. The Strategy shall be pre-approved by the Government (Article 8, paragraph 1). The Government prepares Waste Management Plan on the territory of District which must be consistent with the Solid Waste Management Strategy (Article 9, paragraph 1).

2. The Permit for Waste Management

603. The competent department in cooperation with the department responsible for health protection and other departments conduct waste management activities (Article 11, paragraph 1). It is necessary to obtain the permit issued by department responsible for environmental protection for performing of waste management activities prescribed by this law and bylaws adopted on the base of this law (Article 12, paragraph 1). In addition to town planning consent, approval for construction and environmental permit required by special regulations, permit for waste management is always required (hereinafter, 'the permit') (Article 13, paragraph 1).

727. The provisions of this Law shall apply to: waste resulting from research, extraction, treatment and storage of mineral resources and by the operation of quarries; liquid waste; animal waste and other non-hazardous materials of natural origin that can be used for agricultural purposes; disposed explosives, unless it is regulated by a special regulation (Art. 1, para. 2).

728. For the purpose of achieving the objectives from Art. 2 of this Law, it is necessary to take the following measures: reducing to the minimum of waste generation, especially its hazardous characteristics; reducing the amount of waste; treatment of waste in a way that ensures the return of raw materials from it; incineration or landfill disposal in an environmentally friendly way of those types of waste that are not subject to the component recovery (Art. 3, para. 1).

604. Permits are issued only for certain types of waste and only for performing of certain activities prescribed by bylaw (Article 16, paragraph 3). The permit is issued for a period of five years, while the permit for the landfill and incineration is to be issued for a period of ten years (Article 16, paragraph 4).[729]

3. The Financial Guarantees

605. The responsible persons of facility and landfills with hazardous waste must provide financial guarantees and other forms of guarantees prescribed by special regulations for the settlement of costs related to the reduction of any possible damage to a minimum as well as costs incurred by the activities undertaken after the closure of the facility or landfill (Article 17, paragraph 1). The financial guarantee must be proportionate to the amount of waste, to the expected costs and risk occurrence (Article 17, paragraph 2).[730]

4. Supervision of Waste Management

606. Waste producers and persons responsible for management of waste facilities are required to implement the programme of control, monitoring, and to keep a record about the conditions set out in the permit and other relevant data and annually submit a report to the competent authority for environmental protection (Article 18, paragraph 1).[731]

607. Monitoring over the implementation provisions of this law and the regulations based on it is to be performed by competent department, through the inspectors in charge for environmental protection (Article 19, paragraph 1).[732]

5. Activities and Responsibilities for Waste Management

608. All activities are undertaken in a way to have the least impact on the environment and human health, to reduce the amount and harmful waste impact, to promote the reuse, recycling and safe waste disposal (Article 22, paragraph 1). In order

---

729. The content of the Request for obtaining the permit is prescribed in Art. 15, para. 1 as well as in Art. 42, para. 1. The content of the permit is prescribed in Art. 16, para. 1, as well as in Art. 41, para. 1.
730. Financial guarantees or its part intended for the landfill operation must be valid as long as necessary for the maintenance and operations after closure of the location, at least thirty years (Art. 17, para. 3).
731. Waste producers and responsible persons are obliged to notify the competent department for environmental protection on detected negative impacts on the environment immediately, at the latest up to twelve hours after it is discovered (Art. 18, para. 2).
732. The competent department shall supervise persons responsible for waste management and waste producers when terms of fulfilment the conditions for performing waste management activities are concerned (Art. 19, para. 2).

to use substances or energy from waste, reuse, recycling and substitution of raw materials with waste will be encouraged. If it is not possible, the use of waste as an energy source will be stimulated (Article 22, paragraph 3).[733]

609. The producer will design products and packaging, will use technology, and will develop production in a way that leads to the most efficient use of materials and energy, that stimulates the reuse and recycling of products, while at the end of the product life cycle producer will promote environmentally sustainable treatment, use and disposal (Article 23, paragraph 1).[734]

The producer is obliged to notify the vendor and the consumer on the important characteristics of the product and packaging regarding waste management, as well as on the way of treatment in case of the end of product life cycle and waste arising from it (Article 24, paragraph 1).

610. The responsible person in the facility for which is, according to the Law on Environmental Protection, environmental permit required, prepare and delivers waste management plan (Article 26, paragraph 1). The responsible person of the facility, for which is according to the Law on Environmental Protection required an environmental permit, must determine the person to perform the duties of coordinating of waste management (hereinafter, 'The Coordinator for the waste') (Article 27, paragraph 1).[735]

6. Waste Treatment, Collection and Disposal

611. Communal waste is collected and treated in accordance with a special regulation on providing services by utility companies. Providing services of communal waste management is under the responsibility of the Government department (Article 32, paragraph 1).[736]

612. The company for waste management is considered as a waste producer if the waste is produced during the treatment (Article 36, paragraph 1). The company for waste management shall keep records on the waste that is collected to be treated

733. Waste is disposed only if the use of its materials and energy in the existing technical and economic conditions is not possible, and if the cost of reuse is unreasonably high compared with the cost of disposal. It is forbidden to leave, accumulate, dispose or treat the waste without supervision (Art. 22, para. 5).

734. The producer will stimulate the use of such row materials and basic materials, semi products and packaging that reduce the use of energy and materials and which use reduces waste production. The producer will also stimulate the use of packaging that lasts longer and has a minimum load on the environment when it becomes waste (Art. 23, para. 2).

735. Procedures and the manner in which the vendor of the product or service provider (hereinafter, 'Vendor') shall be obliged to take back or to refund the deposit for used packaging or products, method of selective collection and delivery of used product to the manufacturer or to the authorized person responsible for waste management activities shall be established by bylaw (Art. 28, para. 1).

736. Services may be provided by public or private companies (Art. 32, para. 2).

or which was produced and shall inform the competent department in accordance with special regulations at least once a year (Article 36, paragraph 2).

613. The waste producer or holder collects waste separately in accordance with the need of further treatment. Collection of waste within the site of producer or the holder in such a way as to exclude the negative impact on the environment is time limited and does not require special permission (Article 37, paragraph 1).

614. The waste may be used as a raw material as well as for the production of energy (Article 38, paragraph 1). The waste is transported in a way that excludes environmental pollution (Article 39, paragraph 1).[737]

615. Each landfill must be registered in the Real Estate Cadastre and in the Polluters Cadastre (Article 44, paragraph 1). The competent authority and the court shall order to the landfill owner to take the necessary measures to prevent potential danger or harm to human health as well as to prevent environmental pollution (Article 44, paragraph 5).

7. General Requirements of Transboundary Waste Movement

616. Transboundary waste movement is carried out under the following conditions:

- District as a separate administrative unit in the state of BiH (the exporter) does not have the technical capacity and the necessary facilities, capacities or suitable disposal site, for waste disposal in an environmentally acceptable and efficient way, or if the wastes in question are used as raw materials for recycling industry or return of the components in the District (the importer).
- The waste movement is approved only for special reasons, otherwise the waste transport or disposal is prohibited.
- The waste is packaged, labelled and transported in a way that prevents the environmental pollution in accordance with the best available practices.
- Adequate documentation is needed about the movement from the point where the movement started by the time of disposal in accordance with national and international standards and international regulations related to the beginning of the transboundary movement to the point of disposal (Article 45, paragraph 1).[738]

737. Waste disposal may be carried out: at the landfills; as thermal storage and by the application of chemical, biological or physical processes (Art. 40, para. 1).
738. The transboundary import of waste for disposal in the District is prohibited. Waste can be imported in Brčko District only for the purpose of return of materials (Art. 47, para. 1).

8. Compensation for Damages

617. If an unknown person performs activities in waste management contrary to this law, the Government is obliged to take urgent measures of cleaning, to protect human health, flora and fauna, as well as to protect the environment (Article 55, paragraph 1).[739]

§5. Harmonization with EU Legislation

618. According to the EC Progress Report for 2021 'A consistent countrywide strategy for waste management has yet to be developed to align with the EU *acquis*. Bosnia and Herzegovina needs to pay particular attention to the EU plastic strategy and single-use plastics directive.'[740]

739. The Government has a right to reimburse the cost incurred by performing activities and measures referred to in para. 1 of this article from persons that committed an illegal activity (Art. 55, para. 2).

740. EC, *Bosnia and Herzegovina 2021 Progress Report,* p. 103. In addition, ' Substantial efforts and awareness-raising measures are required to reduce waste generation and promote reuse and recycling. Alignment is furthermore required with the EU *acquis* on sewage sludge, batteries, packaging, polychlorinated biphenyls/ polychlorinated terphenyls and end-of-life vehicles.' *Ibid.*

Chapter 5. Soil Pollution

§1. State of the Soil

619. 'According to the Assessment for Sustainable Development, before the war, about 3,000 hectares of farmland were lost annually (owing to construction, mining, flooding by man-made lakes and the construction of landfills). After the war, according to statistical records, the losses for the past two years amounted to over 10,000 hectares a year. Furthermore, the expansion of karst in Herzegovina (5%–6%) and western Bosnia and Herzegovina results from the misuse of sloping land, clear-cutting of forest, improper agricultural management, etc.'[741]

620. Soil degradation is increasing, and land use changes and loss of agricultural land are caused by sudden urbanization, industrialization and changes to commercial development. Waste is dumped on large areas of fertile agricultural land, thus precluding the possibility of agricultural production. The main characteristics of soils in BiH are: low content of humus and fertilizer nutrients, soils are generally shallow and approximately 14% of the territory contains excess water. Acid soils occupy more than one-third of the land in BiH. As more than 80% of the country consists of terrain with slopes exceeding 13%, water induced erosion is an increasingly present problem.[742]

621. Erosion and flooding of farmlands in BiH endanger harvests and sustainable use of soil. Lijevče polje, Semberija and fertile farmlands along Drina, Bosna, Vrbas, Sana, Una, Sava, Neretva and Trebišnjica rivers are all endangered.[743] Many agricultural activities add nitrogen to soils, thus, increasing the available nitrogen for nitrification and de-nitrification, which has an impact on the amount of N_2O emissions.[744]

622. Seventeen years after the end of the conflict BiH still faces the problem of a high level of landmine and unexploded ordnance (UXO) contamination. BiH is the most landmine contaminated country in Europe and certainly one of the most contaminated in the world. Despite the efforts made and significant improvements

741. As a result of the recent war, the land in Bosnia and Herzegovina is also marked by hundreds of kilometres of trenches, innumerable concrete bunkers, and craters from shells, bombs and missiles and also many agricultural lands are mined. RSMoAFWM, *First national report on the implementation of the United Nations Convention to Combat Desertification/Land Degradation in Bosnia and Herzegovina, supra* p. 20.

742. BiH MFTER, *State of the environment Report of the Bosnia and Herzegovina 2012, supra* p. 35.

743. RSMoSPCEE, *Second National Communication of Bosnia and Herzegovina under the United Nations Framework Convention on Climate Change, supra* p. 31.

744. *Ibid.*, p. 53.

in mine action, management landmines and UXO still represent one of the main threats to the safety of citizens and economic and social development in BiH.[745]

§2. Monitoring

623. Currently there are no specific laws, at the BiH or at the entity level, that directly address soil protection or monitoring. As a result, unified soil monitoring system does not exist at the BiH level. Efforts are limited to ad hoc observations on the scope of projects, soil quality evaluations, studies and other activities performed by such institutions as the Institute for Agropedology in Sarajevo, the Agriculture Institute of Banja Luka, and the Agronomy Institute of Mostar.[746]

§3. Competencies

624. Field of land protection is regulated at the level of the entities and the BD BiH.[747]

§4. Legislation

625. 'Providing there is not implementation of NAP in BIH, the issues of agricultural and forest land protection and controlled use are in general governed by the Laws: Laws on Agricultural Land, on Forests and on Spatial Planning. Soil desertification is not directly addressed in these Laws, but some articles define the action that should be taken to protect the land from degradation.'[748] This includes several measures. For example, a ban on the discharge of harmful substances (e.g., pesticides, oil derivates, radioactive material), a construction ban in the protection zones, the obligatory deposition of humus land, forestation, ground levelling and grass cover after certain land works (e.g., civil constructions, mining and tree cutting).

626. Demining Law (Official Gazette BiH, No. 5/2002) regulates the organizational structure for mine clearance, survey and removal of unexploded ordnance

745. Hodžić-Kovač E., (Ed) *Progress towards the Realisation of Millennium Development Goals in Bosnia and Herzegovina 2013, supra* pp. 123, 124. For more detailed information *see* BiH Council of Ministers, *Bosnia and Herzegovina Mine Action Strategy (2009–2019),* Sarajevo, 2008.

746. UNECE, *2nd Environmental Performance Review, supra* pp. 36–37. 'One example includes the inventory of the post-war land resource situation in BiH, implemented under the Food and Agriculture Organization (FAO) project in 2007. Another example is a pilot project being implemented in several RS municipalities by the RS Agriculture Institute, to identify parameters, plots and pollutants for soil monitoring. A sustained data flow does not exist because all soil monitoring in the country is performed only on a contractual basis (road construction, etc.) or for study and project purposes'.

747. Directorate for European Integration, *Answers to the Questionnaire, Chapter 27, Environment and climate change*, 27 Feb. 2018, *supra* p. 558.

748. MoAFWM, *First national report on the implementation of the United Nations Convention to Combat Desertification/Land Degradation in Bosnia and Herzegovina, supra* p. 21.

(UXO) (hereinafter, 'demining') in Bosnia and Herzegovina. It determines bodies authorized for the conducting of demining, rights and obligations of persons carrying out demining, as well as monitoring over the implementation of this law (Article 1, paragraph 1).[749]

I. The Republic of Srpska

627. The Strategic Plan for the Development of Agriculture and Rural Areas in RS for the period 2016–2020 recognize the relevance of the agricultural land, while measures to protect agricultural land are defined in the Law on Agricultural Land.

628. According to Article 12 of the Law on Nature Protection (Official Gazette of RS No. 20-14), activities in the field of the nature protection from the responsibility of RS authorities performs Ministry for Spatial Planning, Civil Engineering and Ecology. At the RS Ministry for Spatial Planning, Civil Engineering and Ecology, activities in the field of environmental protection are conducted by the Department for Environmental protection.

629. There is no soil monitoring system in place in the RS at the entity level.[750] The RS adopted a Soil Fertility Control Programme carried out through pedological analysis of soil on commercial family farms.[751]

630. Law on Agricultural Land of RS (Official Gazette of RS Nos 93/06, 86/07 and 14/10) regulates planning, protection, regulation and use of agricultural land, as well as other issues of importance to agricultural land as a resource of common interest (Article 1, paragraph 1). According to Article 2, paragraph 1, of said law, agricultural land as a natural wealth and resource of the general interest is to be used for agricultural production and cannot be used for other purposes, except in cases and under conditions determined by this law. The law also defines prohibition of release and disposal of hazardous and damaging substances; decontamination and rehabilitation of agricultural land and anti-erosion measures; and identification of hazardous and harmful substances in agricultural land and irrigation water.

631. Tests based on this law are carried out by authorized institutions, Management monitoring over the enforcement of the law is conducted by the Ministry of

749. Demining under this Law does not include: (a) Removal of unexploded improvised subversive-terrorist devices that are subject to criminal deeds or violations and are subject to the exclusive authorization of Internal Affairs. (b) Specific needs of Entity armies during the process of removal and disposal of used but not exploded ordnance during and after the training of their forces, of the stocks that are out of use. (c) Disposal of debris in the process of production of ammunition and military equipment, reproduction material in the production process and stocked products out of use (Art. 1 para. 2).

750. Directorate for European Integration, *Answers to the Questionnaire, Chapter 27, Environment and climate change*, 27 Feb. 2018, p. 563.

751. *Ibid.*

Agriculture, Forestry and Water Management. Inspection supervision over enforcement of this law and bylaws adopted on the basis of this law, is performed by Agricultural Inspection, which is a part of the RS Inspectorate, and of the inspectors of local self-governments. Pursuant to the Law on the Agricultural Land (Article 18, paragraph 1), testing of agricultural soil and irrigation waters to determine the amount of hazardous and harmful substances is performed according to a programme adopted by the Ministry.

632. According to Article 1, the Law on Nature protection (Official Gazette of RS No. 20/14) regulates the protection and conservation of nature, biological, geological and landscape diversity as a part of the environment.

633. RS Law on Mining (Official Gazette of RS No. 62/18), This Law regulates the conditions and manner of exploitation of mineral raw materials, construction, use and maintenance of mining facilities, mining projects, mining geodetic measurements and plans, protection measures and other issues related to exploitation of mineral raw materials, personnel conditions for performing certain tasks in mining, as well as the conditions for issuing and seizure of licenses in mining.

634. The Law on Geological Exploration of RS (Official Gazette of RS No. 110/13, 91/17, and 107/19) regulates, *inter alia,* subject, purpose and types of geological explorations, conditions for performing of geological researches, preparation and audit of programmes and project of geological researches, professional exam, issuing the decision for performing of detailed geological researches, performing of the geological researches, Geological Information System and other issues related to the area of the geology and geological exploration (Article 1, paragraph 1).

635. In the RS the following laws are also relevant to mention:

(1) The Law on Mineral Fertilisers (Official Gazette of RS No. 24/12).
(2) The Law on Chemicals (Official Gazette of RS No. 21/18).
(3) The Law on Biocides (Official Gazette of RS No. 37/09).
(4) The Law on Spatial Planning and Construction (Official Gazette of RS No. 40/13, 106/15, 3/16).

II. Federation of Bosnia and Herzegovina

636. The FBiH Ministry of Spatial Planning has the principal competence for management of land or land area, which includes protection of land and soil. The FBiH Ministry of Environment and Tourism has direct jurisdiction over protection of nature and biodiversity; soil protection; waste management: noise protection; air protection; as well as, commonly with the FBiH Ministry of Agriculture, Water-Management and Forestry, certain responsibilities of water management and water protection.[752]

637. FBiH Hydrometeorological Institute performs professional and other tasks from the competence of FBiH related to, *inter alia,* environmental quality (soil, air and water).[753]

638. Land policy in the FBiH is defined by the Law on Agricultural Land (Official Gazette of FBiH, No. 52/09) in its Chapter IV. As prescribed in Article 21 of said law, the land policy measures and agricultural land protection affairs are conducted for the purpose of preservation, intended and rational use of agricultural land, preventing the use for non-agricultural purposes, production of healthy food, protection of health of people, animals and plant life, undisturbed use and protection of the environment.

639. Apart from that, Law on Agricultural Land in Article 1, paragraph 1 defines *inter alia* basic principles and management, protection, use and regulation, disposal, records and other issues pertaining to agricultural land at the territory of Federation BiH. Article 2, paragraph 1 of said law defines agricultural land as a natural resource and a resource of public interest that enjoys special protection and is used for agricultural production and may not be used for other purposes except in cases and under the conditions defined by this law. The law divides monitoring competences and powers to FBiH and cantonal agricultural inspection. Article 48, paragraph 1 of the said law prescribes that change of use of agricultural land is to be implemented in accordance with spatial plans and acts prescribed by this law. Agricultural land can be used for non-agricultural purposes with the approval of cantonal ministries and upon payment of fees prescribed by the Law on Agricultural Land.

640. Soil monitoring is done on the basis of the provisions of the FBiH Law on Agricultural Land. FBiH Ministry of Agriculture, Water and Forestry adopted, *inter alia*, the following Rule books:

(1) Law on Chemicals (Official Gazette of FBiH No. 77/20).
(2) Rule book on determining allowed quantities of harmful and dangerous substances in land and methods of testing (Official Gazette of FBiH, No. 72/09).
(3) Rule book on conditions to be met by scientific-expert institutions and laboratories to perform tasks of project development, testing and measurement of land (Official Gazette of FBiH, No. 39/10).

---

752. Directorate for European Integration, *Answers to the Questionnaire, Chapter 27, Environment and climate change*, 27 Feb. 2018. p. 125.
753. *See*: Directorate for European Integration, *Answers to the Questionnaire, Chapter 27, Environment and climate change*, 27 Feb. 2018, p. 683.

(4) Rule book on methodology of monitoring of agricultural soil condition (Official Gazette of FBiH, No. 38/11), etc.[754]

III. Brčko District of Bosnia and Herzegovina

641. In the Brčko District of BiH, following laws apply:

(1) Law on Agricultural Land (Official Gazette of BD BiH, Nos 32/04, 20/06, 19/07).
(2) Law on Spatial Planning and Construction (Official Gazette of BD BiH, No. 29/08).
(3) Law on Environment Protection (Official Gazette of BD BiH, Nos 24/04, 19/07, 1/05 and 9/09).
(4) Law on Waste management (Official Gazette of BD BiH, Nos 25/04, 19/07, 1/05, 2/08 and 9/09).
(5) Law on Utility Activities (Official Gazette of BD BiH, Nos 30/04, 24/07 and 09/13).
(6) Law on Water Protection (Official Gazette of BD BiH, Nos 25/04, 1/05 and 19/07).
(7) Law on Nature Protection (Official Gazette of BD BiH, Nos 24/04, 1/05, 19/07 and 9/09).[755]

A. *The Law on Agricultural Land of Brčko District of Bosnia and Herzegovina*

642. The Law on Agricultural Land of BD regulates issues of property legal rights at agricultural land, planning and preservation of the agricultural land, usage, trade, lease and regulation of the agricultural land, as well as supervision over implementation of provisions of this law and other agrarian operations in Brčko DC BiH. Article 1, paragraph 2 of said law prescribe that the provisions of this law shall be applied at forest land, unless otherwise specified by the law.

754. For more details, *See*: https://fmpvs.gov.ba/poljoprivreda-propisi/ (19 Jul. 2022).
755. *See*: https://skupstinabd.ba/ba/zakon.html (19 Jul. 2022).

Chapter 6. Noise

§1. Legislation

643. There is no general law or policy on noise reduction at the BiH level, as this area is regulated by entity, BD BiH and cantonal legislation. However, a several regulations adopted at the BiH level refer to noise.[756]

I. The Republic of Srpska

644. Jurisdiction over activities in the RS concerning noise, as one of the elements of the environment, is on the Ministry of Spatial Planning, Civil Engineering and Ecology, within which these activities are also performed Division for Environment Protection.

645. The new RS Law on Environmental Protection (Official Gazette of RS, No. 71/12, 79/15, 70/20) regulated the field of noise (Chapter II, Protection of Elements of Environment, Article 15). Article 23 of the same law states: 'A user of a noise source can use noise sources according to prescribed conditions, with the application of the prescribed protection measures that reduce noise emissions, i.e., the use of facilities, equipment, machines, means of transport and apparatuses causing noise. Noise protection is regulated by special legislation adopted by the Minister.' For projects for which, in accordance with this law, an environmental impact assessment is carried out and for facilities for which an environmental permit is issued, noise protection measures are determined in the environmental impact assessment study. For facilities that do not require an environmental permit, noise protection measures are determined by the urban planning and technical conditions, which form an integral part of the location conditions.

II. Federation of Bosnia and Herzegovina

646. In the FBiH noise issue was not regulated by a general law. Individual cantons in FBiH regulated noise issues with their laws.[757] In order to define the general policy in this area, the FBiH Ministry of Environment and Tourism prepared the Law on Protection Against Noise (Official Gazette of the FBiH, No. 110/12).

---

756. Law on aviation of BiH (Official Gazette BiH No. 39/09), Regulation on initial homologation of aircrafts and aircraft components (Official Gazette BiH No. 21/06), Regulation on airports (Official Gazette BiH No. 9/11), Regulation on permitted limits of noise (Official Gazette BiH No. 46/89). *See*: BiH MFTER. *Environmental Approximation Strategy of Bosnia and Herzegovina*, EAS – BiH, Ministry of Foreign Trade and Economic Relations of Bosnia and Herzegovina, May 2017, p. 124.

757. *See*, for example, Law on Protection from Noise (Official Gazette of Central Bosnia Canton, No. 11/00, Official Gazette of Sarajevo Canton, No. 23/16, Official Gazette of Tuzla Canton, No. 3/16).

A. The Law on Noise Protection

647. Basic legal act regulating noise[758] protection in the Federation of Bosnia and Herzegovina is the Law on Protection Against Noise (Official Gazette of FBiH, No. 110/12). It has the following six parts: Part I – General Provisions (Articles 1–3), Part II – The Highest Noise Level in dBA (decibel A-scale) and Protection Measures (Articles 4–20), Part III – Measurement, Monitoring and Noise Recording (Articles 21–26), Part IV – Supervision (Articles 27–28), Part V – Penalty Provisions (Articles 29–30) and Part VI – Transitional and Final Provisions (Articles 31–33).

648. According to Article 1, paragraph 1, this law prescribes permitted noise level, measures for noise protection, the manner of noise measuring and recording, noise limiting values classified according to the ambience, purpose of the space[759] and time of the day (day or night) in order to protect human health, protection of working and living space, as well as protection of the environment in general. The law also regulates other issues of importance for noise protection (Article 1, paragraph 2).

1. The Noise Protection Measures and Noise Maps

649. Noise sources[760] should not cause noise in the surrounding area that exceeds the levels determined by this law (Article 4, paragraph 1.)[761]

650. According to Article 5 noise protection is achieved by:

- Preventing of noise.
- Controlling of the space use and space layout of the actual and potential noise sources in relation to noise sensitive spaces.
- Reducing the number of noise sources.
- Prescribing sound insulation in accordance with the purpose of space in the new buildings.
- Monitoring, controlling and recording the noise level.

758. *Noise* is any sound which value exceeds the permitted level prescribed by this or by other Laws, regarding the time and place where it arises and the environment in which people work and stay (Art. 2, para. 1).

759. *Space* is all indoor and outdoor spaces in settlements and outside settlements in which people work and stay, permanently or temporarily for education, rest, recreation and so on. Under the *space* are implied and protected areas defined by specific Laws that are in any way sensitive to noise (Art. 2, para. 1).

760. *Noise source*, in terms of this Law is any object with the resources for work and transport, devices and installations, noisy activities of humans and animals as well as other objects and actions that produce noise, which exceeds the permitted level for this type of noise (hereinafter, 'noise sources') (Art. 2, para. 1).

761. The highest permitted noise levels in terms of this Law are determined in Tables 1, 2 and 3, while correction of the measured noise levels are shown in Table 4 (Art. 4, para. 2).

- Prohibiting of work for all purposes, i.e., noise sources that cause noise above the limiting values.
- Eliminating or limiting the noise at the permitted level.
- Restricting of work of noise source during the night and on non-working days.
- Drawing up noise maps of existing noise sources and monitoring.
- Drawing up noise maps on the base of the models for all planned changes in space which may endanger or increase noise levels in hazardous areas according to provisions of this law.
- Removing or changing the purpose of the buildings.

651. Noise protection is provided by the competent authorities of the Federation of Bosnia and Herzegovina, cantons, towns and municipalities (Article 6, paragraph 1). Noise protection is also provided by owners of sound sources (Article 6, paragraph 2).

652. The Federation of Bosnia and Herzegovina, cantonal, town and municipal government bodies responsible for spatial planning issues within their jurisdiction provide preparation of noise maps[762] for prediction, recording and monitoring of noise levels (Article 8, paragraph 1).

2. Application of Noise Protection Measures in the Process of Permit Issuing

653. For plants for which is prescribed obligation for environmental impact assessments, as well as for plants that can be built and put into service only if they have an environmental permit-noise protection measures need to be included in the environmental impact study, in action plans, as well as in the environmental permit in accordance with Tables 1 and 2 (Article 10, paragraph 1). For plants and facilities, i.e., for all activities that do not require obtaining of the environmental permits, in process of issue the urban permit, the competent authority is obliged to prescribe conditions for noise protection in accordance with this law (Article 11, paragraph 1).[763]

654. Articles 12–18 of the Law on Noise Protection prescribe measures for noise protection from the following sources:

- Noise from the construction sites.
- Noise from roads and other sources.
- Noise of acoustic devices indoors.
- Noise of acoustic devices outdoors.
- Noise emission produced using devices, machinery, means of transport and other technical equipment.

762. Noise map is a graphical presentation of existing and planned noise levels and is an integral part of the spatial plans (Art. 8, para. 2).
763. Authority responsible for issuing the approval for performing activities cannot issue a permit if conditions for noise protection are not met (Art. 11, para. 2).

Noise sources can also be used when it exceeds the highest permissible noise level only in case of elimination consequences of natural disasters and states that could cause greater material damage or endanger health of people and their surroundings, as well as in cases from Article 12, paragraph 2 of this law (Article 19, paragraph 1).

655. It is forbidden to carry out works, i.e., activities which due to excessive noise, including music reproduction, disrupt nocturnal peace and rest in the settlements in time of 10 PM to 06 AM the next day (Article 20, paragraph 1).

3. Noise Measuring and Monitoring

656. Noise measurements are performed by the legal entity authorized for this activity, which has permanently employed specialist for noise measurement and equipment corresponding to recommendations of IEC 651 and 804 Type 1 and EN 60804 Sound Meter with integrating and averaging (Article 21, paragraph 1).

657. Measuring of noise outdoors is carried out in accordance with BAS ISO 17025:2005 (Article 22, paragraph 4). Measurements are made for the purpose of monitoring and controlling of the noise impact outdoors (Article 23, paragraph 1). For noise monitoring and controlling outdoors a noise study is to be prepared (Article 23, paragraph 2), as well as new and existing spatial-planning documents (Article 23, paragraph 3). Measuring is done according to group of standards BAS ISO 140 for measuring of sound insulation in buildings and in construction elements, for laboratory and for field measurements, as well as for measurements for each specific case (Article 26, paragraph 2).

4. Supervision

658. Supervision over the implementation of this Law within its jurisdiction is performed by relevant administrative bodies of the Federation of Bosnia and Herzegovina, cantons, towns and municipalities (Article 27, paragraph 1).[764]

The authorizations of the competent inspection in performing inspection supervision are prescribed in Article 28, paragraph 1.

III. Brčko District of Bosnia and Herzegovina

659. The Law on Environmental Protection of BDBiH contains several provisions relating to noise. However, it does not prescribe the obligation to adopt detailed bylaws to regulate noise. Regarding noise emissions, the Rulebook on the

764. Supervision over implementation provisions of this Law relating to the noise in period from 10 PM to 06 AM, which disrupts of public order, is performed by responsible police departments (Art. 27, para. 2).

permitted levels of noise and noise intensity of BiH from 1989 (Official Gazette SR BiH No. 46/89) is currently being applied.[765]

765. BD. *Strategija aproksimacije propisa pravnoj stečevini EU u oblasti zaštite životne sredine/okoliša Brčko distrikta BiH*[Strategy for harmonisation of Brčko District BiH environmental legislation with EU *acquis*], EAS Brčko Distrikta, February 2017, p. 63.

Chapter 7. Radiation

§1. Monitoring

660. 'Thanks to the IAEA37 in Vienna, there are 5 automatic stations in BiH in each entity which perform continuous measurement of ionizing radiation in the ambient air. Reporting is done on an annual basis by the Federal Hydro-Meteorological Institute of BiH and the Institute of Public Health of RS. Those institutions measure the absorbed dose of ionizing radiation on a daily basis. According to available data on continuous long-term measurements and test measurements in the region of central BiH, the absorbed dose of ionizing radiation is 0.8 to 1.1 mSv/y. The measured values are below standard world norms ... '[766]

§2. Competences

661. State Regulatory Agency for Radiation Safety and Nuclear Safety is established with the purpose of performing administrative and professional operations in the field of ionizing radiation.[767] In line with the Law on Radiation and Nuclear Safety in Bosnia and Herzegovina (Off. Gazette of BiH, No. 88/07) and other regulations, the agency independently perform regulatory control over safety of radiation sources, radioactive waste safety and transportation safety. The agency is an independent administrative organization and executes its authorizations under direct supervision of the Council of Ministers of Bosnia and Herzegovina.

662. Policy on the safety of ionizing radiation sources in Bosnia and Herzegovina has been adopted by the Council of Ministers of Bosnia and Herzegovina (Official Gazette of BiH No. 55/12). The general objective of the policy is 'establishment of an efficient and transparent radiation protection system, thus ensuring the basis for protection of the people and the environment against harmful effects of ionizing radiation in accordance with international standards'.[768]

---

766. BiH MFTER, *State of the environment Report of the Bosnia and Herzegovina 2012*, *supra* p. 163.

767. For additional information, *see*: http://www.darns.gov.ba/en/EnglishDARNS/AboutAs (19 Jul. 2022).

768. *See*: http://www.darns.gov.ba/en/LegislationAndDocuments/Politika_i_Strategije_en (19 Jul. 2022). The main objective of the safety is 'protection of the people and the environment against detrimental effects of ionizing radiation, and it applies to all circumstances that can give rise to the increase of radiation risks. The safety covers nuclear safety, radiation safety, safe management of radioactive waste, and safe transport of radioactive material'. The main objectives of the security are 'prevention of unauthorized access, loss, theft or unauthorized transfer of radioactive sources; reducing probability of exposure to such sources; reducing probability of misusing the source with the aim of inflicting damage to individuals, society and the environment; and also alleviating and minimizing radiological consequences'. *See also*: Strategy of radioactive waste management in Bosnia and Herzegovina (Official Gazette BiH No. 1/14).

§3. LEGISLATION

I. International Treaties

663. Bosnia and Herzegovina succeeded to the 1963 Vienna Convention on Civil Liability for Nuclear Damage on 30 June 1998, with effect from 1 March 1992. Apart from that, BiH succeeded to the 1979 Convention on the Physical Protection of Nuclear Materials on 30 June 1998 (with effect from 1 March 1992); to the 1986 Convention on the Early Notification of a Nuclear Accident on 30 June 1998 (with effect from 1 March 1991); to the 1986 Convention on Assistance in the Case of a Nuclear Accident or Radiological Emergency on 30 June 1998 (with effect from 1 March 1992). BiH acceded to the 1968 Treaty on the Non-Proliferation of Nuclear Weapons on 15 August 1994. Bosnia and Herzegovina signed the 1996 Comprehensive Nuclear Test Ban Treaty on 24 September 1996.[769]

II. Bosnia and Herzegovina National Legislation

A. *The Law on Radiation and Nuclear Safety*

664. Basic legal act regulating radiation and nuclear safety[770] issues in Bosnia and Herzegovina is the Law on Radiation and Nuclear Safety (Official Gazette of BIH, No. 88/07). It has the following seven parts: Part I – General Provisions (Articles 1–3), Part II – Regulatory Body (Articles 4–12), Part III – Conditions for Conducting of Activities (Articles 13–18), Part IV – Emergency Events,[771] Nuclear Accidents[772] and Nuclear Damage (Article 19), Part V – Regulatory Inspection (Articles 20–21), Part VI – Penalty Provisions (Articles 22–25), Part VII – Transitional and Final Provisions (Articles 26–29).

665. According to Article 1, paragraph 1, this law regulates the control system of ionizing radiation sources, the protection of people, present and future generations, as well as protection of the environment from the exposure[773] or potential exposure[774] to ionizing radiation.[775]

769. BiH is a member of the International Atomic Energy Agency (IAEA). *See*: https://www.iaea.org/about/governance/list-of-member-states (19 Jul. 2022).

770. *Nuclear safety* – set of measures which mitigate the consequences of nuclear accident in the regional countries, which can affect Bosnia and Herzegovina (Art. 3, para. 1, point hh).

771. *Emergency event (Accident)*–shall mean an event resulting, or which might result, in irradiation, i.e., radioactive contamination of working environment, persons working with sources of ionizing radiation, population or material goods, exceeding the limits set forth by the regulations (Art. 3, para. 1, point a).

772. *Nuclear accident* – event or series of events occurring in operations of a nuclear facility, causing one of the consequences that fall under the definition of an emergency event (Art. 3, para. 1, point ii).

773. *Exposure* – process of exposure to ionizing radiation (Art. 3, para. 1, point j).

774. *Potential exposure* – an exposure that is not expected to happen for certainly, but which may result from an accident at a radiation source, from an event or series of events that are likely to happen, and that includes equipment failures or errors during operation (Art. 3, para. 1, point k).

666. The objective of this law is to ensure ionizing radiation protection – radiation and nuclear safety of the citizens of Bosnia and Herzegovina, in the following way:

- To establish and implement a system which enables development and use of ionizing radiation sources in accordance with the requirements for health protection and safety.
- To establish and to maintain a regulatory programme for ionizing radiation sources, and thereby to ensure compatibility with international standards on safety of radiation sources[776] and for protection from ionizing radiation.
- To establish a State regulatory body for radiation and nuclear safety with appropriate set of functions and responsibilities, which also has required resources for the establishment of regulatory control[777] (Article 2, paragraph 1).

1. Regulatory Body

667. The headquarter of the State Regulatory Agency for Radiation and Nuclear Safety (hereinafter, 'the Agency') is to be in Sarajevo, while branch regional offices shall be established in the Republic of Srpska Entity, with office in Banja Luka, as well as in the Federation of Bosnia and Herzegovina Entity, with office in Mostar (Article 5, paragraphs 4 and 5).

2. Conditions for Conducting of Activities: An Approval Request

668. It is prohibited to possess a radiation source and to perform activities with the radiation source without an approval of the competent state body (Article 14, paragraph 1). Every legal entity with the intention to perform activity or to possess the radiation source shall be obliged to submit to the agency in the headquarter or through entity branch offices an approval request which has to be in the form of a registration or a licence (Article 14, paragraph 2). Approval shall be issued for a certain period of time, for the period from one to five years, depending on the type of ionizing radiation sources and the request for its use (Article 14, paragraph 3).[778]

669. The licence holder and registrant shall bear the primary liability for the safety of the radiation source (Article 15, paragraph 1). The licence holder shall be

775. *Ionising radiation* – for the purpose of radiation protection, shall mean the radiation capable of producing ion pairs in biological materials (Art. 3, para. 1, point e).
776. *Radiation source* – anything that may cause radiation exposure, which includes radioactive material and radiation generating equipment (Art. 3, para. 1, point ff).
777. *Regulatory control* – any form of control or of regulation applied by the regulatory body to the facilities or activities for the reasons relating to radiation protection, for safety of radiation sources or for safety of radioactive sources (Art. 3, para. 1, point ee).
778. The Agency shall issue preliminary consent for the purpose of obtaining of the radiation source (Art. 14, para. 4).

liable for safe management of radioactive waste[779] resulting from performing activity involving the radioactive source (Article 15, paragraph 2). Licence holder or registrant shall, at the request of the Agency or at their own initiative, submit the information related to the ionizing radiation source activities (Article 15, paragraph 3).

3. Emergency Events, Nuclear Accidents and Nuclear Damage

670. The Council of Ministers of Bosnia and Herzegovina shall, at the proposal of the agency, issue the state action plan for emergency cases for protection of population from ionizing radiation in the case of emergency event, nuclear accident or occurrence of nuclear damage (Article 19, paragraph 1).[780] In accordance with the international conventions, including the Vienna Convention on Civil Liability for Nuclear Damage, the agency shall be obliged to develop the state nuclear safety plan in case of an accidents in nuclear facilities in other countries, which can affect nuclear safety status in Bosnia and Herzegovina (Article 19, paragraph 3).

4. Regulatory Inspection

a. Inspection

671. All areas of regulatory liability from this law shall fall under the competence of the Agency, which incorporates the Radiation Safety and Nuclear Safety Inspection, which shall perform the activities within its jurisdiction through the agency in headquarter, as well as through entity offices (Article 20, paragraph 1).[781,782] Inspection carried out by the agency, announced or unannounced, must constitute a continuous activities (Article 20, paragraph 4).

b. Radiation Safety and Nuclear Safety Inspectors

672. The radiation safety and nuclear safety control shall be performed by the state inspectors for radiation safety and nuclear safety (Article 21, paragraph 1).

---

779. *Radioactive waste* – material, in any physical form, remaining from activities or interventions, and which no further use is foreseen, and which: (i) contains or which is contaminated with radioactive substances and has an activity or concentration of activities higher than the level of the realize from regulatory requirements and (ii) exposure which is not excluded from regulations (Art. 3, para. 1, Point dd).
780. State action plan shall be reviewed and updated as needed, in relation to the realization of the plan for protection from ionizing radiation in accordance with the international conventions (Art. 19, para. 2).
781. *Inspection* – examination, observation, measurement, or test undertaken to assess structures, components and materials, as well as operational activities, technical processes, organizational processes, procedures, and personnel competence (Art. 3, para. 1, point m).
782. The Agency must define a planned and systematic inspection programme (Art. 20, para. 2).

In case of immediate threat to the life and health of the people, an inspector may order temporary measures. An appeal against the decision on temporary measures shall not postpone its enforcement (Article 21, paragraph 3).

B. Other Relevant BiH Regulations

673.

(1) Rule book on the ionizing radiation protection in medical exposure (Official Gazette BiH No. 13/11).[783]
(2) Rule book on categorization of radiation threats (Official Gazette BiH No. 102/11).
(3) Rule book on radiation protection in occupational exposure and exposure of the population (Official Gazette BiH No. 102/11).
(4) Rule book on inspection supervision in the field of radiation and nuclear safety (Official Gazette BiH No. 65/10).
(5) Rule book on notification and authorization of activities with ionizing radiation sources (Official Gazette BiH No. 66/10).
(6) Rule book on requirements for the transfer and use of sources of ionising radiation (Official Gazette BiH No. 66/10).
(7) Rule book on the authorization of legal entities that perform the medical examinations and the manner of conducting medical examination of persons occupationally exposed to ionizing radiation (Official Gazette BiH No. 25/12).
(8) Rule book on the control of closed radioactive sources of high-activity and sources of unknown owner (Official Gazette BiH No. 62/12).
(9) Rule book on ways of keeping records of legal entities performing activities with ionizing radiation sources (Official Gazette BiH No. 67/12).
(10) Rule book on the safety of Transport of radioactive materials (Official Gazette BiH No. 96/12).
(11) Rule book on the security of nuclear material and radioactive sources (Official Gazette BiH No. 85/13).
(12) Rule book on recognition of the qualified expert status (Official Gazette BiH No. 84/14).
(13) Rule book on the monitoring of radioactivity in the environment (Official Gazette BiH No. 54/14).
(14) Rule book on the concentration limits for radionuclides in food, feed, medicines, items of general use, building materials and other goods placed on the market (Official Gazette BiH No. 54/14).
(15) Rule book on the training in ionizing radiation protection (Official Gazette BiH No. 68/15).
(16) Rule book on radioactive waste management (Official Gazette BiH No. 68/15).

783. *See*: http://www.darns.gov.ba/en/EnglishDARNS/RegulationsDescription (19 Jul. 2022). *See also* Law on Protection from Ionizing Radiation and Radiation safety (Official Gazette of RS, Nos. 52/01, 63/02 and 113/05). The Law on responsibility for nuclear damage (Official Gazette of BiH No. 87/13).

(17) Rule book on the medical surveillance of occupationally exposed workers (Official Gazette BiH No. 68/15).
(18) Rule book for technical services for ionizing radiation protection (Official Gazette BiH No. 68/15).
(19) Rule book on radiation protection officer ('Official Gazette BiH' No. 86/15).
(20) Rule book on the national register of individuals exposed to ionizing radiation (Official Gazette BiH No. 86/15).
(21) Rule book on radiation protection of outside workers (Official Gazette BiH No. 86/15).
(22) Rule book on the radiation protection and medical physics service (Official Gazette BiH No. 86/15).
(23) Rule book on radiological emergency events in practices involving radioactive sources (Official Gazette BiH No. 30/16).

§4. Harmonization with EU Legislation

674. B&H has ratified most of the international treaties, conventions and protocols in this area. 'In terms of meeting international commitments on data submission, the infrastructure available to the agency needs to be improved … ' 'B&H is not a member of the European Community Urgent Radiological Information Exchange system (ECURIE).'[784] According to the Progress Report for 2021, BiH 'made no progress on nuclear energy, nuclear safety and radiation protection,' and 'the country shall consider participating to the European Radiological Data Exchange Platform (EURDEP) and to the European Community Urgent Radiological Information Exchange (ECURIE).'[785]

784. EC, *Bosnia and Herzegovina 2016 Progress Report, supra* p. 62.
785. EC, *Bosnia and Herzegovina 2021 Progress Report,* p. 100.

Chapter 8. Other Sectors

§1. Noxious Substances

I. Chemical Industry

675. 'After all the events between 1990 and present day, the chemical industry in BiH was greatly reduced, and does not have capacities that once existed.'[786] The chemical industry has collapsed, while the food processing industry is facing difficulties because of obsolete plants and the shortage of domestic agricultural products.[787]

II. Reporting

676. There is still no systematic reporting on toxic chemicals and substances in all segments of the environment. There are information sources which clearly state that water, soil and food in BiH contain certain concentrations of harmful substances. The main sources of eco-toxic substances are inadequate disposal of municipal, medical and industrial waste, quarrying waste and a lack of wastewater treatment plants as well as sewage directly discharged into open receiving water bodies.[788]

III. Legislation

677. 'At the state level, there are no law on chemicals and biocides, nor other strategic or legal documents regulating these areas.'[789] Most of the chemicals legislation is at the entity level, and not at the state level. However, there are several regulations related to the chemicals at the state level. According to the Law on Food (Official Gazette of BiH, Nos 50/04) the BiH Food Safety Agency is competent for finding, collecting, analysing and summarizing scientific and technical data in the

786. BiH Council of Ministers, *Answers to the List of EU Questions on Chapter 27, Environment, supra* p. 309.

787. 'The metal-working industry is in a crisis because of its dependence on the defence industry, while the leather and textile production industry cannot achieve adequate competitiveness because of salary levels in BiH'. BiH MFTER, Ministry of Physical Planning, Civil Engineering and Ecology of Republic of Srpska, Federal Ministry of Environment and Tourism, UNDP, *Initial National Communication of Bosnia and Herzegovina under the United Nations Framework Convention on Climate Change, supra* p. 29.

788. Concentrations of toxic substances are being measured, but reporting on findings in most cases is not unified. Usually, food samples are taken and analysed for toxic substance content, but not many studies on eco-toxicology are conducted. BiH MFTER, *State of the environment Report of the Bosnia and Herzegovina 2012, supra* p. 37. For the state of environment in Federation of BiH, *see* FMET, *State of the environment in the Federation of Bosnia and Herzegovina – 2010 Report*, 2010, *supra* pp. 44, 54, 59, 68 79.

789. Directorate for European Integration, *Answers to the Questionnaire, Chapter 27, Environment and climate change*, 27 Feb. 2018, p. 578.

framework of its activities.[790] It is also responsible, in cooperation with the competent bodies in BiH, for the process of health risks assessment. Data collection procedures and risk assessment procedures for contaminants and residues in food are established in the BiH. Rules on maximum allowed levels for specific contaminants in food (Official Gazette of BiH, No. 37/09) prescribe the maximum allowed concentrations of substances.[791]

678. Other activities are performed and regulated at the level of the entities and BD BiH. The main competencies for chemicals management in BiH is given to the Federal Ministry of Health in the FBiH, the Ministry of Health and Social Protection in the RS, and the Department for Health and Other Services of the BD Government. These institutions work closely with environmental ministries when it concerns chemicals and environmental protection. However, there are differences in the level of development of legislation in the field of chemicals and biocides between the two entities.

A. *The Republic of Srpska*

1. Chemicals

679. The RS Ministry of Health and Social Protection is competent in the field of chemicals and biocides in the RS, while in the area of plant protection agents it is responsible for classification, packaging and labelling of these agents, as well as for determining the conditions of their storage in the manufacturing and wholesale distribution.[792]

680. The Republic of Srpska Chemical Safety Strategy for the 2012–2016 period (Official Gazette of RS No. 49/12) was a document comprising goals and measures for environmental protection in terms of ensuring a comprehensive chemical security management in RS.[793]

---

790. *See*: https://fsa.gov.ba/hr/o-nama-2/o-agenciji/sta-radimo/ (19 Jul. 2022).

791. BiH Council of Ministers, *Answers to the List of EU Questions on Chapter 27, Environment, supra* p. 294. *See also*, BiH Law on Phyto-Pharmaceuticals (Official Gazette of BiH, No. 49/04). *See also*: Rule book on the classification, packaging, marking, and equipping of phytopharmaceuticals with the instructions of their use (Official Gazette BiH, No. 10/16), Rule book on the necessary documentation for the assessment of phytopharmaceuticals (Official Gazette BiH, No. 12/16), A list of active substances authorized for use in plant protection products in BiH (Official Gazette BiH, No. 6/16, 63/16, and 86/16). For more information, *see*: Directorate for European Integration, *Answers to the Questionnaire, Chapter 27, Environment and climate change*, 27 Feb. 2018, p. 579.

792. For more information *see*: Directorate for European Integration, *Answers to the Questionnaire, Chapter 27, Environment and climate change*, p. 600.

793. BiH Council of Ministers, *Answers to the List of EU Questions on Chapter 27, Environment, supra* p. 11. *See*: https://www.vladars.net/sr-SP-Cyrl/Vlada/Ministarstva/MZSZ/PAO/Documents/Strategija%20hemijske%20bezbjednosti%20RS%20cirilica%2022.06.2012.pdf (19 Jul. 2022).

a. The Law on Chemicals

681. Basic legal act regulating chemical[794] issues in the Republic of Srpska is the Law on Chemicals (Official Gazette of RS, No. 21/18) It has the following thirteen parts: Part I – General Provisions (Articles 1–6), Part II – Classification, Packaging and Labelling of Chemicals (Articles 7–14), Part III – Safety Data Sheet (Articles 15–20), Part IV – Performing Activities with Chemicals (Articles 21–28), Part V – Integrated Chemicals Inventory (Articles 29–33), Part VI – Restrictions and Bans of Chemicals (Articles 34–37), Part VII – Conditions for Import and Export of Chemicals (Articles 38–39), Part VIII – Conditions for the Placing Detergents on the Market (Articles 40–42), Part IX – Integrated Management of Chemicals (Articles 43–45), Part X – Special Provisions (Articles 46–49), Part XI – Supervision (Articles 50–53), Part XII – Penalty Provisions (Articles 54–55), Part XIII – Transitional and Final Provisions (Articles 56–61).

682. This law regulates the classification, labelling and packaging of chemicals; security-technical sheet; performing of activities with chemicals; integrated chemical inventory; limitations and prohibitions of chemicals; conditions for the import and export of chemicals; placing of detergents on the market; integrated chemical management; monitoring and other issues of importance for the safe chemicals management in the Republic of Srpska (Article 1).

i. Classification, Labelling and Packaging

683. Legal entity as registered producer or importer which puts chemical at market is obliged to classify, label and package[795] chemicals in accordance with this law and regulations adopted on the base of it (Article 7, paragraph 1).[796]

684. A legal entity and importer of chemicals is obliged to report to the Ministry, prior to the commencement of production and import, and shall be responsible

794. *Chemical* means a substance and mixture containing the substance (Art. 6, para. 1, point 1).

795. The process of classification, labelling and packaging of chemicals is carried out in accordance with the Globally Harmonised System (GHS) system in the manner in which this system is applied in the European Union (hereinafter, 'the EU') (Art. 7, para. 2).

796. Classification, labelling and packaging does not apply to following chemicals: (a) which are used in scientific research purposes and development and are not placed on the market, which are used under controlled conditions and with reduced exposure; (b) chemicals that are placed on the market in final form (medicines and medical devices used in human and veterinary medicine; cosmetic products; food and animal feed, additives for food and animal feed, flavourings and additives for animal feed (Art. 5, para. 1).

for the accuracy, completeness and truthfulness of the data submitted in the application to the Ministry (Article 28, paragraph 1).[797] Natural person handling chemicals is obliged to store a chemical so that the chemical does not endanger human health or the environment (Article 22, paragraph 1).[798]

ii. The Security Data Sheet and Integrated Chemical Inventory

685. The supplier of the chemical is obliged to deliver to the recipient of the chemical safety data sheet (hereinafter, 'SDS'), prepared in accordance with this Law and the regulations adopted there under (Article 15, paragraph 1). SDS is provided free of charge in written or electronic form during the first delivery of chemicals (Article 16, paragraph 4).[799]

686. The Integrated chemical inventories that are placed on the market of the Republic, consist of the Chemical Inventory, Biocides Inventory and data on Plant protection products (Article 29, paragraph 1). The Integrated Chemical Inventory is kept by the Ministry as an electronic database (Article 29, paragraphs 5).[800]

687. The Minister shall issue a List of Classified Substances that is harmonized with the Harmonized Classification and labelling for Certain Hazardous Substances in the EU. The list of classified substances shall be published in the Official Gazette of the Republika of Srpska (Article 9, paragraphs 5–6).

iii. Good Laboratory Practice

688. Toxicological and ecotoxicological tests are carried out in laboratories applying the principles of good laboratory practice. The Minister shall issue a Rulebook on the methods of testing chemicals (Article 10, paragraphs 2–3). Good Laboratory Practice (hereinafter, 'GLP') means a quality system that relates to organizational processes and conditions under which health, environmental and human health studies are planned, performed, monitored, recorded, archived and displayed (Article 11, paragraph 1).[801]

797. On the basis of the submitted application, the Ministry shall register in the Register of Manufacturers and Importers of Chemicals (hereinafter, 'the Register') (Art. 28, para. 2).
798. Natural persons who handle chemical are obligated to collect, store and safely dispose of residues of chemicals or packaging of it in accordance with the regulations regarding waste management (Art. 22, para. 2).
799. The Minister shall issue the Rulebook on the contents of the SDS (Art. 17, para. 4).
800. The Minister issues the Rulebook on Integrated Chemical inventory (Art. 29, para. 6).
801. The Minister issues the Rulebook on principles of good laboratory practice and Rulebook on supervision and check of good laboratory practice principles (Art. 11, paras 2–3).

iv. The Conditions for Import and Export of Chemicals

689. Prior notification procedure (PNP) is carried out in accordance with the Rotterdam Convention for the import and export of certain substances for which the restriction or prohibition of production, placing on the market and use, as well as certain Mixtures and products containing that substance are established (Article 38, paragraph 1). For conducting of PNP procedure, exporter of chemicals pays the fee and submits the request to the Ministry (Article 38, paragraph 2 and 4).[802]

v. Supervision

690. The administrative supervision of implementation of this Law and the regulations adopted there under shall be carried out by the Ministry (Article 50, paragraph 1).[803] Inspection supervision over implementation of this Law and the regulations adopted there under, related to the retail or use of chemicals, shall be performed by the health inspector within the body of the local self-government unit, while regulations related to the safety at work shall be performed by Republic Administration for inspection affairs over labour inspection (Article 50, paragraph 3).

691. In order to monitor the market situation and to take adequate measures in the field of chemicals management, the health inspection is obliged to submit to the Ministry reports on the findings and results of the performed inspections in the field of chemicals, and to exchange information in accordance with the regulation governing inspections (Article 53).

b. Other Relevant RS Regulations

i. The Law on Transport of Hazardous Materials

692. Basic legal act regulating transport of hazardous materials in the Republic of Srpska is the Law on Transport of Hazardous Materials (Official Gazette of RS, No. 15/16). It has the following ten parts: Part I – General Provisions (Articles 1–10), Part II – Provisions Relating to all Branches of Land Transport (Articles 11–33), Part III – Advisor for Safety and Persons Participating in the Transport of Materials in Road Traffic, Rail Traffic and on Inland Waterways (Articles 34–37), Part IV – Special Provisions on the Transport of Dangerous Goods in Road Traffic (Articles 38–48), Part V – Special Provisions on the Transport of Dangerous Goods in Railway Traffic (Articles 49–54), Part VI – Special Provisions on the Transport of Dangerous Goods on Inland Waterways (Articles 55–56), Part VII – Records

802. The Minister shall issue the Rulebook on conditions for export and import of chemicals (Art. 38, para. 5).

803. Supervision over the implementation of this Law and the regulations adopted there under is performed by the Republic Administration for Inspection Affairs over health inspection (Art. 50, para. 2).

(Articles 57–58), Part VIII – Supervisions (Articles 59–62), Part IX – Penal Provisions (Articles 63–64), and Part X – Transitional and Final Provisions (Articles 65–71).[804]

693. Following bylaws were adopted on the basis of the Law on Chemicals:[805]

Rulebook on the register of producers and importers of chemicals (Official Gazette of the RS, No. 69/18)
Rulebook on conditions for performing activities with (Official Gazette of the RS, No. 69/18)
Rulebook on the program of additional education for chemical advisers (Official Gazette of the RS, No. 69/18)
Rulebook on Chemical Inventory (Official Gazette of the RS, No. 69/18)
Rulebook on the content of records on chemicals and the method of annual reporting (Official Gazette of the RS, No. 69/18)
Rulebook on the amount of fees related to chemicals (Official Gazette of the RS, No. 69/18)
Rulebook on the content of the safety and technical sheet (Official Gazette of the RS, No. 104/18)
Rulebook on detergents (Official Gazette of the RS, No. 14/19 and 32/19)
Rulebook on the Integral Inventory of Chemicals (Official Gazette of the RS, No. 26/19)
Rulebook on criteria for identification of substances as PBT or vPvB (Official Gazette of the RS, No. 48/19)
List of substances of particular concern (Official Gazette of the RS, No. 72/19)
List of substances that are candidates for inclusion in the List of Substances of Special Concern 2020 (Candidate List)
Rulebook on restrictions and prohibitions of chemicals (Official Gazette of the RS, No. 79/19)
Appendices to the regulations published in the Official Gazette of the RS, No. 2/19
Rulebook on conditions for the import and export of chemicals (Official Gazette of the RS, No. 86/19)
Rulebook on chemical testing methods (Official Gazette of the RS, No. 102/20)

---

804. This law regulates the conditions for the transport of dangerous substances in certain branches of traffic, the rights and obligations of persons participating in the transport, the conditions for packaging and vehicles, the issuance of permits for transport, the conditions for the appointment of safety advisors, the competence and conditions for the training of persons participating in transport, the competence of the ministries in relation to this transport in the Republic of Srpska, and supervision over the implementation of this law (Art. 1). For the text of the Law, see: https://mup.vladars.net/zakoni/rs_cir/ZAKON%20O%20PREVOZU%20OPASNIH%20MATERIJA%20(Sluzbeni%20Glasnik%20RS,%20broj%202015.16).pdf (21 Jul. 2022).

805. *See*: http://www.vladars.net/sr-SP-Cyrl/Vlada/Ministarstva/MZSZ/farmacija/hemikalije/zakoni/Pages/default.aspx (19 Jul. 2022).

Appendices to the rulebook published in the Official Gazette of the RS, No. 5/20
Rulebook on classification, labeling and packaging of chemicals (Official Gazette of the RS, No. 118/20)
Appendices to the regulations published in the Official Gazette of the RS, No. 6/20
List of classified substances (Official Gazette of the RS, No. 119/20)
Appendices to the regulations published in the (Official Gazette of the RS, No. 7/20
Rulebook on the method of chemical safety assessment and the content of chemical safety reports (Official Gazette of the RS, No. 126/20)
Rulebook on principles of good laboratory practice (Official Gazette of the RS, No. 10/21)
Rulebook on supervision and verification of the principles of good laboratory practice (Official Gazette of the RS, No. 10/21).[806]

2. Biocides

694. Ministry of Health and Social Protection is competent in classification, packaging and labelling of biocidal products in the procedure for pesticide registration. This is done as part of the registration process at the Ministry of Agriculture, Forestry and Water Management, in accordance with the instruction for classification, packaging and labelling of pesticides.

a. Law on Biocides

695. Field of biocides (pesticides that are not used in agriculture) in RS is regulated by the Law on Biocides (Official Gazette of RS No. 37/09). This law regulates conditions for placing of biocides on the market and use of biocides, which are related to the following: risk assessment and efficiency of biocides, which are necessary for obtaining a licence for placing of biocides on the market; classification; packaging; labelling; advertising and safety data sheet; licensing procedure; research and development; conditions for import of biocides; safe use; approval for production and transport of biocides; biocides records; prohibitions and restrictions; availability of data; supervision; and other issues of importance for safe placing on the market and use of biocides.[807]

---

806. For more details, *see*: RS MoSPCEE. *Program usklađivanja zakonodavstva Republike Srpske sa pravnom tekovinom EU u oblasti zaštite životne sredine*, [Program of approximation of the Republika Srpska Legislation with the EU environmental *acquis*], Banja Luka, November 2016, pp. 91–98, and 227–229.

807. Directorate for European Integration, *Answers to the Questionnaire, Chapter 27, Environment and climate change*, 27 Feb. 2018, p. 587.

b. Other Relevant RS Regulations

696. The RS Law on Plant Protection Product (Official Gazette of RS, No. 52/10) regulates activities of public interest in the field of plant protection products, establishment of the Plant Protection Commission, registration, transport, import and use of plant protection products in agriculture and forestry, services in the field of plant protection products, records, collection and sharing of data, as well as other issues of importance for application of plant protection products (Article 1, paragraph 1).

697. In accordance with the Law on Biocides several bylaws have been adopted.[808] These are the following:

(1) Rulebook on the conditions to be met by legal entities that use biocides for professional purposes (Official Gazette of RS, No. 79/14 No. 83/14).
(2) Rule book on conditions for performing the production, transport, use and storage of biocidal products (Official Gazette of RS, No. 79/14).
(3) Rule book on the types of biocides (Official Gazette of RS, No. 3/10).
(4) Rule book on the list of active substances allowed in biocidal products (Official Gazette of RS, Nos 32/10 and 72/11, 85/12, 14/15 and 24/16).
(5) Rule book on the list of active substances which are prohibited in biocidal products (Official Gazette of RS, Nos 32/10, 74/11, 85/12, 13/15, and 7/18).
(6) Rule book on content of basic data on biocidal products (Official Gazette of RS, Nos 32/10, 86/13, 33/17, and 12/21).
(7) Rule book on conditions and methods of work of the Commission for Biocides (Official Gazette of RS, No. 23/10).
(8) Rule book on conditions and the procedure for recognition of foreign trade licences for biocides (Official Gazette of RS, No. 49/10).
(9) Rule book on keeping of inventory of biocides (Official Gazette of RS, No. 57/10).
(10) Rules on the manner of keeping of records of biocides (Official Gazette of RS, Nos 99/11 and 86/13).
(11) Rule book on principles and procedures for risk assessment of biocides products (Official Gazette of RS, No. 3/10).
(12) Rule book on content of documents for assessment of active substances in biocides, assessment of biocides, scope and content of dossier and dossier summary (Official Gazette of RS, No. 3/10).
(13) Rule book on content of the report on monitoring procedure on biocides to be imported (Official Gazette of RS, No. 126/11, and 42/16).
(14) Rule book on specific requirements related to classification, packaging, labelling and trade of biocides (Official Gazette of RS, No. 10/11).
(15) Rule book on conditions to be met by legal entities which use biocides for professional purposes (Official Gazette of RS, No. 123/10).

808. *See*: http://www.vladars.net/sr-SP-Cyrl/Vlada/Ministarstva/MZSZ/farmacija/hemikalije/zakoni/Pages/default.aspx (19 Jul. 2022).

(16) Rule book on conditions for performing of production, traffic, usage and storage of biocides (Official Gazette of RS, No. 123/10).
(17) Rulebook on the list of active substances that are allowed in the biocidal product (Official Gazette of RS, No. 35/18)
(18) Rulebook on types of biocides (Official Gazette of RS, No. 32/18). [809]

B. *Federation of Bosnia and Herzegovina*

1. Chemicals

698. FBiH Ministry of Health has the authority to make regulations pertaining to chemicals.[810] The basic law that regulates the area of chemicals management is the Law on Chemicals (Official Gazette of FbiH, No. 77/20).[811]

The law consists of the following chapters: I – Basic provisions (Articles 1–6); II – Sorting, Marking and Packaging Chemicals (Articles 7–14); III – Safety Data Sheets (Articles 15–20); IV – Performing activities with chemicals (Articles 21–28); V – Integral Inventory of Chemicals (Articles 29–33); VI – Restrictions and prohibitions of chemicals (Articles 34–37); VII – Conditions for import and export of chemicals (Articles 38–39); VIII – Placing the detergent on the market (Articles 40–42); IX – Integrated management of chemicals (Articles 43–45); X – Special provisions (Articles 46–49); XI – Supervision (Articles 50–53); XII – Penal provisions (Articles 54–55); XIII – Transitional and Final provisions (Articles 56–61).[812]

a. Classification, Labelling and Packaging

699. The manufacturer and importer who place a chemical on the market are obliged to perform classification, labelling, and packaging in accordance with this

809. For more details, *see*: RS MoSPCEE. *Program usklađivanja zakonodavstva Republike Srpske sa pravnom tekovinom EU u oblasti zaštite životne sredine*, [Program of approximation of the Republika Srpska Legislation with the EU environmental *acquis*], Banja Luka, November 2016, pp. 91–98, and 229–230.
810. *See*: http://www.fmoh.gov.ba/# (21 Jul. 2022).
811. https://www.fmoh.gov.ba/index.php/zakoni-i-strategije/zakoni/zakon-o-hemikalijama.
812. In accordance with Art. 59 of the Law on Chemicals – until the adoption of the regulations from Art. 58 of the new Law, the regulations adopted on the basis of the Law on Trafficking in Poisons ('Official Gazette of RBH', No. 2/92 and 13/94) will be applied if they are not contrary to this law, namely: 1. Rulebook on technical and sanitary-hygienic conditions that must be met by organizations that deal with the trade in poisons ('Official Gazette of RBH', No. 2/92, 13/94, and 'Official Gazette of the FBH', No. 60/07); 3. Decision on establishing the List of poisons that can be put on market in the Federation of Bosnia and Herzegovina ('Official Gazette FBH', No. 50/08); 4. Decision of the Government of the Federation of Bosnia and Herzegovina on the prohibition or restriction of the import, production and use of certain hazardous industrial chemicals in the Federation of Bosnia and Herzegovina ('Official Gazette of the FBH', no. 52/16 and 47/19); 5. Decision of the Government of the Federation of Bosnia and Herzegovina on the procedure for determining conditions for the sale and use of poisons before the Federal Ministry of Health ('Official Gazette of the FBH', No. 66/16). https://www.fmoh.gov.ba/images/federalno_ministarstvo_zdravstva/zakoni_i_strategije/zakoni/dokumenti/LISTA_PROPISA_16112020.pdf (21 Jul. 2022).

law and the regulations adopted on the basis of this law. The process of classifying, labelling, and packaging chemicals is carried out in accordance with the GHS system, in the manner in which that system is applied in the European Union (hereinafter, 'EU') (Article 7).[813]

700. The producer and importer of dangerous chemicals are obliged to ensure the labelling of the hazards and the packaging of chemicals in the manner prescribed by this law and the regulations adopted on the basis of this law. In addition to the provisions of this law and regulations adopted on the basis of this law, the provisions of regulations on consumer protections also apply to the labelling of chemicals (Article 12, paragraphs 1 and 2).[814]

b. The Security Data Sheet and Integrated Chemical Inventory

701. The chemical supplier is obliged to provide the recipient of the chemical with a safety data sheet (STL) prepared in accordance with this law and the regulations adopted on the basis of this law (Article 15, paragraph 1). STL is submitted: (a) if the chemical meets the criteria for classification as dangerous in accordance with this law, or (b) if the substance is persistent, bioaccumulative, and toxic (PBT) or very persistent and very bioaccumulative (vPvB), or c) if the substance is included in the list of substances that are candidates for inclusion on the List of Substances of Special Concern from Article 35, paragraph (3) of this law for reasons other than those listed in point (a) and (b) of this paragraph (paragraph 2).[815] If a chemical safety report has been drawn up, the information specified in the STL should correspond to the information from that report, and the exposure scenario should be listed in the STL annex (paragraph 3).[816]

c. Good Laboratory Practice

702. Good laboratory practice (DLP) is a quality system that refers to organizational procedures and conditions under which tests related to human health and the environment are planned, performed, monitored, recorded, archived and displayed. The Minister regulates the principles of DLP in a special regulation (Article 11, paragraphs 1 and 2).[817]

---

813. The Federal Minister of Health (hereinafter, 'the Minister') regulates the classification, labelling and packaging of chemicals by special regulation (Art. 8, para. 2).
814. Labelling on the packaging must be in one of the languages that are in official use in Bosnia and Herzegovina (hereinafter: BiH) (para. 3).
815. The Minister regulates the criteria for identification of substances as PBT or vPvB by special regulation (para. 5).
816. Chemical safety report is a document on chemical safety assessment and risk reduction and control measures. In order to prepare a report on the safety of the chemical, an assessment of the safety of the chemical is carried out. On the basis of the safety assessment of the chemical, measures are determined to reduce and control the risk posed by the substance (Art. 19, paras 1–3).
817. The Minister regulates the supervision and verification of DLP principles by special regulation (Art. 11, para. 3).

d. Integral Inventory of Chemicals

703. The integral inventory of chemicals that are on the market of the Federation is managed by the Ministry and consists of the Inventory of chemicals, the Inventory of biocides, and data on plant protection products. Data for the Inventory of chemicals is provided by the producer and importer of chemicals based on the provisions of this law. Data for the Biocide Inventory is provided by the manufacturer and importer of biocide based on regulations on biocide. Data on plant protection products shall be submitted to the Ministry by the authority responsible for placing plant protection products on the market based on special regulations (Article 29 paragraphs 1–4).[818] The placing on the market of chemicals registered in the Inventory of Chemicals is free, except if the chemical is under a special import regime when it is necessary to obtain a permit in accordance with special regulations (Article 33).[819]

704. The Ministry provides mechanisms by which certain data obtained in the process of registration in the Inventory of Chemicals are made available to the public (Article 46). Data that must not be made available to the public, for the purpose of protecting the commercial interests of the data owner, and which the Ministry keeps as a business secret are: a) data on the exact composition of the mixture; b) precise data on the purpose and method of application of the substance; c) precise data on the quantities of chemicals produced and placed on the market; d) the relationship between producers or importers and their distributors and further users (Article 47 paragraph 1).[820]

e. Restrictions and Prohibitions of Chemicals

705. For chemicals that pose an unacceptable risk to human health and the environment, restrictions and bans on production, placing on the market, and use (hereinafter, 'restrictions and bans') are prescribed. Restrictions and prohibitions refer to prohibited or permitted ways of using a chemical and define other conditions related to the production, placing on the market, and use of substances, as well as mixtures and products containing that substance (Article 34), paragraphs 1 and 2).[821]

818. The Minister regulates the Integral Inventory of Chemicals by special regulation (Art. 29, para. 6).
819. A detergent may be placed on the market if the surfactant contained in that detergent meets the criteria of complete aerobic biodegradability and if other chemicals contained in the detergent meet the conditions prescribed by this law (Art. 40, para. 1).
820. In addition to the data referred to in Art. 47 of this law, which must not be made available to the public, the person who submits the data in accordance with this law may request that other data be marked as confidential, with the submission of an explanation to the effect that public disclosure of such data would cause damage to the owner data (Art. 48, para. 1).
821. The Minister regulates the restrictions and prohibitions of chemicals in a special regulation (para. 3).

706. In order to ensure the control of the risk of substances of particular concern and to ensure the replacement of these substances with appropriate safer alternatives, the minister shall establish a list of substances of particular concern by special regulation. The list of substances of particular concern is published in the 'Official Gazette of the Federation of Bosnia and Herzegovina'. (3) The Ministry also publishes on its website the List of substances that are candidates for inclusion in the List of Substances of Special Concern (hereinafter, 'Candidate List') (Article 35, paragraphs 1–3).[822]

f. The Conditions for Import and Export of Chemicals

707. In order to improve cooperation and division of responsibility in the international trade in hazardous chemicals, in accordance with the Rotterdam Convention, for the import and export of a certain substance for which a restriction or ban on the production, placing on the market and use, as well as certain mixtures and products, has been established, that contains that substance, the procedure of prior notification, i.e. the procedure of granting consent based on prior notification, is carried out (Article 38).[823] The implementation of the procedures from Article 38 of this law, as well as the implementation of the necessary procedures during the import of chemicals for which the prior notification procedure is prescribed, i.e. the procedure for granting consent based on the prior notification, is carried out in cooperation with the appointed body of BiH for the implementation of the Rotterdam Convention in BiH (Article 39).

g. Integrated Management of Chemicals

708. In order to ensure adequate management of chemicals, the Government of the Federation of Bosnia and Herzegovina (hereinafter, 'the Government of the Federation') establishes a Joint Working Body for the Integrated Management of Chemicals (hereinafter, 'the Joint Working Body'), in the appointment of which it is necessary to take into account equal representation of both sexes (Article 43 paragraph 1).[824] The Parliament of the Federation, on the proposal of the Government of the Federation, adopts the Chemical Safety Strategy of the Federation, with the

822. The lists from paragraphs (1) and (3) of this article are regularly updated (Art. 35, para. 4). The supplier of a product that contains a substance of particular concern or a substance from the Candidate List in a concentration greater than 0.1%, is obliged to provide every other distributor or further user in the supply chain with information sufficient for the safe use of that product, and at least the name of that substance. In addition, the supplier of the products is obliged to provide the information referred to in paragraph (1) of this article free of charge, at the request of the consumer (Art. 37).

823. The Minister regulates the conditions for the import and export of chemicals by special regulation (Art. 38, para. 5).

824. The joint working body is established from representatives of the federal ministries responsible for health issues; agriculture, water management and forestry; environment and tourism; work; internal affairs; industry, energy and mining; trade and entrepreneurship and representatives of the Institute for Public Health of the Federation of Bosnia and Herzegovina. The joint working body can

aim of efficient and transparent policy implementation in the field of safe management of chemicals, protection of citizens' health and environmental protection (Article 44, paragraph 1).[825]

h. Supervision

709. Supervision of the application of this law and regulations adopted on the basis of this law is performed by the Federal Administration for Inspection Affairs through federal sanitary inspectors for the control of poisons. Exceptionally from paragraph (1) of this article, in addition to the inspectors from paragraph (1) of this article, the inspection supervision over the application of this law and the regulations adopted on the basis of this law, which relates to retail, is performed by cantonal sanitary inspectors (Article 50, paragraphs 1 and 2).[826]

2. Bicides

710. There is no specific legislation on biocidal products in FBiH. Draft version of the Law on Biocides has been prepared.[827]

711. Only pesticides which are on the List of Active Substances that are found in the Phyto-pharmaceuticals that can be imported into BiH (Official Gazette of BiH, No. 4/12) can be imported. The list is regularly reviewed and harmonized with the EU legislation. FMAWMF is competent for the issuance of decisions approving putting pesticides on the domestic market.

712. Importer (distributor, agent) must meet all other requirements prescribed by the Law on Companies ('Official Gazette of FBiH' Nos 23/99, 45/00, 2/02, 6/02, 29/03, 68/05, 91/07, 84/08, 07/09 and 75/13) and the Law on Protection of Plants

---

invite to meetings representatives of business entities, scientific and research institutions and representatives of other organizations and institutions, with the aim of consulting and exchanging information necessary for adequate management of chemicals (para. 2).

825. The Ministry submits data from the Integral Inventory of Chemicals to the legal entity responsible for poisoning control, in order to implement preventive measures and treatment measures, especially in emergency cases. In urgent cases, the legal entity referred to in paragraph (1) of this article may also request information on the safety of the chemical from the person who placed the chemical on the market (Art. 45).

826. Legal entities, as well as a person performing an independent business activity – a trade, are obliged to enable the inspector to carry out the inspection and to make available the necessary documentation or the purpose of the inspection, to make available the necessary amount of samples in order to determine the compliance of the content of the chemical or product with the conditions prescribed by this law and regulations adopted on the basis of this law, and provide other necessary information and notifications (Art. 52).

827. *See*: http://parlamentfbih.gov.ba/dom_naroda/bos/parlament/propisi/El_materijali/Prijedlog%20zakona%20o%20biocidima.pdf (19 Jul. 2022). For more information, *see*: Directorate for European Integration, *Answers to the Questionnaire, Chapter 27, Environment and climate change*, 27 Feb. 2018, p. 567.

against Pests and Diseases that threaten the whole country and the rules on the conditions to be met by companies or other legal entities whose activity is trade of pesticides.

713. Before submitting a request to the FMAWMF for issue of an approval to import and request for trade of pesticides, importer (distributor, agent) must obtain a decision issued by the FBiH Ministry of Health proving that conditions for trade of poisons have been met and approving trade of poisons in FBiH, in accordance with the provisions of the Law on Trade of Poisons ('Official Gazette of RBiH', Nos 2/92 and 13/94).

IV. Ratified International Treaties

714. BiH is a member of the Rotterdam Convention on the Prior Informed Consent Procedure for Certain Hazardous Chemicals and Pesticides in International Trade (Official Gazette BiH – International treaties, No. 14/06).[828] Decision of the BiH Council of Ministers (Official Gazette of BiH No. 15/10) appointed the BiH Administration for Plant Health Protection as the state level body to coordinate the implementation of the Rotterdam Convention. Apart from that, BiH ratified the Stockholm Convention on Persistent Organic Pollutants,[829] and the Convention on Transboundary Effects of Industrial Accidents.[830]

V. Harmonization with EU Legislation

715. The alignment of the entities' legislation with the REACH Regulation is uneven, and the country 'still needs to align with the EU regulation on classification, labelling and packaging of substances and mixtures (CLP)'.[831] In addition, BiH 'needs to align with EU legislation on asbestos and on the protection of animals used for scientific purposes'. Further efforts are required to fully implement the Rotterdam Convention. There has been no progress in acceding to the Minamata Convention [832]

828. *See*: http://www.pic.int/Countries/Statusofratifications/tabid/1072/language/en-US/Default.aspx (18 Jul. 2022).
829. *See*: http://chm.pops.int/Countries/StatusofRatifications/PartiesandSignatories/tabid/252/Default.aspx (18 Jul. 2022).
830. *See*: https://treaties.un.org/Pages/ViewDetails.aspx?src=TREATY&mtdsg_no=XXVII-6&chapter=27&clang=_en (18 Jul. 2022).
831. EC, *Bosnia and Herzegovina 2021 Progress Report,* p. 104.
832. Ibid. p. 104.

§2. RATIONAL USE OF ENERGY

I. The Energy Sector in Bosnia and Herzegovina

716. The energy sector is traditionally very important to Bosnia and Herzegovina, which used to be a producer of energy and raw materials for the other parts of the former Yugoslavia.[833] The sector may be divided into four subsectors: power; coal mining; gas; and oil and oil derivates.[834]

717. Currently, there are four thermal power plants in the country with 1,745 MW of installed capacity – in the Republic of Srpska 600 MW and in FBiH 1145 MW. Bosnia and Herzegovina also has significant potential in renewable energy sources, green energy, such as wind, solar energy, biomass and geothermal energy. Their utilization potential is by 30% higher than the EU average, and the highest in the Balkans. This in particular pertains to wind energy potential, estimated at 600 MW, the solar energy, estimated at 67.2 PWh4, and biomass, taking into account the rich forest resources.[835]

718. 'Bosnia and Herzegovina's four incumbents generate electricity predominantly from hydropower and lignite. ... The country is a major exporter of electricity to the regional market, including the European Union. It purchases natural gas imported from Russia through the only interconnector with Serbia. Three wind farms are now operational in the country.'[836]

II. Competencies

719. Based on the constitutional structure of Bosnia and Herzegovina, energy efficiency as a sector is under jurisdiction of entity governments i.e., entity ministries responsible for energy and spatial planning.[837] At the state level, the MFTER is responsible for transposition and implementation of the Energy Performance of Buildings Directive (EPBD) in terms of implementation of carrying out tasks within the jurisdiction of the BiH relating to the definition of policies, the basic principles,

833. 'The authorities believe that the energy sector, and within it, the electricity sector is one of the stronger sectors of the economy with the potential to contribute to economic development in the short and medium term'. Energy Charter Secretariat, *In-Depth Review of Energy Efficiency Policies and Programmes: Bosnia and Herzegovina*, 2012. p. 11.

834. The power and mining sectors are predominantly based on indigenous resources of hydropower and coal. Gas, oil and oil derivates are imported either as raw materials or in processed forms. UNECE, *Environmental Performance Review, Bosnia and Herzegovina*, 2004., *supra* p. 135.

835. Softić A., Glamočić Lj. *National background report on Energy for Bosnia and Herzegovina*, WBC – inco net, Sarajevo, March 2012, p. 4.

836. Energy Community Secretariat, *Annual Implementation Report 2021*, Energy Community Secretariat, Austria, 1 November 2021. p. 37.

837. Energy Community, *Report on the implementation of the Energy Performance of Buildings Directive, Bosnia and Herzegovina* (Update November 2020). p. 1.

coordination of activities and plans of entity authorities and institutions on international level in the field of energy (Law on Ministries and Other Administrative Bodies, Article 9). Also, the ministry is responsible for all the international coordination of the implementation of the Energy Community Treaty, including requirements of EE *acquis communautaire* related issues.[838]

In 2013, both entities adopted Renewable Energy Laws.

III. Legislative Framework

A. The Republic of Srpska

720. The Republic of Srpska Energy Development Strategy by 2030, dated from 2012 lays down the RS energy development policies focused on the use of domestic resources, renewable sources, implementation of energy efficiency measures, use of modern energy technologies, while at the same time preserving the environment and reducing the adverse impacts of the energy sector, and ensuring the energy sector sustainable development under conditions of restricted emissions of greenhouse gases.[839]

1. The Law on Renewable Energy Sources

721. Basic legal act regulating renewable energy sources in the Republic of Srpska is the Law on Renewable Energy Sources (Official Gazette of RS, No. 16/22).[840] It has the following nine parts: Part I – General Provisions (Articles 1–3), Part II – Planning and Encouragement of Production and Consumption of Energy from Renewable Sources (Articles 4–6), Part III – Classification and Certification of Plants for the Production of Electricity from Renewable Sources (Articles 7–10), Part IV – Implementation of Incentives System and Balancing (Articles 11–19), Part V – Guarantee of Electricity Origin Produced from Renewable Sources (Articles 20–22), Part VI – Incentives Measures for Production and Use of Energy from Renewable Energy Sources (Articles 23–64), Part VII – Construction of Energy

838. The State Electricity Regulatory Commission is an independent institution of Bosnia and Herzegovina, which acts in accordance with the principles of objectivity, transparency and equality, and has jurisdiction over and responsibility for transmission of electricity, transmission system operation and international trade in electricity as well as generation, distribution and supply of electricity for customers in Brčko District BIH. *See*: https://www.derk.ba/en/aboutus (15 Jul. 2022).

839. BiH Council of Ministers, *Answers to the List of EU Questions on Chapter 27, Environment, supra* p. 11.

840. In addition, several general regulations in the field of energy should also be taken into account: Law on Energy (Official Gazette RS, No. 49/09), Law on Electricity, (Official Gazette RS, No. 68/20), Law on Gas (Official Gazette RS, No. 22/18), Law on Mining (Official Gazette RS, No. 62/18), Law on Concessions (Official Gazette RS, No. 53/09, 16/18, 70/20, 111/21), etc. For more information, see: https://www.vladars.net/sr-SP-Cyrl/Vlada/Ministarstva/mper/PAO/Pages/ZakoniPravni.aspx (15 Jul. 2022).

Installations and Keeping of Project Register (Articles 65– 68), Part VIII – Supervision and Penalty Provisions (Articles 69–71), Part IX – Transitional and Final Provisions (Articles 72–79).[841]

722. This law regulates the planning and encouragement of the production and consumption of energy from renewable sources, technologies for the use of renewable energy sources, certification of production facilities, incentive measures, the implementation of the production incentive system, the production of electricity by customers-producers individually or within communities, the way of management register and other issues of importance for this area (Article 1, paragraph 1).[842]

a. Classification and Certification of Facilities for Energy Production from Renewable Sources

723. Plants that use renewable energy sources for electricity production, depending on the primary energy source, are classified into plants that use: (1) energy potential of watercourses, (2) wind energy, (3) unaccumulated solar energy, (4) energy obtained from biomass, (5) energy obtained from bio-gas, (6) landfill gas and gas from municipal wastewater treatment plants, (7) energy from geothermal sources, (8) energy from other types of renewable sources, (9) energy from several renewable sources in combination (Article 7).[843]

724. Installations for the production of electricity from renewable sources for which the right to an incentive for electricity production can be exercised, with regard to the installed power, are divided into small and large installations (Article 8).[844]

725. The certificate for the production facility is issued to the electricity producer for the production facility that produces electricity from renewable energy sources in an economically profitable manner with environmental protection and in

841. For more information, see: https://www.vladars.net/sr-SP-Cyrl/Vlada/Ministarstva/mper/PAO/Documents/Zakon%20o%20obnovljivim%20izvorima%20SGRS%2016-22.pdf (15 Jul. 2022). For information about relevant bylaws, *see*: http://www.vladars.net/sr-SP-Cyrl/Vlada/Ministarstva/mper/Pages/Obnovljivi_izvori_energije.aspx (15 Jul. 2022).

842. The objective of this law is to stimulate the production of electricity and thermal energy from renewable energy sources and the use of energy from renewable sources in transport, for consumption on the domestic market and to increase the share in gross final energy consumption, and to ensure the development of incentive mechanisms, regulatory framework and technical infrastructure for renewables. energy sources. (Art. 2, para. 1).

843. Obtaining certificate for production facility is a necessary condition for realization of right on incentive for electricity generation from renewable sources and in efficient cogeneration or for issuing guarantees of origin of electricity (Art. 8, para. 2).

844. Small plants are: 1) hydroelectric power plants, wind power plants, and solar power plants on land with an installed capacity of up to 150 kW, 2) solar power plants on buildings, biomass and biogas power plants, landfill gas and gas from municipal wastewater treatment plants with an installed capacity of up to 500 kW. Large plants are 1) wind power plants and solar power plants on land with an installed capacity of more than 150 kW, including 50,000 kW, 2) solar power plants on buildings and biogas and biomass power plants, with an installed capacity of more than 500 kW

which the measurement of all energy quantities is ensured (Article 9, paragraph 1). Obtaining a certificate for a production facility is a condition for exercising the right to incentives for the production of electricity from renewable sources or for issuing a guarantee on the origin of electricity, except in the case prescribed by this law. The certificate for the production facility is issued by the Regulatory Commission for Energy of the Republic of Srpska (hereinafter, 'the Regulatory Commission'), at the request of the manufacturer (paragraph 4).[845] The Regulatory Commission maintains the Register of issued certificates for production facilities (paragraph 5).[846]

b. Planning and Stimulating of Production and Consumption of Energy from Renewable Sources

726. By using renewable energy sources,[847] the goals of the Republic in the field of energy, taken over by international agreements and strategic documents, and determined by the energy and climate plan of the Republic, are achieved. The goals of the Republic on the share of energy from renewable sources by year, the amounts provided for incentives by technology, an overview of the types and methods of achieving incentives, as well as other issues are regulated by the Programme on the use of renewable energy sources (hereinafter, 'the Programme'), adopted by the Government of the Republic of Srpska (Article 4)[848]

727. The share of energy from renewable sources in the gross final energy consumption is calculated as the gross energy consumption from renewable sources divided by the total final gross energy consumption, expressed as a percentage. Gross final consumption of energy from renewable sources is the sum of (1) gross final consumption of electricity produced from renewable sources, (2) gross final

845. Exceptionally, the certificate for the production plant of the customer-producer or community of renewable energy, with an installed capacity of up to 50 kW, is issued by the competent operator of the distribution system, as an integral part of the declaration on connection, based on the certificate of completion of the works referred to in Art. 52. para. 6 of this law, and with the fulfilment of other criteria prescribed by this law (para. 6).

846. The Regulatory Commission adopts a rulebook that regulates more precisely the criteria for issuing certificates, the issuing procedure, the content of the certificate, its extension, transfer, and modification, keeping the Register of issued certificates, as well as the simplified procedure for issuing certificates for production plants of buyers-producers (Art. 10, para. 2).

847. Renewable energy means energy from the wind, solar (thermal and photovoltaic), and geothermal energy, energy from the environment, hydropower, biomass, biogas, landfill gas, and gas obtained from wastewater treatment plants (Art. 3, para. 1, point 1).

848. The program contains: 1) expected gross final consumption of electricity, heating, and cooling energy, and energy in transport, 2) sectoral goals, i.e. shares of energy from renewable sources in electricity, heating, and cooling and transport, 3) the maximum total installed capacity by year and technology expressed in kW, as well as the maximum annual amount of planned electricity production by technology, 4) the maximum total installed capacity per year for small plants by technology, expressed in kW, as well as the maximum annual amount of planned electricity production by technology (technology quotas), which are subject to incentive measures, 5) technology quotas by technology for renewable energy communities, 6) the method of determining the terms and scope of auctions, 7) other measures of importance for achieving the planned goals. (Art. 5).

energy consumption for heating and cooling produced from renewable sources, (3) gross final consumption of energy from renewable sources in transport (Article 6, paragraphs 1 and 2).

c. Implementation of an Incentives System and Balancing

728. The incentive system operator, as a non-profit organization, performs administrative-financial and other operational tasks of the incentive system for the production of electricity from renewable sources and is established in accordance with the regulations governing the system of public services (Article 11, paragraph 1). The incentive system operator (hereinafter, 'Incentive Operator') has the status of a legal entity with public powers established by this law and is registered in the Register of Business Entities.[849]

729. The operator of the distribution or transmission system is responsible for reading and calculating the electricity delivered to the network, as well as all other energy quantities in the production plant that use renewable energy sources, including gross production, own consumption and consumption for own needs (Article 14, paragraph 1).[850] The incentive operator, the Regulatory Commission, and the operator of the distribution or transmission system have unhindered access to the plants in accordance with the rules that apply to power plants, and all data related to the plant and the energy sources used in it, and for the purpose of fulfilling the obligations prescribed by this law (Article 15, paragraph 1).[851] The supplier of end customers submits reports to the Incentive Operator on the total amount of electricity sold and the total calculated amount of compensation contained in the issued invoices for the electricity consumed (Article 16, paragraph 1).[852]

730. Balancing is regulated by Articles 17 to 19 of the Law.

849. The Government of the Republic of Srpska (hereinafter, 'the Government') makes a decision regulating the establishment, organization, as well as other issues of importance for the work of the Incentive Operator. The incentive operator is financed by the fee for encouraging the production of electricity from renewable energy sources. Supervision of the work of the Incentive Operator is carried out by the Ministry and the Regulatory Commission, within the framework of the competencies established by this law (Art. 11, paras 3–6).

850. The operator of the distribution or transmission system calculates monthly electricity from producers who have exercised the right to incentives and submits a report to the producer and the Incentive Operator, as well as a report on the total delivered electricity to end customers in their area (para. 2).

851. The producer of electricity from renewable energy sources is obliged to provide uninterrupted work to the representatives of the Incentive Operator, the Regulatory Commission, and the operator of the distribution or transmission system.

852. The supplier of end customers is obliged to pay the calculated fee for renewable energy sources to the account of the Incentive Operator. In case of distribution of the planned production of electricity to suppliers of end customers in the Republic, in accordance with Art. 12 point 9) of this law, the supplier is obliged to take over and pay the corresponding share of electricity to the Incentive Operator at the valid reference market price (paras 2 and 3).

d. Warranty on the Origin of Electricity Produced from Renewable Sources

731. A guarantee of the origin of electricity from renewable energy sources (hereinafter, 'Guarantee of origin') is issued at the request of the producer of electricity from renewable energy sources for which he is not entitled to incentives or at the request of the Operator of incentives for electricity for which realized right to incentive (Article 20, paragraph 1). In the case where the production plant is located on the territory of several states, i.e. entities, the guarantee of origin can be issued without obtaining a certificate for the production plant for the corresponding part of the produced electricity, based on the data of the competent institutions and power system operators. The guarantee of origin is issued only once for a unit quantity of electricity produced in a certain period, for which separate records are kept (paragraph 3).[853]

732. The guarantee of origin is issued for electricity produced in a certain period based on data on the produced quantities of electricity determined by measurement (Article 21, paragraph 1). The guarantee of origin can be used within one year from the date of issue, and after its use or expiry, the guarantee of origin is cancelled.[854]

e. Incentive Measures for Production and Use of Energy from Renewable Energy Sources

733. Incentive measures are regulated by Articles 23-64 of the Law. Norms regulating these issues are grouped into the following groups: (1) Measures to encourage the production of electricity from renewable energy sources ((1.1) Benefits when connecting to the network, (1.2) The right to mandatory purchase at a guaranteed purchase price and the right to a premium, (1.3) Pre-contracts and contracts on incentives, (1.4) Funds for incentives), (2) Measures to encourage the use of renewable energy sources for heating and cooling and in transport, (3) Customers-producers and communities of renewable energy, (4) Other measures and information.

f. Building of Energy Facilities and Keeping of Projects Register

734. Pursuant to Article 65 of the Law, the construction of energy plants that use renewable energy sources is carried out in accordance with strategic documents and plans for the development of the energy sector in the Republic. For the construction

853. The Regulatory Commission issues the guarantee of origin, transfers and cancels the guarantee of origin. At the same time, the Regulatory Commission adopts a rulebook on the guarantee of origin for electricity, which regulates the content of the guarantee, conditions and procedure for issuing, transferring and cancelling the guarantee of origin, maintaining the Register of guarantees on the origin of electricity and others (paras 4 and 5).
854. The guarantee of origin issued in other countries is recognized in the Republic according to the principle of reciprocity and in accordance with concluded international agreements (Art. 22).

of energy plants that use renewable energy sources, it is necessary to obtain a concession beforehand in accordance with the regulations governing the field of concessions or in accordance with the regulations governing other types of public-private partnership, when this is regulated by a special regulation (Article 66, paragraph 1).[855]

735. In the event that a location auction procedure is carried out for the construction of a production facility, a concession contract is concluded with the selected bidder without conducting a public call, in accordance with the regulations governing the field of concessions (Article 66, paragraph 2).[856]

736. The Ministry establishes and manages the Register of projects that use renewable energy sources (Article 67, paragraph 1).[857]

g. Supervision

737. Administrative supervision over the implementation of the provisions of this law and the regulations adopted based on it is carried out by the Ministry and the Regulatory Commission, in accordance with the powers prescribed by this law (Article 69).[858]

2. The Law on Energy Efficiency

738. Basic legal act regulating energy efficiency in the Republic of Srpska is the Law on Energy Efficiency[859] (Official Gazette of RS, No. 59/13). It has the following six parts: Part I – General Provisions (Articles 1–4), Part II – Energy Efficiency

855. Except in case of construction: (1) biomass energy plants, biogas, landfill gas and gas from municipal waste water treatment plants, (2) power plants using landfill gas and gas obtained from municipal wastewater, (3) solar plants with photovoltaic cells with an installed power of up to 250 kW on the ground and on buildings, regardless of the installed power.

856. The construction of energy plants is carried out on the basis of a building permit obtained in accordance with the regulations governing the field of construction and environmental protection, except in the case when a customer-producer power plant is being built on a building that has a building permit as part of the adaptation of the building. renewable sources of installed power up to 50 kW (Para. 3).

857. Enrolment of projects in the Register of Projects is carried out by the Ministry ex officio or based on the submitted request of the project owner (Art. 68, para. 1).

858. The inspection supervision over the implementation of the provisions of this law is carried out by the Republic Administration for Inspection Affairs of the Republic of Srpska through competent inspectors, in accordance with the regulation regulating the inspection supervision procedure, this law and the law regulating the performance of electric power activities (Art. 70, para. 1).

859. *Energy efficiency* is the ratio between the actual results in services, goods or energy and for that consumed energy (Art. 4, para. 1, point a). *Energy* is any form of commercially available energy, such as electrical and heat energy, as well as energy products that are on sale, such as natural gas (including liquefied natural gas), liquefied petroleum gas, fuel for heating and cooling, coal and lignite, peat, fuel for motor vehicles and biomass (Art. 4, para. 1, point b).

Policy Documents (Articles 5–9), Part III – Measures for Improving of Energy Efficiency (Articles 10–18), Part IV – Obligations of the Distributor System Operator,[860] Energy Distributor[861] and Energy Supplier[862] (Articles 19–23), Part V – Supervision and Penalty Provisions (Articles 24–26), Part VI – Transitional and Final Provisions (Articles 27–28).

739. This law regulates the energy efficiency in final consumption, making plans for the improvement of energy efficiency and their implementation, the organization of tasks to improve the energy efficiency, measures to improve energy efficiency and ways of energy efficiency financing (Article 1, paragraph 1).

740. This law applies to energy efficiency in final energy consumption and in providing of distribution services and energy supply, as well as the energy performances of energy-using products (Article 2, paragraph 1).[863]

a. The Energy Efficiency Policy Documents

741. Energy efficiency policy is determined by the Energy Development Strategy of the Republic of Srpska (hereinafter, 'the Strategy') (Article 5, paragraph 1).

742. In order to implement energy efficiency policies, the Government of the Republic of Srpska (hereinafter, 'the Government') adopted the Action Plan for Energy Efficiency (hereinafter, 'the Action Plan') (Article 5, paragraph 2). Action Plan adopts Government for period of three years (Article 6, paragraph 1).[864] Action Plan prepares the Ministry of Industry, Energy and Mining (hereinafter, 'the Ministry') and the Ministry in charge for construction and environmental protection affairs, in cooperation with the Ministry of Finance and the Fund for Environmental Protection and Energy Efficiency of the Republic of Srpska (hereinafter, 'the Fund') (Article 6, paragraph 3).

743. A local government unit that has more than 20,000 inhabitants is obliged to adopt its Energy Efficiency Action Plan, which is harmonized with the Action Plan (Article 5, paragraph 3). The Action Plan of the Local Government Units shall be adopted for a period of three years (Article 7, paragraph 1).[865] Sustainable Energy Action Plan of the Local Government Units (SEAP – Sustainable Energy Action

860. *The distribution system operator* is the legal entity responsible for the operation, functioning, maintenance and development of the electricity distribution system, heat energy and natural gas in a given area (Art. 4, para. 1, point c).
861. *Energy distributor* is a legal entity responsible for energy transmission (electricity, heat energy or natural gas) with intention of delivery to the final customer or to distribution stations that transmit energy to the final consumer (Art. 4, para. 1, point đ).
862. *The energy supplier* is a legal entity that sells electricity, gas (liquefied natural gas or liquefied petroleum gas) or heat energy to the final customers (Art. 4, para. 1, point ž).
863. Energy efficiency in sector for construction of buildings shall be regulated in accordance with the regulations for construction of buildings (Art. 2, para. 2).
864. The content of the Action Plan is prescribed in Art. 6, para. 2.
865. The content of the Action Plan of the Local Government units is prescribed in Art. 7, para. 1.

Plan) shall be deemed as an Action Plan within the meaning of paragraph 1 of this article (Article 7, paragraph 5). Activities from the Action Plan of the Local Government Units shall be financed from the budget of the Local Government, the Fund, and from other sources (Article 7, paragraph 2).

744. The Government shall adopt an operational plan to improve energy efficiency in the Republic management authorities for a period of three years (hereinafter, 'the operational plan') (Article 8, paragraph 1).[866]

745. Large customer makes energy efficiency plan for a period of three years (hereinafter, 'plan of a large customers') (Article 9, paragraph 1). Plan of a large consumer contains a comprehensive analysis and the structure of a large consumer spending and characteristics of its consumption, assessment of energy efficiency state, goals, the programme of measures to improve energy efficiency and other necessary information (Article 9, paragraph 2).

b. Measures for Improving of Energy Efficiency

746. Pursuant to Article 10 measures to improve energy efficiency are the following: (a) energy services; (b) energetic management; and (c) other measures (paragraph 1).

747. Energy service in terms of this law shall include activities and actions that lead to measurable or estimatable improve of energy efficiency of buildings and other facilities, technical systems and production processes, i.e., energy savings that can be expressed in money using energy-efficient technologies, i.e., procedures to achieve cost savings energy (Article 11, paragraph 1).[867]

748. Ordering party and the provider of energy service signs contract on energy service in writing (Article 12, paragraph 1).[868] The cost for providing of energy services borne ordering party of energy services or provider of energy services, in whole or in part, from its own resources or through third party financing (Article 12, paragraph 1).

749. Energy management is a system of organizational and technical measures and activities, which are used for monitoring and analysis of energy consumption, to identify measures to improve energy efficiency and the rational use of energy (Article 13, paragraph 1).

866. The content of the Operational Plan is prescribed in Art. 8, para. 2.
867. Energy services provide a legal company for the energy services (Energy Service Company–ESCO) or other legal entity (hereinafter, 'the provider of energy services') on the base of a contract on energy service (Art. 11, para. 2).
868. The content of the contract on energy service is prescribed in Art. 12, para. 1.

750. The use of renewable energy sources[869] to produce electricity or heat energy is considered to be one of the measures to improve energy efficiency in terms of this law, if the electrical or heat energy produced in this way is used in the building or in object in which is partially or completely produced and if it is not intended for sale (Article 15, paragraph 1). Natural persons and legal entities that use renewable energy sources in a way as defined in paragraph 1 of this article may use the funds of the Fund and other funds intended for energy efficiency, if concerned energy production is not already covered by one of the other stimulus measures related to renewable energy sources (Article 15, paragraph 2).

751. Product suppliers are required by each product individually, during delivery process, free of charge, also to provide the energy efficiency label (Article 17, paragraph 2). Energy efficiency label is a visual indicator of the energy class of products[870] which is placed on products in the form of labels (Article 17, paragraph 3).

c. Obligations of the Distribution System Operator, Energy Distributor and Electricity Supplier

752. The Distribution System Operators, energy distributors and energy suppliers are obliged to perform tasks within its competencies so as not to interfere providing of energy services and other measures to improve energy efficiency or the energy services market development and other measures to improve energy efficiency (Article 19, paragraph 1). The entities referred to in Article 19 paragraph 1 of this law submit an annual report to the Fund, not later than 31 March of the current year for the previous year (Article 20, paragraph 1).[871]

753. In order to provide the highest level of availability of information in accordance with this law, the Fund shall establish and maintain a database of energy efficiency (Article 23, paragraph 1). The Fund shall inform the Ministry and the Ministry in charge for construction and environmental protection to provide data access from a database on energy efficiency (Article 23, paragraph 3).

d. Supervision

754. Administrative supervision over the implementation of law and regulations adopted thereunder performs the Ministry and the Ministry in charge for construction and environmental protection affairs (Article 24, paragraph 1).

---

869. *Renewable energy sources* are energy sources that are stored in the nature and are renewed in whole or in part, such as energy of streams, wind, biomass (excluding fuel wood), bio-gas, gas from facilities for treatment of communal waste, agricultural gas, landfill gas, geothermal, not accumulated solar energy and other (Art. 4, para. 1, point l).
870. *Energy class of product* is a product classification according to its energy efficiency (Art. 4, para. 1, point l).
871. The content of the report is prescribed in Art. 20, para. 2.

755. The inspection supervision over the implementation of this law and the regulations adopted thereunder perform Republic Administration for Inspection Affairs, through the authorized state inspectors and inspectors from the local government units, depending on the monitored activity (Article 25, paragraph 1).

B. Federation of Bosnia and Herzegovina

1. The Law on Use of Renewable Energy Sources and Efficient Cogeneration

756. Basic legal act regulating use of renewable energy sources and efficient cogeneration in the Federation of Bosnia and Herzegovina is the Law on Use of Renewable Energy Sources and Efficient Cogeneration (Official Gazette of FBiH, No. 70/13, and 5/14).[872] It has the following thirteen parts: Part I – General Provisions (Articles 1–3), Part II – The Legally Binding Targets (Articles 4–6), Part III – The Projects Registry (Article 7), Part IV – Potential Investigation (Article 8), Part V – The Operator for Renewable Energy Sources and Efficient Cogeneration (Articles 9–10), Part VI – The Guarantee of Origin (Articles 11–17), Part VII – The Dynamic Quotas (Articles 18–19), Part VIII – The Incentive Measures for Using Renewable Energy Sources (Articles 20–30), Part IX – Construction of the Facilities (Article 31), Part X – Informing and Training (Article 32), XI – The Administrative Supervision and Inspection (Articles 33–37), Part XII – Penalty Provisions (Article 38), Part XIII – Transitional and Final Provisions (Articles 39–40).

757. According to Article 1, paragraph 1, The Law on Renewable Energy Sources and Efficient Cogeneration (hereinafter, 'the Law') regulates:

(a) Promoting use of renewable energy sources (RES) and efficiency cogeneration (EC).
(b) Defining the binding targets of RES share in total final energy consumption in the Federation of Bosnia and Herzegovina (hereinafter, 'the Federation').
(c) defining the binding targets of RES share in production of electricity, heating and cooling energy and consumption of renewable energy sources in transport.
(d) defining technology for use of RES and EC.
(e) exploring the potential of renewable energy sources.
(f) incentive measures for production of electricity and heating energy from RES and EC and incentive measures for use of renewable energy sources in transport.

872. In addition, several laws in the field of energy should also be taken into account. For example, Law on Electricity in the FBiH, (Official Gazette FBiH, No. 66/13, 94/15), Law on Energy Efficiency in the FBiH (Official Gazette FBiH, No. 22/17), etc. For more information, see... https://fmeri.gov.ba/zakonodavstvo/ (15 Jul. 2022).

(g) rules on the issuance of guarantees of origin for electricity produced from renewable energy sources[873] and keeping the Register of issued guarantees of origin (hereinafter, 'The Register of guarantee of origin'), their transfers and cancelling.
(h) keeping of RES and EC Register of projects and facilities (hereinafter, 'The Register of projects').
(i) The status of qualified, privileged and potentially privileged electricity producer from RES and EC.
(j) The conditions for establishment and development of the market of electricity produced from RES.
(k) The construction of facilities for electricity production from RES and EC.
(l) Connection of the RES and EC facilities to the electricity grid.
(m) The administrative procedures of the competent authorities for issue of the legal acts prescribed by this law.
(n) Obligations regarding information of the public and improving knowledge of responsible and interested institutions, legal entities and natural persons, as well as other issues of importance to RES and EC usage.

758. The objective of this law is to promote the production of electricity and energy for heating and cooling from RES and EC, as well as the use of RES in transport for the consumption in the domestic market and share increase in total energy consumption, as well as providing development of incentive measures, regulatory framework and technical infrastructure for RES and EC (Article 2, paragraph 1).

a. The Obligatory Targets for the Usage of RES

759. The development and use of RES in BiH, as well as national goals in terms of the share of energy from RES in gross final energy consumption in BiH, in period up to the 2020 year, shall be determined by the National Action Plan for use of RES BiH (NAPRES) (Article 4, paragraph 1).

An integral part of NAPRES is the Action plan for using of renewable energy sources in the Federation (APREF). APREF shall, within the national target for usage of RES, express binding targets of the Federation on the share of energy from RES in gross final electricity consumption, energy for heating and/or cooling and energy for transport (Article 4, paragraph 2).

b. Benefits for Electricity Producers from RES

760. Producers of electricity from RES have the advantage of resolving the requirements for connecting to the electricity grid, compared to facilities that do not

873. *Electricity generated from renewable sources* means electricity produced in power plants using only RES, as well as the proportion of electricity produced from renewable energy sources in hybrid plants that use also conventional energy sources, including electricity generated in renewable energy facilities to be used for filling of reservoir systems, but excluding the electricity that is generated as result of the pump reservoir system (Art. 3, para. 1, point a).

use RES, and in accordance with the current rules and regulations governing the access to the transmission and distribution network (Article 20, paragraph 1).[874]

761. Qualified producers who fully or partly use RES for electricity production, have the right on the guarantee of origin in accordance with Articles 11, 12, 13 and 14 of this law (Article 20, paragraph 4). A qualified producer that has not acquired the status of privileged producer, as well as a qualified manufacturer whose status of privileged producer has expired has the right to redemption of produced electricity at the reference price, if its production was included in the binding quotas prescribed by APREF (Article 20, paragraph 5).

c. Obligation to Takeover the Electricity Produced from RES and Incentives

762. All buyers and suppliers of electricity in the Federation are obliged to takeover part of the electricity produced using of RES in accordance with this law and with acts of the Regulatory Commission (Article 21, paragraph 1).[875]

All end-users of electricity in the Federation are obliged to pay fee for the incentives (Article 22, paragraph 1). At the proposal of the Ministry, the Government of the Federation shall within six months from the date of enactment of this law, adopt the Regulation on Promotion of electricity production from RES and EC and determining of compensations for incentives, prepared in cooperation with the Regulatory Commission (Article 22, paragraph 2).

d. The Status of Privileged Producer and the Production Stimulating in Micro RES Facilities

763. Privileged producer of electricity, in terms of this law, is a qualified producer that has a right at the guaranteed redemption price[876] of the total quantity of produced electricity during the predetermined period (Article 23, paragraph 1). The status of privileged producer can obtain a holder of a work permit, a permit for performing of activity of electricity production. The work permit determines the status of qualified producer, in accordance to Article 20, paragraph 2 of this law (Article 23, paragraph 2).

764. The owners of micro RES facility referred to in Article 3, paragraph 1, point r, are the natural persons or legal entities, which must be the end consumers

874. Producers of electricity acquiring the status of eligible producers in accordance with the Rule book on acquiring the status of eligible producer on the basis of Decision issued by the Regulatory Commission (Art. 20, para. 2).

875. In accordance with APREF and objectives referred to in Art. 2, para. 2, point b of this Law, the Regulatory Commission shall adopt a Rule book on mandatory share and takeover of electricity produced from RES, within six months from the date of entry into force of this Law (Art. 21, para. 2).

876. *Guaranteed redemption price* means the price payable to the privileged producers of electricity from RES and EC for the contract duration for the electricity redemption (Art. 3, para. 1, point e).

of electricity from one of the suppliers from the Federation (Article 27, paragraph 1). The redemption of the electricity produced in micro RES facilities is done by guaranteed purchase prices, which apply to the privileged producers for the same RES (Article 27, paragraph 4).

765. The Construction of the facility for production of electricity from RES and EC under the responsibility of the Federation shall be performed in accordance with the Law on Planning and Land Use at the FBiH level ('Official Gazette of FBiH', Nos 2/06, 72/07, 32/08, 4/10, 13/10 and 45/10) and The Electricity Law ('Official Gazette of FBiH', No. 66/13) (Article 31, paragraph 1). Facilities using RES and EC are built based on Energy Permit[877] obtained in accordance with the Electricity Law (Article 31, paragraph 2).

e. The Administrative and Inspection Supervision

766. Administrative supervision includes supervision over implementation provisions of this law and other regulations, supervision over activities defined by this law, supervision of the legality of administrative and other acts developed by the competent authorities, as well as supervision of their application performs the Ministry and Regulatory Commission, each within their jurisdiction, in accordance with the authorizations prescribed by this law, Electricity Law, the Law on Organization of the Administration Authorities in the FBiH (Official Gazette of FBiH, No. 35/05) and the Law on Administrative Procedure (Official Gazette of BiH, Nos 29/02, 12/04, 88/07, 93/09, 41/13 and 53/16). This does not exclude cooperation with other relevant authorities and organizations (Article 33).

767. The control of facilities construction, technical safety, operational safety of electro energy facilities and plants, the safety of people in electro energy facilities, as well as insight into the technical and operational record performs authorized inspection in accordance with the special law (Article 34, paragraph 1).

IV. International Treaties

768. BiH is party to the Treaty establishing the Energy Community (2000).[878] BiH ratified the Energy Charter Treaty (ECT) and the Protocol on Energy Efficiency and Related Environmental Aspects (PEEREA) in 2001.[879] By ratifying the Protocol, countries commit themselves to formulate and implement policies for improving energy efficiency and reducing the negative environmental impact of the energy cycle (Article 5).

877. *Energy Permit* means an administrative act issued by the Federal Ministry of Energy, Mining and Industry, investors in the process of collecting the necessary permits for construction of the electro energy facility (Art. 3, para. 1, point b).

878. *See*: https://www.energy-community.org/implementation/Bosnia_Herzegovina.html (15 Jul. 2022).

879. *See*: https://energycharter.org/who-we-are/members-observers/countries/bosnia-and-herzegovina/ (15 Jul. 2022).

V. Harmonization with the EU Legislation

769. BiH has yet to adopt 'concrete, comprehensive and binding action plan(s) implementing the 2017 framework energy strategy in line with its commitments under the Sofia Summit Declaration on the Green Agenda for the Western Balkans.'[880] On renewable energy, there is some progress. However, there is still no state-level legal framework and the legislation at the entity level needs to be revised in line with principles of the cost-effective support framework. The Brčko District remains without legislation in this area.[881]

In the area of energy efficiency, although a new national energy efficiency action plan 2019–2021 was prepared, its adoption is still pending. The same is the case for the Republika Srpska entity action plans 2019–2021. The Federation entity adopted its action plan in February 2021. The country needs to complete the transposition of the energy efficiency directive and the framework energy labelling regulation.[882]

880. EC, *Bosnia and Herzegovina 2021 Progress Report,* p. 98.
881. EC, *Bosnia and Herzegovina 2021 Progress Report,* p.99.
882. *Ibid.,* p. 100.

Part II. Nature Conservation and Management

§1. State of Nature

770. Due to its complex geological history, especially during the glaciations periods, its central position in the Balkan Peninsula, access to the Mediterranean Sea, and the Dinaric mountain range, its biodiversity is extraordinarily rich. The most important physical-geographic features that support this biodiversity are a very diverse and developed relief, different climate types, the variety of soils, a developed hydrographic system, and the long and rich cultural history.[883]

771. Since 1954, 153 areas in BiH have some degree of protection. These are usually protected landscapes, natural monuments, or protected habitats (e.g., forest seed stands). However, classification and registration of these areas is still not harmonized with the new legislation. The status of decisions made according to the Law on Natural, Cultural and Historic Heritage of SRBiH (Official Gazette of SRBiH No. 4/1965) 'is still not clear, and those areas cannot be regarded as officially protected'.[884]

772. 'The Strategy and Action Plan for Protection of Biological Diversity of Bosnia and Herzegovina for the period 2015-2020 is a key document for action on all issues of biological diversity, ranging from management of species and ecosystems through research and protection of biological diversity, biosafety, to just and fair distribution of the benefits of ecosystem services and use of genetic resources.'[885] However, National Biodiversity Strategy and Action Plan (NBSAP)

---

883. UNECE, *Environmental Performance Review, Bosnia and Herzegovina*, 2004., *supra* p. 99. The richness of living world that exist on its territory is the result of ecological heterogeneity of Bosnia and Herzegovina, its geomorphologic and hydrological diversity, specific geological past and its eco climate diversity. Flora, Fauna and Fungi of Bosnia and Herzegovina are considered to be among the most diverse in Europe, being especially important in terms of global biodiversity due to its high level of endemism and relicts. *Bosnia and Herzegovina Fourth Report to the United Nations Convention on Biological Diversity*, 2010, *supra,* p. 4.
884. BiH MFTER, *State of the environment Report of the Bosnia and Herzegovina 2012*, *supra* p. 154.
885. BiH MFTER, UNEP, GEF. *Strategy and Action Plan for Protection of Biological Diversity in Bosnia and Herzegovina (2015–2020)*, Ministry of Foreign Trade and Economic Relations of Bosnia and Herzegovina, UNEP, GEF, 2016, p. 10. https://www.fao.org/faolex/results/details/en/c/LEX-FAOC163200/ (13 Jul. 2022).

'has been only partially implemented. Many of the targets contained therein have been implemented only partially, while many of the measures provided have not been implemented at all'.[886]

§2. JURISDICTION

773. The Ministry of Spatial Planning, Civil Engineering and Ecology is responsible for the activities in the field of nature protection within the competences of the RS. The activities in the field of nature protection within the competences of local self-governments are conducted by the administrative bodies for protection of environment.[887]

774. In the FBiH Ministry of Environment and Tourism, two departments were established within the Division for Environment: Department for Preservation of Biological and Landscape diversity, and Department for Preservation of Natural Resources and Eco-Tourism.[888]

775. Nature protection is under the competence of the Department of Spatial Planning and Property Affairs of the Government of BD BiH.

§3. LEGISLATION

776. Biodiversity protection and the sustainable use of natural resources are governed by the Law on Nature Protection of the Federation of Bosnia and Herzegovina (Official Gazette FBiH 66/2013), the Law on Nature Protection of Republic of Srpska (Official Gazette RS 20/2014), and the Law on Nature Protection of BDBiH (Official Gazette of BDBiH 24/04, 1/05, 19/07 and 9/09). In the Republic of Srpska, the Law on National Parks (Official Gazette RS 75/10) also has direct relevance to nature protection. The Federation's cantons are adopting their own laws on nature protection.

I. The Republic of Srpska

777. Competencies in the field of nature protection in the RS is largely entrusted to the Ministry of Spatial Planning, Civil Engineering and Ecology, but also in part

886. For more information, See: MFTER, *Sixth National Report of Bosnia and Herzegovina to the Convention on Biological Diversity*, Ministry of Foreign Trade and Economic Relations of Bosnia and Herzegovina, 2019, p. 215.
887. For detailed information *see*, Directorate for European Integration, *Answers to the Questionnaire, Chapter 27, Environment and climate change*, https://www.dei.gov.ba/en/odgovori-na-upitnik-ek (13 Jul. 2022), pp. 532–534.
888. Competent management bodies are established for the protected areas at the cantonal level in accordance with the cantonal legislation. *See*: *Ibid.*, pp. 531–532, and 534–538.

to the Ministry of Industry, Energy and Mining, the Ministry of Education and Culture and the Republic of Srpska Institute for Protection of Cultural, Historical and Natural Heritage, etc.

A. Law on Nature Protection

778. Basic legal act regulating nature protection[889] in the Republic of Srpska is the Law on nature protection (Official Gazette of the RS, No. 20/14). It has the following thirteen parts: Part I – General Provisions (Articles 1–6), Part II – Planning and Organization of the Nature Protection (Articles 7–15), Part III – The Basic Principles for Nature Protection (Articles 16–22), Part IV – Conservation of Biological Diversity (Articles 23–39), V – Conservation of Geomorphological and Geological Diversity (Articles 40–45), VI – Protected Natural Goods (Articles 46–59), Part VII – Procedure for Promoting of Natural Goods (Articles 60–74), Part VIII – Management and Usage of Natural Goods (Articles 75–88), Part IX – Conditions for Performing Transboundary Movement of Wild Species (Articles 89–90), Part X – Monitoring Conditions and Information System of Nature Protection (Articles 91–92), Part XI – Supervision (Articles 93–95), Part XII – Penalty Provisions (Articles 96–98), Part XIII – Transitional and Final Provisions (Articles 99–105).[890]

779. According to Article 1, the Law on Nature Protection regulates protection and conservation of nature, biological, geological and landscape diversity which are part of the environment.

1. The Objectives of the Law

780. The following objectives are achieved by this Law: (a) conservation and improvement of biological (genetic, special and ecosystem), geological and landscape diversity, (b) harmonization of human activities, economic and social development plans, programmes, bases and projects with the sustainable use of renewable and non-renewable natural resources and the long-term preservation of natural ecosystems and natural balance, (c) sustainable use and management of natural resources and goods, ensuring their function while preserving the natural values and balance of natural ecosystems, (d) timely prevention of human activities and actions which can cause permanent impoverishment of biological, geological and landscape diversity, as well as disorders with negative consequences in nature, (e) identification and monitoring of the situation in nature and (f) improvement condition of disturbed parts of nature and landscape (Article 3).

889. *'Nature'*–is all that exists, the whole world in the diversity of its forms (Art. 6, point š).
890. The provisions of this law shall not apply in case of suppression and prevention of immediate danger to the life or health of people or property, i.e., rescue of people and property, but only during the duration of the stated circumstances (Art. 5).

2. Basic Principles

781. The basic principles of nature protection are the following:

(a) *The principle of a high level of nature protection* – everyone is obliged to contribute to the protection and improvement of nature, biological, geological and landscape diversity, preserving of general nature functions and the natural balance,
(b) *The principle of sustainable use* – the use of natural values can be carried out only to the extent and in a manner that does not jeopardize the diversity and functioning of natural systems and processes,
(c) *The principle of application of measures and conditions of nature protection* – in the use of natural values and protected natural goods, planning and space development shall apply the principles, measures and conditions of nature protection.
(d) *The Polluter Pays Principle* – The polluter of natural resources and protected natural good is required to pay the costs for its usage and bear the cost of its remediation and recultivation of space.
(e) *The Cooperation Principle* – the Republican authorities, local self-government units and other organizations and institutions, as well as all legal entities and natural persons in the performance of their duties and tasks, are obliged to act in accordance with the principles, goals, measures and conditions of protection and permanent conservation of nature, and in doing so, realize mutual and international cooperation and
(f) *The principle of direct application of international Law* – the Republican administrative bodies, local self-government units and other organizations and institutions, as well as all legal and natural persons performing their duties and tasks directly apply generally accepted rules of international Law and ratified international treaties as an integral part of the legal system (Article 5).

3. The Nature Protection Strategy of the Republic of Srpska and Report on the State of Nature

782. The Nature Protection Strategy of the Republic of Srpska (hereinafter, 'the Strategy') is the basic document which determines the long-term goals and guidelines for the preservation of nature and natural values, as well as the manner of their implementation in accordance with the overall economic, social and cultural development of the Republic (Article 7, paragraph 1).[891]

891. In addition to the general strategic objectives, the Strategy shall include: (a) guidelines for the conservation of biological, geological and landscape diversity, for preserving protected natural assets, ecologically important areas, ecological corridors and ecological networks; (b) guidelines for research and monitoring of the situation in nature, (c) guidelines for including nature protection in other sectors, (d) guidelines for the legislative and institutional framework, (e) guidelines for education in order to preserve biological, geological and landscape diversity, (f) guidelines for the

783. The Strategy shall be adopted by the National Assembly of Republika Srpska (hereinafter, 'the National Assembly') at the proposal of the Government of Republika Srpska (hereinafter, 'the Government') for a period of ten years (Article 8, paragraph 1).[892]

784. The Assembly of the local self-government unit shall adopt a local nature protection plan for a period of 10 years defining the objectives of nature protection in its area, in accordance with the Strategy (Article 9, paragraphs 1–2).

785. For the purpose of achieving the objectives of the Strategy and for the complete insight into the state of nature protection, a Report on the state of nature in the Republic of Srpska (hereinafter, 'Report') is prepared. The Report is an integral part of the Environmental Report and is submitted once in two year to the National Assembly, in accordance with the regulation on environmental protection (Article 10, paragraph 1).[893]

4. Subjects of Nature Protection and Public Participation

786. Protection and conservation of nature, within their authorization, provide: (a) Government, (b) Ministry, (c) Institute, (d) local self-government unit, (e) protected area Manager, (f) legal entities and natural persons who use natural resources and protected natural resources in performance of economic and other activities, (g) universities, professional and scientific organizations and other public institutions; and (h) citizen, citizen groups, their associations, professional or other organizations (Article 11).

787. The activities in the area of nature protection within the competence of bodies of the Republic shall be carried out by the Ministry. The activities in the area of nature protection within the competence of local self-government units shall be performed by the local self-government units and local self-government unit department responsible for environmental protection (Article 12, paragraphs 1–2).

788. The Ministry, the bodies of the local self-government unit and the units of the local self-government unit responsible for environmental protection shall, in accordance with this Law, the Strategy and spatial planning documents: (a) take care on preservation of nature, natural values and landscape diversity in its area, (b) declare protected natural goods within their jurisdiction, (c) provide conditions for

---

involvement of the local population u process of protection and improvement of protected areas, (g) guidelines for public information and public participation in decision-making on nature protection, (h) action plans for implementation of guidelines, setting priorities and possible sources of financing, and (i) manner of meeting international obligations in nature protection (para. 2).

892. The Government shall adopt the Plan for implementation of the Strategy for Nature Protection (Art. 8, para. 4).

893. The report is prepared by the Ministry in cooperation with the Institute and other professional and scientific institutions. Local self-government units prepare reports on the state of nature in their area, for a period of two years, and submit reports to the Ministry (Art. 10, paras 3–4).

protection and preservation of protected natural goods within their jurisdiction, (d) participate in proclamation of protected areas declared by the National Assembly or the Government or the Assembly of the local self-government unit, (e) participate in the drafting of a management plan under its jurisdiction, (f) inform the public about the state of nature and natural values in their area and about the taking of protection and conservation measures, (g) provide the necessary assistance to local self-government units for nature protection in their area and (h) perform other tasks prescribed by this Law and regulations adopted pursuant to this Law (Article 13).

789. The Ministry, the local self-government unit and public institutions managing protected natural values shall be obliged to ensure the public information regarding the condition and nature protection (Article 15, paragraph 1).[894]

5. General Measures for Nature Protection

790. General measures for the nature protection are regulated by Articles 16–22 of the Law. Nature protection is carried out by: (a) determining and assessing the state, phenomena and processes in nature, (b) establishment and determining of protected natural goods and systems for monitoring their protection, (c) implementation of nature protection measures, (d) determining conditions and measures for nature protection and protected natural goods in spatial and urban plans, project documentation, bases and programmes for managing natural resources in mining, energy, transport, water management, agriculture, forestry, hunting, fishing, tourism and other influential activities on nature, (e) sustainable use of natural resources and protected natural resources and control of their use, (f) developing a report on the state of nature, adopting and implementing strategies, programmes, action and rehabilitation plans and management plans, (g) mitigating harmful effects that have arisen by activities in nature, using natural resources or natural disasters, (h) linking and harmonizing system of nature protection of the Republic with the international system of nature protection, (i) encouraging scientific and professional work in the field of nature protection, (j) informing the public about the state of nature and public participation in decision-making on nature protection, (k) encouraging and promoting the nature protection, developing awareness of the need for nature protection in the process of upbringing and education and (l) involvement of local communities in state monitoring, protection and promotion of nature (Article 16).

791. The project owner, i.e., the legal person, the entrepreneur and the natural person using natural resources, performs construction and other works, activities and interventions in nature, is obliged to act in accordance with the nature protection measures and conditions laid down in the plans, bases and programmes and in

894. In case of an immediate threat to the nature and health of people or endangering and damaging nature, the public shall be informed of the necessary measures and actions to prevent or mitigate any damage that might result from that danger (Art. 15, para. 2).

accordance with project-technical documentation, in order to avoid or to a minimum reduce the threat and damage to nature (Article 17, paragraph 3).[895]

792. In the process of drawing up plans, bases, programmes, projects, works and activities referred to in Article 17 of this Law, an expert opinion shall be obtained which determines the nature protection conditions adopted by the Institute (Article 18, paragraph 1).[896] If projects or activities in nature are carried out without the established conditions of nature protection or contrary to the given nature protection conditions, resulting in damage to nature and protected natural assets, the project owner, or user of natural resources, is obliged, without delay and at his own expense, remedy the harmful consequences of his action on the principles of objective responsibility (Article 22, paragraph 1).

6. Protected Minerals and Fossils

793. The Ministry, on the basis of the expert opinion of the Institute, proclaims protected minerals and fossils which are significant due to their rarity, size and appearance or educational and scientific importance (Article 73, paragraph 1).[897] Protected natural goods shall be registered in the Register of protected natural goods (hereinafter, 'the Register'), kept by the Institute (Article 74, paragraphs 1–2).

7. Monitoring of the State and Nature Protection Information System

794. The research of strictly protected and protected wild species, protected areas, speleological objects, minerals and fossils and other biological diversity researches are carried out on the basis of expert opinion of the Institute, which determines the conditions of research, at the request of a legal entity or natural person (Article 91, paragraph 1).[898]

795. An information system for nature protection and monitoring of the state (hereinafter, 'information system') is established. The Minister shall issue a Rulebook detailing the management of the information system, monitoring, collecting, registering and analysing of data, facts and other relevant information on the status

895. The legal entity, entrepreneur and natural person referred to in para. 3 of this article after the cessation of works and activities shall be obliged to perform rehabilitation, i.e., recultivation in accordance with this Law and other regulations (para. 4).
896. If the applicant does not start the works and activities for which the expert opinion is issued within two years from the date of delivery of the expert opinion, he is obliged to obtain a new opinion (Art. 18, para. 4).
897. The measures for the protection of protected minerals and fossils and the manner of their use are defined in more detail by the act on the designation of protected minerals and fossils (para. 2).
898. The contractor is obliged to obtain approval of the Manager for the research carried out in the protected area (Para. 2).

and use of nature and measures taken by administrative bodies, institutions, companies and other organizations (Article 92, paragraphs 1–2).[899]

8. Supervision

796. Administrative supervision over the application of the provisions of this Law and the regulations adopted on the basis of it is carried out by the Ministry (Article 93). Inspection supervision over the implementation of the provisions of this Law and the regulations adopted thereunder is carried out by inspectors of the Republic Administration for Inspection affairs and local government unit (hereinafter, 'inspectors') (Article 94).

B. Other Relevant RS Regulations

797. Other relevant regulations include the following:

(1) Rulebook on the inventory of geoheritage objects of the Republic of Srpska (Official Gazette of the RS, No. 65/21)
(2) Regulation on strictly protected and protected wild species (Official Gazette of the RS, No. 65/20)
(3) Rulebook on conditions to be met by the manager of the protected area (Official Gazette of the RS, No. 65/19)
(4) Rulebook on the method of marking protected areas (Official Gazette of the RS, No 3/18, 116/20)
(5) Rulebook on special technical-technological solutions to enable undisturbed movement and safe communication of wild animals (Official Gazette of the RS, No. 66/17).
(6) Rulebook on the nature protection label, procedures and conditions for its use (Official Gazette of the RS', No. 50/16).
(7) Rulebook on the Register of Protected Natural Resources (Official Gazette of the RS, No. 55/15).
(8) Rulebook on the contents, establishment and enforcement of the management measures in protected areas (Official Gazette of the RS, No. 83/15).
(9) Rulebook on interior ordinance in national parks (Official Gazette of the RS, No. 83/11).
(10) Regulation on the Red List of protected species of flora and fauna of the RS (Official Gazette of the RS No. 124/12).

899. The Institute monitors the state, i.e., collects, processes and consolidates data on the state of nature, prepares reports and updates data for the information system of nature protection. The Institute shall submit date to the Ministry by 31 January of the current year for the previous year, making part of a single spatial-information system of the Republic of Serpska, established and maintained by the Ministry in accordance with special regulations (Art. 92, paras 3–4).

(11) Red List of protected species of flora and fauna of the RS (Official Gazette of the RS No. 124/12).[900]

II. Federation of Bosnia and Herzegovina

A. *Law on Nature Protection*

798. Basic legal act regulating nature protection in the Federation of Bosnia and Herzegovina is the Law on Nature protection (Official Gazette of the FBiH, No 66/13). It has the following eighteen parts: Part I – General Provisions (Articles 1–8), Part II – Competence (Articles 9–11), Part III – Conservation of Nature[901] (Articles 12–57), Part IV – Types of Habitats and Ecologically Important Sites (Articles 58–69), Part V – Species and Subspecies (Articles 70–85), Part VI – Protection of Wild Birds (Articles 86–98), Part VII – Transboundary Movement of Protected Wild Species/Subspecies (Articles 99–124), Part VIII – Minerals, Fossils and Speleothems (Articles 125–133), Part IX – Protection of Natural Values[902] (Articles 134–179), Part X – Concession and Concession License in Protected Natural Values and Speleological Facilities (Articles 180–183), Part XI – Nature Protection Planning and Organization (Articles 184–192), Part XII – Inventorying and Monitoring of the State (Articles 193–197), Part XIII – Access to Information and Public Participation (Articles 198–203), Part XIV – Nature Protection Label and Promotion of Upbringing and Education in Nature Protection (Articles 204–207), Part XV – Financing of Nature Protection (Articles 208–209), Part XVI – Inspection Oversight (Articles 210–231), Part XVII – Penalty Provisions (Articles 232–237), Part XVIII – Transitional and Final Provisions (Articles 238–250). The provisions of this Law shall not apply in case of avoiding an immediate threat to life or human health or property, rescuing people and property (Article 7, paragraph 1).[903]

799. According to Article 1, this Law regulates: competences of authorities dealing with the issues of nature protection, general measures of nature conservation, degree of acceptability of activities in nature, types of habitats and ecologically important areas, species and subspecies, protection of wild birds, protection and conservation of biodiversity,[904] forest ecosystems, karst ecosystems, water and

900. *See*: http://www.vladars.net/sr-SP-Cyrl/Vlada/Ministarstva/mgr/PAO/Pages/Podzakonski_akti_-_priroda.aspx (13 Jul. 2022).

901. *Nature* constitutes a fundamental value and one of the most significant resources of the Federation of Bosnia and Herzegovina (FBIH) and enjoys the protection in accordance with this Law (Art. 2, para. 1).

902. *The natural values* determined under this Law are in the interest of the Federation of BIH and Cantons and hence they enjoy a special protection (Art. 2, para. 2).

903. Provisions of para. 1 of this article shall be applied only during the said circumstances.

904. *Biodiversity*-means the variability among living organisms from all sources which are integral part of ecosystems, this includes diversity within species, between species and of ecosystems (Art. 8).

water habitats, protection of marine and coastal natural values,[905] establishment of the European ecological network of particularly protected areas – Natura 2000, protection measures for species and subspecies, transboundary movement of protected wild species[906] and subspecies, protection measures for minerals and fossils, protected natural values,[907] compensation of damage, incentive measures, proposing of concessions on protected natural values and protected natural structures, planning and organization, inventorying and monitoring, access to information and public participation, nature protection label, promotion of upbringing and education, rewards and awards for achievements in the field of nature protection, financing of nature protection, inspection oversight, penalty provisions, transitional and final provisions.

1. Objectives of Nature Protection

800. The aim of nature protection is conservation and restoration of the existing biological and landscape diversity to a state of natural balance and relations harmonized human activities; assessment of the state and monitoring of the natural values; providing the protection system for natural values for the purpose of permanent conservation of their characteristics on the basis of which they were declared protected; providing for a sustainable use of natural estates[908] without significant harm to nature components[909] and with the least possible disturbance to the balance of components, preventing harmful activities and disturbance in nature as consequences of technological development and performance of business operations; ensuring as favourable as possible conditions of conservation and free development of nature during its use for economic purposes, ensuring the right of citizens to a healthy environment, rest and recreation in open (Article 3).

2. Nature Protection Principles

801. Nature protection shall be based on the following principles: everyone must behave in a manner that contributes to conservation of biological and landscape diversity, protection of natural values and conservation of a universally beneficial role of nature; non-renewable natural resources are to be used in a rational manner

---

905. *Natural values* are parts of nature that deserve special protection, due to their sensitivity, for the preservation of biological and landscape diversity, or for serving scientific, cultural, aesthetic, educational, economic and other public interest making an ecological network (Art. 8).
906. *Wild species* of plants, fungi and animals means all species and subspecies whose evolutionary process was not influenced by humans as a consequence of breeding activities (Art. 8).
907. *Protected natural values* means natural values declared protected by the authority defined by this Law and entered in the register of protected natural values, protected plant and animal species and subspecies and fungi as well as protected minerals and fossils (Art. 8).
908. *Sustainable use of natural assets* means the use of natural assets in a way and scope which does not lead to their wreckage but maintains their potential to satisfy needs and aspirations of current and future generations (Art. 8).
909. *Nature component*-means any original component of nature (such as plant, animal, mineral, fossil, water, ground, etc.) (Art. 8);

and those renewable in a sustainable manner; nature protection principles, measures and conditions shall be applied in the usage of natural resources and spatial development; the protection of nature is the right and obligation of every natural and legal person; towards this end they are bound to cooperate in order to avoid and prevent hazardous activities and damage, to eliminate and remedy the consequences of any damage and to restore the natural conditions that existed prior to such damage; the public has the right to free access to information about the state of the natural environment, to timely information about any damage caused to nature and the measures taken to remedy it; the public has the right to free access to information about the state of the natural environment, to timely information about any damage caused to nature and the measures taken to remedy it and to participate in nature-related decision-making (Article 4, paragraph 1).[910]

3. Competences

802. The tasks of nature protection within the competence of the Federation of BIH shall be carried out by the Federation Ministry of Environment and Tourism (the Federation Ministry) (Article 9, paragraph 1).

803. The tasks of nature protection within the competence of cantons shall be carried out by the cantonal environmental Ministry and cantonal nature protection Institute within its competence determined in the charter of foundation and the articles of association (hereinafter, 'The Cantonal Ministry and Cantonal Nature Protection Institute') (Article 9, paragraph 2). These task are including implementation of the BIH Strategy with the action plan for the protection of biological and landscape diversity (hereinafter, 'the State Strategy') and the Federation on natural protection strategy (hereinafter, 'the Federation Strategy') (Article 9, paragraph 3).[911]

804. Regarding nature protection on the inter-entity level, the Inter-Entity Environmental Authority is established on the base of the Law on Environmental protection Federation of BiH (Article 10).[912]

910. With a view to protect nature and by way of the institutions of Bosnia and Herzegovina, the Federation of BIH shall participate along with other states and international organizations in the implementation of international treaties in the field of nature protection to which Bosnia and Herzegovina is a member (para. 2).

911. The tasks of nature protection within the competence of municipalities shall be carried out by municipal services established in accordance with the Law on Local Self-Governance Principles (Art. 9, para. 4).

912. The Inter-Entity Environmental Authority shall also be authorized for: Coordination of work on the issues of nature protection between relevant administrative bodies; Flow of scientific and expert information relative to nature protection towards relevant ministries and other ministries; Agreeing and developing inter-entity cooperation in pursuance of the State strategy implementation; Coordination and cooperation in the establishment of transboundary and inter-entity protected areas proportionate the number of protected natural values.

805. The Environmental Advisory Council established under the Law on Environmental Protection shall have an advisory role in the field of nature protection in accordance with this Law and implementing regulation thereof. The Environmental Advisory Council shall ensure the representation of members of institutions competent for nature protection proportionate to the number of protected values (Article 11, paragraphs 1–2).

4. Nature Protection (General Measures)

806. The conservation of nature shall be carried out by conservation of the overall biological and landscape diversity in the manner prescribed by this Law, special regulations and international treaties of which Bosnia and Herzegovina is a member. The conservation of habitats and wild animal and plant species (biodiversity) shall include a series of measures necessary for conservation and establishment of natural living area (habitats) and populations of species of wild flora, fauna and fungi at the level of favourable state (Articles 12, paragraphs 1, and 2).[913]

807. Owners and trustees of natural assets shall allow the environmental administration authorities' representatives (the relevant authorities) or persons they authorized, to tour and inspect the natural assets for the purpose of research, collection of expert data and expert supervision of the implementation of prescribed requirements and measures for nature protection (Article 13, paragraph 1). The provisions of paragraph 1 of this article shall also pertain to protected natural values (paragraph 2).[914]

808. Any change in the intended use of the land in the protected area shall not be allowed when not in conformity with the spatial development documents (Article 15).[915]

809. In addition to the general measures, this chapter of the law also includes the following issues: Spatial Development and Use of Natural Resources, Assessment of Acceptability to the Ecological Network and Activities in Nature, Mitigation of harmful effects on nature caused by interventions in nature or using natural resources, Landscapes and Ecosystems protection.

913. The protection of forests, waters and other natural assets and protected areas and areas within the ecological network shall be carried out in line with this Law and special regulations (para. 3).

914. In order to prevent degradation of nature, in the areas outside settlement and outside all types of roads, dirt roads, developed paths and driving test ranges (test drives, cross drives, off-road drives, sport, competition and promotional rides, and the like), it shall be forbidden to drive, park or organize motor vehicle rides except when rides are needed in performance of official duty, agricultural, forestry or other allowed activities or when it is in line with this Law and other regulations (Art. 14).

915. The spatial plan may expand the construction area on protected natural values only when there is no threat to biological and landscape diversity of the protected area and if all options of rational use of the existing construction area and existing infrastructure corridors are exhausted. Construction expansion of the area shall be possible after the expert assessment is made by the Federation Institute and relevant cantonal authorities (Art. 16, paras 2 and 3).

5. Nature Protection Planning and Organization

810. The basic nature protection documents are: Strategy of Bosnia and Herzegovina and Action Plan for the Protection of Biological and Landscape Diversity (hereinafter, 'the National Strategy'); the Federation Strategy of Nature Protection (Federation Strategy of Nature Protection is part of the Federation Strategy of Environmental Protection, hereinafter, 'the Federation Strategy'); spatial planning documentation in the Federation of BIH (Article 184, paragraph 1).[916]

811. The Federation Strategy defines long-term objectives and guidelines for conservation of biological and landscape diversity and protected natural values, including implementation methods in accordance with the overall economic, social and cultural development of the Federation of BIH (Article 185, paragraph 1).[917]

812. For the purpose of implementing the Federation Strategy and nature protection programmes, including other documents governing individual issues of nature protection, a report on the state of nature protection in the Federation of BIH shall be prepared and submitted to the Parliament (Article 186, paragraph 1).[918]

6. Protection of Minerals and Fossils

813. Minerals,[919] fossils[920] and speleothems shall be owned by the Federation of BIH (Article 125, paragraph 3). It shall be prohibited to destroy minerals, fossils and speleothems and damage the discover sites (paragraph 4). It shall be allowed in exceptional circumstances if it is in the interest of the Federation of BIH or if there is a significant public interest (paragraph 5). It shall be prohibited to take from

916. Nature protection programs shall be brought by the Cantonal Assemblies, each for its area. The Programs must be harmonized with the Federation Strategy of Nature Protection (Art. 184, para. 2).

917. Every five years objectives and guidelines defined by the Federation Strategy, including implementation of action plans, shall be analysed and the Strategy revised, if required (para. 3).

918. The report on the state of the natural environment referred to in para. 1 of this article shall cover a period of two years and contain in particular: information relating to the state of landscapes, ecosystems, habitat types, wild species/subspecies, indigenous domesticated species/subspecies with an analysis of threats, including the causes of threats and protection difficulties; information relating to impacts of the use of natural resources on biological and landscape diversity; information relating to impacts of individual activities on nature; evaluation of measures taken in connection with the conservation of biological and landscape diversity and protected natural values; analysis of the implementation of the Strategy and other documents of relevance for nature protection; evaluation of the supervision carried out; information relating to the use of nature protection funds, and assessment of the need to prepare new or amend existing documents, including other data of relevance for nature protection and conservation (para. 2).

919. Minerals are naturally occurring homogenous chemical elements or compounds in a form of crystallized or amorphous substances, of a specific structure, shape and system. In terms of this Law, minerals shall not refer to mineral raw materials (Art. 125, para. 1).

920. Fossils represent preserved compounds, parts or traces of extinct organisms and their living activities (Art. 125, para. 2).

nature minerals, fossils or speleothems designated as protected natural values or situated in a protected discovery site (Article 128, paragraph 1).[921]

7. Access to Information and Public Participation

814. The Federation Ministry, cantonal ministries, Federation Institute, cantonal nature protection institutes, administration bodies, public companies and public institutions that manage natural values shall make public the information on the state and protection of nature, unless classified confidential by a special law or a document of a competent body (Article 198, paragraph 1).[922]

815. Public participation shall be ensured in the course of preparing regulations or documents on the designation of protected natural values, spatial development documents, protected area management plans and plans for the use of natural resources, including generally applicable and legally binding regulations and documents in the field of nature protection (Article 200, paragraph 1).[923] For the purpose of nature protection the citizens' associations may: carry out activities educating young people and citizens about the needs of nature protection, benefits of protected areas and similar activities in order to reach the public's attention to the nature and ensure public support to enacting and implementing the regulations on nature protection (Article 201).

8. Inventorying and Monitoring of the State

816. Impacts on the nature shall be monitored through the state of overall landscapes, the state of ecosystems, biological systems and non-living nature components (water, air, land, rocks) (Article 193). The Federation Institute shall establish and carry out an inventory of all components of biological and landscape diversity (biological species/subspecies, habitat types and landscape types), mapping of threatened species/subspecies and habitat types and their permanent and timely

921. Exceptionally, the Federation Ministry may grant a permit for minerals, fossils or speleothems designated protected natural values or situated in a protected discovery site to be taken from nature for the purpose of scientific and expert research, education, displaying in exhibitions and for other purposes (para. 2).

922. The competent bodies and legal entities shall keep records of data relating to the state and protection of nature, and in the event of any degradation of nature they shall immediately inform the public thereof and give instructions for the procedure aimed at nature protection and conservation. In the case of any immediate threat to nature and human health, the public shall be informed about necessary measures and actions to be taken with the view to prevent or offset the damage that might arise from such a threat (Art. 198, para. 2).

923. In the course of procedures referred to in para. 1 of this article, the public shall be informed by a public notification or individually about any act or activity likely to have an impact on the state of the natural environment. Public information is compulsory in cases provided for by this Law and its implementing regulations (Art. 200, para. 2).

updating (Article 194, paragraph 1).[924] In addition, The Federation Institute shall monitor and organize the monitoring of the state of nature conservation (Article 195, paragraph 1),[925] and encourage and promote scientific research into the field of nature protection (Article 196, paragraph 1).

9. Supervision and Financing

817. The inspection oversight of the enforcement of this Law shall be carried out in line with this Law, Law on the organization of administration in the Federation of BIH (the Official Gazette of the Federation of BIH, Vol. 35/05), those pertaining to inspection oversight, and the Law on Inspection of the Federation of BIH (the Official Gazette of the Federation of BIH, Vol. 69/05) (Article 210).[926]

818. The funds necessary for the protection of natural values of international and national importance, including those natural values, funds for financial and other incentives provided for by this Law, funds for compensation due to damage caused by protected animals, for exercising the pre-emption right of the FBIH Government, for indemnification of owners and trustees of property in protected natural values of international, national and Federation importance shall be provided by the budgets of the Federation Government and FBIH Environmental Protection Fund (Article 208, paragraph 1).[927] The resource base for nature protection funding shall also be secured by use of natural resources and protected natural values, unless stated otherwise by this Law or regulations, by charges collected by concession licenses and from other sources provided for by the law or regulations issued pursuant to it (paragraph 3).

B. Other Relevant FBiH Regulations

819. Other relevant regulations include the following:

(1) Rule book on establishing monitoring system of deliberate keeping and killing of protected animals (Official Gazette of FBiH No. 46/05).

924. The data shall be public, unless classified as secret for the purpose of the protection of wild species/subspecies or habitats (para. 2).
925. The data relating to monitoring the state of nature conservation shall be submitted to the Federation Ministry. The data shall be public, unless classified as secret for the purpose of the protection of wild species/subspecies or habitats (Art. 195, para. 3).
926. Inspection oversight of the enforcement of this Law and its implementing regulations in the protected areas of I and II categorise referred to in Art. 134 of this Law, shall be conducted by nature protection inspectors of the Federation Administration of Inspections Affairs and for categorise III, IV, V and VI by the cantonal authority for inspection affairs. The inspection oversight shall be conducted by nature protection inspectors (Art. 211).
927. The funds necessary for the protection of natural values designated protected by a cantons, for financial and other incentives provided for by this Law, for exercising the pre-emption right and for indemnification of owners and trustees of property for restrictions imposed on them in protected natural values, shall be provided by the cantonal budgets (Art. 208, para. 2).

(2) Rule book on establishing and managing an information system for protecting nature and monitoring (Official Gazette of FBiH No. 46/05).
(3) Rule book on the contents and manner of drafting protected areas management plans.
(4) Rule book on new measures for research or preservation for the purpose of preventing significant negative impact on species either by deliberately capture or killing (Official Gazette of FBiH No. 65/06).
(5) Rule book on the contents and manner of preparation of protected areas management plan (Official Gazette of FBiH No. 65/06).
(6) Rule book on the requirements for accessing to the protected area (Official Gazette of FBiH No. 69/06).
(7) Rule book on content and manner of keeping of protected areas registry (Official Gazette of FBiH No. 69/06).
(8) Regulation NATURA2000-protected areas in Europe (Official Gazette of FBiH No. 43/11).
(9) Red list of endangered wild species and subspecies of plants, animals and fungi (Official Gazette of FBiH No. 7/14).
(10) Red list of flora FBiH.
(11) Red list of fauna FBiH.
(12) Red list of fungi of FBiH.
(13) Rulebook on the method of implementation of risk assessment and development of a risk assessment study on the introduction, reintroduction and cultivation of foreign taxa and the procedure for issuing licenses for the importation of foreign taxa in the Federation of Bosnia and Herzegovina (Official Gazette of FBiH No. 102/15, 78/19).[928]
(14) Rulebook on protection measures for strictly protected and protected species and subspecies and protected species and subspecies (Official Gazette of FBiH No. 21/20).
(15) Rulebook on the conditions and manner of establishing and managing the cadastre of speleological objects in the Federation of Bosnia and Herzegovina (Official Gazette of FBiH No. 28/21).
(16) Rulebook on ways, methods, and technical means that least disturb wild species/subspecies or the habitats of their populations, as well as limiting intervention in the habitats of populations of animal species in the time that coincides with their vital periods (Official Gazette of FBiH, No. 87/21)

III. Brčko District of Bosnia and Herzegovina

A. The Law on Nature Protection

820. Basic legal act regulating nature protection in Brčko District of Bosnia and Herzegovina is the Law on Nature Protection (Official Gazette of BD BiH, No. 24/04, 1/05, 19/07 and 9/09). It has the following fourteen parts: Part I – General

928. *See*: https://www.fmoit.gov.ba/bs/zakoni/zakoni-na-razini-fbih (13 Jul. 2022).

Provisions (Articles 1–5), Part II – Definitions (Article 6), Part III – The Basic Principles (Articles 7–13), Part IV – Information System and Public Awareness (Article 14), Part V – Planning of the Nature Protection (Articles 15–16), Part VI – Competences (Articles 17–19), Part VII – General Measures for Nature Protection (Articles 20–23), Part VIII – Special Measures for Nature Protection (Articles 24–37), Part IX – The Wild Species Protection (Articles 38–41), Part X – Protection of Minerals and Fossils (Article 42), Part XI – Supervision (Article 43), Part XII – Financing of the Nature Protection (Articles 44–45), Part XIII – Penalty Provisions (Article 46), Part XIV – Transitional and Final Provisions (Articles 47–49).[929]

§4. Membership in International Treaties

821. BiH is a member of the following international nature protection treaties:

(1) Convention on the Conservation of Migratory Species of Wild Animals, Bonn, 1979.
(2) Convention on Biological Diversity, Rio de Janeiro, 1992.
(3) Convention on International Trade in Endangered Species of Wild Plants and Animals (CITES), Washington 1973, changed in Bonn 1979.
(4) Convention on Wetlands of International Importance Especially as Habitat for Wetland Birds, Ramsar 1971, notification on succession.
(5) Convention on the Protection of European Wildlife Species and Natural Habitats (Bern Convention), Bern, 1979.
(6) Protocol on Biosafety, Cartagena 2000.
(7) UN Convention to Combat Desertification, Paris, 1994.
(8) Convention on the Protection of the World Cultural and Natural Heritage, Paris, 1972.
(9) International Convention for the Protection of Birds, Paris, 1950.
(10) International Convention for the Protection of New Varieties of Plants, 1991.
(11) International Convention on the Plants Protection.
(12) Convention for the establishment of the European and Mediterranean Plant Protection Organization, 1955, 1973, 1999.
(13) Protocol Concerning Mediterranean Specially Protected Areas, 1982.

929. This Law regulates restoration, protection, conservation and sustainable development of landscapes, natural areas, plants, animals and their habitats, soil, minerals, fossils and other natural components, which are part of the environment, in the manner and under the conditions stipulated by this Law (Art. 1, para. 1). The provisions of this Law shall apply to the legal entities, natural persons and associations which might have the rights and obligations according to the provisions of this Law, on the territory of the Brčko District (Art. 5, para. 1).

§5. Harmonization with EU Legislation

822. Alignment with the EU *acquis* on nature protection remains limited.[930]. 'The planning for and investments in renewable energy, including hydropower, wind and solar power plants, requires compliance with the EU's environmental legislation, in particular regarding SEA, EIA, the Birds and Habitats Directives as well as the EU *acquis* on nature protection and water management.'[931] In addition, BiH 'needs to designate institutions, ensure the necessary human and financial resources and establish structures in order to fully implement' CITES Convention, and should prepare the legislation and establish the conditions for ratification and implementation of the Nagoya Protocol on access to genetic resources.

930. EC, *Bosnia and Herzegovina 2021 Progress Report, supra* p. 103.
931. Ibid. The parliaments of both entities have called on their governments (as a result of growing environmental concerns of many NGOs and citizens as regards unrestrained development of hydropower), to impose a moratorium on the construction of small hydropower plants until a review of relevant legislation is completed.

Chapter 1. Monuments and Landscapes

§1. State of the Architectural Heritage, Natural Monuments and Landscapes

823. 'The state of the architectural heritage immediately before the 1992–1995 war in Bosnia and Herzegovina may be analyzed by using the indicators in the inventory of the built heritage conducted by the Republic Statistics Institute of Bosnia and Herzegovina on 31 December 1986. This covered 727 recorded properties, of which 507 were individual monuments and 220 were complexes or groups (with a total area of 272 hectares).'[932] During the war Bosnia and Herzegovina's built heritage was considerably destroyed.

824. Ten areas are designated as Natural Monument (3rd category IUCN), four of which are located in the FBiH, and six in the RS. These are: Skakavac, Prokoško Lake, Vrelo Bosne and Tajan in the FBiH, and Ljubačevo cave, Žuta Bukva, Orlovača cave, Rastuša cave, Dedana pit and Vagan cave in the RS. Apart from these, two protected areas are designated parks of nature (Blidinje and Hutovo Blato), but this category is not envisaged in the Law on Nature Protection in the FBiH.[933]

825. Richness of landscape diversity in BiH can be best explained by geographic zones, which provide prerequisites for different ecosystems and landscapes. Predominant landscapes from the south to the north are as follows: Mediterranean landscapes; Supra-Mediterranean landscapes; Mediterranean-mountainous landscapes; Mountain landscapes; Hilly landscapes; Peripannonian landscapes; Pannonian landscapes.

§2. Competencies

826. The Commission to Preserve National Monuments[934] is an institution of Bosnia and Herzegovina set up pursuant to Annex 8 of the General Framework Agreement for Peace in Bosnia and Herzegovina and the decision of the Presidency of Bosnia and Herzegovina on the Commission to Preserve National Monuments (Official Gazette of BiH, Nos 1/02 and 10/02). Ministry of Civil Affairs of

932. Commission to Preserve National Monuments of Bosnia and Herzegovina, *Report On Assessment Of The Architectural And Archaeological Heritage*, *supra.* Of the 727 recorded monuments, 46 were part of recorded groups. Based on the inventory data, the area under protection was 272 hectares or 0.31% of the total inhabited area of Bosnia and Herzegovina. The inventory covered 162 religious buildings and sites, fifty-two residential buildings and groups, and thirty-six commercial and civil engineering structures, most of which were military structures and groups.
933. BiH MFTER, *State of the environment Report of the Bosnia and Herzegovina 2012*, *supra* p. 154.
934. *See*: http://old.kons.gov.ba/index.php?lang=4 (13 Jul. 2022). The Commission issues decisions on designating movable and immovable property as National Monuments applying the Criteria on the Designation of National Monuments (Official Gazette of BiH, No. 33/02). Responsibility for the enforcement of the Commission's decisions lies with the entity/regional governments and the ministries responsible for regional planning and for culture.

BiH[935] 'performs the tasks and duties within the competences of BiH that are related to the establishment of the basis principles of coordination of activities, harmonisation of the plans of Entity government bodies, and definition of the international-level strategy for culture'.[936]

827. In RS, the Institute for the Protection of the Cultural, Historical and Natural Heritage of RS[937] operates under the auspices of Education and Culture of RS. In the FBiH, the Institute for the Protection of Monuments, part of the Federal Ministry of Culture and Sport, is the body responsible for the protection of cultural and natural heritage.[938] In BD, responsibility for the implementation of the Commission and heritage protection lies with the Commission to Preserve the Heritage of the Education Department and the Department of Spatial Planning and Proprietary Rights.[939]

§3. Legislation

I. Bosnia and Herzegovina

828. The activities on heritage legal protection in BiH as one of the federal states of ex-Yugoslavia started at the end of the Second World War. In 1947 the first Law on Protection of Monuments and natural Rarities was passed. From 1945 to 1992 in the main BiH cities as Sarajevo, Mostar, Tuzla and Banja Luka were founded another four institutes for heritage protection. 'The several laws on legal heritage protection were passed too, that were compatible to all international conventions, among these The Convention of Protection of World Cultural and Natural Heritage passed at UNESCO General Conference at 1972, in Paris.'[940] The latest Law on Protection and Usage of Cultural, Historical and Natural Heritage at the state level of BiH was adopted 1985 (Official Gazette of SRBiH No. 20/1985).

829. The basic legislation include the following:

(1) The General Framework Agreement for Peace in Bosnia and Herzegovina (Dayton Peace Agreement), Annex 8 – Agreement on the Commission to Preserve National Monuments; 1995.

935. http://www.mcp.gov.ba/Content/Read/nadleznosti-ministarstva (13 Jul. 2022).
936. *See*: Directorate for European Integration, *Answers to the Questionnaire, Chapter 26, Education and Culture*, 27 Feb. 2018, p. 442.
937. *See*: http://www.nasljedje.org/ (13 Jul. 2022).
938. *See*: http://fmks.gov.ba/stara/o-ministarstvu/sektor-za-kulturno-historijsko-naslijede-i-kulturu (13 Jul. 2022). Five of the eleven cantons in the FBiH have their own cantonal institutes: Sarajevo, Tuzla, Bihać, Bugojno and Mostar.
939. For more information on jurisdiction with regard to the landscape's management *see* parts of monograph related to the protection of nature.
940. Uzunović Z., *Protection, Documentation and Popularization of Cultural Historical and Natural Heritage of Canton Sarajevo, Bosnia and Herzegovina*. Sarajevo, 2000.

(2) Law on Archival Material and the Archives of BiH (Official Gazette of BiH, No. 16/01).
(3) The Decision of the Presidency of Bosnia and Herzegovina on the Commission to Preserve National Monuments, 2001 (Official Gazette of BiH, Nos 1/02 and 10/02).[941]
(4) The Rules on the Activities of the Commission to Preserve National Monuments with respect to International Cooperation, 2002 (Official Gazette of BiH, No. 29/02).
(5) The Criteria for the Designation of Property as National Monuments, 2002/2003 (Official Gazette of BiH, Nos 33/02 and 15/03; Official Gazette of the FBiH, No. 59/02; Official Gazette of RS, No. 79/02).

II. The Republic of Srpska

A. *Law on Cultural Properties*

830. The Law on Cultural Properties of RS (Official Gazette of RS, No. 38/22) regulates the types of cultural properties, the activity of protection and use of cultural properties and properties that enjoy prior protection, and other issues of importance for the activity of cultural properties protection.[942]

B. *Law on Nature Protection*

831. According to Article 46 of the Nature Protection Act monument of nature[943] belongs to the category of 'protected natural resources', i.e., 'protected areas' – Category III (paragraph 1.a.4). All acts and activities that jeopardize characteristics and values of the monument of nature are forbidden (Article 50, paragraph 3).[944]

941. *See also*: The Law on the Implementation of Decisions of the Commission to Preserve National Monuments Established Pursuant to Appendix 8 of the Dayton Agreement, (Official Gazette of the FBiH, Nos. 2/02, 27/02, 6/04 and 51/07), The Law on the Implementation of Decisions of the Commission to Preserve National Monuments Established Pursuant to Appendix 8 of the Dayton Agreement, (Official Gazette of RS, Nos. 9/02 and 64/08), The Law on the Implementation of Decisions of the Commission to Preserve National Monuments Established Pursuant to Appendix 8 of the Dayton Agreement, (Official Gazette of the BD, Nos. 2/02 and 19/07).
942. Cultural property, in the sense of this law, is any immovable, movable, and intangible property that, in accordance with this law, has been determined to be of permanent historical, artistic, ethnographic, anthropological, archaeological, architectural, natural, scientific, technical or other significance (Art. 2).
943. The monument of nature can be: geological; geomorphologic; speleological; hydrological (whole or part of the watercourse, waterfall, lake, shaking and other); botanical (rare or significant examples of the plant world, individual tree or group of trees, avenues, parks, arboretums, botanical gardens, etc.) (Art. 50, para. 2).
944. Measures for the protection of monument of nature and the manner of its use are defined in more detail by the act promulgating the protected area (Art. 50, para. 4).

832. The Assembly of the local self-government unit, with the consent of the Ministry, and according to the previously obtained opinion of the Institute and the competent ministries, promulgates the protected area's decree: (a) a monument of nature (Article 60, paragraph 3). A monument of nature and a protected area with sustainable use of natural resources whose entire area is belongs to two or more units of local self-government can be promulgated as protected area by the assembly of local self-government units with the consent of the Ministry, and according to the previously obtained opinion of the Institute and competent ministries (Article 60, paragraph 4).[945] The initiative for designation of a protected area may be submitted by the Institute, the state administration bodies and nature protection entities referred to in Article 11 of this Law (Article 61, paragraph 1).

833. The objectives of the Law on Nature Protection are, *inter alia*, following: conservation and improvement of biological (genetic, specie and ecosystem), geological and landscape diversity, and improvement of the state of disrupted parts of nature and landscape[946] (Article 3, points a and đ).

834. 'Protected landscapes – Category V' belongs to the 'protected natural assets'. This term includes the following: protected natural landscapes, protected cultural landscapes, nature park (Article 46, paragraph 1, point 6). Landscape protection implies the planning and implementation of measures to prevent undesirable changes, disturbances or destruction of significant landscape features, their diversity, uniqueness and aesthetic value, and enabling the traditional way of using landscapes (Article 38, paragraph 2).[947]

C. Other Relevant RS Regulations

835.
(1) Law on Museum Activities (Official Gazette of the RS, No. 89/08, 57/12 and 18/17).
(2) Law on Archival Activity (Official Gazette of the RS, No. 119/08).
(3) Law on Culture (Official Gazette of the RS, No. 66/18).
(4) Law on the Protection of the Environment (Official Gazette of the RS, No. 71/12, 79/15, and 70/20).
(5) Law on Spatial Development and Construction (Official Gazette of RS, Nos 40/13, 2/15-CC, 106/15, 3/16-corr, 104/18-CC, 84/19).
(6) Criminal Code of the RS (Official Gazette of RS, No. 64/17).

945. Exceptionally, the act on the designation of a protected area is passed by the Government at the proposal of the Ministry, if the competent authorities do not declare a protected area and if it is determined that the protected area is of exceptional, or republican importance (Art. 60, para. 5).
946. The landscape is a specific territory, homogeneous in its origin and development history, with a unique geological base, relief, climate, and uniform combination of soil (Art. 6, point 4).
947. The Minister shall issue a regulation prescribing the criteria for identification of the landscape and the manner of assessing their significant and characteristic features (Art. 38, para. 5).

(7) Law on the Donja Gradina Monument Site (Official Gazette of the RS, No. 16/96, and 1/09).[948]

III. Federation of Bosnia and Herzegovina

A. Law on the Protection of the Cultural, Historical and Natural Heritage

836. The Law on the Protection of the Cultural, Historical and Natural Heritage of 1985 (Official Gazette of SRBiH, Nos 20/85 and 12/87), is in force in the Federation of Bosnia and Herzegovina and in the cantons that have not enacted their own laws.[949] The heritage is defined as a public asset, and regardless of whether it is in public or private ownership, the law required public investment in its protection and in restoration works.

B. Law on Nature Protection

837. In accordance with Article 3 of the Law on Nature Protection, the objectives of nature protection shall include, *inter alia*, the conservation and restoration of the existing biological and landscape diversity[950] to a state of natural balance and relations harmonized human activities; assessment of the state and monitoring of the natural values; providing the protection system for natural values for the purpose of permanent conservation of their characteristics on the basis of which they were declared protected, etc.

Pursuant to Article 134 of the Law on Nature Protection protected natural values in terms of this Law are, *inter alia*, 'Category IIIa: Nature park – IIIb: Monument of nature and nature characteristics.'[951]

---

948. For more information see: Directorate for European Integration, *Answers to the Questionnaire, Chapter 26, Education and Culture*, 27 Feb. 2018, p. 444. *See also*: https://nasljedje.org/propisi/ (18 Jul. 2022).

949. Cantons that have adopted heritage laws are the following: Sarajevo Canton – Law on the Protection of the Cultural Heritage (Official Gazette of Sarajevo Canton No. 2/00), Herzegovina-Neretva Canton – Law on the Protection of the Cultural Heritage in Herzegovina-Neretva Canton (Official Gazette of Herzegovina-Neretva Canton No. 2/06) and Law on Building Permits Beyond the Boundaries of National Monuments or Interim Boundaries and Implementation of Protection measures (Official Gazette of Herzegovina-Neretva Canton No. 5/08), West Herzegovina Canton – Law on the Protection and Use of the Cultural, Historical and Natural Heritage (Official Gazette of West Herzegovina Canton No. 6/99), Una-Sana Canton – Law on the Protection of the Cultural Heritage (Official Gazette of Una-Sana Canton No. 3/04), and Zenica-Doboj Canton – Law on the Protection of the Cultural Heritage (Official Gazette of Zenica-Doboj Canton No. 2/00).

950. '*Landscape diversity*' is a land of structured natural and anthropogenic landscape elements (biological, geological, geomorphologic and cultural values) (Art. 8).

951. Protected area of category IIIb is separated for the purpose of protecting specific natural features such as special forms of land relief, marine reef, underground caves, geological formations such as caves or form of life such as jungles. Generally, these are small protected areas with a higher potential for tourism (Art. 138).

838. Category Va (*'Protected landscape')*[952] is a protected area that occurred through the interaction of humans and nature, and is characteristic by its significant ecological, biological, cultural and aesthetic values. Maintenance of the humans and nature interaction is of vital importance to the protection and sustainability of the area along with natural and other values (Article 140, paragraph 1).[953]

C. *Other Relevant FBiH Regulations*

839.

(1) Law on the Protection of the Environment (Official Gazette of the FBiH, Nos 33/03, and 38/09).
(2) Law on Spatial Planning and Land Use (Official Gazette of the FBiH, Nos 2/06 and 72/07, 32/08, 4/10, 13/10 and 45/10).
(3) Criminal Code of the FBiH (Official Gazette of FBiH, Nos 35/03, 37/03, 21/04, 69/04, 18/05, 42/10, 42/11, 59/14, 76/16).
(4) Laws on Museum Activities (Cantons).
(5) Laws on Archival Activities (Cantons), etc.

IV. Brčko District of Bosnia and Herzegovina

840. 'In the BDBiH, there is no legal regime that applies to preservation of the cultural heritage.'[954]

A. *Law on Nature Protection*

841. Law on Nature Protection of the Brèko District of BiH prescribes in Article 30 (paragraph 1) that the objectives of the natural monuments[955] management are the following: protection and preservation of natural features of outstanding significance, unique or common qualities, and spiritual values in accordance with specific objectives; providing opportunities for scientific research, education, interpretation and public evaluation; enabling use of the population living in that area which is consistent with the management objectives.

---

952. *'Landscape'* is an area of land that contains a mosaic of ecosystems whose character represents a specific blending of natural and created values characteristic for the given region (Art. 8).
953. Primary objectives are protection and maintenance of important coastal, marine landscapes and nature parks with the values that occurred through the interaction of humans and nature and traditional management practice (Art. 140, para. 2).
954. Directorate for European Integration, *Answers to the Questionnaire, Chapter 26, Education and Culture*, 27 Feb. 2018, p. 471.
955. The natural monument has one or more specific natural/cultural features of outstanding or unique values due to its rarity, natural, representative or aesthetic features or cultural significances (Art. 29, para. 1).

842. According to Article 32 the objectives of protected landscapes[956] are the following (paragraph 1): maintenance compliance of impacts of nature and culture through the protection of land and/or coastal landscapes and traditional land use, construction and social and cultural events; carrying out of economic activities in accordance with nature and preservation of the cultural system of the community; maintaining the diversity of landscapes and habitats, related species and ecosystems; the elimination and prevention of land use and activities those are not consistent with the management objectives; enabling of recreation and tourism appropriate to the category of the area; promotion of scientific and educational activities for the benefit of the population for a longer period of time, public participation in environmental protection of the area; enabling of beneficial effects through the provision of natural products (such as forestry and fisheries products) and services (such as clean water or income from sustainable tourism) for the local community.

B. Other Relevant BD Regulations

843.

(1) Law on monuments and symbols (Official Gazette of BD, No. 22/03).
(2) Law on Environmental Protection (Official Gazette of BD, Nos 24/04, 01/05, 19/07 and 09/09).
(3) Criminal Code of the BD (Official Gazette of BD BiH, No. 33/13 – revised).

§4. International Treaties

844. Bosnia and Herzegovina is member of the following international treaties:

(1) European Cultural Convention (Council of Europe, Paris, 1954).
(2) Convention for the Protection of Cultural Property in the Event of Armed Conflict (UNESCO, The Hague, 1954).
(3) European Convention on the Protection of the Archaeological Heritage (Council of Europe, London, 1969).
(4) Convention for the Protection of the Architectural Heritage of Europe (Council of Europe, Granada, 1985).
(5) Convention concerning the Protection of the World Cultural and Natural Heritage (UNESCO, Paris, 1972).
(6) Convention on the Means of Prohibiting and Preventing the Illicit Import, Export and Transfer of Ownership of Cultural Property (UNESCO, Paris, 1970).
(7) Convention for the Safeguarding of the Intangible Cultural Heritage (UNESCO, Paris, 2003).

956. The landscape is an area of land created by interaction of nature and man with exceptional aesthetic, ecological or cultural values, often with high biological diversity.

(8) Convention on the Protection of the Underwater Cultural Heritage (UNESCO, Paris, 2001).
(9) Convention on the Protection and Promotion of the Diversity of Cultural Expressions (UNESCO, Paris, 2005).
(10) Convention for the Safeguarding of the Intangible Cultural Heritage (UNESCO, Paris, 2003).
(11) European Convention on the Protection of the Archaeological Heritage, revised (Council of Europe, Valletta, 1992).
(12) Framework Convention on the Value of Cultural Heritage for Society (Council of Europe, Faro, 2005).

Chapter 2. Parks and Reserves

§1. The Protected Areas in Bosnia and Herzegovina

845. 'The amount of territories designated as protected areas in BiH are relatively small and extremely low in terms of the percentage of protected territory compared to the total territory of BiH, far below the European standard. The management of existing protected areas is also a matter of considerable concern.'[957] In BiH, 153 areas belong to one of the protection level forms since 1954, including protected landscapes, monuments of nature or protected habitats (e.g., forest seed components). However, the classification and registration of these areas are still not in line with the new legislation, nor is there any clarification for the state of the decisions on protection issued on the basis of the Law on the Natural, Cultural and Historical Heritage of SRBiH, due to which these areas cannot be deemed officially protected.[958]

846. In the period before 1992, the 1965 Law on Nature Protection provided protection to 144 areas of different sizes and levels of protection in the territory of Bosnia and Herzegovina. This Law established sixteen strict nature reserves, nine administered (managed) nature reserves, two national parks, six special reserves, ten reserves of natural landscapes and even 110 nature monuments, among which there were numerous Bosnia and Herzegovina's waterfalls, streams, springs, wells, mountain lakes, grottoes and caves.[959]

847. The protected areas in BiH are classified in accordance with the classification of the International Union for Conservation of Nature (IUCN). Based on the available data, the total percentage of protected areas in BiH is 1.85% (1.4% in the FBiH and 0.45% in the RS). GEF project 'Forest and Mountain Protected Areas', which is implemented by the World Bank in BiH, envisages that the total protected areas in BiH should be about 3%.[960]

848. Bosnia and Herzegovina covers three globally significant ecosystems and several smaller scale globally important sites. It is estimated that BH has the highest proportion of threatened plant species of any European country, and yet by the mid-2000s, it had only 0.55% of land set aside as protected areas – the lowest level

957. Hodžić-Kovač, E. (Ed). *Progress towards the Realisation of Millennium Development Goals in Bosnia and Herzegovina 2013*, Ministry of Finance and Treasury of Bosnia and Herzegovina, Office of the UN Resident Coordinator in Bosnia and Herzegovina, Sarajevo, p. 119. 'These areas are not properly monitored and management remains understaffed and insufficiently supported by the responsible levels of governance, which has resulted in the degradation of these sites and a potential loss of the biological basis for their conservation status.' *Ibid.*
958. BiH MFTER, UNEP, GEF. *Strategy and Action Plan for Protection of Biological Diversity in Bosnia and Herzegovina (2015–2020)*, Ministry of Foreign Trade and Economic Relations of Bosnia and Herzegovina, UNEP, GEF, 2016, p. 72.
959. *Bosnia and Herzegovina Fourth Report to the United Nations Convention on Biological Diversity*, 2010 Biodiversity Targets National Assessments, *supra* p. 32.
960. BiH Council of Ministers, *Answers to the List of EU Questions on Chapter 27, Environment, supra* p. 256.

in Europe. Protected areas were generally underfunded, relying heavily on resource extraction for revenues. Additionally, staff working in protected areas had little or no experience in applied management approaches for ecosystems-based management and new management fields, such as sustainable tourism and participatory conservation. Broad consensus on expanding the protected area network existed in both entities, to protect key biodiversity and cultural assets, as well as to provide new income opportunities for local residents.[961]

849. There are three Ramsar sites in BiH (Bardača, Livanjsko polje, Hutovo Blato).[962] Bardača wetland was designated as a Ramsar site in 2007. It is situated in the floodplain of the Sava River near the border with Croatia. Livanjsko polje was designated as another Ramsar site in 2008. With its territory of 46,000 ha, it is one of the biggest flat limestone depressions in the world.[963]

850. According to the Network of Managers of Marine Protected Areas in the Mediterranean, 'no marine protected areas have been declared and no potential area is currently being discussed along the coast of Bosnia and Herzegovina'.[964]

851. The territory of protected areas in Bosnia and Herzegovina is small, and its percentage share of the total territory of the country is well below the European average. The existing thirty protected areas in the country cover only 2.07% of the national territory (1,063 km^2).[965]

§2. LEGISLATION

852. Protected areas in BiH have been designated in the entities and BDBiH by passing relevant regulations depending on the category of protected area.[966]

I. The Republic of Srpska

A. Law on Nature Protection

853. Pursuant to Article 46 of the Law on Nature Protection protected areas are the following:

(1) strict nature reserve – category Ia (hereinafter, strict nature reserve),

961. World Bank Group – Bosnia and Herzegovina, Partnership Country Program Snapshot, April 2013, p. 18.
962. *See*: https://rsis.ramsar.org/sites/default/files/rsiswp_search/exports/Ramsar-Sites-annotated-summary-Bosnia-and-Herzegovina.pdf?1546474298_ (13 Jul. 2022).
963. UNECE, *2nd Environmental Performance Review, supra* p. 48.
964. UNECE. *3rd Environmental Performance Review, Bosnia and Herzegovina. supra* p. 160.
965. *Ibid.*, p. 188.
966. Directorate for European Integration, *Answers to the Questionnaire, Chapter 27, Environment and climate change*, 27 Feb. 2018, *supra* p. 510.

(2) special nature reserve (wildlife area) – category Ib (hereinafter special nature reserve),
(3) national park – category II (hereinafter national park),
(4) a monument of nature – category III (hereinafter a monument of nature),
(5) protected habitat (area of management of habitat or species) – category IV (hereinafter protected habitat),
(6) protected landscapes – category V,
(7) Protected area with sustainable use of natural resources – Category VI (Article 46, para 1).[967]

854. Strict Nature Reserve is an area of unchanged natural characteristics with representative natural ecosystems, intended exclusively for the preservation of the original nature, genetic resources, ecological balance, monitoring of natural phenomena and processes, scientific research which does not disturb the natural features, values, phenomena and processes (Article 48, paragraph 1). In the strict nature reserve, economic and other activities are prohibited (paragraph 2).[968]

855. The National Park is an area with a large number of diverse natural ecosystems, prominent landscape features and cultural heritage in which man lives in harmony with nature. This area is intended to preserve existing natural values and resources, overall landscape, geological and biological diversity, as well as meeting scientific, educational, spiritual, aesthetic, cultural, tourist, health and recreational needs and other activities in accordance with the principles of nature protection and sustainable development (Article 49, paragraph 1). In the area of the National Park some activities and measures are allowed (which do not endanger the originality of nature, as well as the performance of activities that are in the function of education, health and recreational and tourist needs, the continuation of the traditional way of life of local communities, and in a way that does not endanger the survival species, natural ecosystems and landscapes). These activities and measures have to be in accordance with this Law and the management plan (Article 49, paragraph 2).[969] Protected habitat is an area that includes one or more types of natural habitats significant for the conservation of one or more populations of wild species and their communities (Article 51, paragraph 1).[970]

856. Nature Park is an area of well-preserved natural values with predominantly preserved natural ecosystems and landscapes, intended for the preservation of geological, biological and landscape diversity, as well as satisfying scientific, educational, spiritual, aesthetic, cultural, tourist, health and recreational needs and other

967. Areas with significant geological, biological, ecosystem or landscape diversity and which are significant as habitats of species of birds and other migratory species in accordance with international regulations may be declared as 'protected areas of general interest' (Art. 47, para. 1).
968. However, visits, research and monitoring the state of nature are allowed (Art. 48, para. 3).
969. The measures for the protection of the national park and the manner of its use are prescribed by a special law (Art. 49, para. 3).
970. In the area of the protected habitat all activities which endanger or damage one or more habitat types are forbidden (para. 3).

activities of harmonized with the traditional way of life and the principles of sustainable development (Article 53, paragraph 1).[971]

857. Protected area with sustainable use of natural resources is an area dedicated to the conservation of the ecosystems and habitats and, in addition to this, the accompanying cultural values and traditional ways of managing natural resources (Article 54, paragraph 1).[972] Minerals and fossils with remarkable scientific and educational significance or which are significant due to their rarity, size and appearance are declared to be protected (Article 59).

858. The ecological network consists of: (a) ecologically significant areas; (b) ecological corridors and (c) protective zone (Article 25, paragraph 1).[973] The preservation of the ecological network shall be ensured by implementation of the prescribed measures of protection in order to preserve biological and landscape diversity, sustainable use and restoration of natural resources and goods and improvement of protected areas, habitat types and habitats of wild species in accordance with this Law, other regulations, generally accepted rules of international rights and confirmed international agreements (Article 26, paragraph 1). In the area of the ecological network, measures, methods and technical and technological solutions are applied with the aim of preserving ecologically significant areas and improving disturbed state of parts of the ecological network.[974]

859. Ecologically significant areas are: (a) areas of habitat types that are biologically highly diverse or well preserved, where habitats are endangered or endemic biological species and other ecological systems that are internationally significant according to international criteria or otherwise contribute to the conservation of biological diversity, (b) areas of habitat types, which significantly contribute to the preservation of natural balance because they form parts of the ecological network, (c) areas of endangered and rare habitat types, (d) Preserved forests, (e) habitats of species protected under international treaties, (f) migratory pathways of animals, (g) ecological corridors, (h) areas that significantly contribute to the genetic linkage of populations of biological species (Article 28, paragraph 1).[975]

971. In the nature park, economic and other activities are permitted provided that its essential characteristics and values are not threatened (Art. 53, para. 2).
972. The protected area with sustainable use of natural resources is: (a) forest park and (b) nature-designed objects (Art. 54, para. 2).
973. Institute in cooperation with other professional and scientific the institutions prepare the documentation for the establishment ecological network. The government adopts a regulation establishing the ecological network, as well as the manner of its management and financing, and identify ecologically important areas of the European Union that will become part of the European ecological network Natura 2000 (Art. 25, paras 2 and 3).
974. Monitoring of the state of the ecological network shall be performed by the Institute and other professional and scientific institutions under the authority of the Ministry (Art. 26, para. 4).
975. The preservation of ecologically important areas shall be ensured by implementation of the prescribed measures and conditions of nature protection in order to preserve biological and landscape diversity and protection of natural values in accordance with the provisions of this Law (Art. 28, para. 2).

1. Procedure for Declaring Protected Natural Goods

860. National Park shall be proclaimed by the National Assembly by the Law (Article 60, paragraph 1). On the proposal of the Ministry, according to the previously obtained opinion of the competent Ministry by the act on the proclamation of the protected area, the Government proclaim as protected: (a) a strict nature reserve, (b) a special nature reserve, (c) protected habitat and (d) protected landscapes (Article 60, paragraph 2).

861. The Law on National Parks (Official Gazette of RS, No. 75/10) governing issues relevant to for protection, development, improvement, management, financing and sustainable use of national parks.[976]

862. The Assembly of the local self-government unit, with the consent of the Ministry, and according to the previously obtained opinion of the Institute and the competent Ministries, promulgates the act on the designation of the protected area as protected: (a) a monument of nature and (b) a protected area with sustainable use of natural resources whose entire area is in the area of the local self-government unit (Article 60, paragraph 3).[977]

2. Management and Use of Protected Areas

863. The management of a protected area is an activity of general interest. The protected area shall be managed by a legal entity (hereinafter, 'Manager'), which fulfils the professional, personnel and organizational conditions for carrying out activities of preservation, improvement, promotion of natural and other values and sustainable use of the protected area (Article 75, paragraphs 1, and 2).[978]

864. A management plan shall be adopted for each protected area for a period of ten years (Article 77, paragraph 1). The Management Plan shall determine the manner of implementation of the protection, use and management of the protected area, guidelines and priorities for the protection and preservation of the natural values of protected area, as well as development of guidelines, while respecting needs of local

976. *See also*, Law on the National Park 'Kozara' (Official Gazette of RS, No. 121/12), Law on the National Park 'Sutjeska' (Official Gazette of RS, No. 121/12), Law on the National Park 'Drina' (Official Gazette of RS, No. 63/17).

977. A monument of nature and a protected area with sustainable use of natural resources whose entire area is in the area of two or more local self-government units can be consensually declared by the protected area of the Assembly of local self-government units, with the consent of the Ministry, and according to the previously obtained opinion of the Institute and the competent Ministries (Art. 60, para. 4).

978. The Manager shall be determined by the Protection Act (Art. 75, para. 3).

population. Legal entities, entrepreneurs and natural persons are obliged to perform activities in the protected area in accordance with the management plan (Article 77, paragraphs 3–4).[979]

865. Works and activities in the protected area are prohibited, i.e., implementation of projects that damage, distort and change the properties and values for which the area is protected. For the works and activities, i.e., the implementation of projects in the protected area, an environmental impact assessment procedure shall be conducted in accordance with the Law on Environmental Protection (Article 81, paragraphs 1–2). In addition, the use of plant protection products in the protected areas is prohibited in accordance with the Law on Plant Protection Products (Article 82, paragraph 1).

3. Financing of Protected Areas

866. The financing of protected natural good shall be provided from: (a) the budget of the Republic, (b) the budget of the local self-government unit, (c) funds of the Fund for Environmental Protection and Energy Efficiency of the Republic of Srpska, (d) own revenues,[980](e) funds provided for implementation of programmes, plans and projects in the field of nature protection, (f) donations, gifts and assistance, and (g) other sources in accordance with the Law (Article 87, paragraph 1). The annual report on the spending of funds shall be submitted by the Manager of the protected area to the Ministry or to the local self-government unit, depending on the source of funding (Article 88, paragraph 4).

II. Federation of Bosnia and Herzegovina

A. Law on Nature Protection

867. In accordance with Article 134 of the Law on Nature Protection of FBiH, protected natural values in terms of this Law are (1) Category Ia: Strict nature reserve, Category Ib: Wilderness area, (2) Category II: National park, (3) Category IIIa: Nature park, IIIb: Monument of nature and nature characteristics, (4) Category IV: area of habitats/species management, (5) Category V: (a) protected landscapes: coastal landscapes, and marine landscapes, (b) regional park and (6) Category VI: Protected areas with sustainable use of natural resources.

979. The Minister shall issue a regulation prescribing in more detail the content, determination and manner implementation of measures for the management of protected areas (Art. 77, para. 10).
980. Revenues from services that Manager provides to the visitors of protected natural goods (tourism, catering, sales, etc.) (Art. 87, para. 2).

1. Strict Nature Reserve

868. According to Article 135 Category Ia is strictly protected area separated for the protection of biodiversity and possible geological/geomorphologic occurrences, where visits, use and impacts are strictly controlled and limited for the sake of protection of natural values. Such protected areas are irreplaceable reference places for scientific research and monitoring. (Primary objective: protection of regional, national or globally important ecosystems, species (individual or group) and/or specific characteristics of geodiversity: these attributes shall be maintained mainly or completely without human activity and shall be degraded or destroyed with even minor human influence.)[981]

2. Area of Wilderness

869. Category Ib is a protected area which is completely unchanged or very slightly changed, which kept its natural character and impacts with permanent or significant human settlements that are managed for the purpose of protection and conservation of its natural conditions. (Primary objective: Long-term protection of ecological integrity of natural areas that are not disturbed by significant human activities, without modern infrastructure and with predominant natural forces and processes so that present and future generations have a possibility to feel them as such.)

3. The National Park

870. Protected areas of Category II are vast natural or almost natural areas, separated for the protection of wide-range ecological processes, and relevant species and ecosystems characteristic for the area, which constitute ground for spiritual, scientific, educational, recreational and touristic purpose compatible with the protection of cultural and natural heritage. (Primary objective: protection of natural diversity together with ecological structures and accompanying ecological processes with the promotion of education and recreation.)

4. Procedure of Designating Protected Natural Values

871. Protected natural values shall be designated by the FBIH Parliament in a form of a law in compliance with the provisions of Article 134(1) lines (1) and (2)

981. Other goals are following: conservation of ecosystems, species and geomorphological specific characteristics in the way which does not disturb human activities in as much as possible; conservation of specimens of natural environment for scientific research, ecological monitoring and education, covering the common areas which can help in avoiding impacts; minimizing nuisances by way of cautious planning and implementation of research, as well as other allowed activities; preservation of cultural and spiritual values therein.

of this Law (Article 144, paragraph 1). Protected natural values referred to in Article 134(1) lines (3), (4), (5) and (6) shall be designated by the Cantonal Assembly in a form of a law. Protected natural values referred to in Article 134(1) lines (3), (4), (5) and (6) which are locate in the territory of two or more cantons shall be designated by the FBIH Parliament in a form of a law, with the approval of cantonal legislative authorities.[982]

872. The Law designating a protected area shall contain: name and category of the protected value; a precise description of the spatial determination of borders; a name of the category referred to in Article 134(2) of this Law; indication of the scale of the cartographic presentation; a cartographic presentation showing the boundaries or a site denotation forming a constituent part of the designation document (Article 145, paragraph 1).[983] The boundaries of the protected area shall be determined in accordance with the relevant spatial development documents, the Law on Spatial Planning and Use of Land at the level of the Federation of BIH (Article 145, paragraph 2).

873. The Law on Designation shall be based on an expert explanation specifying the values of the area or its components proposed for protection, the methods of managing that area and a statement of the authority issuing the designation document confirming that funds necessary for the management of the protected area have been secured (Article 145, paragraph 4).[984]

874. The public shall be informed about any proposal to designate a protected area (Article 146, paragraph 1). Public information implies providing public access to the proposed document designating the area of a protected value and an expert explanation with cartographic documentation.[985]

875. Protected natural values shall be entered into the Register of Protected Natural Values. The Register of Protected Natural Values shall be kept by the relevant Ministry and Institute (Article 148, paragraphs 1, and 2).[986]

---

982. If the natural value referred to in this article is located in both Entities, the proposal for protection is made by the Federation Ministry and relevant RS Ministry in compliance with the Inter-entity environmental protection program (Art. 144, para. 4).
983. For the purpose of preventing threats to the protected values referred to in the document referred to in para. 1 of this article may provide for a buffer zone outside the protected natural area and lay down measures for the protection thereof.
984. The expert explanation shall contain a detailed description of features and values of the area to be protected, the assessment of the state of that area, consequences that will arise from the adoption of the document of designation, the decision of the relevant body relative to the protection, and evaluation and sources of funds necessary for the enforcement of the document designating the protected area.
985. Public access to the proposed document designating a protected area shall be provided in local self-governance units in the area in which the protected area is located. Public access under para. 2 of this article shall be provided for at least thirty days. The public access procedure shall be laid down by the FBIH Government in a regulation at the proposal of the Ministry (Art. 146, paras 3 and 4).
986. The contents and methods of keeping the Register of Protected Natural Values shall be determined by the Federation Minister by way of the Instruction (Art. 148, para. 3).

III. Brčko District of Bosnia and Herzegovina

A. Law on Nature Protection

876. Law on Protection of Nature of the BD BiH (Articles 24 and 25) defines special measures of environmental protection, through the declaration of protected areas. Regional Spatial Plan of the BD BiH determines protected areas of protected landscape (parks-forests), parks and natural reserves. BD BiH does not have the level of nature reserve protected areas or national parks (Article 54 of the Spatial Plan of BD BiH).[987]

877. The protected area is the land area defined for the protection and maintaining of biological diversity, natural and cultural resources (Article 24, paragraph 1). Protected areas are the following:

- Natural protected areas established for scientific purposes or for wildlife protection.
- National parks established in order to protect the ecosystem and recreation.
- The nature monuments, established for the purpose of conservation of specific natural features.
- Protected landscapes established for the purpose of conservation of terrestrial landscapes, coastal areas and recreation (paragraph 2).

1. Natural Protected Areas

878. Natural protected area is:

- An area of land with outstanding or representative ecosystems, geological or physiological features and types, and that is used primarily for scientific research and environmental monitoring.
- Unmodified or slightly modified large land area that has retained its natural character and influence, without permanent or significant habitats, established to preserve natural conditions.
- An area of land exposed to the active construction intervention on which it is necessary to ensure the maintenance of habitats and meet the requirements of specific species (Article 25, paragraph 1).

2. The National Parks

879. The national park is a natural area of land declared for:

987. BiH Council of Ministers, *Answers to the List of EU Questions on Chapter 27, Environment, supra* p. 261.

(a) Protection of the ecological integrity of one or more ecosystems for present and future generations.
(b) Excluding exploitation or visits which may cause changes and damage to the nature.
(c) Providing foundation for spiritual, scientific, educational, recreational, and visitor's opportunities, which must be in accordance with the principles of environmental protection (Article 27, paragraph 1).

880. The objectives of the national parks management are the following:

- Protection of natural areas of outstanding value, of national and international significance for spiritual, scientific, educational, recreational or for tourist purposes.
- Preserving the original state of representative examples of physiographic regions, biotic communities, genetic resources and species.
- Ensuring environmental stability and diversity.
- Ensuring of usage for inspirational, educational, cultural and recreational purposes in a way that will maintain natural or near-natural state of the area.
- Excluding exploitation or visits which may cause changes and damage to the nature.
- The maintenance of ecological, geomorphological, or aesthetic features due to which the area was declared protected (Article 28, paragraph 1).

Chapter 3. Wildlife Protection

§1. Biodiversity in Bosnia and Herzegovina

881. The variability of wildlife in BiH is the result of ecological heterogeneity of space, geomorphologic and hydrological diversity, specific geological past and climate diversity. BiH wildlife is characterized by a high degree of endemic and relict life forms. More than 5,000 species and subspecies of vascular plants, more than 100 species of fish and more than 320 species of birds and other elements of biological diversity have been identified in BiH.[988]

882. Living world that inhabit different places of BiH compose numerous communities and ecosystems at present day, which are specific for this area, the Balkan Peninsula and entire Europe. High level of floristic diversity is based upon diversity of cyanophytes, algae and vascular plants. By undertaken investigations, till now it is identified 1,859 species from 217 genera within group of cyanophytes and algae. The most diverse groups are Charophyta, i.e., Charophyceae and Chlorophyceae classes, and Heterokontophyta, i.e., Bacillariophyceae class.[989]

§2. Monitoring

883. 'Data on the majority of identified indicators for monitoring the biological diversity state are not available in BiH. Systematic collection and analysis of biological diversity data are almost non-existent.'[990]

§3. Jurisdiction

884. The Law on the Protection and Welfare of Animals (Official Gazette of BiH, No. 25/09) at the level of BiH prescribes the general conditions for the protection of wild animals. Prescribing detailed conditions is under the competences of the entity ministries responsible for protection of nature.[991]

---

988. BiH MFTER, *State of the environment Report of the Bosnia and Herzegovina 2012*, *supra* p. 149. However, BiH wildlife is 'poorly researched at the moment'.

989. *Bosnia and Herzegovina Fourth Report to the United Nations Convention on Biological Diversity*, *supra* p. 4. Main factors responsible for high diversity of BiH are: 1) Diversity of terrestrial habitats caused by: occurrence of rocks of different age, diversity of bedrocks, diversity of soil types, unique and diverse forms of relief, and diversity of climate conditions; 2) Diversity of aquatic habitats reflected by: rich and diverse hydrological network (mountain lakes, springs, mountain torrents, brooks, rivers, sinking streams, ponds, marshes, underground water, thermal sources, brackish water and sea).

990. BiH MFTER, *State of the environment Report of the Bosnia and Herzegovina 2012*, *supra* p. 157. Expert institutions responsible for the collection of biological diversity data do not exist at the state level or at the level of the FBiH, the RS and the BD, and neither do databases.

991. For more information, *see* BiH Council of Ministers, *Answers to the List of EU Questions on Chapter 27, Environment*, *supra* 2012. pp. 273–277.

§4. LEGISLATION

I. Bosnia and Herzegovina

885.

(1) Law on Animal Protection and Welfare of Bosnia and Herzegovina (Official Gazette of BiH, No. 25/09).
(2) Rules on conditions for establishment and operation of zoos (Official Gazette of BiH, No. 27/10).
(3) Rules on animal health conditions for imports of specific species of birds and quarantine conditions (Official Gazette of BiH, No. 17/11).

II. The Republic of Srpska

A. *Law on Nature Protection*

886. Conservation of biological diversity is achieved by implementing measures for protection and improvement of species, their populations, natural habitats and ecosystems (Article 23). The preservation of the habitat shall be carried out by implementing measures and activities for protection and conservation of nature, the sustainable use of natural resources and protected natural goods and the preservation of ecologically important areas (Article 24, paragraph 1).[992] The habitat map shall be published on the website of the Ministry and the Institute (Article 24, paragraph 3).[993]

887. The conservation of wild species is achieved by implementing measures and activities for preserving the species, their populations and habitats, ecosystems and corridors that link them (Article 29, paragraph 1).[994] The protection of wild birds refers to birds, their eggs, nests and habitats (Article 31, paragraph 1). In order to preserve the populations of all types of wild birds, all necessary measures shall be taken, taking into account ecological, economic and recreational requirements (Article 31, paragraph 2).

888. Protected spaces are: strictly protected wild species, and protected wild species (Article 46). Areas that have significant geological, biological, ecosystem or landscape diversity and which are significant as habitats of bird species and other

992. The Minister shall issue a rulebook prescribing the criteria for allocation of endangered, rare and vulnerable habitats and habitat types of special importance for the conservation and protection measures for their conservation according to the previously obtained opinion of the Institute (Art. 24, para, 2).
993. The collection of data on habitats and continuous updating shall be provided by the Ministry in cooperation with the Institute and other professional and scientific institutions, in accordance with the regulation referred to in Art. 94, para. 2 of this Law (Art. 24, para, 4).
994. Conservation of wild species means prevention of all acts affecting the disturbance of the favourable condition of wild populations, destruction or damage to their habitat, litter, nests or disturbance of their life cycle or favourable condition (Art. 29, para. 2).

migratory species in accordance with international regulations may be designated as protected areas of general interest. Protected areas may be cross-border linked to protected areas of neighbouring countries or entities (Article 47, paragraphs 1, and 2). Wild species that are endangered or can become endangered, which have special significance from the genetic, ecological, ecosystem, scientific, health, economic and other aspects, are protected as strictly protected wild species or protected wild species (Article 58, paragraph 1).

889. The Government adopts the Red List Regulation, which establishes a list of endangered wild species classified according to the categories of vulnerability, and the Red Book on Endangered Wild Species and Habitats, which contains more detailed data on the basic characteristics of the species, its degree of vulnerability, and proposals for measures for the protection of the species itself, upon the proposal of the Ministry, and according to the obtained opinion of the competent Ministries and the Institute (Article 67, paragraph 1).[995]

890. On the territory of the Republic is not permitted introduction of non-native wild species and their hybrids into free nature, except in case submission of scientific and expert evidence regarding nature protection and sustainable management, i.e., if the natural habitat of autochthonous wild species is not endangered by the introduction (Article 35, paragraphs 1, and 2).[996] Reintroduction of wild species into free nature on the territory of the Republic may be carried out on the basis of a permit issued by the Ministry, with the previously obtained opinion of the Ministry responsible for agriculture, forestry and water management (Article 36, paragraph 1).[997]

891. For the purpose of import, export, entry, removal or transit and breading of endangered and protected plant and animal wild species, their parts and derivatives protected under the Laws, ratified international treaties and generally accepted rules of international Law, in accordance with special regulations, the Ministry issue a Decision on fulfilment of conditions, with the prior consent of the Ministry responsible for agriculture, forestry and water management (Article 89, paragraph 1).[998] Import, export, entry, removal and transit of protected wild species, their parts and derivatives shall be reported to the customs authority in accordance with special regulations (Article 90, paragraph 1).

---

995. The regulations referred to in para. 1 of this article shall be adopted in accordance with the international methodology for determining the contents and measures for the conservation of species and habitats from the Red Book (Art. 67, para. 2).
996. The Ministry shall issue the permit on the basis of the opinion of the Ministry responsible for agriculture, forestry and water management and expert opinion of the Institute (Art. 35, para. 3).
997. Together with request for issuing the permit, it is necessary to submit a reintroduction program prepared by the Institute in cooperation with expert and scientific institutions and on the basis of conducted research (Art. 36, para. 2).
998. During the import, export, entry, and transit of live animals they shall be transported and kept in accordance with the legislation governing the protection and welfare of animals (Art. 89, para. 5).

B. Other Relevant RS Regulations

892.

(1) Law on the Protection and Welfare of Animals (Official Gazette of RS, No. 111/08).
(2) Law on Hunting (Official Gazette of RS Nos 4/02, 34/08 60/09).
(3) Law on Veterinary in the RS (Official Gazette of RS, Nos 42/08, 6/12).
(4) Law on Forests (Official Gazette of RS, Nos 53/05, 91/06 and 75/08).
(5) Order on time of hunting season for wildlife protected during closed season (Official Gazette of RS, No. 3/10).
(6) Order defining birds and mammals that are useful for agriculture and forestry (Official Gazette of RS, No. 3/10).
(7) Rule book on conditions for establishment and operation of zoos (Official Gazette of RS, No. 85/10).
(8) Rule book on animal health conditions for imports of specific species of birds and quarantine conditions (Official Gazette of BiH, No. 17/11).[999]
(9) Regulation on strictly protected and protected wild species (Official Gazette of RS, 65/20)

III. Federation of Bosnia and Herzegovina

A. Law on Nature Protection

893. According to Article 70 of the Law on Nature Protection wild species and subspecies of plants, fungi and animals (hereinafter, 'wild species/subspecies') shall be: live and dead specimens of wild plants and fungi and free living animals and their bred specimens; their development shapes (egg, larvae, pupae, seeds, fruits, mycelia, etc.); their parts; and easily recognizable products produced out of them (paragraph 1). It is prohibited to exterminate an indigenous wild species/subspecies (paragraph 1). It is prohibited to exterminate an indigenous wild species/ subspecies.[1000] When carrying out activities in nature and using natural resources that affects habitats of wild species/subspecies, the manner, methods and technical means shall be used which shall not endanger a good conservation status of species/ subspecies (Article 72, paragraph 1).[1001]

999. *See*: http://www.vladars.net/sr-SP-Cyrl/Vlada/Ministarstva/mps/%d0%b1.%d0%ba%d0%b5%d1%86%d0%bc%d0%b0%d0%bd/Pages/default.aspx (10 Jul. 2022).

1000. It shall be prohibited to reduce the number of population of wild species/subspecies, destroy their habitats or change their living conditions to the extent which would lead to their endangerment (para. 3).

1001. The Federation Minister, with a previously obtained approval of the Federation Minister of Agriculture, Water Management and Forestry, shall render the Rulebook prescribing the manner, methods and technical means referred to in para. 1 of this article which least disturb wild species/ subspecies or habitats of their populations and limiting the activities in the habitats of animal populations at times synchronized with their important life cycles.

894. Protection of wild birds shall refer to birds, their eggs, nests and habitats (Article 86).[1002]

895. The Federation Ministry shall render the decision on entry, exit and import or export an introduction from the sea, and shall issue an approval for re-export of wild species/subspecies, their parts and derivatives protected under this Law (Article 99, paragraph 1).[1003] Import, export or transit of protected species/subspecies, their parts and derivatives shall be mandatorily reported to the customs service in line with the provisions of this Law and the implementing regulations along with adequate implementation of customs regulations (Article 100, paragraph 1).[1004]

896. The endangered wild species/subspecies shall be the species/subspecies the long-term survival of which is endangered or the one which is rare or specified as such in the red list of endangered plant, fungi and animal species/subspecies (Article 108, paragraph 1). Threatened wild species and subspecies shall be determined and listed in the red list by the Federation Minister based on scientifically determined professional foundations made by the Federation Institute.[1005]

897. Protection measures for strictly protected wild species and subspecies[1006] and protection measures of their habitats shall be prescribed by the Minister in a Rulebook (Article 110, paragraph 3). If some area is a temporary habitat of strictly protected species/subspecies and its protection cannot be ensured otherwise, the Federation Minister may declare that are or part thereof as temporarily protected for not longer than six months, with a prior opinion of the Federation Minister of Agriculture, Water Management and Forestry (paragraph 4).

1002. The Government of the Federation of BIH shall enact the regulations determining the measures needed to maintain populations of all bird species which naturally occur in the wild state in the European territory at the level which corresponds primarily to ecological, scientific and cultural demands at the same time taking into account economic and recreational demands, or to adjust those species populations to that level (Art. 87).

1003. The decision and approval referred to in para. 1 of this article shall be given only of it does not endanger respective populations of animals, fungi or plants. The decision and approval shall also be obtained in the case of a hybrid of which one or both parents belong to a protected wild species/subspecies (Art. 99, paras 2 and 3).

1004. Veterinary inspection and control of consignments referred to in para. 1 of this article that are the responsibility of the relevant veterinary inspection shall be conducted in accordance with special regulations. Protected wild species/subspecies, their parts and derivatives shall be imported, exported, transited across determined border crossing points with phytosanitary and border veterinary inspection (para. 2, and 3).

1005. Red books shall be developed based on red lists of endangered plant, fungi and animal species/subspecies (Art. 108, para. 3).

1006. Strictly protected species/subspecies shall refer to: Wild species/subspecies faced with extinction in the territory of the Federation of BIH; Narrowly distributed endemic species; Wild species/subspecies the appropriate protection of which is prescribed by the international treaty of which Bosnia and Herzegovina is a member. Certain wild species/subspecies may be strictly protected in the entire FBIH territory or in some parts of the territory (Art. 110, para. 1, and 2).

898. Introduction of foreign species/subspecies into nature at the territory of the Federation of BIH shall be prohibited (Article 77, paragraph 1).[1007] In addition, introduction of foreign types of fish into nature and near-nature waters, as well as their transfer from fisheries to other wetlands shall be prohibited. The Federation Minister shall render the Rulebook to prescribe the manner of making the risk assessment and developing the risk assessment study relative to the introduction, reintroduction and breeding and the procedure of permit issuance (paragraph 5).[1008]

899. Reintroduction (re-population) of disappeared wild species/subspecies into nature on the territory of the Federation of BIH shall be conducted with a permit of the Federation Ministry which is issued based on the risk assessment study relative to reintroduction, with a prior approval of the Ministry of Agriculture, Water Management and Forestry (Article 79, paragraph 1).[1009]

B. Other Relevant FBiH Regulations

900.

(1) Law on Hunting (Official Gazette of FBiH, Nos 4/06 and 8/10).
(2) Law on Veterinary Medicine (Official Gazette of FBiH, No. 46/00).
(3) Regulation on Forests (Official Gazette of FBiH, Nos 83/09, 26/10, 38/10 and 60/11).

IV. Brčko District of Bosnia and Herzegovina

A. Law on Nature Protection

901. In accordance with Article 38 (paragraph 1) of the Law on Nature Protection of Brčko District of BiH (Official Gazette of BD BiH, Nos 24/04, 1/05 and 17/07) when the plants and fungi listed in the Red Book are concerned it is forbidden to do the following: deliberately pick, collect, cut and remove the roots or damage such plants in their natural extent in the wild; store, transport, sell or exchange such species located in the wild, except for those that are required prior to the entry into force of this law (Article 6, paragraph 1).

1007. Exceptionally to para. 1 of this article, the introduction shall be allowed if it is scientifically and professionally founded and acceptable from the point of view of nature protection, expert opinion of an expert authority and sustainable management (para. 3). The relevant Ministry shall issue the permit referred to in para. 3 of this article based on the risk assessment study related to the introduction into nature, and with a prior approval of the relevant Ministry of Agriculture, Water Management and Forestry. The permit shall be issued in a form of a decision (para. 4).

1008. For the purpose of preventing unintentional introduction of foreign species/subspecies into the territory of the Federation of BIH, and with a prior approval of the Ministry of Agriculture, Water Management and Forestry, the Federation Minister shall render the Rulebook to prescribe the preventive protection measures (Art. 78, para. 1).

1009. Costs of the study development and implementation of the risk assessment procedure shall be borne by the legal or natural person who filed a request for the permit (para. 2).

902. It is forbidden to do the following with the animal species including birds listed in the Red Book: intentionally keep or kill protected animals in the wild; intentionally disturb, especially during breeding, hibernation and migration; intentionally damage or remove the nests; damage or destroy of nests and habitat; store, transport, sell or exchange species from the wild, except for those acquired before the entry into force of this law; use actions that can cause loss or disturbance of populations of such species (Article 39, paragraph 1).

903. It is forbidden to deliberately introduce new plant and animal species that do not originate from the territory of the Brčko District. The competent department responsible for environmental protection shall by special act determine otherwise, under condition that it is not damage for natural habitats within their natural scale or for the wild plant and animal species (Article 41, paragraph 1).[1010]

1010. Reintroduction of extinct plants and animals in the Brčko District of BiH can be done only with the prior approval of the competent department and with prior obtained opinion of the department responsible for agriculture and forestry (Art. 41, para. 2).

Chapter 4. Agricultural Resources

§1. Agriculture in Bosnia and Herzegovina

904. 'All natural conditions & production factors, except capital, are very suitable for sustainable development of agriculture and food processing industry in BiH.'[1011] The agriculture sector is a small but important part of the Bosnia and Herzegovina (BH) economy. It decreased from 15.1% in 1999 to 9.8% in 2007, while services and industry sectors now make up 63.9% and 26.2% of the economy, respectively. Institutional constraints prevent BiH's agro-food sector from reaching its full potential.[1012]

905. Around 52% (2,600,000 ha) of the total land area is suitable for agriculture with the remaining considered as forestland. Although the total agricultural land area in FBIH and RS is similar, when the population of each are considered – 2,250,000 for FBIH and 1,450,000 for RS – the division of agricultural land per capita in FBIH is at 0.56 ha whereas in RS it amounts to approx. 0.90 ha per capita. Furthermore, when the areas of fertile fields and gardens are considered, the situation in FBIH declines further and at 0.23 ha per capita is half that in RS.[1013]

906. Only 1% of arable land is irrigated, which is insignificant in comparison to most EU countries. Production of cereals, vegetables, industrial crops and fodder has significantly decreased compared to the pre-war period. Even though organic production is not widespread, it is constantly increasing every year. Impact of agriculture on the environment is reflected in soil and water pollution and it contributes to global warming due to GHG emissions. Since BIH agriculture is characterized by small and fragmented estates, inadequate equipment on estates and poor use of agricultural inputs, it is estimated that the current impacts of this sector on the environment are not significant in comparison to certain other sectors.[1014]

§2. Competencies

907. The most of agriculture legislation including all legislation affecting animal and plant health as well as food safety, but also harmonization with EU agricultural legislation and EU standards for the agricultural sector, is transferred to BiH

1011. Foreign Investment Promotion Agency, *Bosnia and Herzegovina Agriculture and Food Processing Industry*, Sarajevo, 2013. p. 7.

1012. World Bank Group – Bosnia and Herzegovina, Partnership Country Program Snapshot, April 2013, p. 17. BH's comparative advantages in agriculture, especially for niche products, are due to its close proximity to the European Union (EU), moderate continental climate, fairly rich and cultivable soils, clean and abundant natural water resources, natural upland pastures, and good availability of labour. There is a long tradition of small-scale farming and organic production.

1013. RSMoAFWM, *First national report on the implementation of the United Nations Convention to Combat Desertification/Land Degradation in Bosnia and Herzegovina, supra* p. 26.

1014. BiH MFTER, *State of the environment Report of the Bosnia and Herzegovina 2012, supra* p. 33.

state level.[1015] MFTER is responsible for tasks and duties falling within the jurisdiction of the State of BiH including defining policies and basic principles, co-coordinating activities and consolidating entity plans with those of international institutions in the field of agriculture.[1016] The Strategic Plan for Rural Development of Bosnia and Herzegovina (2018–2021) sets out programmes, measures and other activities to achieve these goals, establishes monitoring and evaluation mechanisms and the necessary funding and procedures for its use.[1017] In the field of fisheries, the study 'Fisheries and Aquaculture Sector in Bosnia and Herzegovina' was completed in 2015. Study was funded by the European Commission and implemented by the FAO and national competent institutions and experts.[1018]

908. Specific jurisdictions over protection of agriculture are assigned to BiH MFTER under the Law on Ministries and other administrative bodies of BiH.[1019] The Plant Health Protection Administration of BiH (PHPA) is an administrative organization of the MFTER, responsible for protection of plant health, production and sale of seeds and seedlings, protection of new plant varieties, market and use of phytopharmaceutical products (PPP) and mineral fertilizers.[1020] The Veterinary Office of Bosnia and Herzegovina was established by the decision of the Council of Ministers on 18 December 2000. The Food Safety Agency of BiH (FSA) is an independent administrative organization established by the decision of the Council of Ministers ('Official Gazette of BiH', No. 22/05).[1021]

909. RS Ministry of Agriculture, Forestry and Water Management is responsible for, *inter alia*, defining and implementing of policies for development and improvement of agriculture, rural development, land policies, protection of plants, seeds and planting materials; it is also in charge of preventing introduction and spread of quarantine and economically harmful organisms, etc.[1022]

1015. Foreign Investment Promotion Agency, *Bosnia and Herzegovina Agriculture and Food Processing Industry*, Foreign Investment Promotion Agency, *supra* pp. 28–30.
1016. *See*: http://www.mvteo.gov.ba/Content/Read/poljiprivreda-i-ruralni-razvoj (13 Jul. 2022).
1017. *See*: http://www.mvteo.gov.ba/data/Home/Dokumenti/Poljoprivreda/Strategic_Plan_for_Rural_Development_of_BiH___Eng.pdf (13 Jul. 2022).
1018. *See*: https://europa.ba/wp-content/uploads/2015/05/delegacijaEU_2015020309341807bos.pdf (13 Jul. 2022).
1019. According to the Art. 9: 'This Ministry shall also be responsible for carrying out tasks and discharging duties which are within the competence of BiH and relate to defining policy, basic principles, coordinating activities and harmonizing plans of the Entity authorities and bodies at the international level in the fields of *agriculture*, energy, protection of the environment, development and use of natural resources'. Art. 10 of the Law on Agriculture, Food, and Rural Development (Official Gazette of BiH, No. 50/08) prescribes that administrative organizations within the Ministry are the following: (a) BiH Veterinary Office, (b) BiH Plant Health Protection Administration, and (c) Office for Harmonisation and Coordination of Payment Systems.
1020. By the Decision of the Council of Ministers of BiH the Plant Health Protection Administration has been appointed to coordinate the implementation of the Rotterdam Convention in BiH (Official Gazette of BiH, No 15/10).
1021. *See also* Art. 11 of the Law on Agriculture, Food, and Rural Development.
1022. In addition, the Ministry is in charge of hail protection, veterinary, medicines and biological agents used in the veterinary, including products, materials and animal waste, feed, food safety, registration and operation of facilities for the production of food of animal origin, manufacturing and

FBiH Ministry of Agriculture, Water Management and Forestry has the responsibilities in the field of the agriculture, water management and water protection. Together with the FBiH Ministry of Environment and Tourism and FBiH Ministry of Spatial Planning, carry the principal competence for management of land or land area, which includes protection of land and soil.[1023]

§3. LEGISLATION

I. Bosnia and Herzegovina

910. There is no policy document on agriculture at the state level.[1024]

911. Agricultural legislation includes the following:

(1) Law on Agriculture, Food and Rural Development (Official Gazette of BiH, No. 50/08).
(2) Law on Plant Health protection (Official Gazette of BiH, No. 23/03).
(3) Law on Veterinary medicine (Official Gazette of BiH, No. 34/02).
(4) Law on Food (Official Gazette of BiH, No. 50/04).
(5) Law on Protection of new plant varieties of BiH (Official Gazette of BiH, Nos 14/10, 32/13).
(6) Law on Seeds and Seedlings of Agricultural Plants of BiH (Official Gazette of BiH, No. 03/05).
(7) Law on Mineral Fertilizers (Official Gazette of BiH, Nos 46/04, 76/11).
(8) Law on wine, brandy and other products of grapes and wine (Official Gazette BiH No. 25/08).
(9) Law on Phyto-pharmaceutical Products (Official Gazette of BiH No. 49/04).
(10) General Law on Cooperatives (Official Gazette of BiH, Nos 18/03 and 55/06).
(11) Law on Genetically Modified Organisms (Official Gazette of BiH, No. 23/09).

912. Law on Agriculture, Food and Rural Development (Official Gazette of BiH, No. 50/08) encompasses definitions of terms to be used within the agriculture, food and rural development sector legislation, the objectives, principles and mechanisms for development of strategies and policies, the structures and competencies at all

marketing of drugs and biological agents used in veterinary; the Ministry competences also cover forestry, hunting and fishing, protection and use of agricultural and forest land, food industry, tobacco industry, integrated water management, including establishment and control over the implementation of measures to prevent deterioration of surface waters and ground waters, water supply conditions in RS, etc. BiH Council of Ministers, *Answers to the List of EU Questions on Chapter 27, Environment, supra* p. 13.

1023. At the cantonal level there are 7 Ministries of Agriculture, Forestry &Water Management, and 3 Agriculture Departments within Ministries of Economy. Directorate for European Integration, *Answers to the Questionnaire, Chapter 11, Agriculture and Rural Development,* 27 Feb. 2018, p. 39.

1024. UNECE. *3rd Environmental Performance Review, Bosnia and Herzegovina, supra* p. 24.

levels of authority, institutional support structures and services, their functions and linkages, monitoring and evaluation mechanisms and administrative and inspection supervision (Article 1.2).[1025]

913. The law also outlines the initial legal and institutional framework required to gradually prepare the sector for EU integration. The law provides for the establishment of a wide range of new institutional structures and mechanisms which can ensure effective coordination and communication between all stakeholders. Many of them are essential foundations to attract future EU pre-accession and structural funds, and include: BiH Agriculture Market Information Service, BiH Administration for Harmonisation of Payment Systems, BiH Farm Registry and Land Parcel Identification System, BiH Agricultural Report.[1026]

II. The Republic of Srpska

914. The Strategy for Agricultural Development of RS by 2015, dated from 2006, was a document establishing goals and projections for the long-term development of agriculture in the RS, the optimal use of agricultural resources (land, water, forests, genetic resources, etc.), increasing of productivity and competitiveness through improvement of technical and technological levels, environment protection and sustainable development.[1027] In addition, the Strategic Plan for the Development of Agriculture and Rural Areas of Republika Srpska 2021–2027 has been prepared.[1028]

915. In RS several laws govern the field of agriculture. These are the following:

(1) Law on Agriculture (Official Gazette RS Nos 70/06, 20/07, 86/07, 71/09).[1029]
(2) Law on Plant Health Protection (Official Gazette of RS, No. 25/09).
(3) Law on Agricultural Land (Official Gazette of RS, Nos 93/06, 86/07, 14/10, 5/12, 58/19).

1025. Pursuant to the Art. 2 'Agriculture, Food and Rural Development sector includes: a) Agriculture and Food (primary production, processing & distribution of food & food stuffs), b) Rural Development, c) Forestry and forestry products (as this relates to EU integration), d) Fisheries and fish products, e) Water Management (as this relates to agriculture and rural development), f) Agricultural machinery, equipment and buildings, g) Agricultural Land, h) Agri-Environment, i) Agri-food trade (domestic and international), j) Veterinary medicine and animal health (livestock), k) Plant health and protection' (Art. 2).

1026. Foreign Investment Promotion Agency, *Bosnia and Herzegovina Agriculture and Food Processing Industry*, *supra*, pp. 28–30.

1027. BiH Council of Ministers. *Answers to the List of EU Questions on Chapter 27, Environment.* Sarajevo. 2012, p. 11.

1028. https://www.vladars.net/sr-SP-Cyrl/Vlada/Ministarstva/mps/%d0%bc%d0%b8%d0%bd%d0%b8%d1%81%d1%82%d0%b0%d1%80%d1%81%d1%82%d0%b2%d0%be/Documents/strategija%202021%202027.pdf (13 Jul. 2022).

1029. The Law on Agriculture of the RS regulates the objectives and measures of agricultural policy, beneficiaries, family agricultural holding, institutional support to agriculture, keeping of registers, monitoring and reporting in agriculture, as well as administrative and inspection supervision.

(4) Law on organic agriculture (‘Official Gazette of RS’, No. 12/13).
(5) The Law on inspections in RS (‘Official Gazette of RS’, No. 18/20).
(6) Law on Mineral Fertilisers (Official Gazette of RS No. 24/12).[1030]
(7) Law on Planting Material (Official Gazette of RS, Nos 37/09).
(8) Law on Agricultural Plant Seeds (Official Gazette of RS, Nos 37/09, 100/11).
(9) Law on Genetically Modified Organisms (Official Gazette of RS, No. 103/08).
(10) Law on Food (Official Gazette of RS, No. 19/17).
(11) Law on Tobacco (Official Gazette RS No. 72/12).
(12) Law on Wine (Official Gazette of RS, No. 80/15).
(13) The Law on Alcoholic Drinks (Official Gazette of RS, No. 81/15).
(14) Law on Veterinary Medicine (Official Gazette of RS, No. 75/17).
(15) Law on Animal Husbandry (Official Gazette of RS, No. 44/15).
(16) Law on Waters (Official Gazette of RS, Nos 50/06, 92/09, 121/12, 74/17).
(17) Law on Forests (Official Gazette of RS, No. 75/08, 60/13, 70/20).
(18) Law on Hunting (Official Gazette of RS, Nos 60/09, and 50/13).
(19) Law on Agricultural Cooperatives (Official Gazette RS Nos 73/08; 78/11, 106/09).

A. The Law on Agriculture

916. Basic legal act regulating agriculture in the Republic of Srpska is the Law on Agriculture (Official Gazette of RS, No. 70/06, 20/07, 86/07 and 71/09). It has the following eight parts: Part I – General Provisions (Articles 1–2), Part II – The Objectives and Measures of Agricultural Policy and Beneficiaries of the Right (Articles 3–26), Part III – Family Agricultural Household (Articles 27–29), Part IV – Institutional Support in Agriculture (Articles 30–38), Part V – Keeping the Registry, Monitoring and Reporting in Agriculture (Articles 39–44), Part VI – The Administrative and Inspection Supervision (Articles 45–51), Part VII – Penalty Provisions (Articles 52–53), Part VIII – Transitional and Final Provisions (Articles 54–59).[1031]

1030. The Law on Mineral Fertilizers (Official Gazette of RS No. 24/12) regulates requirements for classification, quality and labelling of mineral fertilizers, testing, sampling and phytosanitary control in transport, import and application, as well as other issues of importance for mineral fertilizers. In its Art. 15, the Law on Mineral Fertilizers indicates that the mineral fertilizers are used in accordance with good agricultural practices in the amount that is consistent with fertility of land and plant needs, taking into account the climate conditions of the area and conditions of sowing and planting.

1031. This Law regulates the objectives and measures of agricultural policy, beneficiaries of the right, family agricultural household, institutional support in agriculture, keeping the registers, monitoring and reporting in agriculture, as well as administrative and inspection supervision (Art. 1, para. 1).

1. The Objectives and Measures of Agricultural Policy

917. For the purpose of implementation of economic, spatial, environmental and social conditions of agriculture, as well as its sustainable development, the objectives of the agricultural policy of the RS are: (a) ensuring food safety of population as much as possible with domestic agricultural products; (b) increasing of agricultural production and exports in order to strengthen the competitiveness at the domestic and world markets; (c) providing of adequate levels of production, supply of quality food at affordable prices for consumers; (d) providing of adequate living standards of farmers using modern technical-technological solutions in production, as well as providing of stable income for producers; (e) developing and preserving rural areas and rural values; (f) the rational use and preservation of natural resources, environmental protection and promotion of integral and organic agriculture (Article 3, paragraph 1).

918. Measures of structural policy is a set of measures to support the efficiency of agricultural production in order to ensure a stable income and a satisfactory standard of farmers in rural areas, as well as an equal development of agricultural regions and rural areas (Article 13, paragraph 1).[1032]

2. Support Development of Agriculture That Does Not Pollute the Environment

919. Article 15 provides that support development of agriculture that does not pollute the environment and ensures the preservation of biodiversity is intended to: (a) support of integrated and organic agriculture production that cares for the protection of natural resources such as agricultural land and water as well as on the environment in general; (b) the environmental protection in affected areas and preventing the formation of barren, uncultivated and unsustainable agricultural areas on agricultural farms; (c) the conservation of biodiversity of ecosystems (paragraph 1).[1033]

3. The Administrative and Inspection Supervision

920. The administrative supervision over implementation of this law and regulations adopted on the base of it, as well as administrative supervision over the institutions, establishments and organizations that perform the duties specified by this law performs the Ministry (Article 45, paragraph 1). Inspection supervision over implementation of this laws and regulations adopted on the base of it perform agricultural inspections (Article 45, paragraph 2).

1032. Measures of the structural policy are support, i.e., for development of agriculture that does not pollute the environment, as well as that ensure preservation of biodiversity (Art. 13, para. 2, point b).

1033. The Minister shall adopt Rulebook on integrated agricultural production (Art. 15, para. 2).

B. The Law on Plant Health Protection

921. The RS Law on Plant Health Protection (Official Gazette of RS No. 25/09) regulates activities of public interest in the field of pesticides, establishment of the Plant Protection Commission, registration, transport, import and use of pesticides in agriculture and forestry, services in the field of plant protection products, records, collection and sharing of data, as well as other issues of importance for application of pesticides. Ministry of Agriculture, Forestry and Water Management is competent for implementation of this law and the related legislation. Inspection monitoring over the implementation of the legislation is carried out by the RS Administration for Inspection, through its phytosanitary and agricultural inspectors and agricultural inspectors of the units of local self-governments.[1034]

III. Federation of Bosnia and Herzegovina

922. The list of legislation governing agriculture sector in FBiH includes the following:

(1) Law on Agriculture (Official gazette FBiH Nos 88/07, 4/10, 27/12, 7/13, 82/21).
(2) Law on Agricultural Land (Official Gazette FBiH No. 52/09).
(3) Law on Agricultural Organic Production (Official Gazette of FBiH, No. 72/16).
(4) Veterinary Law of the FBiH (Official Gazette of FBiH No. 46/00).[1035]
(5) Law on Payments in Agriculture and Rural Development (Official Gazette of the FBiH, No. 42/10).
(6) Law on Freshwater Fisheries (Official Gazette FBiH No. 64/04).
(7) Law on Payments in Primary Agricultural Production (Official Gazette FBiH No. 28/04).
(8) Law on Recognition and Protection of Agricultural and Forest Plant Varieties (Official Gazette FBiH No. 31/00).
(9) Law on Wine (Official Gazette FBiH No. 55/12).
(10) Law on Tobacco ('Official Gazette of FBiH' Nos 45/02, 42/04 and 51/07).
(11) Law on Forestry ('Official Gazette of FBiH', Nos 20/02, No. 29/03 and 37/04).
(12) Law on Waters ('Official Gazette of FBiH', Nos 18/98, 33/03, 54/04 and 70/06).
(13) Law on Cooperatives FBiH ('Official Gazette of FBiH', Nos 28/97, 28/98 and 18/03).
(14) Law on Seeds and Propagating Material of Agricultural Plants ('Official Gazette FBiH', No. 55/01, 31/14)

1034. BiH Council of Ministers, *Answers to the List of EU Questions on Chapter 27, Environment*, *supra* pp. 299–230.

1035. For the complete list of regulations governing veterinary sector, *see* https://fmpvs.gov.ba/veterinarstvo-propisi/ (10 Jul. 2022).

(15) Law on Agricultural Advisory Services (Official Gazette FbiH, No. 66/13, 25/22.[1036]

A. *The Law on Agriculture*

923. Basic legal act regulating agricultural issues in the Federation of Bosnia and Herzegovina is the Law on Agriculture (Official Gazette of FBiH, Nos 88/07, 4/10, 27/12, 7/13).[1037] It has the following ten parts: Part I – General Provisions (Articles 1–3), Part II – The Objectives and Measures of the Agricultural Policy (Articles 4–28), Part III – The Users-Clients (Articles 29–30), Part IV – The Family Agricultural Household (Articles 31–32), Part V – The Farmer (Articles 33–34), Part VI – The Institutional Support (Articles 35–43), Part VII – The Informing on the Agriculture and Keeping the Register (Articles 44–52), Part VIII – The Administrative and Inspection Supervision (Articles 53–60), Part IX – Penalty Provisions (Articles 61–65), Part X – Transitional and Final Provisions (Articles 66–73).

1. The Objectives and Measures of the Agricultural and Structural Policy

924. The objective of the agricultural policy in the Federation is *inter alia* rational use and preservation of the natural resources, protection of the environment and improvement of integrated and organic agriculture (Article 4, paragraph 1, point 6).

925. The measures of the structural policy are *inter alia* to support the agriculture[1038] that does not pollute the environment and ensures preservation of the biological diversity (Article 17, paragraph 1, point 2).

1036. For the complete list of regulations, *see* https://fmpvs.gov.ba/poljoprivreda-propisi/ (10 Jul. 202 2).

1037. The Law on Agriculture of the FBiH governs: the objectives and measures of agricultural policy, the beneficiaries of rights, definition of agricultural holding, determination of the farmer's concept, institutional support, information in agriculture and keeping of registers, administration and inspection supervision, penalty provisions, as well as other issues of importance to agriculture.

1038. *Agricultural activity* means an economic activity, including plant and animal production and related service activities in accordance with the standard classification of economic activities in BiH, as well as preservation of land in good agricultural and environmental condition (Art. 3, para. 1, point a). *The rural development* means a set of policies, measures and activities aimed at a comprehensive economic, social and cultural development of population in rural areas that are planned and implemented respecting the principles of sustainable development, conservation and improvement of environmental quality (Art. 3, para. 1, point g).

2. Support for the Development of the Agriculture That Does Not Pollute the Environment and Measures of the Land Policy

926. Support for the development of the agriculture that does not pollute the environment and ensures the preservation of the biological diversity are intended for:

- Supporting the introduction of such technologies in agricultural production, which provides the protection and preservation of natural resources such as agricultural land and water, as well as the protection and preservation of the environment in general.
- Preserving for the environment threatened areas and taking measures for prevention formation of unplanned, uncultivated and non-maintained agricultural land of agricultural household.
- Preserving of the agricultural biological diversity of ecosystems (Article 19, paragraph 1).[1039]

IV. Brčko District of Bosnia and Herzegovina

927. Department of Agriculture, Forestry and Water Management of the Government of Brčko District of BiH is in charge for the domain of agriculture and forests.[1040]

928. Agricultural regulations of BD include the following:

(1) Law on Agricultural Land of BD (Official Gazette of BD BiH Nos 32/04, 20/06 and 19/07).[1041]
(2) Law on Financial Support to the Agricultural Production (Official Gazette of BD BiH Nos 11/06, 19/07, 15/10, 21/20, 30/20, 4/21).
(3) Law on Agricultural Cooperatives (Official Gazette of BD BiH Nos 19/02, 19/07 and 2/08).
(4) Law on Land Consolidation (Official Gazette of BD BiH Nos 7/06, 19/07 and 2/08).
(5) Law on Waters protection (Official Gazette of BD BiH Nos 25/04, 1/05 and 19/07).
(6) Law on Fresh Water Fishery of BD (Official Gazette of BD BiH Nos 35/05 and 19/07).

1039. Measures of land policy is a set of measures that affect the proper and rational management of agricultural land as good of interest to the Federation in accordance with applicable regulations, including the systematic environmental protection (Art. 27, para. 1).

1040. BiH Council of Ministers, *Answers to the List of EU Questions on Chapter 27, Environment, supra* p. 74.

1041. The Law on Agricultural Land of the BD of BiH regulates for the Agricultural Land: protection, usage, improvement, development of agricultural land, traffic and rental as well as other agricultural operations in the Brčko District of BiH. The provisions of this Law shall be used for forest land, unless otherwise specified by the Law.

(7) Law on Brandy and Wine (Official Gazette of BD BiH Nos 35/05 and 19/07).
(8) Law on forests of Brčko District BiH (Official Gazette of BD BiH No. 14/10 and 26/16).
(9) Law on Tobacco (Official Gazette of BD BiH Nos 35/05 and 19/07).

§4. Harmonization with EU Legislation

929. BiH 'is at an early stage of preparation in the area of agriculture and rural development'.[1042] There was no progress in establishing the necessary administrative structures required for the common agricultural policy (CAP), including a paying agency. At the same time, there was no progress in developing elements of an integrated administration and control system (IACS), a land parcel identification system (LPIS) or a farm accountancy data network (FADN). The country delayed the reporting on the implementation of the 2018-2021 strategic plan for rural development. Regarding food safety, veterinary, and phytosanitary policy BiH 'has some level of preparation in this area'.[1043]

1042. EC, *Bosnia and Herzegovina 2021 Progress Report, supra* p. 106.
1043. Ibid, p. 107.

Chapter 5. Forests

§1. The State of Forest Resources and Forest Degradation

930. Forest lands cover about 2.5 million ha, or 49% of the total land area, which is among the highest forest coverage in Europe.[1044] Forest ecosystems cover 41% of the territory, and a relatively high number of species are endemic. Bosnia and Herzegovina ranks among the territories with the highest level of biological diversity in Europe. Therefore, forestry in BH is a very important industrial sector, and the sustainable management of forest resources is a significant factor in environmental, climate and biodiversity protection.[1045]

931. However, the recent war and subsequent unregulated development has resulted in heavy at all levels. In certain areas illegal logging operations occurred, along with forest clear-cuts and degradation, which have led to the occurrence of many diseases, forest fires, ice and wind breaks.[1046] It is also important to emphasize the fact that a large portion of the forested areas are under mines, which makes any forest protection and rehabilitation activities impossible to conduct. As an overall result, the sustainability of forest management and the stability of forest ecosystems are threatened.[1047]

932. 'Forests have been significantly degraded, due to mismanagement of deciduous forests and uncontrolled logging and clear cutting across a wide area, especially of beech forests in the pre-war period when trees of higher quality were logged and those of poorer quality were left behind.'[1048]

1044. The first forest inventory in BiH was implemented in the period between 1964 and 1968. After this, no new forest inventory was performed until the new state inventory that was initiated in 2006 and it is now in its final phase. It is expected that published data, the result of a new forest inventory, will ensure relevant information on the state of forest resources for stakeholders at the state and entity level. BiH MFTER, *State of the environment Report of the Bosnia and Herzegovina 2012, supra* p. 115.
1045. BiH MFTER, Ministry of Physical Planning, Civil Engineering and Ecology of Republic of Srpska, Federal Ministry of Environment and Tourism, UNDP, *Initial National Communication of Bosnia and Herzegovina under the United Nations Framework Convention on Climate Change, supra* p. 27.
1046. For detailed information, *see Illegal Logging in SEE and EE (Governance, Implementation and Enforcement), Illegal logging activities in Bosnia and Herzegovina*, A. DIAGNOSTIC AUDIT, Kingdom of Belgium, Federal Public Service, Foreign Affairs, Foreign Trade and Development Cooperation, REC, Envsec, June 2010.
1047. RSMoAFWM, *First national report on the implementation of the United Nations Convention to Combat Desertification/Land Degradation in Bosnia and Herzegovina, supra* p. 28.
1048. UNECE. *3rd Environmental Performance Review, Bosnia and Herzegovina, supra* p. 213.

§2. Competencies

933. According to the BiH Constitution, forests come under the mandate of the entities, as forming part of their natural resources and with regard to environmental issues.

934. The FBiH Ministry of Agriculture, Water Management, and Forestry is responsible for forests and forestry at entity level. The Ministry is also responsible for providing guidance to the cantonal forestry directorates and forest management enterprises. It also oversees the Federal Forest Institute, which provides capacity for producing documents (including strategies, programmes and plans), expert support, collection and processing of forestry data (including information provided by cantons) and a variety of forestry projects for the Ministry.[1049]

935. Authority for management of forests and hunting resources in the RS is on the Ministry of Agriculture, Forestry, and Water Management through the Division of Forestry and Hunting and the RS Forestry Agency.[1050]

936. Municipalities are responsible for the development and approval of management plans for all private forests on their territory.

§3. Legislation

937. BiH has very long tradition of forest legislation. The first institutional legal foundation was the Forest Law in 1286. Between 1878 and 1929, the Forest Law (1852) of the Austro-Hungarian Monarchy was in force. In this period, the provisions of the following laws were also in force: the Forest Law of the Kingdom of Serbia (from 1891 to 1904), the Forest Law of Vojvodina (from 1879 and 1898), Amendments to the Forest Law of the Kingdom of Croatia and Slavonia (from 1894 and 1901), Law on the Protection of Forest Ownership in Bosnia and Herzegovina (1913), Amendments to the Forest Law of the Kingdom of Yugoslavia (passed in 1927).[1051]

1049. The cantons hold a number of responsibilities for forests: the cantonal governments (forestry directorates) are responsible for the observation, reporting and organization of fire fighting and disease control, as well as for preparation and adoption of forest management plans for all private forests within their canton.

1050. The RS Agency for Forests performs professional and technical activities relating to: making FMPs (forestry management plans), long-term programme of management of rocky areas, programme of use of non-timber products; monitoring the implementation of planning documents, keeping their registry; ensuring the implementation of forest inventory in large areas; keeping records and the forest cadastre; monitoring forest health, monitoring the use of special purpose funds for forests, etc. BiH Council of Ministers, *Answers to the List of EU Questions on Chapter 27, Environment, supra* p. 72.

1051. In 1929, a unique Forest Law of the Kingdom of Yugoslavia was enacted. In 1947, the General Forest Law of the FNRY was passed and in 1948 the Forest Law of the NR BiH. The Forest Law of the NR BiH in 1956 prescribed that forests and forest land in social ownership were administered by forest enterprises, scientific and other organizations. The Law on Wood Saving of the

I. The Republic of Srpska

938. In RS, the Law on Forests (Official Gazette of RS Nos 75/08 and 60/13) is the key legal document in the area of forestry, with subsequent regulations. Republika Srpska adopted the Forestry Development Strategy for the period 2011–2021.[1052]

A. The Law on Forests

939. Basic legal act regulating forest[1053] issues in the Republic of Srpska is the Law on Forests (Official Gazette of RS, Nos 75/08 and 60/13). It has the following eight parts: Part I – General Provisions (Articles 1–8), Part II – Policy and Planning (Articles 9–30), Part III – The Forest Management and Governance (Articles 31–86), Part IV – Financing and Value of the Forests (Articles 87–96), Part V – Property and Legal Relations (Articles 97–98), Part VI – Supervision (Articles 99–100), Part VII – Penalty Provisions (Articles 101–103), Part VIII – Transitional and Final Provisions (Articles 104–109).

940. This law regulates the policy and planning, governance and management of forests[1054] and forest land, forest protection, financing and the forest value, cadastre of forests and forest lands, forestry information system, property and legal relations, as well as other issues of importance to the forest and forest land for the purpose of improving and sustainable use of forests and forest lands and forestry development (Article 1, paragraph 1). The provisions of this law shall apply to all forests and forest land,[1055] regardless of the form of ownership (Article 1, paragraph 2). Forests and forest land on the territory of the Republic of Srpska (hereinafter, 'the Republic') are ownership of the Republic, legal entities and natural

NR BiH (1957) prescribed the measures for rational utilization of wood raw material. By the Law on Amendments to the Forest Law of the NR BiH (1960) forest enterprises were transformed from the status of institutions into economic organizations. Ferlin F., *Forest Legislation, Institutional Development and Forest Policy Study of the Republic of Srpska*, PHARE, Technical Assistance to the Implementation of the Bosnia and Herzegovina Forestry Programme, Banja Luka & Ljubljana, 2001. http://www.slideshare.net/francferlin7/forest-legislation-institutional-development-and-policy-study-executive-summary (13 Jul. 2022).

1052. *See*: https://www.vladars.net/sr-SP-Cyrl/Vlada/Ministarstva/mps/Documents/%D0%A1%D1%82%D1%80%D0%B0%D1%82%D0%B5%D0%B3%D0%B8%D1%98%D0%B0%20%D1%80%D0%B0%D0%B7%D0%B2%D0%BE%D1%98%D0%B0%20%D1%88%D1%83%D0%BC%D0%B0%D1%80%D1%81%D1%82%D0%B2%D0%B0%20%D0%A0%D0%A1%202011-2021_393893095.pdf (13 Jul. 2022).

1053. *The forest* is a complex community or biogeocenosis (ecosystem) of forest trees and forest land that affects each other, as well as the environment in which they are located (Art. 7, para. 1).

1054. *Forests* in the terms of this Law are areas covered with forest tree species, on area larger than 0.16 ha, a minimum width of 20 meters, with the degree of land covered area with treetops at least 20% and more, regardless of whether it is the offspring or adult trees either from seeds or sprouts from stumps or roots (Art. 7, para. 2). In terms of this Law, parks, alleys, orchards, boundary trees, cemetery trees, etc. shall not be considered as forest (Art. 7, para. 5).

1055. Forests and forest land are natural resource of common interest and enjoy special care and protection of the Republic (Art. 2, para. 1).

persons (Article 3, paragraph 1). The right to use forests and forest lands may be limited when it is in the public interest (Article 2, paragraph 2).

941. The total area of forest owned by the Republic cannot be reduced, except in special cases referred to in Article 42 of this law (Article 3, paragraph 2). Forests and forest land owned by the Republic cannot be alienated, except in cases of land consolidation and in cases determined by the Law (Article 3, paragraph 3). Forests and forest lands shall be managed in accordance with criteria and principles of sustainable management (Article 4, paragraph 2). The Ministry of Agriculture, Forestry and Water Management (hereinafter, 'the Ministry') administrates and manages forests and forest land owned by the Republic (Article 4, paragraph 1).[1056]

1. The Politic and Planning

942. National Assembly of the RS adopts Forestry Development Strategy, which is the basis for the development of the Forestry Programme of the Republic (Article 9, paragraph 1). Forestry Development Strategy is a document that promotes the development of the forestry sector as part of economic and rural development in order to create and maintain employment, environmental protection, forest heritage protection and restoration of damaged forests, environmental improvement, economic and social functions of forests, encouraging of environmental values of wood and other forest products, ensuring the competitiveness of the wood industry, etc. (Article 9, paragraph 2).[1057]

943. The Forestry Programme of the Republic is the basic document that provides a participatory, comprehensive, cross-sectoral and permanent process of planning, implementation, monitoring, and evaluation of forestry policy in order to achieve sustainable forest management of all property types, together with the Action Plan for its implementation (Article 10, paragraph 1).[1058]

1056. Article 6 para. 1 provides that 'Functions of forests are the following: a) Commercial (economic) function which includes the wood production and other forest products, including hunting wild animals in order to generate revenues and b) Generally useful forest functions, including ecological and social function. According to the determined functions and management measures, the forests can be: a) Commercial forests; b) Protective forests; c) Forests of special purposes' (Art. 6, para. 2). More detailed regulations on the manner of proclamation, marking, financing, method of management of protective forests and forests for special purposes shall be adopted by the Minister (Art. 6, para. 3).

1057. Pursuant to the Art. 16 'For the purposes of management and forest administration the following planning documents are produced: (a) Forest economic plan; (b) Long-term program management in karst areas; (c) Investment program management of industrial and other forest plantations; (d) Implementation project of forest management (hereinafter, 'Implementation project'); (e) Program for utilization of other forest products' (para. 1).

1058. The Forestry Program of the Republic is to be adopted by the National Assembly of the RS for a period of twenty years (Art. 10, para. 2).

2. Forest Management and Administration

944. Forests are managed on the base of forest management basis[1059] (hereinafter, 'basis') and implementation projects (Article 17, paragraph 1). Management and administration of forests and forest land owned by the Republic is the activity of general interest (Article 31, paragraph 1). Forests and forest land in private ownership are administered and managed by their owners (hereinafter, 'forest owner') (Article 39, paragraph 1).[1060]

945. The user of forest and forest land owned by the Republic is responsible 'for monitoring of forest health through reporting and forecasting services within it, and inform the Ministry and the public' (Article 48, paragraph 2).[1061]

946. The protection of forests and forest land includes measures and activities to be implemented for the protection of biotic, abiotic and other factors that may cause harmful effects on forest and forest land (Article 50, paragraph 1). The owners and users of forests and forest land owned by the Republic are obliged to adopt plan for forest protection from fire (Article 55, paragraph 1).

947. Natural persons and legal entities who cause damage to the forest are obliged to compensate the damage to the forest owner or to the forest users and forest land owned by the Republic according to the forest-compensation price list to be applied for all forests irrespective of the form of ownership (Article 57, paragraph 1). Disposal of waste, toxic substances and other waste in the forest, as well as on forest land, is prohibited (Article 58, paragraph 1).

3. Production of Forest Reproductive Material

948. Maintenance of seed facilities, except seed facilities for the production of seed of known origin, is performed by users of forest and forest land owned by the Republic in a way that ensures maximum production of quality forest seeds and allows for easier picking, i.e., seed collection (Article 66, paragraph 1). Management measures of starting material for the production of forest seeds are prescribed by planning documents developed by the user of forest and forest land owned by the Republic and approved by the Ministry (Article 66, paragraph 2).

949. Forest reproductive material is forest seeds and seedlings (Article 68, paragraph 1). The production of forest seeds is carried out in seed objects through the activities of their separation or the establishment, arrangement, maintenance, and

1059. The basis is made for period of ten years (Art. 17, para. 3).
1060. The owners perform the protection, preservation and use of forests in private ownership (Art. 39, para. 2).
1061. The Minister shall prescribe the method for monitoring of forest health (Art. 48, para. 3).

collection and vintage, processing and storage of seeds and fruits, method of quality testing and organization of the trade (Article 68, paragraph 2).[1062]

950. Facilities necessary for the management of forest and wildlife can be built in the forests in accordance with the planning documents in forestry and hunting, if this law is not otherwise regulated (Article 78, paragraph 1).

4. Cadastre of Forests and Forest Land and Forestry Information System

951. User of the forests and forest land owned by the Republic and forest owners through the perpetrator of professional-technical jobs are obliged to keep and update the cadastre of forests and forest lands at the prescribed manner and report to the Ministry on changes no later than March 31 for the previous year (Article 85, paragraph 1).[1063]

952. An information system in forestry, managed by the Ministry, which provide all necessary information on the status and changes of forest fund for the purpose of planning, state monitoring and reporting is to be established (Article 86, paragraphs 1 and 2). The detailed regulations on the form and content, way of management, maintenance and usage of information systems, as well as an cadastre of forests and forest lands, the way of keeping records of performed works and reports will be issued by the Minister (Article 86, paragraph 3).

5. Financing and Values of the Forests

953. In order to achieve long-term goals based on the principles of sustainable forest management set out in the Forestry Programme of the Republic, in the Strategy of forest development and in the Forest management plans (Basis), are provided funds for forest protection, policy and planning and forest management, forest cadastre unification and improvement of forests, as well as a means of special purpose for forests (Article 87, paragraph 1).

954. Fees for the use of forests and forest land owned by the Republic (means for simple reproduction) set aside from the realized total revenue of forest users and forest land users owned by the Republic, while the allocated funds cannot be less than 10% of the value of sold forest assortments determined according to the prices in the woods on a stump, on the base of the price list of forest users and forest land users owned by the Republic (Article 89, paragraph 1).[1064]

1062. Forest planting material are plants multiplied and raised at the nursery garden as separate arranged land area on which through the system of technological-technical seedling production procedure are produced seedlings for the appropriate purpose (Art. 68, para. 3).

1063. The Ministry combines the cadastre of forest users and forest land owned by the Republic and forest owners (Art. 85, para. 2).

1064. The control of income and expenditure of funs performs Ministry (Art. 89, para. 1).

955. The compensation shall be paid into a special account of forest users and forest land users owned by the Republic monthly and will be used within forest business area, i.e., lumber camp (Article 89, paragraph 2).

956. Compensation for performing of services of general interest in privately owned forests pay private forest owners in the ratio of 80% to the account of perpetrators of professional-technical jobs in the forests in private ownership and 20% to the account of local government wherefrom originate assortments (Article 90, paragraph 1).

957. Compensation for improving of generally useful forest functions (extended reproduction) is used to finance the development and realization of the Forestry Programme of the Republic, Forestry Development Strategy of the Republic, Long-term programme of karst area management, financing of management of forests and forest land in karst areas, to carry out the activities of the Forestry Council of Republic, the establishment and maintenance of an information system in forestry, establish and maintain an cadastre of forests and forest land, financing of determining the boundaries of forests and forest land owned by the Republic, the development and implementation of forest inventory in large areas, support for protected areas through the promotion and development of forest social functions and implementation of projects improvement of forest in all forms of ownership of forests and forest lands, etc. (Article 95, paragraph 1).

958. The value of forests must be defined in Basis (Article 96, paragraph 1). The value of forests in terms of this law makes value of: trees (wood), soil, other forest products and generally useful forest functions (Article 96, paragraph 1).

6. Property Legal Relations

959. The sale or other ways of alienation of forests and forest land owned by the Republic (Article 97, paragraph 1).[1065] Forests owned by the Republic cannot be leased (Article 98, paragraph 1). Leasing of forest land owned by the Republic is performed by the Ministry with the consent of forest users and forest land owned by the Republic (Article 98, paragraph 4).[1066] Forest land owned by the Republic may be leased up with an intention of bringing it to the purpose established by planning documents and under conditions set forth by this law (Article 98, paragraph 2).[1067]

1065. The Ministry may part of the forest and forest land owned by the Republic in which cannot be organized a rational management (less isolated forest, enclaves or semi-enclaves) exchange with owners whose forests are isolated, i.e., as enclaves or semi-enclaves in the forest complex owned by the Republic, with the consent of the Government (Art. 97, para. 2).

1066. The Minister prescribes terms and method for leasing of forest land owned by the Republic (Art. 98, para. 5).

1067. Leased forest land owned by the Republic cannot be used to build permanent structures, except in special cases of public interest, on the base of the Government decision (Art. 98, para. 3).

7. Supervision

960. The Ministry performs administrative supervision over implementation of this Law and the regulations adopted on the base of it (Article 99, paragraph 1). Inspection supervision over implementation of this law and bylaws adopted on the base of it is performed by the Inspection for forestry and hunting as part of the Republic Administration for Inspection Affairs (Article 99, paragraph 2).

B. Other Relevant RS Regulations

961.

(1) *Law on Enterprises* (Official Gazette of RS Nos 24/98, 62/02, 66/02, 38/03, 97/04 34/06, 127/08, 58/09, 100/11 and 67/13).
(2) The Law on control of help to the legal entities (Official Gazette of RS No. 106/09).
(3) *Law on Public Enterprises* (Official Gazette of RS Nos 75/04 and 78/11).
(4) Law on Reproductive Material of forest trees (Official Gazette of RS No. 70/09).
(5) Law on Hunting (Official Gazette of RS Nos 34/08 and 60/09).
(6) Law on Tourism (Official Gazette of RS Nos 70/11 and 67/13).
(7) The Labour Law (Official Gazette of RS No. 55/07).
(8) Law on Protection at Work (Official Gazette of RS Nos 01/08, 13/10), etc.

C. Subordinate Legislation

962. Subordinate legislation include, *inter alia*, following:

(1) Rule book on inventory of forests over large areas (Official Gazette of RS No. 13/09).
(2) Rule book on the forest and forest land cadastre (Official Gazette of RS No. 47/09).
(3) Rule book on the registry of performed protection operations, silviculture operations and growing and using (cutting) of forests (Official Gazette of RS No. 47/09).
(4) Rule book on the manner of developing, maintaining and submitting data from the hunting registry (Official Gazette of RS No. 107/09).
(5) Rule book on the manner of proclaiming, marking, financing and managing of protected forests and special purpose forests (Official Gazette of RS No. 57/09).
(6) Rule book on the contents and procedure for drafting a forest fire protection plan (Official Gazette of RS No. 107/09).
(7) Rule book on the requirements, deadlines and manner of notification of pests occurrence and damage to forests and forest land (Official Gazette of RS No. 98/09).

(8) Rule book on establishing a forest plant gene bank (Official Gazette of RS No. 107/09), etc.

II. Federation of Bosnia and Herzegovina

A. The Law on Forests

963. Regarding forests, in spite of their economic and environmental relevance, the Federation BiH does not yet have a forest law, although an advanced draft is currently in the approval process.[1068] Basic legal act regulating forest issues in the Federation of Bosnia and Herzegovina was the Law on Forests (Official Gazette of FBiH BiH, Nos. 20/02, 29/03 and 37/04). It has the following eleven parts: Part I – General Provisions (Articles 1–3), Part II – Conservation and Protection of Forests and Their Functions (Articles 4–16), Part III – Forestry Programs, Plans for Forests Management and Forest Management Areas (Articles 17–22), Part IV – Forests and Forest Land Management (Articles 23–37), Part V – Forests and Forest Land with Special Management Regime (Articles 38–43), Part VI – Ownership, Management, Forests Cadastre, Administrative and Economic Functions (Articles 44–55), Part VII – Forests Institutions (Articles 56–59), Part VIII – Financing (Articles 60–62), Part IX – Supervision of Law Enforcement (Articles 63–68), Part X – Penalty Provisions (Articles 69–72), Part XI – Transitional and Final Provisions (Articles 73–81).

964. However, the Forest Law (Official Gazette of FBiH No. 20/02, Nos 20/03 and 37/04) was abolished by the Constitutional Court (verdict ref: U-26/08, Official Gazette of FBiH No. 36/09) in 2009 (ceased in November 2009). This decision was based on a petition submitted by the mayor of the Konjic municipality and the Council of Municipalities and Cities of FBiH for the protection of the right to local self-governance. Thus, forest management in FBiH is currently governed by a temporary regulation on forests (with amendments) and a set of regulations adopted since 2003 as complementary regulations to the Forest Law. This temporary decree was extended from 30 March 2010 to 30 June 2010 and will be extended further until the new forest law is approved. 'A draft forest law has been prepared and submitted to the Federal Government of FBiH.'[1069]

B. Other Relevant FBiH Regulations

965.

(1) Law on Seeds and Propagating Material of Forest and Horticultural Species of Trees and Bushes (Official Gazette FBiH, Nos 71/05 and 8/10).[1070]
(2) Law on Plant Health Protection (Official Gazette FBiH, No. 23/03).

1068. UNECE. *3rd Environmental Performance Review, Bosnia and Herzegovina, supra* p. 62.
1069. UNECE, *2nd Environmental Performance Review, supra* p. 120.
1070. *See*: https://fmpvs.gov.ba/sumarstvo-zakoni/ (13 Jul. 2022).

(3) The Law on Hunting (Official Gazette FBiH, Nos 4/06 and 8/10).
(4) Law on Requirements and Procedures of Wood Cutting Activities (Official Gazette FBiH Nos 27/97 and 25/06).

C. Subordinate Legislation

1. Rule Books

966.

(1) Rule book on the Programme of Falconry Exam and Hunting method with Predatory Birds (Official Gazette FBiH No. 31/09).[1071]
(2) Rule book on the Hunting Exam Programme, Requirements and Procedures (Official Gazette FBiH Nos 63/06 and 05/08).
(3) Rule book on the form of the certificate on origin of wild animals and its parts and the conditions under which can be performed wild animals taxidermy and keeping the trophies publicly exposed in the building and on use of wild animal's meat in restaurants.
(4) Rule book on types of uniform, designations and requirements for carrying guns, types of guns and size of hunting guard area.
(5) Rule book on use of hunting guns and ammunition.
(6) Rule book on types and number of hunting dogs for individual wild animal species in defined areas.
(7) Rule book on demarcation and delineation of hunting area borders and the procedure for establishment of hunting areas in the Federation of Bosnia and Herzegovina.
(8) Rule book on open and closed hunting seasons, inventory of mammals and birds considered to be of benefit for agriculture and forestry.
(9) Rulebook on the conditions which ensure the retention of seed quality (Official Gazette FBiH No. 75/12).
(10) Rule book on the amount of the fee for the performed expert review of the production of seed and planting material and the determination of the quality and declaration of seeds and planting material (Official Gazette FBiH No. 75/12).
(11) Rulebook on the method and methodology of the professional examination of the production of planting material (Official Gazette FBiH No. 79/07).
(12) Rule book on conditions for pasture, acorn feeding, browsing, lopping of branches and foliage, collection of rustling and moss (Official Gazette FBiH No. 42/08).

2. Decisions

967.

1071. *See*: https://fmpvs.gov.ba/sumarstvo-pravilnici/ (13 Jul. 2022).

(1) Decision on Establishment, Management, Maintenance and Use of the Forestry Information System in the Federation of Bosnia and Herzegovina (Official Gazette of FBiH Nos 69/18).
(2) Decision on drafting, content and application of forest management bases (Official Gazette of FBiH Nos 15/14 and 45/18).
(3) Decision on the manner of transformation of forest land into a construction land (Official Gazette of FBiH Nos 108/12).
(4) Decision on sale of forest wood varieties from state forests on the territory of the Federation of BiH (Official Gazette of FBiH Nos 52/09 and 25/10).

3. Regulations and Instruction

968.
(1) Instruction on accounting methods, deadlines and procedures for payments of charges for forest protection and improvement (Official Gazette of FBiH No. 44/10).
(2) Regulation on Forests (Official Gazette of FBiH Nos 83/09, 26/10, 38/10, and 60/11).
(3) Regulation amending Regulation on the application of powers of the authorities of FBiH in enterprises with the state capital share (Official Gazette No. 44/15).

III. Brčko District of Bosnia and Herzegovina

A. *The Law on Forests of Brčko District of Bosnia and Herzegovina*

969. Basic legal act regulating forest issues in Brčko District of Bosnia and Herzegovina is the Law on Forests of Brčko District BiH (Official Gazette of BD BiH, No. 14/10, and 26/16). It has the following nine parts: Part I – General Provisions (Articles 1–4), Part II – Forests Protection (Articles 5–18), Part III – Forest-Commercial Base and Annual Forest Management Plan (Articles 19–23), Part IV – Forest and Forest Land Management (Articles 24–42), Part V – Forests and Forest Land with Special Way of Management (Articles 43–46), Part VI – Way of Forest Administration and Management, Administrative and Economic Forest Functions (Articles 47–58), Part VII – Supervision over Implementation of the Law (Articles 59–61), Part VIII – Penalty Provisions (Articles 62–65), Part IX – Transitional and Final Provisions (Articles 66–69).[1072]

1072. The Law regulates the preservation, protection and strengthening of the generally beneficial forest functions, forestry planning, forest management, economic functions, financing of reconstruction and improvement of forests at the territory Brčko District of BiH, the supervision of the Law implementation and other issues related to forest management (Art. 1, para. 1). *See also* Law on Hunting of BGBiH (Official Gazette of BDBiH, No. 1/15).

Chapter 6. Subsoil and Minerals

§1. State of Mineral Resources

970. Total geological reserves of coal in BiH are estimated at 5,647 billion tons. The most important reserves of brown coals are located in central BiH, Banovići, Ugljevik, Miljevina and Kamengrad, and of lignite in Kreka, Gacko, Stanari, Bugojno, Livno and Duvno (Tomislavgrad). These basins are existing and future potential for thermal energy generation. There are significant lead ore deposits in BiH, with estimated reserves of 450 million tons. The explored salt reserves amount to 370 million tons, while exploitable reserves amount to an estimated 54.72 million tons. Besides these deposits, other types of metal ores (lead, zinc, silver, manganese, antimony, copper, mercury) and non-metallic ores (magnesite, barite, bauxite) are present in BiH.[1073]

971. Mining and ore-processing are an important sector in BiH. 'The significant reduction in industrial operating capacity has led to a similar reduction in activity within the mining and ore sector. The production rate for mining and ore-processing has declined to about 33% of its pre-war level. Coal and other ore and stone production have been reduced to 40% and 23%, respectively.'[1074]

§2. The Impact of Mining on the Environment

972. Surface exploitation of mineral ores (coal, iron ore, bauxite and clay) has resulted in 15,000 ha of affected land.[1075]'The main consequence of this kind of exploitation is not only the direct land loss due to the mining, but also the additional land loss due to disposal of waste material adjacent to the mining area.'[1076]

973. Very few studies on the impact of mining on the environment have been carried out. Major issues concern damages resulting from mining and the effects of mining areas on some habitats. Therefore, there are no comprehensive measures for

1073. BiH MFTER, *State of the environment Report of the Bosnia and Herzegovina 2012*, *supra* p. 36. For more information about investment opportunities in the territory of the Republic of Srpska *see*: https://investsrpska.vladars.net/investment-opportunities/ (13 Jul. 2022). *See also*: Stuhlberger C. (Ed) *Mining and environment in the Western Balkans*, Zoi Environment Network (UNEP, ENVSEC), January 2010, pp. 56–59.

1074. UNECE, *Environmental Performance Review, Bosnia and Herzegovina*, 2004. *supra* p. 92. *See also*, Brininstool M. *The Mineral Industry of Bosnia and Herzegovina*. 2008 Minerals Yearbook, US Department of the Interior, US Geological Survey, December 2010.

1075. Disposals of fly ash and slag occupy an area of approximately 250 ha. BiH MFTER, *State of the environment Report of the Bosnia and Herzegovina 2012*, *supra* p. 35.

1076. RSMoAFWM, *First national report on the implementation of the United Nations Convention to Combat Desertification/Land Degradation in Bosnia and Herzegovina*, *supra* p. 42.

protection and adequate monitoring of possible impacts on the environment. Processes of land reclamation and remediation of mined out areas have generally not been implemented in accordance with legislation.[1077]

974. Laws on Environmental Protection in the FBiH and the RS prescribe an obligation to implement strategy assessments of the environmental impact for the purpose of urban planning and to develop an assessment of the environmental impact at the project level. The procedure for assessing environmental impacts and the contents of the Environmental Impact Study are defined by the Rule book on plants and facilities which require an environmental impact assessment on plants and facilities that can only be built and commissioned if an environmental permit has been issued (Official Gazette of FBiH, No. 19/04) and by the Decree on projects that must undergo an environmental impact assessment and on the criteria for deciding on the obligation of implementing the environmental impact assessment and the scope thereof (Official Gazette of RS, No. 7/06).[1078]

§3. Competencies

975. RS Ministry of Industry, Energy and Mining is the competent to participate in activities in the field of use of natural resources, geological exploration and exploitation of natural and technogenic mineral resources, groundwater (potable, industrial, mineral, thermal, thermo-mineral), as well as geothermal resources and concession operations. Activities in the field of geological exploration and exploitation of groundwater are conducted by the Division for Mining and Geology, i.e., the Department of Geology.[1079]

976. The Federal Ministry of Energy, Mining and Industry performs administrative, professional and other tasks established by law related to the realization of the Federation's competence in the fields of industry, energy, mining, geological research and entrepreneurship (Article 8 of the Law on Federal Ministries and other bodies of the Federal Administration).[1080]

1077. BiH MFTER, *State of the environment Report of the Bosnia and Herzegovina 2012*, *supra* p. 76.

1078. The Law on Environmental Protection defines an environmental impact assessment as an obligatory precondition for obtaining an environmental permit and consequently a planning permit, together with other permits that are necessary for building new energy plants and mines. Further, it is prescribed by the law that existing mines shall prepare activity plans containing measures and requirements for a complete reduction of emissions, i.e., pollution, and that they shall synchronize with the Best Available Techniques – BAT, which include obligatory plans for waste management, which is one of the preconditions for obtaining an environmental permit. Waste management plans must also be prepared for new plants and facilities. *Ibid.*, pp. 77–78.

1079. *See*: http://www.vladars.net/sr-SP-Cyrl/Vlada/Ministarstva/mper/OMin/Pages/Splash.aspx (13 Jul. 2022).

1080. *See*: https://fbihvlada.gov.ba/bosanski/sastav%20vlade/zakon%20o%20ministarstvima.php (13 Jul. 2022).

§4. LEGISLATION

I. The Republic of Srpska

A. The Legal Framework

977. The legal grounds for exploration and exploitation of mineral resources in the Republic of Srpska include the following basic laws:

(1) The Law on Mining (Official Gazette of RS, No. 62/18).
(2) The Law on Geological Explorations (Official Gazette of RS, No. 110/13, 91/17, and 107/19).
(3) The Law on Concessions (Official Gazette of RS, No. 59/13, 16/18).
(4) The Law on Oil and Oil Derivatives (Official Gazette of RS, Nos 36/09 and 102/12).
(5) The Law on Gas (Official Gazette of RS, Nos 86/07 and 121/12).
(6) The Law on pipeline transport of gaseous and liquid hydrocarbons and distribution of gaseous hydrocarbons (Official Gazette of the RS, No. 52/12).
(7) The Energy Law (Official Gazette of the RS, No. 49/09).
(8) The Electricity Law (Official Gazette of the RS, Nos 8/08-revised text, 34/09, 92/09 and 01/11).
(9) The Law on Renewable Energy Sources and Efficient Cogeneration (Official Gazette of the RS, No. 16/22).
(10) The Law on Energy Efficiency (Official Gazette of the RS, No. 59/13).
(11) The Law on public-private partnerships (Official Gazette of the RS, No. 59/09), etc.[1081]

978. The RS Law on Mining (Official Gazette of RS, No. 62/18), governing conditions and methods of exploitation of mineral raw materials, construction, use and maintenance of mining facilities, mining projects, mining geodetic measurements and plans, protection measures and other issues related to exploitation of mineral raw materials, personnel conditions for performing certain tasks in mining, as well as the conditions for issuing and seizure of licenses in mining.[1082]

1081. For more information *see*: http://www.vladars.net/eng/vlada/ministries/MIEM/legalframework/Pages/default.aspx (13 Jul. 2022).

1082. Article 5 of the RS Law on Mining prescribed what is considered under mineral resources. Mineral raw materials are considered to be: (1) All types of coal, hydrocarbons (petroleum and natural gas) and other natural gas, asphalt, oil shale and radioactive ore, (2) Metallic mineral raw materials and their usable compounds, (3) Non-mineral mineral raw materials, raw materials for industrial processing and for obtaining building material, 4) all types of salt and salt water, 5) Water below the surface of the earth: mineral, technical and thermomineral water, geothermal sources, thermal waters and gases that come with them (groundwater), 6) Mineral raw materials which are the result of exploitation and processing of mineral raw materials, 7) all other mineral raw materials of natural origin. Exploitation of these, and other mineral resources, is regulated by the Law on Mining. The mining waste has been exempted in the Law on waste management (Official gazette RS, No 111/13), as it is the subject of special act, i.e., the current Law on mining. The current Law on mining regulates the issue of the mining waste, in the Arts 74–76. Disposal and management of mining waste shall be carried out on the basis of the mining waste management

979. The Law on Geological Researches (Official Gazette of RS, No. 110/13, 91/17, and 107/19) regulate the subject, purpose, and types of geological exploration, requirements for performing of geological research, preparation and audit of programmes and projects for geological researches, expert exam, research area, issuing of decision to perform detailed geological surveys, performing of geological researches, preparation and audit of the elaborates on reserves and elaborates on performed researches, cadastres in the field of geology, geological information systems, Technical Documentation Fund, Bank of core drill holes, and other issues related to the field of geology and geological researches (Article 1).[1083]

980. The Law on Oil and Oil Derivatives (Official Gazette of the RS, Nos 36/09 and 102/12) and the Law on Pipeline Transportation of Gaseous and Liquid Hydrocarbons and Distribution of Gaseous Hydrocarbons (Official Gazette of the RS, No. 52/12), which regulate activities in the fields of oil and oil derivatives, transportation and distribution of gaseous and liquid hydrocarbons, conditions for security of supply and transport; construction, use and maintenance of energy facilities in accordance with the environmental protection regulations.[1084]

B. Subordinate Legislation

981. A large number of bylaws in this area have been adopted. Following deserve to be mentioned:

(1) Rulebook on the procedure for issuing and revoking licenses for geological researches, forms of license and keeping and publishing of the license registry (Official Gazette of the RS, No. 20/18).
(2) Rulebook on Execution of Mining Surface Works (Official Gazette of RS, No. 7/14).
(3) Rule book on the performance of surface mining operations (Official Gazette of the RS, No. 7/14).
(4) Rule book on conditions, method and programme for taking of professional exam in the geological profession (Official Gazette of the RS, No. 111/14, 28/18).

---

license issued by the Ministry, subject to the opinion of the Ministry responsible for environment protection, in accordance with the Waste Management Plan and other supporting documentation defining the type, manner of management and reporting, as well as other duties related to the management of mining waste (Art. 74, para. 1).

1083. Mineral resources are concentrations, i.e., accumulations of geological natural (geogenic) and technogenic materials of economic interest in/or on the Earth's crust (surface), which, in an appropriate form, quantity, as well as in quality characteristics justify the real chances that can be profitably exploited (Art. 2b).

1084. The Law on Gas (Official Gazette of the RS Nos. 86/07, and 121/12) governing activities in the field of natural gas, conditions for security of supply, construction, use and maintenance of energy facilities in accordance with the environmental protection regulations.

(5) Rule book on procedure for approving of exploitation field and the way of keeping records on approved exploitation fields (Official Gazette of the RS, No. 42/13).
(6) Rule book on the content, the audit process and approval of mining projects (Official Gazette of the RS, No. 1/13).
(7) Rule book on technical norms during the exploration and exploitation of petroleum, natural gases and layered water (Official Gazette of SFRY, No. 43/79, 41/81 and 15/82).
(8) Rule book on rinsing of precious metals and river sediments (Official Gazette of SR BiH, No. 24/78).
(9) Rule book on technical measures for the safety at work during underground mining works (Official Gazette of SFRY, No. 11/67, 35/67, 60/70, 9/71 and 3/73), etc.[1085]

II. Federation of Bosnia and Herzegovina

A. *The Legal Framework*

982. The most important laws adopted are as follows:

(1) The Law on Mining (Official Gazette of FBiH, No. 26/10).
(2) The Law on Geological Survey (Official Gazette of FBiH, Nos 9/10 and 14/10).
(3) The Law on Concessions (Official Gazette of FBiH, Nos 40/02, 61/06).
(4) The Law on the Use of Renewable Energy Sources and Efficiency Cogeneration (Official Gazette of FBiH, No. 70/13).
(5) The Law on Electricity in FBiH (Official Gazette of FBiH, No. 66/13, and 94/15).
(6) The Law on the Exploration and Exploitation of Oil and Gas in the Federation of Bosnia and Herzegovina (Official Gazette of FBiH, No. 77/13), etc.[1086]

983. 'The concepts of environmental sustainability including the protection of habitats and species have been integrated in the mining sector policy: the FBiH Law on Geological Survey and the FBiH Mining Law include clear and precise provisions stipulating mandatory environmental protection at the designing, geological survey and exploitation stages, as well as technical and biological recultivation of exploited areas upon completion of the exploitation.'[1087]

1085. For the complete list of mining and geology regulations of the Republic of Srpska *see*: http://www.vladars.net/sr-SP-Cyrl/Vlada/Ministarstva/mper/PAO/Pages/Tehnicki_propisi_iz_oblasti_rudarstva_i_geologije.aspx (13 Jul. 2022).
1086. For detailed information, *see*: https://fmeri.gov.ba/zakonodavstvo/ (13 Jul. 2022).
1087. BiH Council of Ministers, *Answers to the List of EU Questions on Chapter 27, Environment, supra* p. 279.

984. The Law on Mining (Official Gazette of FBiH No. 26/10) regulates: the legal status of mining wealth, i.e., mineral resources, methods and conditions for mineral resources management, protection, performing of mining works, safety at work measures, the suspension of the execution and permanent discontinuation of mining works, technical documentation and design, mining measurements and mining plans, inspection supervision, space protection and development, penalty provisions and other matters related to the management of raw mineral at the territory of the FBiH. Mining wealth is the good of general interest and under special protection (Article 1).

985. The Law on Geological Survey (Official Gazette of FBiH Nos 9/10, and 14/10) regulates: geological researches, stages for performing of geological researches, geological research of interest to the Federation of BiH, activities that use the results of geological researches, production and distribution of geological maps, research area, keeping the cadastre, making and revision of the geological documentation, approval for dealing with registered activity in the field of geology, approval process and what is determined by approval for performing of geological researches, performing of geological researches, reports on geological researches, issuing of decision on the recognition of raw mineral reserves, procedure after the research completion, collection and preparation of geological databases, financing of geological researches of interest to the Federation, the abolition of approval for geological researches, taking of professional exam, establishing of professional chamber, validation of geological documentation and international agreements, inspection supervision over implementation of the Law on Geological Researches in the FBiH, administrative supervision, penalty provisions and other issues related to the geological researches (Article 1).

B. Subordinate Legislation

986. Bylaws in this area include the following:

(1) Rule book on content of the elaborates, method and procedure for classification of the coal seam and pit categorization, i.e., pit areas according to the threat level of the explosive coal dust (Official Gazette of the FBiH No. 104/13).
(2) Rule book on technical measures with protection measures during the exploitation of raw minerals by deep drilling.
(3) Rule book on conditions to be fulfilled by legal persons for preparation of Elaborate on categorization of coal seams and pits and classifying of pit rooms according to the threat level of methane, Elaborate on classification and categorization of the pit, i.e., pit rooms according to the threat level of explosive coal dust in terms of qualification and amenities, and procedure for their approval (Official Gazette of FBiH No. 68/11).

(4) Rule book on way of collecting, recording, processing, usage and sharing of data for Geological database and establishing of technical documentation fund on geological researches and geoinformation systems organization (Official Gazette of the FBiH No. 51/12).
(5) Rule book on the way for keeping the evidence and preparation of raw minerals deposits cadastre, geological phenomena and approved research areas (Official Gazette of the FBiH No. 38/11).
(6) Rule book on the contents and method for preparation of the strategy for management of raw minerals (Official Gazette of the FBiH No. 31/12).
(7) Rule book on technical norms for performing of mining measurements, preparation of mining plans and maps, their scale, the selection of the coordinate system and the keeping of mining-measuring and other documents used during the preparation of mining technical documentation (Official Gazette of the FBiH No. 14/12).
(8) Rule book on taking of professional exam for certain jobs in the area of mining (Official Gazette of the FBiH No. 76/11).
(9) Rule book of categorization, classification, calculation of reserves of subterranean waters and keeping evidence of them (Official Gazette of the FBiH No. 36/12).
(10) Rule book on keeping of approved exploitation fields cadastre, way of management of the documents collection and census of legal entities which have issued permits for the exploitation of raw minerals (Official Gazette of the FBiH No. 79/11), etc.[1088]

III. Brčko District of Bosnia and Herzegovina

A. The Legal Framework

987. There are very few laws adopted by Brčko District Government that could make a legal base for exploration and exploitation of mineral resources in BD. Some of them are the following:

(1) The Law on Concession (Official Gazette of BD Nos 41/06, 19/07 and 2/08).
(2) The Law on Electricity (Official Gazette of BD Nos 36/04, 28/07, 61/10, 04/13, 27/21).
(3) The Law on Transport/Transfer of Explosive Materials and Flammable Liquids and Gases (Official Gazette of BD No. 27/07).
(4) The Law on General Conditions for Electricity Supply (Official Gazette of BD Nos 36/04, 3/06, 28/07, 25/08 and 04/13).
(5) The Law on Tariff System for Sale of the Electricity (Official Gazette of BD Nos 37/04, 28/07 and 04/13).

1088. *See*: http://www.fmeri.gov.ba/legislativa.aspx?cat=7 (13 Jul. 2022).

(6) The Law on Public-Private Partnerships (Official Gazette of BD No. 7/10), etc.[1089]

1089. *See*: https://skupstinabd.ba/sr/zakon.html (13 Jul. 2022).

Part III. Zoning and Land-Use Planning

§1. Evolution of Spatial Planning

988. Development of spatial planning in BiH started after the Second World War in the framework of 'new Yugoslavia'. The Law on Social Planning System and Social Plan of the Socialist Republic of Bosnia and Herzegovina was enacted in 1978. 'The procedure of making the Spatial plan of the Republic had, however, to be formally reconciled with the new concept of spatial planning as an integral part of social planning. The same was with the other Republics of the SFRJ.'[1090] After enacting the Spatial Plan of SR BiH (1981), spatial plans for municipalities, towns, small settlements and special purpose areas, were prepared.

§2. Spatial Plans and Competencies

989. Increased urban sprawl and high rates of poverty are also an important driving force of environmental degradation. Urban areas are constantly developing, so, despite the decrease of total population, these areas and their transport corridors have a continuing trend of population concentration. Regarding spatial planning, BiH is still missing a major number of its spatial and urban plans. The RS has adopted a spatial plan (Spatial Plan of RS 2008–2015), while the Draft Spatial Plan of FBiH 2008–2028 is still in the adoption procedure.[1091] Four out of ten cantons, in the FBiH have prepared and adopted spatial plans.[1092]

990. There is no responsible body for spatial planning at BiH level. However, the FBiH, the RS and the BD have authorities for developing and implementing

1090. UNEP, PAP/RAC, *National Report on Current Policy, Procedures, Legal Basis and Practice of Marine Spatial Planning in Bosnia and Herzegovina, supra* p. 2.

1091. BiH MFTER, *State of the environment Report of the Bosnia and Herzegovina 2012, supra* p. 32. 'Illegal construction is a major issue in the whole of BiH, which is a result of missing planning mechanisms, insufficient implementation and control and significant socio-economic factors and population displacement during the war'.

1092. Data on the number of spatial and urban development plans in the FBiH are not available. In late 2000, 22 municipalities in the RS had no spatial or urban development plan, 32 municipalities had no spatial plan, and 30 municipalities had no urban development plan. The situation has not improved significantly since 2000, judging by new data showing that almost 80% of municipalities in the RS have no planning documents or have outdated planning documents that are not in line with the existing Spatial Plan. *Ibid.*, p. 97.

legal regulations in this sector, as well as adopted laws that regulate the issues of spatial and urban planning in these territories.

§3. Legislation on Spatial Organization and Construction

I. The Republic of Srpska

991. The Department of Urban and Spatial Planning (in RS Ministry of Spatial Planning, Civil Engineering and Ecology) performs activities in the field of urban and regional planning, as well as other professional activities related to integrated planning and development of space, application of RS Spatial Plan, administrative supervision, review and approval of regional plans of local governments and special areas, urban and regulatory plans, audit of spatial planning documents, development programmes, investment and technical documentation of particular interest for RS urban planning, establishment of a unified central database on RS space, etc.[1093]

A. The Law on Spatial Development and Construction

992. Basic legal act regulating spatial development[1094] and construction in the Republic of Srpska is the Law on Spatial Development and Construction (Official Gazette of the RS, No. 40/13, 2/15-CC, 106/15, 3/16, 104/18-CC, 84/19). It has the following nine parts: Part I – General Provisions (Articles 1–9), Part II – Spatial Planning (Articles 10–66), Part III – Buildable Land (Articles 67–85), Part IV – Construction (Articles 86–150), Part V – Legalization (Articles 151–168), Part VI – Supervision (Articles 169–171), Part VII – Chamber of Engineers of the Republic of Srpska (Articles 172–175), Part VIII – Penalty Provisions (Articles 176–188), Part IX – Transitional and Final Provisions (Articles 189–199).

993. This law regulates the system of spatial planning and spatial development, preparation, drafting and adoption of spatial planning documents,[1095] location conditions, buildable land regulation, issuing of the construction permits, types and

1093. BiH Council of Ministers, *Answers to the List of EU Questions on Chapter 27, Environment, supra* pp. 34, 35. *See also*: https://www.vladars.net/sr-SP-Cyrl/Vlada/Ministarstva/mgr/OM/sektori/supp/Pages/splash.aspx (18 Jul. 2022). Within the Department of Construction, administrative tasks (administrative-legal and administrative-supervisory tasks), testing and professional training tasks, construction, and tasks related to the development of construction land, production of construction materials, development, and services in the field of construction, residential construction are performed, etc. https://www.vladars.net/sr-SP-Cyrl/Vlada/Ministarstva/mgr/OM/sektori/gradjevinarstvo/Pages/Home.aspx (18 Jul. 2022).

1094. *Spatial development* is the planned deployment of activities and structures in a particular area (Art. 2, para. 1, Item c).

1095. *Spatial planning document* is a planning document that defines the organization, purpose and method of use and space management, as well as the criteria and guidelines for the arrangement and space protection (Art. 2, para. 1, Item dj).

content of the technical documentation, construction of structures and interrelationships between participants in the construction, structure using and removal, structure legalization, performing of supervision over implementation of this law, the competency and work of the Chamber of Engineers and other issues of importance for spatial development, buildable land and construction of structures (Article 1, paragraph 1).

994. The construction of cities, settlements[1096] and structures is planned in spatial regulation documents issued in accordance with the provisions of this law (Article 3, paragraph 1). Structure must be designed and constructed in a way to achieve its security as a whole, as well as in its every part separately (Article 4, paragraph 1). Every new building, depending on the type and purpose, must be designed, constructed and maintained in a way that during the use it has prescribed energy performances[1097] (Article 5, paragraph 1).

995. The preparation of spatial development documents, as well as preparation, review and nostrification of technical documentation, construction and supervision over the structure construction and conducting of energy audits of constructions, under conditions prescribed in this law, can be provided by natural persons and legal entities only if they possess an appropriate licence (Article 8, paragraph 1).[1098] The licence to a natural person shall be issued by the Minister on the proposal of the Commission upon submitting the request (Article 8, paragraph 2).[1099]

1. The System of the Spatial Planning

996. Spatial planning is an integral part of a unified system of planning[1100] and programming of the development[1101] and is a mandatory and continuous activity of

1096. *Settlement* is built and functionally unified space where conditions are provided for the life, work and meet the common needs of the population, and may have the character of urban or rural settlements (Art. 2, para. 1, Item o).
1097. *Energy performance of the buildings* is calculated or measured amount of energy needed to meet the energy requirements associated with typical use of the building, including the energy used for heating, cooling, ventilation, hot water preparation and for lighting (Art. 2, para. 1, Item d).
1098. Records on issued construction and use permits are kept in the process of its issuance, while the structures constructed on the basis of this licence shall be recorded in the public records in accordance with the provisions of this Law and other regulations (Art. 7, para. 1).
1099. The licence to the legal entity shall be issued by the Minister on the proposal of the Commission after submitting the request, if the legal entity is recorded in the register for that type of work (Art. 8, para. 4).
1100. Planned spatial development includes (Art. 13, para. 1): (a) The construction and development of settlement and surrounding area; (b) The use and protection of natural, as well as built resources and (c) The construction of other structures in accordance with the spatial development documents and other prescribed conditions from this Law.
1101. Spatial development includes (Art. 12, para. 1): (a) Research, check and assessment of possibilities for sustainable development in the area of the Republic of Srpska; (b) Protective measures and manner of space management; (c) Preparation of spatial planning documents and (d) Implementation and control of implementation of spatial development documents.

the Republic and of all local government units, which includes permanent and multidisciplinary process that is performed on the base of the study of natural conditions, especially seismic, demographic, economic, social, technical and other conditions which ensure functional and rational organization and use of the available space,[1102] goods in general use, natural resources, material, cultural and ecological values, the rational use of energy, protection and improvement of the environment and harmonizing of the interests of all space users (Article 10, paragraph 1).

997. Some of the spatial planning principles are following (Article 11, paragraph 1): space protection in accordance with the principles of sustainable development,[1103] integrated planning, harmonization of the natural values with human activities, environmental protection, protection of cultural and natural heritage, harmonization of spatial development documents of the Republic of Srpska and the Federation of Bosnia and Herzegovina, harmonization of spatial development of the Republic of Srpska with spatial development of neighbouring countries, the public and free access to the information and documents relevant for the spatial development and establishment of a unified information system about the space of the Republic for the purpose of planning, land use and protection of the Republic area.

998. The Government and the National Assembly of the Republic of Srpska are competent for spatial planning in the Republic, as well as the Assembly of the local governments, while planning is done by adopting of spatial development documents and other documents and regulations specified in this law (Article 22, paragraph 1). The Ministry is responsible for preparation of spatial development documents relevant for the Republic, as well as for their implementation, while local government authorities, performing spatial development activities, are responsible for the preparation and implementation of spatial development documents of importance for the local government unit (Article 23, paragraph 1).

999. Spatial development documents define the organization, purpose and way of use and management of space, as well as the criteria and guidelines for the development and space protection of the Republic (Article 25, paragraph 1). Spatial development documents can be strategic and executive (Article 25, paragraph 2). The strategic documents of spatial development are adopted for the planning period[1104] of twenty years (Article 25, paragraph 6). Executive spatial development

---

1102. *Space* is a collection of natural and built structures on the surface, above or below ground and water, until reaching the immediate impacts of human activities (Art. 2, para. 1, Item u).

1103. *Sustainable development* means enabling the use of such space which beside preservation of the environment, nature and permanent use of natural resources, as well as protection of the cultural heritage and natural assets, meet the needs of present generations without compromising the needs of future generations (Art. 2, para. 1, Item s).

1104. *Planning period* is the period of time expressed in years for which are performed the analysis and assessment of needs and opportunities for spatial development, as well as set goals and program, i.e., concept of the area development in the scope of spatial planning documents (Art. 2, para. 1, Item s).

documents are technical-regulatory documents of spatial development based on which are defined the requirements for design and construction of buildings (Article 25, paragraph 8).[1105]

2. Implementing of the Spatial Development Documents

1000. Zoning Plan is an implementing spatial development document that is adopted for spatial units, sub units or individual zones[1106] within the urban area of the local government units, for which it is prescribed in urban or other plan of higher order or the wider area and must be harmonized with that plan (Article 34, paragraph 1). The basic purpose of a particular area, i.e., zone is defined in Zoning Plan and it provides an inventory of compatible purposes for that zone (Article 34, paragraph 3).

1001. The regulation plan is adopted for mainly constructed urban areas based on urban plan, as well as areas of common interest of the local government unit for economic development or construction of structure of the social infrastructure on the base of the urban plan or documents of a higher order or wider area, while it is necessary to define in detail the conditions for design and construction of new structures, as well as reconstruction of the existing (Article 35, paragraph 1).

3. The Spatial Development Documents and Unified Spatial-Information System

1002. Spatial Plan of the Republic of Srpska,[1107] Spatial Plan of the area of special purpose of the Republic of Srpska and the implementing documents of spatial development of the area of the Republican importance for which the Government was declared the public interest are adopted by the Government of the Republic of Srpska (Article 38, paragraph 1).

1003. Spatial plan of the Local Government Unit, urban plan,[1108] special purpose area plans of the local government units and the implementing documents of

1105. Executive spatial development document shall be adopted for planning period up to ten years, and is valid until its modification or adoption of a new one, if it is not contrary to the spatial development document of a higher order (Art. 25, para. 9).

1106. *Zone* is a spatial unit or part of spatial unit, graphically and numerically determined by spatial planning documents and in accordance with special regulations (Art. 2, para. 1, Item z).

1107. Spatial Plan of the Republic of Srpska defines long-term objectives and measures of spatial development of the Republic in accordance with overall economic, social and cultural-historical development, sector strategies and other development documents, based on the developmental importance and priority given in the process of harmonization of objectives and relativization of conflict of interest in development of the area (Art. 29, para. 1).

1108. Urban plan is to be adopted for the urban area of the local government on the basis of the local Government spatial plan (Art. 33, para. 1).

spatial development of the local government units adopts the Assembly of the Local Government Unit (Article 38, paragraph 2).

1004. The Ministry performs supervision and coordination over the establishment and maintenance of a unified spatial-information system of the Republic (Article 53, paragraph 1). The unified spatial-information system includes data and information with electronic support in the entire territory of the Republic (Article 53, paragraph 2). Funding for the establishment and maintenance of the unique spatial-information system shall be provided from the budget of the Republic (Article 53, paragraph 4).

4. Buildable Land

1005. The local government unit takes care on the development of city buildable land[1109] in accordance with the law (Article 67, paragraph 2). In order to provide conditions for the development of city buildable land, the local government unit may establish a public enterprise or otherwise provide performing of such activities in accordance with the law (Article 67, paragraph 3).

1006. City buildable land can be developed or undeveloped (Article 71, paragraph 1). Developed city buildable land is land that has the utility infrastructure for construction in accordance with the implementing space development document, i.e., which has a built access road, provided electricity supply, water supply and provided other special conditions (Article 71, paragraph 2).[1110]

5. Construction

1007. All structures must be designed and constructed in accordance with the spatial development documents (Article 86, paragraph 1). Compliance of the structures with spatial development documents is ensured by the designing in accordance with the requirements from site conditions, audit of the project prior to the procedure for issuing of the construction permit, performing of the works in accordance with the approved main project and control in the process of issuing of the occupancy permit (Article 86, paragraph 2).

1008. Prior to the issuance of the occupancy permits, approvals for probation work, i.e., before the changing of ownership or lease of a new building constructed

1109. *The city buildable land* is developed and undeveloped land in cities and in urban settlements which, according to the appropriate spatial development documents, is intended for the construction of facilities in accordance with the provisions of this Law, as previously defined by the Law and other regulations, i.e., that was determined by decision of the Local Government Unit Assembly (Art. 2, para. 1, Item v). Buildable land is used according to its purpose and in a manner that ensures its rational use in accordance with the Law (Art. 67, para. 1).

1110. An undeveloped city buildable land is land that is not fully communally equipped pursuant to para. 2 of this article (Art. 71, para. 3).

after the entry into force of this law or its special part, must be obtained the energy certificate issued in accordance with the provisions of this Law and the regulations related to the energy efficiency[1111] (Article 90, paragraph 4). The energy certificate of the building includes integrated results of an energy audit of the building as a whole, which is made according to the regulations of this law, including its technical systems (Article 90, paragraph 5).[1112]

1009. Building energy audit performs a legal entity that has the proper licence to perform energy audits issued by the Minister (Article 91, paragraphs 1 and 2). Licence to perform energy audits issued to the natural person with licence for preparation or audit of the technical documentation and construction, acquired under the provisions of this law and have completed special training to perform energy audits in accordance with the provisions of the laws and regulations on energy efficiency (Article 91, paragraph 3).[1113]

1010. The Ministry shall keep a single register of persons who have been issued a licence to carry out energy audits (Article 92, paragraph 1). Local Government Unit keeps a register of issued energy certificates in their area (Article 92, paragraph 2).[1114]

1011. An authorized person, who has made energy audit, shall submit a report to the Fund on conducted review and determined energy class of the building, within eight days from the audit (Article 94, paragraph 1). Fund on the base of the submitted report issue energy certificate and delivers it to an authorized person who has performed an energy audit, to the Ministry, as well as to the competent authority of the Local Government Units, within eight days of the receipt of the report (Article 94, paragraph 2).[1115]

1012. The construction, i.e., execution of the works on the structure under this law may be performed by a legal entity that has a licence to perform these activities

1111. *Certification of the energy performance of the buildings (hereinafter, 'energy certificate')* is a certificate issued by the authority specified in this Law on the basis of the energy audit report performed by an authorized person, showing the energy performances of a building or part thereof which forms an independent usable unit (Art. 2, para. 1, Item dž).

1112. The public sector which use building with a usable area greater than 500 m^2 is obliged to apply energy management system into these buildings in accordance with provisions of the regulations related to the energy efficiency (Art. 90, para. 6).

1113. Special professional training for conducting of the energy audits is organized by the Fund for Environmental Protection and Energy Efficiency (hereinafter, 'the Fund') (Art. 91, para. 5).

1114. Registers from paras 1 and 2 of this article are public, and shall be published on the website of the Ministry and of the local government units or on other appropriate way (Art. 92, para. 3).

1115. The energy certificate has a validity of ten years and is subject to independent control system (Art. 94, para. 4). The costs for issuing of the energy certificate shall be borne by the investor (Art. 94, para. 5).

(hereinafter, 'the contractor') (Article 116, paragraph 1).[1116] The licence for the legal entity for construction of the structure is to be issued by the Minister (Article 116, paragraph 3).

Licences for companies issued pursuant to this law shall be valid for four years from the issue date (Article 120, paragraph 1). Upon the expiration of that period, a new licence shall be issued to the legal entity that has had a licence, at its request and on the basis of the evidence presented, in accordance with the provisions of this law (Article 120, paragraph 2).[1117]

6. The Building Permit

1013. Construction of the structure can be started only on the basis of the decision for issuing of the building permit, unless in cases when in accordance with the provisions of this law is not required to obtain a building permit (Article 124, paragraph 1). Building permit[1118] is to be issued for the construction of the entire building or part of a building that makes technical, technological or functional unit (Article 124, paragraph 2).

1014. Building permit is to be issued by the administrative authority in charge for the construction affairs in the local government unit in whose area the building is constructed (Article 127, paragraph 1). Notwithstanding from paragraph 1 of this article, the Minister shall issue a building permit[1119] for the facilities referred to in Article 60, paragraph 2 of this law (Article 127, paragraph 2).[1120]

7. The Use Permit and Removal of the Structure

1015. Constructed structure cannot be used, i.e., cannot be put to use before the competent authority issues a use permit by the decision, based on previously completed technical inspection of the structure (Article 140, paragraph 1). Technical inspection includes the control of compliance of the performed works with the building permit and with technical documentation based on which the structure was built, as well as with technical regulations and standards that apply to certain types of works, materials, installation, equipment, devices and structures (Article 140, paragraph 2).

1116. Exceptionally from para. 1 of this article, building of the individual housing and individual residential-commercial structures of gross floor area up to 200 m^2 for the needs of their household, as well as construction of structures for which, in accordance with the provisions of this Law, construction permit is not required, may perform the investor directly (Art. 116, para. 2).
1117. Licence to the natural person shall be issued without validity period (Art. 120, para. 3).
1118. Building permit expires if construction of the structure for which it was issued is not started within three years from the date the building permit became enforceable (Art. 136, para. 1).
1119. Content of the building permit is prescribed in Art. 132, para. 1.
1120. Temporary prefabricated structures that are placed for fair and public events, which will not be removed within ninety days of their placement, shall be placed only on the base of the building permit (Art. 134, para. 1).

1016. Use permit may be issued for part of the building which is a separate technical and functional unit, prior to the completion of construction of the entire structure (Article 140, paragraph 5). Technical inspection[1121] performs an expert commission formed on the base of the decision by the authority which issued the building permit (hereinafter, 'the Commission')[1122] within three days from the receipt of a complete application (Article 142, paragraph 1). Use permit of the structure is permanently kept by the administrative authority which issued the construction permit, as well as the owner of the structure (Article 146, paragraph 2).

1017. The structure is used in accordance with its purpose (Article 148, paragraph 1). The owner of the structure can remove the structure or part thereof only on the base of the permit for removal, if other than the removal based on the inspection decision (Article 149, paragraph 1). The permit for removal is issued by the authority responsible for spatial development in the Local Government Unit, while for the structures referred to in Article 60, paragraph 2 of this law permit for the removal shall be issued by the Ministry (Article 149, paragraph 2).[1123]

8. Legalization

1018. Legalization, in terms of this law, meets a subsequent issuing of the site conditions, building permits and use permits for structures, i.e., parts of the structures constructed, started or reconstructed without a building permit, as well as structures constructed on the basis of the building permit on which changes were made during construction from the building permit and final design, which were constructed or which construction was commenced up to the entry into force of this Law (Article 151, paragraph 1).[1124] Legalization of buildings is a general interest for the Republic of Srpska, which is achieved by applying the provisions of this Law governing the legalization (Article 151a).

1019. Notwithstanding from Article 151 of this law, for individual housing and individual housing-business structures with a gross building area less than 400 m^2, except for complex structures in terms of this law, when the authority responsible for issuing of the building permits determines that a structure which is the subject

1121. Costs for performing of the technical inspection shall be borne by the investor, i.e., owner of the structure (Art. 146, para. 3).
1122. The Commission shall consist of at least three members (Art. 142, para. 2).
1123. Permit for removal of the structure shall be permanently kept by the administrative authority that issued the permit and the owner of the structure (Art. 149, para. 7).
1124. Notwithstanding from para. 1 of this article, procedure for legalization of the completed structures under the provisions of this Law shall be carried out without subsequent issuance of locational conditions, unless if needed for legalization of the facilities on state land (Art. 151, para. 3). *See also*: Law on Legalization of Illegally Build Buildings (Official Gazette of the RS, No. 62/18).

of legalization is completed and that meets the prescribed requirements for the construction and use, the subsequent building and use permit are issued by the same decision[1125] (Article 152, paragraph 1).

1020. The decision on the subsequent issuance of building permits for individual residential and individual residential-commercial structures with a gross building area less than 400 m^2, except for complex structures in terms of this law, which are not fully completed, but for which the structure of the building was completed, the roof and facade walls, shall be issued under the conditions set out in Article 156 of this law, provided that it is not necessary to submit evidences referred to in paragraph 1, item d) of the said article (Article 157, paragraph 1).

9. Supervision

1021. Administrative supervision over the implementation of this law and the regulations adopted on the basis of this law is to be performed by the Ministry (Article 169, paragraph 1). Inspection supervision over the implementation of this law and the regulations adopted on the basis of this law performs the Republican Administration for Inspection Affairs through Republican urban-construction inspectors, i.e., urban-construction inspectors in local government unit (Article 169, paragraph 2).

10. Chamber of Engineers of the Republic of Srpska

1022. In order to improve the conditions for performing of professional activities in the field of spatial and urban planning, design, structure construction and other areas relevant to the planning and construction, the protection of general and individual interest in doing business in these areas, the organization of services in these areas as well as to achieve other goals in the field of Spatial Planning and Construction, the Chamber of Engineers of the Republic of Srpska is established, in accordance with the law governing the issues of citizens' associations (hereinafter, 'the Chamber') (Article 172, paragraph 1).[1126]

B. Other Relevant RS Regulations

1023.

1125. Procedure for legalization of the structures from Art. 151, para. 1 of this Law shall be initiated at the request of investors or owner of illegally constructed structure or part of a structure constructed illegally (Art. 153, para. 1).

1126. The Ministry performs supervision over work legality of the Chamber (Art. 175, para. 3).

(1) Law on Waste Management ('Official Gazette of the RS', Nos 111/13, 106/15, 16/18, 70/20, 63/21).[1127]
(2) Law on the implementation of the Decisions of the Commission for Preservation of National Monuments ('Official Gazette of the RS', No. 7/06).
(3) Law on National Parks ('Official Gazette of the RS', No. 75/10).
(4) Law on the Nature Protection ('Official Gazette of the RS', No. 20/14).
(5) Law on Privatization of business buildings, business premises and garages ('Official Gazette of the RS', Nos 98/ 04, 71/10, 30/12 and 67/13).
(6) Law on the Construction Products ('Official Gazette of the RS', No.: 05/12).
(7) Law on state apartments with no tenancy rights ('Official Gazette of the RS', No. 98/11).
(8) Law on the Building Maintenance ('Official Gazette of the RS', No. 101/11).
(9) Law on Privatization of State-owned Apartments ('Official Gazette of the RS', No. 118/11, 67/13 and 45/18).
(10) Law on Public Utility Activities ('Official Gazette of the RS', No. 124/11, and 100/17).

C. Basic Bylaws/Rule Books/Decrees/Instructions

1. Acts–Spatial Development and Construction

1024. Based on the Law on Spatial Planning and Construction ('Official Gazette of the RS' No. 40/13, 106/15, 3/16, 84/19), the following bylaws were enacted:

(1) Rule book on the general rules of town planning regulations and parcelling ('Official Gazette of the RS' No. 115/13).
(2) Rule book on the performing of technical inspection of the facility and observation of the terrain and facilities during their usage ('Official Gazette of the RS', No. 100/13).
(3) Rule book on the content and control of technical documentation ('Official Gazette of the RS', No. 101/13).
(4) The Regulation on amount of fee for the costs of taking professional exams and the amount of fee for members of the Commission ('Official Gazette of the RS' No. 99/13, and 23/16).
(5) The Regulation on the amount of fee for licence issuing ('Official Gazette of the RS' No. 99/13).
(6) Rule book on way of issuing, content and forming of the spatial development documents ('Official Gazette of the RS' No. 69/13).
(7) Rule book on the development and adoption of spatial development documents in shortened procedure ('Official Gazette of the RS', No: 69/13).
(8) Rule book on forms, content and way of issuing of location conditions ('Official Gazette of the RS', No: 69/13).

1127. *See*: http://www.vladars.net/sr-SP-Cyrl/Vlada/Ministarstva/mgr/PAO/Pages/Splash.aspx (11 Jul. 2022); http://www.vladars.net/sr-SP-Cyrl/Vlada/Ministarstva/mgr/PAO/Pages/Zakoni_-_stambeno-komunalne_djelatnosti.aspx (11 Jul. 2022).

(9) Rule book on conditions and manner of taking of the professional exam ('Official Gazette of the RS', No: 69/13, 99/19).
(10) Rule book on the conditions for granting and revoking of licences to the participants in construction ('Official Gazette of the RS', No. 70/13, and 24/15).
(11) Rule book on the content, the holders of the spatial-information system and methodology for data collection and analysis ('Official Gazette of the RS', No. 93/13).
(12) Rule book on the requirements for the planning and design of structures for the smooth movement of children and persons with reduced physical abilities ('Official Gazette of the RS', No. 93/13).
(13) Rule book on the calculation of the costs for the arrangement of city buildable land ('Official Gazette of the RS', No. 95/13, and 34/14).
(14) Rule book for calculating of surface and capacities of facilities ('Official Gazette of the RS', No. 95/13).
(15) Regulation on conditions, method of calculation and payment of the fee for legalization of the structures ('Official Gazette of the RS', No. 97/13, and 23/16).
(16) Rulebook on Performing Energy Inspection of Buildings and Issuing Energy Certificates (Official Gazette of Republika Srpska, No. 30/15 and 93/16).
(17) Rulebook on Minimum Requirements for Energy Performance of Buildings (Official Gazette of the Republic of Srpska, No. 30/15).
(18) Rulebook on the methodology for calculating energy characteristics of buildings (Official Gazette of the Republic of Srpska, No. 30/15).[1128]

2. Bylaws-Housing and Public Utilities Activities

1025.

(1) Rule book on entry into registry of community buildings with the forms of acts for a unified application of the Law on Building Maintenance ('Official Gazette of the RS' No. 27/12).[1129]

II. The Federation of Bosnia and Herzegovina

1026. Federal Ministry of Spatial Planning performs administrative, expert and other tasks falling under competence of the Federation BiH related to: planning and improvement of space; policy of land utilization at the Federal level; drafting, enforcing and applying of the Spatial Plan of the Federation BiH; harmonizing of the spatial plans of the Cantons with the Spatial Plan of the Federation BiH; directing a long-term development in utilization of natural resources; geologic researches; drafting of basic maps – geophysical, seismological, geothermal, minerogenetic,

1128. For more information, *see*: http://www.vladars.net/SR-SP-CYRL/VLADA/MINISTARSTVA/MGR/PAO/Pages/Prostorno_uredjenje_i_gradjenje.aspx (11 Jul. 2022).
1129. *See*: http://www.vladars.net/sr-SP-Cyrl/Vlada/Ministarstva/mgr/PAO/Pages/Stambeno-komunalne_djelatnosti_-_podzakonski_akti.aspx (11 Jul. 2022).

geochemical, geomorphological, and other; preparing geological backgrounds for physical improvements; supervising appropriate institutions in this sector and other tasks as set out by the applicable legislation.[1130]

A. *The Law on Spatial Planning and Land Use at the Federation of Bosnia and Herzegovina Level*

1027. Basic legal act regulating spatial planning and land use issues at the Federation of Bosnia and Herzegovina level is the Law on Spatial Planning and Land Use at the Federation of Bosnia and Herzegovina level (Official Gazette of the FBiH, Nos 2/06, 72/07, 32/08, 4/10, 13/10, 45/10, 85/21, 92/21). It has the following nine parts: Part I – General Provisions (Articles 1–5), Part II – Planning (Articles 6–22), Part III – Preparation of Planning Documents (Articles 23–30), Part IV – Documentation (Articles 31–33), Part V – Using of the Land for Construction (Articles 34–77), Part VI – Removal of Structure (Articles 78–81), Part VII – Supervision (Articles 82–98), Part VIII – Penalty Provisions (Articles 99–110), Part IX – Transitional and Final Provisions (Articles 111–118).

1028. According to Article 1, paragraph 1, this law regulates: land use planning[1131] at the Federation of Bosnia and Herzegovina level (hereinafter, 'the Federation') through the development and adoption of planning documents and their implementation, the types and content of planning documents, land use at the Federal level, monitoring of the planning documents implementation of the importance for the Federation, monitoring implementation of this Law, as well as penalties for legal entities and natural persons.

1029. Planned management, land use and space protection (hereinafter, 'planned spatial development') are ensured by implementation of planning documents based on an integrated approach to the planned spatial development, as well as the sustainable development principles (Article 2, paragraph 1). Planning at all authority levels in the Federation must be in accordance with special regulations in the field of environmental protection, cultural-historical, architectural and natural heritage, soil, air, forest, water, health, as well as protection of energy, mining and industrial buildings, infrastructural facilities and liaison facilities, as well as protection of sports, touristic, objects of special purpose and security facilities and their infrastructure (Article 4, paragraph 1).

1130. *See*: https://fmpu.gov.ba/en/ministry/competencies/ (19 Jul. 2022).

1131. *Planning*, in terms of this Law, is a planned management, land use and protection of the Federation territory as a particularly valuable and limited good (Art. 1, para. 2).

1. Planning

1030. Planning documents define organization, usage and land use, as well as the measures and guidelines for the spatial protection (Article 6, paragraph 1). Planning documents are the following (Article 6, paragraph 2):

(1) The Spatial Plan.[1132]
(2) The Urban Plan.
(3) Detailed planning documents.[1133]

1031. It is mandatory to adopt the following planning documents:

(1) For the territory of the Federation – The Federation Spatial Plan.
(2) For the territory of Cantons – The Cantonal Spatial Plan.
(3) For the cities of Mostar and Sarajevo – The City Urban Plan.
(4) For the municipalities in the area of cities of Sarajevo and Mostar – The Municipality Spatial Plan.
(5) For the area of interest for the Federation – Spatial Plan of the area of special features.
(6) For the urban area of the municipality in which is located the Cantonal headquarters – the Urban Plan.
(7) For the area for which such obligation is determined by the plan of the wider area – Regulatory Plan and the urban project (Article 7, paragraph 1).

1032. The Federation Spatial Plan determines long-term goals and measures of spatial development in accordance to overall planned economic, social and historical development of importance to the Federation (Article 9, paragraph 1).[1134] The Federation Spatial Plan contains land use policy and directs the development of functions and activities on the Federation territory (Article 9, paragraph 2). Spatial base of the Federation, the programme of measures and decisions on the implementation of the Spatial Plan of the Federation are integral parts of the Federation Spatial Plan (Article 9, paragraph 6). The land use[1135] at the Federation level shall be in accordance with the planning documents of the Federation (Article 34, paragraph 1).

1132. Spatial plan of the Federation of Bosnia and Herzegovina (hereinafter, 'the Federation Spatial Plan'); The Cantonal spatial plan; Spatial plan of the area of special features; Spatial plan of the municipality (except for the municipalities that are part of the cities of Sarajevo and Mostar).
1133. Regulatory plans; Urban projects.
1134. The Federation spatial plan is adopted by the Parliament, on the Government's proposal for a period of twenty years (Art. 9, para. 7).
1135. The land use, in terms of this Law, means the construction of structures and performing of other operations in the area of jurisdiction of the Federation (Art. 34, para. 2).

2. Preparation of Planning Documents

1033. Decision on beginning of preparation of a planning document is to be made by the Parliament, by the legislative Cantonal body or by Municipal council (Article 23, paragraph 1).[1136]

1034. The bearer for the document preparation shall be appointed for preparation of a planning document (Article 24, paragraph 1).[1137] The Ministry is bearer for the preparation of a planning document for which adoption is competent the Parliament (Article 24, paragraph 2).

1035. The process of adoption and enactment of a planning document from the jurisdiction of the Federation is identical to the process of adoption and enactment of the Federal Laws (Article 29, paragraph 1). The procedure of enactment of a planning document from the Cantonal jurisdiction will be determined by Cantonal regulation (Article 29, paragraph 2).

3. Unified Information System

1036. For the purpose of o collecting, processing and using of information relevant for planning, the Ministry in conjunction with other Ministries in charge for the area of importance for planning shall establish and maintain a unique information system (Article 31, paragraph 1).[1138] The Government, at the proposal of the Ministry shall prescribe the content and the holders of the information systems, a methodology for data collecting and processing, as well as unique forms for keeping the evidence (Article 31, paragraph 3).

4. The Land Use for Construction

1037. Construction may be approved if the previously determined that the related construction is in accordance with planning documents and other conditions laid down for that space, special laws and regulations adopted on the base of those laws, by issuing of the urban consent (Article 37, paragraph 1). The investor shall submit to the Ministry request for issuing of the urban consent for structures[1139] and

1136. The content of the Decision is prescribed in Art. 23, para. 2.

1137. Preparation of a planning document may be entrusted to the legal entity registered for conducting of such tasks (hereinafter, 'the bearer for the document preparation') (Art. 26, para. 1).

1138. A unique information system covers the area of data and information for the entire Federation territory (Art. 31, para. 2).

1139. In terms of this Law, the structure is considered as: (1) structure permanently attached to the ground, which consist of the construction assembly or of construction assembly and installed equipment, as well as independent facilities permanently attached to the ground; (2) transport, water management and energy structures and the areas with associated installations, telecommunication structures and installations, the structures and installations of utility infrastructure; (3) production and other economy structures and facilities, warehouses, fairs and similar structures;

requests from Article 40, paragraph 1, items from (1) to (5) (Article 38, paragraph 1). The Ministry shall issue an urban consent on the base of previously obtained opinion of the Cantonal Ministry of Spatial Planning, (Article 40, paragraph 1).

1038. The urban consent for temporary structures[1140] shall be issued only in exceptional circumstances and for a limited validity period (Article 44, paragraph 1). The urban consent for temporary structures is valid for one year from the date it becomes legally binding. The request for approval for construction must be submitted in that timeframe (Article 46, paragraph 1). Exceptionally, the validity of the urban consent for temporary structures may be extended, for justified reasons, for an additional year (Article 46, paragraph 2).

5. The Buildable Land, Approval for Construction and Technical Inspection

1039. Land use is possible only at arranged buildable land[1141] (Article 47, paragraph 1). The parcelling of buildable land is done on updated geodetic-cadastral plans certified by a competent authority or administration, according to a planning document that is the basis for approval of the construction at the related land (Article 50, paragraph 1).

1040. Construction of structures can be accessed only on the basis of issued construction consent. Construction consent is not necessary to be provided for routine structure maintenance works and for repair of damaged structures that can be classified as ongoing maintenance works (Article 53, paragraph 1).

1041. The Ministry shall perform technical inspection of the structure, within thirty days of receipt of a proper request for issuing of consent for use (Article 68, paragraph 1).[1142] Structure for which is not issued construction permit and consent for use cannot be entered in the land register (Article 77, paragraph 2).

---

(4) structures on the water surfaces (fish farms, floating platforms, etc.); (5) squares, public areas, public green areas, playgrounds, sport structures, cemeteries, landfills, public markets, shelters and similar structures (Art. 36, para. 1).

1140. *Temporary structures*, in terms of this Law, shall be considered as structures built or placed at a temporary designated location for construction site purposes and/or for the application of appropriate construction technology, performing of research activities, etc. (Art. 44, para. 2).

1141. *Arranged buildable land* is considered to be the land on which are completed works of land preparation for the construction and equipping of the land as prescribed in the Law on Construction Land ('Official Gazette of Federation of BiH', No. 25/03) (Art. 47, para. 2).

1142. During technical inspection will be determined that the structure was constructed in accordance to the technical documentation, technical regulations and standards, as well as in accordance to the conditions for the related structure determined by special regulations. Approval for the construction was issued on the base of technical documentation (Art. 68, para. 2).

6. Removal of Structures and Supervision

1042. Removal of structures or part thereof, unless it is a removal based on the inspection decision, can be accessed only on the base of authorization for removal (Article 78, paragraph 1). The request for issuing of authorization for the removal of structure shall be submitted by the owner of the structure (Article 79, paragraph 1).

1043. The Ministry performs supervision over the implementation of planning documents within the jurisdiction of the Federation, this Law and regulations adopted on the base of this law (Article 82, paragraph 1). The tasks of inspection supervision perform Federal urban-construction inspection (Article 83, paragraph 1).[1143]

B. Other Relevant FBiH Regulations

1044.

(1) Law on taking over the Law on housing relations ('Official Gazette of FBiH', Nos 11/98, 38/98 and 19/99).
(2) Law on sale of the apartments covered with the tenant's right ('Official Gazette of FBiH', Nos 27/97, 11/98, 22/99, 27/99, 7/00, 32/01, 15/02, 54/04, 36/06, 51/07 and 72/08).
(3) Law on Suspension of application of the Law on abandoned apartments ('Official Gazette of FBiH', Nos 11/98, 38/98, 12/99, 27/99, 43/99, 54/01 and 29/03).
(4) Law on restitution, granting and sale of apartments ('Official Gazette of FBiH', Nos 28/05 and 2/08).
(5) Law on Implementation of Decisions of the Commission for Preservation of National Monuments ('Official Gazette of FBiH', Nos 2/02, 27/02, 6/04 and 51/07).[1144]

1. Decrees/Rule Books/Decisions

a. Decrees

i. Spatial Planning

1045.

1143. The tasks of the Federal urban inspections in the field of planning shall be conducted by the Federal urban inspector (Art. 83, para. 2). The tasks of the Federal construction inspections in the field of land use at the Federal level shall be conducted by the Federal building inspector (Art. 83, para. 3).

1144. *See*: http://fmpu.gov.ba/zakoni (18 Jul. 2022).

(1) Decree on uniform methodology for preparation of spatial planning documents ('Official Gazette of FBiH', Nos 63/04 and 50/07).[1145]
(2) Decree on special requirements to be fulfilled by companies and other legal entities to be eligible for registration for performing of professional activities for developing of planning documents ('Official Gazette of FBiH', Nos 29/07 and 71/08).
(3) Decree on contents and carriers of the uniform information system, methodology for data collecting and processing, and on uniform forms for keeping the record ('Official Gazette of FBiH', No. 33/07).

ii. Land Use

1046.

(1) Decree on Interventions in Spaceband Building Structures, for which the urban development consent and/or location information is issued by the Federal Ministry of Spatial Planning ('Official Gazette of FBiH', No. 32/14).
(2) Decree on technical features that building structures must comply with in terms of their safety and manner of usage and maintenance thereof ('Official Gazette of FBiH', Nos 29/07, 51/08 and 99/14).
(3) Decree on development of building site, compulsory documentation at building sites and participants in the construction ('Official Gazette of FBiH', Nos 48/09 and 75/09 and 93/12).
(4) Decree on type, content, marking and storing, control and validation of investment-technical documents ('Official Gazette of FBiH', No. 33/10).
(5) Decree on standards, criteria and manner of construction of the shelters and technical norms for safety control of shelters ('Official Gazette of FBiH', Nos 21/05 and 59/07).
(6) Decree on spatial standards, urban-technical conditions and standards for preventing formation of urban-architectural barriers for persons with reduced physical abilities ('Official Gazette of FBiH', No. 48/09).

iii. National Monuments

1047.

(1) Decree on the performance of previous work of investigating character at the national monuments ('Official Gazette of FBiH', No. 36/08).

1145. *See*: *ibid*.

b. Rule books

i. The Construction Sector

1048.

(1) Rule book on technical inspection of the building structure ('Official gazette of FbiH' No. 58/14, 89/18, 44/20, 42/21).[1146]
(2) Rule book on technical characteristics for concrete to be built in concrete constructions ('Official gazette of FBiH' No. 38/08).
(3) Rule book on technical characteristics for chimneys in building structures ('Official Gazette of the FBiH', No. 49/08).
(4) Rule book on technical characteristics for steel and steel products to be embedded in steel construction ('Official Gazette of the FBiH', No. 69/08).
(5) Rule book on technical regulations for construction products to be built in masonry constructions ('Official Gazette of the FBiH', No. 86/08).
(6) Rule book on technical regulations for construction products to be built in concrete constructions ('Official Gazette of the FBiH', No. 86/08).
(7) Rule book on the technical properties of windows and doors ('Official Gazette of FBiH' No. 6/09).
(8) Rule book on conditions for persons who carry out activities of conformity assessment of construction products ('Official Gazette of FBiH', Nos 49/10, 64/11, 94/17, 97/17).
(9) Rule book on conformity assessment of construction products ('Official Gazette of FBiH', Nos 88/10, 64/11, and 44/16).
(10) Rule book on the labelling of construction products ('Official Gazette of FBiH', No. 88/10).
(11) Rule book on technical approvals for construction products ('Official Gazette of F FBiH', No. 2/11).
(12) Rule book on control procedures and the manner of implementing of control procedures for construction products ('Official Gazette of FBiH', No. 28/11).
(13) Rule book on the technical characteristics of the ventilation system, partial air conditioning and air conditioning in building structures ('Official Gazette of FBiH', No. 49/09).
(14) Rule book on the technical characteristics of the heating and cooling systems of building structures ('Official Gazette of FBiH', No. 49/09).
(15) Rule book for geotechnical researches and investigations, organization and content of missions of geotechnical engineering ('Official Gazette of FBiH' No. 60/09, 80/15, 73/21).
(16) Rule book on energy certification of building structures ('Official Gazette of FBiH', No.: 50/10).
(17) Rule book on conditions for persons who carrying out the energy certification of buildings ('Official Gazette of FBiH', No. 28/10).
(18) Rulebook on minimum requirements for energy characteristics of buildings ('Official Gazette of FBiH', No. 81/19).

1146. *See*: *ibid.*

(19) Rulebook on the energy efficiency information system in the Federation of Bosnia and Herzegovina ('Official Gazette of FBiH', No. 2/19).
(20) Rulebook on the procedure for calculating the optimal costs of the minimum requirements for the energy properties of buildings ('Official Gazette of FBiH', No. 31/21).

ii. The Guidelines from the Field of Construction

1049.

(1) Guidelines for conducting of energy inspection for new and existing objects with simple and complex technical systems (August 2009).
(2) Guidelines for disposal of construction waste (May 2009).

c. Decisions

i. Spatial Plan of the Federation of BiH

1050.

(1) Decision on Spatial Plan preparation for the FBiH for the period 2002–2022 ('Official gazette of FBiH' Nos 20/04, 2/08).[1147]

ii. Areas with Specific Characteristics

1051.

(1) Decision on designation of river Una basin area as the area of significance for the F BiH ('Official Gazette of FBiH' Nos 32/04, 80/07).
(2) Decision on Spatial Plan preparation for the areas with specific characteristics of significance for the FBiH – river Una basin for the period 2007–2027 ('Official Gazette of the FBiH' No. 79/07).
(3) Decision on designation of Igman, Bjelasnica, Treskavica and canyon of Rakitnica river (Visocica) as areas with specific characteristic of significance for the Federation of Bosnia and Herzegovina ('Official gazette of the FBiH' Nos 8/05 and 66/08).
(4) Decision on the Regulatory plan preparation for the historical urban area of Mostar for the period 2007–2017 ('Official Gazette of the FBiH', No. 38/08).
(5) Decision on designation of area 'Highway at Vc Corridor' as an area of specific characteristics of significance for the FBIH ('Official Gazette of the FBiH', No. 56/08).

1147. *See*: *ibid*.

(6) Decision on preparation of spatial plan for the areas with specific characteristics of significance for the FBIH 'Highway at Vc Corridor' ('Official Gazette of the FBiH', No. 48/08).
(7) Decision on establishing of body for preparation of Parcelling Plan for the areas of significance for the Federation of BiH ('Official Gazette of the FBiH' No. 25/08).

C. *Cantons of the Federation of BiH*

1052. Federation of Bosnia and Herzegovina, as the entity, consists of ten cantons (which, in administrative terms are further split into eighty municipalities) as follows: Una-Sana Canton, Posavina Canton, Tuzla Canton, Zenica-Doboj Canton, Bosnia – Podrinje Canton, Central Bosnia Canton, Herzegovina-Neretva Canton, West Herzegovina Canton, Sarajevo Canton, and Canton 10.[1148] Basic laws related to the urbanism, spatial planning and environment include the following:

1. Bosnia-Podrinje Canton Goražde

1053.
(1) Law on Communal Activities of BPC (Official Gazette of BPC Goražde No. 9/13).[1149]
(2) Law on non-profit social habitation in BPC Goražde (Official Gazette of BPC Goražde No. 9/13).
(3) Law on Spatial Planning and Construction of BPC Goražde – Revised text (Official Gazette of BPC Goražde No. 7/13).
(4) Law on apartment renting in BPC Gorazde (Official Gazette of BPC Goražde No. 7/04).
(5) Law on Maintenance of the common parts of buildings and on building management.
(6) The Law on Environmental Protection of BPC (Revised text: Official Gazette of BPC Goražde Nos 5/05, 11/10 and 8/11-corrective).
(7) Law on Water of BPC (Official Gazette of BPC Goražde No. 6/10).

1148. As already mentioned, it should be kept in mind that cantons, in addition to the regulations that are adopted at the cantonal level, also apply the regulations of the Federation of BiH. For example, six cantons implement Law on Environmental Protection of the FBiH (Official Gazette FBiH, No. 33/03, 38/09) (Sarajevo Canton, Canton 10, Posavina Canton, Tuzla Canton, Una-Sana Canton, Zenica-Doboj Canton). They do not have their own environmental protection law. However, cantonal law on environmental protection is in force in four cantons (Herzegovina-Neretva Canton, Bosnia-Podrinje Canton, Central Bosnia Canton, and West Herzegovina Canton). In these cantons, their own environmental protection laws are applied (for some issues), in addition to the law passed at the level of the FBiH. The situation is similar in some other areas (spatial planning and construction, waters, air protection, etc). A list of the basic laws is given below.
1149. *See*: http://mu.bpkg.gov.ba/preuzmanja/71/zakoni-i-propisi (18 Jul. 2022).

(8) Law on Noise Protection (Official Gazette of BPC Goražde No. 9/13 – revised text).

2. Sarajevo Canton

1054.

(1) Law on Spatial Planning (Official Gazette CS No. 24/17).[1150]
(2) Law on Environmental Protection (Official Gazette CS No. 33/03, and 38/09).
(3) Law on Nature Protection (Official Gazette CS No. 66/13).
(4) Law on Waste Management (Official Gazette CS No. 33/03, 72/09, and 92/17).
(5) Law on Noise Protection (Official Gazette CS No. 23/16).
(6) Law on Forestry (Official Gazette CS No. 05/13).
(7) Law on Waters (Official Gazette CS No. 18/10, and 43/16).
(8) Law on temporary use of public surfaces at the cantonal area (Official Gazette CS No. 20/04, 26/12, 32/12 and 24/15).[1151]

3. Herzegovina-Neretva Canton

1055.

(1) Law on Spatial Planning (Official Gazette HNC No. 4/04).[1152]
(2) Construction Law (Official Gazette HNC No. 5/04).
(3) Law on Concessions (Official Gazette HNC Nos 2/03, 1/06).
(4) Law on Environmental Protection (Official Gazette HNC No. 7/04).
(5) Law on Waste Management (Official Gazette HNC No. 6/06).
(6) Law on Nature Protection (Official Gazette HNC No. 3/05).
(7) Law on Air Protection (Official Gazette HNC No. 7/14).
(8) Law on Environmental Protection Fund of HNC (Official Gazette HNC No. 6/12).

1150. Authority: Ministry of Communal Economy, Infrastructure, Spatial Planning, Construction and Environmental Protection; *See*: https://mkipgo.ks.gov.ba/ (18 Jul. 2022).
1151. For the complete list of relevant regulations, *see*: https://mkipgo.ks.gov.ba/legislativa (18 Jul. 2022).
1152. Authority: Ministry of construction, and spatial planning; Ministry of trade, tourism and environmental protection. *See*: https://www.vlada-hnz-k.ba/hr/ministarstvo-trgovine-turizma-i-zastite-okolisa, https://www.vlada-hnz-k.ba/bs/ministarstvo-gradenja-i-prostornog-uredenja (18 Jul. 2022).

4. Canton 10 (Livno)

1056.
(1) Law on Spatial Planning (Official Gazette HBC No. 12/14).[1153]
(2) Construction Law (Official Gazette HBC No. 3/16).

5. Posavina Conaton

1057.
(1) Law on Spatial Planning (Official Gazette PC Nos 5/99, 7/00).[1154]
(2) Construction Law (Official Gazette PC Nos 5/99, 7/00, 5/01).
(3) Law on Concessions (Official Gazette PC No. 6/03).
(4) Law on Environmental protection (Official Gazette PC No. 4/00).
(5) Law on Waters (Official Gazette PC No. 2/00).
(6) Law on Agricultural Land (Official Gazette PC No. 2/00).

6. Central Bosnia Canton

1058.
(1) Law on Spatial Planning (Official Gazette CBC No. 11/14).[1155]
(2) Construction Law (Official Gazette CBC No. 10/14).
(3) Law on Waters (Official Gazette CBC No. 11/09).
(4) Law on Environmental Protection (Official Gazette CBC No. 04/05).
(5) Law on Protection of Nature (Official Gazette CBC No. 04/05).
(6) Law on Waste (Official Gazette CBC No. 04/05).
(7) Law on Air Protection (Official Gazette CBC No. 11/00).
(8) Law on Noise Protection (Official Gazette CBC No. 11/00).
(9) Law on Concessions (Official Gazette CBC Nos 08/09, 6/13 and 9/15).
(10) Law on Forestry (Official Gazette CBC Nos 14/02, 2/05).

7. Tuzla Canton

1059.

1153. Authority: Ministry of construction, reconstruction, spatial planning and environmental protection. *See*: http://www.vladahbz.com/ministarstvo-graditeljstva-obnove-prostornog-uredenja-i-zastite-okolisa/propisi-ministarstva/ (18 Jul. 2022).

1154. Authority: Ministry of economy and spatial planning; Ministry of traffic, connections, and environmental protection; municipal departments for urban affairs. *See*: https://www.zupanijaposavska.ba/ministarstvo-gospodarstva-rada-i-prostornog-uredenja/, https://www.zupanijaposavska.ba/ministarstvo-prometa-veza-i-zastite-okolisa/ (18 Jul. 2022).

1155. Authority: Ministry of physical planning, construction, environmental protection, returns and housing *See*: http://sbk-ksb.gov.ba/bs/ministarstvo-prostornog-ure%C4%91enja,-gra%C4%91enja,-za%C5%A1tite-okoli%C5%A1a,-povratka-i-stambenih-poslova.html#osnovni-dokumenti-koji-reguliraju-rad (18 Jul. 2022).

(1) Law on Spatial Planning and Construction (Official Gazette TC No. 6/11, 4/13, 15/13).[1156]
(2) Law on Conditions and Procedures for Legalization of Illegally Constructed Objects (Official Gazette TC Nos 3/06, 1/07, 5/08, 10/11).
(3) Law on Communal Activities (Official Gazette TC Nos 11/05, 7/07, 8/12).
(4) Law on Concessions (Official Gazettes TC Nos 5/04, 7/05, 6/11, 1/13 and 11/14).
(5) Environmental Protection Plan 2015–2020 (Official Gazette TC No. 5/15).
(6) Law on Environmental Protection (Official Gazette TC Nos 6/98, 15/00).
(7) Law on Nature Protection (Official Gazette TC No. 10/04).
(8) Law on Forestry (Official Gazette TC No. 9/12).
(9) Law on waters (Official Gazette TC No. 11/08).
(10) Law on Protection from Noise (Official Gazette TC No. 3/16).

8. Una-Sana Canton

1060. Basic construction and other relevant laws:[1157]

(1) Law on Spatial Planning and Construction (Official Gazette USC Nos 10/11, 13/11, 19/11 and 8/13).
(2) Law on use, managing and maintenance of common building facilities and equipment (Official Gazette USC No. 32/12).
(3) Law on Communal activities of Una-Sana Canton (Official Gazette USC No. 4/11, 11/11, 6/12 and 13/12).
(4) Law on Waste Management (Official Gazette USC No. 4/12, and 8/14).
(5) Law on Concessions (Official Gazette USC No. 10/03, and 7/09).
(6) Law on Forests of Una-Sana Canton (Official Gazette USC Nos 22/12, and 16/16).
(7) Law on Water of Una-Sana Canton (Official Gazette USC No. 4/11).
(8) Law on Noise Protection (Official Gazette USC No. 3/13).

9. West-Herzegovina Canton

1061.
(1) Law on Spatial Planning (Official Gazette ZHC Nos 4/99, 15/01, 10/03 and 18/11).[1158]

1156. Authority: Ministry of spatial planning and environmental protection; *See*: http://www.vladatk.kim.ba/dokumenti-mpuzo (18 Jul. 2022). *See also*: https://www.kuiptk.ba/index.php/zakoni/zakoni1/zastita-okolice.html (18 Jul. 2022).
1157. Authority: Ministry of construction, spatial planning and environmental protection; municipal departments for urban affairs. *See*: http://vladausk.ba/v4/index/ministarstvo-za-gradjenje-prostorno-uredjenje-i-zastite-okolisa/5# (18 Jul. 2022).
1158. Authority: Ministry of spatial planning and environmental protection; municipal departments for urban affairs. https://www.mpugzo-zzh.com/hr/prostorno-uredjenje-i-gradjenje (18 Jul. 2022).

(2) Law on Construction (Official Gazette ZHC Nos 4/99, 15/01, 10/03 and 18/11).
(3) Law on Environmental Protection (Official Gazette ZHC No. 8/13).
(4) Law on Concessions (Official Gazette ZHC Nos 7/01, 7/03, 13/07).
(5) Law on Protection from Noise (Official Gazette ZHC No. 17/14).

10. Zenica-Doboj Canton

1062.
(1) Law on Spatial Planning and Construction (Official Gazette ZDC No. 1/14).[1159]
(2) Law on management and maintenance of residential and residential/business buildings (Official Gazette ZDC No. 2/08).
(3) Law on Noise Protection (Official Gazette ZDC No. 1/14).
(4) Law on Waters (Official Gazette ZDC No. 17/07).
(5) Law on Concessions (Official Gazette ZDC No. 5/03).
(6) Law on Environmental Protection (Official Gazette ZDC No. 1/00).
(7) Law on Communal Activities (Official Gazette ZDC No. 17/08).

III. Brčko District of Bosnia and Herzegovina

A. *Basic Law*

1063. Basic law is Law on Spatial Planning and Construction (Official Gazette BD BiH, No. 29/08, 18/17, 48/18, 54/18, 10/20, 29/20, and 40/20).[1160]

B. *Other Related BD Regulations*

1064.
(1) Law on Legalization of the Illegally Built Constructions (Official Gazette BD BiH', Nos 21/03, 3/04, 29/04, 19/07, 54/18).
(2) Law on Environmental Protection (Official Gazette BD BiH, Nos 24/04, 1/05, 19/07 and 9/09).
(3) Law on Air Protection (Official Gazette BD BiH, Nos 25/04, 1/05; 19/07 and 9/09).
(4) Law on Protection of Waters (Official Gazette BD BiH, Nos 23/06, 25/04, 1/05 and 19/07).

1159. Authority: Ministry of spatial planning, traffic, communications and environmental protection; municipal departments for urban affairs. https://www.zdk.ba/propisi/category/9-prostorno-uredenje-promet-i-komunikacije-i-zastita-okoline (18 Jul. 2022).

1160. *See*: https://skupstinabd.ba/ba/zakon.html?lang=ba&id=/Zakon%20o%20prostornom%20planiranju%20i%20gradjenju (18 Jul. 2022).

(5) Law on Waste Management (Official Gazette BD BiH, Nos 25/04, 1/05, 19/08, 9/09, 22/18).
(6) Law on Roads (Official Gazette BD BiH, Nos 43/04, 19/07, 17/9, 9/13, and 22/18).
(7). Law on Agricultural Land (Official Gazette BD BiH, Nos 32/04, 20/06, 19/07).
(8) Law on Land Registry and Rights over Land (Official Gazette BD BiH, Nos 11/01, 1/03, 14/03, 19/07 and 2/08).
(9) Law on Ownership and Other Rights (Official Gazette BD BiH, Nos 11/01, 8/03, 40/04, 19/07, and 26/21).
(10) Law on Forests of BDBiH (Official Gazette BD BiH, Nos 14/10, and 26/16).
(11) Law on Administrative Proceeding (Official Gazette BD BiH, Nos 48/11, 21/18, and 23/19).

C. Basic Bylaws/Rule Books/Decrees

1065.

(1) Rule book on plants and machineries which must have estimation of the environmental impact and on plants and facilities which can be built only with the environmental permit (Official Gazette BD BiH, No. 30/06).
(2) Rulebook on the content of the environmental impact study (Official Gazette BD BiH, No. 2/07).
(3) Rule book on conditions for submission of the requests for issuance of ecological permit for plants and facilities which have environmental permits issued before entering into force of the Law on Life Environment Protection (Official Gazette BD BiH, No. 2/07).
(4) Rule book on deadlines for submission of the requests for issuance of ecological permit (Official Gazette BD BiH, No. 2/07).

Part IV. Liability Questions

Chapter 1. Civil Liability

§1. The Republic of Srpska

I. Law on Environmental Protection

1066. Law on Environmental Protection (Chapter XI, Articles 118–126) regulates civil liability for damage caused to the environment by any legal entity or natural person. Articles 118–120 stipulate the obligations of legal entities and natural persons to ensure environmental protection while performing their activities, as well as liabilities and obligations of polluters. A legal entity or natural person is responsible for the environmental pollution if it enables or allows environmental pollution by illegal or improper activities (Article 119, paragraph 2). The pollutants that by their acts or by omissions cause environmental pollution shall immediately take the necessary measures to reduce damage to the environment or eliminate further risks, hazards or remediation of the damage to the environment, at their own expense (Article 120, paragraph 1).[1161]

1067. Articles 121–124 are of special importance, as they define the obligation of a polluter responsible for damage caused to the environment to cover the costs of damage assessment and remedying, and the liability of legal entities involved in a business that poses threat on the environment for damage to persons, property and the environment caused by the business activity, as well as financial guarantees and liability exemptions. The polluter[1162] is liable for the damage caused to the environment and space, and bears the costs of damage assessment and its remediation (Article 121, paragraph 1).[1163]

1161. If the damage made to the environment cannot be remedied by appropriate measures, the polluter which caused the damage is responsible for compensation in amount of the destroyed property value (Art. 120, para. 2).

1162. Polluter that causes environmental pollution is responsible for resulting damages under the principle of strict liability (Art. 119, para. 1).

1163. The polluter is obliged to provide financial or other guarantee to secure the payment of compensation costs under para. 1 of this article, during and after carrying out the activities (Art. 121, para. 2).

1068. A legal entity engaged in activities dangerous to the environment is responsible for the damage caused by the activities to people, property and the environment (Article 122, paragraph 1).[1164]

The responsible person performing the activity dangerous to the environment is required to provide funds for the compensation of potential damage (Article 124, paragraph 1). Any person who has suffered damage has the right to compensation (Article 125, paragraph 1).

II. Law on Waters

1069. RS Law on Waters defines water pollution liabilities. Article 64 of the Law on Waters stipulates operator's obligations and liabilities in case of an accident. If a water pollution threat has occurred, a person or operator is obliged to immediately take all required actions to prevent or mitigate the impact of the accident, to prevent reoccurrence of the accident, and to inform the nearest police station, water inspection or agency (paragraph 1).[1165] Costs of the actions taken shall be covered by the legal entity or natural person that caused the pollution or pollution threat by their action or failure to take action (paragraph 8).[1166]

§2. Federation of Bosnia and Herzegovina

I. Law on Environmental Protection

1070. Chapter XII 'Financing Environmental Damages and Liability for Environmental Damage' of the FBiH Law on Environmental Protection regulates Civil Liability for Environmental Damage (Articles 114-122). Legal and natural persons are obliged to ensure environmental protection in the performance of their activities, namely (a) application and implementation of regulations on environmental protection, (b) sustainable use of natural resources, goods and energy, (c) introduction of more energy-efficient technologies and renewable natural resources, (d) using products, processes, technologies and practices that pose less risk to the environment, (e) taking measures to prevent or eliminate the consequences of endangerment and damage to the environment, (f) keeping records of raw materials and

1164. Activities dangerous for the environment are those activities that pose a significant risk to people, property or the environment, including (Art. 122, para. 2): (a) The management of sites that are dangerous to the environment, (b) The release of genetically modified organisms, and (c) The release of microorganisms.

1165. Immediately upon learning of water pollution or pollution threat, the relevant Agency for Waters shall take actions to eliminate or prevent pollution (Art. 64, para. 4).

1166. Articles 161–164 of the Law on Waters define conditions and procedures for temporary and permanent revoking of a water law act, if the user of the act fails to take action within the time frame determined in the water act causing immediate threat on life and health of people, if conditions specified in the water act were seriously violated, or if an activity causes impacts prohibited by the Law on Waters.

energy consumption, pollutants and energy, classification, characteristics and quantities of waste, (g) control of activities and operation of facilities that may pose a risk or cause danger to the environment and human health, (h) other measures in accordance with this Law (Article 115).[1167]

1071. The operator is not responsible for damage caused by: (a) war; (b) natural disaster or other force majeure; (c) by a third party intending to cause harm; or (d) due to the implementation of special orders and measures of the competent authorities that affected the occurrence of damage (Article 117, paragraph 1).[1168]

1072. An operator performing an activity dangerous to the environment shall be liable for damage caused by that activity to people, property and the environment. The possibility that an activity dangerous to the environment causes damage shall be assessed on the basis of the mode of operation, facilities used, type and concentration of substances used or generated by that activity, use of genetically modified organisms or microorganisms, meteorological conditions and time and place of damage (Article 116, paragraphs 1, and 2).[1169]

1073. If the dangerous activity causes damage to the environment, the operator is obliged to compensate the costs of damage assessment and the costs of measures to restore the state that was immediately before the damage occurred or to mitigate the damage caused to the environment, as well as compensation for damage caused to persons and property caused by the dangerous activity (Article 120, paragraph 1).[1170] If the damage caused to the environment cannot be remediated by appropriate measures, the person who caused the damage is liable for compensation in the amount of destroyed property (Article 121, paragraph 1).[1171]

1167. The environmental protection measures referred to in paragraph (1) of this article shall be performed by a legal and natural person independently or through an authorized legal entity (Art. 115, para. 2).
1168. The operator shall be released from liability for damage if he proves that he has applied appropriate protection measures in order to prevent or mitigate the damage (Art. 117, para. 2).
1169. Plants and plants such as mines, mineral oil or refinery deposits, gas supply and smelting plants, thermal power plants, coke ovens, metal and mineral production and processing plants, chemical plants, treatment plants, heat treatment and storage wastewater treatment plants, slaughterhouses, dyehouses and tanneries, papermaking plants, dams and hydropower infrastructure, gas or oil pipelines and storage facilities and liquefied atmospheric gases are hazardous to the environment due to the way they are managed, the materials they use or the activities which is performed in them (Art. 116, para. 3).
1170. The costs referred to in paragraph (1) of this article shall be borne by the operator whose activity caused the damage (Art. 120, para. 2). However, the provisions of this article shall not apply to activities whose main purpose is national defence or international security, nor to activities whose sole purpose is protection against natural disasters (para. 3).
1171. An operator performing an activity dangerous to the environment shall be obliged to provide funds for compensation of damage caused to the environment through insurance or by allocating a monetary amount for special purposes (Art. 119, para. 1).

II. The Law on Waters

1074. The Law on Waters defines liabilities for damages caused by water. In case of existence of a water pollution threat, the legal entity or natural person, which activity or failure caused such risk, must immediately take all precautions to prevent or mitigate accident-caused impacts, to prevent reoccurrence of the accident, and notify the nearest police station, water inspection, FBiH Environmental Inspection, Agency for Waters or the operative civil protection centre without delay (Article 61, paragraph 1).[1172]

1075. Articles 135–138 of the Law on Waters define conditions and procedures for temporary and permanent revoking of a water act, if the user of the act fails to take action within the time frame determined in the water act, thus causing immediate threat on life and health of people, if conditions specified in the water act were seriously violated, or if an activity which causes impacts is prohibited by the Law on Waters.

§3. Brčko District of Bosnia and Herzegovina

1076. Brčko District of BiH Law on Environmental Protection (Chapter XVI, Civil Liability for Environmental Damage) defines the liability and obligation of legal entities and natural persons for causing environmental damages (Articles 99–107).

1172. The relevant Agency for Waters shall take actions to eliminate or prevent pollution immediately after finding out of water pollution or pollution threat (Art. 61, para. 4). The Costs of the actions taken (elimination of consequences) shall be covered by the legal entity or natural person that caused the pollution or pollution threat by their action or failure to take action (Art. 61, para. 8).

Chapter 2. Criminal Liability

1077. The protection of the environment through criminal law is regulated by the criminal codes of the RS, FBiH and BDBiH.[1173]

§1. Criminal Code

1078. Criminal legislation includes criminal provisions contained in the criminal laws of Bosnia and Herzegovina, the Federation of Bosnia and Herzegovina, the Republic of Srpska and the Brčko District of Bosnia and Herzegovina, and, to a lesser extent, the provisions on criminal responsibility prescribed in other laws.[1174] Criminal offences against the environment are stipulated in the criminal laws of the FBiH, RS and BD. These are the following:

(1) Criminal Code of the RS (Official Gazette of RS, No. 64/17, 104/18-CC, 15/21, 89/21) – Chapter XXIX – Criminal offences against environment.[1175]
(2) Criminal Code of the FBiH (Official Gazette of FBiH, Nos 36/03, 37/03, 21/04, 69/04, 18/05, 42/10, 42/11, 59/14, 76/14, 46/16, 75/17) – Chapter XXVI, – Criminal offences against environment, agriculture and natural resources.[1176]

1173. For additional information, *see*: Directorate for European Integration, *Answers to the Questionnaire, Chapter 27, Environment and climate change*, 27 Feb. 2018, pp. 312–326.
1174. Criminal Code of Bosnia and Herzegovina does not specify offences against the environment.
1175. Environmental Pollution (Art. 370), Environmental pollution with waste materials (Art. 371), Endangering the environment by noise or non-ionizing radiation (Art. 372), Illegal construction and putting in function facilities and plants (Art. 373), Damaging of facilities and devices for environmental protection (Art. 374), Destruction or damage of protected natural resource (Art. 375), Destruction of habitat (Art. 376), Production of harmful substances for treatment of animals (Art. 377), Contaminating of fodder and water used for feeding the animals (Art. 378), Illegal removal and introduction of strictly protected plants or animals or genetically modified organisms (Art. 379), Ozone Layer Endangering (Art. 380), Failure to comply with regulations for suppressing of animal and plant diseases (Art. 381), Unconscientious action in trade with pesticides (Art. 382), Unconscientious providing of veterinary assistance (Art. 383), Unauthorized providing of veterinary services (Art. 384), Destruction of plantations (Art. 385), Non enforcement of decision on environment protection measures (Art. 386), Importing of dangerous substances into the Republic of Srpska (Art. 387), Forests devastation (Art. 388), Causing fire (Art. 389), Torturing and killing of animals (Art. 390), Illegal occupation and exploitation of natural resources and goods of general importance (Art. 391), Illegal hunting (Art. 392), Illegal fishing (Art. 393).
1176. Chapter XXVI prescribes criminal offences against the environment and the related penalties, as follows: Art. 303–Environmental Pollution, Art. 304–Endangering the Environment with devices, Art. 305 – Endangering the Environment by Waste, Art. 306 – Endangering the Environment by Noise, Art. 307–Production of harmful substances for the treatment of animals, Art. 308–Veterinary Malpractice, Art. 309–Unauthorized Rendering of Veterinary Services. Art. 310–Failure to Comply with Regulations for Suppressing Animal and Plant Diseases, Art. 311–Concealing the Existence of a Contagious Animal Disease, Art. 312–Contaminating Fodder or Water Used by Livestock, Art. 313–Destruction of Plantations, Art. 314–Careless Actions in Circulation of Pesticides, Art. 315–Devastation of Forests, Art. 316–Forest Theft, Art. 317–Causing Forest Fire, Art. 318–Torturing and Killing an Animal, Art. 319–Illegal Hunting, Art. 320 – Illegal Fishing, Art.

(3) Criminal Code of the BD (Official Gazette of BD BiH, No. 33/13, 26/16, 13/17, 50/18, 19/20) – Chapter XXVI, Articles 297–316 – Criminal offences against environment, agriculture and natural resources.

1079. The following types of criminal sanctions are prescribed by the criminal legislation: punishments,[1177] warning measures/sanctions,[1178] security measures[1179] and educational measures[1180] (The Law on Criminal Code of FBiH, Article 6; and The Law on Criminal Code of RS, Article 41).

1080. In the five-year period from 2007–2011 courts in Bosnia and Herzegovina resolved 3,646 criminal cases in the field of environment out of which 97%, i.e., 3,570 cases were related to criminal offences of forest stealing. The proceedings were suspended, charges dropped or acquitted in 13% or 459 cases. Suspended sentences are issued in 72% or 2,618 cases, fines in 9% or 311 cases and prison sentences in 7% or 253 cases, while in four cases court citations and in one case corrective measure were issued.[1181] Not a single case was processed in accordance with the Law on Waters and the Waste Management Law.

§2. Criminal Provisions in Specific Laws

1081. Environmental legislation in RS, FBiH and BDBiH defines offences only (only administrative responsibility is envisaged).

§3. Minor Offence Responsibility

1082. In addition to criminal liability under criminal justice legislation in BiH, the legislation that regulates the minor offences prescribes responsibility of natural persons and legal entities for violations of public order or rules on economic and

321–Damage, Destruction and Illicit Export of Cultural Monuments and Protected Natural Objects, and Art. 322–Illicit Research and Appropriation of Cultural Monuments.

1177. The following punishments may be imposed on perpetrators of criminal offences that are criminally responsible: imprisonment, long-term imprisonment and fine.

1178. Warning measures are: measures of suspension and judicial admonition.

1179. The following security measures may be imposed on perpetrators of criminal offences: (a) mandatory psychiatric treatment, (b) mandatory medical treatment of addiction, (c) ban on carrying out a certain occupation, activity or duty, (d) ban on driving a motor vehicle, (e) forfeiture.

1180. Educational measures are imposed on juvenile perpetrators of criminal offences.

1181. BiH Council of Ministers, *Answers to the List of EU Questions on Chapter 27, Environment, supra* p. 105. Average fines amounted BAM 628 and the collection rate was 46% in the above mentioned period. Average prison sentence imposed was 4.6 months and average proceedings costs amounted BAM 89. Average period of time from starting the proceedings until the first instance sentence lasted ten months. In case of appeals the second instance sentence was passed by an average of six months. For more information, *see*: Directorate for European Integration, *Answers to the Questionnaire, Chapter 27, Environment and climate change*, 27 Feb. 2018, pp. 326–339.

financial operations specified by law or regulation, which are determined by the characteristics and prescribed sanctions.[1182]

1083. The minor offence laws stipulate that the perpetrator may be imposed by the following sanctions: (a) fine, (b) reprimand, (c) conditional sentence and (d) protective measures (seizure of items, ban on performing occupation, activity or duty, full or partial prohibition to operate a motor vehicle and out-patient treatment of addiction).[1183]

§4. Minor Offence Responsibility in Environmental Laws

1084. All the environmental laws include minor offence provisions, which provide for civil liabilities for violation of these laws. Minor offence provisions are listed below, which describe infringements in the field of environmental protection and the ranges of fines for such violations.

I. The Republic of Srpska

1085.

(1) RS Law on Environmental Protection (Official Gazette of RS, Nos 71/12, 79/15, and 70/20 – Articles 132–133).
(2) RS Law on Nature Protection (Official Gazette of RS, No. 20/14 – Articles 96–98).
(3) RS Law on Air Protection (Official Gazette of RS, No. 124/11, and 46/17 – Articles 75–78, and 78a).
(4) RS Law on Waste Management (Official Gazette of RS, No. 111/13, 106/15,16/18, 70/20, 63/21 – Articles 92–95).
(5) RS Law on Waters (Official Gazette of RS, No. 50/06, 92/09, 121/12 and 74/17– Articles 210–213).

II. Federation of Bosnia and Herzegovina

1086.

(1) FBiH Law on Environmental Protection (Official Gazette of FBiH, No, 15/21 – Article 141-145).

1182. The following laws on minor offence are applicable in BiH: BiH Law on Minor Offence (Official Gazette of BiH, Nos 41/07, 18/12, 36/14, 81/15, 65/20), FBiH Law on Minor Offence (Official Gazette of FBiH, No. 63/14), RS Law on Minor Offence (Official Gazette of RS, Nos. 63/14, 36/15-CC, 110/16, 100/17, 19/21-CC), Law on Minor Offence of the BDBiH (Official Gazette of BDBiH, Nos. 24/07, 29/16, 6/22).

1183. In addition to the above sanctions for the minor offences, the following measures may also be imposed: (a) seizure of property gain, (b) mandatory compensation of damage, (c) negative points, and (d) deprivation of liberty in order to collect fine.

(2) FBiH Law on Nature Protection (Official Gazette of FBiH, No. 66/13 – Articles 232–235).
(3) FBiH Law on Air Protection (Official Gazette of FBiH, No 33/03, 4/10 – Articles 35 and 36).
(4) FBiH Law on Waste Management (Official Gazette of FBiH, Nos 33/03, 72/09, 92/17 – Article 53).
(5) FBiH Law on Water FBiH (Official Gazette of FBiH, No. 70/06 – Articles 204–206).

III. Brčko District of Bosnia and Herzegovina

1087.
(1) Law on Environmental Protection of BD BiH (Official Gazette of BDBiH, Nos 24/04, 19/07, 1/05, 9/09 – Article 112).
(2) Law on Nature Protection of BD BiH (Official Gazette of BDBiH, Nos 24/04, 1/05, 19/07, 9/09 and 10/18 – Article 46).
(3) Law on Air Protection of BD BiH (Official Gazette of BDBiH, Nos 25/04, 19/07, 1/05, 9/09, 17/22 – Article 45).
(4) Law on Waste Management of BD BiH (Official Gazette of BDBiH, Nos 25/04, 19/07, 1/05, 2/08, 9/09, 22/18
– Article 56).
(5) Law on Water Protection of BD BiH (Official Gazette of BDBiH, Nos 25/04, 1/05, 19/07 – Article 63).

§5. Liability of Legal Entities for Criminal Offences and Minor Offences

1088. Criminal Codes of FBiH, RS and BD envisage criminal liability of domestic and foreign legal entities for the offences stipulated in these laws, which include crimes against the environment.[1184]

1089. The minor offence laws prescribe that the provisions of the criminal laws related to the criminal liability of legal entity shall be applied *mutatis mutandis* to the entity accused of committing a minor offence, unless otherwise prescribed by minor offence legislation.[1185]

1184. The following punishments may be imposed upon legal entities for criminal offences: fine; seizure of property; dissolution of the legal entity.

1185. The following sanctions may be imposed on a legal person due to the liability for a minor offence: seizure of property gain, mandatory compensation of damage.

Part V. Juridical Actions of Individuals

§1. Structure of Judicial System

1090. Taking into account the specific constitutional and territorial organization, there are four court systems in Bosnia and Herzegovina: the court system of BiH,[1186] the court systems of the Entities (RS, and FBiH)[1187] and the court system of the BD BiH.[1188]'In accordance with complex constitutional arrangements, the legal system in BiH is also organized in a complex way. ... As it was pointed out in the 2010 and 2011 European EC Progress Report, these complexities pose serious challenges to the functioning of the judicial system.'[1189] The Council of Ministers of Bosnia and Herzegovina, at the 25th session held on 3 February 2021 adopted the Decision on the formation of a Working Group for drafting the Strategy for the

1186. At the level of BiH, there are the Constitutional Court of BiH, the Court of BiH and the Prosecutor's Office of BiH. *For more detailed information, see EU – Bosnia and Herzegovina, SAA structured dialogue on justice, technical information requested by the European Commission,* Sarajevo, 2011, pp. 1–57. The judicial branch established by Dayton consists of a State-level Constitutional Court. The High Judicial and Prosecutorial Council, as well as a State Court and Prosecutor Office, were established later. EC, *Bosnia and Herzegovina 2013 Progress Report, supra* p. 3.

1187. In the Federation of BiH there are: the Constitutional Court of FBiH, the Supreme Court of FBiH, the FBiH Prosecutor's Office, the municipal and cantonal courts and the cantonal prosecutor's offices. In Republic of Srpska there are the courts of general and of special jurisdiction. The courts of general jurisdiction are: basic courts, district courts and the Supreme Court of the Republic of Srpska. The courts of special jurisdiction are the district commercial courts and the Higher Commercial Court.

1188. Brčko District has the Appellate and the Basic Court and the Prosecutor's Office of BD.

1189. Sali-Terzić, S. *Study on the capacities of the judicial institutions (courts) to address the needs and demands of specific groups: Persons with Disabilities, Roma, and women in Bosnia and Herzegovina, Strengthening Judicial Integrity through Enhanced Access to Justice*, UNDP, 2011. p. 13. *For detailed information see* EC, *Bosnia and Herzegovina 2011 Progress Report,* accompanying the document, Communication from the Commission to the European Parliament and the Council, Enlargement Strategy and Main Challenges 2011–2012, COM(2011) 666 final, European Commission, Brussels, 12 Oct. 2011. EC, *Bosnia and Herzegovina 2010 Progress Report,* accompanying the document, Communication from the Commission to the European Parliament and the Council, Enlargement Strategy and Main Challenges 2010–2011, {COM(2010) 660}, European Commission, Brussels, 09 Nov. 2010.

reform of the justice sector in Bosnia and Herzegovina and the Action Plan.[1190] However, Bosnia and Herzegovina is at an early stage and has some level of preparation as regards its judiciary.[1191]

1091. 'One of the key impediments to efficiency and effectiveness in the courts is the backlog of cases, which at the end of 2006 stood at 1.9 million cases. Around 56% of this total related to execution cases for small value claims, and around 20% for violation cases.'[1192]

§2. Legal Aid

1092. The following legislation on legal aid is in force in BiH: Law on Free Legal Aid of the BiH (Official Gazette of BiH, No. 83/16); Law on Exercise of the Right to Free Legal Assistance in the Republic of Srpska (Official Gazette of RS, No. 67/20); Law on the Cantonal Free Legal Aid Institute of the Zenica-Doboj Canton (Official Gazette of the ZDC, No. 1/14); Law on the Cantonal Free Legal Aid Institute of the West-Herzegovina Canton (Official Gazette of the West Herzegovina Canton, No. 5/08); Law on Free Legal Aid of the Tuzla Canton (Official Gazette of the TC No. 10/08); Law on Free Legal Aid of the Sarajevo Canton (Official Gazette of the SC No. 1/12, 26/14, 40/17); Law on Free Legal Aid of the Una-Sana Canton (Official Gazette of the USC No. 22/12); Law on Free Legal Aid Office of the BD BiH (Official Gazette of the BD BiH, No. 19/07, 23/19).[1193]

1093. 'The country needs to develop a comprehensive strategic framework on human rights and on the protection of minorities, including on transitional justice.'[1194] 'Without comprehensive coverage and clear minimum common standards, the right to legal aid continues to be upheld unevenly, to the detriment of the most vulnerable. The legal framework needs to be completed by adopting laws in the Federation entity and the Central Bosnia Canton. A needs assessment is required to

1190. See: http://www.sluzbenenovine.ba/page/akt/lvelUWiXkR0= (26 Jul. 2022).

1191. EC. *Bosnia and Herzegovina 2021 Progress Report*, European Commission, Strasbourg, 19.10.2021, p. 4. 'Lack of commitment to judicial reform from political actors, and the poor functioning of the judicial system continued to undermine the citizens' enjoyment of rights and the fight against corruption and organised crime'. Ibid. In addition, 'the length of proceedings remains a major concern.' *Ibid.*, p. 19.

1192. BiH, Ministry of Justice, *Bosnia and Herzegovina Justice Sector Reform Strategy, 2008–2012*, Sarajevo, June 2008, p. 19.

1193. Free legal aid beneficiaries are exclusively indigent individuals. Types of free legal aid are the following: provision of general information about the rights and obligations, legal advice and assistance in completing the forms, providing legal assistance in the preparation of all types of documents, representation in court, etc. Free legal aid is provided, among others, in litigation and in administrative disputes.

1194. EC. *Bosnia and Herzegovina 2021 Progress Report,* p. 25. *See also*, Human Rights Watch, Bosnia and Herzegovina, Events of 2021. https://www.hrw.org/world-report/2022/country-chapters/bosnia-and-herzegovina (26 Jul. 2022). Bosnia and Herzegovina, *National report submitted in accordance with paragraph 5 of the annex to Human Rights Council resolution 16/21*, Human Rights Council, General Assembly, A/HRC/WG.6/34/BIH/1, 22 Oct. 2019, https://documents-dds-ny.un.org/doc/UNDOC/GEN/G19/310/04/PDF/G1931004.pdf?OpenElement (1 Aug. 2022).

identify and address the main gaps and ensure effective equal access to justice for all, irrespective of the place of residence.'[1195]

1195. *Ibid.*, p. 32.

Chapter 1. Administrative Remedies

1094. In the cases of environmental damage, NGOs and individuals are entitled to access the courts through administrative dispute in the following two ways: (1) instigating an administrative dispute,[1196] (2) getting involved in an ongoing administrative dispute. Apart from that, according to the general rules with regard to damages, any person may request from the court in a civil action to be awarded compensation for damages suffered as a result of damage to the environment by another natural person or legal entity.[1197]

1095. The right of NGOs and individuals to instigate administrative dispute before the competent court is expressly prescribed by the following laws on environmental protection: Articles 43, and 42 of the FBiH Law on Environmental Protection (Official Gazette of FBiH, No. 15/21) and Article 12 of the RS Law on Environmental Protection (Official Gazette of RS, Nos 71/12, 79/15, and 70/20).[1198]

1096. Representatives of the concerned public have the right to challenge, before the court, the legality of administrative acts passed by the authorities or conduct that is inconsistent with the provisions of environmental laws by initiating the proceedings before the competent court to protect their rights.

1097. In both entities, under the respective Laws on Administrative Procedure and the Laws on Environment, the developer, interested agencies, organizations and the public have the right of appeal against all decisions made by the respective ministries and local government bodies responsible for carrying out an EIA procedure.

1098. A court decision that was made in an administrative dispute, in accordance with Article 40 of the FBiH Law on Administrative Disputes (Official Gazette of FBiH, No. 09/05) and Article 34 of the RS Law on Administrative Disputes (Official Gazette of RS, No. 109/05), may not be appealed. However, it is possible to

1196. In accordance with Art. 17 of the Federation of Bosnia and Herzegovina Law on Administrative Disputes, Art. 14 of the Republic of Srpska Law on Administrative Disputes and Art. 16 of the Brčko District of Bosnia and Herzegovina Law on Administrative Disputes BD, initiation of an administrative dispute, as a rule, shall not stay the enforcement an administrative act.

1197. *See*: BiH Council of Ministers, *Answers to the List of EU Questions on Chapter 27, Environment*, *supra* p. 146.

1198. The Law on Environmental Protection of the BD BiH does not contain provisions on the right of members of the concerned public to initiate legal action if they believe that the provisions of the Law were violated. *Ibid.*, p. 133.

submit an application for an extraordinary review of court decisions in administrative disputes to the Supreme Courts of the entities due to violation of law, regulation or general act or a breach of the rules of procedure that would have influenced the resolution of the matter.[1199] Another possibility is to file a motion for retrial to the entities Supreme Courts.[1200]

1099. With regard to the right to get involved in the administrative disputes instigated in connection with the damage to the environment, NGOs dealing with the protection of the environment and interested individuals may exercise their right of access to justice under the general statutory provisions of the following laws governing administrative dispute: Article 15 of the BiH Law on Administrative Dispute (Official Gazette of BiH Nos 19/02, 88/07, 83/07, 74/10); Article 12 of the RS Law on Administrative Dispute; Article 15 of the FBiH Law on Administrative Dispute; Article 13 of the BD BiH Law on Administrative Dispute (Official Gazette of BD BiH, Nos 4/00, 1/01).

§1. The Republic of Srpska

1100. All interested persons, including organizations and NGOs in the RS have the right to protection in administrative and judicial proceedings (access to administrative and judicial proceedings) in all environmental issues and related proceedings.[1201]

1101. The Law on Environmental Protection and the Law on General Administrative Procedure regulate the procedure of reviewing the decisions issued by the competent authorities for the protection of the environment.[1202] The public and/or concerned public may file an appeal or instigate an administrative dispute proceedings or any other proceeding before the court against a decision made in proceedings conducted in accordance with the Law on Environmental Protection (Law on General Administrative Procedure).[1203]

1199. It should be noted that, pursuant to Art. 32 of the Law on Administrative Disputes of BD BiH, the decisions rendered by the Basic Court of the BD BiH in administrative proceedings may be appealed to the Appellate Court of the BD BiH.
1200. Decisions of Supreme Courts are final.
1201. BiH Council of Ministers, *Answers to the List of EU Questions on Chapter 27, Environment, supra* p. 153. According to the provisions of the Law on Administrative Disputes (Official Gazette of RS, no. 109/05) administrative dispute may be instituted by any natural or legal person if considered that an administrative act violates their right or direct personal interest based on law.
1202. Against the decision on the termination of the environmental permits a responsible person may appeal to the Ministry or initiate administrative proceedings before the competent court (Art. 98 para. 4).
1203. Article 42 of the Law on Environmental Protection stipulates that representatives of the interested public, concerned parties or authorities that participated in the decision-making process may use legal remedies against the decision.

§2. FEDERATION OF BOSNIA AND HERZEGOVINA

1102. According to Article 42 of the Law on Environmental Protection (Official Gazette of the FBiH, No. 15/21) 'if they participated in the first instance procedure, members of the public concerned have the right to appeal and to initiate a review procedure before the court to challenge the substantive and/or procedural legality of any decision, act or omission'.

1103. If the dangerous activity causes damage to the environment, the operator is obliged to compensate the costs of damage assessment and the costs of measures to restore the state that was immediately before the damage occurred or to mitigate the damage caused to the environment, as well as compensation for damage caused to persons and property caused by the dangerous activity (Article 120, paragraph 1).[1204]

§3. BRČKO DISTRICT OF BOSNIA AND HERZEGOVINA

1104. The Law on Environmental Protection in the BD (Official Gazette of BD, Nos 24/04, 01/05, 19/07 and 09/09) provides a right to appeal in case of denial of access to information (Article 37) and to the inspector's decision (Article 87). In both cases, the complaint is sent to the Appellate Committee of the Government of BD.[1205]

1204. If the damage caused to the environment cannot be remedied by appropriate measures, the person who caused the damage is responsible for compensating the damage equal to the value of the destroyed property (Art. 121, para. 1).

1205. In case of occurrence of harm or the existence of the danger to the environment public prosecutor has the right to file the lawsuit in order to impose ban or limitations of activity (Art. 43).

Chapter 2. Judicial Remedies

§1. Procedure Before the Civil Court

1105. With regard to judicial protection of victims of discrimination in Bosnia and Herzegovina, protection in the civil proceeding has the primary role. The Law on the Prohibition of Discrimination (Official Gazette of BiH 59/09, and 52/21) gives special attention to the civil proceeding aimed at anti-discrimination protection, for which, compared to the general rules for civil proceedings, it stipulates certain procedural specificities.[1206]

I. The Republic of Srpska

1106. The Civil Procedure Code of the RS (Official Gazette of RS, Nos 58/03, 85/03, 74/05, 63/07, 105/08-CC, 45/09-CC, 49/09, 61/13, 109/21-CC) prescribes in Chapter VII ordinary legal remedies (appeal against the first instance judgment, Articles 203–232) and appeal against the first instance court decision (Articles 233–236).

1107. Extraordinary legal remedies are revision (Articles 237–254) and reopening of the proceedings (Articles 255–264).

II. Federation of Bosnia and Herzegovina

1108. According to Article 203 of the Civil Procedure Code (Official Gazette of FBiH, Nos 53/03, 73/05, 19/06, 98/15) parties may file an appeal against the first instance judgment within thirty days from the day of rendering the judgment, or, if the judgment is served in accordance with provisions on service of this law, within thirty days from the service of the judgment, unless a different time limit is set by this law. In disputes concerning bills of exchange and cheques, the time limit is fifteen days.[1207]

1109. An appeal against the first instance court decision is allowed unless this law prescribes otherwise (Article 233).[1208]

1206. *For detailed information, see* Hanušić A. *Judicial Protection from Discrimination in Bosnia and Herzegovina Analysis of Legislative Solutions and Practice in Light of the First Cases in this Field*, Analitika –Centre for Social Research, Sarajevo, 2013. p. 11. *See also*, ćerimović E., Hrlović Dž, *From Collection to Prevention, Preconditions for Comprehensive Gathering of Information on Discrimination in Bosnia and Herzegovina*, Analitika –Centre for Social Research, Sarajevo, June 2013.

1207. Appeals filed within the prescribed time limits prevent the finality of the judgment in the part contested by the appeal (para. 3).

1208. If this Law explicitly sets forth that a separate appeal is not allowed, the decision of the first instance court can be contested only in the appeal against the final ruling (Art. 233, para. 2).

1110. Extraordinary legal remedies are revision (Articles 237–254) and reopening of the proceedings (Articles 255–264). The parties may file the request for revision of the final second instance judgment within thirty days from the day of the service of the judgment (Article 237). The revision shall not be allowed if the value of the contested part of the final judgment does not exceed BAM 10,000.[1209]

1111. Proceedings completed by a final court ruling may be reopened at the party's motion in the following cases: if a judge, who should have been exempted according to the provisions of this law, participated in the rendering of the ruling; if a party was not given the possibility to be heard before the court due to the unlawful conduct of the court; if a person who cannot be a party in the proceedings participated in the proceedings in capacity of plaintiff or defendant; if a legal person in capacity of party has not been represented by an authorized person; if a party which has no litigation capacity was not represented by a legal representative; if a legal representative or an agent has not had necessary authorization for conducting the proceedings or performing particular procedural actions, unless conducting the proceedings or carrying out particular procedural actions has been subsequently approved; if the court ruling has been based on a false testimony by a witness or an expert or a forged document or a document where the false content has been certified; if rendering the court ruling involved a criminal act of the judge, the legal representative or the agent of a party, adverse party or a third party; if a party learns new facts, finds or gains the possibility to use new evidence which would have led to a more favourable ruling if those facts or evidence had been presented in the previous proceedings (Article 255).

§2. Criminal Procedure

I. Bosnia and Herzegovina

1112. According to the Law on Criminal Procedure (Official Gazette of BiH, Nos 3/03, 32/03, 36/03, 26/04, 63/04, 13/05, 48/05, 46/06, 76/06, 29/07, 32/07, 53/07, 76/07, 15/08, 58/08, 12/09, 16/09, 93/09, 72/13 and 65/18) regular legal remedies in criminal procedure are the following: appeal against the first instant verdict

1209. Exceptionally, the Supreme Court may also allow revision in all cases if it finds that deciding on revision is important for the application of law in other cases (para. 3).

(Article 292),[1210] appeal against second-instant verdict (Article 317a),[1211] and an appeal against the decision (Article 318).[1212]

1113. An extraordinary legal remedy is reopening the criminal proceedings (Articles 324–333). Pursuant to Article 329 a petition to reopen a criminal proceeding may be filed by the parties and the defence attorney, and following the death of the accused the petition may be filed in his favour by the Prosecutor and by the persons cited in Article 293(2) of this Code. A petition to reopen a criminal proceeding in favour of a convicted person may be filed even after the convicted person has served his sentence and regardless of the statute of limitation, amnesty or pardon.[1213]

1114. The final verdict may also be modified without the reopening of the criminal proceedings if several penalties have been imposed on the same convicted person by two or more final verdicts, while the provisions pertaining to the meting out of a single compound sentence for the crimes in concurrence were not applied (Article 324 a).[1214]

II. The Republic of Srpska

1115. Pursuant to the provisions of Article 222 of the Criminal Procedure Code of RS (Official Gazette of RS, No. 53/12, 91/17, 66/18, and 15/21), a citizen is

1210. An appeal may be filed against the verdict rendered in the first instance within fifteen days from the date when the copy of the verdict was delivered. In complex matters, the Court may, on the motion of the parties or the defence attorney, extend the deadline for filing an appeal for a maximum of fifteen days. Until the Court renders a decision on a motion referred to in para. 2 of this article, the deadline for filing an appeal shall not run. An appeal filed on time shall stay the execution of the verdict.

1211. An appeal against the verdict of the Appellate Division shall be allowed in the following cases: if the Appellate Panel modified the first-instance verdict of acquittal and pronounced a verdict finding the accused guilty, if on the basis of the appeal from the verdict of acquittal the Appellate Panel in a hearing pronounced a verdict finding the accused guilty (para. 1). An appeal against the second instance verdict shall be decided in the third instance by the Panel composed of three judges (para. 2).

1212. The parties, the defence attorney and persons whose rights have been violated may always file an appeal against the decision of the Court rendered in the first instance unless when it is explicitly prohibited to file an appeal under this Code (para. 1). A decision rendered in order to prepare the main trial and the verdict may be contested only in an appeal against the verdict (para. 2).

1213. If the Court learns that a reason exists for reopening a criminal proceeding, the Court shall so inform the convicted person or the person authorized to file the petition on his behalf (para. 3).

1214. In this case, the court shall, with this new verdict, modify the previous verdicts with respect to the decision on sentence and impose a single penalty. The new single verdict shall be rendered by the first-instance court that imposed the most severe type of penalty; if the penalties were of the same type it shall be the court that imposed the heavier penalty; and if the penalties are equal in that respect, the court that issued the most recent penalty (para. 2). The new verdict shall be rendered by the court in a session of the panel on petition of the prosecutor or the convicted person or the defence attorney, upon hearing the adverse party (para. 3).

entitled to report a criminal offence. All persons shall report commission of a criminal offence in those instances where failure to report such a criminal offence itself constitutes a criminal offence.[1215]

1116. The Criminal procedure code of the Republic of Srpska prescribes that regular legal remedies are the following: appeal against First Instance Verdict (Articles 306–332), appeal against Appellate Court Verdict (Article 333), and appeal against decision (Articles 334–339).

1117. According to Article 307 the parties, the defence attorney and the aggrieved party may file an appeal. An appeal on behalf of the accused may also be filed by his legal representative, spouse or cohabitee, relatives by blood in a direct line, brother, sister, adoptive parent or adopted child.[1216] The prosecutor may file an appeal in favour or against the accused. The injured party may contest the verdict only with respect to the decision of the court on costs of the criminal proceedings and with respect to the decision on the property claim. An appeal may also be filed by a person whose item was forfeited or from whom the property gain obtained by a criminal offence was forfeited.[1217]

1118. The parties, the defence attorney and persons whose rights have been violated may always file an appeal against the decision of the court rendered in the first instance unless it is explicitly provided that an appeal is not allowed under this Code. An appeal is not allowed against any decision rendered during the investigation, unless this Code provides otherwise. A decision rendered in order to prepare the main trial and the verdict may be contested only in an appeal against the verdict (Article 334, paragraphs 1–3).[1218]

1119. Extraordinary legal remedies are the following: reopening Criminal Proceedings (Articles 340–349), and motion for Protection of Legality (Articles 350–357).

1120. Pursuant to Article 345, paragraphs 1–2a motion to reopen criminal proceedings may be filed by the parties and the defence attorney, and following the death of the accused the motion may be filed in his favour by the prosecutor and by

---

1215. The report must be filed with the prosecutor in writing or orally (Art. 223, para. 1).
1216. In this case, the period allowed for the appeal shall run from the day when the accused or his defence attorney was delivered a copy of the verdict.
1217. The defence attorney and persons referred to in para. 2 of this article (legal representative, spouse or cohabitee, adoptive parent or adopted child) may file an appeal even without a special authorization of the accused, but not against the will of the accused, unless a sentence of long period imprisonment was pronounced on the accused (para. 6).
1218. No appeal is allowed against a decision issued by the Supreme Court unless otherwise provided by this law (Art. 334 para. 4).

the persons from Article 307, paragraph 2, of this Code. A motion to reopen criminal proceedings in favour of a convicted person may be filed even after the convicted person has served his sentence and regardless of the statute of limitations, amnesty or pardon.[1219]

1121. A motion for protection of legality may be filed by a prosecutor, convicted person and defence attorney. After the death of the convicted person, persons referred to in Article 307 paragraph 2 of this Code may file the motion in his favour. The prosecutor may file a motion for protection of legality both in favour and to the detriment of the convicted person (Article 351, paragraphs 1–2).[1220]

III. Federation of Bosnia and Herzegovina

1122. In accordance with the Criminal Procedure Code of the FBiH (Official Gazette of the FBiH, Nos 35/03, 37/03, 56/03, 78/04, 28/05, 55/06, 27/07, 53/07, 9/09, 12/10, 8/13, 59/14, and 74/20) regular legal remedies are the following: appeal against the first instance verdict (Articles 307–332),[1221] appeal against the second instance verdict (Article 333),[1222] and appeal against decision (Articles 334–339).[1223]

1219. If the court learns that a reason exists for reopening criminal proceedings, it shall so inform the convicted person or the person who is eligible to file the motion on his behalf (Art. 345, para. 2).

1220. A motion for protection of legality shall be filed within three months of receipt of the final and binding verdict (Art. 351, para. 3).

1221. Pursuant to the Art. 308 the parties, the defence attorney and the injured party may file an appeal (para. 1). An appeal on behalf of the accused may also be filed by his legal representative, spouse or extramarital partner, direct blood relative, adoptive parent, adopted child, brother, sister and foster parent. In this case, the period allowed for the appeal shall run from the day when the accused or his defence attorney was delivered a copy of the verdict (para. 2). The prosecutor may file an appeal to the detriment or to the benefit of the accused (para. 3). The injured party may contest the verdict only with respect to decision of the court on costs of the criminal proceedings and with respect to decision on a claim under property law (para. 4). An appeal may also be filed by a person whose item was forfeited or from whom the property gain obtained by a criminal offence was forfeited (para. 5). The defence attorney and persons referred to in para. 2 of this article may file an appeal even without the separate authorization of the accused, but not against the will of the accused, unless a sentence of long-term imprisonment was pronounced against the accused (para. 6).

1222. An appeal is permitted against the verdict of the second instance court if the second instance court altered the first instance verdict in which the accused has been released from the charge and pronounced the guilty verdict (para. 1). The Supreme Court of the Federation shall decide the appeal against the second instance verdict referred to in para. 1 of this article in the session of the Panel pursuant to provisions of the proceedings before the second instance court (para. 2).

1223. According to the Art. 334 the parties, the defence attorney and persons whose rights have been violated may always file an appeal against the decision of the court rendered in the first instance unless explicitly prohibited to file an appeal under this Code (para. 1). An appeal is not allowed against a decision of the Panel rendered during the investigation, unless otherwise provided by this Code (para. 2). A decision rendered in order to prepare the main trial and the verdict may be contested only in an appeal against the verdict (para. 3).

1123. Extraordinary legal remedy is 'reopening the criminal proceeding' (Articles 340–439). In accordance with the provision of Article 345 a motion to reopen the criminal proceedings may be filed by the parties and the defence attorney, and following the death of the accused the motion may be filed in his favour by the prosecutor and by the persons referred to in Article 308, paragraph 2, of this Code.

A motion to reopen criminal proceedings in favour of a convicted person may be filed even after the convicted person has served his sentence and regardless of the statute of limitations, amnesty or pardon (paragraph 2).[1224]

IV. Brčko District of Bosnia and Herzegovina

1124. Criminal procedure code of the Brčko District BiH (Official of the BD BiH, Nos 48/04, 6/05, 14/07, 19/07, 21/07, 2/08, 17/09, 9/13, 33/13-Revised text, 27/14, 3/19, and 16/20) defined in the Chapter XXIII following regular legal remedies: appeal against the first instance judgment (Articles 292–317), appeal against appellate division verdict (Article 317a), appeal against decision (Articles 318–323).

1125. Repeating the criminal proceedings is extraordinary legal remedy prescribed in the Chapter XXIV (Articles 324–333). Pursuant to Article 324 a criminal proceeding that was terminated by a legally binding decision or judgment may be repeated upon the petition of an authorized person only in cases and under the conditions provided by this Code.[1225]

§3. Constitutional Court Procedure

1126. In BiH there are three constitutional courts: the Constitutional Court of BiH,[1226] the Constitutional Court of FBiH[1227] and the Constitutional Court of RS.[1228]

1224. If the court learns that a reason for reopening criminal proceedings exists, the court shall so inform the convicted person or the person authorized to file the motion on his behalf (para. 3).

1225. A petition to reopen a criminal proceeding may be filed by the parties and the defence attorney, and following the death of the convicted person, the petition may be filed in his favour by the Prosecutor and by the persons from Art. 293, para. 2, of this Code (Art. 329 para. 1). A petition to reopen a criminal proceeding in favour of a convicted person may be filed even after the convicted person has served his sentence and regardless of the statute of limitations, amnesty or pardon (para. 2). (3) If the Court learns that a reason exists for reopening a criminal proceeding, the Court shall so inform the convicted person or the person authorized to file the petition on his behalf (para. 3).

1226. For more information *see*: https://www.ustavnisud.ba/en/home (10 Jul. 2022).

1227. *See*: http://www.ustavnisudfbih.ba/bs/index.php (10 Jul. 2022).

1228. *See*: http://www.ustavnisud.org/ (10 Jul. 2022).

I. Bosnia and Herzegovina

1127. The Constitutional Court of BiH has 'appellate jurisdiction over issues … arising out of a judgment of any court in Bosnia and Herzegovina' (Article VI.3b of the Constitution of BiH).

1128. According to the Constitution, the Court serves as the protector of, among others, the following human rights: the right to life, the right not to be subjected to torture or to inhuman or degrading treatment or punishment, the right not to be held in slavery or servitude or to perform forced or compulsory labour, the rights to liberty and security of person, the right to a fair hearing in civil and criminal matters, other rights relating to criminal proceedings, the right to private and family life, correspondence, freedom of thought, conscience, and religion, freedom of expression, freedom of peaceful assembly, freedom of association with others, the right to marry and found a family, the right to property, the right to education and the right to liberty of movement and residence.

1129. Pursuant to Article 15 of the Rules of Procedure of the Constitutional Court of BiH, the participants in the proceedings shall be: (a) the initiators of proceedings referred to in Article VI.3 (a) of the Constitution and the adopters of the acts which are the subject of the dispute; (b) the parties to the proceedings which ended in a decision challenged by the appeal and the court and/or the authority which adopted the judgment or decision which is the subject of an appeal under Article VI.3 (b) of the Constitution; (c) the Chair of the House of Peoples, in case of a dispute according to Article IV.3 (f) of the Constitution; (d) the court which referred the issue to the Court and the adopter of the law the validity of which the court's decision determines under Article VI.3 (c) of the Constitution.

1130. 'The country's Constitution, which is Annex 4 to the Dayton/Paris Peace Agreement, established a complex institutional architecture that remains inefficient and which is subject to different interpretations …. A number of Constitutional Court decisions are yet to be implemented at various levels across the country.'[1229]

II. The Republic of Srpska

1131. Article 115 of the Constitution of the RS (Official Gazette of RS, Nos 6/92, 8/92, 15/92, 19/92, 21/92, 28/94, 8/96, 13/96, 15/96, 16/96, 21/96, 21/02, 26/02, 30/02, 31/02, 69/02, 31/03, 98/03, 115/05 and 117/05) prescribes that the Constitutional Court shall decide on: conformity of laws, other regulations and general enactments with the Constitution; the compliance of laws, other regulations and enactment of the National Assembly with the provisions of the Constitution on the protection of vital interests of the constituent peoples; conformity of regulations and general enactments with the law; conflict of jurisdictions between bodies of legislative, executive and judicial branch; conflict of jurisdiction between agencies of the

1229. EC, *Bosnia and Herzegovina 2018 Progress Report,* p. 4.

Republic, city and municipality; conformity of programmes, statutes and other general enactments of political organizations with the Constitution and the law.[1230]

1132. Pursuant to Article 120 of the Constitution of the RS 'anyone can give an initiative to start the proceedings for assessing the constitutionality and legality' (paragraph 1). Apart from that proceedings with the Constitutional Court may, without restriction, be initiated by the President of the Republic, by the National Assembly and by the Government, while other bodies, organizations and communities may do so under conditions prescribed by law (paragraph 2). The Constitutional Court may initiate the proceedings itself to assess the constitutionality and legality (paragraph 3).[1231]

1133. According to the provisions of Article 4(2) e) of the Law on the Constitutional Court of RS, the procedure of assessing the constitutionality and legality may be initiated by, among others, municipality, city, company, political organization or association of citizens and other organizations if their rights established by the Constitution or the law are violated. In accordance with the above provision, NGOs may initiate proceedings in the capacity of a party to the proceedings before the competent authorities (courts and administrative bodies) and the proceedings to review the constitutionality and legality before the Constitutional Court.

III. Federation of Bosnia and Herzegovina

1134. Constitution of the Federation of BiH (Official Gazette of the FBiH, Nos 1/94, 13/97, 16/02, 22/02, 52/02, 60/02, 18/03, 63/03, 9/04, 20/04, 33/04, 71/05, 72/05 and 88/08) prescribes that the Constitutional Court shall: (a) at the request of the President, of the Vice-President, of the Prime Minister, of the Deputy Prime Minister, or of one-third of the members of either House of the Legislature, determine whether any proposed law that has been adopted by either House of the Legislature, or any law or proposed law that has been adopted by each House of the Legislature, is in accord with this Constitution; (b) at the request of the Prime Minister, of the canton concerned, or of one-third of the members of the Legislature of a Canton, determine whether any law or proposed law that has been adopted by that Legislature (including the Cantonal Constitution and any amendments thereto), is

---

1230. The Constitutional Court shall monitor events of interest for the achievement of constitutionality and legality, and inform the highest constitutional bodies of the Republic on the status and problems in that area, offering them opinions and proposals for adopting laws and undertaking other measures for the purpose of ensuring constitutionality and legality, as well as the protection of freedoms and rights of citizens, organizations and communities. The Constitutional Court may assess the constitutionality of laws and both the constitutionality and legality of regulations and general enactments, which have ceased to be effective, provided that not more than one year has elapsed from the date of the cessation of validity to the date of initiating the proceedings.

1231. When the Constitutional Court assesses that a law is not in accordance with the Constitution, or that another regulation or general enactment is not in accordance with the Constitution or law, such law, regulation or general enactment shall cease to be effective on the day of the publication of the Constitutional Court's decision (para. 4).

in accord with this Constitution; (c) at the request of the President, of the Vice-President, of the Prime Minister, of the Deputy Prime Minister, determine whether any regulation enacted or proposed regulation to be enacted by any organ of the Federation Government is in accord with this Constitution; (d) at the request of the Prime Minister, of the canton concerned, determine whether any proposed law that has been adopted by a body of the Canton, city or municipality authority, is in accord with this Constitution (Article C.10.2).[1232]

1135. Pursuant to the Article C.10.1. the primary function of the Constitutional Court shall be to resolve the following disputes: (a) between any Cantons; (b) between any Canton and the Federation Government; (c) between any city, its Canton or the Federation Government; (d) between any municipality and any city; (e) between any Municipality and its Canton or the Federation Government; and (f) between or within any of the institutions of the Federation Government.

§4. Human Rights Ombudsman of Bosnia and Herzegovina

1136. According to Article 18 of the Law on Human Rights Ombudsman of Bosnia and Herzegovina (Official Gazette of BiH, Nos 32/00, 19/2002, 35/2004 and 32/2006) 'any natural person or legal entity claiming a legitimate interest may complain to the Institution without any restriction. Nationality, citizenship, residence, gender, minority, ethnicity, religion, legal incapacity, imprisonment of any kind, and, in general terms, a special relationship with, or dependence on, a government body may not restrict the right to lodge a complaint with the Institution'.[1233]

1137. The institution has begun to operate in two offices, with the seat in Sarajevo and the main Office in Banja Luka, and from the end of 2000 with the branch-office in Brčko District of BiH. The institution is set up in order to protect the rights and liberties of natural and legal persons and to promote good governance and the rule of law in Bosnia and Herzegovina. For that purpose the Institution is analysing individual complaints, investigations and undertaking different active measures.[1234]

1232. Apart from that, the Constitutional Court shall also decide constitutional questions presented by the Supreme Court or a Cantonal court that arise in the course of a proceeding currently pending before that Court. The Constitutional Court shall decide questions, which arise under legislation regulating immunity in the Federation (para. 3).

1233. Basis for work and functioning of BiH Ombudsman are enshrined by Annexes IV and VI of the General Framework Agreement on Peace for Bosnia and Herzegovina (14 Dec. 1995) and, based on mentioned documents, the institution has started function in 1996. For more information *see*: http://www.ombudsmen.gov.ba/Default.aspx?id=14&lang=EN (10 Jul. 2022).

1234. Initial report on Implementation of the International Covenant on Civil and Political Rights in Bosnia and Herzegovina for the period from 1994 to 2004, CCPR/C/BIH/1, 24 Nov. 2005, p. 76.

1138. Importance of environment protection is confirmed by citizens' addressing various problems they encounter in this area.[1235]'In 2011 there were 8 complaints related to issues of ecology and environment protection. In 5 cases Ombudsmen Institution acted ex officio concerning issue of animals' protection, that is, problem of stray dogs. 'Processing of cases, following investigation conducted, resulted in 5 recommendations issued by the Ombudsmen.'[1236] During 2017, the Ombudsman Institution registered 755 complaints pertaining to violation of economic, social and cultural rights, including 11 in the fields of 'ecology and environmental protection'.[1237]

1235. For more information *see*: Institution of Human Rights ombudsman of Bosnia & Herzegovina, *Annual report on result of the activities by the Human Rights Ombudsman of Bosnia and Herzegovina for 2012*. Banja Luka, 2013. pp. 48–49.

1236. Institution of Human Rights ombudsman of Bosnia & Herzegovina, *Annual report on result of the activities by the Human Rights Ombudsman of Bosnia and Herzegovina for 2011*. Banja Luka, 2012. p. 64.

1237. Institution of Human Rights ombudsman of Bosnia & Herzegovina, *2017 Annual Report on the results of the activities of The Institution of the Human Rights Ombudsman of Bosnia and Herzegovina*, Banja Luka, March 2018, p. 42. During 2020 the Ombudsmen received 15 complaints in the field of ecology, i.e., environmental protection and one recommendation was issued. *2020 Annual Report on the results of the activities of The Institution of the Human Rights Ombudsman of Bosnia and Herzegovina*, Banja Luka, March 2021, p. 88.

Selected Bibliography

Abolmasov, B. *Landslide Risk Management Study in Bosnia and Herzegovina.* UNDP, 2016. http://www.ba.undp.org/content/dam/bosnia_and_herzegovina/docs/Research&Publications/Democratic%20Governance/Landslide%20Risk%20Management%20Study%20in%20BH.pdf (7 February 2022).

Ademović, N., J. Marko &G, Marković. *Ustavno pravo Bosne i Hercegovine* [*Constitutional Law of Bosnia and Herzegovina*]. Sarajevo: Fondacija 'Konrad Adenauer', Predstavništvo u Bosni i Hercegovini, 2012.

Bassuener K. (pr) Bosna i Hercegovina: između paketa mjera za EU-integraciju i izlazne strategije međunarodne zajednice [*Bosnia and Herzegovina: Between EU-Integration Toolbox and International Community's Exit Strategy*]. Sarajevo: Fondacija Heinrich Böll, Ured za Bosnu i Hercegovinu, 2010.

BD. *Strategija aproksimacije propisa pravnoj stečevini EU u oblasti zaštite životne sredine/okoliša Brčko distrikta BiH* [*Strategy for Harmonisation of Brčko District BiH Environmental Legislation with EU* Acquis], EAS Brčko Distrikta, February 2017. http://www.mvteo.gov.ba/data/Home/%D0%94%D0%BE%D0%BA%D1%83%D0%BC%D0%B5%D0%BD%D1%82%D0%B8/%D0%92%D0%BE%D0%B4%D0%BD%D0%B8%20%D1%80%D0%B5%D1%81%D1%83%D1%80%D1%81%D0%B8/Strategija_aproksimacije_propisa_pravnoj_ste%C4%8Devini_EU_oblasti_za%C5%A1tite_%C5%BEivotne_sredine_BD.pdf (26 July 2022).

BiH Council of Ministers. *Answers to the List of EU Questions on Chapter 27, Environment.* Sarajevo. 2012. https://www.dei.gov.ba/en/odgovori-na-upitnik-ek (6 February 2022).

BiH Council of Ministers. *Bosnia and Herzegovina Mine Action Strategy (2009-2019).* Sarajevo, 2008.

BiH Council of Ministers. *Bosnia and Herzegovina Mine Action Strategy 2018 – 2025*, http://bhmac.org/?page_id=624&lang=en (27 July 2022).

BiH Council of Ministers. *EU Integration Strategy of Bosnia and Herzegovina.* Directorate for European Integration, 2004.

BiH, *Implementation of Agenda 2030 and the Sustainable Development Goals in Bosnia and Herzegovina, Voluntary Review*, April 2019, p. 38. https://sustainabledevelopment.un.org/content/documents/23345VNR_BiH_ENG_Final.pdf (26 July 2022).

Selected Bibliography

BiH Ministry for Human Rights and Refugees (MHRR). *Housing and Urban Profile of Bosnia and Herzegovina.* Sarajevo: Ministry for Human Rights and Refugees 2006, http://www.mhrr.gov.ba/PDF/default.aspx?id=243&langTag=bs-BA (26 July 2022).

BiH MFTER. *State of the Environment Report of the Bosnia and Herzegovina 2012.* Sarajevo: Ministry of Foreign Trade and Economic Relations, Millennium Development Goals Achievement Fund, 2012.

BiH MFTER. 'Ministry of foreign trade and economic relations, Ministry of Physical Planning, Civil Engineering and Ecology of Republic of Srpska, Federal Ministry of Environment and Tourism, UNDP'. *Initial National Communication of Bosnia and Herzegovina under the United Nations Framework Convention on Climate Change.* Banja Luka: Ministry of foreign trade and economic relations, Ministry of Physical Planning, Civil Engineering and Ecology of Republic of Srpska, Federal Ministry of Environment and Tourism, UNDP 2009, http://unfccc.int/resource/docs/natc/bihnc1.pdf (27 July 2022).

BiH MFTER. *Environmental Approximation Strategy of Bosnia and Herzegovina.* EAS – BiH, Ministry of Foreign Trade and Economic Relations of Bosnia and Herzegovina, May 2017. http://www.mvteo.gov.ba/data/Home/Dokumenti/Vodni%20resursi/Environmetal.pdf (6 February 2022).

BiH MFTER, UNEP, GEF. *Strategy and Action Plan for Protection of Biological Diversity in Bosnia and Herzegovina (2015-2020).* Ministry of Foreign Trade and Economic Relations of Bosnia and Herzegovina, UNEP, GEF, 2016. https://www.cbd.int/doc/world/ba/ba-nbsap-v2-en.pdf (26 July 2022).

BiH Ministry of Justice. *Bosnia and Herzegovina Justice Sector Reform Strategy, 2008 – 2012.* Sarajevo: Ministry of Justice June 2008.

BiH. *Nationally Determined Contribution of Bosnia and Herzegovina (NDC) for the period 2020-2030.* https://www.vladars.net/sr-SP-Cyrl/Vlada/Ministarstva/mgr/Documents/NDC%20BiH%20_170460761.pdf (29 July 2022); https://unfccc.int/sites/default/files/NDC/2022-06/NDC%20BiH_November%202020%20FINAL%20DRAFT%2005%20Nov%20ENG%20LR.pdf. (29 July 2022).

BiH Vijeće ministara Bosne i Hercegovine, Ministarstvo vanjske trgovine i ekonomskih odnosa. *Nacrt vodne politike u BiH* [*The Draft Water Policy in BiH*]. Oktobar / Listopad 2011, http://www.voda.ba/udoc/projekti/ppvbih/strategija/vodna_politika_-_finalna-_bih.pdf (26 July 2022).

Bobić, M. & D. Todić. '"National" and "Supranational" in the EU Accession Process and Harmonisation of National Regulations with EU Regulations (Example of Regulations in the Field of Environment)'. In *Thematic Proceeding: National and European Identity in the Process of European Integration*, edited by P. Petrović& M. Radaković. Belgrade: International Conference, 28–29 June 2012; Belgrade: Institute of International Politics and Economics, 2013, 97–110.

Bogdanović, S. 'Good Governance of the Sava Basin – Legal Realities and Practical Prospects'. *Journal of Water Law* 15, no. 3 (2004):93–99.

Bogdanović, S. 'Water Law after Dayton'. Water International 25, no. 4 (2000):534–543.

Bosnia and Herzegovina and the United Nations Sustainable Development Cooperation Framework, A Partnership for Sustainable Development, 2021-2025, Sarajevo 2021, p. 19. https://unece.org/sites/default/files/2021-05/2021-2025_UNSDC_BiH.pdf (27 July 2022).

Bosnia and Herzegovina, *National report submitted in accordance with paragraph 5 of the annex to Human Rights Council resolution 16/21*, Human Rights Council, General Assembly, A/HRC/WG.6/34/BIH/1, 22 October 2019, https://documents-dds-ny.un.org/doc/UNDOC/GEN/G19/310/04/PDF/G1931004.pdf?OpenElement (1 August 2022).

Bosnia & Herzegovina. *Assessment of Sustainable Development in Bosnia and Herzegovina.* The Report of BiH for The World Summit on Sustainable development (WSSD), Project of preparation of Bosnia and Herzegovina for participation on The World Summit on Sustainable Development Rio+10, Johannesburg 28 August–4 September 2002, Sarajevo: Banja Luka, Mostar-jun 2002.

Bosnia and Herzegovina Fourth Report to the United Nations Convention on Biological Diversity. 2010 Biodiversity Targets National Assessments, April 2010, www.cbd.int/doc/world/ba/ba-nr-04-en.doc (27 July 2022).

Bose, S. 'The Bosnian State a Decade after Dayton'. In *Peace Without Politics? Ten Years of International State-Building in Bosnia*, edited by D. Chandler. *International Peacekeeping* 12, no. 3 (2005), 322–335. DOI: 10.1080/13533310500074028.

Brčko District of BiH, *Development Strategy of Brčko District BiH 2021-2027*, Brčko 2020, p. 10.

Bratović, E. & S. Lepić. *Education for Sustainable Development, Bosnia and Herzegovina, Research Report.* Sarajevo: Promente, 2011.

Brininstool, M. *The Mineral Industry of Bosnia and Herzegovina. 2008 Minerals Yearbook.* U.S. Department of the Interior, U.S. Geological Survey, December 2010.

CEC. *Report from the Commission to the Council on the preparedness of Bosnia and Herzegovina to negotiate a Stabilization and Association Agreement with the European Union*, COM(2003) 692 final, Commission of the European Communities, Brussels, 18 November 2003, http://eur-lex.europa.eu/LexUriServ/LexUriServ.do?uri=COM:2003:0692:FIN:EN:PDF (26 July 2022).

CEC. *Bosnia and Herzegovina 2006 Progress Report*, COM(2006) 649 final, Commission of the European Communities, Brussels, 8 November 2006, https://eur-lex.europa.eu/legal-content/PT/TXT/?uri=CELEX:52006SC1384 (26 July 2022).

CEC. *Bosnia and Herzegovina 2007 Progress Report*, accompanying the Communication from the Commission to the European Parliament and the Council, Enlargement Strategy and Main Challenges 2007–2008, COM(2007) 663 final, Commission of the European Communities, Brussels, 6 November 2007, https://eur-lex.europa.eu/legal-content/EN/TXT/?uri=CELEX:52007SC1430 (26 July 2022).

CEC. *Bosnia and Herzegovina 2008 Progress Report*, accompanying the Communication from the Commission to the European Parliament and the Council,

Enlargement Strategy and Main Challenges 2008-2009, COM(2008)674, Commission of the European Communities, Brussels, 5 November 2008, https://europa.ba/wp-content/uploads/2015/05/delegacijaEU_2011121405151330 eng.pdf (26 July 2022).

CEC. *Bosnia and Herzegovina 2009 Progress Report*, accompanying the Communication from the Commission to the European Parliament and the Council, Enlargement Strategy and Main Challenges 2009-2010, COM(2009) 533, Commission of the European Communities, Brussels, 14 October 2009, https://ec.europa.eu/neighbourhood-enlargement/bosnia-and-herzegovina-progress-report-2009_en (26 July 2022).

Cenić S. *Resource Efficiency Gains and Green Growth Perspectives in Bosnia and Herzegovina.* Friedrich Ebert Stiftung, September 2012.

Commission on Security and Cooperation in Europe, The Referendum on Independence in Bosnia-Herzegovina February 29-March 1, 1992. A Report Prepared by the Staff of the Commission on Security and Cooperation in Europe, 29 February 1992. https://li.proquest.com/elhpdf/histcontext/CMP-1992-CSC-0012.pdf (26 July 2022).

Commission to Preserve National Monuments of Bosnia and Herzegovina. *Report on Assessment of the Architectural and Archaeological Heritage.* AT03 132 rev. Sarajevo, 2010, http://old.kons.gov.ba/main.php?mod=vijesti&extra=1075460574&&id_vijesti=254&lang=4&action=getExternal&id=200 (26 July 2022).

Constitution of Bosnia and Herzegovina. The General Framework Agreement: Annex 4, 14 December 1995, http://www.ohr.int/?page_id=63255 (26 July 2022).

Council Decision of 30 January 2006 on the principles, priorities and conditions contained in the European Partnership with Bosnia and Herzegovina and repealing Decision 2004/515/EC, OJL 35, 7 February 2006, pp. 19–31, https://eur-lex.europa.eu/legal-content/EN/TXT/PDF/?uri=CELEX:32006D0055&from=EN (26 July 2022).

Council Decision of 18 February 2008 on the principles, priorities and conditions contained in the European Partnership with Bosnia and Herzegovina and repealing Decision 2006/55/EC, OJL 80, 19 March 2008, pp. 18–31, http://eur-lex.europa.eu/LexUriServ/LexUriServ.do?uri=OJ:L:2008:080:0018:0031:EN:PDF (26 July 2022).

Cerimović E. & Hrlović Dž. *From Collection to Prevention, Preconditions for Comprehensive Gathering of Information on Discrimination in Bosnia and Herzegovina.* Sarajevo: Analitika – Centre for Social Research, June 2013.

DIKTAS. *Protection and Sustainable Use of the Dinaric Karst Transboundary Aquifer System.* National Report – Bosnia and Herzegovina, GEF, UNDP, UNESCO, December 2012.

Directorate for European Integration. *Answers to the Questionnaire, Chapter 27, Environment and Climate Change*, 27 February 2018. https://www.dei.gov.ba/en/odgovori-na-upitnik-ek (7 Feb. 2022).

Directorate for European Integration, *Answers to the Questionnaire, Chapter 26, Education and Culture*, 27 February 2018, https://www.dei.gov.ba/en/odgovori-na-upitnik-ek (26 July 2022).

Directorate for European Integration, *Answers to the Questionnaire, Chapter 15, Energy*, 27 February2018, https://www.dei.gov.ba/en/odgovori-na-upitnik-ek (26 July 2022).

Directorate for European Integration, *Answers to the Questionnaire, Chapter 11, Agriculture and Rural Development*, 27 February 2018, https://www.dei.gov.ba/en/odgovori-na-upitnik-ek (26 July 2022).

Directorate for European Integration of Bosnia and Herzegovina. Division for the legal harmonization, Smjernice za usklađivanje propisa Bosne i Hercegovine s pravnom tečevinom Evropske unije *[Hand book for harmonization of Bosnia and Herzegovina legislation with European Union legislation]*. Sarajevo, 2020. https://www.dei.gov.ba/uploads/documents/smjernice-za-uskladivanje-propisa-bih-s-pravnom-tecevinom-evropske-unije_1606812865.pdf (26 July 2022).

Doing Business 2014, Economy Profile: Bosnia and Herzegovina. Washington: The International Bank for Reconstruction and Development / The World Bank, 2013.

EBRD. *Commercial Law of Bosnia and Herzegovina, An Assessment by the EBRD*, October 2010, European Bank for Reconstruction and Development, http://www.ebrd.com/downloads/sector/legal/bosnia.pdf (26 July 2022).

EC, *Bosnia and Herzegovina 2021 Progress Report*, accompanying the document Communication from the Commission to the European Parliament, the Council, the European Economic and Social Committee and the Committee of the Regions, 2021 Communication on EU Enlargement Policy, European Commission, SWD(2021) 291 final, Strasbourg, 19 October 2021.

EC, *Commission Opinion on Bosnia and Herzegovina's application for membership of the European Union*, COM(2019)261 final, European Commission, Brussels, 29 May 2019.

EC. *Bosnia and Herzegovina 2018 Progress Report*, accompanying the document Communication from the Commission to the European Parliament, the Council, the European Economic and Social Committee and the Committee of the Regions, 2018 Communication on EU Enlargement Policy, COM(2018) 450 final, European Commission, Strasbourg, 17 April 2018.

EC. *Bosnia and Herzegovina 2016 Progress Report*, accompanying the document Communication from the Commission to the European Parliament, the Council, the European Economic and Social Committee and the Committee of the Regions 2016 Communication on EU Enlargement Policy, COM(2016) 715 final, Brussels, 9 November 2016.

EC. *Bosnia and Herzegovina 2014 Progress Report*, accompanying the document Communication from the Commission to the European Parliament, the Council, the European Economic and Social Committee and the Committee of the Regions, Enlargement Strategy and Main Challenges 2014-2015, COM(2014) 700 final, Brussels, 8 October 2014.

EC. *Bosnia and Herzegovina 2013 Progress Report*, accompanying the document, Communication from the Commission to the European Parliament and the Council, Enlargement Strategy and Main Challenges 2013–2014, COM(2013) 700 final, European Commission, Brussels, 16 October 2013.

EC. *Bosnia and Herzegovina 2012 Progress Report*, accompanying the document, Communication from the Commission to the European Parliament and the Council, Enlargement Strategy and Main Challenges 2012–2013, COM(2012) 600 final, European Commission, Brussels, 10 October 2012, https://ec.europa.eu/neighbourhood-enlargement/bosnia-and-herzegovina-progress-report-2012_en (26 July 2022).

EC. *Bosnia and Herzegovina 2011 Progress Report,* accompanying the document, Communication from the Commission to the European Parliament and the Council, Enlargement Strategy and Main Challenges 2011–2012, COM(2011) 666 final, European Commission, Brussels, 12 October 2011, https://ec.europa.eu/neighbourhood-enlargement/bosnia-and-herzegovina-progress-report-2011_en (26 July 2022).

EC. *Bosnia and Herzegovina 2010 Progress Report,* accompanying the document, Communication from the Commission to the European Parliament and the Council, Enlargement Strategy and Main Challenges 2010-2011, COM(2010) 660, European Commission, Brussels, 9 November 2010, https://ec.europa.eu/neighbourhood-enlargement/bosnia-and-herzegovina-progress-report-2010_en (26 July 2022).

EC–Directorate-General for Economic and Financial Affairs. *2013 Economic and Fiscal Programmes of Albania and Bosnia and Herzegovina: EU Commission's overview and country Assessments*, Occasional Papers 157, European Commission, Directorate-General for Economic and Financial Affairs, Brussels, July 2013, pp. 20–28, http://ec.europa.eu/economy_finance/publications/occasional_paper/2013/pdf/ocp158_en.pdf (26 July 2022).

EEA, European Environment Agency, https://www.eea.europa.eu/soer/2010/countries/ba/country-introduction-bosnia-and-herzegovina (18 July 2022)

EEA. *Bosnia and Herzegovina, Country Profile – Distinguishing Factors.* European Environment Agency, https://www.eea.europa.eu/soer/2015/countries/bosnia-and-herzegovina (26 July 2022).

EEA. *The European Environment – State and Outlook 2010: Synthesis.* Copenhagen: European Environment Agency, 2010.

EEA. *Environmental Trends and Perspective in the Western Balkans: Future Production and Consumption Patterns.* EEA Reports, No. 1/2010. European Environmental Agency, Copenhagen, 2010, http://www.eea.europa.eu/publications/western-balkans (26 July 2022).

Energy Charter Secretariat. *In-Depth Review of Energy Efficiency Policies and Programmes: Bosnia and Herzegovina*, 2012, https://www.energycharter.org/fileadmin/DocumentsMedia/IDEER/IDEER-BosniaandHerzegovina_2012_en.pdf (26 July 2022).

Energy Charter Secretariat. *Follow-Up Review of the Investment Climate and Market Structure in the Energy Sector of Bosnia and Herzegovina.* Brussels, Belgium, 2011, https://www.energycharter.org/what-we-do/investment/investment-climate-and-market-structure/investment-in-bosnia-and-herzegovina-2011/ (26 July 2022).

Energy Community. *Report on the implementation of the Energy Performance of Buildings Directive, Bosnia and Herzegovina*, 2013.

. Energy Community Secretariat, *Annual Implementation Report 2021*, Energy Community Secretariat, Austria, 1 November 2021.

EU – Bosnia and Herzegovina, SAA Structured Dialogue on Justice, Technical Information Requested by the European Commission. Sarajevo, 2011. http://europa.ba/?page_id=553 (26 July 2022).

Efendic A., G. Pugh & N. Adnett. 'Confidence in Formal Institutions and Reliance on Informal Institutions in Bosnia and Herzegovina-An empirical investigation Using Survey Data'. *Economics of Transition* 19, no. 3 (2011): 523, doi: 10.1111/j.1468-0351.2010.00408.x.

Fagan A. 'Global–Local Linkage in the Western Balkans: The Politics of Environmental Capacity Building in Bosnia-Herzegovina'. *Political Studies* 56, no. 3 (2008): 629–652, doi: 10.1111/j.1467-9248.2007.00711.x.

FAO. *Global Forest Resources Assessment, Country Report, Bosnia and Herzegovina.* Rome: Food and Agriculture Organization of the United Nations, 2010, http://www.fao.org/docrep/013/al462E/al462e.pdf (26 July 2022).

Federal Office of Statistics, *Statistical Yearbook 2017, ('SY FBiH 17').* Sarajevo, 2017. http://fzs.ba/index.php/publikacije/statisticki-godisnjaciljetopisi/ (26 July 2022).

Federal Office of Statistics, *Statistical Yearbook 2021, ('SY FBiH 21')*, Sarajevo, 2021, p. 34. http://fzs.ba/index.php/publikacije/statisticki-godisnjaciljetopisi/ (18 July 2022).

Foreign Investment Promotion Agency. *Bosnia and Herzegovina Agriculture and Food Processing Industry.* Sarajevo, 2013, http://www.fipa.gov.ba/publikacije_materijali/brosure/Agriculture%20and%20Food%20Industry.05.06.2013.pdf (26 July 2022).

FMET. *State of the Environment in the Federation of Bosnia and Herzegovina – 2010 Report.* Federal Ministry of Environment and Tourism, June 2010.

FMET. *Program aproksimacije propisa Federacije Bosne i Hercegovine sa pravnom stečevinom EU u oblasti okoliša*[*Program of Approximation of the Federation of Bosnia and Herzegovina Legislation with the EU Environmental* Acquis]. Sarajevo, December 2016, http://www.mvteo.gov.ba/data/Home/%D0%94%D0%BE%D0%BA%D1%83%D0%BC%D0%B5%D0%BD%D1%82%D0%B8/%D0%92%D0%BE%D0%B4%D0%BD%D0%B8%20%D1%80%D0%B5%D1%81%D1%83%D1%80%D1%81%D0%B8/Program_aproksimacije_propisa_FBiH_sa_pravnom_stecevinom_EU_u_oblasti_okolisa.pdf (26 July 2022).

Ferlin F. *Forest Legislation, Institutional Development and Forest Policy Study of the Republic of Srpska.* PHARE, Technical Assistance to the Implementation of the Bosnia and Herzegovina Forestry Programme, Banja Luka & Ljubljana, 2001, http://www.slideshare.net/francferlin7/forest-legislation-institutional-development-and-policy-study-executive-summary (26 July 2022).

Filipović O. (ed.). *Parliamentary Assembly of Bosnia and Herzegovina.* Sarajevo: Parliamentary Assembly of Bosnia and Herzegovina, 2010.

Gaeta P. The Dayton Agreements and International Law. *European Journal of International Law* 7, no. 2 (1996): 147–163.

General Assessment of the Water Supply Sector and its Human Development Function in Bosnia and Herzegovina, Prepared within the MDG-F DEG programme in BiH by HEIS and Prism research, MDG Achievement Fund, January 2011, https://www.undp.org/bosnia-herzegovina/publications/general-assesment-water-supply-sector-and-its-human-development-function-bosnia-and-herzegovina (26 July 2022).

Grbić, V. & D. Todić. Ekonomski instrumenti za upravljanje otpadom u ruralnim regionima jugoistočne Evrope [Economic Instruments for Waste Management in Rural Region of Southeast Europe], *Ekonomika poljoprivrede*, Naučno društvo agrarnih ekonomista Balkana, Knjiga 2, 2011, Specijalni broj, str. 55-61.

Legislative Advocacy Resource Guide, Promoting Human Rights in Bosnia and Herzegovina, Washington: Global Rights, 2005,

Hanušić A. *Judicial Protection from Discrimination in Bosnia and Herzegovina Analysis of Legislative Solutions and Practice in Light of the First Cases in this Field*. Sarajevo: Analitika –Centre for Social Research, 2013.

Hodžić-Kovač E. (ed.). *Progress towards the Realisation of Millennium Development Goals in Bosnia and Herzegovina 2013*. Sarajevo: Ministry of Finance and Treasury of Bosnia and Herzegovina, Office of the UN Resident Coordinator in Bosnia and Herzegovina, 2013.

Human Rights Watch. *World Report 2012: Bosnia and Herzegovina*. Country Summary, January 2012, http://www.hrw.org/sites/default/files/related_material/bosnia_2012.pdf (26 July 2022).

Human Rights Watch. *World Report 2013*. New York: Human Rights, 2012, 411–417, http://www.hrw.org/sites/default/files/reports/wr2013.pdf (26 July 2022).

Human Rights Watch, Bosnia and Herzegovina, Events of 2021. https://www.hrw.org/world-report/2022/country-chapters/bosnia-and-herzegovina (26 July 2022).

Ibrahimbegovic, A. & M. Zlatar (eds). *Damage Assessment and Reconstruction after War and Natural Disaster*. Proceedings of the NATO Advanced Research Workshop on Damage Assessment and Reconstruction after War and Natural Disasters and Previous Military Activities, Sarajevo, 5–9 October 2008.

Ignjatić, M. & D. Todić. 'Directive of the European Parliament and of the Council on Promotion of the Use of Energy from Renewable Sources'. *European Legislation*, no. 35–36/2011, 106–115.

Illegal Logging in SEE and EE (Governance, Implementation and Enforcement), Illegal Logging Activities in Bosnia and Herzegovina, A. DIAGNOSTIC AUDIT, Kingdom of Belgium: Federal Public Service, Foreign Affairs, Foreign Trade and Development Cooperation, REC, Envsec, June 2010,

Initial report on Implementation of the International Covenant on Civil and Political Rights in Bosnia and Herzegovina for the period from 1994 to 2004, CCPR/C/BIH/1, 24 November 2005.

Institute for Statistics of FBiH. *Federation of Bosnia and Herzegovina in Figures*. Sarajevo, 2017, http://fzs.ba/wp-content/uploads/2017/07/F-BiH-u-brojkama-2017.pdf (26 July 2022).

Institution of Human Rights ombudsman of Bosnia & Herzegovina. *2017 Annual Report on the results of the activities of the Institution of the Human Rights Ombudsman of Bosnia and Herzegovina*. Banja Luka, March 2018.

Institution of Human Rights ombudsman of Bosnia & Herzegovina. *Annual Report on Result of the Activities by the Human Rights Ombudsman of Bosnia and*

Herzegovina for 2012. Banja Luka, 2013, http://www.ombudsmen.gov.ba/documents/obmudsmen_doc2013040401341524eng.pdf (26 July 2022).

Institution of Human Rights ombudsman of Bosnia & Herzegovina. *Annual Report on Result of the Activities by the Human Rights Ombudsman of Bosnia and Herzegovina for 2011*. Banja Luka, 2012, http://www.ombudsmen.gov.ba/documents/obmudsmen_doc2013012811550655eng.pdf (26 July 2022).

Institution of Human Rights ombudsman of Bosnia & Herzegovina. *Annual Report on Result of the Activities by the Human Rights Ombudsman of Bosnia and Herzegovina for 2020*. Banja Luka, 2021, https://www.ombudsmen.gov.ba/documents/obmudsmen_doc2021030808580995eng.pdf (10 July 2022).

Juelich R. *Progress in Environmental Law Drafting in South Eastern Europe*. Szentendre: Regional Environmental Centre, December 2005.

Knežević, A., et al. *Strategija prilagođavanja na klimatske promjene i niskoemisionog razvoja za Bosnu i Hercegovinu* [*Climate Change Adaptation and Low Emission Development Strategy for BiH*], June 2013, http://www.unfccc.ba/site/publikacije/spkp.pdf (19 July 2022); http://www.ba.undp.org/content/bosnia_and_herzegovina/en/home/library/environment_energy/climate-change-adaptation-and-low-emission-development-strategy-.html (19 July 2022).

Letter dated 3 March 1994 from the permanent representatives of Bosnia and Herzegovina and Croatia to the United Nations Addressed to the Secretary General, S/1994/255, UN Security Council, 4 March 1994.

MFTER, *Sixth National Report of Bosnia and Herzegovina to the Convention on Biological Diversity*, Ministry of Foreign Trade and Economic Relations of Bosnia and Herzegovina, 2019. http://bih-chm-cbd.ba/wp-content/uploads/2020/11/Sixth-National-Report-BiH_ENG.pdf (29 July 2022).

Ministry of Human Rights and Refugees. *The Second Periodic Report of Bosnia and Herzegovina on International Covenant on Economic, Social and Cultural Rights*. Sarajevo, 2010.

Nagradić, S. National minorities in legislation of Bosnia and Herzegovina, *Politea*, 10/2015, pp. 181-207. https://scindeks-clanci.ceon.rs/data/pdf/2232-9641/2015/2232-96411510181N.pdf (26 July 2022).

Negotiating Justice? Human Rights and Peace Agreements. Geneva, Switzerland: International Council on Human Rights Policy, 2006.

Nalog supervizora o urbanističkom planiranju [Supervisory Order on Urban Planning], (Official Gazette of BD BiH No. 10/07), http://www.ohr.int/?ohr_archive=supervisory-order-on-urban-planning (26 July 2022).

Nixon N. (ed.). *Progress Towards the Realization of the Millennium Development Goals in Bosnia and Herzegovina 2010*. Sarajevo: The Ministry of Finance and Treasury of Bosnia and Herzegovina, the United Nations Country Team in Bosnia and Herzegovina, 2010, https://www.undp.org/bosnia-herzegovina/publications/progress-towards-realization-millenium-development-goals-bosnia-and-herzegovina-2010 (26 July 2022).

Pickard, R.D., A.M. Cousin & B. Coussey. *Sustainable Development Strategies in South-East Europe*. Strasbourg: Council of Europe (CoE). Directorate of Culture and Cultural and Natural Heritage, 2008, 23–48.

Selected Bibliography

Porej D. & S. Matić. *Protected Area Management Effectiveness in Bosnia and Herzegovina.* Final Report of the RAPPAM analysis, FMET, 2009, http://awsassets.panda.org/downloads/bosnia_and_herzegovina_rappam_report.pdf (26 July 2022).

REC. *Doors to Democracy Current Trends and Practices in Public Participation in Environmental Decisionmaking in Central and Eastern Europe.* Szentendre: The Regional Environmental Center for Central and Eastern Europe, June 1998, 93–108.

Regional Environmental Centre for BiH. *Regional Centre Report on the Status and Needs of the Environmental Legislation in BiH.* 25 January–15 March 2002.

Republic of Srpska Institute of Statistic. *Statistical Yearbook of Republic of Srpska, 2013.* Banja Luka, November 2013, http://www.rzs.rs.ba/front/article/866/ (26 July 2022).

Republic of Srpska's Tenth Report to the UN Security Council, 8 November 2013, http://www.vladars.net/eng/Documents/Republic%20of%20Srpska%2010th%20Report%20to%20the%20UN%20Security%20Council.pdf (26 July 2022).

RSMoAFWM. *First National Report on the implementation of the United Nations Convention to Combat Desertification/Land Degradation in Bosnia and Herzegovina.* Republic of Srpska, Banja Luka: Ministry of Agriculture, Forestry and Water Management, 2007.

RSMoSPCEE. *Second National Communication of Bosnia and Herzegovina under the United Nations Framework Convention on Climate Change.* Banja Luka: Ministry for Spatial Planning, Construction and Ecology, 2013 https://unfccc.int/resource/docs/natc/bihnc2.pdf (26 July 2022).

RS MoSPCEE. *Program usklađivanja zakonodavstva Republike Srpske sa pravnom tekovinom EU u oblasti zaštite životne sredine*[*Program of Approximation of the Republika Srpska Legislation with the EU Environmental* Acquis]. Banja Luka, November 2016, http://www.vladars.net/sr-SP-Cyrl/Vlada/Ministarstva/mgr/PAO/Pages/Strategije.aspx (26 July 2022).

Sali-Terzić, S. *Study on the Capacities of the Judicial Institutions (Courts) to Address the Needs and Demands of Specific Groups: Persons with Disabilities, Roma, and Women in Bosnia and Herzegovina, Strengthening Judicial Integrity through Enhanced Access to Justice.* UNDP, 2011.

Seizović Z. A Need for a Comprehensive Administrative Reform in Bosnia and Herzegovina with an Emphasis on the Modernisation of Administrative Procedure. *HKJU – CCPA*, god. 12. (2012), br. 2., str. 409–432.

Softić A. & Lj. Glamočić, *National Background Report on Energy for Bosnia and Herzegovina.* WBC – inco net, Sarajevo, March 2012.

Statute of the Brčko District of Bosnia and Herzegovina–5 June 2008, http://www.ohr.int/?ohr_archive=statute-of-the-brcko-district-of-bosnia-and-herzegovina (26 July 2022).

Stuhlberger C. (ed.). *Mining and Environment in the Western Balkans.* Zoi Environment Network (UNEP, ENVSEC), https://www.researchgate.net/publication/262312336_Mining_and_Environment_in_the_Western_Balkans (6 26 July 2022).

Strategija razvoja Brčko Distrikta BiH za razdoblje 2008-2017. godina [Development Strategy of the Brčko District BiH for the Period 2008 to 2017. year], Brčko, June2009, http://www.vlada.bdcentral.net/Content/Read/strategije (26 July 2022).

Strategy for Bosnia and Herzegovina. Document of the European Bank for Reconstruction and Development, 15 January 2014, http://www.ebrd.com/downloads/country/strategy/bosnia2014.pdf (26 July 2022).

Šehić A., et al. *Access to Justice in Bosnia and Herzegovina, Collection of Public Policy Analyses in the Field of Judiciary.* Sarajevo: Justice Network in Bosna and Herzegovina, 2011.

Todić D. Multilateral Environmental Agreements and EU Integration of Western Balkan States (Status of Bosnia and Herzegovina, Montenegro, Serbia and Croatia in Multilateral Environmental Agreements), *European Energy and Environmental Law Review*, February 2019, Vol. 28, No. 1, pp. 17–27.

Todić D. Zaključivanje i izvršavanje međunarodnih ugovora u pravnom sistemu BiH, Crne Gore i Hrvatske [Conclusion and Implementation of International Treaties in the Legal Systems of BiH, Montenegro, and Croatia]. *Strani pravni život,* 2/2018, pp. 103–119, https://www.stranipravnizivot.rs/index.php/SPZ/article/view/425 (26 July 2022).

Todić D. & M. Zlatić. Transboundary Cooperation of Western Balkan states in the Field of Water Resources Management: Between the Existing Treaties and a New International Treaty. *Environmental Science & Policy* 89 (November 2018): 67–72.

Todić D. & V. Grbić. 'Natural Disasters: Legal Framework for Cooperation Between the Republic of Serbia and Bosnia and Herzegovina'. In *Soil and water resources protection in the changing environment*, edited by M Zlatić & S Kostadinov (Advances in Geoecology, Vol. 45). Stuttgart, Germany: Catena Soil Sciences, Scheizerbat Science Publishers, 2018, 301–311.

Todić D&M. Ignjatić. 'Analiza zakonodavstva Republike Srbije, Bosne i Hercegovine (Republike Srpske i Federacije BiH) i Crne Gore u oblasti upravljanja otpadom – u svetlu evropskih integracija' ['Comparative Analysis of the Republic of Serbia, Bosnia and Herzegovina (The Republic Srpska and Federation of BiH), and Montenegro Waste Management Legislation – In the Light of European Integration'], *Evropsko zakonodavstvo*, 52-53 (2015): 222–239.

Todić D. 'Komparativna politika i pravo klimatskih promena: Bosna i Herzegovina, Crna Gora, Hrvatska i Srbija (osnovni elementi)' ['Comparative politics and climate change law: Bosnia and Herzegovina, Montenegro, Croatia and Serbia-Basic Elements']. *Strani pravni život*, br. 1 (2014):str. 181–194.

Todić D., V. Grbić & M Antevski. *Pridruživanje Evropskoj uniji i održivi razvoj* [*EU Accession and Sustainable Development*]. Beograd: Institut za međunarodnu politiku i privredu, 2014.

Todić D. & V. Grbić. 'Ekonomsko-geografski aspekti analize prelaznih rokova u ugovorima o pristupanju Evropskoj uniji' ['Economic and Geographical Aspects of the Transitional Periods Analysis in the EU Accession Treaties']. *Megatrend revija* 11, no. 1 (2014): str. 53–72.

Todić D. 'Globalna politika u oblasti klimatskih promena i politika država najvećih emitera gasova sa efektom staklene bašte'. *Međunarodna politika* br. 1150 (April-June 2013): str. 80–91.

Todić D. 'Montenegro', in *International Encyclopaedia of Laws: Environmental Law,* edited by K. Deketelaere. Alphen aan den Rijin, NL: Kluwer Law International, 2013.

Todić D. 'Social and Environmental Issues Related to the Security in SEE Countries'. In *Environmental Security in South – Eastern Europe,* edited by M. Montini & S. Bogdanovic. Springer Science + Business Media B.V., 2011, 43–58.

Todić D. & D. Božanić. 'Elements of the Climate Change Policy in South-East Europe (Serbia, Montenegro, Bosnia and Herzegovina and Croatia) and EU Climate Change Policy'. In *Challenges of the 21st Century and the Region,* edited by D. Dimitrijević & I. Lađevac. Beograd: Institute of International Politics and Economics, 2013, 199–215.

Todić D. & D. Dimitrijević. Energetska bezbednost u međunarodnom pravu životne sredine [Energy Security in International Environmental Law]. *Teme* 2 (2012):703–721.

Todić D., et al. *Međunarodni ugovori u oblasti životne sredine u funkciji evropskih integracija i region jugoistočne Evrope*. Beograd: Evropski pokret Srbija, 2011.

Todić D. & V. Vukasović. 'Regional Security and International Legal Regulation of Water Protection and Use – The Case of Serbia'. In *Energy and Environmental Challenges to Security*, edited by S. Stec & B. Baraj. Budapest, Hungary: Proceedings of the NATO Advanced Research Workshop on Energy and Environmental Challenges to Security, 21–23 November 2007; The Netherlands: Springer, 2009, 141–156.

Thompson, S. Status of the Environment in Bosnia and Herzegovina: Current Assessment. *Georgetown International Environmental Law Review* 12, no. 1 (1999):247–268.

UNCTAD. *Investment Policy Review, Bosnia and Herzegovina.* New York and Geneva, 2015.https://unctad.org/en/PublicationsLibrary/diaepcb2015d1_en.pdf (26 July 2022).

UNDP. National Human Development Report 2013, United Nations Development Programme (UNDP). *Rural Development in Bosnia and Herzegovina: Myth and Reality*. Sarajevo: Bosnia and Herzegovina, 2013.

UNDP. *Assessment of Development Results, Evaluation of UNDP Contribution, Bosnia and Herzegovina*. May 2009.

UNDP. *MDG Update Report for Bosnia and Herzegovina, PRSP, Europe and Beyond*. Sarajevo: United Nations Development Programme, Office in Bosnia and Herzegovina, 2013, https://www.undp.org/bosnia-herzegovina/publications/mdg-update-report-bosnia-and-herzegovina (26 July 2022).

UNDP. *National Human Development Report 2005, Better Local Governance in Bosnia and Herzegovina*, UNDP, 2005, http://hdr.undp.org/en/content/better-local-governance (26 July 2022).

UNDP. *National Human Development Report 2009, The Ties That Binds, Social Capital in Bosnia and Herzegovina*, 2009, http://hdr.undp.org/en/content/ties-bind (26 July 2022).

UNDP. National Human Development Report 2013, Rural Development in Bosnia and Herzegovina: Myt and Reality. Sarajevo, 2013, http://hdr.undp.org/en/content/rural-development-bosnia-and-herzegovina-myth-and-reality (26 July 2022).

UNDP in Bosnia and Herzegovina. *Third National Communication and Second Biennial Update Report on Greenhouse Gas Emissions of Bosnia and Herzegovina under the United Nations Framework Convention on Climate Change*, GEF, UNDP, MFTER, MSPCEE, FMET, DSPPABD, July 2016, https://www.undp.org/bosnia-herzegovina/publications/third-national-communication-tnc-and-second-biennial-update-report-greenhouse-gas-emissions-sbur-bosnia-and (26 July 2022).

UNDP in Bosnia and Herzegovina. *Human Development Report 2016, Risk-Proofing the Western Balkans: Empowering People to Prevent Disasters*. Sarajevo, 2016, 52, https://www.undp.org/bosnia-herzegovina/publications/human-development-report-2016-risk-proofing-western-balkans-empowering-people-prevent-disasters (26 July 2022).

UNECE. *Environmental Performance Review, Bosnia and Herzegovina*. New York, Geneva: United Nations, 2004.

UNECE. *2nd Environmental Performance Review, Bosnia and Herzegovina*. New York & Geneva: United Nations, 2011.

UNECE. *3rd Environmental Performance Review, Bosnia and Herzegovina*. New York & Geneva: United Nations, 2018.

UNEP. *Depleted Uranium in Bosnia and Herzegovina Post-Conflict Environmental Assessment*. Nairobi, March, 2003.

UNEP. *Desk Review of the Legal and Institutional Framework of Environmental Protection in Bosnia and Herzegovina*, [FINAL DRAFT], UNEP Bosnia and Herzegovina, April 2011, http://aarhus.ba/sarajevo/images/docs/pregled_okvira_za_zastitu_okolisa-bh.pdf (26 July 2022).

UNEP, PAP, PC. *National Report on Current Policy, Procedures, Legal Basis and Practice of Marine Spatial Planning in Bosnia and Herzegovina*, Mostar, May 2007.

UNICEF. *Bosnia and Herzegovina, Country Programme Document 2010-2014*. United Nations Children's Fund, 2009.

Uzunović Z. *Protection, Documentation and Popularization of Cultural Historical and Natural Heritage of Canton Sarajevo, Bosnia and Herzegovina*. Sarajevo, 2000.

Vučić M. & D. Todić. Članstvo država sukcesora SFR Jugoslavije u međunarodnim ugovorima u oblasti životne sredine ['Membership of Former Yugoslavia's Successor States in International Environmental Treaties']. In *Regulisanje otvorenih pitanja između država sukcesora SFR Jugoslavije* [*Settlement of Open Issues between Successor States of SFR Yugoslavia*], edited by D. Dimitrijević, Ž. Novičić& M. Vučić. Beograd: Zbornik radova sa međunarodne naučne konferencije 29–30 November 2012; Beograd: Institut za međunarodnu politiku i privredu, 2013, str. 337—355.

Vukasović V. & D. Todić. *Environmental Law in Serbia*. The Netherlands: Kluwer Law International BV, 2021.

World Bank Group. *Bosnia and Herzegovina, Systematic Country Diagnostic Update*, Report No. 148573-BA, Washington, 2020.

Selected Bibliography

World Bank Group – Bosnia and Herzegovina, Partnership Country Programme Snapshot, April 2015. https://documents1.worldbank.org/curated/en/657201468193766472/pdf/105238-WP-PUBLIC-BH-SNAPS.pdf (26 July 2022).

WB. https://data.worldbank.org/indicator/SI.POV.NAHC?locations=BA (26 July 2022).

WB. *Air Pollution Management in Bosnia and Herzegovina.* Report No: AUS0001227, October 2019. https://documents1.worldbank.org/curated/en/117281576515111584/pdf/Air-Quality-Management-in-Bosnia-and-Herzegovina.pdf (1 August 2022).

WB. *International Development Association and International Finance Corporation Country Partnership Strategy for Bosnia and Herzegovina for the period FY12-FY15*, 30 August 2011. Report No. 64428-BA, http://www-wds.worldbank.org/external/default/WDSContentServer/WDSP/IB/2011/09/12/000370910_20110912084943/Rendered/PDF/644280CAS0P12502011002820BOX361537B.pdf (26 July 2022).

World Bank. 'Bosnia and Herzegovina, from Aid Dependency to Fiscal Self-Reliance, a Public Expenditure and Institutional Review'. WB Report No. 24297-BIH, Poverty Reduction and Economic Management Unit Europe and Central Asia Region: The World Bank, 2002.

Zavod za vodoprivredu. *Water Management Strategy of the Federation of Bosnia and Herzegovina.* Sarajevo, Mostar: Zavod za vodoprivredu, March 2012, http://jadran.ba/strategija/SUV_FBiH_eng.pdf (26 July 2022).

Index

The numbers here refer to paragraph numbers.

Index

Index

Index